LORCA

LORCA

A DREAM OF LIFE

LESLIE STAINTON

FARRAR · STRAUS · GIROUX

NEW YORK

Farrar, Straus and Giroux
19 Union Square West, New York 10003

Library of Congress Cataloging-in-Publication Data
Stainton, Leslie, 1955–
    Lorca, a dream of life / Leslie Stainton.
        p.   cm.
    Includes bibliographical references and index.
    ISBN 0-374-19097-6 (alk. paper)
    1. García Lorca, Federico, 1898–1936—Biography. 2. Authors.
    Spanish—20th century—Biography.   I. Title.   II. Title: Dream of life.
    PQ6613.A763Z8856   1999
    868´.6209—dc21
    [B]   98–51194

ACKNOWLEDGMENTS
Grateful acknowledgment is made for permission to quote from the following sources:
To Herederos de Federico García Lorca and the respective translators of the English translations of poems from: Federico García Lorca, *Collected Poems*, ed. Christopher Maurer (New York: Farrar, Straus and Giroux, 1990), and Federico García Lorca, *Poet in New York*, ed. Christopher Maurer (New York: Farrar, Straus and Giroux, 1988);
To the publishers for extracts from: Federico García Lorca, *Deep Song and Other Prose*, ed. and trans. Christopher Maurer, 3rd ed. (New York: New Directions, 1980, and London: Marion Boyars, 1980); Federico García Lorca, *Selected Letters*, ed. and trans. David Gershator (New York: New Directions, 1983); Francisco García Lorca, *In the Green Morning: Memories of Federico*, trans. Christopher Maurer (New York: New Directions, 1986); *How a City Sings from November to November*, limited edition (San Francisco: Cadmus Editions, 1982);
To the Fundación Gala-Salvador Dalí, Figueres (Spain), with thanks, for extracts from the writings of Salvador Dalí;
To the President and Fellows of Harvard College for extracts from two poems by Antonio Machado, reprinted by permission of the publisher from *Antonio Machado: Selected Poems*, ed. and trans. by Alan S. Trueblood (Cambridge, Mass.: Harvard University Press), copyright © 1982 by the President and Fellows of Harvard College;
To the Houghton Library Harvard for extracts from: Letter from Guillermo de Torre to Jorge Guillén (shelf mark bMS Span 100 (484)) and "Federico García Lorca" by Pedro Salinas (shelf mark, bMS Span 100 (1060)), both by permission of the Houghton Library, Harvard University.
Please note: every effort has been made to trace copyright holders of material in this book. The Publishers apologize if any material has been included without permission and would be pleased to hear from anyone who has not been consulted.

FOR MY PARENTS

ANN SCARLETT PETTIGREW STAINTON

AND

WILLIAM WHITFIELD STAINTON

CONTENTS

I remember a certain thunderstorm when we were young. The two of us were walking from Valderrubio to Fuente Vaqueros, and all of a sudden, without our even noticing it, a storm came up. Halfway between the two villages, as we were going through the tall poplars that border the Cubillas, day turned to night. The fields were deserted and silent. A few heavy raindrops fell, and the wind began to rock the trees. Then, suddenly, there was a dry, formidable clap of thunder. An unsaddled runaway horse almost ran over us. Then came another more distant clap and the typical odor of ozone. Federico ran over to me, his face pallid, and told me that his cheek was burning. He said he had been touched by a spark of the lightning, which had, in fact, been blindingly bright. I drew near him, looked at his cheek, calmed him down, and we began our return in silence.

Francisco García Lorca
In the Green Morning: Memories of Federico

LORCA

On the evening of March 17, 1918, four days before the German army launched its final assault on the Western Front, Federico García Lorca, a nineteen-year-old university student, stood before a small crowd of friends in the Arts Center of Granada, Spain. He was of average height and weight, with pitch-black hair and mournful eyes. A smattering of moles sprinkled his face. His clothes hung awkwardly from his shoulders.

He had agreed to read that night from his forthcoming book, *Impressions and Landscapes*, a prose account of his travels through Spain with one of his professors and a group of fellow students. It was his first public recital. For months he had been reading his poetry and prose to friends as they sat together in local cafés. He carried copies of his work on folded slips of paper in his pockets, even though he knew much of it by heart. But he had never given a formal reading of his work before now.

He was uncertain about the book—his first. In a prologue to the volume he described *Impressions and Landscapes* as "just one more flower in the poor garden of provincial literature." He feared readers would laugh at the work or, worse, ignore it. Within a month of its publication he confessed to a friend that he thought his new book was "very bad."

But that evening in the Arts Center, the audience applauded him warmly, and the following day, two local newspapers published favorable reviews of his recital. The *Defensor de Granada* announced that *Impressions and Landscapes*

revealed "a most vigorous literary temperament." The *Noticiero Granadino* predicted that the book was merely a "prologue" to greater work.

Two weeks later, Lorca received his first copy of the 264-page paperbound
volume. He found the experience of publication oddly disappointing. Once a
book "hits the streets, it's not mine anymore, it belongs to everyone," he said.
That evening, he marked the arrival of his book by drafting a five-page poem
entitled "Vision," a melancholy work about youth and love, one of dozens he
would write that spring. Midway through the poem he asked, "What will become of my passion?" On the final page of the manuscript, almost as an after-
thought, he wrote, "April 3, 1918. Night of my book."

The Armistice was still seven months away. During its final offensives, between
March and November of 1918, the German army sustained nearly one million
casualties. On even a quiet day on the Western Front, hundreds of German
and Allied soldiers lost their lives. A total of nine million men died in uniform
during the four years of the Great War—one in eight of those who served. Another eighteen million were wounded. Throughout Europe, veterans of the war
returned home blind, limbless, gassed, or as "scar throats"—men whose faces
were so crudely disfigured by wounds that sometimes even their own families
could not recognize them.

Lorca hated war. He hated the nationalistic sentiments that gave rise to it.
"In a century of zeppelins and stupid deaths," he told a friend in the spring of
1918, "I sob before my piano, dreaming in a Handelian mist, and I create verses
very much my own, singing the same to Christ as to Buddha, to Muhammad,
and to Pan." Humanity was his only concern. "Why fight against the flesh
when the terrifying problem of the spirit exists?"

At home, his family supported the Allies. Although Spain was officially neutral, people across the country took sides in the conflict according to their political and religious beliefs. Spanish newspapers were filled with accounts of
the fighting. On June 5, 1918, Lorca's twentieth birthday, the *Defensor de
Granada* described a battle that had raged the previous night between German
and French troops along the Aisne river, some sixty miles east of Paris. The paper also reported on the victims of "shell shock" who were allegedly subject to
"barbarous" treatment in German military hospitals.

The carnage of World War I moved Lorca to denounce patriotism as "one of
humanity's greatest crimes." In elementary school, he had been taught to love
his country unreservedly, and to honor its military and political heroes. As he

remembered it, his teacher, a gloomy man who struck his pupils' hands with a cane whenever they misbehaved, talked repeatedly about the virtues of war and the glories of the Spanish Inquisition. Pounding his chest with his hand, he reminded Lorca and his classmates that Spain was their "second mother. As good sons, you must be willing to give her your last drop of blood." In his teens, Lorca recoiled at the memory of these exchanges: "Instead of teaching us to love one another and help each other in our sorrow, they teach us the deplorable history of our countries, which are steeped in hatred and blood."

Late at night, while his family slept, he composed long, prayerlike treatises calling for peace and love. Often he worked until morning. He had made his first strides "toward the good of literature," as he phrased it, in 1916, at eighteen. Since then he had filled hundreds of pages with his haphazard scrawl. He wrote on whatever was handy—the margins of books, leftover voting ballots, his father's calling cards, his brother's high school drawings. Sometimes he drafted as many as five poems in a single night. At the end of some compositions, as though weighing their merit for publication, he jotted the word "Good." He stored his work in a wooden box beneath his bed.

He thought of himself as a passionate "romantic," an iconoclast who refused to conform to what society expected of him. He often neglected to comb his hair, and he wore unfashionably long cravats and patched trousers. He dreamt of becoming a writer. He persuaded his father, a wealthy landowner who was inherently skeptical about such things, to pay for the publication of his first book. At the end of *Impressions and Landscapes*, Lorca listed his forthcoming books. They included a poetry collection of "eulogies and songs," a series of "mystical writings," and a hybrid work about a lovesick monk, "Friar Antonio (Strange Poem)."

To a friend he acknowledged that *Impressions and Landscapes* "contains only a great emotion that flows from my sadness, and the ache I feel in the presence of Nature." He thought the book mediocre. For a time after its publication he continued to give copies to friends and acquaintances. But eventually he retrieved all the unsold volumes from Granada's bookshops and piled them in his family's attic. He later claimed to have burnt them.

He expected to fail. "There is within me an ideal so lofty that I will never achieve it. And I mean never," he wrote, "because I have a cruel and deadly enemy—society." Society was responsible for the slaughter in the trenches of France. Society was to blame for history's darkest crime, the murder of Jesus Christ, "who filled the world with poetry!" More particularly, Spanish society was to blame for the ignorance and bigotry that surrounded Lorca in Granada.

Spain was "a desert where great ideas die," a "soulless" nation that turned its back on "the Christs" who sought to redeem it. At times, Lorca saw himself as a twentieth-century Don Quixote, consumed by insatiable passions. In such an enormous world, he wondered, would anyone be able to see the goodness in his heart?

CHAPTER 1

FOUNTAINS

1898-1905

In the confusion of adolescence, Lorca turned to the past for clarity. At nineteen, he drafted "My Village," a prose account of his daily life as a boy in rural Spain. He described the narrative as "the vague remembrance of my crystalline soul."

He recalled his childhood as a time of pure, unambiguous emotion, free from the destructive powers of politics and time. In childhood, his parents had loved him unconditionally. Each morning before dawn, his father had come into the room where Federico and his brother and sister slept, and gently kissed their faces. "There was a trembling at his mouth and a brightness in his eyes," Lorca remembered. "Back then I laughed to see the expression on his face. Today I think I would weep." His father then tiptoed off and rode out to his fields for the day. Shortly afterward, Lorca's mother would stride into the room and, with a brisk "May the grace of God enter," open the shuttered windows, cross herself, and lead her children in prayer.

They lived in a white house in the center of the village of Fuente Vaqueros, some ten miles from Granada and thirty miles from the Mediterranean, in the heart of Andalusian Spain. The town had fewer than 2,500 inhabitants. It was built over deep underground springs and flanked by two rivers, the Cubillas and the Genil. Water poured from a fountain in the center of the village and coursed through an elaborate web of irrigation channels in the surrounding countryside. To Federico, it seemed that each morning the moisture in the air "kissed" all the houses and cloaked the village in a cold, silver gauze. Water had given the town its name: Fuente Vaqueros, "Fountain of the Cattlemen." Or simply "la Fuente," "the Fountain."

His home was spacious for its day, and far more comfortably appointed than most other houses in the village. Lorca was acutely aware of the difference between his family's standard of living and that of his neighbors. His family's house had tiled floors and beamed ceilings. By contrast, one of his friends, a young blond girl, lived in a house with dirt floors and reed ceilings. On wash days Federico was not allowed to visit the girl and her family, because they were "naked and stiff with cold, washing their rags, the only ones they owned." When he thought of all the "clean, fragrant clothes" hanging in his wardrobe at home, he felt "a cold weight" in his heart.

His father, Federico García Rodríguez, one of the richest men in the village, owned hundreds of acres of farmland in and around Fuente Vaqueros. A large man with a thick, coppery face and a broad smile, Don Federico began each workday with a shot of brandy and a cigar at the local café while the sun was still rising. As he sat at the table, he often talked to himself and occasionally laughed out loud. He had grown rich farming sugar beets in the wake of the Spanish-American War and the subsequent loss of the Cuban sugar crop, and each season hired dozens of men to work in his fields. But unlike other landowners in the region—most of them absentee landlords who left the administration of their property up to their agents, or *caciques*, who controlled local employment and ensured political calm—Don Federico lived in town and looked after his own land. His generosity to his workers was fabled. He always took on extra men when he knew they needed a job, and he kept some hands all year round.

Lorca adored his father. He loved his mother, too. She was well-read and refined, and from her, he said, he acquired "intelligence." But he was closest in temperament and looks to his father. Both men had round faces, coarse features, and dense black eyebrows. Both loved music. His mother bragged that before Federico was able to talk, he could hum popular tunes. He learned many of them from his father, who played the guitar at night while his family sang. It was his father, Lorca said later, who gave him his "passion."

A blunt, jocular man with a cigar-stained mustache and fingers, Don Federico García Rodríguez was, according to his son Federico, a "farmer, a rich man, an entrepreneur, and a good horseman." He was born in Fuente Vaqueros in 1859 and lived in the town for the first forty years of his life. He was the oldest son of Enrique García Rodríguez, a modest landowner, and his wife, Isabel, both of whom enjoyed long-standing ties to the region. The couple had nine children. The Garcías were comfortable but not rich, bright but informally schooled. Unusual for that time and place, all nine of Enrique García's children knew how to read, as did their parents, and all, thanks to their father, learned to play the guitar.

In 1880, at age twenty-one, Federico García Rodríguez married for the first time. His bride was Matilde Palacios Ríos, then twenty, the daughter of a neighboring landowner whose wealth far surpassed Enrique García's simple holdings. Upon his marriage, Don Federico's fortunes prospered. He obtained a house in the center of Fuente Vaqueros, on Calle Trinidad, went to work for his father-in-law, and began purchasing farmland of his own. He became town clerk of Fuente Vaqueros, a post both his father and grandfather had held. In 1891, at the age of thirty-two, he was elected municipal judge by the town council, a position contingent upon its occupant's social, moral, and economic standing.

But his life was marred by loss: the deaths of his father and of Matilde's parents in the early 1890s, the fact that he and Matilde remained childless. In the fall of 1894, six days after her mother's death, Matilde Palacios died from a sudden illness. The previous day, from her bed in the white house in Fuente Vaqueros where she and her husband had lived for fourteen years, she dictated her last will and testament. In it she ordered that the whole of her estate, save a token bequest to a maid and the inheritance due her sister, be left to her thirty-five-year-old husband, Federico García Rodríguez. His wealth was assured. Within months of his wife's death, Don Federico had purchased a second home in Fuente Vaqueros, thirty-five acres of farmland outside the neighboring village of Asquerosa, and a sizable new home in the center of Asquerosa. If to his first marriage he had brought "only the clothes on his back"—as the wording in Matilde's will quaintly phrased it—to his second marriage he brought considerable property and wealth.

Three years after Matilde's death, Don Federico chose as his new bride a soft-spoken young woman named Vicenta Lorca, who worked as a schoolteacher in Fuente Vaqueros. At first his family questioned the match, judging Vicenta neither rich nor particularly talented. But her quick mind and gentle ways appealed to Don Federico. The first time he approached the window of her home in Fuente Vaqueros and began to speak to her through its grille, as was the custom in village courtship, he was smitten. "Vicenta," he exclaimed, "you talk just like a book." From that moment on he tried to polish his own rough speech in her presence.

Nothing she had known in her brief, difficult life could have prepared Vicenta Lorca for the prosperity she would enjoy as the wife of Federico García Rodríguez. She was a Granadan by birth, and something of that city's melancholy had settled in her eyes—or perhaps it was the strain of poverty that had quietly left its mark on her face. Her father died one month before Vicenta's birth on July 25, 1870. She grew up an only child in her mother's care, dependent on family charity for her existence. By the time she was thirteen, Vicenta and her mother had lived in four different homes in Granada, each belonging to some relation.

At thirteen, she was sent to a convent school for poor children. The experience horrified her. Behind cloistered walls the nuns bickered among themselves and forced the child to eat food she loathed. The sisters' piety was more than offset by the envy and rancor with which they treated one another and their charges. Vicenta Lorca never forgot the ugliness she saw in the convent, and although she remained a devout Catholic throughout her life, she avoided any show of zealotry.

She spent five years with the nuns, then several more years in Granada training to be a schoolteacher—one of the few jobs, besides motherhood, then available to women. She worked hard at her studies and graduated with glowing marks as a licensed *maestra* of elementary education. Her first and only job sent her ten miles away, to the girls' primary school in Fuente Vaqueros. The salary was meager, and the village a far cry from her cherished Granada, but Vicenta dutifully packed her belongings and moved to the countryside with her mother to begin her career. By the age of twenty-two she was installed as a professor of primary instruction in Fuente Vaqueros.

Her relative good fortune lasted little more than a year. In the fall of 1893, her mother suddenly died. Vicenta was inconsolable. Time did little to blunt her grief. Years later she could still remember the desperation of those days, and with the candor that often characterized her words, she told a niece, "After all that struggle and effort, I finally got my degree, and then what happened? My mother died." Four years later Vicenta Lorca became the bride of Federico García Rodríguez.

The pair were married in the parish church of Fuente Vaqueros on August 27, 1897, two days before Don Federico's thirty-eighth birthday and one month after Vicenta's twenty-seventh. Nine months and nine days later, their first child, Federico, was born, on Sunday, June 5, 1898, in the plain white stucco house on Calle Trinidad where his father had lived, childless, for the past two decades. The infant arrived at midnight, a fitting hour for a boy who would grow up loving the night. At six days old he was carried to the church around the corner from his house and baptized Federico del Sagrado Corazón de Jesús. More simply, he was known as Federico García Lorca.

Overseas, the once-resplendent Spanish empire was in its death throes. One month before Lorca's birth, the United States declared war on Spain. The brief, catastrophic engagement that followed was to be Spain's last imperial war in the Americas. The result of a complex set of circumstances—the Cuban independence movement; persistent economic and trade difficulties involving Cuba, the United States, and Spain; the United States government's commitment to manifest destiny; and the ineptitude of an aging and authoritarian Spanish regime—the Spanish-American War lasted barely four months and shattered Spain's centuries-old status as a world power. Within a week of the declaration of war, Admiral George Dewey had destroyed Spain's Pacific squadron in a single hour's battle off the Philippine coast. In early July 1898, Spain's Caribbean fleet was defeated by the United States Navy in the waters off Santiago, Cuba, in what many consider one of the worst naval catastrophes of modern times. In a single gruesome day of battle, 2,129 Spaniards died; just one American perished. The only Spanish ship fast enough to slip away ran out of coal. Its lifeline to the Iberian peninsula cut, Cuba yielded at once to the American army. Two weeks later, against token resistance, the United States invaded Puerto Rico. In August 1898, Spain signed a peace protocol ending the war.

Few Spaniards could forgive their government its folly. At home, citizens dubbed the year 1898 "the Disaster." By 1899 the Spanish empire had evaporated, its last remaining colonies—Cuba, Puerto Rico, the Philippines—jettisoned with the stroke of a pen. The Spanish mainland was visited by the depressed, fever-ridden remnants of its military, whose pitiable specter accelerated an already bitter process of national soul-searching. Only a handful of Spaniards gained anything from the losses of 1898. Among them was Federico's father, whose sugar-beet business prospered.

When Lorca was two, his mother gave birth to a second child, Luis. Twenty months later, the boy died of pneumonia and was buried in a tiny casket in the town cemetery. Lorca never forgot the ghostly child. At nineteen he signed a poem "Federico Luis," and at twenty-four he recalled an infant lost in limbo,

"my little brother Luis / in the meadow / with the tiny babies." At thirty-one he
was still imagining the dead boy, this time as his son.

At first, the theatrics of death enthralled him—the white casket festooned in
flowers and crepe, the candles and cross. But by adolescence his delight had
turned to horror, and he could not face a burial procession without closing his
eyes. Haunted by the thought of the cold body decomposing inside its chaste
coffin, he repeatedly asked himself, and others, what happened to people after
they died. What became of the soul after the body had dissolved into a putrid
mass of fluids? Was there, as the Church promised, a "great beyond," or merely
interminable darkness, a void? In his struggle to reconcile himself to the
fragility of human existence, his heightened imagination probed the very
essence of death. He envisioned the process of decay: the stains, the pus, the
"streams of black blood" that spilled from the nose, the glassy eyes with their
unforgettable "look of terror." His father, similarly perturbed by the death of his
second son, took a more pragmatic approach to matters and began compulsively carrying medications with him whenever he and his family went on excursions.

Lorca learned early on that life and death were two halves of an indecipherable whole. Barely three months after Luis's death, Vicenta Lorca gave birth to
a third son, Francisco Enrique, nicknamed Paco. The following year a daughter, María de la Concepción, or Concha, was born. The girl, like Federico, resembled their father. Paco, with spare, lean features and an air of fragility, took
after their mother.

By the summer of Concha's birth, in 1903, the family had moved into a new
home in Fuente Vaqueros, close to the village church. To Federico, the sound
of the church bells seemed to rise straight from "the heart of the earth." By
seven o'clock, he was usually up and pulling on his acolyte's robes so that he
could get to church and dress the altar in time for Mass. He thrilled to the
charged world of martyrs and orations. Sometimes, as he sat beside his mother
at High Mass in the cold damp of a winter morning and fixed his eyes on the
altar, he felt his soul go "into ecstasy" at the sound of the organ's first chords.

He studied the catechism, learned liturgical phrases in Latin, and became
thoroughly schooled in Catholic ceremony. Although he sometimes arrived
late for Mass and was scolded by his mother, once inside the sanctuary he gave
himself fully, imaginatively, to the service. When his mother bowed her head
devoutly in prayer beside him, he did the same, his gaze fixed on a likeness of
the Virgin and the Christ child, "blessing us with his fingerless little hands." It
was principally the spectacle he enjoyed, the Mass as high drama. The sound
of the organ and "the smoke of the incense and the tinkling of the tiny bells

would excite me," he recalled in his teens, "and I would be terrified of sins which today no longer disturb me."

The Church suffused his boyhood. At school a plaster statue of Christ stood watch over his classroom. The walls were hung with posters bearing moral and religious axioms. Federico sat in the second row of benches, beside two poverty-stricken village boys whom he kept supplied with sweets and sugar lumps from home. A lackluster student, he disliked his teacher and was bored by the routines of the classroom. What he remembered best from primary school, and relished most, was the soft, virginal sound of girls singing in the classroom next door to his, and the pleasures those voices implied. At school, as at church, boys were kept separate from girls and taught to assume their re-spective roles. But to Lorca and his young classmates the muted voices next door were a constant source of awe. One day as the girls were singing, an older boy leaned over to Federico and whispered, "Hey, what if all the girls were naked and we were all naked, would you like that?"

Dumbfounded, Federico stammered, "Yes, yes, I'd like it a lot." The school-master heard them talking and slammed his cane down on the table. In the si-lence that followed, the girls next door went on singing. For Lorca, the incident, and the memory of their voices, came to signify his awakening both to "the mysteries of the flesh" and to all the "truths and disappointments" the flesh had to offer.

When school was not in session he and his friends often played together in the Lorca family's attic, gorging on dried fruit and engaging in a grisly, make-believe game of hide-and-seek that involved a ravenous wolf in search of inno-cent sheep prey. The rite provoked in Federico a strange, incomprehensible mingling of suffering and pleasure, and he later identified these moments as one of the "greatest emotions" of his early life.

He lived at a high emotional pitch. He craved sensation—the keener the better. When the real world disappointed him, he made up a more interesting one. Physically neither graceful nor athletic, he preferred the life of the imagi-nation to that of the body. One of his legs was slightly shorter than the other, and this gave him, he said, a "clumsy gait." He did not enjoy sports. The one time his father managed to get him to mount a horse, Lorca simply sat on the motionless animal while his brother and sister looked on and giggled.

He liked fiction best. One of his first toys was a little theater; he broke open his pottery bank to pay for it. The miniature stage came without plays, so Fede-rico made them up. One day, after watching an itinerant puppet troupe per-form in the village square, he persuaded an aunt to fashion a set of cardboard figures so that he and a neighbor could put on a puppet show. With friends he periodically carried out mock funeral processions, bearing dead birds through the streets while intoning the Ave Maria. At home he set up improvised altars, donned priestly robes, and conducted Mass before his aunts, cousins, siblings, and neighbors. He urged his makeshift congregations to weep in response to his sermons and even showed them how.

For the most part, his family indulged his fantasies. His mother, in particular, humored his passion for the dramatic and, long after he might have outgrown such pastimes, encouraged him in his theatrical and literary pursuits. She shared his fondness for literature. One January night, Lorca sat in the kitchen listening to his mother read Victor Hugo's *Hernani* aloud to a group of farmhands and servants. "I was shocked to see the maids crying," he recalled years later, "even though obviously I didn't understand anything . . . anything? . . . yes, I understood the poetic atmosphere, although not the human passions of the drama."

His family owned a deluxe edition of *Don Quixote* and a complete set of Hugo's works, bound in red with gold-tipped pages and color illustrations. His father had bought the set on the occasion of Hugo's death in 1885, and the beautiful tomes accompanied the family wherever they lived. Both Lorca and his brother, Paco, read Hugo as boys. At times Lorca crept off by himself to a corner of his home to pore over one of Hugo's novels. He admired the Frenchman's pacifism and his compassion for the maligned. He was not the first in his family to idolize Hugo. His paternal grandmother, Isabel, an ardent reader, once kept a life-size plaster bust of the novelist in her room.

At night, Lorca's parents, aunts, and uncles often read books out loud or told stories—local tales of passions, kidnappings and murders, or accounts of cruelty by the Civil Guard, who patrolled the countryside around Fuente Vaqueros. Federico relished their stories and begged to hear more. He loved it equally when his family sang. He had eight aunts and uncles and nearly forty first cousins on his father's side of the family, and all of them lived within a few miles of Fuente Vaqueros. Most worked the land, but "within their simplicity," as a friend of Lorca's later observed, they were remarkably sophisticated. Many in the huge clan were musical. Federico's father and his aunt Isabel were both spirited guitarists, and his uncle Luis, who stood witness at Lorca's baptism, was a splendid pianist known throughout the region for the speed of his playing. From his father, uncles, and other relatives who knew flamenco guitar, Lorca learned dozens of Gypsy songs—*seguidillas, soleares, peteneras*—and countless ballads. He listened time and again to popular Andalusian tunes such as "El café de Chinitas" and "Los cuatro muleros."

The songs Lorca heard in the village—ballads, flamenco lyrics, love songs—

were his introduction to poetry, and he later used the medium of poetry to recall them, writing in adolescence of village field hands who used to gather in
their doorways at night to drink wine, eat cheese, and dance "the fandango /
with religious unction" while guitars "wept their / rhythm quietly or with thunderous ardor." He responded instinctively to the dense, allegorical images and
concise lines of popular Spanish songs, and to the harsh, often tragic nature of
Spanish lullabies, which he heard not only from his family but from household
servants.

At birth he was given a wet nurse, and for the rest of his life he was tended by
maids, housekeepers, cooks, caretakers, and chauffeurs—men and women
whose presence he took for granted, although he later spoke rapturously of the
cultural debt wealthy children owed their servants. "The rich child listens to
the lullaby of the poor woman, who gives him, in her pure sylvan milk, the
marrow of the country," he said. He failed to mention that for most poor
women, servitude was an economic necessity.

With some irony, Lorca later characterized his childhood as being that of "a
rich little boy in the village, a bossy child." As his father's firstborn and name-
sake, he was indeed the object of countless attentions while growing up, more
so than either his brother or his sister. His father served as paterfamilias to the
entire García clan, dispensing money and advice to those who needed it, and
the family, in turn, revered him. Each year on July 18, they celebrated Don
Federico's saint's day, and eventually that of his son Federico. Relatives and
friends brought gifts of ice cream and anisette, baskets of candied fruit, live
roosters, iced drinks made from almonds and hazelnuts.

As he matured, Lorca chafed at being "a rich little boy in the village." In adolescence he wrote movingly of the misery he had witnessed as a child. His accounts of poverty spared few details. He recalled winter days when his
classmates dressed in threadbare clothes while he wore a fur-trimmed red cape
to school. He told of a six-year-old village boy who fell gravely ill and was
forced to drink a folk remedy made of mule dung cooked with beetles. As
neighboring children looked on from the window, adults held the boy down
and forced him to swallow the foul mixture. Shortly afterward he died, prompting the woman who had prescribed the cure to snort, "Such a delicate child!
He wasn't fit to belong to a poor family."

The lot of rural women, in particular, dismayed Lorca. In Andalusia, he
wrote, "all poor women die of the same thing, of giving lives and more lives."
The cycle was relentless. More than once in boyhood he glimpsed the body of

a woman lying in a coffin with a dead child between her legs, both having perished from "misery and neglect." Childless women fared no better. Lorca was profoundly moved by the plight of one woman in his village, a recluse and spinster born with froglike hands. He asked himself how often this pitiful woman must have cursed her parents for having conceived her—"without thinking"—during an instant of pleasure.

Little that he saw or heard as a child was lost on him. He spent hours exploring the countryside around Fuente Vaqueros, roaming his father's property or daydreaming beside one of the shallow rivers that flowed past the town. The landscape of his birthplace—the *vega* of Granada, a lush river plain ringed by hills and watered by snows from the Sierra Nevada mountains—stirred him as few locations could. He was intimately familiar with the sensations of the place. As a teenager he wrote of the echo of birds in the *vega*'s sprawling poplar groves and the smell of straw burning in autumn fields. Momentarily neglecting its more troubling aspects—poverty, death, the cruelties of fate and the mysteries of desire—he described his childhood as "shepherds, fields, sky, solitude. Simplicity itself." For Lorca, the *vega* embodied these. Uninhibited and pagan, it provided a vivid contrast to the tedium of the classroom and the constraints of the catechism.

He was keenly attuned both to the agricultural rhythms of the landscape and to its human legacy. Hints of past civilizations—Greek, Iberian, Roman, Arab—littered the countryside. To the north of Fuente Vaqueros, along the road to Asquerosa, stood a crumbling brick residence that Renaissance courtiers had used as a hunting lodge during the reigns of Ferdinand and Isabella, and Carlos V. A few hundred yards to the south were the remains of an Arab watchtower, a vestige of the eight-hundred-year Muslim occupation of Andalusia. Beyond it was the tiny village of Romilla, "Little Rome," a reminder that for nearly seven centuries before the Arabs invaded Spain, the country—Hispania—had belonged to the Roman Empire, and from it derived both a religion and a language. Time and again, Andalusia had passively absorbed foreign cultures, then quietly imposed its own sophisticated customs and character. From the eighth until the late-fifteenth centuries—what to the rest of Europe was a "dark age"—the region sustained one of the most spectacular civilizations in history, the Arab kingdom of al-Andalus, a model of ethnic tolerance in which Christian, Muslim, and Jewish traditions and residents not only coexisted but flourished. The era gave to the region an artistic, scientific, linguistic, and agricultural heritage that endured well into the twentieth century.

With his brother, Lorca pondered the origin of local names and pored over the deeds to certain of their father's properties. The oldest documents were written in Arabic. Roman relics occasionally turned up on neighboring farms, and one day their father's own land yielded a set of small unpainted vases of unknown origin, which the two brothers subsequently kept in their bedroom.

As a boy, Lorca once watched a plow unearth a fragment of Roman mosaic from one of his father's fields. He later recalled "how the huge steel plowshare cut gashes into the earth, and then drew forth roots instead of blood." The rugged blade tore deep into the soil, so deep that according to Lorca it scraped the foundations of ancient buildings. As he watched, the tool struck "something solid and stopped. The shiny steel blade had turned up a Roman mosaic." The mosaic bore an inscription whose precise subject Lorca could not remember. "But for some reason I think of the shepherds Daphnis and Chloë," he said. "So the first artistic wonder I ever felt was connected with the earth."

CHAPTER 2

NEW WORLDS

1905-15

At the age of seven or eight, Lorca moved with his family to the small village of Asquerosa, a mile or so to the northwest of Fuente Vaqueros. The word *asquerosa* means "repulsive," which disturbed Lorca, who in later years deemed the name unworthy of his biography and went out of his way to avoid using it. (Eventually the town was renamed Valderrubio.) In fact, Lorca viewed Asquerosa, with its pristine white buildings and placid streets, as "one of the prettiest towns in the *vega*."

His father owned two homes in the village, a sprawling farm on the edge of town, the Cortijo de Daimuz, and a large two-story house in the center. It was to the second of these that Don Federico moved his family in 1905 or 1906. A lavish residence by village standards, the new home had stables, a corral, four bedrooms, a kitchen, a dining room, and an imposing pair of lightning rods on its roof. By moving to Asquerosa, Lorca's father gained closer access to his properties, the train stop, and the sugar-beet refinery where much of his business took place.

To Federico, the move was a slight but nonetheless dramatic change. Built on dry land, not wet, Asquerosa was older and smaller than Fuente Vaqueros. It sat low and bleached on the earth, with green fields and poplar groves at its edge. There were few trees to shade its streets and no public fountain. More so than Fuente Vaqueros, Asquerosa revealed to Lorca the cloistered, provincial nature of life in a tiny rural community. Within the privacy of his own home he could sense the presence of his neighbors. On summer afternoons, with the shutters drawn against the sunlight and flies, he could hear people passing by on the street outside the living room and see their silhouettes reflected on the ceiling. Little in the town went undetected or unremarked. Years later, while visiting Asquerosa, Lorca complained peevishly to his brother about daily life in the town: "It's full of stupid etiquette. You have to greet people and say good night. You can't go out in your pajamas or they'll stone you, and it's full of malice and bad will."

Within a year or two of settling in Asquerosa, his parents abruptly sent Federico to school in Almería, a thriving Mediterranean seaport nearly a hundred miles to the southeast. They wanted him to prepare for his entrance examinations to secondary school under the tutelage of their good friend Antonio Rodríguez Espinosa, the former schoolmaster of Fuente Vaqueros. Rodríguez Espinosa had witnessed Federico's baptism in 1898, and although he had left Fuente Vaqueros four years later, he remained in close touch with the boy's parents. Don Federico and Vicenta admired their friend's pragmatism and devotion to work, as well as his liberal outlook and quiet anticlericalism—traits they hoped Don Antonio might instill in their son.

Lorca was eight or nine when he was sent to Almería; he had never been separated from either his parents or the *vega*. The sudden move deepened his sense of estrangement from other children. Aware that he was now about "to embark on another life," as he later put it, he realized as never before the degree of his economic and social isolation from everyday village existence. When he heard his classmates mutter that "the boss's kid" was going off to school, he felt homesick and depressed. When he said goodbye to them, he wept.

His father accompanied him on the long journey east. They were joined by two cousins and a fourth boy from the *vega*, all of whom were to live and study that year with Rodríguez Espinosa and his wife. Don Antonio later remembered that of the four children, Lorca was the smallest and the "most turbulent." In school, he was an indifferent student who distinguished himself chiefly by coining puns and clever nicknames for his classmates. Nevertheless, he managed to complete his schoolwork with Rodríguez Espinosa, and at age ten he passed his entrance exam for the General and Technical Institute of Almería, a public secondary school.

Almost immediately afterward he contracted a gum infection. His face swelled and his temperature rose alarmingly. Terrified, Don Federico hurried to Almería to tend to his son. Lorca later recalled the episode with pride. He claimed his father feared he would die. He also claimed the infection inspired his first verse. "I asked for a mirror and saw my face all swollen, and since I couldn't talk I wrote my first funny poem, in which I compared myself to the fat sultan of Morocco, Muley Hafid."

At home in Asquerosa, Lorca gradually recovered from his illness. His face still bloated, he sat in an armchair by the window, occasionally strumming a guitar. Although in time he regained his health, his parents were so shaken by the incident that they elected not to send him back to Almería, and instead enrolled him in the General and Technical Institute of Granada, in the provincial capital, fifteen miles from Asquerosa. So that they could remain together as a family, they also decided to take a home for themselves in the center of Granada, and in the spring of 1909, shortly before Lorca's eleventh birthday, they settled into a rented, three-story house on Granada's Acera del Darro, a street named for the slender Darro river that wound past it. With the windows open in their living room, the family could hear the murmur of water below.

If Almería was bright light and the din of a Mediterranean harbor, Granada was cypress trees, rivers, and the toll of church bells through the night. The word granada means "pomegranate," an image whose poetic implications were not lost on Lorca. The fruit, he would write, is hard and skull-like on the outside, but inside it contains the "blood of the wounded earth."

He responded passionately to his new surroundings. Located at the base of two mountain spurs well above sea level, Granada fed on the waters of the Darro and Genil rivers. The second of these skirted the southern edge of town before making its way out into the vega, to Lorca's birthplace and his father's farmlands. The sound of water permeated the city. Lorca would boast that Granada "has two rivers, eighty bell towers, four thousand irrigation ditches, a thousand and one jets of water." Mountains anchored the town on three sides, most spectacularly the snow-clad Sierra Nevada to the south, whose gray peaks dominated the horizon. Unlike other Spanish cities, Granada turned in on itself, not out to the world—or so Lorca came to believe. He felt that Granada's beauty lay not in monumental vistas but in small things: houses, patios, music, water, "everything reduced and concentrated, so that a child can feel it."

He made frequent, often solitary visits to the city's most celebrated monument, the Alhambra, which sat high above town on a steep hill covered with cypress and sycamores. From its heights, Arab sultans had presided in luxury over the final two centuries of Muslim rule in Spain. Their reign ended in

1492, after a long siege, when the Catholic king and queen, Ferdinand II of Aragon and Isabella I of Castile, swept into Granada on horseback and toppled the fabled kingdom of al-Andalus. The victory capped a four-hundred-year Christian reconquest of Islamic Spain, a militant holy war conducted by the infant Christian kingdoms of the country's north, which in 1469, with the marriage of Ferdinand and Isabella, had combined to form a fledgling Spanish nation-state. Granada was the last outpost of Muslim Spain; during its two-hundred-year tenure as the capital of al-Andalus, the city and surrounding province enjoyed a level of religious freedom and artistic and scientific brilliance unmatched elsewhere in Europe. Poetry, music, and architecture prospered; scholars pursued questions of philosophy, religion, astronomy, and medicine. Granada's Arab rulers developed an elaborate irrigation system—still used in Lorca's time—by which the waters from the Sierra fed the city and neighboring *vega*, yielding bountiful orchards and fields.

Although at first they tolerated the Arab presence, within months of their victory in 1492 the Spanish monarchs embarked on a violent campaign to "purify" the blood of Christian Spain. They ordered the expulsion of all Jews who refused to convert to Christianity. Both Arabs and Jews became disadvantaged minorities, subject to prejudicial racial laws. By 1610 the country's Muslim population had been eradicated. Meanwhile, Ferdinand and Isabella, whose bodies lay buried in Granada's massive cathedral, instituted what Lorca, at nineteen, called the "great crime of the Inquisition": a savage system of control meant to forge a single, monolithic Christian ideology through the arrest, torture, imprisonment, and public execution of alleged heretics. The system endured into the eighteenth century. Coincidentally, the Catholic reconquest in 1492 inaugurated the era of Spain's greatest expansion, and the start of the country's role as a world power. That year, in the town of Santa Fe (not far from Lorca's birthplace), which had been built to house the army laying siege to Granada, Ferdinand and Isabella authorized Christopher Columbus to investigate new trade routes to Asia.

Lorca's boyhood visits to the Alhambra "tensed Federico's soul," his brother recalled. The ornate, long-empty citadel reminded him of what had been lost with the reconquest, when a tolerant, cultured civilization had given way to one marked by oppression and war. Throughout his life, Lorca voiced his support for the persecuted and talked of the "fatal duel" between Arab and Christian cultures "that throbs in the heart of every *granadino*." In his teens he sometimes donned a white turban and robes and masqueraded as a Muslim sultan. A sense of loss colored his understanding of Granada from the outset. Nowhere was that sense more palpable than in the grounds of the Alhambra.

In the fountains of the Generalife gardens, he would write, the water "suffers and weeps, full of tiny white violins."

His mother decorated the family's new home in typical Granadan fashion, with dainty slipcovers and embroidered tablecloths, antique prints, family portraits, and a crystal lamp sheathed in pink crepe—surroundings as genteel as Vicenta Lorca herself. Like many Granadan women, she kept a canary. She also allowed her son Paco to keep a brood of pigeons in the small stable at the back of the garden. He and Lorca shared a bedroom in the new house. From their balcony they saw Halley's comet blaze overhead in the spring of 1910.

Soon after settling in Granada, Vicenta Lorca gave birth, at home, to a fifth child and second daughter, Isabel, a name shared by several women in the García clan. Following Isabel's birth, Vicenta, then thirty-nine, fell sick and was taken with the infant to the region's best hospital, in Málaga, more than eighty miles from Granada, where they remained for months. Federico, Paco, and Concha occasionally visited their mother and sister by train, and between visits kept in touch by letter. "Mama I want to see you very much and I hope you come home soon," Lorca wrote on an ink-stained card that appears to be his earliest correspondence. "Greetings all the way from the goatherd to the Gypsies your son who loves you very much. Federico."

At eleven, Lorca became an official student in Granada's General and Technical Institute, despite having failed a part of the school's entrance exam. He most likely began attending classes in the fall of 1909 as one of 442 students, all but one of them boys, enrolled in five separate grades at the public institute. Each was pursuing his *bachillerato*, or secondary school degree.

During his second year at the Institute, he began taking supplementary afternoon classes at the Academy of the Sacred Heart of Jesus, a private school run by one of Vicenta Lorca's relatives, Don Joaquín Alemán. The option to attend private school, either in place of or in addition to public school, was available to most Spanish schoolchildren, but generally only rich families could afford the tuition. Despite the piety of its name, Alemán's Academy was a secular institution. Located on the ground floor of a rambling nineteenth-century Granadan house, its classrooms were chilly, damp, and dark. In the winter, students' hands turned numb with cold. Like many of his classmates, Lorca suffered from chilblains.

He was an odd, shy student, whose fellow pupils, with their city-bred ways, intimidated him. Some of them poked fun at his eccentric dress—a flowing cravat instead of a tie—and at his mannerisms and interests, which they deemed effeminate. "Federica," they jeered, with an emphasis on the feminine *a*. They ridiculed his ungainly stride. He walked "like a sailor on deck," remembered classmate José Alemán, the director's son, who thought Lorca far less attractive, less "normal," than his younger brother, Paco, who started school not long after Federico.

Although neither brother especially liked school, Paco sailed through his classes, passing every exam and earning prizes and honors along the way. Lorca struggled. He lacked his brother's "schoolboy pride." He ignored subjects that did not interest him, rarely studied for exams, and paid no attention to penmanship, then a required course. His erratic handwriting went from bad to worse; in time, Lorca called it "vile." Often he skipped classes and wandered off by himself to some corner of Granada—to the Alhambra or to the Albaicín, the Gypsy quarter. Although his parents knew about some of his absences, they were ill-prepared for the extent of his truancy. His mother urged him to follow the example set by his younger brother. "Federico, study!" she pleaded. Lorca ignored her.

He received the standard schooling of his day: courses in Spanish language and literature, mathematics, history, geography, Latin, and French. Most of these subjects confounded him. Although Lorca learned to read French, he never managed to say so much as "good afternoon" in that or any foreign tongue, according to his brother. Somehow he contrived to take the final examinations for his *bachillerato* in October 1914, at age sixteen. After failing and retaking the mathematics part of the test, he passed the exam and received his diploma the following May. His apathy was such that he waited another twelve years before requesting a copy of his certificate.

On his own, away from school, he read avidly. His father opened an account for his children at a local Granada bookstore, and although it was intended for the exclusive purchase of "useful" books, Lorca bought whatever he liked. Together he and Paco amassed a small but impressive library complete with new editions, liberal texts, and works thought to be scandalous, among them Voltaire's *Candide* and Darwin's *Origin of Species*. The classics were well represented and well thumbed. With a tenacity that might have stunned his schoolteachers, Federico pored over such works as the Platonic dialogues, Hesiod's *Theogony*, and Ovid's *Metamorphoses*, about which he later exulted, "It has everything."

Thick underlinings crisscrossed his copies of Shakespeare (he and Paco owned the complete works in Spanish translation) and the *Rubáiyát of Omar Khayyám*, whose hedonistic invocations to love enthralled Federico. From Maeterlinck's essay *The Treasure of the Humble*, this line caught his eye:

"Everything that can be learned without anguish belittles us." Pencil marks underscored a similar passage in his copy of Oscar Wilde's *De Profundis*, written, as Lorca surely learned, during the Irishman's brutal imprisonment on the charge of indecent behavior with men: "Now it seems to me that love of some kind is the only possible explanation for the extraordinary amount of suffering that there is in the world."

In his growing quest to understand himself and his place in the world, Lorca turned to the Spanish mystics, Augustine's *Confessions*, Goethe's *Faust*, works of Indian philosophy, and the poetry of Rabindranath Tagore. It was chiefly his exposure to Hispanic *modernismo*, though, with its call to Beauty and Art as the highest absolutes, that nourished his emerging sense of himself as an artist. A Latin American phenomenon that eventually took hold in Spain, where it held sway from 1890 to 1910, Hispanic *modernismo* was a late and decadent flowering of romanticism, a poetic and artistic revolt against both the prosaic nature of late-nineteenth-century art and verse and the materialism and philistinism of bourgeois society. In contrast to Anglo-American modernism, Hispanic *modernismo* coincided roughly with the fin de siècle art nouveau or modern style. Inspired by Baudelaire and the French symbolists Verlaine, Rimbaud, and Mallarmé, its literary practitioners forged a new and expanded poetic language characterized by exotic imagery, unconventional meters, technical virtuosity, a darkly pessimistic view of reality, and a concomitant belief in art, women, and love as transcendent ideals.

By the time he was eighteen, Lorca had adopted a new literary idol, the Nicaraguan poet Rubén Darío, father of Hispanic *modernismo* (he coined the term), whose embrace of symbolist and Parnassian technique had led to a revolution in Spanish prosody in the late-nineteenth and early-twentieth centuries. Darío's lush imagery, expansive vocabulary, and metrical innovations and revivals had freed the Spanish language from conventional versification, much as Whitman's unorthodox meter and line liberated English. Darío sought to effect a "musical miracle" in poetry. He believed that art was "not a set of rules but a harmony of whims," a view Lorca admired, and in his two most important books, *Azul* (1888) and *Prosas profanas* (1896), Darío evoked an aristocratic, fairy-tale world brimming with swans, roses, champagne, pearls, and peacocks, a Dionysian existence peopled with mythological figures. Darío's radical verse inspired a generation of Spanish writers, among them Juan Ramón Jiménez and Antonio Machado. Likewise enthralled by the brilliant Nicaraguan, who died in his late forties in 1916 from poor health and alcohol abuse, Lorca looked for spiritual and aesthetic guidance to "Rubén Darío, 'The Magnificent.'"

At night Federico often stayed up late in his bedroom, reading. Because the light kept his brother awake, the two struck a compromise: Lorca would read on alternate evenings only. On the nights when he did not read, his brother would recite a brief dialogue with him. The ritual drew its inspiration from Victor Hugo's "Legend of the Handsome Pécopin and the Beautiful Baldour," a tale about two lovers separated, on the eve of their wedding day, for the next one hundred years. When at last they are reunited, Pécopin is still a young man, while Baldour has become an old woman. The story fascinated Federico, who would gently call out to Paco from his bed, "Pécopin, Pécopin."

"Baldour, Baldour," his brother would answer.

"Turn off, turn off . . ."

"The light, the light."

Only then would Lorca "put out the light without reading," Paco remembered. "But even when he was reading, if he saw that I was not completely asleep, he would softly say, 'Pécopin, Pécopin,' before turning off the light. Sometimes I took this with a grain of salt, and sometimes I answered with an expletive."

By day Lorca drafted his siblings into more elaborate entertainments. He costumed his brother, sisters, and the family maids in towels to look like Arabs, or dressed them in Vicenta Lorca's clothing when she was gone from the house. He dusted their faces with rice powder and led them in short pantomimes or recitals of poems and ballads that he had adapted into plays. Sometimes he staged plays on the patio for his youngest sister, Isabel, whom he cherished. In a room next door to his bedroom he set up makeshift altars and shrines and delivered prayers, sermons, and lectures on the Passion of Christ to his family and servants. The trappings of Christian doctrine appealed to him as much as its stories, with their powerful lessons on good and evil, charity and faith. He presented puppet performances and took part in local pageants. Once, during Carnival, he dressed up as a bullfighter, coated his legs with fake blood, and allowed his friends to carry him through the streets on their shoulders as though he were mortally wounded. By simulating death he sought to dispel its mystery.

His hunger for ritual stemmed partially from his mother, who attended Mass faithfully in Granada and instructed Lorca and his siblings in the Catholic liturgy. She taught them to regard the Church as a thing of beauty, independent of its theological function. "We're not going to that church," she sometimes announced. "It's ugly." Occasionally the family prayed together at home.

During the month of May, "Mary's month," Vicenta Lorca recited the rosary in Latin after dinner every night, and Lorca periodically preached a sermon. His more skeptical father suffered such activities with forbearance. Don Federico once told his wife as she was about to leave for Mass, "Only stay a little while."

"What do you mean?" Vicenta asked.

"I mean, I think that a little while won't hurt you much."

The entire family went regularly to the theater in Granada, where the offerings ranged from Shakespeare to comic folk operas known as *zarzuelas* to realistic drawing-room comedies by such popular Spanish playwrights as Jacinto Benavente and the Quintero brothers. But although Lorca delighted in the theater, his greatest love was music. His father saw to it that all four of his children received piano lessons. Lorca later recalled rapturously that in his teens he "took the Holy Orders of Music and donned its robes of passion." From the start, he proved a gifted player, blessed with an innate understanding of the art. The piano allowed him to express himself with a candor that no other medium could match. "No one," he observed, "can reproduce with words the shattering passion that Beethoven expressed in his Appassionata Sonata."

Hunched over the piano, his dark hair falling onto his forehead, he surrendered easily to the music of Chopin, Schubert, Mendelssohn, and Beethoven—composers he had admired since childhood. (As a boy he had fallen in love "like a madman" with the sound of young village girls practicing Beethoven and Chopin on the piano.) After hearing Federico perform one day, his piano teacher, Antonio Segura Mesa, turned to Vicenta Lorca and begged her to hug the boy. "It wouldn't be proper if I were to do it," he said. "It's just that he plays so divinely!"

His father bought Lorca his first piano, an upright that his uncle Luis, the pianist, auditioned and approved. In time Don Federico replaced this instrument with a shiny black baby grand. "*I love you more than anything else in the world,*" Lorca confessed to his piano in writing, underlining the words for emphasis. He envisioned the instrument as "a woman who is always asleep, and in order to wake her one must be filled with harmonies and grief." Like a woman, he suggested—his understanding of the gender shaped almost exclusively by his reading—"she is unpredictable."

Music became his idiom. He sought to emulate Beethoven, whose genius, he said, had been to translate his life into musical language, to convey through sound the "painful song of impossible love." By age eighteen, Lorca was composing. His first works were inspired by Granada. He titled one composition "Serenade on the Alhambra," then shortened it to "Granada." His piano teacher encouraged him. A spare, timid man in his seventies, Segura Mesa had consecrated his life to music in the hope of becoming a great artist. He had composed a number of works, including an opera that was booed at its Granada premiere. He never played publicly, and outside his native Granada he was unknown. "Just because I haven't reached the clouds," he often reminded Federico, ". . . doesn't mean the clouds don't exist." Lorca repeated the statement to himself like a mantra.

Keenly sensitive to criticism, and painfully shy, Segura Mesa rarely ventured from his house, except to teach Federico. A forlorn figure, with a domed forehead, buttonlike ears, and a thick mustache that trailed sadly down either side of his mouth, the older man made his way each day through Granada's noisy streets to the Lorca apartment. Federico regarded him as a "saint." As they sat together at the piano Segura Mesa frequently talked about famous composers, recounting their struggles as well as their achievements. More so than anyone else, he taught Lorca to view art as a grave calling, not a hobby. Sometimes, after a long session of rules and exercises, Segura Mesa would pull out samples of his own work for Lorca to analyze and perform. Neither man cared that these compositions had failed to attract a following. What mattered was the work itself. Inspired by the example of his teacher, Lorca set his sights on a musical career.

The piano stool became his favorite seat at home. In addition to his own compositions, he entertained family and friends with classical as well as popular works. He began performing in public. He joined Granada's Arts Center, the hub of the city's cultural life, and quickly established a name for himself in the institution by giving private recitals, helping to form a chamber music society, and providing background music for a life drawing class. He was the only outsider permitted to enter that particular classroom. While students sketched from human models, Lorca accompanied them on the piano with works by Beethoven.

His academic career continued to founder. In the fall of 1914, shortly before completing his *bachillerato*, he had enrolled as a student of Philosophy and Letters at the University of Granada. Although he survived his first year, the classwork soon became more difficult. Before long Lorca was no more than a nominal student. He fled subjects that perplexed him, such as Hebrew and Arabic, without so much as attempting to learn the material.

During his second year as a university student he switched from Philosophy and Letters to Law, then a conventional discipline for the sons of good Spanish families, or for undecided students like Lorca who were eager to please their fathers. Again, he passed a few easy courses before stumbling over the difficult ones that inevitably followed. Unwilling to abandon his interest in Letters, in 1916 he enrolled in both programs, and for the next three years took courses in literature as well as law. He did poorly in both. On the first day of an economics class, he burst out laughing at the professor's odd mannerisms and was expelled from class. He never returned, and consequently failed the course. His brother, Paco, enrolled in the same university in 1918 and sailed through his studies, earning stellar marks in every class.

Daunted by mandatory courses in such topics as civil, canonical, and administrative law, Lorca shunned the classroom and spent much of his time exploring Granada by himself or with a group of like-minded friends. He rarely prepared for class and seldom studied. He soon gained a reputation as a prankster in school, an inventor of nicknames. Only a handful of professors saw him as anything but a wayward dreamer with tousled black hair and a faraway gaze. The university's elderly librarian liked Lorca enough to let him spend hours in the library reading classical texts in lieu of the law books he had been assigned. Long after the building officially closed, the two men would sit together in the vast book-lined space overlooking the school's botanical gardens, reading and discussing literature.

Lorca also managed to impress Fernando de los Ríos, a distinguished young law professor who had joined the university faculty in 1911 at age thirty-three. While Federico was playing a Beethoven sonata one day at the Granada Arts Center, de los Ríos, then vice-president of the organization, happened to walk by and hear him. Struck by the teenager's skill, he introduced himself. Before long, Lorca was traipsing out to the professor's home, along with other young protégés, to talk about literature and to borrow books.

Fernando de los Ríos was a familiar sight in Granada. As he strode through the city in a top hat and morning coat, an assortment of young men often trailed behind. Occasionally the entourage would pause to browse in a bookstore or to buy *churros* before moving on to the professor's house, where his pupils helped themselves to books from Don Fernando's extensive private library. As unpretentious as he was kind, de los Ríos treated his students as peers. Through his "eloquence, wisdom, and honesty," as one of them remembered, he awakened his young disciples to the social and political issues of the day and taught them to be critical of provincial Spanish society.

De los Ríos regarded himself as a "spiritual grandson" of the eminent nineteenth-century educator Francisco Giner de los Ríos, a distant relative whose commitment to the renovation of Spanish education had led him in 1876 to found the unorthodox and influential Free Teaching Institution in

Madrid. This was a private secular school devoted to intuitive methods of instruction—discussions, field trips, tutorials, student papers—instead of authoritarian lectures and tests. The school's guiding pedagogical ethos, derived from the German philosopher Karl Christian Friedrich Krause, emphasized freedom of conscience and discussion, an ecumenical view of philosophy, and a pantheistic spirituality. Its graduates included some of the finest minds in Spain, among them the philosophers Miguel de Unamuno and José Ortega y Gasset. As a young man, Fernando de los Ríos had attended the Institution and come to embrace its liberal and anticlerical ideals. He subsequently studied in Germany and returned to Spain an avowed "European," inflamed by socialist thought and persuaded that his country's future depended on education.

He was a handsome man, with dark eyes and black hair, a mustache and goatee. A native Andalusian, he loved both Gypsy song, which he occasionally performed, and bullfights. He played the guitar, wrote, lectured, and was conversant in several languages, ancient as well as modern. He also engaged in politics. Shortly after settling in Granada in 1911, he founded the city's Socialist Party and boldly aligned himself with the working class in its struggle to end the region's corrupt political system, *caciquismo*, whereby local powerholders, or *caciques*, controlled political life, fixed elections, and obtained graft from political transactions. Many of Granada's more prominent citizens treated de los Ríos with contempt. "Respectable" women crossed the street to avoid him. His daughter, Laura, had difficulty finding playmates. One of the few children to befriend her was Lorca's sister Isabel, who became Laura's closest friend.

Although nearly twice their age, Don Fernando took both Federico and Francisco García Lorca under his wing, and counseled them on practical as well as philosophical and spiritual matters. He urged Paco to "listen" for his true vocation by heeding his "inner voice" and being true to himself. Lorca received similar advice. Despite the teenager's scholastic failings, de los Ríos admired Federico and did what he could to ease his passage through the university. He recognized Lorca's superb musical talent and encouraged him to pursue a career in the arts. He also nurtured his budding awareness of social injustice.

He believed in Lorca at a time when few others did—least of all his family. At school, his brother surpassed him in everything but music; lately, Paco had begun writing poetry and appeared to excel at that, too. At home, their father complained daily about Federico's lack of discipline and focus. "I don't know what's going to become of the boy," he grumbled to a sister-in-law. "He won't get anywhere like this." Even Vicenta Lorca had begun to fret.

Pushed toward an adulthood he neither wanted nor understood, Lorca took refuge in music and books, in long, often solitary walks, and in those rare teachers and friends who saw beyond his indolence. He missed the simplicity of life in the *vega*. Much as he loved Granada, he believed that by moving to the city he had forsaken his true and legitimate roots, had severed his bond with the people. He risked becoming an Andalusian *señorito*—a young man who wallows in his own pleasure and privilege. Whenever he visited Asquerosa, he felt like an outsider. "The children who were in my grade school are field-workers now, and when they see me they scarcely dare to touch me with those great stony hands of theirs, filthy from work," he brooded. Years later, reminiscing about his life at the University of Granada and his daily struggle against "the enormous mustachioed face of Mercantile Law," Lorca noted wistfully that his "life of fun and practical jokes" as a student had in fact concealed "a true but charitable melancholy."

CHAPTER 3

YOUNG SPANIARD

1915-16

The Alameda Café stood a few blocks from the Lorca home in the middle of Granada. Inside the café, the walls were mirrored and the music refined. Most evenings a piano and string quintet performed until midnight, at which point Federico sometimes took over the keyboard and played until dawn.

He met nightly in the Alameda with a group of friends who called themselves El Rinconcillo, "The Little Corner." Seated around marble-topped tables in a corner beneath a staircase, they listened to music and talked. Several members of the group were university students, who sought in these informal gatherings a more candid form of discourse than that available to them in the university's staid lecture halls. Within the Rinconcillo, Lorca and his friends traded anecdotes and books, sparred over ideas, criticized each other's work, debated the latest trends in literature and art, and discussed the progress of the Great War, then raging across Europe. All of them sided with the Allies. They fancied themselves bohemians. Of the dozen or so young men who belonged to the group, most, like Lorca, preferred Granada's lyrical sites to its classrooms, and thought nothing of forsaking their work to spend a sunny morning in the Alhambra or a moonlit night in the Albaicín, reading poems by Darío or listening to Gypsy song.

Both Lorca and his brother joined the Rinconcillo in their mid-teens, but while Paco resisted the group's more wayward tendencies, Lorca embraced them. It was the first set of friends with whom he had felt a genuine affinity since childhood, and he spent as much time with them as he could. His par-

ents despaired. Don Federico blamed the Rinconcillo for Lorca's growing
delinquency at school, and lectured them on their responsibility toward his
son. Vicenta Lorca likewise begged them to reform. "Why can't you just study
and let Federico study, too?" she pleaded. They ignored her. When Lorca
failed a grammar course, one of his Rinconcillo friends published a note in the
local newspaper reprimanding the university for its shameful treatment of an
outstanding student.

The Rinconcillo included two painters, a poet, and at least three local journalists. One of these, José Mora Guarnido, was in his late twenties when he
met Federico, who was seventeen at the time. At their first encounter, Lorca
wore a poorly knotted tie beneath a loose piqué collar and a black hat with a
brim so flimsy it fluttered in the wind like "a huge butterfly wing," Mora recalled. He noted Lorca's dark face and thick eyebrows, lustrous eyes, the delicate mole above his lip, and his smile, which was "full of kindness." Over
glasses of sweet Málaga wine, the two talked about Granada and found they
had much in common, including a shared contempt for artistic mediocrity and
bad taste, two sins of which, in their view, the city's painters and writers were
eminently culpable. Mora Guarnido had long used his clout as a reporter to
rail against pretension. In 1915, the year he met Lorca, he published, in collaboration with another Rinconcillo member, a slim work entitled *The Book of
Granada*, in which he called for a rediscovery of the authentic "Granadan
spirit."

During their first meeting, Lorca sat at a piano and idly ran his fingers over
the keyboard, producing, to Mora's mind, a "distant murmur that echoed our
words." The journalist realized he was in the presence of an uncommon talent—one capable, perhaps, of fulfilling the aims he had set forth in *The Book
of Granada*. He became one of Federico's most devoted fans. Not long after
they met, he inscribed a copy of his book for Lorca. "To my friend Federico
García Lorca," Mora wrote, "admirable interpreter of Granada's music, with all
the fervor and admiration I can muster."

Lorca received similar encouragement from another Rinconcillo journalist,
Melchor Fernández Almagro, a portly, good-natured young man whose
breadth of knowledge and prodigious memory prompted one friend to call him
a "living archive." A critic and historian as well as a reporter, "Melchorito," as
friends knew him, was five years older than Lorca. He was deeply impressed by
Lorca's musical gifts, and together with Mora Guarnido, regarded him as a
likely means of reviving Granada's ailing cultural life.

In their passion for Granada, both Fernández Almagro and Mora Guarnido echoed the late-nineteenth-century Granadan author Ángel Ganivet, whose small book *Granada the Beautiful* had inspired readers since its publication in 1896. Ganivet had committed suicide in 1898, furthering the notion of that year as a "disaster" in Spain's intellectual and political life. But his little book survived and became a clarion call to young men of Lorca's age and outlook. In *Granada the Beautiful*, Ganivet sketched a portrait of a Granada "that could and ought to exist," one where the old blended harmoniously with the new, and the local with the universal. He praised the city's humble, diminutive beauty—a sentiment Lorca endorsed—but decried Granada's ongoing "epidemic of expansion." He believed such innovations as electric lights and broad streets threatened the city's physical and spiritual well-being. Lorca shared this view, and later proclaimed Ganivet "the most illustrious *granadino* of the nineteenth century."

Ganivet belonged to the "Generation of '98," a circle of writers, scholars, and theorists whose informal alliance was born of the disillusionment that followed Spain's military defeat in 1898. In addition to Ganivet, the Generation included the philosopher Miguel de Unamuno, the poet Antonio Machado, the essayists Azorín and Ramiro de Maeztu, and the novelist Pío Baroja. All were politically and intellectually progressive, with strong ties to Giner de los Ríos's Free Teaching Institution in Madrid. All had spent their formative years in an atmosphere of pessimism and soul-searching sparked by the sense of despair and isolation that gripped Spain in the wake of the Spanish-American War. They came together as a generation to address what they viewed as the country's degeneration and decadence, and in their creative writings and political and social polemics they both analyzed and criticized the country's predicament. If Spain was to avoid slipping permanently into the realm of nations whose past grandeur outweighed their present and future achievement, something had to be done—spiritually as well as practically. Through their outspoken work, the Generation of '98 sought to define the essence of the Spanish soul, and in doing so to help bring about the spiritual and ideological regeneration of individual Spaniards, and, in turn, of Spain itself. Convinced that this could be achieved, in part, by invoking the past as a model for the future, several members of the Generation turned to the seventeenth-century story of Don Quixote as a framework for Spain's twentieth-century revitalization. Their ideals inspired Lorca and his friends in the Rinconcillo, who saw themselves as logical heirs to the older generation.

The young group launched a vigorous campaign to reform and revitalize Granada. They organized homages to overlooked artists from the city's past.

They talked of founding an avant-garde magazine, and openly scorned much of what passed for art in Granada. Despite his association with the institution, Lorca joined his Rinconcillo peers in attacking the Granada Arts Center, which the group perceived as a symbol of bourgeois pretension. Eventually, Lorca and two others from the Rinconcillo officially resigned from the Arts Center in protest against its provincial artistic "direction."

Increasingly, he saw himself as a visionary waging a noble fight for artistic purity. Thanks to his friends in the Rinconcillo, who praised his expertise on the piano, he also viewed himself as a serious musician and composer with a budding future. But at the university he continued to flounder. Except for one or two sympathetic teachers, no one on the faculty paid much attention to him. At home, he drifted further away from his parents. Matters came to a head each spring when he invariably failed one of his university exams, and his father was forced to postpone the family's annual seaside vacation in Málaga so that Federico could stay home and study.

In 1915, at the age of seventeen, Lorca took an art history course from Martín Domínguez Berrueta, a charismatic professor in his mid-forties, whose passion for his subject caught Federico by surprise and prompted him to reassess his attitude toward school. Lorca quickly fell under the man's spell. Like de los Ríos, Berrueta was one of a very few university professors who sought to breach the divide between faculty and students. He cultivated friendships with his pupils, invited them home to meet his wife and children, and took select groups of them on exhaustive trips through Spain. Devoted to art, he spoke enthusiastically to his classes about aesthetics. Lorca found him deeply inspiring. The two shared a romantic temperament and a sentimental view of the artist as a melancholy soul. Both loved Granada. Don Martín routinely took his students on outings to city monuments—a novel concept in Spanish education. At the same time, he recognized Granada's shortcomings, and in words familiar to Federico from the Rinconcillo, he decried Granada's "lazy atmosphere."

A small, headstrong man with a spare frame and a long, angular face, Berrueta was the author of more than half a dozen books, among them *Mysticism in Poetry* and *The Religious Problem from Within*. Obsessed with his mission as a teacher, he concerned himself with all aspects of his students' lives, including their love affairs. To those who challenged his ideas, he reacted furiously, his pointed gray beard flapping with indignation. His detractors thought him pompous and meddlesome. José Mora Guarnido despised Berrueta's "cheap histrionics and vanity," and tried to steer Lorca away from him. But Lorca dismissed his friend's warnings.

Twice yearly, in the hope that select students could experience life beyond the confines of provincial Granada and could "know and love Spain," Berrueta organized sightseeing expeditions to different regions of the country. The professor chose his travelers carefully, seeking those—such as Lorca—who were artistically or intellectually inclined, or who, as Mora Guarnido cynically concluded, were both skilled and docile enough to mimic Don Martín's aesthetic theories. In June 1916, one week after his eighteenth birthday, Lorca set out on the first of four expeditions he would make with Berrueta. His father paid his travel costs. The excursions permanently altered Lorca's perception of himself. "For the first time," he remembered years later, "I became fully aware of myself as a Spaniard."

He was one of six young men to accompany Berrueta on a weeklong journey through Andalusia that June. The group traveled north by train to the hill towns of Baeza and Úbeda, then west to Córdoba, and south to Ronda before returning home. Every day they set out before dawn for an arduous morning's tour of local monuments. In the evenings, Berrueta, and occasionally his students, gave lectures and informal talks to local hosts and dignitaries. Lorca sometimes played the piano.

Each student was expected to keep detailed notes on everything he saw and heard. Lorca applied himself to the task with unaccustomed zeal. On pages crowded with misspelled words and meandering lines, he logged his daily activities, noted the history of ancient sites, and traced the ancestry of Spanish kings and queens. He wrote exuberantly, his ear tuned to the melody and rhythm of words as if to music. In Baeza he observed rapturously, "Here among these golden stones, one is always drunk on romanticism." He described the town's cathedral as a "solemn black chord." Upon his return to Granada the following week, he read some of his notes to the Rinconcillo. His friends were startled by Federico's observant eye and unexpectedly graceful style.

He had until then remained intent on a career in music, and in recent weeks had become more than ever convinced of his calling. Shortly before his trip through Andalusia with Professor Berrueta, his beloved piano teacher, Antonio Segura Mesa, had died. Wishing to consecrate his life to his teacher's memory, Lorca had promptly asked his father to send him to Paris to study the piano. The landowner refused. Dismayed, Lorca turned impulsively toward a new vocation—one that would not require his father's financial endorsement. He later described this period in a brief, dispassionate autobiographical note: "Since his parents did not permit him to move to Paris in order to continue his initial studies, and his music teacher had died, García Lorca turned his (dramatic) pathetic creative zeal toward poetry." He never wholly reconciled himself to the choice. As an adult he once remarked, "Never in poetry will I be able to say as much as I would have said in music."

Berrueta became his new idol. The art history professor taught Lorca to write and introduced him to writers. During their visit to Baeza in the summer of 1916, Lorca met the poet Antonio Machado. Then forty-one, Machado was known throughout Spain for *The Castilian Country*, a collection of poems drawn from the poet's extended residence in central Spain. Published to wide acclaim in 1912, *The Castilian Country* revealed Machado's preoccupations with time, death, and the spiritual calm of childhood—issues that had begun to absorb Lorca.

As a member of Berrueta's ensemble, Lorca received a warm welcome from Machado. Whenever the art history professor visited Baeza, he and Machado engaged in long conversations and joint poetry recitals. During their brief visit in 1916, Lorca and his fellow students heard Machado read a selection of his verse as well as several poems by Rubén Darío. Following the reading, Lorca gave a short piano recital. His encounter with Machado so enthralled him that on returning to Granada he reenacted the episode for his parents, gravely imitating the poet's measured voice.

Machado exemplified Lorca's idea of a writer. A sad, reclusive man whose shabby black suit habitually bore traces of cigarette ash on its lapels, Machado had quietly observed the desolate landscapes of Castile and memorialized them in his poems. Born in Andalusia but educated at the Free Teaching Institution in Madrid, he had spent several years as a teacher in the small Castilian town of Soria. While there he married a beautiful woman in her teens. Their brief, blissful union ended in 1913 with his young wife's sudden death. Near mad with grief, Machado fled south to the isolated town of Baeza, where he took a job teaching secondary-school French and wrote mournful poems steeped in the Andalusian landscape. Neighbors grew accustomed to the sight of him roaming the streets alone like a vagrant. Sometimes Machado wandered fifteen miles of twisting road to the nearby town of Úbeda for a cup of coffee, then returned, on foot, to Baeza.

He described his poetry as a "borderline song," on the other side of which lay death. He resisted both artistic and intellectual fads, calmly drafting a body of work whose almost casual tempo and tone yield brief, surprising epiphanies. He was influenced by Hispanic *modernismo* but withstood its decadent excesses; he shunned free verse and avant-garde poetics. His work is marked by an acute consciousness of landscape and time, a subtle irony, and a receptiveness to both folklore and traditional verse and song—the latter a trait Machado acquired from his father, who collected popular Spanish folk songs and lore.

One of the most celebrated writers of his time, Machado spoke modestly of the poet as "a poor creature in a dream / groping for God perpetually in the mist." He viewed poetry as "neither hard and timeless marble, / nor painting nor music / but the word in time." Through verse he aimed to effect a "deep pulsing of spirit." His *The Castilian Country* offers a harsh critique of provincial Spanish life and a bleak assessment of the country's state of mind and role in history. Machado never fully resolved his ambivalence toward Spain.

By example, he taught Lorca to regard poetry as a melancholy medium and to view the poet's mission as a solitary one. When a new edition of Machado's *Complete Poems* appeared in 1917, Lorca borrowed a copy from a friend. Smitten by the collection, he drafted a seventy-nine-line poem that began, "In this book I would set down / my entire soul." With a purple pencil he copied the poem out in its entirety on the title page of his friend's book and signed his name at the bottom. The work conveys his understanding of the writer's task:

> The poet is the medium
> of Nature
> who explains her grandeur
> by means of words.
>
> The poet comprehends
> all that is incomprehensible,
> and it is he who calls things
> that despise each other, friends.
>
> He knows that every path
> is impossible, and thus
> he walks them calmly
> in the night.

Poetry "is the impossible / made possible," Lorca wrote. Not unlike music, it is the visible record of invisible desire, the mystery of the spirit made flesh, a mournful relic of what the artist once loved. "Poetry is the life / we traverse in anguish / awaiting the one who leads / our boat adrift."

Lorca made his second trip with Professor Berrueta in October 1916. This time the group traveled to northern Spain—to Machado's Castile, and from there to Galicia. The excursion lasted twenty-one days and included stops in Madrid, Ávila, Burgos, and Berrueta's hometown of Salamanca.

Like Machado, Lorca was transfixed by Castile, and in his journal described the region's windswept fields as "all red, all kneaded with the blood of Abel and Cain." Its towns were "full of melancholy charms, memories of tragic loves." Throughout the trip Lorca kept a record of his impressions in which he blended fact with emotional fancy. He sprinkled his prose with musical terms. Of his arrival in Ávila he wrote, "There were few stars in the sky, and the wind was slowly glossing the infinite melody of the night."

In Ávila, the group traced the route of Saint Teresa and received special permission to tour the cloistered convent where the sixteenth-century mystic had lived and worked. A veiled nun led them through the building, sounding a bell in order to warn the other sisters of the group's approach. Lorca could scarcely subdue his curiosity. In a letter to his parents he explained that he and his friends "took photographs of the nuns on the sly (they didn't want us to). It was a real coup." In the midst of the tour, Professor Berrueta told Federico to cut tiny splinters from "everything the Saint used," so that he could take souvenirs of Teresa home with him to Granada.

That evening, Berrueta gave a lecture on art at a local school and arranged for a few of his students to do the same. Luis Mariscal, a plump teenager known for his academic prowess, spoke on "artistic cities." Lorca talked briefly about Andalusian music, then played the piano. The next day *El Diario de Ávila* praised the "young musician," suggesting that his piano composition "Albaicín" proved him a worthy heir to Isaac Albéniz. Someone copied the long article by hand onto six separate sheets of paper and mailed the account home to Lorca's parents.

He received similar notices in both Santiago de Compostela and Burgos, where the weather was so cold that his face and lips became chapped. "But I'm stronger and more agile, and I must have gained two or three kilos, so clearly this suits me," he assured his parents. Throughout the three-week journey he sent letters and telegrams to his family and telephoned them at prearranged times. He repeatedly asked his father to wire him more money. From Ávila he complained that his funds were "dwindling" because he was spending money on souvenirs; in Burgos the story was the same.

"I'm in Salamanca extremely happy this is beautiful I'm visiting monuments," he informed his family by telegram soon after reaching the ancient university town where Professor Berrueta had been born and later taught. Lorca basked in his teacher's attentions and strove hard to please him. Berrueta is more like "an eighteen-year-old boy" than a middle-aged man, he told his parents. "He runs, he laughs, he sings with us, and he treats us as equals . . . I am delighted." In Salamanca, the professor took his students on a silent tour of the city and introduced them to his friend and former colleague Miguel de Unamuno, professor of Greek language and literature at the University of Salamanca and its former rector. An essayist, poet, novelist, playwright, and philosopher of international renown, Unamuno, at fifty-two, was the leading member of the Generation of '98 and one of the most brilliant men of his time. His square face, aquiline nose, and round, wire-rimmed spectacles gave him the appearance of a vigilant owl. Antonio Machado referred to him as the rector "not only of Salamanca" but of Spain itself.

Although he left no record of his meeting with Unamuno in 1916, within two years of the encounter Lorca eagerly recommended the professor's work to friends. He underlined a number of passages in his copy of Unamuno's *Essays*, and inside the book wrote:

> At the crossroads of blurred death
> I will be quiet and sweet,
> singing my song.
> And my intense bitterness
> for my fruitless life
> will be like the sunsets of Autumn.

At eighteen, Lorca was beginning to grapple with the same topics that had beset Unamuno in his youth. Despite a deeply pious Catholic upbringing, the philosopher had undergone a profound spiritual crisis in adolescence and eventually lost what he called the "serene intuition" of his childhood faith. In his controversial 1913 book, *The Tragic Sense of Life*, Unamuno explored the human fixation on death, noting its close bonds with love, and questioned the existence of God. Stirred by what he had seen on his travels — in particular, the sight of so many veiled nuns in Ávila who had consecrated their physical and spiritual lives to Christ — Lorca found himself similarly plagued by doubt. Like Unamuno, he resolved to gauge his uncertainty through writing.

By the time he returned home in early November 1916, his life had subtly shifted course, and Lorca knew it. On the night of October 15, 1917 — precisely one year from the date he had left Granada with Berrueta to tour Castile — he scribbled a note to himself: "One year since I sallied forth toward the good of literature." In his poem "Proverbs and Song-Verse," first published in *The Castilian Country* in 1912, Antonio Machado articulated the challenge as well as the predicament facing those of Lorca's generation:

Think of it: a Spaniard
wanting to live, starting in
with a Spain on one side of him dying
and a Spain all yawns on the other.
Young Spaniard entering the world,
may God preserve you.
One of these two Spains
will make your blood run cold.

CHAPTER 4

CRUCIBLE

1917-18

⁓

Late at night, after his family had gone to bed, Lorca wrote. He worked compulsively, crowding his thoughts onto small sheets of paper. Often the sun was rising when he stopped. "Another day," he observed at the end of an essay. "Jesus! Let the star of your soul descend upon mine so that I can be with you forever. Dawn is breaking. Already I can see it growing light."

His early writings were a beginner's passionate efforts to find a subject and a voice. Many works took the form of Augustinian confessions or prayers in which Lorca strove to decipher his feelings toward God and toward his fellow human beings, especially women. Quintessentially romantic, his writings were filled with an adolescent thirst for spiritual purity, for oneness with nature and reconciliation with society. Lorca saw himself as an artist in search of beauty but trapped by the vulgar reality of everyday life. "Am I to blame for having a heart, and for having been born among people interested only in comfort and money?" he asked, overlooking the fact that it was his father's money that made it possible for him to indulge his fantasies. At home and in school he cultivated a romantic pose. Acquaintances took note of his "strange opinions," his unkempt clothes, unruly hair, and sorrowful eyes.

He drew on a variety of sources: romanticism, symbolism, Hispanic *modernismo*, Catholic liturgy, and above all music, which he, like Verlaine, considered a more perfect art than literature. Through writing, he sought to achieve the condition of music. He applied musical terms and titles to his works, and structured a number of early writings according to musical tempi and forms. The result was an often clumsy mingling of the arts. In this, and in his fondness for exotic imagery and florid language, he was deeply influenced by Rubén Darío, and to a lesser extent by the Spanish poet Juan Ramón Jiménez. Although years later Lorca would gently flout Darío's "delightful bad taste and his shameless use of excessive poetic phrasing," he prized these qualities in his teens.

Because it lacked the formal constraints of both poetry and drama, and therefore freed him to give full vent to his feelings, Lorca turned first to prose, and in a series of nearly forty meditations entitled, variously, "Emotional States," "Altarpieces," and "Mystical Writings," he tried to fathom the jumble of sensations that gripped him in adolescence. He wrote compulsively about sex, women, God, sorrow, love, and the bittersweet loss of his childhood innocence. He proclaimed his scorn for the Catholic Church and its suppression of human instinct. He described his contempt for the Old Testament God and his corresponding love for Jesus, with whom he clearly identified. "When will my carnal Calvary end?" he pleaded. His soul-searching accounts built on his youthful readings of works as disparate as the Bible, Saint Teresa's *Life*, Unamuno's essays, Hindu philosophy, the poems of Saint John of the Cross, the *Rubáiyát of Omar Khayyám* (which he read in a Spanish translation from the Persian original), and Wilde's *De Profundis*.

Like the Spanish mystics and his *modernista* idols, Lorca yearned to reconcile his erotic and spiritual selves. Sex was a demon that prevented his pure self—"my spirit, which is me"—from prospering. "From on high, my spirit contemplates my body's actions, and I become two during the great sacrifice of semen." He convinced himself that he was in love with women. But it was the idea of woman he loved, not flesh-and-blood women themselves. By day he indulged in unrequited crushes on his pretty young Granadan neighbors, to whom he occasionally read his work. By night he imagined himself being kissed by a woman in white, with "lips that burn," her bare legs girded by turquoise snakes, her breasts so large they drowned him.

Intrigued by homoeroticism, he drafted a fictive dialogue between Sappho and Plato in which he explored the ancient Greek notion that all kinds of love are permissible. About his own sexuality, he was both naive and ambivalent. Although he craved carnal experience, it repulsed him. He spoke wistfully of his desire "to be a flower . . . and to enjoy the reproductive act in a spiritual way." He vacillated between a passive wish to remain celibate and an aggressive need to flaunt his virility. "An exotic and distant virgin and a muscular and powerful man dance together inside me," he confessed in a prose text on Pierrot, a favorite modernist emblem of poetic fantasy, a figure Lorca claimed he resembled "most of the time." As he aged, he would return often to the image of Pierrot, the mournful clown whose contradictory nature both reflected and revealed the dichotomies in his own personality.

In page after page of ornate schoolboy script, Lorca dramatized his plight. At nineteen, he complained of being old. Viewed from a distance of only twelve years and as many miles, his *vega* boyhood came to signify a lost paradise, a transcendent era when the world, as he remembered it, had been good and whole. In "My Village," a sentimental attempt at an autobiography, he recalled the "quiet, fragrant little village" of Fuente Vaqueros, where he had been born and where he hoped to die. "Its streets, its people, its customs, its poetry, and its evil are the scaffolding where my childhood ideas once took shape and then melted in the crucible of puberty."

"My Village" includes a lengthy account of the final illness, death, and funeral of one of Lorca's closest boyhood friends, a fifty-five-year-old man known as Compadre Pastor, or "Shepherd Godfather." During Compadre Pastor's burial, Federico, then seven, had glimpsed his friend's body in its casket. Recalling the scene twelve years later, Lorca described the dead man's rigid form, his folded hands, the silk handkerchief that hid his decaying face. The episode proved to Lorca that death was neither a liberation, nor a transition to some new phase of existence, but the complete physical annihilation of life. Unamuno had reached the same conclusion in *The Tragic Sense of Life*, a work whose blunt admission of doubt helped fuel Lorca's growing agnosticism.

Neither he nor Unamuno romanticized death. But Lorca did romanticize his friendship with Compadre Pastor. The dead man, a former shepherd, epitomized everything Lorca had lost at puberty: virtue, harmony with nature, the unconditional love of his parents and friends. Compadre Pastor was an "angel come down from heaven," a hero, a saint. At night, the young Federico used to sit in his lap and listen to Compadre Pastor tell stories, until the boy fell asleep and was carried to his mother, "who pressed me against her bosom and covered me with kisses." "My poor Compadre Pastor," Lorca reminisced. "You were the one who made me love Nature. You were the one who shed light on my heart."

Vicenta Lorca nurtured her son's dreams of a writing career. Some years later, in a confidential letter, she suggested to him that the "things" he had written in adolescence were "beautiful" and ought to be more widely known. "If all this is a secret, well and good. But if not, tell me and no one else. Write a little note and I'll keep it to myself and not show it to anyone."

His father was more practical. "Good God!" the landowner sputtered when told that his oldest son intended to become a writer. "Imagine trying to earn a living writing poetry!" He warned Lorca to expect failure. Don Federico's own uncle Baldomero, a gifted but unsuccessful poet and minstrel, had ended his days roaming the *vega* in poverty, dependent for survival on family charity. "You're just going to turn into another Baldomero!" Don Federico accused his son.

"If only I could!" Lorca said.

Determined to prove himself, Lorca published his first work in February 1917, four months after sallying forth "toward the good of literature." A vignette of the nineteenth-century Granadan poet José Zorrilla, the piece appeared in a special edition of the Granada Arts Center bulletin, published on the centenary of Zorrilla's birth. In contrast to the more conventional essays submitted by others, Lorca contributed a short, highly romantic dialogue entitled "Symbolic Fantasy," in which a variety of elements—among them a bell, a river, and the spirit of Zorrilla himself—pay homage to the city of Granada.

A few months later, in early summer, Lorca embarked on another of Professor Berrueta's Andalusian tours. In Baeza, he overcame his earlier reserve and confessed to Antonio Machado his love of poetry and music. The poet thought Lorca like "a young olive tree." Machado admired the teenager's piano playing, and took mental note of their encounter. Later in the evening Lorca and his fellow travelers went for a moonlit stroll through town. Seized by the poetry of the setting, Federico dramatically "baptized" the group with imaginary, "moon-filled water" from a dry fountain in the cathedral square. His companions marveled at his ability to turn an ordinary occasion into a moment of pure lyricism.

While in Baeza, Lorca renewed his acquaintance with a young man named Lorenzo Martínez Fuset, whom he had met the previous year during his first visit to the town. The two had subsequently struck up a correspondence. Thin and dark-haired, with delicate features and a pensive smile, Martínez Fuset aspired to a writing career and for a time labored on a novel he intended to dedicate to Lorca. He was certain that no one understood or loved him. "I want a friendship, one friendship, yours alone," he told Federico. Despite this bold assertion, Martínez Fuset claimed to be in love with a girl named Lina, while Lorca carried on about a variety of young women. Together the two struggled to make sense of the female sex. Martínez Fuset once urged Federico to visit him in Baeza so that, among other things, they could talk about "woman. She is lovely because we spiritualize her . . . But she is inherently dirty, her ele-ments are lustful and black, and her menstrual periods diminish her in my eyes. Nevertheless, I revere women, I love them."

Neither man had any genuine understanding of the female sex. Both had grown up in a largely segregated society, separated from girls in school and at church, taught to assume gender-specific roles, told to prize virginity, and left to speculate about the physical and emotional realities of women's lives. Lorca's few friendships with young women were confined largely to long walks and conversations about art. In late 1916 he became infatuated with a young neighbor in Granada named Amelia, who shared his interest in poetry and re-portedly read him "her dramas and stories." But nothing came of their friend-ship.

By the summer of 1917, he had abandoned his quest for Amelia and taken up a new love, a pretty blonde named María Luisa Egea González, who enjoyed playing duets with Lorca on the piano in his parents' living room. Her very name inspired him. "And I, like the saints / love only María," he declared. Martínez Fuset teased Lorca about his prowess as a "*Don Juan!*" and urged him to renounce his "schoolboy scruples," to love Mariá "without timidity, without that monastic reserve that impedes and diverts you." But María Luisa ignored what overtures he was able to muster and Lorca despaired. He longed to retreat from puberty, to crawl back in time to the sanctity and safety of child-hood. "Let the goblet of my semen / spill over and empty completely," he wrote in an early poem.

> I want to be like a child
> rosy and silent,
> who, in the ermine thighs
> of his loving mother,
> can listen to a star
> speaking with God.

In July 1917, Lorca set out on the fourth, and last, of his cultural expeditions with Domínguez Berrueta. This time the group toured Castile, with a brief visit to Madrid and a prolonged stay in the city of Burgos, where they spent three hours every day writing up their notes in libraries and archives. Lorca pol-ished his observations with an eye toward publication. He and fellow student Luis Mariscal each published several articles in rival Burgos dailies. Lorca's first effort, an elliptical description of a visit to a local convent, appeared on Au-gust 3. An accompanying note informed readers that the article was adapted from a book "under preparation, *Long Romantic Walks through Old Spain*, with a prologue by Señor Berrueta."

The group's itinerary in Burgos included an overnight stay in the remote monastery of Silos, south of the city. Lorca spent the night in a white room with a single bed, a table, and a crucifix. As he lay in bed in the dark, he heard dogs barking. Their howls filled him with "intense fear," and he felt the presence of death. By morning his terror had passed, and he was able to enjoy the "tragically solemn theatricality" of High Mass and the beauty of the monks' Gregorian chant.

After Mass he spoke to the organist, a monk who had spent most of his life in the monastery. To his astonishment, Lorca learned that the man, an able musician, had never heard of Beethoven. Impulsively, Federico sat down at the organ and played a passage from the Allegretto of the composer's Seventh Symphony, a movement Lorca regarded as a "work of superhuman grief." During his performance, a second monk came quietly into the organ loft and hid his face beneath his hands. Deeply moved, he begged Lorca to keep playing. Shaken by this unexpected confrontation between plainsong and romanticism, between the spirit and the flesh, Lorca's memory failed him. Later, when the second monk had regained his composure, he cautioned Federico against a life in music. "It is lust itself," the man warned. Lorca found the remark both intriguing and sad. But the encounter merely reinforced his devotion to art.

Nearly a month into their Castilian tour, three of the students on Berrueta's trip returned home to Granada. Lorca remained alone in Burgos with his professor during August. He was the only student whose father was able to afford the additional month's expense. His parents were pleased with the progress Lorca had shown during his travels. "Father says for you to get three or four more newspapers like the one you sent, because your uncles are eager to have copies," his mother wrote after receiving one of Lorca's published articles. She asked if he had a good hat and enough warm clothing for the city's cool climate. She missed him intensely.

In Burgos, Lorca continued to write. He published two articles in August, the first a descriptive account of a Castilian inn—part of his forthcoming book on "Old Spain"—and the second a reflective essay entitled "Rules in Music," in which he examined a number of issues that would continue to engage him for years: the rules of creative expression, the role of the critic, the profound unity of the various arts, and the relationship between an artist and his public. Rules, Lorca argued, are created chiefly for the mediocre. While it is important to learn rules at the outset of one's career, ultimately an artist must discard them, because art springs from the soul, not from some preexisting code. "How are you going to lock one person's heart inside a prison belonging to somebody else?" He cited the example of his idols—Beethoven, Wagner, Darío—men who had broken the rules and triumphed because of it. By implication he counted himself among them.

He was certain of his power and promise as an artist. More so than his three previous expeditions with Professor Berrueta, his tour of Castile in 1917 confirmed Lorca's determination to write. During the trip he saw his name in print not once but several times, an intoxicating experience for any beginner. While in Burgos he enjoyed the undivided attention of his teacher, and he basked in his parents' praise. He emerged from his monthlong visit newly persuaded of his extraordinary talent, and keen to publish his first book. Some years later he told a friend that whenever he thought of Burgos, tears overcame him. "For the cathedral's gray towers of air and silver showed me the narrow door through which I had to pass in order to know myself and to know my soul . . . My heart will never again be so alive, so full of pain and eternal grace."

The pain he referred to stemmed in part from another infatuation. In Burgos, Lorca evidently fell in love with a girl whose cool response so crushed him that at the end of August he fled the city, and in a melodramatic display of emotion went directly home to Granada. He refused to stop in Madrid, where his friend José Fernández-Montesinos had been expecting him. Montesinos responded calmly to Lorca's histrionics. "I suppose all this is a consequence of your emotional state," he wrote. "Your hasty departure portends an unhappy outcome, and if that's the case, I sympathize with you."

At home, Lorca's friends were equally solicitous. "Are you grieving, sad?" Lorenzo Martínez Fuset asked. "Then come to my fountain and refuge." Lorca resolved instead to heed Beethoven's example and transform his grief into art.

By the time Lorca rejoined his family late in the summer, his parents had moved into a new home in the center of Granada, a roomy apartment overlooking one of the city's most fashionable promenades, the Acera del Casino. Cheerfully decorated with flowered wallpaper and slipcovered furniture, the apartment remained the family's primary residence for the next decade.

Lorca settled into his new surroundings and began work almost immediately on a novel, "Friar Antonio (Strange Poem)," about a "romantic" man whose sexual torment impels him to enter a monastery. In the wake of his recent visits to Castilian convents and monasteries, Lorca was drawn to the idea of monkhood. Initially he saw it as a refuge from both society and the anguish of sexual desire, and for a time he apparently considered it for himself, to such an extent

that he studied San Juan Clímaco's *The Spiritual Ladder,* a treatise outlining
the route to perfect monkhood. But in the end Lorca loved the world too much
to renounce it, and he came to view monasticism as an unhealthy subversion of
carnal instinct.

He completed fifty pages of "Friar Antonio," then abandoned the novel. Narrative was not his medium. By the summer of 1917 he had begun to experiment
with both poetry and drama, frequently in combination with one another or
with prose. By mixing genres he sought to tap deeper wells of creativity. Increasingly, he thought of himself as a poet. He wrote his first poem a few weeks
after his nineteenth birthday. Within a year his output was so prolific that a
friend referred to him in a book dedication as "the *poet,*" underlined twice. "I
am a poet and cannot help it," Lorca told his family and friends. Even his
handwriting changed. As if liberated by verse, it grew looser, more careless than
the large, curling script he had cultivated in prose.

From the start, he conceived of poetry as music. When he read his poems to
others, he drew his hands through the air, stretching and modulating individual lines of verse, playing "with a word as if it were an accordion," a friend remembered. He did not commit himself to a rigorous study of metrics, but
instead picked up the "mysteries of prosody" from conversations with his Rinconcillo friend José Fernández-Montesinos, a scholar of literature. Lorca was
timid about showing his poems to Montesinos and generally reluctant to publish his verse—not so much because he feared public disapproval but because
he believed that poetry was first and foremost an oral art. When even close
friends asked him for copies of his poems, he often turned them down.

He believed that "poetry" and "melancholy" belonged to the same "kingdom." He said he could not conceive "of any kind of poetry but lyric." Thematically, his first poems were indistinguishable from his prose. Throughout
1917 and 1918, Lorca's verse dwelt on his ongoing, increasingly desperate search
for love. Consumed by desire, he spoke of his "tragic weddings / without bride
or altar." He asked pointedly why "the roses that smell of woman / wither at my
slow sob?" His poems suggest that by early 1918 Lorca was on the verge of an
emotional breakdown. Sometime that spring Lorenzo Martínez Fuset complained that Lorca had become as "sensualized" as a mindless animal, and he
begged him to cease his "amorous ravings."

In late April 1918, a month short of his twentieth birthday, Federico wrote:
"The spring of my life, / perhaps the last one . . ." The following month he
again referred obliquely to suicide: "My life / wants to sink in the channel's /
sweet song." He felt old beyond his years. His plump face was becoming

more angular, and he had dark whiskers. He sensed life slipping inexorably through his grasp. "What a huge sorrow / it is to be young, but not to be!" he exclaimed.

Shortly after returning from Castile in the late summer of 1917, Lorca had announced to his family that he intended to bring out a book, and had asked his father to defray the costs of publication. His Rinconcillo friends endorsed the project, and immediately began offering advice. They urged Lorca to rid his writing of Professor Berrueta's overblown romantic style, and Lorca complied, reworking various passages of his book to include negative remarks about artworks that in Berrueta's company he had once admired.

His father meanwhile debated the merits of publication. He cornered Lorca's friend José Mora Guarnido on the street one night and demanded to know what the journalist thought of his son's writing. "As I'm sure you'll understand, I don't mind wasting one or two thousand pesetas to give him the pleasure of publishing a book. It would cost me more if he asked for an automobile or something worse," the landowner said, chewing on a cigar. "But I don't want every idiot in Granada laughing at him because of the book." He worried in particular that his cronies in the town casino would mock his son's "little poems." Mora assured him that Lorca's book was worthy of publication.

Still skeptical, Don Federico consulted others: Professor Berrueta, Fernando de los Ríos, the editor of the local newspaper, Lorca's grade school teacher. All agreed that Lorca had talent and deserved a chance. In the end, his father yielded. Arrangements were made with a local press to print the book, and Lorca began assembling a manuscript. The work he had originally envisioned, however, an assortment of essays culled from the material he'd written while traveling with Berrueta, was too sparse. To pad the book he dashed off several additional impressions about Granada as well as a series of lyrical "Themes," some of which he extracted from his prose meditations. By the time he delivered his first chapters to the printer in late 1917 or early 1918, Lorca was still rushing to complete his manuscript.

He gave a public reading from his forthcoming book at the Granada Arts Center on March 17, 1918. Two weeks later he received his first bound copy of *Impressions and Landscapes*, as he had chosen to title the book. The next day he began signing copies for family and friends. He approached the task with gravity. "To my great friend Antonio, delicate and sentimental, who dreams

with his flesh overflowing in another, distant flesh," read one of his more opulent inscriptions.

Impressions and Landscapes received two local reviews. Critic Aureliano del
Castillo, of the *Defensor de Granada*, hailed the book's skill and sincerity, despite its syntactical errors and what del Castillo called its "unnecessary trivialities." Luis de Luna, of the literary journal *El Éxito*, termed the work a "portrait
of the artist, with his desires, his anathemas, his aspirations, and his dreams of
Art and Poetry." Luna, who knew Lorca personally, described him as a man so
deeply preoccupied with life's graver issues that he often neglected to "comb
his hair and knot his tie."

Like its author, *Impressions and Landscapes* was rambling and unkempt.
Grammatical, syntactical, and punctuation errors littered the text. The narrative itself consists of a loosely structured sequence of travel essays followed by a
series of random prose meditations. The book's cover, an art nouveau illustration designed by one of Lorca's Rinconcillo friends, shows a framed painting of
a landscape beside a floor lamp and a spider's web. The image suggests the
work's prevailing motif: the Spanish landscape, illuminated by the author's soul
and ravaged by time. But the book's underlying subject is art. Where does it exist? How is it made? What comprises it? Building on ideas he had set forth the
previous summer in "Rules in Music," Lorca argues in *Impressions and Landscapes* for an art derived from the soul and founded on personal sentiment.
"Poetry exists in all things, in the ugly, in the beautiful, in the repugnant," he
advises in the book's prologue. "The difficult thing is knowing how to discover
it, how to awaken the deep wells of the soul."

From both Domínguez Berrueta and the romantics, Lorca had learned to
interpret existence by applying his own feelings and senses to things. Throughout *Impressions and Landscapes* he filters the Spanish countryside through his
consciousness, so that, as Luis de Luna observed, the work is less a portrait of a
place than of the artist as a young man. Lorca understood this and warned
readers that the book's scenes are more accurately "passionate internal states"
than objective renderings of external reality.

Acutely aware of the book's flaws and of its overall insignificance to Spanish
literature, Lorca spoke of the work's "vagueness" and "melancholy," qualities
that owe as much to the book's sources as to his own sensibility. Most of *Impressions and Landscapes* is derivative, an amalgam of romanticism, symbolism, and Hispanic *modernismo*, tempered by a keenly felt social consciousness
whose most immediate inspiration is the Generation of '98. In his haphazard
attempts to paint an emotional and geographical portrait of Spain, Lorca was

trying on styles, seeking a voice. His descriptions of Castile borrow thematically and stylistically from Machado and Unamuno. A section on "Gardens" draws heavily on Darío and Jiménez. The book is a miscellany of voices and styles. Passages of intense introspection follow mannered accounts of regional customs and scenes. Pedantic critiques of monuments alternate with lyrical, often synesthetic impressions of sunsets, landscapes, and mood. Musical terminology and references to Lorca's favorite composers fill the text.

His first book reveals far less about the author's public travels through Spain than about his private obsessions: the destructive powers of time and death, the constraints of faith, the lure of sex. Recounting his visits to Castilian monasteries, Lorca imagines the frustrations of monks and nuns who have renounced the flesh, and he questions their sexual identity. He recoils at the sight of a pair of crudely masculine monks with coarse hands who press their lips to the Holy Sacrament, but at the same time he derides a male passenger in a carriage who sighs with "monklike effeminacy." He celebrates the carnal. In a markedly bacchanalian episode whose imagery is rooted in both popular tradition and classical mythology, Lorca describes a group of village women bathing in a river while young men watch from some nearby underbrush. "Nature hopes for a gigantic copulation," he writes. "The young men roll about among the flowers and the elder as they see a girl emerge from the water, naked, her breasts erect."

Reviewing *Impressions and Landscapes*, Aureliano del Castillo noted that its exuberant young author was only nineteen years old. The critic predicted that before two years had passed, the stylistic excesses and "tiny blemishes" that mar the volume "will have disappeared from his work. The cleansing of style, like the cleansing of color, is the final phase in the artist's formation." Despite its faults, Lorca's first book announced his presence as a writer and introduced the issues that would dominate his subsequent work. To Lorca, the volume served as a tangible symbol of his conversion from musician to writer. He assumes a number of guises in the book: poet, teacher, social critic, playwright, and, above all, romantic. The narrator of *Impressions and Landscapes* is a melodramatic figure, a modern-day Quixote in search of the impossible. Oppressed by society and by the needs of his flesh, enamored of nature and beauty, haunted by the past, he seeks a spiritual and aesthetic absolute that persists in eluding him.

His primary mode is elegiac. He longs in vain for what is absent or lost, for what cannot be named. He is painfully aware that he will never fulfill his quest "for something spiritual or beautiful to ease our soul from its principal sorrow.

We go bounding off in search of an impossible happiness . . . But we almost never find it." The object of human desire changes constantly. Its essence, Lorca writes, "is immutable."

Shortly after the book's publication, Lorca took a signed copy of *Impressions and Landscapes* to Martín Domínguez Berrueta. The small, gray-haired man opened the volume and glanced inside. Suddenly he hurled the book at Lorca and ordered the teenager to leave his house. Two weeks later, Berrueta returned the volume to Lorca with a curt note explaining that although it grieved him to act with such "violence," he did not wish to keep the book in his possession.

He had expected that Lorca would dedicate *Impressions and Landscapes* to him. But Lorca had instead consecrated the book to "the venerable memory" of another man, his former piano teacher, Antonio Segura Mesa. Berrueta was furious. His own name appeared just once in the book, in a brief afterword where Lorca paid tribute to his "dear teacher D. Martín D. Berrueta" and the "dear companions" who had accompanied him on his travels. Otherwise there was no mention of the professor whose expeditions had in large part enabled Lorca to write *Impressions and Landscapes*.

His traveling companions were shocked. They rebuked Lorca for his selfishness, reminding him that it wasn't Berrueta who had accompanied Lorca on his journeys, but Lorca who had accompanied Berrueta. Worse, he had neglected to ask the professor to contribute a prologue to the book, as originally planned, and in a number of passages had callously challenged Berrueta's cherished ideas about art. Not long after the book's publication, Lorca further snubbed the professor by evidently contributing to some derisive remarks about him in a local newspaper. These "domestic flatteries," as Berrueta called them, were the final straw that drove him to sever all ties with Lorca.

Berrueta and his wife mourned the rupture, as did Lorca's parents. But Lorca was impenitent. Berrueta was merely a critic of art, not an artist, and in his quest for greatness Lorca sought to identify himself with the latter. He wanted to follow in the footsteps not of a teacher but of a genuine creator—an artist like his former piano teacher, Segura Mesa, a disciple of Verdi, a dreamer who despite the failure of his work had never compromised or abandoned his dreams. That his choice might devastate Berrueta did not concern Lorca. He was blinded by ambition.

The two men never reconciled. Two years later, at age fifty-one, Martín Domínguez Berrueta died. As an adult Lorca took pains to express in public the debt he owed Berrueta. In private, he confided to the professor's son that he regretted the events of 1918. "I'll never forgive myself," he said.

Besides its principal dedication to Antonio Segura Mesa, five chapters in *Impressions and Landscapes* bore dedications to Lorca's friends. Among them were María Luisa Egea González, the young blonde from Granada with whom he remained infatuated, and his devoted admirer in Baeza, Lorenzo Martínez Fuset, who promptly launched a one-man campaign to promote the book. In Baeza, Martínez Fuset spoke about Lorca's book to Antonio Machado, who expressed a desire to see the work. After scrutinizing the text, Machado advised Lorca, through Martínez Fuset, to "abandon his law studies, since being an artist entails separation, the breaking of Harmony, and divorce from the systematic." The older poet also urged Lorca to prove himself outside his hometown. "One's first successes ought to be measured in places where it's harder to triumph."

Lorca was quick to heed at least some of Machado's advice. He took no university exams in the spring of 1918, and the following autumn dropped out of school completely. His breach with Berrueta had intensified his dislike of the university, and he saw no need to continue. Besides, he had other, more useful teachers. In addition to Machado, Miguel de Unamuno perused *Impressions and Landscapes* and, according to Lorca, published an insightful review of the book. "No one has taught me as much about my art as Unamuno did on that occasion," Lorca said later of the review, whose existence has never been proven.

At the end of *Impressions and Landscapes*, Lorca listed his forthcoming works. They included a volume of poems, which he falsely claimed was "at press," as well as a series of books "in preparation." Some of these existed; some did not. Lorca drew no distinction between the two: to conceive of a work was to create it. "Whenever he found himself with a friend," a colleague remembered, "he'd discover a new project, he'd invent his next tragedy."

CHAPTER 5

DEBUT

1918-20

On June 5, 1918, Lorca turned twenty. He could no longer fend off adulthood or, with it, the possibility of death. Three days after his birthday he learned that one of his childhood friends, a young man his age, had died. That evening Lorca wrote a poem in his friend's memory. All summer long he thought about death, a process fueled in part by contemporary events. By fall, the worst flu epidemic in history had struck Europe, afflicting 150,000 people in Spain alone. Within a year the so-called Spanish flu had claimed twenty million victims worldwide. In France, the disease assailed a country already ravaged by four years of trench warfare—a murderous deadlock that killed, maimed, or wounded nearly half of those who took part in it. "One eats, one drinks beside the dead, one steps in the midst of the dying, one laughs and one sings in the company of corpses," wrote French surgeon Georges Duhamel in the midst of the Battle of Verdun, which lasted ten months and claimed more than 700,000 lives.

The Granada press issued daily reports of the fighting, as it had since the outbreak of war in 1914. By September 1918, Allied soldiers, having stemmed repeated German attempts to advance, were on the verge of rupturing the once-impregnable Hindenburg Line. In Berlin, starving citizens sifted through heaps of garbage in search of potato rinds.

In early September Lorca wrote a poem, "Dawn of the Twentieth Century," in which he described war as the "failure of the soul / and the failure of God." He believed the world had lost both its innocence and its faith, had entered a brutal new era: "Dawn! Ancient hour of Apollo. / Today it is the hour of Horror." On November 11, jubilant crowds poured into the streets of Granada to celebrate the signing of the Armistice. Two days later Lorca attended a tea in honor of the Allies. Among his fellow guests was Fernando de los Ríos, who earlier in the week had given a speech extolling the League of Nations and calling for an end to the Spanish monarchy as well as a suspension of the military's power in Spain.

Lorca shared de los Ríos's contempt for the monarchy and his distrust of the military. The matter was more than theoretical. At twenty, Lorca was eligible for service in the Spanish army and, like thousands of his compatriots, at risk of being sent to Morocco to defend the Spanish protectorate against tribal attacks. In the aftermath of the country's humiliating defeat in 1898, and the loss of its remaining colonies, Spain's young king, Alfonso XIII, had sought to salvage the army's honor by dispatching thousands of troops to Spanish Morocco, the nation's last remaining field of military action, where they took part in an endless and deadly series of cleanup operations in the Atlas mountains. Because military duty in Spain was at the time a class affair, Lorca's parents were able to purchase his freedom from service by arranging for a local doctor to pronounce him "totally unfit" for the army. The physician noted that besides problems in his legs, chest, and "light symptoms of spinal sclerosis," "Youth Number 63" (who measured thirty-four inches around the chest and stood five-foot-seven) possessed legs of somewhat uneven length—hence his slight limp. The report spared Lorca from combat.

But it did not shield him from violence. In early 1919, two months after the Armistice, labor strikes and political demonstrations erupted across Spain. In streets and squares, workers echoed de los Ríos's cry for an end to the monarchy and a limit to military power. Weary of the irresponsible Alfonso XIII, who cared more for martial pomp than for running the country, Spaniards clamored for greater democratization and an end to *caciquismo*, the degenerate political system that kept vast segments of the rural population mired in poverty. The phrase "Viva Lenin" turned up on whitewashed walls throughout Andalusia.

Lorca and his friends in the Rinconcillo joined the campaign for workers' rights. They denounced *caciquismo*, and in early February commenced a drive to commemorate its victims by installing a plaque on City Hall. During the first two weeks of that month, workers and bosses clashed openly in Granada. Houses burned and shots were fired. Fernando de los Ríos began receiving anonymous threats and nighttime visits from the Civil Guard.

On February 11, members of the Guard opened fire on a group of university

students who were demonstrating in Granada not far from Lorca's home. A
medical student was killed in the crossfire. By the end of the day two more citizens were dead and seven wounded. Martial law was declared. Shops and
businesses closed, the trams shut down, and Granadans hung black bunting
from their balconies in a show of solidarity with the victims. Fearing reprisals,
authorities ordered the Civil Guard to stay out of the city until the situation
cooled.

Throughout the two-week period of civil unrest Lorca cowered inside his
parents' apartment. Although willing to voice his support for workers' rights, he
was fundamentally apolitical and, more to the point, he was terrified of violence. For two weeks he refused to venture onto the balcony of his parents'
home for so much as a glimpse of the streets below. He relied for news on his
Rinconcillo friend Manolo Ángeles Ortiz, who shuttled back and forth between his house and the Lorca apartment with reports of new developments.
Each day, Ángeles Ortiz stood on the sidewalk beneath Lorca's window and
shouted information up to Federico, who was so frightened he remained hidden from even his close friend.

Lorca sought refuge in a different Granada, one far removed from the contentious city that engulfed him with its troubles in 1919. Four months after the
labor disturbances he published a poem, "Granada: Humble Elegy," in a local
journal. The work, though derivative in manner and tone, underscored his ab-
sorption in the city's past, and in doing so hinted at his dissatisfaction with its
present. In the poem, Lorca mourned Granada's ancient grandeur. Time, he
suggested, had robbed the city of its glory. Time had rendered Granada a ghost
of its former self, had transformed it into a "giant skeleton . . . before whom the
Spanish poet keeps vigil and weeps."

Having earned a name in his hometown—or so he thought—Lorca understood
that it was now time to prove himself elsewhere, as Machado had admonished.
By the spring of 1919, several of his Rinconcillo friends had moved to Madrid,
among them José Mora Guarnido, who urged Lorca to join him. "Tell your father I said he'd be doing you a bigger favor by sending you here than he would
by taking you around the world."

Lorca needed little encouragement. During his travels with Berrueta he had
been impressed by Madrid and was eager to try his luck in the capital. The city
promised new friends, boundless opportunity, and a welcome change from the
parochialism of life in provincial Andalusia. But his mother was reluctant to let

him go. The three-hundred-mile trip from Granada to Madrid took more than twelve hours by train and even longer by road. Doña Vicenta worried that Lorca could not look after himself so far away from home. His father thought otherwise. He told his son Paco that since Lorca was bound to do "whatever he feels like doing, which is precisely what he's done since the day he was born," the landowner had no option but to send him to Madrid. "He's determined to be a writer. I don't know if he'll be any good at it, but since that's the only thing he wants to do, I've got no choice but to help him."

Equipped with a full wallet, several letters of introduction, and a set of new clothes—including a black suit, an assortment of starched white shirts, and a pair of patent-leather shoes—Lorca set off for the capital in the spring of 1919. Once there he moved into a pension with his friend José Mora Guarnido and immediately claimed Madrid as his own. Nothing about the city perturbed him—not its size (ten times that of Granada), not its traffic, not its tall build-ings or its new subway system. "I feel as if I come from here," he announced shortly after arriving. "There's nothing strange about it. Nothing shocks me, es-pecially not all this hubbub. It gives one strength and courage."

His mother sent letter after letter to Mora Guarnido, imploring the journal-ist to watch after her son. "Don't let him spend nights without sleeping." "Make him write to me every week." "Send me a telegram if he gets sick." If a week passed without hearing from her son, Doña Vicenta demanded to know what he was doing and why the family had received no news from him. Lorca did his best to appease her. But he was far more interested in pursuing his new life in Madrid than in writing letters to his mother. He quickly made the rounds of the city's cafés, and through his Granada colleagues met key individ-uals at the university, in the newspaper world, and in the Atheneum, the site of one of Madrid's finest libraries and the center of the city's intellectual life. His friends heralded his arrival as if he were a national celebrity. Lorca endeavored to prove them right.

His theatrical personality drove itself "like a wedge into [Madrid's] artistic world," Mora Guarnido recalled. For the first time, Lorca grasped the seductive power of his own charm. He impressed several of the city's most illustrious artists. Playwright and director Gregorio Martínez Sierra took note of the tal-ented youngster from Granada. The Catalan dramatist Eduardo Marquina talked of arranging a public reading of Lorca's work. Juan Ramón Jiménez, the great poet from Andalusia, welcomed Lorca into his apartment, listened to his poems, and invited him to come back "so we can read and play the piano," an exuberant Lorca reported afterward to his parents.

He was thrilled by his encounter with Jiménez. The celebrated poet had been seated in a "stupendous" armchair when Lorca arrived at his home bearing a sheaf of poems and a letter of introduction from Fernando de los Ríos. In *Impressions and Landscapes*, Lorca had described Jiménez as a "great poet of mist." The image befitted the poet's intensely lyrical verse as well as Jiménez himself, a moody, taciturn man plagued by spells of depression, who so craved silence that he once tried to insulate his office walls with sacking and esparto grass so that he could work undisturbed. Strikingly handsome, with brooding eyes, a black mustache and goatee, and a long, angular face that El Greco might have painted, he was introspective, self-absorbed, and petulant. His enemies called him Narcissus—a term Jiménez deemed accurate. On the afternoon of his meeting with Lorca he wore a black dressing gown trimmed in silver. Lorca sat on a nearby sofa and fixed an ecstatic gaze on the older man. Jiménez stared back at his dark-haired, "snub-nosed" guest.

The two talked about literature. To Lorca's delight, "Juan Ramón"—as most called him—gossiped about Madrid's literary elite and heaped scorn on the city's "young little poets," from whose ranks Lorca understood himself to be excluded. He was in awe of the older poet. Then thirty-seven, Jiménez was one of Spain's two reigning poets in the first years of the twentieth century; the other was Machado. At nineteen, Jiménez had published his first poetry collections, a pair of flamboyantly *modernista* works. He later turned his back on these volumes and sought to hone his style, progressively shedding the effusive, sentimental language of his earlier work in favor of a more concise, hermetic idiom stripped of ornament, a poetry Jiménez christened "naked verse." A perfectionist, he labored daily, arduously, to create his *obra*; he spoke of poetry as his "discipline and oasis," his "caprice and crucible." By 1916 he had published fifteen books; he would produce four more by 1923. He agonized over each one, seeking the most beautiful typeface and cover, the perfect paper. It grieved him to publish his work. "The moment I receive the first printed copy . . . I tear off the cover and begin all over again," he confessed. "Letting go of a book is always, for me, a provisional solution, reached on a day of weakness." Lorca would adopt the same attitude.

As a member of the Generation of '98, Jiménez aspired to "remake" Spain by remaking the Spanish language, specifically, by reshaping its poetry—eliminating the rhetoric of imperial Spain, the hollow idioms of politics, and introducing a quieter, more intimate and memorable form of discourse. He believed, with Shelley, that "poets are the unacknowledged legislators of the world," and he devoted much of his life to the creation of a "political poetics," an "ethical aesthetics"—an art that, while not explicitly political, nonetheless wields a subtle and profound effect on public sensibility.

In this, as in his conviction that poetry is a spiritual rather than a materialistic pursuit, and in his constant efforts to renew traditional forms of Spanish poetry—ballad, folk song, sonnet—Jiménez was to prove an exemplary teacher to Lorca. He taught through his poems, as well: works suffused with the lore and landscape of his native Andalusia, lines that chart Juan Ramón's love of nature and music, and his intense, prodigious, morbid fascination with death.

That afternoon, Lorca read a handful of his own poems to Jiménez. The older poet expressed admiration for the works. He asked Lorca to leave a few poems behind so that he could show them to his wife, Zenobia. Afterward, Jiménez wrote to Fernando de los Ríos: "Your poet came, and he made an excellent impression on me. He seems to possess a very fine temperament and what I judge to be the essential virtue in art: enthusiasm. He read me some very beautiful compositions. A little long, perhaps, but concision will come on its own. I hope I don't lose sight of him."

A second letter from de los Ríos introduced Lorca to Alberto Jiménez Fraud, director of the Residencia de Estudiantes, a prestigious men's residence hall where de los Ríos had suggested Lorca try to live the following autumn. Admission to the Residencia was selective, and dependent chiefly on recommendations from prominent citizens.

Jiménez Fraud took an instant liking to Lorca. During their interview, the director asked him what his father did for a living. "My father is just rich," Lorca shrugged. Charmed, Jiménez Fraud asked the "dreamy-eyed" poet if he would agree to give a reading of his work at the Residencia, as a kind of informal audition for admission to the institution. Lorca said yes, and days later gave a triumphant recital before an enthusiastic crowd that included several of his Granada friends—one of whom remarked afterward that in the previous six months Lorca had "improved enormously."

Lorca's confidence soared. He had expected to conquer Madrid, but not so quickly, and certainly not so easily. "This business about how difficult it is to do well here isn't true with me," he bragged to his family. "I'm having real success." He ridiculed Madrid's "little writers" and brashly characterized the level of the city's artistic life as "rock bottom." "If I don't come back here next year," he threatened, "I'll throw myself off the towers of the Alhambra."

Flushed with achievement, he returned to Granada in the late spring of 1919. On June 15, ten days after his twenty-first birthday, he attended a tribute to Fer-

nando de los Ríos in the Alhambra's Generalife gardens. As a result of his support for local workers earlier in the year, de los Ríos had recently won election
to the Spanish Parliament.

During the evening, Lorca and another local writer gave a poetry reading.
Among their listeners was Gregorio Martínez Sierra, a small, impeccably
dressed man in his late thirties, with a domed brow and black eyes. Although
Martínez Sierra had met Lorca a few weeks earlier in Madrid and been impressed by him, there was something about Lorca's recital that evening in the
Generalife's lush gardens that prompted him to pay closer attention. A writer,
editor, publisher, and stage director, Martínez Sierra was in Granada with his
theater company, the Teatro Eslava, to present a series of plays, among them Ibsen's revolutionary drama *A Doll's House*. The director had founded the Eslava
three years earlier with the express intent of combating the trite bourgeois theater then so popular in Spain, and he had shaped the company's repertoire accordingly. Typically the Eslava offered both classical and contemporary works,
with an emphasis on poetic drama, especially the work of the Belgian symbolist Maurice Maeterlinck.

As he listened to Lorca read, Martínez Sierra detected hints of Maeterlinck,
particularly in Lorca's allegorical poems about the Granadan landscape. The
director may have recognized something of himself, too, in the passionate
young Granadan. Like Lorca, Martínez Sierra had published his first book in
his teens, a lyrical tome filled with nostalgic descriptions of nature. As a child
he had staged amateur theatricals. As a teenager, he had dropped out of college, bored with its formalities. Throughout his adolescence he believed he
was "destined to die young and live sadly." But he survived, fell in love, married
at eighteen, and embarked on a promising theatrical career with his wife,
María, who collaborated with him on his plays. Sometime after founding the
Eslava, Martínez Sierra left his wife for the company's leading actress, an attractive brunette named Catalina Bárcena, who was with the director that
evening in Granada.

Bárcena shared her companion's enthusiasm for Lorca's poetry. After the
recital, Martínez Sierra approached Lorca and asked if he might be willing to
give the couple a private reading. Lorca consented and, in an ancient Arab
tower overlooking the Generalife, regaled the director and his companion with
more poems. Martínez Sierra was spellbound. "This poem is pure theater!" he
exclaimed after hearing one particular work, a sentimental account of animal
life in the *vega*. "What you must do now is expand it and turn it into true theater. I give you my word, I'll premiere it at the Eslava."

The offer was irresistible. Lorca had already tried his hand at a number of scripts, most of them static dramas about familiar topics, barely indistinguishable from his poems. Except for the amateur productions he had staged at home for family and friends, he had no practical theater experience. But he loved the stage and was determined to write plays. He accepted Martínez Sierra's proposal on the spot, and within weeks began trying to draft a script. The process turned out to be more difficult than he had anticipated, however, and despite Martínez Sierra's repeated encouragements by letter, Lorca failed to complete a play that summer. When he returned to Madrid in the late fall of 1919, he went back empty-handed.

The threat of another flu epidemic kept Lorca in Granada until the end of November. Because he reached Madrid late in the term, he was unable to move into the Residencia, as planned, and instead took a room in a boarding-house surrounded by "unendurable" street noise and vagrants whose presence was so distracting, he said, that it prevented him from writing letters home. He assured his parents that once he moved into the Residencia, "with my silent little room and my beloved books," he would write regularly.

His parents worried about him. His mother fretted about his well-being, and his father about his career prospects. The landowner demanded to know "the truth" about Lorca's literary affairs. He distrusted his son's incessant declarations of success. Even Lorca's brother nagged him. When their parents sent Federico a pair of shirts by rail, Paco reminded him to "please pick them up and don't do what you usually do with your things." He then apologized for his outburst. "You're no doubt resting up from all the sermons you get here about your indolent temperament."

But Lorca needed reminding. In Madrid he answered to no one. He lived spontaneously, indulging in fun, heedless of his obligations to his parents—or, more critically, his promise to Martínez Sierra, who had now announced that he intended to produce Lorca's play early in 1920. During the first weeks of December, Lorca worked halfheartedly on a script in a friend's apartment. At Christmas he went cheerfully home to Granada, assuring Martínez Sierra that he would be back in Madrid by January 7. But without bothering to inform the director, he then prolonged his stay. Shortly afterward Martínez Sierra sent a tart letter demanding to know "a firm date by which time I will have the finished work in my hands so that rehearsals can start."

Lorca ignored him. He had no appreciation of the everyday workings of the theater, and was insensitive to the artistic, financial, and scheduling pressures Martínez Sierra faced. At twenty-one, Lorca had never taken responsibility for himself or his affairs. Money meant nothing to him; in matters of art, he preferred to let inspiration, not deadlines, be his guide. Convinced of his own genius and virtue, he blithely elected to delay work on his script for Martínez Sierra until it suited him to resume drafting the play.

He could conceive of no reason why anyone should fault his behavior. Months earlier he had told his parents there was "so much literary deadwood" in Madrid that success was his for the asking. "For me, the field is richly primed." With little effort, he had been asked to write a play by one of the country's leading directors, and another distinguished man of the theater, Eduardo Marquina, had volunteered to contribute a prologue to a published edition of his poems. Although the edition ultimately failed to materialize, Lorca remained buoyant. "I'm in no hurry to 'arrive,' as they say. In literature it's extraordinarily prudent to proceed with leaden feet," he informed his family. ". . . I am convinced that the doors will open for anyone who creates good work."

His long Christmas holiday in Granada ended in late January 1920, when Lorca returned to Madrid and took a room at the Residencia de Estudiantes. From the instant he arrived, he gloried in the place. Founded in 1910 by royal order, and based on the tenets set forth in the 1870s by Francisco Giner de los Ríos and his Free Teaching Institution, the Residencia was an informal residential college where cultured young men could live and learn at leisure. Director Alberto Jiménez Fraud called it a "spiritual home" for Spaniards, and it was that: a rarefied setting in which a generation of men was meant to forge the new and liberal Spain envisioned by the country's leading intellectuals. Foreigners nicknamed it the "Oxford and Cambridge" of Madrid.

At the Residencia, Lorca enjoyed the same pampered existence he had always led at home. A full complement of housekeepers, cooks, and maids was on hand to clean his room, make his bed, wash his clothes, and prepare and serve his meals. There were no academic requirements and few rules. Residents were expected to wear proper dress in the dining hall, to arrive punctually for meals, and to sit in assigned seats, but were otherwise at liberty to come and go as they pleased, to study or not, to pursue whatever avenues they deemed useful to their scientific, artistic, and intellectual advancement.

Lorca moved into a spacious room, "bathed in sunlight from dawn to dusk," with magnificent views of Madrid. He felt immediately at home. Days after settling in, he told his parents that his new life in Madrid was healthier than the old one in Granada, "because I have to get up early and eat breakfast." Although his room was spartan, with scrubbed wooden floors, pine furniture, and a single radiator for heat, he thought it a "happy" place and, in a poem written a few months after his arrival, observed that it had become

> saturated with the aroma
> of my new heart.
> The chairs now smile at me.
> And the mirror knows me.
> (At times
> the mirror says I'm handsome.)

He flourished at the "Resi," as occupants called the place. Built on a hilltop on the northernmost edge of Madrid, the peaceful campus was planted with flowering shrubs and hundreds of poplar trees, whose leaves rustled so loudly in the spring that Lorca compared the effect to the sound of "whales frying." To his family he stressed the benefits of living in such relative seclusion. "You get absorbed in your studies and you forget completely about Madrid." He neglected to mention that he did little studying himself while living there. His room possessed few of the academic tomes that filled his fellow residents' quarters, and although he registered for a few university classes, he rarely attended them. Lorca "did practically nothing in Madrid," a friend recalled. He was a hopeless student, "always on vacation."

At the Residencia he took part in excursions to the Prado and other museums, and he attended in-house concerts and lectures. During his first years there, guest speakers included H. G. Wells, Albert Einstein, Paul Valéry, and Louis Aragon. A decade later Lorca claimed to have attended "nearly one thousand lectures" at the Residencia, all of which, he teased, left him gasping for "air and sunshine." Among friends he parodied those speakers whose "literary accent" and "delicate pedantry" annoyed him. But despite his mockery, he learned from the Residencia's speakers to regard teaching as a crucial component of what every artist must do.

Wherever Lorca went in Madrid, he took center stage with his music-making, poetry recitals, and stories, both real and invented, which he told with laughter and joyous slaps of the hand on his listeners' backs. He cultivated friends and admirers with the instincts of an impresario compelled to fill an empty theater night after night. His daily life was a performance. He constantly sought new audiences to mirror his thoughts, to provoke and encourage his creativity, to fuel his sense of importance, to stave off loneliness.

Lorca was a mixture of "strength and weakness, country boy and decadent youth," a friend remembered. He wore his black hair combed back from his

forehead, revealing a tiny widow's peak, and he dressed in pseudo-bohemian attire: dark suits, carelessly knotted ties, and gauche, broad-brimmed hats. He
sometimes wore high-cut trousers and spats. At night he often gathered with
others in the Residencia salon to talk, read, recite poetry, or play the piano. He
astonished his fellow residents with impromptu recitals of Chopin, Mozart, Debussy, and Ravel. His fingers were "electric." He "gave the impression that music flowed from him," that music "was the source of his power, his fascinating
secret," an admirer recalled.

"Play Schumann!" someone would shout, and Lorca would instantly invent
a Schumann-like passage. Someone else might request a popular song, and
Lorca would lift his head, lean back, extend his arms, grin, and begin to play
and sing. He had a coarse, earthy voice. He once remarked that he sang the
way a "farmboy sings while nudging his oxen along." One song followed another. Between pieces he bantered and wisecracked and dabbed at his mouth
with a handkerchief. In the mornings he sometimes sat by himself in the salon
to practice the piano. Down the hall, Residencia director Alberto Jiménez
Fraud would prop his office door open so that visitors could hear the talented
musician.

He soon enjoyed a circle of devoted friends at the Residencia. One of these
was Luis Buñuel, then nineteen, a brawny student from Aragón who spent
more time with a punching bag and a pole vault than he did with books. By his
own account Buñuel was an "uncouth, provincial athlete" when he met Lorca
in early 1920. Besides sports, he devoted himself to practical jokes, women, and
jazz. He cared nothing about either literature or film, his eventual métier. But
Lorca's "dark, shining gaze" and prodigious creativity intrigued him, and
Buñuel spent hours listening to him recite his poetry. Lorca "made me know
another world," he recalled. Before long the athlete was writing verse of his
own. He and Lorca drank brandy and wine together, listened to jazz, and
roamed Madrid in search of eccentric places and personalities.

Another young resident, Emilio Prados, an aspiring poet, was so smitten by
Lorca that he confessed to his diary in early 1920, "My one great joy has been to
find in Federico the friend I so desired. I opened my heart to him, and he knew
how to understand it." A bashful science student from Málaga, Prados had met
Lorca briefly in his teens during one of Lorca's holiday visits to his hometown,
but the two did not become close friends until Lorca moved into the Residencia.

An introvert with a long face and round spectacles who suffered from
chronic poor health, Prados spent much of his time alone, reading, listening to
music, and writing poetry. Hopelessly in love with a woman in Málaga who

spurned his attentions, he confided in Lorca, "with whom I can discuss my most private affairs without his laughing at them," Prados told his diary. "His way of being and thinking is very similar to my own, his same manly childishness, his eagerness to reach the summit of glory. Not that he fully understands it, but he desires it because he desires the new and the revolutionary: in everything he is like me. His political ideals, which undermine his own well-being, are the same as mine. This makes me love him all the more."

Fueled by a mutual love of poetry and disappointment in women, their friendship deepened. Prados became obsessed with Lorca. The following year Prados left Madrid to seek treatment for tuberculosis at a sanatorium in Switzerland. From there he sent Lorca a poem, one he pointedly described as his "farewell":

> Federico
> you go along your road
> a cold road
> Federico you go along your road
> and I along a river
> A deep
> and turbid river
> Will I be left alone . . . ?

By then their friendship had begun to wane, but Lorca nevertheless preserved the poem. He also kept a handful of subsequent letters in which Prados again professed his love. At one point Prados suggested the two live together, "ridding ourselves of people, emotions, bonds, and breaking the ties of responsibility . . . Do you have the nerve?" Lorca left no record of his response to the proposal.

He was ill-prepared for the intensity of Prados's pursuit and uncertain of his own feelings toward men. He continued to fear sex. Two years before moving into the Residencia, he had described himself to another young poet as "a poor, impassioned, and silent fellow who, very nearly like the marvelous Verlaine, bears within himself a white lily impossible to water, while to the foolish eyes of those who look upon me I seem to be a very red rose with the sexual tint of an April peony, which is not my heart's truth." It is unclear if by invoking Verlaine he was making a veiled allusion to homosexuality, and thus hinting at his own sexual ambiguity, or merely restating his discomfort with the notion of physical love. What is clear is that Lorca found the subject of sex disturbing, and he longed to settle it. He spoke wistfully of his desire to unravel "the enigma of myself."

At the Residencia young men like Prados and Lorca, both of whom had

spent years convincing themselves they were in love with women, had ample
opportunity to forge passionate, sometimes volatile friendships. Residents did
everything together: lived, ate, bathed, studied, socialized. Luis Buñuel later
characterized it as a hothouse atmosphere, where a certain homoerotic promis-
cuity evolved, "although it never amounted to more than kisses or the like."
Freed from the social and religious strictures that elsewhere constrained
Spaniards, the young men who lived at the Residencia were at leisure to explore the emotional, intellectual, and physical breadth of human existence.
Twice in the 1920s, the eminent Spanish physician Gregorio Marañón, author
of *Essays on Sexual Life* (1926), lectured at the Residencia on human emotion
and sexuality. As one resident said later, the institution and its liberal outlook
"freed us forever from the mental severity and the moral indecency of sectari-
anism." For Lorca, life at the Residencia was both an emancipation and a revelation.

Madrid itself inspired him. In verse, Lorca described the Spanish capital as a
"strange and modern, / almost cubist, Madrid." Inside the city's cafés, people
met nightly to exchange gossip and ideas, hear jazz, and discuss current events:
the Treaty of Versailles, the Russian Revolution, the Socialist Republican
movement in Spain. A new aesthetic was taking hold. Hispanic *modernismo*,
with its extravagant images and ponderous approach to reality, was in decline;
writers and artists now talked of playful new movements: ultraism, creationism,
cubism, futurism, Dada.
    Lorca showed up regularly at Madrid's more popular literary gatherings,
known as *tertulias*. He met the eccentric Galician playwright Ramón del Valle-
Inclán, renowned as much for his foot-long beard as for his innovative theater.
He met the doyen of the city's *tertulia* scene, the loquacious Ramón Gómez de
la Serna, whose brisk aphorisms taught Lorca to prize concision of language.
He befriended the young Chilean poet Vicente Huidobro, the chief proponent
of creationism, a short-lived literary movement whose adherents championed
an extreme form of art-for-art's-sake, with an emphasis on nonfigurative images
and a contempt for verisimilitude. Lorca also befriended Rafael Pérez Barradas, a painter and leading advocate of ultraism, a more durable, image-based
movement that held sway in Spain's avant-garde circles through 1923. Barradas
and his ultraist followers viewed art as a game without rules, and experimented
with free verse, scant punctuation, and unorthodox typography. They scorned
Hispanic *modernismo* and, in their attempt to forge a uniquely Spanish "ism"
akin to other European movements, such as futurism, sought to rid poetry of

anecdote and romantic sentiment by audaciously juxtaposing natural and man-made images, and adding a heavy dose of humor. Lorca often dropped in on Barradas's *tertulia* at the Café del Prado. But although intrigued by ultraism and drawn to its avant-garde sensibilities and machine-age metaphors, he refrained from joining this or any other movement.

His exposure to the avant-garde strengthened Lorca's growing determination to rejuvenate his writing. Even before coming to Madrid, he had begun to distance himself from the florid excesses of his earliest work. But he found it hard to do any actual writing in the capital. At the Residencia he worked intermittently, distractedly. Propped in bed or hunched over a table, he scribbled lines of verse on pieces of paper, which he then carried in his pockets and subsequently lost.

Although he had nothing more than a preliminary draft of the script with which to work, Gregorio Martínez Sierra began rehearsals for Lorca's unfinished play in early March 1920. The untitled work was a full-length poetic drama about a young male cockroach who dreams of an "impossible" love and dies when he finds it in the guise of a wounded white butterfly. Aesthetically the subject was both outmoded and preposterous. Lorca was sensitive to its shortcomings, but hoped nonetheless to profit from the work. "According to Martínez Sierra's calculations, if the cockroaches succeed, I'll earn a respectable sum of money," he told his parents.

Once rehearsals were under way, Lorca took an active role in the play's production and made a concerted effort to finish his script. He paid close attention to Martínez Sierra's work each night, offered frequent suggestions, and submitted fresh revisions of the script by day. He found the business of staging a play compelling work. After years of watching puppet shows and pageants, of attending plays and Mass, and then staging his own versions of these activities at home, he had a sharp, if untutored, sense of the theater and its power to move an audience. He had never forgotten the effect his mother had achieved in his childhood with her dramatic reading of Victor Hugo's *Hernani* to the family servants. At the end of Doña Vicenta's recital the maids had wept, much as Martínez Sierra's actors cried after hearing Lorca read his play to them for the first time—or so Lorca boasted. He described his reading as "the greatest success I have had in my short literary life." To a friend he later confessed, "I have to do theater. In the theater passions are expressed with a strength one cannot find in lyric poetry."

Victor Hugo was both an indirect and a direct influence on Lorca's play about cockroaches. Lorca had long subscribed to Hugo's Franciscan belief in the spiritual superiority of animals and, like the French novelist, wrote movingly of small animals, plants, and insects in his work. In one of his earliest plays, an unfinished "dramatic poem" called "On Love. Animal Theater," he composed a long dialogue between a dove and a pig.

But if Hugo, and by extension Saint Francis, inspired the subject matter of Lorca's play for Martínez Sierra, its principal argument—"that love springs forth with equal intensity on all planes of life"—came from Shakespeare's *A Midsummer Night's Dream*, a play Lorca once claimed had "poisoned" his soul. In fact, Shakespeare's comedy nourished his imagination, for it prompted him to see love as a haphazard phenomenon, a conceit that in turn bolstered his dawning suspicion that all kinds of love are valid.

Lorca acknowledged his debt to Shakespeare in the prologue to his play, a long exposition by the work's "author," a poet, on the drama's origins and significance. The "poet" explains to his audience that even the most repulsive of nature's creatures can experience love—hence the appearance of an ungainly cockroach, Curianito, in the play's leading role. Curianito displays many of the qualities that marked Lorca as a teenager. He possesses a "yellow mole" on his leg and "a poet's dreamy eyes." His fellow cockroaches taunt him. A poet and a visionary, Curianito dreams of love but fails to attain it. He struggles to comprehend the cruelty of a God ("Saint Cockroach") who deliberately wills his creatures to suffer. He longs to return to childhood, to "call my mother as I did when a boy."

The object of Curianito's passion is a beautiful white butterfly with a broken wing, whose true identity is revealed during an eerie moonlight soliloquy. "For I am death / and beauty," she says, plaintively moving her wings. The butterfly's words confirm what the poet has suggested in the prologue, that "Death disguises itself as Love!"—a concept central both to the play and to Lorca's vision. By the end of the drama both Curianito and his beloved butterfly have died, proving that love brings only suffering, never joy.

Little actually happens in the play. Written in verse, the work is a protracted investigation of the same themes that dominate Lorca's adolescent poetry and prose. Occasionally a musical or dance interlude interrupts the dialogue, and the insects' lavish costumes offer some visual distraction. But the characters speak in one voice, Lorca's, and there is virtually no conflict, merely suffering. Despite his ripe theatrical imagination, Lorca did not yet know how to compose for the stage. He drew many of his ideas for plot and stagecraft from Maeterlinck, whose lyrical style, use of allegory, and preoccupation with death appealed to his sensibility. But Lorca lacked the means to invoke these devices in any but the most plodding of ways. His trite use of symbolist iconography —moonlight, dusk, stars, dawn, flowers—only heightened the play's unintentional humor. Although he meant his fable about insect life to express profound human truths, Lorca failed to see how funny it was.

Rehearsals did not go smoothly. Despite the play's flaws, Lorca's father had agreed to pay Martínez Sierra's costs, and the director was keen to rush the script into production. Lorca himself was now ambivalent about the work. Well into rehearsals, he was still unable to come up with a title for the play. The company's producers complained that without a title they could not advertise the drama.

There were further problems. The first set designs, by Rafael Barradas, were unacceptable, and new ones had to be substituted. Lorca watched with increasing alarm as Martínez Sierra forged ahead with the production, the director's faith in the troubled play intact. As opening night drew near, Lorca felt what he later described as a "mute anguish" at the thought of his name being plastered across town on posters advertising the work. Eventually he lost all confidence and convened a meeting of his Rinconcillo colleagues to appraise the situation. He told his friends he intended to withdraw the work from production. He had already drafted a letter to his father, asking Don Federico to reimburse Martínez Sierra's expenses to date. His friends argued against it. If he were to back out now, they advised, he would be hard put to find another producer in the future. Reluctantly, Lorca agreed to persevere. But he declined an offer from Madrid's *La Tribuna* to contribute a self-critique of his play to the paper's theater section.

Confusion surrounded the work up to its premiere. On March 11, 1920, the *Heraldo de Madrid* announced the opening of "*The Star of the Meadow*, the first dramatic work by a new and most interesting poet, Federico García Lorca." The same day, a rival daily, *El Sol*, said that *The Star of the Meadow* would open the following week. The next day, the *Heraldo de Madrid* informed readers that the premiere of Lorca's new play had been postponed. Meanwhile, Martínez Sierra telephoned Federico at the Residencia with a last-minute suggestion for a new title. In exasperation, Lorca told the director to call the play "anything you like, whatever you think best."

The following day the *Heraldo de Madrid* announced a new opening date for the work, March 18, as well as a new title: *The Butterfly's Evil Spell*.

Martínez Sierra's sentimental tastes had prevailed; the title would endure. But the play's opening date continued to change. In the end, Lorca's dramatic fable made its debut in the Teatro Eslava on March 22, 1920, at ten-thirty in the evening.

Little about the theater in Madrid in the early 1920s was innovative. Companies routinely gave two performances nightly, often of different plays. Audiences demanded a steady menu of realistic bourgeois comedies, performed by mediocre actors in unimaginative settings. Works were formulaic and predictable. "Any comedy that's a tiny bit risqué is considered pornographic," observed one disgruntled theatergoer in the mid-1920s. "Any drama where two ideas are presented in succession without a cup of tea between them is regarded as a play to be read at home." The era's reigning playwrights were the prolific Jacinto Benavente, known for his bourgeois melodramas, and a pair of equally productive brothers, Álvarez and Serafín Quintero, renowned for their jovial, cliché-ridden scripts set in Andalusia. Even Gregorio Martínez Sierra had a decided penchant for morally uplifting, light comedies. "The public today comes to the theater to forget the worries with which real life . . . crushes the spirit," he said in 1921, a year after premiering *The Butterfly's Evil Spell*.

In an effort to shore up support, Lorca booked a large number of seats in the Eslava for his friends on opening night. As curtain time approached they began filing into the theater's upper stalls—new friends from Madrid as well as old ones from Granada, including María Luisa Egea, Lorca's adolescent passion, who now lived in Madrid. Backstage, Lorca waited nervously. Most of the city's theater critics were in the audience, pens poised. The crowd around them was lively, even obstreperous, as was often the case with opening night audiences in Madrid. Earlier in the evening Martínez Sierra's company had presented a French farce; following Lorca's play, they were to premiere a new Spanish comedy.

At ten-thirty the house lights dimmed, and Lorca's "poet" took the stage. "Ladies and Gentlemen," he began. "The play you are about to hear is humble yet disturbing, a failed comedy about one who wished to scratch the moon but whose heart was scratched instead." A moment later the curtain rose on a green "meadow" peopled by actors wearing dark capes meant to resemble cockroaches' shells. The audience started to murmur. When Catalina Bárcena, in the role of Doña Cockroach, came onstage sporting a round helmet with two antennaelike feathers, a spectator muttered something about her "little horns."

Within minutes chaos erupted. A man in a box seat began shouting, "This is for Atheneumites! Intellectuals go home!" Jeers and insults rattled the small theater. People stomped their feet. Lorca's friend Manolo Ángeles Ortiz feared the balconies would collapse. He and Lorca's other companions tried to drown out the noise with applause. "We can't hear the work!" someone cried out. Moments later, when an actor costumed as a scorpion announced that he had just eaten "ten flies," the crowd burst out laughing. Somebody called for insecticide. The cast struggled valiantly on.

Lorca tried to make light of it. "I'm visibly moved," he joked backstage to a friend, seizing on a journalistic cliché. "But 'invisibly' I'm very calm. I don't care a bit about the audience." He later claimed to have spent the evening in the theater basement, near the actors' dressing rooms, where the clamor from the audience was so loud he felt as though the crowd was "stomping on my head!" During the intermission he slipped into the lobby to see his friends, who were having an "awful time." They marveled at Lorca's apparent serenity.

In the middle of the second act a beautiful young dancer named Encarnación López Júlvez, "La Argentinita," appeared as the wounded butterfly, and her beguiling performance, to music by Edvard Grieg, briefly pacified the audience. Lorca later credited her with having redeemed the evening. Still, hisses and snide remarks continued to mar the production. During the final curtain call, theater personnel barred Lorca from joining the cast onstage because they feared for his safety.

Afterward, as Martínez Sierra's company geared up for its third performance of the evening, Lorca and his friends went off to a café to drink hot chocolate and go over the night's events. On his way out of the theater, Melchor Fernández Almagro ran into Lorca's elementary school teacher, Antonio Rodríguez Espinosa, who now lived in Madrid and was eager to know how his former pupil had fared. "I didn't want to go inside. I could not have withstood the vicissitudes of the opening night," Espinosa confided.

In Granada, Lorca's family waited with equal anxiety for word of the play's debut. Don Federico had arranged with a banker friend to wire them with news of its reception. "The work was not a success," the banker wrote in his telegram, adding tactfully, "All agree Federico is a great poet."

Critics shared the banker's perception. "In order to create poetic theater, one must think first about creating theater," wrote one reviewer, who characterized *The Butterfly's Evil Spell* as a fine lyric poem but not a stage play. Manuel Machado, brother to the poet Antonio and critic for Madrid's *La Libertad*, suggested that "Señor García Lorca" should in the future stick to writing verse.

Other reviewers savaged the work. They called it elitist, a play for snobs; they attacked its vague language and weak allegory, its "conventional" symbolism and vulgar choice of subject matter. The *Heraldo de Madrid* compared the drama to a night at the zoo. Many noted the fractious nature of the opening night. One writer complained that he was unable to judge a work that, strictly speaking, he had not heard. He blamed the disaster on "the highly esteemed poet Señor García Lorca," who could have prevented the fiasco by not writing his play in the first place. Lorca may have taken heart from the words of *El Sol's* José Alsina, who urged the young dramatist not to be discouraged by his bad luck, for his aspirations were "extremely noble and his versification noteworthy."

On the surface Lorca took the debacle in stride, and even laughed about it. Privately, it shook him. After months of believing that celebrity was within his reach, he had failed on a grand and highly public scale. He later refrained from listing *The Butterfly's Evil Spell* as his first theatrical production. To a friend he said it was "the classic debut of every new author. The work wasn't very good."

The Butterfly's Evil Spell closed on March 25, 1920, after four performances. Years afterward Lorca remarked dryly that his first play received "one consecutive performance."

CHAPTER 6

PORTRAIT OF YOUTH

1920-21

Within weeks of the play's opening, Lorca's father demanded that he leave Madrid and return home at once to finish his university degree. The landowner had had enough of theater and poetry. Years earlier he had watched his uncle Baldomero ruin himself on dreams of art and glory, and he had no desire to see his son do the same. He threatened to go to Madrid in person to fetch Lorca if he refused to obey.

Lorca panicked. In a four-page letter crowded with exclamation points and misspelled words, he begged his "dear Papa" to reconsider. "What am I supposed to do in Granada? Listen to a lot of foolish conversation, and be the butt of envy and dirty tricks (naturally, this only happens to men of talent)." Although his father may have lost confidence in his future after the fiasco of *The Butterfly's Evil Spell*, Lorca had not. "Someday I will probably have a great name in literature," he said. If his career seemed momentarily stalled, it was merely because he was proceeding "with leaden feet in order to give birth to a sensational book."

"You cannot change me. I was born a poet and an artist, just as others are born lame, or blind, or handsome." Like Don Quixote, with whom Lorca compared himself, he had embarked on a path, and "neither wolves nor dogs" could make him turn back. Seizing on a new image, one he would repeatedly invoke, he implored his father to let him keep his "wings. I can assure you I will know how to use them . . . And don't consult about all this with friends who are lawyers, doctors, veterinarians, etc.—mediocre, nasty little people—

but with Mother and the children." He closed his letter by reminding his sixty-year-old father how much he loved him.

Don Federico relented. Worn down by years of argument, and by the sheer force of his son's ambition, he agreed to let Lorca stay in Madrid until late June 1920. A giddy Federico wrote home to ask that pictures of his family be sent to him. He particularly wanted a portrait of his father, he said, so that "I can have the pleasure of putting it over my bed."

In early May, he began work on a new play. He was determined to put the experience of *The Butterfly's Evil Spell* behind him. Years later Lorca gave this timeworn advice to a young writer whose first play had fared poorly: "You must force yourself to write something immediately. The first thing horseback riders do when they take a spill is to get right back on the horse. Go back and ride again, believe me."

His new play, a derisive portrait of Jehovah in old age, told of a wrathful God who orders his son Christ to be bound in chains because the young man's "lunatic" behavior endangers the status quo. Lorca completed twelve pages of the script, then abandoned it. But the effort, the third in an early series of patently autobiographical attempts to dramatize Christ's life, allowed him to romanticize his own domestic squabbles. Despite his father's concessions to his demands, Lorca continued to chafe at the constraints he felt his parents—and, more generally, society—imposed on him, and he sought ways of saying so. In late May, in a brief profile of a young guitarist for a Granada newspaper, he purposefully described his subject as a restless and melancholy youth, "like all of us who are unable to flaunt the splendid wings that God has placed on our shoulders."

He returned home in late June to find himself under renewed pressure from both parents to finish his university degree. This time his father tried bribery. "If you'd pass some exams this September," he told Federico, "I'd let you go to Madrid with more joy than if you had crowned me emperor." Lorca realized he had no choice but to comply. "Little by little the domestic mole of family love has been undermining my innocent heart, convincing me that out of duty and civility I ought to complete my shipwrecked career as an undergraduate," he confided wryly to Antonio Gallego Burín, a former Rinconcillo colleague who had recently joined the faculty of the University of Granada. "It pains my father to see me with no career other than my emotion about things."

He worried about the detrimental effect school might have on his writing. In the quiet of his father's farm in Asquerosa, where he and his family were to spend the summer, he had begun work on a number of projects, including a series of innovative poems, the concision, subtlety, and optimism of which revealed a new Lorca, one whose adolescent angst had been tempered by age and by his contact with other poets in Madrid: "I am thirsty . . . for new songs / without moons and without irises, / and without dead loves."

"Must I, Antonio of my heart, abandon my children without raising them, tears of my spirit and flesh of my heart, to caress the cold tomes of dead histories and moribund concepts?" he asked Gallego Burín. "Or will I be able to bear both burdens with ease?"

Lorca pressed his friend for information on which university courses were easiest to pass. His plan was simple but devious: he intended to show his father "a few passing grades in September to give him a thrill," then go to Madrid and publish books. He coerced another Rinconcillo friend, literature scholar José Fernández-Montesinos, into helping him cheat in an exam in Spanish literature. Montesinos warned Lorca that if he were caught, "there'd be hell to pay." But Lorca persisted. In September he took and passed examinations in both world history and Spanish literature. Although he failed an exam in the history of the Spanish language, his father was sufficiently impressed with his performance that he consented to let his son return to Madrid.

Lorca's Rinconcillo friends sent a curt note to the professor who had issued his only failing grade that September, informing the man that by his deed he had earned a "memorable place in the biography of a great poet, whose work will do more for the Castilian language than all [your] years of ordinary and incompetent teaching." A short-lived scandal ensued.

On his return to Madrid, Lorca transformed himself into a model son. He settled into the Residencia and promptly enrolled in two philosophy courses. "I am utterly engrossed in the things I'm doing, because I have resolved to renew myself, to renew myself constantly," he assured his parents. He promised to let them know "everything I do, buy, and think."

To friends at the Residencia, Lorca extolled his family's charms. "My father is extraordinary, and my mother—what can I say? And Paquito is so talented! Jesus! And my sisters!" He was especially fond of his youngest sister, Isabel, a frail, dark-eyed eleven-year-old whom he called *"mi niña Isabelita."* In letters home he asked anxiously if she was eating properly and had put on weight. He told of toothaches and other afflictions, projects and ideas. At one point he announced the "great news" that he had just purchased a Gillette razor. When his father suggested that he wrote home only for money, Lorca grew indignant. Such an accusation, he said, "does not befit your esteem for me."

He was closest to his mother, to whom he sent bonbons on her saint's day, and in letters addressed her as "my child." Vicenta Lorca not only understood her son's aspirations but embraced them. While she applauded his decision to study philosophy, for instance, she reminded him that his writing "is more important than all the careers in the world, or, better yet, is the best career of all, both for you and for me." In dozens of neatly scripted letters, his mother praised Lorca's talent and cautioned him not to lose time or abandon hope. "I am positive that, God willing, you will see your dreams come true." But Doña Vicenta knew her son well. Midway through the fall semester she observed, "I can see you've made yourself into a real student, at least in appearance. You know that way we'll stop bothering you."

In letter after letter, she talked of the extent to which she and her husband missed Lorca when he was away. His father, she informed him, was so desperate to hear from Lorca that he rarely left home until the morning post had arrived, and he spent a portion of every afternoon waiting outside his club in Granada for the second post. As for Vicenta, she so longed to see her son that she claimed she was capable of boarding an airplane—"forgetting that it could kill me"—and flying to Madrid.

Lorca shared their nostalgia. As winter approached and Madrid turned damp and cold, he felt increasingly homesick for Granada. He asked his family to send him more pictures of themselves. To Emilia Llanos, a fashionable *granadina* in her early thirties whom he had known for several years, he remarked that he remembered his hometown "as one should remember a sweetheart who has died and as one recalls a sunlit day of childhood." His friendship with Llanos was another of Lorca's chaste attachments to women, founded largely on a shared passion for literature and art. He asked Llanos if the leaves had fallen yet in Granada. "Here in Madrid, the trees are already skeletal and cold. On only a few does a little leaf remain, and it moves in the sad wind like a golden butterfly." He too was sad. "In my soul I feel the bitterness of being bereft of love. I know this gloom will pass . . . , but the telltale sign remains forever!"

He was conscious of time passing, of another generation coming to replace his own. In November one of his oldest friends, Manolo Ángeles Ortiz, a former member of the Rinconcillo who now lived in Madrid with his wife, Paquita, became the father of an infant daughter. Throughout Paquita's pregnancy, Lorca doted on the couple. One day he took Paquita to the park to "look at pretty things so that your baby will notice them, too." Asked to be the child's godfather, he accepted with enthusiasm, and at her baptism gravely promised to instruct tiny Isabel Clara Ángeles Ortiz in the Christian doctrine.

His own children, he said, were his poems, "and I love them very much." But although he had written more than a hundred poems by early 1921, he had published fewer than twelve. He was shy about his verse, so much so that Juan Ramón Jiménez took it upon himself to arrange for the publication of several of Lorca's poems in two prestigious literary journals. "He is so timid that in spite of what I've said to encourage him, he hasn't dared send the poems directly himself," Jiménez told the editor of one of the journals. Jiménez regarded Lorca as one of the country's "true" young writers.

Others also urged him to publish. Playwright Eduardo Marquina and director Gregorio Martínez Sierra each talked of bringing out a collection of Lorca's verse. Lorca spoke brightly to his parents about the prospect of a book, but at heart he was ambivalent about publication. His mother was keen for him to bring out a book and wrote, "You mustn't content yourself with the admiration of a few. That isn't enough. Many, many people must know of you—everyone." Lorca was skeptical. He had rushed into publication with *Impressions and Landscapes* and then regretted it; shortly after the book's release he told a friend that when it came to publication, no writer should compromise his ideals. The disastrous premiere of *The Butterfly's Evil Spell* had only confirmed his thinking—and taught him, besides, to loathe what a friend called "the precarious publicity of newspapers and magazines." To his parents Lorca acknowledged that "irresponsibility and impetuosity" were lethal to fine art.

He was eager to do justice to his poetry, which at this stage of his career meant more to him than either his prose or his plays. Asked once why he insisted on reading his poems aloud, he slapped his hand against his chest as though pressing a sheaf of verse to his heart and answered, "To defend them." He was fundamentally an oral poet who preferred the direct response of a live audience to the filtered rewards of publication. On those rare occasions when he did surrender a poem to a magazine or journal, he did so "with a sense of rupture and a secret repugnance, like a mother who sends her son off to the army," remembered José Mora Guarnido. Lorca was more succinct. "I publish only for my friends," he said.

In 1921 it was a friend who ultimately persuaded Lorca—"almost by force"—to publish his poems in book form. Gabriel García Maroto, then twenty-nine, was an enterprising painter and publisher who owned a small print shop in

Madrid. Maroto was known for the elegance of his publications, a fact that pleased Lorca, who told his parents he had no intention of issuing an "ugly" edition. "I want the book to come out to my liking, since I'm its father." His own father agreed to fund the costs of publication. Maroto offered to let Lorca edit the book himself—a condition Jiménez had advised him to seek, for by doing so he could control both its content and design.

Lorca asked his brother, Paco, to help him select and assemble a collection of poems from the mass of verse he had written since 1917. He found the selection process itself torturous because, as he told his parents, "you're confronting your own work and every line becomes an immense wave that engulfs you." He worked fastidiously, rejecting poems with too many literary allusions and toiling over revisions to those that remained. As he reread his work and corrected proofs, he felt increasingly like a poet, "a pure poet, an exquisite artist, which is what one ought to be." Unwilling to settle for "cheap popularity and the applause of the ignorant," he viewed himself as a lone crusader for lyrical purity. "The fight I must wage is enormous, for on the one hand I have before me the old school, and on the other I have the new school. And here I am, from the newest school, chopping and changing old rhythms and hackneyed ideas."

His mother offered her customary support. "As far as the public is concerned, you must be cold-blooded," she warned, "because unfortunately people's tastes are old-fashioned, and therefore you moderns will have to fight hard until you prevail." She assured Lorca that she would pray to the Virgin "to help you and to make everything turn out well, and to grant you peace of mind, and not to let you suffer for any reason."

Throughout the first months of 1921, Lorca worked on his book. He devoted much of his spare time to helping Juan Ramón Jiménez organize an upcoming visit to Spain by the Bengali poet and Nobel laureate Rabindranath Tagore, whose work Lorca had long admired. It was soon apparent to both his parents that Lorca was neglecting his studies. When at the last minute Tagore's visit was canceled, his mother scolded him for having let the project distract him from his real work: "Federico, don't waste time, for these are the best years of your life. Be more like your brother, who works hard, and you see how he is rewarded. Give each thing its due, but no more than that." Vicenta begged Lorca to publish his book and finish his degree, if only to please his father, for "if he's happy, then I am too." She urged him not to waste time with friends.

But it was useless. Despite assurances that he socialized only on Sundays, when he and his friends went to the park ("I'm turning blacker than a genuine Angolan"), Lorca in fact squandered hours with his companions. He had a new roommate at the Residencia that semester, an impish teenager named Pepín Bello, who cared as little, if not less, for school than Lorca did. Bello seldom passed an exam and in time abandoned his studies altogether, dismissing his chosen field of medicine as nothing but "dissection and putrefaction." He preferred to carouse with friends and dabble in nonsense. Blond and boyishly lean, he was, according to a friend, "a mischievous genius . . . happy, electric, a maker-inventor of a thousand silly remarks and situations."

He and Lorca became firm friends. Years later Bello recalled their days together at the Residencia as having been tinged with a "special aura." "You're my best friend, the one I love most," he told Federico, whom he nicknamed "cherry," a probable pun on "chéri." Like others, he was dazzled by Lorca's ingenuity. At night Lorca sometimes sat in their room and read plays by Lope de Vega to friends, or he gave impromptu sketches of contemporary authors. Occasionally Bello would come home to find his roommate so absorbed in writing or revising a poem that he failed to notice his presence, even when Pepín spoke to him. Lorca went through virtual "labor pains" in order to write, Bello remembered. No poem was complete until he had shaped it to perfection.

Lorca spent much of the spring correcting proofs and rewriting individual poems for his book. He also began work on a new series of poems, a set of "suites" whose short, elliptical style differed radically from the poems he was about to publish. Sharply aware of the distinction between the two sets of verse, he told his parents his new poems were the "the most perfect thing" he had ever produced. "I'm very happy. Happy with myself and happy with my . . . future work!"

On June 15, ten days after Lorca's twenty-third birthday, Maroto published *Book of Poems* "by Federico G. Lorca." His mother sent her congratulations, and reminded Lorca to distribute copies of the book to every newspaper, politician, and man of letters in Granada. "I know that you know more than we do about these things," she conceded, "but, my son, when it comes to matters of importance, parents can't help thinking of their children as little boys and girls."

Stacks of *Book of Poems* piled up in Lorca's room at the Residencia. As Federico watched, Bello inscribed copies of the volume for their friends. The teenager signed Lorca's name as if it were his own. It was the sort of joke both men loved.

Maroto had produced *Book of Poems* with meticulous care, setting the volume's sixty-eight poems in handsome typography and beginning each poem on a new page. Both the cover and the frontispiece featured a small *modernista* image of a nude woman bathing. Lorca dedicated the 298-page book to his brother, "Paquito," then eighteen, whose help in preparing the collection had been crucial. Despite their temperamental differences and the constant comparisons between the two at home, Lorca adored his younger brother and had come to rely on his astute critical eye.

It was Paco who had persuaded him to include samples of his earliest verse in *Book of Poems*, so that readers could get an accurate picture of the poet's artistic evolution. As a result, many poems in the collection were more than three years old by the time the book appeared, and illuminate the process of self-criticism and self-censorship Lorca had undergone in assembling the book. To underscore their age and aesthetic disparity, as though documenting an archive, he dated each work and in many instances noted the place of its composition. He was conscious of the collection's "limitations" and "irregularities," and in an apologetic prologue to the volume cautioned readers, "I offer, in this book, which is all youthful ardor, and torture, and measureless ambition, the exact image of my days of adolescence and youth." Each poem in the volume reminded him of his passionate childhood, he said, "running about naked through the meadows of a *vega* against a mountainous background."

Book of Poems is the largest, most wide-ranging collection of poetry Lorca was to publish in his lifetime. Culled from the vast outpourings of his adolescence, it is, together with *Impressions and Landscapes* and *The Butterfly's Evil Spell*, a portrait of his youth. Like those works it announces Lorca's talent and introduces the primary themes of his art: love, death, childhood, nature, God, the character of the poet and of poetry. Although in time Lorca would learn to transform the reflective, vaguely melancholy quality of these first works into acute drama, he never strayed far from their subject matter.

Nature is the chief source of inspiration in *Book of Poems*, and the *vega* its principal setting. From the volume's first stanza to the last, Lorca delights in the region, lovingly cataloging its insects and sunsets, moonscapes and wheatfields, forcing readers to view the collection's author in the context of his native Andalusia, and thereby stressing his ties with the region's more celebrated turn-of-the-century poets: Jiménez, Manuel and Antonio Machado, Salvador Rueda, and Francisco Villaespesa, whose melodramatic reworkings of symbolist idioms and emotions struck a resonant chord in Lorca. He clearly saw himself as one in a distinguished line of Andalusian poets. Of the water that courses through the *vega*'s streams and irrigation canals, he writes:

> It is the intimate sap
> that ripens the fields,
> the blood of poets
> who loosed their souls
> to wander all the ways
> of Nature.

Formally, *Book of Poems* resembles a metrical exercise book, with lines ranging from the conventional alexandrines of high-art verse to the brief lyrics of the Spanish oral tradition. In the collection's best poems, Lorca discards the Hispanic *modernismo* of his earliest writing and invokes the sparse language of popular verse. Lines shorten, metaphors replace similes, and Lorca reveals his startling gift for images, one sharpened by his contact in Madrid with the creationist and ultraist movements. A welcome note of irony and playfulness appears. Trees, he writes, are "arrows / fallen from blue." The half-moon is a "fermata" that "marks a pause and splits / the midnight harmony."

The poems in this "disordered" collection, as Lorca described it in his prologue, span the years 1917 to 1920 and show a writer straining to find himself. Lorca draws heavily on the authors he most admired in adolescence: Darío, Unamuno, Hesiod, Hugo, Goethe, Jiménez, and above all Antonio Machado, with whom Lorca shares a nostalgia for childhood, a love of traditional Spanish song, and a predilection for such images as the unknowable "road of life" and the terrible "waterwheel of time." In the volume's older, more discursive poems, he adopts a declamatory tone he later shunned. In newer works he is far briefer and more personal. The ill-defined melancholy that marks much of the collection gives way to an acute perception of what suffering and loss entail: "And the real soul awakens in death? / And the thoughts we think now are swallowed by night?"

In several of the book's newer poems, Lorca borrows images and refrains from traditional children's songs, works whose abbreviated lines and fragmentary plots he had known since boyhood. Although his use of children's songs is often superficial—a parody of the real thing rather than a deeply imagined reworking of its elements—the effort nevertheless points to a new direction in his work, a new way of envisioning childhood. "Who showed you the road / of the poets?" a group of children asks the narrator in "Ballad of the Little Square."

"The fountain and the stream / of the old song," the poet replies.

Throughout *Book of Poems*, Lorca explores the familiar *modernista* dialectics of sin and innocence, carnal and celibate existence, flesh and spirit. He pits the pagan splendor of ancient Rome against the dull morality of Catholic Spain. Venus becomes "the world's harmony" and God a capricious being in a "boring old blue heaven" who plays with human beings "like toy soldiers." Satan is a friend: "we took an exam in Lust together." The book's young narrator mourns the loss of his arcadian youth and seeks comfort in nature and in language. Baffled by sex, scorned by women, racked by desire, he weeps his passion "like a lost child" and wanders alone down the street,

> grotesque, without solution,
> with the sadness of Cyrano
> and Quixote,
>   redeeming
> infinite impossibles
> with the rhythm of the clock.
> My voice is stained with bloody light,
> and I see irises dry up
> at its touch;
> in my song
> I wear the finery
> of a white-faced clown. Love,
> sweet Love, hides
> under a spider.

Lachrymose and derivative, sensual and elegiac, *Book of Poems* is plainly the work of a gifted but immature writer. Lorca rightly complained that parts of the collection were "oppressive," even "terrible." But the book was a turning point in his career. It captured an era and, in doing so, freed Lorca to move forward. As he acknowledged in the prologue to the collection, "It would be cruel to scorn this work, which is so intertwined with my very life."

Lorca left Madrid in late June 1921, within weeks of the book's publication, and went home to Granada. He joined his parents on their farm in Asquerosa and settled into the familiar rhythms of country life. "I'm very happy to be surrounded by my family, who love me so much," he told a friend. The sights and sounds of the *vega* soothed him. Here, he said, "I scoff at the same passions which in the tower of the city hound me like a herd of panthers." Removed from the distractions of Madrid and the petty rivalries of the city's literary life, he could relax and focus on his work: "I believe I belong among these melodic poplars and lyrical rivers."

But there were annoyances. He arrived home to find that copies of *Book of*

Poems had only begun to trickle into Granada's bookstores, and no mention of the collection had yet been made in either the local or the national press. Lorca himself was largely to blame, for he had left Madrid without telling anyone where to send the book. Discouraged, his parents pressed him to do what he could to generate interest in the volume. Lorca turned to friends for help. From Madrid, José Mora Guarnido rallied with an effusive review for the *Noticiero Granadino*, which the paper published on the front page of its July 3 edition. In his review, Mora trumpeted the release of *Book of Poems* and hailed Lorca as "a singer of stars, a hunter of dreams."

On July 30, a second friend, Adolfo Salazar, a plump, dark-haired *madrileño* in his early thirties, published a long review of *Book of Poems* in the influential Madrid daily *El Sol*. A distinguished critic as well as musician, Salazar usually wrote about music, not books. But he made an exception with *Book of Poems*, for although he had not known Lorca long, he was deeply impressed by his talent and infatuated by his personality. In the headline to his review, Salazar proclaimed the advent of "A New Poet: Federico G. Lorca." The critic enumerated Lorca's gifts: the vivid emotion and sonority of his verse, the poet's sense of childlike astonishment at nature's beauty, his affinity with the popular tradition. While noting the collection's flaws—its "inevitable reminiscences," "forced attempts," and "high-sounding and artificial expressions"—Salazar advised readers that *Book of Poems* was a "book of transition," and did not represent Lorca's current work. It contained, instead, the "simple fruits of his dawning," and as such constituted the poet's "farewell" to the "naive hours" of his early career.

The review was a breakthrough, the first wholly positive notice Lorca had received in the Spanish national press. The day after its appearance, Salazar wrote to Lorca to clarify a few of the points he had made in the piece and to remind him of the great affection he bore him. "I'm longing to see you and to hear your frank and hearty laughter." He warned Lorca to expect envy—"in your case the numbers will grow"—but cautioned him to remember that "those of us who love you" would remain constant. Lorca wrote back quickly. His gratitude to Salazar was immense, and he turned warmly to the critic. "The only way to repay you is to tell you that as you already know my affection is sincere, and my heart will always be loyally yours." He thanked Salazar for his "high praise" and acknowledged his own misgivings about *Book of Poems*. "What's bad stands out . . . but, dear Adolfo, when the poems were at the printers they seemed to me (or they seem to me) all equally bad . . . If only you knew! I don't find myself in my book."

In Salazar, Lorca saw that he had a crucial new ally as well as a generous friend and confidant to whom he could look for encouragement and advice—both of which he dearly needed. He asked Salazar's help in securing additional publicity for his book, complained of his difficulties with his parents, and paid elaborate tribute to Salazar himself. "If you could only see how I remember you! There are friendships that slip through the fingers like clear water, others are like a rose that one absent-mindedly sticks in his lapel, but true friendships are . . . limpets placed silently over the heart."

Salazar replied at once. He chided Lorca for not having done more to publicize his book and urged him not to lose faith in his family. Parents, he advised, "are oblivious to the intrigues and petty details of the literary world." He invited Lorca to join him on a three-month tour of Europe the following year. "Tell your parents how splendid this trip would be for your spirit." But Lorca declined. It is not clear whether he did so because his parents objected to the trip, or because he himself was uncomfortable with the idea.

Book of Poems received three additional reviews. One, by Guillermo de Torre, an ultraist poet, was unfavorable. Torre took issue with the collection's mostly traditional, nineteenth-century tone. The book's other reviewers, Spanish critic Cipriano Rivas Cherif and British musicologist and Hispanist John B. Trend, sang its praises. Rivas Cherif noted the volume's "intensely romantic aroma" and "lyrical pantheism." Trend, who had met Federico briefly in Granada in 1919, wrote that *Book of Poems* seemed "less reminiscent than many first books of verse." Trend's review appeared in the British journal *The Nation and the Athenaeum* and gave Lorca his first foreign press coverage.

Aside from these reviews, *Book of Poems* "languished in silence, like all first books," as Lorca was to reflect. Disappointed by the volume's meager reception, his parents resumed their campaign to get him to finish his university degree. According to Lorca, they regarded him as "a failure because no one talks about me." Nonetheless, he was beginning to acquire a name. In Granada, his friend and longtime champion Fernando de los Ríos now introduced him to visitors as "our local poet."

Between June and September 1921, Lorca plunged into an intense period of work on the suites he had begun earlier in the year in Madrid. He planned to publish them in the fall. The series revealed his growing esteem for popular song as well as his new taste for shortened lines and heightened metaphor, as exemplified both by the recent work of Juan Ramón Jiménez and by Japanese haiku.

In Madrid, where Asian verse forms were the latest rage, Lorca had tried his hand at a series of haiku (he sent the set to his mother as a gift), and from the experiment had learned to say more with less. To his brother he explained, "Haiku must convey emotion in two or three lines." His new poems, terse and keenly personal, did precisely that. Through his suites Lorca sought to effect the condition of music, or, as he told Salazar, to "render in words the sublime sensations of a reflection, removing from the tremor whatever it has of baroque undulations."

An avid fan of haiku as well as a versatile musician and composer, Salazar was ideally suited to appreciate what Lorca was trying to do. In his correspondence with the critic, Lorca tried out phrases and ideas that subsequently found their way into poems. Describing the *vega* to Salazar he wrote: "Especially at nightfall one lives in complete fantasy, in a half-forgotten dream . . . there are times when everything evaporates and we're left in a desert of pearl gray, of rose and dead silver." Days later, in the suite "Shadow," he distilled the scene:

> The night sky
> is a desert,
> a desert of lamps
> with no owner.

During the summer of 1921, Lorca composed some seventy-five short poems, works he then grouped thematically into suites with titles reminiscent of both art and music: "Palimpsests," "Six Songs at Nightfall," "Vignettes of the Wind," "Seaside Prints." Themes from earlier poems—lost childhood, impossible love, time, death—surface in fresh and provocative ways. "When we die," Lorca writes in "Memento,"

> we'll take with us
> a series of shots
> of the sky.
>
> (Skies around daybreak
> and skies in the night.)
>
> Though they've told me
> that dead
> we don't have any memories
> past a sky in midsummer,
> a black sky
> shaken up
> by the wind.

New preoccupations emerge, most noticeably a growing fascination with the question of identity. Language becomes a prism through which Lorca is able to capture and explore the shifting nature of the self. "The reflected is / the real. / . . . / The real / is the reflected," he suggests in "Moments of Song." In "Confusion," one of fourteen poems—some as brief as three lines—that constitute "Mirror Suite," he asks:

> Is my heart
> your heart?
> Who is mirroring my thoughts?
> Who lends me this un-
> rooted passion?
> Why are my clothes
> changing color?
> Everything is a crossroads!
> Why does this slime
> look so starry?
> Brother, are you you
> or am I I?
> And these cold hands,
> are they his?
> I see myself in sunsets
> and a swarm of people
> wanders through my heart.

In his review of *Book of Poems*, Salazar had announced that Lorca intended to publish a new collection of verse in the fall of 1921. He was referring to the suites. But although Lorca continued to work on the series for the next two years, he failed to publish the collection in its entirety. He did publish a handful of individual suites in late 1921 and early 1922 in the fledgling literary journal *Índice*, edited by Juan Ramón Jiménez. Shortly after the poems appeared, Lorca, like all other contributors to the issue, received a letter from the journal's editorial staff, asking him to help offset the magazine's printing costs.

Throughout the hot, dry days of July and August, Lorca's febrile imagination bolted from one idea to the next. Eager to immerse himself in the popular Spanish tradition, he spent hours learning to play the guitar from two Gypsies who gave him daily lessons in the art of flamenco.

He also revived his boyhood love of puppetry. By late summer he was "*hammering* away" at a new interpretation of the "Billy Club Puppets," Spain's version of the Punch-and-Judy show. He pumped his elderly neighbors in Asquerosa for information about the itinerant puppet shows they had witnessed at the turn of the century—shows Lorca himself had seen as a child. By 1921 the puppet tradition had all but vanished from the countryside, but, as Lorca told Salazar, the "old people" in the village were full of picturesque memories that "would make you collapse with laughter." "I'm very much loved by the workers, especially by the young lads, with whom I stroll and talk and everything," he added, his happiness at being accepted by the people undiminished by the fact that as the son of one of the town's wealthiest landowners and biggest employers, he was unlikely to be snubbed.

Fall arrived, and Lorca moved back to Granada with his family. He had hoped to return to Madrid and the Residencia, but his father insisted he remain in Granada to finish his university degree. This time there was no arguing. His father also demanded that Lorca change his major from literature to the far more practical subject of law.

Lorca surrendered. At twenty-three, he settled despondently into his family's apartment in Granada and prepared to resume his hapless undergraduate career. It had been two years since he last enrolled in school. He had completed fewer than half the courses necessary for his degree. "I see life is now casting its chains upon me," he had told Salazar earlier in the summer. "Life has its reason, too much reason, but . . . my wings, what a pity! My dried-up childhood, what a pity!" In a poem called "The Return," part of a suite he composed in August, he was more direct:

> I'm coming back
> for my wings.
>
> O let me come back!

CHAPTER 7

FALLA

1921-23

Lorca's fall semester class list read like a courthouse directory: canonical law, administrative law, public housing, penal law, civil law, judicial proceedings, mercantile law, legal practice. He struggled to make the best of it. His brother, then nineteen and on the verge of completing his own law degree, tutored him.

Lorca made light of his situation. He told former Rinconcillo colleague Melchor Fernández Almagro that he was "neither sad nor happy; I'm inside autumn; I am '. . . Oh, heart, heart! / Cupid's Saint Sebastian!' " Fernández Almagro encouraged him to leave Granada and return to Madrid: "You're not doing anything there. Let me know what train you take." Adolfo Salazar teased Lorca about his new vocation and counseled him to do the minimal amount of work necessary in order to pass his exams. "I don't like to think of you as . . . serious, or formal," Salazar said, "because you're not like that. You're the bad Residencia student full of sunshine and brimming with songs."

Bored by the classroom and exasperated by its routines, Lorca renewed his acquaintance with those members of the Rinconcillo who still remained in the area. As a group they were particularly interested in the city of Granada, which they had now seen evolve from a quaint rural outpost into a noisy urban center filled with cars, banks, apartment buildings, and avenues. Lorca feared that "architects and junk dealers" might ultimately change their city into a "population without color or ambience." He and his friends resolved to preserve Granada's heritage. They talked excitedly about building a monument to the geniuses of Granada's Arab past, men whom Lorca called "*granadinos* of pure stock," but their plans never crystallized, and Lorca and his friends looked for another project. They found it in traditional Andalusian song.

At dusk, in a small tavern inside the walls of the Alhambra, they gathered nightly to hear the tavern owner, Polinario, and his guitarist son, Ángel Barrios, perform *cante jondo,* or "deep song," a form of Andalusian song, most often associated with Gypsies, that had graced Granada's caves and hillsides for centuries. Convinced that "true" deep song had been supplanted by its nineteenth-century successor, flamenco, played to gawking tourists in gaudy revues, Lorca sought to know *cante jondo* in its "original" state. Night after night, surrounded by the Alhambra's ghostly towers, he and his friends sat in Polinario's tavern, listening to the wails of deep song. Other artists, writers, and singers joined them, including a diminutive, bald-headed musician and composer, Manuel de Falla, who had moved to Granada with his sister in 1920. A gaunt man, with pale, delicate features and dark eyes, Falla lived in a tiny white house, or *carmen,* on the slopes of the Alhambra. He shared Lorca's fascination with Gypsy culture and love of Andalusian song. When Lorca's group talked of founding a musical café, Falla proposed a more ambitious idea: Why not stage a *cante jondo* festival in Granada, a festival of national scope and importance, one that would illuminate the distinction between "true" deep song and its "vulgar" cousin, flamenco?

Long before moving to Granada, Manuel de Falla had embraced the city imaginatively. He set his 1905 opera, *La vida breve,* in Granada, and in 1915 named the first movement of his celebrated *Nights in the Gardens of Spain* after the Generalife gardens. A native of Cádiz, Falla was a passionate Andalusian whose work sprang directly from the traditions of southern Spain. Like Lorca, he had grown up hearing nursemaids croon folk songs, the words and melodies of which now filled his mind and fueled his music.

He and Lorca had met briefly in 1919, during one of Falla's periodic visits to Granada, but their friendship did not take root until 1921, when both found themselves living more or less permanently in the city—Falla by choice, and Lorca by paternal edict. On the face of it they had little in common. Lorca, twenty-three, was impulsive and undisciplined. Falla, in his mid-forties, was a timid, methodical man, who so regulated his life that he timed himself brushing his teeth. He slept in a cell-like white room on a narrow bed with a cross suspended above the headboard. Each morning before starting his day's work at the piano he attended Mass. He viewed his talent as a God-given gift to be diligently honed, and he scolded Lorca for not doing the same. "When you're dead, you'll be sorry you didn't work," he warned. Lorca was both amused and awed by the composer's quest for perfection. He called Falla "a saint"—the same term he had used to describe his former piano teacher, Antonio Segura Mesa.

Their friendship, marked by an age difference of more than twenty years, was cordial. Falla remained "Don Manuel" to Lorca. He addressed Federico as "my dear son" and reproached him when he succumbed to childish pranks. More than once, Lorca was forced to board a tram and make the noisy uphill trek to Falla's *carmen* to beg the composer's forgiveness for some misdeed. But each accepted the other's quirks. Lorca regaled friends with accounts of Falla's compulsive need for silence (the sound of a fly buzzing could make him stop work entirely), while Falla relished Lorca's madcap sense of fun. One day the composer looked out his window to see Lorca approaching his house on foot with his stylish friend Emilia Llanos in tow. Lorca walked in front, solemnly holding a lantern in each hand. Llanos, wearing a huge hat, trailed behind. At the sight of their sober procession, Falla burst out laughing.

From the moment he first heard Lorca play a Debussy prelude on the piano, Falla knew he was in the presence of an artist whose love of music and powers of invention rivaled his own. Lorca became a regular guest in the composer's home. Falla's small house sat high on the northwest edge of the Alhambra, overlooking the sand-colored sprawl of Granada and, beyond it, the *vega*. The composer thought the view from his *carmen* "the most beautiful panorama in the world." He and his sister, María del Carmen, who served as his amanuensis, lived here in relative seclusion. The site gave Falla the "silence, above all silence," he needed in order to work. He found the place so inspiring that each night before drifting off to sleep "new ideas and new projects," he said, "assault me."

Lorca and his Rinconcillo companions frequently joined Falla in the afternoon for a "frugal" meal of tea and toast after the composer had finished his day's work. While his sister poured tea, Falla would slowly and deliberately light a cigarette—one of the few he allowed himself daily—and ask questions of his guests. He smiled politely as they answered. Occasionally he played the piano for his visitors, but rarely his own work. Modesty forbade it. (He thought it pretentious when people called him "Maestro.") Although he could have basked in his considerable fame, Falla chose not to. During a seven-year stint in Paris, from 1907 to 1914, he had known and worked with the great musicians of his day: Debussy, Ravel, Stravinsky, Albéniz. Both Picasso and Diaghilev had collaborated on the London premiere of his *Three-Cornered Hat* in 1919. (Picasso's costume sketches for the production hung above the piano in the living room where Lorca and his friends sat chatting.) But Falla shrank from celebrity. His only aim, Lorca observed, was "to become better each day and to create works of art. Anyone else who had achieved what he has achieved would take a break . . . but not Maestro Falla."

From Falla, Lorca learned to strive for perfection in his work and to experiment constantly. The composer nurtured Lorca's growing passion for traditional Spanish song, and through the example of his own work proved to Lorca, at a time when he was struggling to make sense of such issues, that stylization, not direct imitation, was the most persuasive means of interpreting traditional material. One need only look at Debussy and Ravel, Falla maintained, to see how effectively an artist could suggest the sounds of Spain without once setting foot in the country. Falla taught Lorca that in working with traditional material one must seek "truth without authenticity."

Years earlier Falla had evoked the Gypsies' untamed world in *El amor brujo* ("Love the Magician") and *La vida breve* ("Brief Life"), and his understanding of Gypsy music shaped Lorca's understanding of traditional Andalusian song. In his quest for what he believed to be "authentic" deep song, as opposed to its corrupt descendant, flamenco, Falla took Lorca on exploratory visits to the Gypsy caves that lined Granada's Sacromonte hill. In fact, neither man was correct to think there was any distinction between "ancient" deep song and "modern" flamenco; the two were intertwined. Nevertheless, both Falla and Lorca clung to the notion that they could unearth and revive *cante jondo* in a pure, uncontaminated state, and they set out to do so. As they listened to Gypsy singers, Lorca seized on the stunning simplicity of Gypsy song, the concision and imagery of the three- and four-line lyrics or *coplas* that were the bedrock of *cante jondo*, gemlike poems that spoke eloquently of love:

> Your eyes and mine
> have become entwined,
> like blackberry bushes
> in the hedges.

And death:

> The moon has a halo,
> my love has died.

Struck by the "naked" emotion of deep song, Lorca later said that "all the passions of life" could be found in its abbreviated form, that it "comes from the first sob and the first kiss." He understood *cante jondo* intuitively and interpreted it romantically, both as a poet and as an Andalusian whose great-grandmother had been part Gypsy—or so he claimed. Deep song contained the wellsprings of his own writing: love, pain, and death. It embodied the essence of the Andalusian temperament. He admired the pagan tones of the form, the candor of its language, its pantheism, and the fusion of cultures—Indian, Jewish, Byzantine, Islamic—implicit in its sounds. The poems in deep song, he said, "consult the wind, the earth, the sea, the moon, and things as simple as a violet, rosemary, a bird." Later critics would observe that deep song also spoke of hunger, protest, and complaint.

Plans for a *cante jondo* festival soon dominated Lorca's life. His university work forgotten, he spent the last months of 1921 and first weeks of 1922 helping Falla and others circulate a petition throughout Granada requesting local funding for the event. In Madrid, Adolfo Salazar circulated a similar petition among the city's writers and intellectuals; Juan Ramón Jiménez signed the document, as did the composer Joaquín Turina, Fernando de los Ríos, and the Mexican writer Alfonso Reyes. Organizers envisioned the festival as a matter of national as well as international significance, an occasion whereby Spain could pay formal tribute to the country's rich musical heritage. Falla planned to bring both Stravinsky and Ravel to Granada for the event.

Their work on the festival drew Lorca and Falla closer. On New Year's Eve 1921, Falla's saint's day, Lorca hired a quartet of street musicians to serenade the composer. Late at night the revelers crept on tiptoe to Falla's *carmen*, positioned themselves under his window, and, with Lorca conducting, burst into a noisy rendition of *El amor brujo*. Falla laughed so hard he could scarcely open the door to let them in. Later that night he asked the ensemble to repeat their performance four separate times while he accompanied them on the piano. He remarked to Lorca that "not even the great Don Igor" Stravinsky could have devised such an ingenious instrumentation.

To his family and companions, Lorca spoke possessively of his friendship with "Manuelito." Years later he boasted that in 1922 he and Falla had single-handedly organized Granada's first *cante jondo* festival. He told how one night, as he and Falla were walking along a Granada street, discussing the "degeneration, neglect, and discredit that surrounded our old songs," they had suddenly heard the "pure" strains of an ancient Andalusian song wafting from an open window. They approached the window and inside glimpsed two men, a guitarist and a singer. The "liturgical" simplicity of this private performance so moved them that, according to Lorca's story, Falla decided on the spot to found a deep-song festival. Casting their work in an epic light, Lorca subsequently declared that no two people were better equipped for the task "than a musician like Falla . . . and a poet like Lorca, a Gypsy, a *granadino*, black and green like a thoroughbred pharaoh."

In truth, dozens of other people took part in planning the festival, as Lorca knew. In early 1922, after receiving funding for the project, its organizers began preparing in earnest for the event. One of their most crucial tasks was to find *cante* singers to perform at the festival, which was to be a competition. The job fell largely to Lorca, who was only too willing to exchange his law books for long forays into the countryside in search of performers.

Although Falla and others occasionally joined him in his hunt for Gypsy singers, Lorca's most frequent companion on these expeditions was his childhood friend Manolo Ángeles Ortiz, who, like Lorca, had grown up in the *vega* and knew the region intimately. For weeks the two crisscrossed Granada province in search of performers. They scoured taverns, neighborhoods, towns, and farms. Arriving in a village where singers were said to reside, the two friends would first wander the streets, then sit in a public square in the fading afternoon light and wait. As Lorca later described it, two elderly men might be seated on a bench across from them, talking, when suddenly one or both would start to sing. Lorca could recognize what he called the "bloodcurdling" sound of pure *cante jondo* instantly.

His search for singers and song carried him back to his roots, to the distant nights of his *vega* boyhood when he used to sit by the fire in Fuente Vaqueros and listen to villagers sing while his father played the guitar. His innate fondness for popular song had gradually evolved into a sophisticated understanding of the art. At twenty-two, he had helped the renowned Spanish historian Ramón Menéndez Pidal collect ballads in Granada's Gypsy quarters. Lorca knew dozens of popular Spanish songs by heart. He once claimed to have collected more than three hundred songs in the province of Granada alone. Seated at a piano, his head thrown back, hands stretched wide on the keyboard, he was capable of spending a whole evening playing and singing songs from each region of the country without repeating a single example. He owned several ballad books, and like many of his contemporaries, including Falla, he was an aficionado of composer Felipe Pedrell's *Cancionero musical popular español*, a massive compendium of traditional Spanish song published in four volumes between 1918 and 1922. For many in Lorca's generation, Pedrell's *Cancionero* served as a secular "book of hours."

For Lorca, songs brought the past back to life. "While a cathedral is always fastened to its own epoch, giving the ever-shifting landscape a ceaseless expression of yesterday, a song leaps out of that yesterday into our own moment," he said. He viewed popular songs as "magnificent poetry." As he and Ángeles Ortiz traveled through Granada province in 1922, the two men, both in their early twenties, bellowed lines of *cante* back and forth to one another. Brashly, Lorca insisted that he was the better singer, and an amiable rivalry developed. But there was a poignant undercurrent to their game. Weeks earlier, Manolo's young wife, Paquita, had died following a long illness brought on by the birth of their only child, Isabel Clara, Lorca's goddaughter. Shattered, Ángeles Ortiz had left Madrid and returned home to Granada with his year-old daughter. At night, the artist slept with his arms wrapped around his wife's death mask. He sometimes sobbed so loudly that his neighbors heard him.

During their trips in search of *cante* singers, Lorca watched devotedly over his friend. In February he reported to a mutual acquaintance that although Manolo was now "much calmer," he had been "in a bad way, because it was all memories." As they roamed the Andalusian countryside, Lorca was acutely moved by his companion's grief, all the more so because it underscored the inherent sorrow of the music they were seeking. In subsequent years, he liked to tell about a *cante* singer named Silverio Franconetti who mourned his son's death by spending an entire night singing deep song. To Lorca, the story captured the essence of *cante jondo*.

Not all Granadans approved of the festival. Informed that city monies were to be used to fund the event, a number of residents sent angry letters to the local newspaper denouncing the project in particular and Gypsy culture in general. Their response reflected a general antagonism in Spain toward traditional Andalusian song and dance. One detractor argued that the competition would be nothing more than a "festival full of dirty straw hats and shabby clothes performed by a bunch of riffraff."

Advocates of the competition rallied to its defense. Several citizens submitted letters of support to the local press. The *Defensor de Granada* published a lengthy justification of the festival by Manuel de Falla, in which the composer reminded naysayers that a *cante jondo* festival would bring international prestige to their city. In addition to his piece for the newspaper, Falla published an essay in pamphlet form outlining what he believed to be the origins, values, and contemporary significance of deep song.

Spurred by Falla's example, Lorca also drafted a lecture on the topic of *cante jondo*, which he gave late one February night in the Granada Arts Center. At twenty-three, his black hair combed back from his face, he looked more student than teacher. Uncomfortable with the role of lecturer, he warned his audience that his speech—which bore the unimaginative title "Historic and Artistic Importance of the Primitive Andalusian Song Called *Deep Song*"—was a "poor, badly constructed lecture." Nevertheless, he hoped his remarks would be sufficiently "luminous and profound" to convince his listeners of deep song's "marvelous artistic truth."

He drew much of his talk directly from Falla's pamphlet on *cante jondo*, lifting quotations, phrases, and occasionally whole passages from the composer's essay. As Falla had done, Lorca outlined the origins and evolution of deep song as he saw them, and discussed the form's use by contemporary artists. He reiterated Falla's belief that the most effective means of interpreting traditional material was stylization, not direct imitation. "Nothing but the quintessence and this or that trill for its coloristic effect ought to be drawn straight from the people," Lorca advised.

He referred frequently to Falla, whom he called "Maestro Falla," "the Maestro," and even "the great Maestro." His talk was at once a protracted homage to an admired friend and a tribute to the Gypsy music they both loved. And yet the voice was unmistakably Lorca's. Incapable of delivering a strictly academic lecture, he seasoned his long speech with personal anecdotes and allusions. He described the late Claude Debussy as a musician who early in his career had "engaged in the fight all we young artists must carry on, the fight for what is new and unforeseen, the treasure hunt, in the sea of thought, for inviolate emotion." He mentioned "the marvelous *Omar Khayyám*," renounced "the over-luxuriant tree" of romanticism, described himself as "an incurable lyrist," and declared his allegiance to a new aesthetic, one inspired by the brevity and raw emotional power of popular verse.

His audience applauded warmly throughout the talk. Two days later, the *Noticiero Granadino* pronounced the event a "grand success," and subsequently published the lecture in serial form. Equally enthusiastic, the *Defensor de Granada* hailed this new facet of Lorca's career. In Madrid, Adolfo Salazar published a short synopsis of the talk in *El Sol*.

His debut as a lecturer heightened Lorca's stature in Granada. But at home the old battles continued. In early February, Lorca confessed to Salazar that he had recently undergone "some family storms," and although these had died down, he longed to escape to Madrid. He found Granada stifling. From his desk he could see the snowcapped Sierra Nevada in the distance, but he was weary of "so much beauty." Granada inspired and at the same time constrained him. By contrast, Madrid—big, noisy, prosaic Madrid—offered the liberty he craved.

Twice that spring (once by telegram from Luis Buñuel) he received word from the Residencia that a room was waiting for him, but his father refused to let him go. Lorca managed to escape Granada in April for a quick visit to Seville during Holy Week with his brother and Falla, where the trio reveled in the spectacle of the city's magnificent Easter week processions and listened to more Gypsy song. Otherwise, he stayed put in Granada. He told guitarist Regino Sáinz de la Maza, with whom he had recently struck up a correspondence, that he needed to remain home because he was tackling projects whose "Andalusian character" warranted his being in the south. In addition to his work on the *cante jondo* festival and his lecture on deep song, he had embarked on a new series of poems, verse that had at first seemed to him "unattainable" but whose "riddles" he had eventually managed to solve. Jubilant, he proclaimed to Sáinz de la Maza, "Poetry has become master of my soul."

He had begun drafting the new series in November 1921 in a blaze of inspiration, completing thirty-two poems in just ten days. By the end of the month he had finished nearly eight additional poems. In early January 1922 he told Adolfo Salazar he was putting the finishing touches—"the little golden roof tiles"—on the series, and hoped to publish it later that year in conjunction with Granada's *cante jondo* festival. He called the series *Poem of the Deep Song*.

The new poems sprang directly from Lorca's suites of the previous summer and were in fact themselves "suites" linked thematically by the concept of Gypsy deep song. And yet, as Lorca told Salazar, the series was "distinct from the suites, and full of Andalusian implications. Its rhythm is stylized popular, and in it I bring out the old singers and all the fantastic flora and fauna that fills these sublime songs." The poems were part and parcel of his work on the *cante jondo* festival. During his search for Gypsy singers, he had occasionally been struck by a particular turn of phrase and, pulling a scrap of paper from his pocket, had paused to scribble a line of verse.

He sensed that he was on to something new—"*another orientation of mine,*" he informed Salazar, "and I don't know yet what to tell you about it . . . but novelty it has!" In one breath Lorca described the series as both an altarpiece and a jigsaw puzzle. Although its precise nature eluded him, he knew the effort was audacious. He teased Salazar: "If only for its daring I deserve a smile, which you'll send me right away." He claimed, inaccurately, that Spanish poets had "never *touched* this theme." In fact, a host of nineteenth- and early-twentieth-century regional poets had created a dense body of poetry in imitation and celebration of traditional Andalusian folk song, notably Lorca's immediate contemporaries Manuel Machado and Francisco Villaespesa, each of whom had sought to evoke Gypsy song through verse. But their efforts had resulted in *modernista* pastiches of the form, contrived and melodramatic replications of standard topics and phrases, that simulate the effect of deep song without penetrating its spirit. In his poem "Cante hondo," Machado dutifully lists, rather than evokes, the components of his source material: "*Malagueñas, soleares* / and gypsy *siguiriyas* . . . // It is popular wisdom / that contains all wisdom: / to know how to suffer, love, / die and hate." By contrast, Lorca hoped to effect a radical new synthesis of the traditional and the avant-garde. Stylization, not imitation, was the key to his approach. In his lecture on *cante jondo* he had argued that artists should never seek to copy the ineffable modulations of traditional material, for "we can do nothing but blur them. Simply because of education."

Stirred by the briefness and density of authentic *cante*, Lorca strove in his new verse to compress language as he had never done before. The resulting poems are even shorter and more enigmatic than his suites, and a far cry from the often self-indulgent lyrics of *Book of Poems*. In the stark modulations of Gypsy song Lorca had found a new idiom.

At the heart of the work are four suites he completed in November 1921, each a series of poems based on one of four specific types of Gypsy song: *soleá, petenera, siguiriya,* and *saeta.* In mood and subject Lorca's suites suggest their real-life sources. "Poem of the Soleá" and "Graphic of the Petenera" dwell on death and mourning, as do traditional *soleás* and *peteneras*. "Poem of the Gypsy Siguiriya" evokes a form that Lorca described in his lecture on deep song as a lament that begins with "a terrible cry," then halts, giving way to an "impressive and measured silence." Lorca's version of a "Gypsy Siguiriya" includes a poem called "The Silence," which reads in its entirety:

> Listen, my son, to the silence.
> The undulating silence
> where valleys and echoes slip,
> bending foreheads
> to the ground.
> Listen.

In "Poem of the Saeta," a suite inspired by the *coplas*, or *saetas*, sung during Andalusia's Holy Week processions, Lorca summons the ethereal world of Easter week in Seville, the most famous of Spain's Holy Week celebrations, which he had witnessed that spring in Falla's company. Transforming its ritual cast of Virgins and hooded penitents into an incongruous set of archetypal figures, he transcends the everyday circumstances of Holy Week to offer a unique vision of Christ's Passion:

> Strange unicorns are advancing
> through the narrow street.
> From what forests of myth,
> from what mythological fields?
> Up close, they're astronomers,
> fantastic Merlins
> and the *Ecce Homo*,
> Durandarte bewitched,
> Orlando furioso.

Some of his deep-song poems have real-life antecedents: a family anecdote, a scene glimpsed during a Holy Week procession or on a hillside above the Alhambra. (One night as he stood in the Arab fortress gazing at the surrounding landscape, Lorca cried, "The olive trees are opening and closing like a fan!" He worked the phrase into the poem "Landscape" in "Poem of the Gypsy Siguiriya.") Other works draw on Lorca's ample knowledge of Andalusian topography and lore. The series pits the Dionysian grandeur of Seville against the mournful beauty of Granada, with its two slender rivers, "one of blood, one of tears. // Ay, the love / that went off on the breeze!"

Grief and its progeny, lament, dominate the collection. Lorca writes of the persecuted and disgraced, of desire and despair, of imprisonment and death. He borrows liberally from authentic Gypsy song, sprinkling his deep-song poems with the heartrending *Ay*'s and plaintive refrains of true *cante*, thus giving an idea of what it is like to hear *cante jondo* performed in a cave on Sacromonte hill or in a village square. Through Falla he had learned to draw sparingly on traditional sources, fusing the past to the present through metaphor and in the process creating a mythic Andalusia, a half-real, half-imagined place of epic proportion, where Gypsy singers are blind "like Homer," and Christ evolves from "Judea's iris" into "Spain's carnation." Even something so humble as a guitar—a common motif in Andalusian poetry— bears novel traces of Calvary: "Oh, guitar! / Heart gravely wounded / by five swords."

The Andalusia of Lorca's deep-song poems is a spiritual as well as a physical entity, a palimpsest of vanished civilizations. In a sense, Lorca was re-creating the Andalusia of his boyhood—a land whose fields held Roman mosaics and Arab towers, Catholic spires and Renaissance palaces. His is an Andalusia of "immense nights" and "deep cisterns," a "land of arrows / and death without eyes," an "Andalusia of grief!" where death and love are intertwined:

Beneath the dry earth
the hundred lovers sleep
Andalusia has long, red roads;
Córdoba, green olive trees,
a place for a hundred crosses
to remember
the hundred lovers
that forever sleep.

Martyrs all, Lorca's Gypsies dream of an impossible love but encounter only death. Their sorrow is ancient, their song primal. In drafting *Poem of the Deep Song*, Lorca sought to capture the Gypsy world not from the outside, as his predecessors had done, but from within, to suggest rather than to explain. He aimed to create a body of work that Gypsies themselves would find authentic. Metrically irregular, terse, often truncated, his poems give the impression of sung prose. From the lyrical excesses of *Book of Poems*, to the abbreviated lines of his suites, to the concentrated images and avant-garde sensibility of his deep-song poems, Lorca had traveled far. And yet his understanding of human destiny had not changed. "The labyrinths / that time creates / disappear," he writes in "And After That":

(Only the desert
remains.)

The heart,
fount of desire,
disappears.

(Only the desert
remains.)

The illusion of dawn
and kisses
disappear.

Only the desert,
the undulating desert,
remains here.

Although he completed much of *Poem of the Deep Song* while preparing for the *cante jondo* festival in 1922, Lorca did not issue the collection in book form that year, as planned, and the work remained unpublished until 1931, while other projects took precedence. But his deep-song poems did not languish in silence. Lending his husky voice to Spain's oral tradition, he recited the new works compulsively as he wrote and refined them in the spring of 1922. Friends such as Ángeles Ortiz responded warmly to the collection, but Lorca's best audiences were, as he had hoped, Gypsy singers themselves. When he read *Poem of the Deep Song* to one group of Gypsies, they were so dazzled by his impassioned performance that afterward they swarmed around him, kissing and hugging him as though he were one of their own.

To fan interest in the *cante jondo* festival Lorca gave a public reading of *Poem of the Deep Song*—his first official poetry recital—in Granada's opulent Alhambra Palace Hotel on June 7, 1922, one week before the competition and two days after his twenty-fourth birthday. Accompanied by two guitarists, one of them a plump young Andalusian named Andrés Segovia, Lorca read his work to a "distinguished and aristocratic" crowd. Local reviewers raved. "Granada has a poet," exclaimed the *Defensor de Granada*. "This dreamy young man who is so in love with the beautiful and the sublime will soon be a glory."

The following week nearly four thousand people attended Granada's first Deep Song Competition. The event took place over the course of two nights in the moonlit grounds of the Alhambra. Audiences wore nineteenth-century Andalusian costume: straw hats, embroidered shawls, flounced skirts. Although controversy had continued to rage up to the end, ticket sales were brisk and the event itself was an unrivaled success. Lorca later boasted to a reporter that while watching the competition he kept imagining "all of its detractors sitting off in a corner, biting their fingernails."

In his lecture on *cante jondo*, he had said that deep song "knows nothing but the night, a wide night steeped in stars," and this was the case with Granada's Deep Song Competition of 1922. The singing began each evening at ten-thirty and lasted until two the following morning. Among the performers were Diego Bermúdez, "El Tenazas," an old, nearly forgotten singer from Córdoba province, whose formidable voice riveted the crowd, and an eleven-year-old prodigy named Manuel Ortega, "El Caracol," who later became one of the century's finest *cantaores*.

One witness observed that the first Gypsy cry of the competition pierced the night air like a "wound from a traitor's hand." A "terrible silence" then descended, followed by another, softer cry. Guitars throbbed and castanets clicked. Gypsies of all ages sang and danced as hundreds of spellbound listeners murmured their approval and clamored for more. Even a downpour on the second night of the competition failed to shatter the spell. People simply covered their heads with their chairs and continued to listen in the rain.

Reviewing the event for the *Noticiero Granadino*, Lorca's Rinconcillo friend Antonio Gallego Burín pronounced the competition a "festival of great Truth." Word of its success reached as far as Paris and London. Asked by a local journalist to give his opinion of the festival, Lorca replied brightly, "I told you, dear friends, that the Deep Song Competition would be unique." Its lyricism delighted him. "It was a competition with moonlight and rain. Just like the sun and shadow of the bullfight," he said.

In the aftermath of the competition and his public triumph as both a lecturer and a poet, Lorca found himself feeling "very happy, but terribly emotional." He did not know why. By early July he and his family had moved to Asquerosa for the summer. To his loyal correspondent Melchor Fernández Almagro, he confessed that he felt an irresistible urge to weep every morning. He described the impulse in melodramatic terms:

> Anything moves me (the emotion of dawn) . . . It seems to me as though I am recuperating from some illness and I'm as weary as if I had crossed deserts blurred with fever. I'm thinking now of doing a lot of work beneath my eternal poplars and beneath "the pianissimo of gold."

The last phrase came from a suite he had written the previous year. He resumed work on his suite series that July, completing what he described as several "little plaintive poems that I feel inside, in the deepest part of my unhappy heart."

He was vague about the source of his unhappiness. Although he longed to write, to produce a "calm and serene work this summer," his attempts at poetry disappointed him. In the wake of *Poem of the Deep Song*, the confessional verse he had once turned out with alacrity had become an embarrassment. "You have no idea how much I suffer when I see myself portrayed in these poems," he told Fernández Almagro shortly after completing a handful of new suites. "Stitch and stitch . . . like a shoemaker, stitch, stitching away, and nothing to show! These days I feel pregnant."

Midway through the summer he was gripped with passion for a new project, an "admirable book" that he intended to call "The Meditations and Allegories of Water." He envisioned the work as a vast "Life of Water" in both verse and prose, with many chapters, a poem at once Eastern and Western, in which water's "impassioned life," water's "martyrdoms" would be sung. If he attacked the project boldly he felt he could achieve something. "And if I were a great poet, what one calls a great poet, I might find myself face to face with my great poem."

Water had "penetrated" him. The great rivers and waterways of Andalusia "flow into Federico García Lorca, modest dreamer and son of the water," he said. His childhood worship of the *vega's* streams and canals, together with his enduring awe of the sea and fear of drowning, had led him at last, he thought, to his magnum opus. "Oh what a water obsession I suffer!" But for unspecified reasons, Lorca set aside his "Meditations and Allegories of Water" after a few brief attempts at composing parts of the book. He never returned to the project, although his preoccupation with its subject continued to nourish his imagination and to pervade his poetry.

The *cante jondo* festival had given Lorca a chance to collaborate with other artists, to experience the excitement of live performance. He had spent most of the previous year consumed with preparations for the event. Now that it was over, he missed it more than he realized. Toward the end of the summer of 1922 he conceived a new project, one that would gratify his need for theatrical performance: he and Falla would create a traveling Andalusian puppet show. "Enough of Castile!" he exclaimed. His immediate literary forebears, notably Antonio Machado and Miguel de Unamuno, had already championed that arid part of Spain. It was time to exalt Andalusia.

Falla endorsed the idea at once and agreed to collaborate with Lorca on the project. The composer was so excited by the notion that he could scarcely sleep. As a child growing up in Cádiz he had thrilled to the raucous fun of the puppeteers who periodically set up shop in that city's streets and squares, and like Lorca he longed to revive the magic of those occasions. Falla had recently been at work on an operatic interpretation of Cervantes' *Don Quixote*, which he called *Master Peter's Puppet Show*; he hoped to premiere the composition within the year. By collaborating with Lorca on a traveling puppet company he could try out some of his ideas and techniques for the opera. Falla envisioned a company of international standing, one that would tour not only Granada but Europe and South America. He told Lorca that both Stravinsky and Ravel could be counted on to take part in the endeavor.

While Falla considered the logistics of the operation, Lorca turned to the question of repertoire. Drawing on memories of the puppet shows he had seen in childhood, as well as the conversations he had held in 1921 with his neighbors in Asquerosa, he concluded that the troupe should offer a tragedy from the popular tradition as well as several farces of "our own invention," a series of crime ballads and holy miracles, and "the savage idyll of Don Cristóbal and Miss Rosita," Andalusia's Punch and Judy. "If we put a little love into this matter, we'll be able to produce a clean and faultless art," he remarked to Falla.

Lorca admired the puppet theater precisely because it ruptured so thoroughly the deadly conventions of the bourgeois stage: its invisible fourth wall, decorous manners, and polite language. Filled with coarse talk and violent action, the puppet theater epitomized the kind of directly confrontational, vigorous spectacle Lorca longed both to see and to create onstage. So keenly did he revere this homely form that he later described it as the very "backbone" of the theater. If the theater is to be saved, he argued, it must return to its puppet roots.

In the summer of 1922 he began drafting a farce for the "Billy Club Puppets of Granada," as Falla proposed to call their troupe. The name came from the protagonist of the classic Andalusian guignol, Don Cristóbal, a billy-club wielding brute who takes a reluctant bride. The character of Cristóbal was so well known that throughout southern Spain puppets were known generically as "cristobalitos" or "cristobicas"—billy-club puppets.

By August Lorca had completed three scenes of his play. Although he failed to finish the farce that summer, he returned to it the following year and eventually completed several different versions of the work. He described the endeavor as "the dream of my youth." Two decades earlier, in the same tract of *vega* land, he had persuaded an aunt to make him a set of cardboard puppets so that he could put on plays. Hints of that vanished era surfaced both in the plot of Lorca's "Billy Club Puppets," a variation on the traditional Cristóbal story, and in its details, many of which Lorca drew from childhood recollections of Fuente Vaqueros.

He titled his short play *The Billy Club Puppets. The Tragicomedy of Don Cristóbal and Miss Rosita. A Guignolesque Farce in Six Scenes and an Announcement.* The vigor of the puppet theater and the bawdy content of the classic Cristóbal story freed Lorca to explore his lewder, more comic side. The play opens with a high-spirited prologue in which a puppet named Mosquito, who "represents the joy of free living, the grace and poetry of the Andalusian people," bluntly commands his audience to pay attention. "Son, shut your little mouth. And you, little girl, sit down at once."

Although Lorca was not the only Spanish playwright of his day to embrace the rough-hewn world of the puppet stage, his interest in the form was nonetheless unusual. Most Spanish audiences preferred the drawing-room dramas of Jacinto Benavente to the rustic antics of the puppeteer, an attitude Lorca found incomprehensible. He favored the true art of the puppet stage over the more pretentious theater of Benavente, and in his prologue to *The Billy Club Puppets* he said as much. Lorca's Mosquito describes the bourgeois stage as a "theater of counts and marquises, a gold and crystal theater where men . . . and ladies . . . go to fall asleep."

The ensuing farce incorporates stock lines, characters, and situations from the puppet theater, as well as popular Andalusian lyrics, and the grunts, groans, and salacious dialogue typical of the Cristóbal tradition. As he sets out to woo his reluctant bride, Rosita, a drunken Cristóbal drools, "She's a juicy little woman! What a pair of little hams she has!" Later he brags about the number of men he has killed with his billy club. Still later, distraught by his discovery that Rosita loves another man, Cristóbal ruptures his grotesque belly and dies. At his funeral a priest intones, "Whether or not we sing, / we'll earn our five pesetas."

The puppet tradition had led Lorca to see that action, not words, is the theater's principal medium, and in *The Billy Club Puppets* he demonstrates his new appreciation for theatrical technique. Rudely comic scenes are punctuated by moments of startling visual and aural beauty. As a snoring Don Cristóbal is being shaved for his wedding, a young girl dressed in yellow, with a crimson rose in her hair, sings a wistful love song, accompanying herself on castanets while an elderly beggar plays an accordion. At the close of this lyrical scene a ravishing Spanish *maja* appears at a tavern window and silently fans herself.

But Lorca's farce is not without the more conventional poetry of words. Midway through the play a character named Hour counsels the distressed Rosita to "be patient . . . How can you know what winds will spin the weather vane on your little roof tomorrow? Since I come here every day, I will remind you of this when you are old and have forgotten this moment." Elsewhere, a young man who once loved Rosita is shocked to hear of her impending marriage to Cristóbal. In an exchange reminiscent of Hugo's "Legend of Pécopin and Baldour," he reflects, "It isn't possible. She loved me so much, and that was only . . ." His voice trails off. "Five years ago," a village boy reminds him. Lorca's implication is clear. Love—true and abiding love between two individuals—is merely a chimera. The true steward of human destiny is time.

By the fall of 1922, Lorca had spent an entire year in Granada, chipping away at his long-postponed university degree. That autumn his twenty-year-old brother graduated from the University of Granada with honors. In early October, Lorca informed a friend that he had passed ten courses himself and planned to graduate in January. "Then my Señor Papá will let me travel. I'm thinking about going to Italy." He later changed his mind and settled on Paris. Either way, he was confident his first trip abroad would be "brilliant."

Confined once more to his parents' apartment in Granada, his puppet play momentarily set aside and college again the focus of his attention, Lorca amused himself by playing the piano in the evening for friends or sipping anisette with them in local bars. He missed Madrid—"that dandyish and absurd Madrid," he called it—but Don Federico insisted that he stay in Granada, and Lorca capitulated. Despite their differences, he admired his father. One night while playing the piano at home for friends, he glanced out the window and saw the stout, balding landowner below him in the distance, running pell-mell through the streets of Granada on his way home. As Don Federico reached the square in front of his apartment, he stopped, composed himself, and resumed walking at a measured pace. Lorca roared with laughter. "My father's so funny!" he cried. "He's such an Andalusian, such a poet, so wonderful!"

By December, Lorca had devised a new project: a private puppet show, to be staged at home during the holidays as a gift for his sister Isabel and her young friends. Falla was jubilant. As Lorca reported to Melchor Fernández Almagro in mid-December, they were both "terribly happy"—Lorca because the show would delight his sister, distract him from school, and advance his theatrical career, and Falla because it would allow him to try out some of the ideas he hoped to implement in *Master Peter's Puppet Show*. "Falla is like a little boy, saying, 'Oh, it's going to be something unique!' Last night he stayed up until all hours working and copying out the instrumental parts with a child's enthusiasm."

While Falla pored over his score for the production—a sophisticated blend of traditional songs and carols, Latin chant, and his own arrangements of music by Stravinsky, Ravel, Debussy, and others—Lorca prepared to direct the show. It was the first time since childhood that he had staged anything on his own. Now, as then, he drew his friends and family into the effort, enlisting both his brother and sister Concha as amateur puppeteers. The family apartment soon resembled the backstage of a busy theater, with Falla pounding away at the piano nearly every morning, and Hermenegildo Lanz, a lanky young artist who had agreed to design the production, tearing up and down the stairs, making adjustments to the stage and set. Lanz was thrilled to be part of such a distinguished undertaking, and informed his parents that he and his two colleagues hoped to perfect their "Andalusian Puppet Theater" and take it abroad.

On Saturday afternoon, January 6, 1923, the Feast of the Epiphany, a small crowd assembled in the Lorca family drawing room for the company's debut performance. Scattered among the "curls and ribbons of the rich children" were a handful of newsboys whom Lorca had spotted on the street outside his home and spontaneously asked inside. He was to remember their "smiling faces" for years.

Brightly colored souvenir programs announced the day's fare: an interlude attributed to Cervantes, a thirteenth-century mystery play, and a short script by Lorca himself, *The Girl Who Waters the Basil Plant and the Inquisitive Prince*, a poetic retelling of an old Andalusian folktale. As the curtains parted on the first act and Lanz's wooden-headed puppets began to speak, it seemed to Paco García Lorca that the spirit of Cervantes himself was smiling "upon that roomful of giggling children." When he wasn't backstage working puppets, Paco took photographs of the spectacle with a black-and-white camera. In a calculated attempt to publicize their achievement, Lorca and Falla subsequently sent copies of these pictures to their friends in the press.

By all accounts, the production was exquisite. From Lanz's vibrant cardboard sets to Lorca's poetic text and Falla's elaborate score, each of its components had been meticulously crafted. Intent on perfection, Falla covered the strings of Lorca's piano with tissue paper so that the instrument would sound like a harpsichord. For Lorca, the spectacle was a boyhood dream come true. Between acts he poked his puppetclad hand through the curtains of the stage and, in the role of his favorite puppet character, the boorish Don Cristóbal, bantered with his audience. To their glee, he called out to children by name. His brisk exchanges were the highlight of the day.

The production received three reviews, two by Lorca's close friend José Mora Guarnido, who after witnessing the event termed it "the first sophisticated attempt to recover the 'billy-club' theater." Mora compared the novelty of the undertaking to a "cubist poem," and suggested that the future of the Spanish theater depended upon this sort of experimental work. Mora's two accounts appeared in consecutive weeks in the prominent Madrid daily *La Voz*. After learning of the first of Mora's reviews, an ecstatic Hermenegildo Lanz begged his parents to buy "six, eight, or ten" copies of the paper.

In February 1923 Lorca took the last examinations in his long and lackluster university career. As usual, he relied on charm to carry him through. During an oral exam in political law, his friend and teacher Fernando de los Ríos asked him to define "the State." Lorca replied that it was a "great spider." Shrewdly, de los Ríos steered the exam away from politics. He suggested that Lorca discuss ancient mythology. The Greek myths, Lorca told him, were dreams. De los Ríos gave him a passing grade.

Lorca's final examination was in mercantile law, a topic about which he knew nothing. At the appointed hour for the test, he failed to appear. His professor, an older man on the verge of retirement, did not wish to end his career on such a sour note, and offered Lorca a second chance. In a private session, the professor asked him a few rudimentary questions about the subject. Lorca answered in generalities and passed.

He celebrated the end of his academic career by dining with friends at a cheap seafood restaurant in downtown Granada. It had taken him nine years to complete his university degree. He was three months shy of his twenty-fifth birthday. For the first time in his life, he was free to do as he pleased.

CHAPTER 8

GARDEN OF POSSIBILITIES

1923-24

W ithin weeks Lorca set off for Madrid. He was accompanied by his handsome younger brother, Paco, who had never been to the capital. As the two traveled north by train through the olive groves of Jaén and the blood-red fields of La Mancha, they talked about the future. Paco intended to pursue a doctorate in law; Federico had no specific plans, other than to resume his old life in Madrid and to continue writing.

A crowd of friends stood waiting for them on the platform at Madrid's Atocha Station. Lorca was overwhelmed. During the next few weeks he found himself "feted and pursued by everyone." Adolfo Salazar published a discreet tribute to him in *El Sol*. Declining to name the object of his praise, Salazar spoke coyly of a "little poet" who had recently returned to the capital, bringing with him a profusion of vitality and "exquisite good taste" with which to counter the "decadence" and "torpor" of metropolitan life.

Lorca carefully informed his parents that each day he felt "happier to have followed my own path, for I believe I will reach the goal I have set for myself." Aware of his father's continued misgivings about his career choice, he told his mother, "I think he'll be convinced when he sees how many things I've done, and how well I've done them."

The two brothers moved into a sunny room in the Residencia, where despite a full house Lorca's friends had managed to find a spot for them. Paco adapted quickly to city life. In the mornings before breakfast he exercised outdoors with

Luis Buñuel, who, according to Lorca, was "unbelievably kind" to both brothers. Later in the day Paco often toured Madrid with his brother. The two were such inseparable companions that friends referred to them as "Paco" and "Pico" García Lorca, an allusion to an old children's rhyme about a rich boy (*chico rico*) named "Paco Pico." Lorca smilingly signed some of his own letters as "Pico."

In time Paco settled down to work and began studying for his doctorate, while Lorca resumed his usual desultory existence, drifting from one social event to the next. He met a number of new friends during his first weeks in Madrid, among them Pedro Salinas, a lanky young poet and literature professor, who at their first encounter was astounded by Lorca and his poems. Salinas described the latter to fellow poet Jorge Guillén as "lively, fresh, and spontaneous, even those that are recherché. Like nothing else. He has a way of treating popular Andalusian themes that at times reminds one of Góngora . . . He's a boy who still lacks severity and refinement, but the basic material is splendid and most abundant. In short, a discovery of this spring."

The real discovery of the spring, however, was not Lorca but a nineteen-year-old artist who had come to Madrid the previous fall from Catalunya and taken a room at the Residencia. Tall and slender, with pale, almost feminine features and long hair, he was an enigma to most. He wore knee-length velvet coats, silk cravats, and leather leggings. He spent most of his time shut away in his room, painting. He seldom spoke to anyone except when he needed help with some practical matter, such as buying stamps at the post office, and then he got confused and managed to deposit both his change and his letter in the post box.

Residents called him the "Czechoslovak painter" and gossiped about him. But one day a maid accidentally left the door to his room ajar, and Pepín Bello glanced inside. Bello saw enough of the artist's work to realize that it was exceptional. Word of the discovery spread quickly, and Buñuel, Lorca, and others offered the young man their friendship at once. The painter accepted. Years later he remarked that at the time he thought Lorca and his crowd were nothing more than a group of "intellectual snobs."

He thought of himself as a prodigy. His name, Salvador Dalí Domenech, meant that he was destined, he said, to be the "savior" of contemporary painting. Born May 13, 1904, exactly nine months and nine days after the death of his two-year-old brother, Salvador, for whom he was named, Dalí produced his first oil painting at the age of six. At fourteen he took part in his first official art exhibition, for which he received glowing reviews in the local press and the more lucrative financial encouragement of a rich family friend who bought two of his paintings. At sixteen he wrote his first novel. By the time he moved to Madrid in 1922 at age eighteen, Salvador Dalí was known in his native Catalunya as an artist of formidable potential.

In Madrid he settled into the Residencia and began taking classes at the city's Academy of Fine Arts. Although his father expected him to receive a teaching degree from the institution and then become a drawing instructor, Dalí had other ideas. Two years earlier he had confided to his diary that he planned to work "like mad" at the Academy for three years and then, "by sacrificing myself and submitting to truth, I will win the prize to study for four years in Rome; and coming back from Rome, I'll be a genius, and the world will admire me. Perhaps I'll be despised and misunderstood, but I'll be a genius, a great genius, I am sure of it."

At the Residencia, Dalí sketched and painted incessantly. Drawings littered the floor of his room—sheets of paper covered with bold images inspired by futurism and fauvism, and above all by cubism, whose clean geometrical lines and objectivity Dalí sought to emulate. He revered his compatriot Pablo Picasso.

He said later that during this period of his life freedom mattered less to him than his work, to such an extent that he would have welcomed confinement in a prison cell. But although content to renounce the world, he did not want the world to renounce him. One of his chief aims in life was to be found fascinating, and he was willing to do almost anything to succeed. To attract attention to himself in high school he had leapt from tall staircases in front of classmates and had feigned affection for a young woman who was in love with him. He enjoyed deluding her. "In a short time I've made great advances along the path of farce and deceit," he wrote in his diary, noting his pleasure at being "a great actor in the even greater comedy that is life, the farcical life of our society." In truth, Salvador Dalí was devoted to one person alone. "I am madly in love with myself," he said.

Everything Dalí did and said—his velvet coats and broad-brimmed hats, his manic pursuit of solitude, his brashly avant-garde work—was calculated to provoke admiration. When Lorca first set eyes on the painter, he had to disguise his amazement at Dalí's attire. The artist, in turn, was captivated by Lorca. He sensed at once that the olive-skinned Andalusian was somehow distinct from others at the Residencia. During their first meeting, Dalí later recalled, "the poetic phenomenon in its entirety and 'in the raw' suddenly appeared before me in flesh and blood." As their friendship grew, Dalí became so smitten by Lorca's poetic "fires" that he had to work consciously to "extinguish" them with his own prosaic talk so as not to fall under the poet's sway.

Still, he found Lorca difficult to resist. Soon after their first encounter, the painter cut his hair, clipped his sideburns, and bought a sports suit so that he could better fit into Lorca's crowd. He gave Lorca one of his paintings and sketched his portrait sitting in a café. The two engaged in long discussions about literature, art, and aesthetics, often talking until dawn. At times they disagreed violently. But they always treated each other with sincerity, and Dalí came to rely on Lorca's superior knowledge of such matters as music. Once, at a concert, he inquired, "Should I be liking this?" Yes, Lorca said, and Dalí promptly burst into wild applause.

In many ways Lorca's antithesis, Dalí was so shy—despite his flamboyant appearance—as to be "almost mute," while Lorca was vigorous and outgoing, a font of laughter and music. Whenever Lorca took Dalí to a *tertulia*, the painter refrained from talking. Lorca reproached him for his reserve and devised a scheme for breaking the ice at such gatherings. "I'll say you're a great painter and that you're here working," he told Dalí.

But when silence descended in the midst of the next *tertulia*, Dalí panicked. Before Lorca could say anything, he blurted, "I'm also a very interesting painter."

On several occasions Lorca took Dalí to dinner at the home of the Residencia director, Alberto Jiménez Fraud. As usual, Lorca talked and laughed through the evening, while Dalí kept to himself. When he did speak, it was with a deep, nervous voice and a heavy Catalan accent. He smiled rather than laughed, a furtive smile that exposed a row of tiny, sharp teeth. Jiménez Fraud's wife, Natalia, thought the artist "nothing more than Lorca's echo."

As the months wore on, Dalí shed his inhibitions. Shortly before the end of the spring 1923 term, he took part in a student protest at the Academy of Fine Arts and was expelled from school. Unrepentant, he went home to Catalunya, where he immediately took part in an illegal political demonstration and was sent to jail for a month. In prison, he bragged, "We drank lousy local champagne every evening."

With the approach of summer, Lorca prepared to go home for his yearly stay in the *vega*. He ordered his family to see to it that someone whitewash his bedroom in Asquerosa, paint the ceiling blue, hang white curtains, and deliver a

piano *"that plays"* to his father's country house, "even if we're only there for fifteen days." He had hoped to join Falla in Italy for a brief vacation before returning to Granada, but his parents wouldn't allow it. Nor was he able to attend
a performance in June of Falla's *Master Peter's Puppet Show* in Paris, despite
the composer's repeated insistence that both Lorca and his brother be there.

Falla was eager to see Lorca again. Earlier in the year, while rehearsing their
holiday puppet show, the two had begun work on a comic operetta featuring elements of Italian opera and Andalusian folk song. Lorca had immediately
started drafting the libretto, but he had become distracted from the project in
Madrid and neglected to finish the script. His mother caught wind of the situation and sent Lorca a chastening note. "Even if you don't need the money
because you have a father who supports you," she reminded him, "this gentleman"—Falla—"must earn his own living, and I would be extremely sorry if you
were to hinder his plans instead of helping him."

During the summer of 1923 the two men resumed work on the operetta,
"Lola the Stage Actress," a bittersweet love story set in rural Andalusia. At his father's country home in Asquerosa, Lorca pored over the libretto. He confessed
to being "in love" with his protagonist, a clever actress who enjoys outwitting
others with her feminine wiles and wardrobe of disguises. But despite his desire
to finish the script so that Falla could "put his hands on my operetta" and begin
composing the score, Lorca failed to finish, and the following year he and Falla
abandoned the project.

It was the last time the two were to collaborate. The older, more disciplined
composer could not tolerate Lorca's haphazard approach to work, nor his utter
inability to meet a deadline—either his own or one imposed by someone else.
Lorca's friends shared Falla's frustration. Privately, Adolfo Salazar suggested
to Falla that Lorca lacked the necessary "control" to succeed in his career.
He writes poetry, Salazar observed, "as one heaves a deep, emotional sigh. It's
charming, of course, but it frightens me because I don't think it's enough to
'make him into' a real artist."

Others expressed similar qualms. In Madrid, Gregorio Martínez Sierra, who
had premiered *The Butterfly's Evil Spell* in 1920, wanted to stage a second
Lorca work and was considering the still-unfinished puppet play *The Tragicomedy of Don Cristóbal and Miss Rosita*. But although convinced of Lorca's talent
and eager to present his work, Martínez Sierra remembered the difficulties he
had endured while preparing *The Butterfly's Evil Spell*, and told Lorca, "My
fear is that . . . you'll never finish the puppet play." Lorca continued to putter
with the script, and eventually managed to complete the work, but he failed to

do so in time to meet Martínez Sierra's needs, and the director gave up on the play.

Lorca spent the summer of 1923 much as he had the two previous summers, flitting from one idea to the next. He tinkered with his puppet farce and operetta; he talked of writing a new play and of finishing his suites, some of which were now three years old. For the third consecutive year he attempted to master the guitar. In desperation, his mother tried to hide the instrument from him.

"I'm going through a feverish and bitter summer, pursued by a crowd of poems that make my life impossible," Lorca wrote to a friend in Madrid. Nothing resolved itself. For twenty days and nights he worked "feverishly" on a new suite, "In the Garden of the Lunar Grapefruits," a dreamlike account of a poet's journey into the "garden" of his own creative psyche. But in spite of his efforts to perfect the poem, Lorca managed only to "pin it down." Words came to him filled with "mysterious sounds and meanings." Lines of verse eluded him. His poetry seemed both "fugitive and *alive*." He found himself in a desperate struggle against his "two secular enemies (and those of all poets), Eloquence and Common Sense." He felt "penetrated by everything. At times I imagine that I've got a small crown of glow-worms, and that I am something other than what I am. I believe we'll never be pure because we're able to distinguish and judge . . . , but no matter how much I try, the wind doesn't want to instruct me . . . and I must remain here until I'm an old man, seeking the true and ineffable little card of the breeze." Even his name bothered him: he could not endure it when people called him "Lorca! I am Federico but I'm not Lorca."

For the third year in a row he completed nothing. His work confounded him. "I feel a real panic when it comes to writing!" he told José de Ciria y Escalante, a friend and fellow poet in Madrid. The notion of possibility, of potential, consumed him. In "Garden of the Lunar Grapefruits" he acknowledged the "garden / of all I am not, all / I could and should have been!" His "garden," he said, "is the garden of possibilities . . . the garden of the theories that went away without being seen and of the children who have not been born." He was haunted by the specter of what he had failed to create: "My unborn children / pursue me."

Unable to publish or even finish his suite collection as he had hoped, frustrated by the mystery of his work and the impossibility of charting its future, he waited for some sort of revelation. It may have been during this, his twenty-fifth summer, that Lorca told the guitarist Regino Sáinz de la Maza: "Now I've dis-

covered something terrible (don't tell this to anyone). I haven't been born yet."
A few days earlier, while sitting in his grandfather's easy chair brooding about
his past, he had come to the sudden realization, as he told Sáinz, that

> none of the dead hours belonged to me because it wasn't I who had lived them, nei-
> ther the hours of love, nor the hours of hate, nor the hours of inspiration. There were
> a thousand Federico García Lorcas, stretched out forever in the attic of time and in the
> storehouse of the future; I contemplated another thousand Federico García Lorcas,
> very tightly pressed, one on top of the other, waiting to be filled with gas in order to fly
> off without direction. This moment was a terribly fearful moment, my mother Lady
> Death had given me the key of time and for a second I understood everything. I'm liv-
> ing on borrowed time, what I have within is not mine; let's see if I'm going to be born.

He drifted from project to project. Everything attracted him: old and new,
somber and comic. As he worked on "In the Garden of the Lunar Grapefruits"
he immersed himself in the poetry of the Spanish Golden Age ("and what great
pleasure our old poets give me!"). Spurred by his deepening zeal for the avant-
garde, he sat in cafés with friends in Granada and mocked the vulgar tastes of
the local bourgeoisie.

In particular, Lorca and his friends ridiculed the claptrap bourgeois verse
that permeated the local press: rhapsodic poems celebrating the beauty of the
Alhambra and the quaint charms of the Albaicín. Although many Granadans
adored this sort of sentimental drivel, Lorca and his companions loathed it. In
their scorn they invented an apocryphal poet of their own, a fictitious balladeer
named "Isidoro Capdepón Fernández," whose pedestrian verse sang praises to
"Granada, Granada . . . / oh, beautiful Granada!" The group concocted
Capdepón's poems in unison while sitting at café tables, then surreptitiously
submitted them to the local press. In 1923, Capdepón's flowery verse began ap-
pearing in the *Defensor de Granada*. That same year one of Lorca's friends
nominated the nonexistent poet to the prestigious Royal Spanish Academy in
Madrid, where, according to a bogus newspaper article, the distinguished Don
Isidoro gave a talk on "Rhetorical Menopause, or The Decadence of Civic Poetry in Contemporary Spain." On his own, Lorca scribbled and circulated innumerable poems "by Capdepón"; he even compiled a page-long biography of
the poet. The game went on for years.

While sitting in cafés with his friends, Lorca also began doodling on scraps
of paper—an impulse evidently due in part to his new friendship with Dalí.
Lorca made dozens of drawings in 1923: comic portraits, grotesque caricatures
prompted by funny names ("Trop-long," a Frenchman with a long, phallic
nose) or peculiar professions (archbishops' hairdresser, cornucopia salesman).

His big hands were remarkably agile. On the backs of calling cards, magazine subscription forms, pages torn from books, Lorca turned out sketch after sketch in pencil and pen. At home, he began keeping a set of colored pencils on his desk. His drawings were deliberately provocative. He sketched bearded women and big-breasted men, spotted monsters, an orator crying "Shit!," and an androgynous figure with tentaclelike growths on its face, which he titled "The Demon of Masturbation." Although he'd had no formal training except for a few drawing classes in secondary school, his sketches possessed a naive charm and were clearly the work of an astounding visual imagination. Lorca drew as spontaneously as he wrote.

By the fall of 1923, he had established enough of a reputation as a draftsman for his friend Melchor Fernández Almagro to make reference to his new avocation in a tribute to Lorca in the Madrid press. The article, "The Lyrical World of García Lorca," appeared in the magazine *España* and was the first of its kind to offer an overview of the young writer's literary output. Lorca was profoundly touched. "I know that you love me, and most of all you encourage me in a way for which I cannot thank you enough," he told Fernández Almagro. For years the portly critic had been one of Lorca's closest friends and advisers. Born and raised in Granada, and now a respected figure in Madrid's most important literary circles, Fernández Almagro had successfully bridged the cultural abyss separating provincial Granada from metropolitan Madrid, and as such was to Lorca an ideal reader. Lorca deliberately sought his reaction to projects and ideas, and the two exchanged frequent letters—a testament to the depth of their friendship, for Lorca was at best a selective correspondent and once told Fernández Almagro, "When I'm not on close terms with the person I'm writing to, I don't know what to say!"

In September, Lorca sent word to "Melchorito" of yet another new literary undertaking. In addition to his other activities, he had recently become obsessed with the figure of a woman who had "strolled through the secret little road of my childhood" and later haunted his adolescence. She was Mariana Pineda, a real-life resident of early-nineteenth-century Granada, who had borne two children by her husband and a third, illegitimate child by a lover, seven years after her husband's death, before taking part in a conspiracy to overthrow Spain's despotic King Fernando VII. For her role in the conspiracy Mariana was condemned to death and hanged in a public square in Granada on May 26, 1831, at the age of twenty-seven.

Legend had subsequently transformed this complex and worldly woman into a beautiful widow who had embraced freedom and died for it. To Lorca, Mariana Pineda epitomized both the romantic age and the romantic spirit he claimed as his own. A statue of Mariana, a perfect "symbol of a revolutionary ideal," stood in a square directly below his bedroom in Granada. As a young man he had stared so often at her gray stone presence that he felt compelled to "exalt" her. She stirred his most distant memories. In childhood he had heard maids and old-timers "very close to the event" sing ballads and tell stories about Mariana Pineda, and he had later thumbed a leatherbound edition of her biography in his family's library. He confessed to having loved her "at the age of nine." He told Fernández Almagro, "If I'm afraid of doing this play, it's precisely because I am disturbing my most delicate memories of this martyred blond widow." That he risked creating hagiography rather than biography did not occur to him.

At first he was unsure how to proceed. Months earlier he had asked Rinconcillo companion Antonio Gallego Burín, a professor at the University of Granada, for a "few notes" on the subject because "I don't want to bungle it, do you understand?" But Gallego Burín turned him down, fearful that Lorca might plagiarize his own research on the topic. Lorca pronounced his friend's attitude "absurd" and resolved to seek a different kind of truth by investing the past with "poetry" and "emotion," as he phrased it. He aimed to depict Mariana as he believed she was "in reality"—Lorca's version of reality. Instead of presenting the Mariana Pineda of history, the sensual lover and courageous activist executed for her political ideals, he would reveal the Mariana of legend, the romantic heroine of the tales and ballads he had heard as a child, the saintly Granadan beauty who died not for politics but because she loved a fellow conspirator and sacrificed her life to his cause. In order to achieve his guileless vision of Mariana, Lorca planned to invent and conflate characters, reshaping the facts of the original story to suit both his aesthetic and emotional needs. "Since childhood," he said, "I've been hearing these lines, so very suggestive: 'Marianita went out for a walk / and a soldier stepped out to meet her . . .' "

The air in Granada smelled of jasmine as he set to work on his new play, and Lorca's mind soared with lyrical images of "Mariana the lover," a "Juliet without Romeo." In his heart he felt he had found the right approach. Fernández Almagro praised him for having chosen to pursue the "poetic truth" over historical accuracy. He also praised Lorca's timing. Although Lorca had turned to Mariana's story primarily as a means of ennobling the past—his own as well as Granada's—his choice of subject matter took on unexpected political overtones shortly after he began drafting the play. On September 12, 1923, General Miguel Primo de Rivera of the Spanish army seized control of the nation in a bloodless military coup. The country's thirty-seven-year-old king, Alfonso XIII, yielded to him at once. Within a week, Primo de Rivera had dissolved Parliament, abolished trial by jury, imposed martial law, and suspended citizens' rights. Thick black censorship notices began to riddle the Spanish press.

"The political circumstances of the present moment exalt the figure of Mariana Pineda," a weary Fernández Almagro wrote to Lorca just three days after Primo's coup. "Our grandparents' century is returning."

Spain's new dictator was a hard-drinking, cigar-smoking Andalusian in his early fifties with a taste for bullfights, wine, and women. Two days after assuming power the general issued a proclamation stating that his new government was "a man's movement. Anyone who feels his masculinity is not yet fully defined should wait patiently for the good days we are preparing for the Fatherland. Spaniards! Long live Spain and long live the King!"

Many citizens welcomed the change in government. Under Alfonso XIII the country had suffered years of labor unrest at home and military incompetence overseas; even Lorca, who normally paid scant attention to such things, had complained about the nation's hapless leaders. In the summer of 1921, Alfonso's disastrous policy in the country's Moroccan protectorate, where Spain's government sought to pacify Berber tribes through a combined program of political bribery and military occupation by ill-trained conscripts, had led to a brutal rebel attack at Anwal, in which nearly nine thousand Spanish soldiers died. The political repercussions of the event had irreparably damaged the monarchy. Primo's coup appeared to promise a return to stability. Like his idol, Benito Mussolini, the new Spanish dictator planned to impose discipline and order on his wayward nation by unifying "People, King, and Military."

But for Spain's intellectual and artistic life, the coup was an appalling "step backward," as Fernández Almagro termed it. The dictator quickly demonstrated his anti-intellectual bias. Within months of his coup he closed down the Madrid Atheneum with the excuse that the institution, one of Lorca's favorite sanctuaries in the capital, was promulgating "strident politics." At the same time Primo accused Miguel de Unamuno of spreading antigovernment propaganda, and expelled the philosopher from Spain. Incensed, Lorca's friend and former professor Fernando de los Ríos sent a letter of protest to the dictator. The government promptly prosecuted de los Ríos. Ultimately he was acquitted—but the ideological battle lines were drawn.

To his parents Lorca bemoaned the country's dreadful political situation. The following year, at the behest of friends, he signed a manifesto voicing support for the Catalan language, which Primo de Rivera sought to suppress. But unlike the socialist de los Ríos, Lorca had no appetite for organized politics. Its meetings, petitions, documents, and other formalities bored him. He cared about broader issues: human rights, social justice, subjects he could address through poetry and plays.

Two months after Primo's coup, Lorca returned to Madrid and to the Residencia, where he continued to work on his play about Mariana Pineda. He hoped to premiere the drama the following spring. In late December he attended an Italian production of Luigi Pirandello's *Six Characters in Search of an Author*, presented in Madrid as part of a rapprochement between the new regimes of Italy and Spain. Spanish critics hailed Pirandello's unconventional dramaturgy and his ingenious play-within-a-play, which one reviewer called "a reality more real than reality itself." The work exemplified the kind of radically innovative theater Lorca longed to see on the Spanish stage, and although he left no record of his response to *Six Characters*, months after attending the production he began drafting his own version of a play-within-a-play.

He remarked to his parents that he was optimistic about his future and grateful to be in Madrid. To remain in Granada, he said, invoking a favorite image, would be to clip his wings, and he wanted none of that. Despite the parochialism of the country's new government—or more probably because of it—Madrid's cultural life was as vital as ever. During the spring of 1924 Lorca met and befriended a number of poets his own age, men who shared his antipathy to artistic mediocrity and his aspirations for a renaissance of Spanish literature.

Together with Lorca, this eclectic assortment of young, mostly male writers was beginning to be seen as a "generation," even outside Spain. Born with the century and baptized in the waters of despair that followed the collapse of the Spanish empire in 1898, they had come of age during World War I and launched their careers in the Roaring Twenties. Like their European contemporaries, they eschewed pessimism. They saw each other regularly in Madrid—at cafés, in theaters, at the Residencia—and although linked by little more than age, friendship, and circumstance, they began to think of themselves as a cohesive whole. Lorca had known at least two members of the group, the Malagan poets Emilio Prados and Manolo Altolaguirre, since childhood, and he was familiar with the work of others. In 1923, while attending Pirandello's *Six Characters*, he met Vicente Aleixandre, a tall, pale blond from Seville, whose fragile health made him one of the more reclusive poets of their generation, but who warmed nonetheless to Lorca's spontaneity and "tremendous dark laugh."

A few months after meeting Aleixandre, Lorca was introduced to the poet Jorge Guillén, a literature professor in his early thirties, who lived, taught, and wrote in the city of Valladolid, a few hours north of Madrid. Guillén was struck by Lorca's vibrant personality and histrionic gifts. After spending an evening chatting in Lorca's room at the Residencia and later hearing him recite his short play *The Billy Club Puppets*, Guillén wrote excitedly to his wife, "Stupendous, perfect, the *Petrouchka* that modern art has been searching for; lyrical, very musical, funny, dramatic, abundantly inventive, completely *réussie*, popular, Andalusian, with extraordinary strength and sap. Lorca reads his work as if playing each and every part of a stage company and an orchestra. He's a poet and then some. Lorca is the best among us, I have to believe it."

Guillén found Lorca irresistible—his charm, his effervescence, his apparently constant creativity. "Federico's here," he used to cry whenever Lorca arrived at a gathering. "Now we'll go on a poetry bender." He cautioned others against trying to resist the ebullient *granadino*: "It's no use . . . Federico will devour you." After one of many visits with Lorca in the 1920s, Guillén remarked to his wife, "Federico continues to make us laugh, in a state of true, superhuman, poetic happiness." He described the "court of friends" who invariably surrounded the charismatic Andalusian.

Lorca's room at the Residencia soon became one of the most popular meeting spots in Madrid. So many people used to crowd into it to hear him read that his friends called the place "the tram." Lorca relished the attention. Night after night he sat enthroned on his daybed, a crowd of young men massed around him—standing, sitting, lying curled up beneath the table—while he read from his work, pulling pages of poetry from a notebook he kept bound with red tape. He was a sensation, a "modern minstrel," the "last bard."

He read simply but with commanding authority. Some maintained that the secret to his power lay in his eyes, which conveyed all the mystery and emotion of his verse. Others claimed it was his voice, with its dark sounds and rustic accent. He could be pompous. As he read, his chest swelled and he punctuated words with gestures. To suggest the moon opening and closing "its tail," he moved his thick hands back and forth like a fan. To signal the end of a poem he sometimes held a rolled napkin to his forehead and let it fall like a curtain over his face. Occasionally, to heighten the effect of an image, he tugged at someone's arm. Audiences clung to his words. Whenever Lorca read his poems, a friend remembered, "he gave the impression that he was writing them. It was like attending a birth. His own poems surprised him."

He preferred reading his poetry to publishing it. "When I correct proofs, I experience the inevitable sensation of death," he complained. "The poem no longer lives." He cared so little about preserving his work that he gave away copies of poems at random. At *tertulias* he taunted admirers by destroying manuscripts before their eyes. "Here's a poem I've written for you," he would shout to some friend, an accomplice familiar with the routine, who would then put a match to Lorca's work and use it to light a cigarette. Luis Buñuel once salvaged what he could of some of these charred poems; years later they turned out to be the only extant copies of Lorca's suite "Water Jets."

Because he refrained from publishing his poetry, it began to circulate informally, and what one journalist called a "García Lorca state of mind" evolved. Few writers had published less and were more celebrated. In virtually no time, Lorca emerged as the leading poet of his generation. He did so as much by force of personality as by the quality of his work. Other writers began to imitate his ostentatious recital style. The phenomenon took on a name: *lorquismo*, "that Lorca business." As Lorca's circle of fans grew, so did his ego. He began to view himself in historic terms. When he agreed to pose for a series of sketches by the artist Gregorio Prieto, he told Prieto, "With these portraits of me we'll both be immortalized. They're every bit as good as the ones Velázquez did of Góngora."

Hungry for praise, and eager to share his work, he courted new listeners, "virgin" audiences. A consummate performer, he knew precisely how to woo a crowd. Rafael Martínez Nadal, a university student who met Lorca in 1923 at the home of a mutual friend, recalled that during their first encounter someone asked Lorca to play the piano. "Oh, I feel terrible!" Lorca muttered, taking a handkerchief from his suit pocket and dabbing at his face, before sitting down at the piano and plunging into a series of popular Spanish songs. For his final tune he sang a bawdy habanera:

> My father's cu-chu-cha
> is bigger than mine,
> for last night I took a peep
> when he was fast asleep.

Lorca's voice crackled with amusement. He then swung around from the piano and launched into a sequence of dramatic sketches. To Martínez Nadal's delight, he improvised a dialogue between two Granadan gossips, followed by a make-believe Mass, for which he imitated a priest with a cold, a dozing altar boy, and a squeaking door. Someone asked if he could read some of his poetry. Lorca paused momentarily, composed himself, then embarked on a recital of his latest work. His audience was enthralled.

Shortly afterward, Martínez Nadal, an impetuous teenager with a ramlike face and coiled blond hair, told Lorca that while he liked his poems, he wasn't sure if it was because they were "really good or because you read them so well." Lorca was caught off guard by the young man's candor. "You rotten little bastard!" he cried. "Tomorrow I'm going to leave a stack of poems at your house and next week I'm coming back to hear you criticize them." To Lorca's surprise, Nadal turned out to be a perceptive critic, and Lorca began taking poems to him on a regular basis. He enjoyed Rafael's brash humor and irreverent take on life, and he welcomed his literary insights. From Nadal, Lorca accepted criticism that from others he might have dismissed. The two shared secrets, nicknames, inside jokes. Alone with Nadal, Lorca relaxed, ceased his theatrics, and revealed a more private, solitary self, one preoccupied with death and with the enduring sadness of the human condition.

He became a regular guest at Nadal's home and a friend to Rafael's mother, Lola. The entire Nadal household succumbed to his wiles. Whenever Lorca arrived for dinner, the cook would hug him with her floury arms and send him to the table to see what she'd made. When Nadal wasn't home, Lorca sometimes dropped by to visit his friend's mother or to browse in Rafael's library. Left on his own, he once sketched a young man's face inside Nadal's copy of *The Picture of Dorian Gray*. "Don't say anything to Rafael," he cautioned Doña Lola, "but when he comes home he's going to find a surprise or two." It didn't occur to Lorca that Nadal might object to having his book defaced, for among disciples like Rafael, he knew he could do no wrong. And in fact, when Nadal came home and discovered the drawing, he was charmed.

But even Nadal acknowledged his friend's constant need to show off. In *tertulias* Lorca flaunted his knowledge of literature. He once broke into a conversation about Goethe's *Faust*—a work that had long intrigued him—to offer his own, highly personal interpretation of the book. On another occasion he delivered a complex appraisal of Joyce's *Ulysses*, despite the fact that he had never read the book. Days earlier he had heard a friend summarize the novel in conversation, and from that synopsis he had absorbed enough information to feign knowledge of the work.

To those who were pretentious about their scholarship Lorca was merciless. "Jesus, you know a lot!" he would exclaim in a show of mock admiration. His own approach to literature, as to life, was serendipitous. Blessed with a nimble mind and a prodigious memory, he drew much of what he knew about books, especially foreign ones, from talk with friends. He could recite obscure literary passages at a moment's notice. But he was coy about the source and scope of his erudition; it was part of his mystique. He once claimed to have read only two books in the world, the Bible and *A Thousand and One Nights*. ("The Bible has Heaven and *A Thousand and One Nights* has Earth. Who needs more?") On another occasion he bragged of having gone through periods when he read two books a day "as an intellectual exercise."

Martínez Nadal eventually concluded that Lorca read far more than anyone suspected. But he was no pedant. He culled from books, and from conversations about books, only what he needed for his writing. According to another friend, whenever a literary work was discussed in his presence, "Lorca would deftly separate the grain from the chaff, invent whatever was lacking in order to complete the picture, and store the whole thing away in his mind for future reference."

Brimming with confidence, Lorca returned home for the summer in late June 1924. He brought with him the poet Juan Ramón Jiménez and his wife, Zenobia. The couple had decided to spend a brief holiday touring Granada in Lorca's company. Together with Paco García Lorca, the three traveled south by rail from Madrid. As their train entered Granada province, the Andalusian-born Jiménez murmured, "Oh, I can smell the thyme!" Eager to please his distinguished guest, Lorca leapt from his seat to open the window so that the balmy scent could suffuse the car.

In Granada, he introduced his visitors to his family and friends and, with his family in tow, took the couple on a tour of the city's principal sights: the cathedral, the Albaicín, the Alhambra, and the Generalife gardens, where Jiménez fell into rapture at the sound of so much running water. Along a cypress-lined path in the gardens, the ensemble paused to have their picture taken. While others in the group stared straight at the camera, Lorca glanced shyly at Jiménez, his young face a radiant blend of reverence and pride.

Although the two men had seen each other frequently in Madrid and had collaborated on a handful of projects, it was not until his visit to Granada that Jiménez came to appreciate the full scope of Lorca's mercurial personality. The older poet watched with amusement as Lorca raced through the city on his stocky legs, laughing obstreperously and pausing from time to time to sing ballads with his sister Isabel, by then a charming fourteen-year-old. The childless Jiménez found the entire Lorca family enchanting and Granada itself a marvel. Not long after his visit he sent a letter to Isabel, in which he vowed to return to the city in order to fill himself "to the gills with Granada." He added that as a result of his stay, his "fondness" for Lorca had "turned into a deep affection."

Lorca was jubilant. Having now dealt "intimately" with the great Jiménez, he told Melchor Fernández Almagro: "I've been able to observe what a profound sensitivity and divine quantity of poetry his soul possesses. One day he told me, 'We'll go to the Generalife at five in the afternoon, the hour in which the gardens begin to *suffer.*' This paints a full-length portrait of him, doesn't it?" In subsequent months, Lorca endeavored to render his own portrait of Jiménez in two brief poems, "Juan Ramón Jiménez," and a second, "shadow" poem, "Venus." Coolly impersonal in tone, both works reflect the older poet's stated devotion to a pure, unsentimental verse, and allude to his mania for silence and isolation, "the infinity of white. / Snow. Spikenard. Salt flat."

Jiménez's presence lingered long after his departure from Granada and the Lorca family's annual retreat to Asquerosa. In his letter to Isabel, the poet had urged the girl to persuade her brother to work hard that summer, and as it happened, Lorca did. He began a new play, a farce about an Andalusian shoemaker's wife. Its cast list so pleased him that he sent it to Fernández Almagro, "since I believe you can tell if a play is good or bad by simply reading the cast list."

He also wrote a sonnet in memory of a twenty-year-old friend, José de Ciria y Escalante, who had died on June 4, 1924, the day before Lorca's twenty-sixth birthday. For ten days Lorca tried but failed to summon the poem. His "fountain," he confessed to Fernández Almagro, was uncustomarily dry. But at last, one August afternoon as he stood in the midst of a poplar grove trying to commune with his dead friend, inspiration had arrived. "I was able to give birth in an instant to the sonnet I am mailing you," he told the critic. He explained that he had chosen the difficult form because in its austerity the sonnet "preserves an eternal feeling, one that does not fit into any other flask than this apparently cold one."

The rigor of the form allowed Lorca to confront emotions that might otherwise have overwhelmed him, and although not by nature disciplined, he found the act of yielding to the sonnet's constraints both gratifying and safe. The poem led him beyond grief:

> And you above, so high, so green and cold
> forget me! And forget the foolish world,
> my sad, sad Giocondo, my sweet friend.

After completing the sonnet Lorca told Fernández Almagro, "From time to time I'm seized by a strange happiness that I had never felt before. The very sad happiness of being a poet! And nothing matters to me. Not even death!"

Newly infatuated with his craft, he turned to another traditional meter, that of the ballad, a form whose narrative thrust and eight-syllable line Lorca judged "the vessel best shaped to my sensibility." In a much-quoted phrase, Juan Ramón Jiménez once decreed the ballad the "river of the Spanish language," because of its significance to the nation's literature. Its practitioners included medieval minstrels and Golden Age poets, anonymous balladeers and some of Lorca's more famous contemporaries, among them Antonio Machado and Jiménez himself, both of whom sought through their work to revive and revitalize the form.

On July 29, 1924, scarcely a month after Jiménez's visit to Granada, Lorca penciled the words "Gypsy Ballads" on a sheet of notepaper and beneath them jotted the text to a poem he later titled "Ballad of the Moon, Moon." A sensual tribute to a longtime obsession, the poem told of a seductive moon with "breasts of tin, / shiny and pure and hard," whose pale light illuminates a scene of death and mourning among a band of Gypsies.

In writing the poem, Lorca sought to fuse the ballad form with the mystical world of the Andalusian Gypsy, and in doing so to convey the essence of southern Spain, much as Machado had used the ballad to evoke central Spain in *The Castilian Country*. Lorca hoped to render Andalusia as myth, and the Gypsy as the region's archetypal hero. He viewed the Gypsy not with scorn or disgust, as many of his compatriots did, but romantically, as the "truest and purest thing in Andalusia"—and because Andalusia exemplified life, the Gypsies, with their nomadic, impassioned, violent existence, were a paradigm for all humanity, the embodiment of raw human instinct.

Visually, his new poem was a departure from Lorca's most recent work. The ballad's long, slender silhouette bore little resemblance to the haikulike stanzas of his suites and deep-song poems. Years of casual contact with the form had taught Lorca to relish the ballad's traits: its shortened line and elliptical style, its abrupt beginnings and ends. At home, his multivolume copy of Pedrell's *Cancionero musical popular español*, which abounds with traditional Spanish ballads, was worn with use. Many of the ballads he knew best were anonymous songs that had been worked and whittled from one century to the next until, in Lorca's words, they were "worn away by time." Palimpsests, they aroused in him the same sense of wonder he had felt as a boy, combing through his father's fields in search of relics.

On July 30, one day after drafting "Ballad of the Moon, Moon," Lorca wrote a second Gypsy poem, "Romance de la pena negra," or "Ballad of the Black Sorrow." The work's primary focus is *pena*, a term Lorca found difficult to define. "*Pena* is not anguish," he observed, "because with *pena* one can smile, nor is it a blinding ache, since it never produces weeping; it is a longing without object, a keen love for nothing, with the certainty that death (the eternal preoccupation of Andalusia) is breathing behind the door." As such, the word coursed through Lorca's work like an underground stream.

Three days later he composed a third poem in the series, "Sleepwalking Ballad," a chronicle of the love and death of a Gypsy smuggler and his girlfriend. In the poem's refrain, a phrase inspired by a popular lyric, Lorca produced one of his most celebrated lines of verse: "Green oh how I love you green, / green wind, green boughs."

His initial spree of ballad-making ended with "Sleepwalking Ballad." But Lorca soon resumed work on the series. Within three years he had drafted nearly two dozen Gypsy ballads. To Fernández Almagro he confessed that he had written the first three ballads "completely for my own enjoyment." There was more to it, however. In their novel blend of form and content, traditional motifs and stark metaphors, lyrical and narrative voice, the poems were his most ingenious work to date, and Lorca sensed it. Although he had practiced writing ballads in his teens and had published a handful of ballads in *Book of Poems*, nothing he had previously written could rival the power and innovation of these new works. Years later, looking back on his Gypsy ballad collection, Lorca noted that it was here, with these poems, that his poetic countenance appeared "for the first time with its own personality, a virgin untouched by any other poet."

CHAPTER 9

DALÍ

1924-25

Hours after returning to Madrid that fall, Lorca read his ballads to a group of friends and admirers who crowded into his Residencia room to welcome him back to the capital. His face darkened by the summer sun, a stray lock of black hair on his forehead, Lorca leaned back on his bed and joyfully declaimed his Gypsy poems. Among his listeners was Rafael Alberti, a twenty-one-year-old painter and poet from the Andalusian city of Cádiz, who thought Lorca looked like a peasant from the south.

That evening Lorca and Alberti dined together and afterward strolled through the Residencia gardens. There, Lorca launched into a second, impromptu recital of his new poems. "Green oh how I love you green," he intoned dramatically in the darkness. Alberti was struck by his warmth and spontaneity. At one point Lorca turned to Alberti and impulsively asked the handsome young poet to create a painting, one with a likeness of the Virgin beside a stream, and the legend "Apparition of Our Lady of Beautiful Love to the poet Federico García Lorca." Alberti was flattered. By the time the two parted, well after midnight, a soft rain had begun to fall. "Goodbye, cousin," Lorca said.

A few days later Alberti returned to the Residencia bearing the painting Lorca had requested, as well as a sonnet, "To Federico García Lorca, Poet of Granada." Lorca waved his hands effusively and told Alberti, "You've got two things going for you as a poet: a great memory and the fact that you're Andalusian."

Within a year of meeting Lorca, Alberti admitted to him that he felt like his "younger brother," and he suggested they stay in close touch with each other by letter. He became a regular visitor at the Residencia—one of dozens of young men pulled irresistibly into Lorca's orbit.

In Madrid, Lorca continued to work on his ballad series. His new roommate at the Residencia, José Antonio Rubio Sacristán, a law student, remembered that one winter night Lorca lay in bed with the covers pulled up to his neck and his fingers poking out from the blankets, scribbling onto a sheet of paper. The window was open—it was thought admirable at the Residencia to endure extremes of cold and heat—but despite the chill, Lorca pushed on, scratching out lines, turning the paper sideways to add stanzas, placing wavy marks beside passages he intended to revise. Occasionally he paused to recite a line of verse to Sacristán, who thought Lorca read with "an ardor capable of melting the snows." When at last he had completed a draft that satisfied him, Lorca stopped writing.

Drawn from the Old Testament story of Thamar and Amnon, the poem told of a brother who rapes his sister. Because the Gypsies of Andalusia themselves sang the story of Thamar and Amnon, Lorca considered his ballad "Gypsy-Jewish." But his version of the story owed less to the Bible than to traditional Spanish ballads and to plays by Tirso de Molina and Calderón. In contrast to the straightforward narrative of the Old Testament, Lorca imbued his "Thamar and Amnon" with powerful erotic imagery, relying on metaphor to convey the story's darkest truths:

> Now he takes her by the hair,
> now he tears her underthings.
> Warm corals drawing little creeks
> across a map of blonde.

The poem's subject matter betrayed Lorca's growing fascination with sexual instinct. Among those who later praised the work was Salvador Dalí, who told Lorca it was "the best" of his Gypsy ballads. The painter especially admired the poem's "chunks of incest."

Dalí was back at the Residencia that year. In the wake of his expulsion from Madrid's Academy of Fine Arts in 1923, and his subsequent imprisonment in Catalunya, he had shed his timorous ways and embraced the avant-garde with maniacal zeal. He dared others to dispute his passion for the new.

Lorca and fellow residents rallied to Dalí's cause. They proclaimed anything modern good—automobiles, telephones, airplanes, radio. Luis Buñuel bought a gramophone and a stack of American records. Lorca, Dalí, and others spent hours in Buñuel's room listening to jazz while sipping rum grog, a drink strictly against house rules. They attended films by such new stars as Buster Keaton, and at the Residencia they practiced their own brand of goofball humor.

Late in the afternoon they often spilled into Lorca's room to drink tea, read, talk, and smoke. Lorca dubbed these improvised gatherings "meetings of the desperation of tea." The evenings typically lasted until midnight and culminated in a reading from some book. As a rule, Lorca reserved the final passage for himself; when he spotted a line that moved him, he stopped to repeat it. Once, after reading a scene in which a character rolled about on the floor, he and former roommate Pepín Bello suddenly dropped to the floor, laughing, and began to roll around together.

Dozens of pranks, jokes, antics, and games evolved. Lorca hosted mass poetry-writing sessions in his room, during which he and his friends invented four-line nonsense poems called "anaglyphs." "Tea, / tea, / hen / and Teotocópuli," read one. Someone came up with the idea of a "fart meter": a wooden box with a hole, a candle, and a piece of string. Lorca and his friends held private tournaments to see who could expel the most wind. According to Rafael Alberti, who sometimes participated in these competitions, "It took a very strong fart to make the flame swell high enough to light the string."

With Luis Buñuel, Lorca staged innumerable practical jokes. They once coated their faces with rice powder, donned bogus nuns' habits, and boarded a city tram, where they cast lascivious glances at their neighbors and rubbed obscenely against male passengers. One drunken evening Buñuel inaugurated the "Order of Toledo," an informal fraternity whose primary purpose was to make inebriated excursions to the city of Toledo, two hours south of Madrid by train. Lorca was among the founding members; Dalí, Bello, and Alberti eventually joined the Order. In Toledo, the group's ritual activities included kissing the ground and climbing the cathedral bell tower, then wrapping themselves in bedsheets and wandering the streets, drunk, all night long.

As perpetrators of the outlandish, Lorca, Buñuel, Dalí, and Bello became the nominal leaders of the Residencia avant-garde. Of the four, Bello was often the most ingenious. Buñuel called him a "surrealist at heart"; Lorca compared him to El Greco. Lifting a phrase from his medical studies, Bello coined the term "putrefaction" to refer to anything outmoded, sacred, or anachronistic— anything, in short, that blocked the onset of modernity. He and his friends immediately began using the word as a label for people and things that offended them. Dalí told Bello that at heart "putrefaction" meant "EMOTION. And therefore it's inseparable from human nature." In Dalí's hierarchy, the pope was a "putrefaction"; so was the current Spanish king, the artist Henri Rousseau, and a whole raft of critics, books, paintings, and fashions.

Together with Lorca, Dalí began planning a book of putrefactions, to which Lorca was to contribute prose entries and Dalí illustrations. The artist turned out a number of sketches for the book—whimsical drawings of buffoons reminiscent of the grotesque caricatures Lorca had begun producing two years earlier in Granada. But Lorca reneged on his end of the bargain and never drafted so much as a prologue. To Dalí's annoyance, the project died. Yet the friendship prospered.

The two men wandered Madrid together. They gazed at paintings by Velázquez and Raphael in the Prado and listened to jazz in cafés. At the Residencia they once leaned out of a bedroom window and waved white handkerchiefs to passersby while shouting "Heeeelp! Lost at sea!" Forever low on cash, they schemed for ways to supplement their allowances from home. According to Lorca, who may have been lying (he "lied a lot and with pleasure," recalled Pepín Bello), he and Dalí once sold a mediocre painting to an unsuspecting couple from South America. The two friends celebrated the deed by hiring a pair of taxis to take them home to the Residencia. As they sat together in the first taxi, puffing on Havana cigars, the second car followed behind, empty. Lorca later explained that the second taxi was a *taxi de respeto*—a car hired exclusively for the sake of "respect." The idea, he added, quickly became a fad among rich young men in Madrid.

By the spring of 1925, he and Dalí were near-constant companions. They made several weekend excursions to Toledo, and in March they took a trip to the mountains north of Madrid. Each found in the other a reflection of his own beliefs and ambition and, most of all, talent. There was an element of idolatry to their friendship, of mutual awe, but also, increasingly, of love. They understood each other in ways no one else did or could, and as time wore on, they came to need one another with growing urgency.

That spring Dalí invited Lorca to spend Easter week in Catalunya with his family. Lorca begged his parents to let him make the trip. He outlined the various reasons why he had to go: the distinction and wealth of the Dalí family, the fact that Dalí's sister, Ana María, was "one of those girls who is so beautiful she drives you crazy." Clearly, he thought that his parents might relent if they detected a love interest. Furthermore, the visit would give him time to work on at least two new plays. "You know how the countryside and its silence give me all the ideas I have."

His final, and most compelling, justification for the trip was financial. He told his parents that the Barcelona Atheneum had asked him to give a reading during his stay in Catalunya and had agreed to pay his travel expenses. Given both the money and prestige he stood to gain from the event, he would be foolish to refuse. He did not mention the fact that the Atheneum invitation came from one of Dalí's friends, nor that he and Dalí had apparently persuaded the friend to issue the offer in order to bolster Lorca's case with his parents. The scheme worked: Lorca received permission to go to Catalunya.

The village of Cadaqués lies a hundred kilometers north of Barcelona, in a rocky cove beside the Mediterranean. Traveling by taxi with Dalí from the nearby town of Figueres, Lorca first glimpsed the town from the hills above it and was struck by the purity of what he saw: a crescent of bright white buildings hugging the sea. He later described the setting as "both eternal and actual, but perfect."

As a boy Dalí had spent summers and holidays here with his family. He loved Cadaqués. The town's angular contours and brilliant Mediterranean light filled his canvases in much the same way that the Granadan *vega* filled Lorca's poems. Lorca instinctively understood Dalí's attachment to the place, and within days of his arrival he, too, felt as though he were treading on sacred ground when he walked among the olive trees that skirted the tiny village.

More than anything it was the warmth of the welcome he received from the Dalí family that made him fall in love with Cadaqués. He and Salvador arrived in time for lunch and immediately sat down at the table with Dalí's father, stepmother, and sister. "My friend Federico, whom I've told you about," Dalí announced. By dessert Lorca was on such good terms with the family that it seemed to seventeen-year-old Ana María Dalí "as if we had always known one another."

To his astonishment, Lorca learned that Dalí's father, Salvador Dalí Cusí, a stout, cigar-smoking lawyer, knew a number of his poems by heart. Lorca was even more astonished by Dalí's sister, Ana María, whom he pronounced "without doubt, the most beautiful girl I have seen in my life." Her long, dark hair fell to her shoulders in such a cascade of curls that he was reminded of the angel Gabriel. She had a cherubic face, limpid brown eyes, and a soft, coquettish smile. There was both a girlishness to her and a budding sensuality to which Lorca was not immune. One day, as he watched her nap in the sun, he turned to Dalí and exclaimed, "What pretty breasts Ana María has!"

Dalí grabbed Lorca's hands. "Well, touch them, man. Touch them!"

Dalí himself was entranced by his sister's beauty and repeatedly asked her to pose for him. Eventually this phase of his career became known by Ana María's presence in his canvases. She spent hours standing patiently beside windows in Cadaqués and Figueres, studying the landscape while her brother painted her. They were unusually close—a situation owing to their mother's death four years earlier, when Dalí was nearly seventeen and Ana María twelve. At the time they had turned to one another in grief and bewilderment, and now, four years later, at twenty-two and seventeen, they continued to dote on each other. They played infantile games together, as if by doing so they could somehow re-create the childhood they had so abruptly lost to death. Ana María had a teddy bear named "Little Bear," which she dressed in toy clothes and carried with her wherever she went. When she, her brother, and Lorca were together in a room, the bear often sat near them on a chair. Dalí sometimes placed a philosophy book between its paws, "so that it can learn." He and Lorca adopted the bear as a mascot, and long after leaving Cadaqués, Lorca sent messages to the animal. "Give plenty of kisses to the little bear," he once instructed Ana María. "Four days ago I found him smoking a cigar."

In Cadaqués, Lorca behaved as childishly as the two Dalí siblings. He and Salvador had their photograph taken wearing white beach robes and top hats, and posing rakishly beside a table where Ana María stood with a watering can, pretending to sprinkle them. Like a small boy, Lorca frequently taunted his friends. Pouting, he would cry, "You don't love me! Well, then, I'm going away!" He would then run off and hide until Dalí and Ana María dutifully be-gan hunting for him, at which point Lorca would reappear, giggling. He drew immense pleasure from these episodes, Ana María remembered, "because then he felt loved."

At the same time he fell prey to sudden and frequent bouts of gloom. His smile would vanish, and a hard, expressionless look would grip his face. Both Ana María and her brother were startled by Lorca's brusque mood changes and by his apparent obsession with death. At the Residencia, Dalí had often heard Lorca refer to his own death—sometimes more than once in a given day. On a number of occasions the painter witnessed a bizarre ritual in which Lorca imagined himself dead. The rite always began late at night, with Lorca calling out to a group of friends, "Hey everyone, this is how I'll look when I die!" He would then throw himself across the bed, feign rigor mortis, and direct his companions in a boisterous enactment of his funeral procession through the streets of Granada. The performance invariably ended with Lorca's burial. Afterward he would leap up, laughing, and herd his friends through the door so that he could sleep in peace. Death thus became a familiar presence in his life, an event to be viewed with calm, to be milked for inspiration.

In Cadaqués, Lorca once stretched out on the floor in Dalí's studio and closed his eyes in a death pose. Ana María took his picture while her brother sketched him. Dalí later incorporated Lorca's lifeless face into his painting *Honey Is Sweeter than Blood*.

Both men worked during the Easter holiday. Lorca began a new play, *The Sacrifice of Iphigenia*. Dalí painted from sunrise to dusk in his cluttered gray studio. As he worked, the artist sang to himself through closed lips. To Lorca, the sound resembled "a hive of golden bees." He loved to watch his slender young friend at work.

At night, he and the two Dalís took walks through Cadaqués. Ever in search of new details for his paintings, Dalí scrutinized the light, clouds, and sea. Lorca talked of the work he had done that day, and later, as moonlight danced across the Mediterranean, recited his poems. His voice mingled with the sound of waves lapping against fishing boats. It was then, recalled Ana María, that the poet entered "his element" and became "perfectly elegant." His husky voice softened into a thing of beauty. "Everything around him was transformed." Language had purified him.

In Cadaqués, as elsewhere, Lorca craved the limelight. In addition to reciting poetry he read his new three-act play about Mariana Pineda to the Dalí family one afternoon as they sat around the dining room table. He had finished a draft of the work in January. Ana María was so moved by the drama that she wept. Her father let out a triumphant cry and proclaimed Lorca the greatest poet of the century. From that moment on, the plump attorney treated Lorca like a second son.

At the end of Easter week the Dalí family returned to their winter home in Figueres, where Dalí's father arranged for Lorca to give a second reading of *Mariana Pineda* before a group of his friends; they included the editor of one of Barcelona's daily newspapers. Lorca was grateful for the chance to read his drama before such a distinguished audience. To his parents he described the crowd as "the cream of the progressive and intellectual set of Figueres."

In recent months he had made several unsuccessful attempts to find a producer for *Mariana Pineda*. No one seemed willing to commit to a production of the work, in part because the drama's political content made it read like a tract against Primo de Rivera's regressive dictatorship, and censorship was likely. Lorca tried to be optimistic. He vowed to remain a pure artist, despite the current political climate. But he quaintly acknowledged the difficulty of doing so. "It requires as much effort as young ladies need in order to preserve their honor," he told his parents.

He wanted his play to be judged on its poetic merits, not its political subtext. From the outset he had resolved to treat the saga of Mariana Pineda as a love story, and he fervently defended his use of romantic "clichés and devices" throughout the play. Both the tone and language of *Mariana Pineda* are romantic, often excessively so, and its drawing-room settings and sentimental plot are conventional. Lorca was unapologetic. "My play is naive, like the soul of Mariana Pineda," he declared.

But even this most conventional of dramas bears signs of Lorca's ingenuity. His enduring interest in hybrid genres had led him to subtitle the work "A Popular Ballad in Three Engravings." The concept allowed Lorca to define a unique visual and aural approach to his otherwise simple story line, and ultimately gave the play its novelty. He sought to endow each of its three acts with the look of a nineteenth-century engraving by painstakingly composing its setting to resemble an old print. He also sought to link the play to the popular musical tradition by framing it with the folk ballad he had learned as a boy. At both the beginning and the end of *Mariana Pineda*, a chorus of children chants:

> Oh, what a sad day in Granada,
> when even the stones were made to cry,
> for on the scaffold stood Marianita
> who would not talk and therefore must die!

In effect, Lorca was forcing his audience to receive the story of Mariana in much the same way he first had, through a child's eyes and ears. He later said that in writing the drama he had followed his own vision, "a nocturnal, lunar, childlike vision."

Written in verse, the play recounts the events for which Mariana Pineda had become famous: her involvement in a plot to overthrow the king, her subsequent arrest, her refusal to betray her co-conspirators, her conviction and execution. Lorca deliberately altered the historical record, exaggerating his protagonist's bravery in order to shape a clear-cut tale of heroism and villainy, set among the streets and monuments of his native Granada. As such, the work is another elegy to his hometown. The particular twist he gave to the story—about which a number of obscure nineteenth-century poets had also written—was to have Mariana discover in the end that her lover, the dashing young revolutionary who lured her into abetting his cause, had in fact deceived her, so that Mariana's life and death are but another illustration of the futility of human desire. The heroine's final words, uttered as she makes her way to the scaffold, confirm this bleak understanding:

> I am Freedom itself, wounded by mankind!
> Love, love, love, and eternal solitude!

Don Salvador Dalí Cusí's friends were astounded by *Mariana Pineda* and by its talented twenty-six-year-old author. A few days after the reading they honored him with a lavish banquet in a Figueres hotel. There, too, Lorca dazzled his audience with a reading of his poems. A local journalist noted the "intense maturity" Lorca had achieved, despite his relative youth.

Shortly after the banquet Lorca left Figueres with Dalí, and the two went to Barcelona. They spent a few blissful days in the city, listening to jazz and visiting friends. Lorca gave a private poetry recital at the Atheneum. He then said goodbye to Dalí and boarded a train for Madrid. His stay with the Dalí family had lasted just over two weeks, but its effect was abiding. Nearly ten years later he would list Cadaqués among the four places in the world where he had "loved the most."

He returned home to Granada in June. He missed Catalunya desperately and sent letters to both Salvador and Ana María Dalí, urging them to visit him. Neither came. Dalí insisted that he could not leave his work.

With Ana María, Lorca struck up a flirtatious correspondence. "I have a portfolio of memories of you and of your laughter that is unforgettable," he confessed to her soon after leaving Catalunya. He remarked on her sunburnished beauty and called her a "little daughter of the olive trees and niece of the sea!"

But his true passion was for her brother. Within weeks of his visit to Cadaqués, Lorca began drafting an "Ode to Salvador Dalí," in which he revealed his affection for the painter:

> I sing a common belief
> that unites us in the dark and golden hours.
> It is not Art, this light that blinds our eyes.
> It is first love, friendship, or fencing.

As he worked on the ode, Lorca sent passages of the poem to Dalí, who praised its brilliance and begged to see more. "AH, MY ODE!" he scrawled exuberantly across the top of a letter hailing Lorca as "the only genius of our time."

He signed the document, "Dalí Salvador, painter of certain talent and friend (close) of a great POET who is VERY handsome. Goodbye. Oh, your recently shaved face. WET! Your shoehorn, your SUITCASE . . . ! Your socks."

Already the two shared a private vocabulary that soon evolved into an encoded language all but indecipherable to outsiders. Week after week letters went back and forth between Catalunya and Granada, and later Madrid. "What are you doing? Are you working?" Dalí asked Lorca in November 1925. "Don't fail to write to me—you, the only interesting man I've ever known." He referred to himself repeatedly as Lorca's "little son" and sent him drawings, collages, photographs, postcards, and even a florid valentine—the essence of putrefaction—stamped "My Beloved Darling."

By January 1926, Lorca could boast to Melchor Fernández Almagro that he enjoyed "an abundant correspondence [with] my friend and inseparable companion Salvador Dalí." Elsewhere he spoke reverently of "the ineffable Dalí." He had not been so intoxicated by another human being since adolescence, when he had pined after María Luisa Egea. She had spurned his love; Dalí did not.

To Lorca, the painter's extravagant, adoring letters were a godsend. But Lorca wanted more. In the summer of 1925, in the weeks following his visit to Cadaqués, he talked anxiously of his desire to see Dalí, and in letters to their mutual friend Benjamín Palencia, a painter, he hinted at the depth of his attachment to "Salvadorcito." Through Palencia, Dalí had promised to send him a pair of his paintings. "They will live in my house and next to my heart," Lorca said.

To admit to himself that he loved Dalí as much as he did was to confront matters Lorca had long sought to suppress. It was a troubling summer. Frustrated by his stalled theatrical career and increasingly mesmerized by Dalí's radical ideas, he questioned the direction of his work. At home, his parents had once more begun lamenting his apparent unwillingness to make something of himself. Lorca mourned his absent friends. Each evening at dusk he watched the sun cast its golden light across the *vega*. He saw birds glisten like bits of metal in the sky, and he felt as though he had died. "I'm going through one of the toughest crises I've ever experienced," he told Palencia. "Both my literary and emotional work are failing me. I don't believe in anyone. I don't like anyone. I dream of a constant dawn, as cold as a spikenard, full of cold smells and exact emotions. An exact tenderness and a hard, intelligent light. We'll see how I escape!"

Lorca knew the perils of homosexual love. He knew about Oscar Wilde's imprisonment, and he had read *De Profundis*; his copy of Wilde's book was heavily marked. He could scarcely have been ignorant of his own country's attitude toward same-sex love. The Arabs who settled Andalusia had sanctioned it. But the Inquisition had persecuted homosexuals, and the Catholic Church continued to regard them as deviants of the worst sort. Lorca knew how people gossiped; as a teenager he had been ridiculed for his peculiar dress and effeminate ways. At twenty-one he had gone weeping to a friend's house after learning that someone was spreading a rumor that he, Lorca, was homosexual.

For years he had tried to convince both himself and his friends that he was "normal." Although he lacked his brother's polish with women, he made a show of desiring. While vacationing with his family in Málaga in 1918, he complained to an acquaintance, "The hotel is lively but there are no girls." In truth, Lorca was intimidated by the notion of physical intimacy with women. His closest friends and confidants had almost always been men. He loved the frank badinage of the all-male *tertulia*, the high jinks of masculine camaraderie at the Residencia. His poetry revealed his growing fascination with the beauty of the male form.

He would later admit that since boyhood an "impassioned force" had driven him toward men, not women. He claimed to have idolized a particular village boy during his childhood, a younger neighbor whose friendship Lorca sought to monopolize: "I wanted him to play only with me." Decades later Lorca still remembered that early love with an acute sense of joy as well as privation. "When I eventually realized my preference," he recalled, "I came to understand that what I liked, others thought perverse."

He learned to veil the truth, to flaunt a socially acceptable facade. Even in the summer of 1925, in the midst of his turbulent awakening to a new emotional, sexual, and aesthetic self, he understood intuitively that he must dissemble. To his lifelong friend Melchor Fernández Almagro he said only, "I'm getting into problems I should have addressed long ago." Newly consumed by the notion of masquerade, he began sketching clowns and harlequins whose sad faces belied the merriment of their dress.

He turned to metaphor as a means of both veiling and articulating the truth. To Ana María Dalí he confessed that he'd had a difficult summer and longed to be near the sea. More than ever, landlocked Granada epitomized his repressed desires, and the sea his longing for emotional and sexual freedom. "The young ladies of Granada go up to their whitewashed terraces to see the mountains and *not* see the ocean," he wrote delicately to Dalí's sister. "In the afternoon they dress in gauze and vaporous satiny things and go down to the promenade where the fountains flow like diamonds and there is an old anguish of roses and amorous melancholy . . . The young ladies of Granada have no love for the sea. They have enormous nacre shells with painted sailors and that is the way they see it; and great conch shells in their salons, and that is the way they hear it." A trip to Málaga with his family toward the end of the summer "saved" his life. There, as in Cadaqués, Lorca basked in the life-giving force of the Mediterranean. The moment one reaches Málaga, he told Benjamín Palencia, "Dionysus rubs your head with his sacred horns and your soul turns the color of wine."

By late September, he had begun writing what he called "erotic poetry." The effort invigorated him. He wrote eight poems in all, each a brief, ironic work depicting a particular woman and the sexual trait by which she is known. The poems suggest Lorca's deepening aversion to the female anatomy. He describes the breasts of a spinster as "black melons." Of another woman he writes, "Beneath the moon-dark rosebay / you looked ugly naked." In the short poem "Lucía Martínez" he assumes the voice of a predatory Don Juan:

> Here I am, Lucía Martínez.
> I've come to devour your mouth
> and drag you off by the hair
> into the seashells of daybreak.
>
> Because I want to and I can.

The poems were a departure for Lorca, his first foray into what he called "a distinguished field." They made him feel young again. "Am I backward?" he asked Fernández Almagro. "What is this? It seems as though I've only just come into my youth. That's why when I'm sixty I won't be old . . . I'm never going to be *old*."

Age frightened him nearly as much as heterosexual sex. Both were the subject of a new play he began that summer, *The Love of Don Perlimplín for Belisa in Their Garden*, the story of a marriage between an elderly man and a beautiful young woman whose seductive appearance on their wedding night so intimidates her husband that he is unable to consummate the marriage. Lorca subtitled the work an "Erotic *Aleluya*"—a reference to the popular Spanish broadsheets, or *aleluyas*, printed with colorful vignettes of stock characters, which he and his brother had read as children. Again Lorca was mixing genres. The plot of *Perlimplín* enabled him both to revisit an art form he had loved in boyhood and to explore a favorite and familiar theme, the conflict between spiritual and sensual love. Perhaps for that reason the short play flowed quickly from his pen. Lorca finished a first draft by January 1926.

He remained restless. In the midst of his work on *Perlimplín* he began writing a series of short, highly experimental dialogues. "Pure poetry. Naked," he said of them. Terse and unorthodox, the miniature works sketched an amusing portrait of the life Lorca had known the previous year in Madrid with Dalí and their friends. He titled one work "Dialogue of the Residencia." Others included "Dialogue with Luis Buñuel," a conversation over tea at the Residencia; "Buster Keaton's Stroll," a short homage to Keaton and the silent films Lorca had grown to love; and "Mute Dialogue of the Carthusians," a wordless conversation—expressed principally through punctuation marks—between two Carthusian monks. Dalí's presence in the dialogues, explicit as well as implicit, was pervasive. On the manuscript of "Buster Keaton's Stroll," Lorca wrote, "Goodbye Dalilaitita / Daliminita / Dalipiruta / Damitira / Demeter / Dalí." And then: "Write to me at once. / At once. / At once. At once."

To Fernández Almagro he described the dialogues as "more *universal* than the rest of my work . . . (which, in parentheses, I don't find acceptable)." Lorca later pronounced both the dialogues and *Perlimplín* "very poor." He drew little comfort from his work. "I've gone through a terrible, dark time of grave emotional depths which neither my lyric nor my innate happiness has been able to combat," he told another friend. Professionally, he was drifting. He had completed two full-length plays since 1920—*Mariana Pineda* and *The Billy Club Puppets*—both of which remained unproduced. He had not published a poetry collection since 1921.

At twenty-seven, he was under renewed pressure from both family and friends to prove himself. "My parents are angry with me," he told Fernández Almagro. The critic was unsympathetic. "You don't tell me why your parents are angry with you, but I can imagine why. And in your conscience you know we're right when we reproach you for your 'things' . . . Everyone who loves you laments your idleness." He urged Lorca to "discipline and manage" himself.

But Lorca yearned to escape. He felt that time was closing in, dissolving him "the way water dissolves lumps of sugar." He longed to travel abroad, to go to Paris or "to Italy, which is my dream." Instead, it was his enterprising brother who went to France in the fall of 1925 as the recipient of a government scholarship—Paco's second visit to the country in two years. Lorca stayed home. Newly worried about his oldest son's floundering career, Don Federico refused to let him leave Granada until he had shown he could support himself. Lorca toyed with the idea of a teaching career. He told Fernández Almagro he was thinking about taking "some qualifying exams, and if not . . . we'll see! I don't think I'll lack for money as long as I'm strong."

Both friends and admirers nagged him. The Madrid critic Enrique Díez-Canedo remarked publicly in 1926 that Lorca had shown "unspeakable lazi-

ness" in refusing to publish anything since *Book of Poems*. Rafael Alberti told
Lorca that, given his abilities, he should have published five or six books by
now. "You've been too distracted." Benjamín Palencia, the painter in whom
Lorca had confided his feelings toward Dalí, also scolded him. "It's not right
that the best young poet in Spain should be unknown and unpublished." The
poet Gerardo Diego spoke of "the impossible and doubtful and problematic
Federico García Lorca." Even Lorca's mother reprimanded him, arguing that
"without realizing it you get tired of your work and drop it, because nothing
pleases you, and that's the source of your apathy and neglect."

Chastened, Lorca plotted his literary salvation. "I work in order to die living," he told Fernández Almagro. "I don't want to work to live dying. I'm re-
newing myself. Thank God, in whom each passing day I place my desire and
my dreams."

CHAPTER 10

INCORRIGIBLE POET

1926-27

In 1924 the *Revista de Occidente* had announced the appearance of a new movement, surrealism, "one of the latest inventions of the French literati." In 1925 the journal published André Breton's "Surrealist Manifesto," a plea for the resolution of "dream and reality into a sort of absolute reality, a *surreality*."

The news intensified Lorca's desire to visit France, to establish himself as a player in the avant-garde. "Foreign waters," he told a friend in early 1926, would refresh his poetry as well as his heart. He begged his brother to send him "all the news" from France—"your impressions of Bordeaux, of the surrealist youth, etc." From other friends in Paris, among them Luis Buñuel, he learned of further artistic and intellectual developments in the French capital.

He resolved meanwhile to demonstrate his mettle by publishing not one but three books of poetry: *Suites, Poem of the Deep Song,* and a new collection to be called *Songs* ("the best one!"), consisting of nearly ninety poems composed between 1921 and 1926. He had no publisher, and no one to help him prepare his manuscripts, but he felt capable nonetheless "of creating a great, original *oeuvre,* and have *faith* I can do so," he told his brother. As soon as the books came out he intended to go to Madrid and then to France. "In four months time I could put French under my belt."

Because they possessed a "rare, surprising *unity,*" he planned to issue the three collections simultaneously in a cardboard slipcase. He labored over the arrangement of the poems, sifting through the disordered mass of papers he had accumulated since the publication of his last book in 1921. He sought to winnow each book until it contained only those poems that "belonged" to it. To his amazement, he found he enjoyed the process of collating and ordering his poetry. "I have seen *completed* things I couldn't see before, and I've given balance to poems which were limping but which had heads of gold." He also envisioned a fourth book, a Gypsy ballad collection, and in his apparent haste to complete that series, he wrote four new ballads in early 1926. These included "The Unfaithful Wife," a work Lorca described as an "erotic ballad."

Convinced that he had entered a new phase of his career, he sent exultant reports to friends. "You can't say I waste time!" he wrote breezily to Jorge Guillén. "I'm *hacking* away . . . a hardworking *guy*. I'm a gentleman who's a *knockout*." To Melchor Fernández Almagro he confided, "I want to be a Poet through and through, living and dying by poetry. I'm starting to *see clearly*. A high awareness of my future work is taking hold of me, and an almost dramatic sense of my responsibility constrains me . . . it seems to me I'm giving birth to new forms and an absolutely defined balance."

Dalí remained his most important audience. Lorca hoped the painter would design the covers for his new books. He worked on his long ode to the artist even as he rushed to complete his poetry collections. He finished the "Ode to Salvador Dalí" in March and published it the following month in Madrid's progressive *Revista de Occidente*, edited by José Ortega y Gasset. The poem's twenty-eight stanzas filled six pages of the journal. Critic Guillermo de Torre described it as a perfectly balanced "poetic transcription of cubism's visual norms," and later hailed the ode as "the most important work of 1926."

It was as much an exaltation of cubism as of Dalí, for to Lorca the two were vitally linked. Although Dalí was not a cubist per se, he embraced cubist ideals in his paintings. Lorca sought to effect the same dispassionate, analytical approach to reality in his ode. His poem presents an Apollonian Dalí, an artist who paints with a light "that the loving vines of Bacchus / and the chaotic force of curving water fear," a man whose "astronomical and tender heart" is afraid of emotion, but who inspires the poet nevertheless: "I sing your restless longing for the statue, / your fear of the feelings that await you in the street."

The ode, like Dalí's art of the period, is rigid, ordered, classical. Lorca wrote the poem in alexandrines, a meter he believed "must be clear, well constructed, and weighty," as opposed to shorter forms, which, he said, "can be winged." Dalí judged certain lines of the ode to be "almost ARITHMETIC." He praised the poem's objectivity. A prescriptive as well as a descriptive work, it stakes Lorca's claim to a new aesthetic, effectively renouncing the romanticism of his past. In the ode, he outlines the evolution of Dalí's art, from its inception in the "white ateliers" in Paris, where the first cubists practiced their craft, to its ripening in Cadaqués, whose angular shapes and horizon remind the poet of "wounded handkerchiefs."

Provocative metaphors combine with traditional metrics to give the ode a startling sense of newness. Guillermo de Torre called the poem a brilliant embodiment of the "two aesthetics of humanized and dehumanized art"—a reference to Ortega y Gasset's 1925 essay "The Dehumanization of Art," a work aimed at clarifying the chief traits and tenets of post–World War I movements such as cubism and expressionism. Having noted the tendency of these movements to avoid reality and eliminate living forms, Ortega coined the phrase "dehumanized art" to describe the phenomenon. His essay helped steer a generation of writers toward a "depersonalized" art devoid of the pathos of romanticism and naturalism and devoted to a spirit of play. Lorca had toyed with the new aesthetic in his dialogues and erotic poems, but in the "Ode to Salvador Dalí" he went further, blending form and content to exalt the revolutionary art of his contemporaries. With its dispassionate tone and wild flights of metaphor—a tool Ortega defined as "the most radical instrument of dehumanization"—Lorca's ode exemplified the new.

And yet, as Torre observed, the poem is also a personal, "humanized" work of art designed to pay tribute to a beloved companion. Throughout the work Lorca extols Dalí's "olive-colored voice" and "honest eyes," his extraordinary talent and steadfast ideals. The poem ends with a prayerful appeal to his friend:

> May fingerprints of blood on gold
> streak the heart of eternal Catalunya.
> May stars like falconless fists shine on you,
> while your painting and your life break into flower.
>
> Don't watch the water clock with its membraned wings
> or the hard scythe of the allegory.
> Always in the air, dress and undress your brush
> before the sea peopled with sailors and with ships.

Despite his infatuation with the French avant-garde and his longing to go abroad, Lorca found things to admire in Spain. In February 1926, he made a two-day trip to the Alpujarras, south of Granada. "I'll never forget the village of Cáñar (the highest in Spain), full of singing laundresses and somber shepherds," he told his brother. "*Literarily* speaking, there is nothing newer." On February 13, during the inaugural ceremonies for Granada's new Atheneum, Lorca delivered a lecture on a once-renowned sixteenth-century Cordoban poet, Luis de Góngora, whom he proclaimed "the father of the modern lyric." Ostensibly a speech about a neglected baroque master, the lecture, "The Poetic Image of Don Luis de Góngora," was in effect a statement of Lorca's own evolving poetics.

He applauded the older poet's "legacy of objectivity and his sense of metaphor." In essence, Góngora had written "dehumanized" verse three hundred years before Ortega y Gasset defined the term. By stripping his poetic images of spontaneous emotion and what Lorca called "realities that die," Góngora had created a lasting body of work. A genius at metaphor, he had memorably transformed the Straits of Magellan into an "elusive silver hinge," and a grotto into a "melancholy yawn of the earth." "A poem's eternity," Lorca said, "depends on the quality and coherency of its images."

Long overlooked, except for a brief vogue among the French symbolists and Hispanic *modernistas*, Góngora exemplified for Lorca and his generation their growing quest for a "pure" poetry, detached from reality and uncontaminated by ordinary usage. Góngora's work—chiefly sonnets, ballads, and his four-part unfinished masterpiece, *Solitudes*—was objective, clear, and technically brilliant, just like Dalí's paintings. Both men had striven to distance themselves from the Dionysian fires of creation and take refuge in an Apollonian world of order and control—a world Lorca also sought to inhabit, despite his impulsive, essentially emotional nature. "I do not believe any artist works in a state of fever," he said in his lecture. "Even the mystics begin working only after the ineffable dove of the Holy Spirit has already abandoned their cells and is vanishing among the clouds. One returns from inspiration as from a foreign land. The poem is the narration of the voyage. Inspiration supplies the image but not its clothing."

In its front-page review of the talk, the *Defensor de Granada* called Lorca's speech a "brilliant dissertation" and described Lorca as a "restless and delicate spirit, full of emotion." An accompanying photograph showed his dark face staring moodily into the camera. Shocked by the uncharacteristic solemnity with which he had addressed his audience, Lorca, then twenty-seven, told Jorge Guillén, "My voice was another's. It was a serene voice and full of years . . . as old as I am! It grieved me a little to see that I'm capable of giving a lecture without making fun of the audience. I'm becoming serious. I spend a lot of time in pure sadness. At times I surprise myself when I see that I'm *intelli-*

gent. Old age!" Aware that Guillén had written a doctoral dissertation on Góngora, Lorca promised to forward a copy of his talk. "You tell me *as a teacher* what critical blunders it has," he urged.

By March, he had made some progress with his poetry books, but he still lacked a publisher and a secretary to help him prepare his manuscripts. In the meantime, he had resumed the dismal task of trying to find a producer for *Mariana Pineda.* Although confident that once he prevailed in the theater ("as I believe I will," he told his parents) the doors to success would open wide, he had yet to find anyone willing to take on the play. Gregorio Martínez Sierra ("that bastard") had withdrawn his initial offer to stage *Mariana.* Lorca had also sent a copy of the script to the Catalan playwright Eduardo Marquina, whom he had known since 1919, but Marquina had not responded. Lorca despaired. "Will anyone want to produce it?" he asked Melchor Fernández Almagro. "I'd like that for my family's sake. There's no doubt that I really have a *feeling for the theater.*"

Confined to home until he published his books or otherwise persuaded his parents to let him leave, Lorca groped for ways to withstand the tedium of provincial life. At times he believed Granada had a *"deadly"* effect on his work. He harbored few illusions about the city. The older he became, the more he decried its faults. The *granadino,* he once said, is a man of "few friends," because he withdraws from the world instead of embracing it. In words reminiscent of Unamuno, Lorca called for the "Europeanization" of his hometown. "We must love Granada, but we must think in European terms. Only in this way can we unearth our finest and most secret local treasures."

For years he and his Rinconcillo friends had flirted with the idea of publishing a small magazine in Granada, partly as a means of needling their complacent bourgeois neighbors. In recent years a number of Lorca's poet friends had started literary magazines elsewhere in Spain. Eager to be part of the trend, Lorca announced in early 1926 that he, too, intended to found a magazine — "a joyful, lively, anti-local, anti-provincial review belonging to the whole world, as Granada does." He planned to call the magazine *gallo,* or "cock," because the cock "is a symbol of youth, whose song everywhere heralds the dawn." If he couldn't be part of the Paris vanguard, he would forge his own version of the avant-garde at home.

He had no funding for the magazine and little idea how to proceed, other than to launch a letter-writing campaign to friends soliciting material for the first issue. Dalí agreed to design its cover. But even he had more business sense than Lorca. "I'll make you all the covers you want for any magazine you like,

but you've got to be *more specific*," he said. "Give me the facts: / size / black—
color, etc. / the magazine's *degree* of putrefaction."

In early April, Lorca's parents paid his way to Madrid so that he could try to
locate a producer for *Mariana Pineda*. Although he failed to find one, he secured a commitment from the *Revista de Occidente* to publish his Gypsy ballads in book form.

From Madrid, he traveled north to Valladolid to visit Jorge Guillén and to
give a public poetry reading, one of his first outside Granada. For Guillén,
Lorca felt "*total* admiration, if not veneration." Since their first meeting in
Madrid two years earlier, he had come to know both Guillén and his lovely,
French-born wife, Germaine, as well as their two small children, with whom
Lorca struck up a playful correspondence. He admired Guillén's calm and disciplined demeanor, his patent devotion to his family, and he was awed by the
poet's erudition. A gifted writer as well as scholar, Guillén had received his doctorate in literature from the University of Madrid and had taught at the Sor-
bonne before joining the faculty of the University of Valladolid. He looked like
the professor he was: tall and lean, with round spectacles and a probing gaze.
Guillén's presence reminded Lorca of his own academic failings. He confessed
sheepishly to the older writer, "I'm not intelligent, it's true! But I'm a poet."
Guillén countered with unqualified praise for Lorca's work. In response to a
self-deprecating remark by Lorca, he once sent a postcard addressed "to the
Poet Federico García Lorca." On the back he wrote, "Poet, yes, always. (Impossible, *utterly impossible*, the notion of 'ex-poet.')"

Lorca relied on Guillén's advice and encouragement, and looked for inspiration to the poet's "clean and beautiful verse," a highly refined, "pure poetry"
that, while intelligent, was not "excessively cerebral." In fact, Lorca argued,
Guillén's verse possessed "the gift of tears," a phrase he borrowed from Saint
Teresa. By contrast, he sometimes felt his own poetry lacked clarity and light. "I
have too much chiaroscuro," he complained to Guillén. "You're generous with
me. Ge-ne-rous."

At his poetry reading in Valladolid, Guillén introduced Lorca as a magnificent writer destined to enter the annals of history. "As the years go by," he told
the audience, "we'll be able to say, 'We saw in Federico García Lorca the great
and glorious poet he later became. We were among the makers, not the grave
diggers.' " Guillén enumerated Lorca's gifts as a poet, playwright, artist, and
musician, and praised Lorca's oratorical skills. Lorca himself then took the
stage. To local critic Francisco de Cossío he seemed "almost adolescent," with
his clumsy walk and engaging smile. But the moment he began reading,

Cossío knew he was in the presence of a master. The critic praised Lorca's poetry and predicted his eventual fame. Someday, he wrote, children will sing
Lorca's ballads, and young girls will "whisper his songs in secret." The *Defensor
de Granada* reprinted Cossío's flattering review, together with excerpts from
Guillén's introduction, under the heading "A Granadan Poet in Castile." By
letter Lorca took pains to inform his parents that he had been "well taken care
of" in Valladolid and had passed several agreeable days *"gratis."*

On his way home from Valladolid he stopped in Madrid, where he appears
to have met up briefly with Salvador and Ana María Dalí. The two had just
made their first trip to Paris. From the French capital they had sent a joint postcard to Lorca. "We think of you constantly," it read. Alone, Dalí sent a second
card with an image of the Eiffel Tower. On the back he scrawled a single
phrase: "Another hug."

Dalí's fame, like Lorca's, was growing. In late 1925 he had held his first painting exhibition in Barcelona, at the prestigious Dalmau Galleries. A critical as
well as a commercial triumph, the show caught the eye of Pablo Picasso. When
Dalí visited Paris, the two artists spent several hours together in Picasso's studio.
During his stay in Madrid that spring Dalí provoked another of his short-lived
scandals. Having reenrolled in Madrid's Academy of Fine Arts after his expulsion in 1923, he showed up at the school in mid-June 1926 for a final examination. Dressed in a checked coat with a gardenia in its lapel, and bolstered by a
glass of absinthe, he curtly told his examiners, "Given that none of the professors at the school . . . has the competence to judge me, I withdraw." For the second time in his life, he was expelled from the institution. Dalí went home to
Catalunya, intent on persuading his father to send him to Paris. He believed
that in France he would "definitively seize power!"

Lorca continued to idolize him. Each viewed the other as his most discern-
ing audience. After his Barcelona exhibition, Dalí sent Lorca press clippings
from the show, but only "the harshest criticism." The other reviews, he explained, were of no interest "because they are so unconditionally enthusiastic."
In March 1926, Dalí confessed to Lorca that he had spent the whole of one
Sunday afternoon rereading Lorca's letters to him. "Little son! They're extraordinary. In each line there are suggestions for numerous books, theatrical works,
paintings, etc., etc., etc., etc." A week or so later he sent another note. "Do you
love me?" he asked.

He still wanted Lorca to collaborate with him on a book of putrefactions,
and they discussed the project during Dalí's visit to Madrid that spring. But
Lorca had more pressing matters to address—chiefly the business of finding a
producer for *Mariana Pineda*. He told his parents he intended to remain in

Madrid until he had resolved the issue. After Dalí's departure, Lorca lingered in the capital, but without results. Eduardo Marquina could not find a producer for the play, and no one else to whom Lorca showed the script was willing to take on the work. Lorca blamed the theater establishment. "This business of dealing with impresarios is one of the most repugnant things in the world, because they're all a bunch of idiots," he said to his parents. "The Spanish theater is in the hands of the worst riffraff, actors as well as playwrights."

He assured his family he hadn't the "slightest worry or the least bit of depression. I'm naturally optimistic. And I am entirely certain that at the end of the day everything will turn out just as I want it to and as it ought to be. I have a wonderful thing called faith! I have faith in myself, as do a number of other people." In another letter home, he blithely announced that the trick to conquering despair was to live an active life—to play tennis, to bathe every morning, and to eat prudently. "That's how I've freed myself at times in Madrid from becoming too sad because of some (always *small*) setback."

After a couple of months in Madrid, Lorca left the capital empty-handed and went home to Granada for the summer. He invited Dalí to join him, but the painter declined, citing the need to prepare for his next exhibition. Unlike Lorca, who yearned for Dalí's physical presence, the artist was content with a mostly cerebral friendship. He needed Lorca imaginatively, not physically. At least four canvases in Dalí's upcoming exhibition bore hints of Lorca's heart-shaped face.

In their letters the two began to make cryptic, homoerotic references to Saint Sebastian, by coincidence the patron of Cadaqués. Dalí referred to Sebastian's "delicious" agony and, invoking another shared icon, the fish, invited Lorca to embrace "my new type of Saint Sebastian, consisting of the pure transmutation of the Arrow by the Sole." Both men viewed the figure of Sebastian as a provocative one, at once inviting and impassive, a perfect emblem of the emotional control each now sought to achieve in his work. Dalí called Sebastian "Saint Objectivity." In a letter to Jorge Guillén, Lorca defined true poetry as "love, effort, and *renunciation*. (Saint Sebastian)."

More so than Dalí, Lorca struggled to find a balance between his old work and his new. He continued to be inspired by Andalusia, even as he looked to Catalunya and to France for enlightenment. But it was a constant battle. While on holiday in the *vega* with his family that summer, he told his brother he was sick of the village of Asquerosa and its petty inhabitants. "In the country one seeks innocence," he grumbled. "I attribute all this to the fact that there are no cows here, and no grazing of any sort."

Luis Buñuel wrote from Paris to ask if Lorca would consent to write a screenplay for his cinematic debut. The former athlete had decided to become a filmmaker. "You know this is a lucrative business, and I know you intend to make money, come what may," Buñuel advised. But despite his numerous requests, Lorca refused to collaborate, and eventually Buñuel gave up.

Late in the summer the Lorca family moved into a new summer home on the outskirts of Granada, a two-story white house that Don Federico had bought the previous year and christened the "Huerta de San Vicente" in honor of his wife, Vicenta. Lorca instantly fell in love with the place and in doing so rekindled his passion for Andalusia. Although the house stood barely half a mile from the center of Granada, it was surrounded by the damp green fields of the *vega* and adorned with flowers. There was so much jasmine in the garden that each morning he and his family suffered "a lyrical headache," he told Jorge Guillén. "And yet, nothing is excessive! That's the beauty of Andalusia!"

His mother kept the house filled with roses. His father planted fruit trees and rows of vegetables in the garden. In time Lorca and his brother sunk three cypresses into the soil beside the dirt path that led to the house, so that from a distance the site was marked by their mournful silhouettes. From the balcony of his bedroom upstairs, Lorca could see both the *vega* and the towering Sierra Nevada in the distance, a view he thought "the most beautiful . . . panorama of mountains in Europe."

At night the perfume of flowers suffused his room, and the air became "divinely unbreathable." Inspired by his bucolic surroundings, Lorca returned to Andalusian themes and resumed work on two of his more conventional projects, the Gypsy ballads and a popular Andalusian farce called *The Shoemaker's Prodigious Wife*, which he had begun two years earlier. Years afterward he described the circumstances that prompted him to complete *The Shoemaker's Prodigious Wife* in the summer of 1926:

> I was in the city of Granada, surrounded by black fig trees, spikes of wheat, and little crowns of water . . . The restless letters I was receiving from my friends in Paris, who were engaged in the handsome and bitter struggle to create abstract art, led me to produce this almost banal fable with its direct reality.

In contrast to his friends' experiments with abstraction, *The Shoemaker's Prodigious Wife* "was like slamming my fist down on the table," he said. Brief and raucous, like the drama *Don Perlimplín*, which he had finished earlier in the

Federico García Lorca in 1899, at age one.
He was later ashamed of the pampered
existence he had enjoyed as a child.

Lorca at age six, 1904.

Lorca (*standing, left*) with his mother, sister Concha, father, and brother, *c.* 1912.

With his youngest sister, Isabel, in 1914. As a teenager, Lorca liked to lie on his back on the floor and "play games with my little sister (she's my delight)."

ABOVE Antonio Segura Mesa, the piano teacher to whom Lorca dedicated his first book, "with pious devotion."

LEFT Antonio Rodríguez Espinosa, who witnessed Lorca's baptism in 1898 and was later his elementary school teacher in Almería.

Students from the University of Granada inside the Alhambra. Lorca (*first row, second from right*) sits at the feet of his art history professor, Martín Domínguez Berrueta, with gray hair and glasses. Unlike most professors of the time, Berrueta regularly took his classes on field trips.

Lorca heeded the example of his sometime mentor Juan Ramón Jiménez in paying careful attention to the design of his books. "I want the book to come out to my liking, since I'm its father," he said of his first poetry collection, *Book of Poems*. LEFT Ismael Gómez de la Serna's *modernista* cover for the first edition of *Impressions and Landscapes* (1918).

Lorca, in his family's apartment in Granada, *c.* 1919–20.

BELOW Although he claimed to find letter writing difficult ("When I'm not on close terms with the person I'm writing to, I don't know what to say!"), Lorca sent lyrical, often whimsically illustrated letters to good friends, such as Benjamín Palencia (*below*).

Monsieur Troplong, 1923, pencil. Spurred on by his friends, Lorca sketched dozens of irreverent, often grotesque caricatures in the early 1920s.

With Dalí at a fair in Barcelona, mid-1920s. "May stars like falconless fists shine on you, / while your painting and your life break into flower, " Lorca wrote in his 1926 "Ode to Salvador Dalí."

Luis Buñuel, c. 1920. "Through the strength of our friendship, he transformed me, he made me know another world," Buñuel said later of Lorca.

Emilio Prados, early 1920s. Prados inscribed this photograph, "For my dear brother Federico, upon sealing or forever opening our interior book. I embrace you with all my heart, Emilio." In 1926, Prados published three of Lorca's gypsy ballads in the first issue of the literary magazine *Litoral*, which he edited with the poet Manuel Altolaguirre.

Sailor, 1925, colored pencil. The image appeared on the cover of the magazine *Litoral* in March 1927. The band on the sailor's cap indicates that he is a crew member of the ship *Love*.

"The melancholic and contemplative man goes to Granada," Lorca wrote, "to be all alone . . . near the bonfire of saffron, deep gray, and blotting-paper pink—the walls of the Alhambra."

BELOW Lorca, on his back in a death pose, wearing Arab dress, surrounded (*left to right*) by Rinconcillo friends Miguel Pizarro, Manuel Angeles Ortiz, and Angel Barrios, in a sequence from "The History of the Treasure," a brief story the four men filmed in 1918. Throughout his teens and early twenties, Lorca drew pleasure from ritual enactments of his own death.

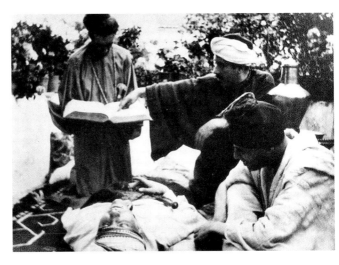

ABOVE Lorca (*rear seat*), during a 1926 excursion into the Andalusian countryside with friends, among them the composer Manuel de Falla, who sits in front, wearing a cap and white scarf.

LEFT Beside Granada's Genil river, 1924. Lorca once called himself "Federico García Lorca, modest dreamer and son of the water."

In the Generalife gardens, 1924: (*left to right*) Lorca, Zenobia Camprubí, wife of Juan Ramón Jiménez; Isabel García Lorca; Lorca's good friend Emilia Llanos; Juan Ramón Jiménez; and Concha García Lorca, during Jiménez' visit to Granada.

At home in Granada, 1925, beneath one of several paintings Dalí gave him in the mid-1920s. Lorca said that Dalí's paintings would live "in my house and next to my heart."

year, Lorca's farce dealt with one of the Spanish theater's more traditional themes: the marriage of a young girl to an old man. But the play lacked the tragic overtones of *Perlimplín*, and was, in fact, closer in spirit and technique to his puppet theater. Lorca later recalled that while writing the play during his first summer at the Huerta de San Vicente, he felt "as though I were holding happiness in my hands. I felt I was the intimate friend of all the roses in the garden."

The idyll did not last. He and his family moved back to their Granada apartment in the fall, and Lorca renewed his search for a producer for *Mariana Pineda*. He called the play, which had now consumed nearly three years of his life, "the exceedingly tiresome *Mariana Pineda*." Most recently, playwright Eduardo Marquina, then in his late forties, and one of the country's best-known writers, had given the script to Margarita Xirgu, a prominent Catalan actress who ran her own theater company. Marquina, who had long supported Lorca's literary efforts, believed Xirgu might be interested in staging the work. But weeks passed without a response from the actress. "I know her mother died," Lorca griped to Marquina, "but that was some time ago, and besides, she's not going to retire from the stage on account of that."

He knew that the theater was the only way he stood to make any money as a writer—and yet he could not seem to break into its insular world. To make matters worse, his brother had recently gone to England, where he was enjoying further success in his lustrous academic career. "My parents see *nothing practical* in my literary endeavors," Lorca reported wearily to Marquina. "They are displeased with me and do nothing but point to the example of my brother Paquito, a student at Oxford loaded with laurels."

By late fall he had lost patience with himself, with his play, and with Marquina, whom he had never completely trusted. He lamented the time he had spent on this "disastrous venture of mine into the den of the theater." He told Melchor Fernández Almagro that he had been a victim of "bad faith," of "rotten people and cretinism." He begged Fernández Almagro to speak to Marquina on his behalf—"the shameless and cavalier Marquina." "Naturally, if *Mariana* were produced, I'd gain everything with my family."

Granada turned cold and damp. The first snows fell, and Lorca felt even more trapped. "What do I do?" he asked Fernández Almagro. "My family, annoyed with me because they say I don't do anything, won't let me leave Granada. I'm unhappy, as you can imagine. Granada is a hateful place to live. Here, in spite of everything, I'm *drowning*." Relations with his parents had rarely been worse. "For the first time, they are opposed to my writing poetry without thinking of anything else," he revealed to Jorge Guillén.

In early September, Lorca abruptly announced his decision to become a literature professor. "I think I have a vocation for it (it's slowly growing in me) and the capacity for enthusiasm," he wrote weakly to Guillén. He claimed that his parents had "promised, if I begin to study promptly, to give me the money for a trip to Italy, which I've dreamt about for years." He asked Guillén for advice on his new career. Guillén replied with amusement, "You have to start by buying yourself a card file! A CARD FILE. This practical first step will make a huge impression on your family: 'He's begun a card file! And index cards!' That is, *evidently* you're going to work in earnest."

Lorca dutifully ordered a card file ("What fantastic notes will fill it!") and asked Guillén what he should do next. "Because I need to have a job. Just suppose I wanted to get married. Could I do that? No. And this is what I want to resolve. I'm beginning to see that my heart seeks a garden and a little fountain as in my first poems." Lorca assured Guillén that as yet there was no "*particular* girl, but isn't it imminent?"

His own sister Concha, then twenty-three, had announced her engagement that fall to Lorca's friend Manuel Fernández-Montesinos, a medical student and former member of the Rinconcillo. The news had jolted Lorca, who suddenly now yearned for a conventional life, for a career that would please his parents, and for the respectability of marriage and fatherhood. In one of his earliest plays he had portrayed an adolescent Christ who dreams of "a tranquil and sweet life" he knows will never be his. Lorca, too, dreamt of a happy existence, "a garden and a little fountain." But the events of the past two years—above all, his infatuation with Dalí—pointed in a different direction.

Caught between his desire for propriety and his urge to flout convention, to acknowledge his sexuality, he looked wistfully back to the innocence of childhood. "Let me stay a little longer in the playground," he wrote plaintively to Guillén, recalling a popular childhood rhyme ("To the garden of happiness / my mother sends me"), "since I'll have plenty of time to put on gray flannel and the cold airs of meditation." He talked idly of obtaining a position abroad as a lecturer in Spanish literature. "Paris would be ideal." In Paris he would be free of his family and could indulge his whims, sexual or otherwise. He could go off by himself to watch the sun rise over the mountains, "with no need to be home on time. Dawn of responsibility. I'll be responsible for the sun and the breezes. Threshold of fatherhood." At the same time, he worried that he lacked the "aptitude" to be a professor. "Because I'm neither intelligent nor hardworking (a good for nothing!)."

Guillén persuaded their mutual friend Pedro Salinas to look into the possibility of a teaching position for Lorca in France. But Salinas was skeptical. "My private opinion is that your true career is your vocation: poet," he told Lorca. "But your father will never see that as a responsible career as long as you are not known and acclaimed publicly. And you would achieve that with books or stage productions."

From Cadaqués came even sterner advice. "You won't take examinations for *anything*," Dalí wrote. "Convince your father to let you live in peace without all those worries about guarantees for the future, work, personal effort and other things . . . , publish your books, for that can make you famous . . . with a real name and not a legendary one like you have now." The painter reminded Lorca that he loved him "very much. One day we'll see each other again, and what a great time we'll have!"

A few weeks after receiving Dalí's letter, Lorca abandoned his plans for a university career. His flirtation with the academy had lasted just over two months. In a letter to Jorge Guillén written shortly after reaching his decision, he signed himself "Federico (incorrigible poet)."

His three books of poetry—*Songs, Suites,* and *Poem of the Deep Song*—remained unpublished. In the ten months since announcing his plan to publish them, Lorca had come to doubt the wisdom of issuing the three simultaneously, and on the advice of friends had elected to stagger their publication. In late October 1926, he surrendered the manuscripts for the collections to fellow poet Emilio Prados, who with Manolo Altolaguirre had recently founded both a literary magazine, *Litoral,* and a small press by the same name in his native Málaga and was looking for material. Both men had known Lorca for years— Prados most notably in the early 1920s, when he had developed an intense crush on Lorca at the Residencia. Although the two had subsequently drifted apart, both geographically and emotionally, Prados continued to admire Lorca.

He spent several days visiting Lorca in Granada that October. The two toured the province by car and took part in a local homage to the seventeenth-century Granadan poet Pedro de Soto de Rojas, another neglected figure from the city's past, whose work Lorca and his Rinconcillo colleagues sought to revive. Dressed in a bulky suit, Lorca gave a short, highly poetic talk at the homage. He praised the baroque poet and his inspired vision of Granada as a "paradise closed to many."

Days later, Prados returned to Málaga, brandishing Lorca's manuscripts. But his joy at having procured the collections paled the moment he inspected the handwritten documents. It was not unusual for Lorca's manuscripts—even those he submitted for publication—to contain misspelled words, faulty punctuation, accentless syllables, coffee and tobacco stains (which he sometimes ringed with tiny drawings), in short, as Prados described it in a panic-stricken letter to Jorge Guillén, "twenty thousand unknown and indecipherable muddles . . . I didn't count on this when I brought his papers with me. What's to be done?"

The following month, Prados and Altolaguirre published the first volume of their new literary magazine, *Litoral.* The issue contained three of Lorca's Gypsy ballads. These, too, had proved difficult to transcribe, for when Lorca opened his copy of the magazine he found "more than ten! enormous errata" in the poems. The sight so grieved him that he wept. "What great anguish it caused me," he told Guillén, ". . . to see them broken, damaged, without that strength and flintlike *grace* that to me they seem to have!"

Both Guillén and Prados scolded Lorca for his carelessness. Prados returned the manuscript of *Songs,* the first of the poetry books Litoral intended to release, and demanded that Lorca prepare a fair copy of the book himself. His nerves were shattered, Prados said, "after translating you from the Chinese." Lorca at first misinterpreted the gesture to mean that Litoral no longer wished to publish his books. In desperation he told Guillén that "even if it's just the book of *Songs,* I want to publish it. After all, if I try to publish it's only to please a few friends and nothing else. I'm not interested in seeing my poems definitively *dead* . . . that is to say published."

Late in the year Lorca received word from Melchor Fernández Almagro that the actress Margarita Xirgu had agreed to produce *Mariana Pineda.* By then Lorca was so weary of the play that he could only muster a perfunctory thank you to his friend and confess his revulsion at the process he'd been forced to endure. "It's disgusting, the theater," he said. Fernández Almagro had to remind him to thank the many people who had helped secure the production.

In Figueres, Dalí rejoiced at the news and begged Lorca to let him design the show. But Lorca was ambivalent about the work. He remarked gloomily to Guillén that while it had been fine to write a romantic verse drama three years earlier, he now viewed *Mariana,* his lyrical account of the life and martyrdom of a love-struck nineteenth-century *granadina,* as "peripheral to my work." Nevertheless, he went to Madrid in March to meet with Margarita Xirgu and read his drama to her company.

In Málaga, the pace of work on *Songs* quickened. With a production of *Mariana* looming, Prados and Altolaguirre hoped to capitalize on Lorca's impending renown by issuing his new poetry collection in time for the play's premiere.

Lorca scrutinized the copy for the book until he had each poem "just where it wants to be." Proud of his workmanship, he told Fernández Almagro, "I'm happy. I've omitted [some of the] rhythmic songs despite their success because I want the book to have the high air of the sierra." He thought *Songs* "great poetry (great in the sense of nobility and quality, not of worth)," and he predicted the book would provide "surprises for many and happiness for a few."

Songs appeared on May 17, 1927, three weeks before Lorca's twenty-ninth birthday, in a handsome paperbound edition. Lorca dedicated the collection to the three friends who had been his most trusted confidants while preparing the book: Jorge Guillén, Melchor Fernández Almagro, and Pedro Salinas. Privately, Lorca called them "my three weaknesses."

He described the volume itself as a "book of friends." Many individual poems carried inscriptions to friends or to the children of friends. Leafing through his new copy of the book, Jorge Guillén was charmed to find a poem dedicated to his young daughter, "Mademoiselle Teresita Guillén, playing her six-note piano." Guillén slipped a photograph of the child into the book at that spot. He told his wife that *Songs* was "formidable. Brilliant. The best one of all. It contains the most offbeat, most adorable things." Lorca's poetry, he said, was "divine."

The collection included nearly ninety poems written between 1921 and 1926. Their short lines and airy refrains were redolent of popular Spanish songs, especially children's songs, but their veneer of childlike innocence was deceptive. Even the most impish of works in the collection reveals Lorca's poignant understanding of human nature:

> Mama.
> I wish I were silver.
>
> Son,
> you'd be very cold.
>
> Mama.
> I wish I were water.
>
> Son,
> you'd be very cold.
>
> Mama.
> Embroider me on your pillow.
>
> That, yes!
> Right away!

Awash with traditional Andalusian settings and motifs, *Songs*—like *Book of Poems* and *Poem of the Deep Song*—shows how completely Lorca had absorbed the lore of his region. But the collection is more than simply an exercise in the neopopular. Through a combination of humor and obscurity, coupled with an emphasis on metaphor and a studied avoidance of the personal, Lorca reveals his infatuation with the trends of his day: pure poetry, haiku, Góngora. The collection exudes a sense of confidence and delight: in the possibilities of structure and rhythm, in the sorcery of words. One contemporary reviewer pronounced it "new, new, new. Terribly new. Avant-garde!"

Above all, *Songs* exemplifies the notion of a "dehumanized" art. By avoiding the confessional tone and romantic clichés of his earliest work and replacing these with what Ortega y Gasset called "the higher algebra of metaphors," Lorca achieved a new level of poetic composure, in which he neither hides nor confesses anything. Relatively few poems in *Songs* possess any sort of narrative voice, and those that do are evasive. "The song / I will never say, / has fallen asleep on my lips," says the unnamed speaker in the poem "Verlaine."

Language allowed Lorca to do on paper what he longed to do in life: prevaricate. *Songs* is filled with terms such as "mute," "echo," "shadow," and "mirror"—words that enabled Lorca to stress the layered nature of truth. Throughout the collection surfaces mislead, shadows contradict, and personality is mutable. "I used to be. / I once was. / But I am not," confides the narrator of "Monday, Wednesday, and Friday." (While at work on the collection, Lorca admitted to Melchor Fernández Almagro that in "everything" he found "a painful absence of my *own* and true person.")

Lorca's interest in concealment sprang partly from his growing need to suppress certain aspects of himself. In *Songs* he hints at his ambivalent feelings toward love and sex. His evocations of heterosexual love are occasionally tinged with a sense of regret:

> The girl goes through my brow.
> Oh, what ancient feeling!
> . . .
> Full moon brunette.
> What do you want of my desire?

The collection includes the series of "erotic poems" Lorca wrote in 1925 in the wake of his first, impassioned visit to Dalí in Cadaqués, poems that exude a triumphant—if ironic—male sexuality. In "Song of the Fairy," part of another series called "Games," Lorca writes with amusement of a "fairy" homosexual in a silk dressing gown who "arranges / the curls on his head" while his neighbors watch from their windows and smile.

In a complex series of six poems entitled "Three Portraits with Shadow," Lorca intimates his unease with the female sex ("No one would love you like me / if you'd only change my heart!") and seems to embrace love of the self, or those like the self. True to the overall concept of the book, it is only in the so-called shadow poems—"Bacchus," "Venus," and "Narcissus," each of which appears in smaller type after its "portrait," respectively, of Verlaine, Juan Ramón Jiménez, and Debussy—that Lorca ventures to signal the truth, and then he does so obliquely, relying on metaphor to convey what he cannot speak. "Boy! / You'll fall into the river," he warns in "Narcissus." "Deep down there's a rose / with another river inside."

As in all of Lorca's work, there is an undertow of loss and sorrow in *Songs*, and a sometimes acute consciousness of human mortality, but despite the collection's occasional sobriety, it is the most buoyant volume of poetry Lorca was to create. Individual poems have titles like "Silly Song," "Useless Song," "Sung Song." Many are dedicated to Lorca's friends at the Residencia (one inscription reads: "to Luis Buñuel's head. En gros plan"), and the collection as a whole is marked by the sort of high-spirited fun that characterized life at the Madrid institution.

In shaping the book, Lorca had sifted through almost six years' worth of poems, many of which he had originally written for other collections, chiefly *Suites* and *Poem of the Deep Song*. As a consequence he had also had to rethink each of those books. The process caused him "genuine anguish." But in the end he was pleased with the results. "The songs remain girded to my body and I am master of the book," he told Jorge Guillén. "A bad poet . . . very well! But master of my bad poetry!"

Any doubts he had about the collection were groundless. *Songs* was Lorca's first definitive book, a leap forward in the evolution of his style, and while it received scant critical notice at the time, those who did review it were struck by its originality. *El Sol*'s Ricardo Baeza praised *Songs* as "a poetry of codes and arabesques." Luis Montanyá, writing in the avant-garde Catalan journal *L'Amic de les Arts*, called *Songs* "pure poetry . . . an authentic book of poems." Enrique Díez-Canedo, who the year before had criticized Lorca for his sloth in getting his work into print, extolled Lorca's "penetrating poetic vision."

Dalí voiced his qualified approval of the book. Although he claimed to prefer the poetry of "a nickel-plated motor" to that of an old Granadan song, he nevertheless admired Lorca's "delightful songs." Yet he could not refrain from noting that Lorca's lyrical vision of a timeless Andalusia no longer suited a world that had just seen Lindbergh cross the Atlantic. "Your songs are Granada without trams, without even airplanes," Dalí wrote. He conceded, however, that Lorca would go on doing whatever he wished. "That much we already know!"

CHAPTER II

CELEBRITY

1927

$\smile$

At twenty-three, Dalí was on the brink of international fame. In late 1926 he held his second painting exhibition in Barcelona. The show drew buyers from Paris and a representative from Pittsburgh's Carnegie Institute, who purchased two Dalí canvases.

In February 1927 the Spanish army drafted the artist for nine months of military service. "*Carísimo amigo,*" Dalí wrote to Lorca in March. "You can't imagine. I've been a soldier for one month!" Being in the army was a lark. "I'm strong from boxing and very suntanned," he reported in May. He missed Lorca: "Now we're beginning to need our madnesses, our wanderings about, our tears and our laughter, and our hunger!"

Nearly a year had passed since their last rendezvous in Madrid. With *Mariana Pineda* slated to open that summer in Barcelona, they expected to see each other soon. In late March Lorca went to Madrid to meet with Margarita Xirgu to finalize plans for the production. From there he intended to go to Barcelona to begin rehearsals. He told Pepín Bello it was the start of a new era for him: "I'm saying goodbye to Segovia and Toledo. That's how it must be. I dream of Paris and another, more enjoyable life."

But he needed money for the trip, and his father, exasperated with Lorca's spending habits, hesitated to give it. His parents were especially put out with him because during his brief stay in Madrid in March, he had squandered a large amount of money. He claimed it wasn't his fault. Upon his arrival the Residencia had been full, he explained, and he had been forced to eat in cafés and stay in a costly hotel (the cheaper places were too far away to accommodate his "theater life"). He had also found it necessary to send a bouquet of roses to Xirgu and to host a banquet for several journalist friends in order to persuade them to go to Barcelona later in the season to review *Mariana*. "The money disappears like water," he said. "I'm not a spendthrift."

His father viewed matters differently. For years he had indulged Lorca financially. A two-month allowance sometimes vanished in three days—spent on little more than outings with friends. In letters home, Lorca invariably asked for money, time and again insisting that his expenses were "necessary." His requests could be blunt: "Send me fifty pesetas in your next letter. I need it." Usually his parents obliged him. They sent money so that he could buy food, shoes, hats, a new winter coat. "You know that we want you to be decently dressed and not to have to beg things from people," his mother wrote.

But in the spring of 1927 his father balked, and threatened to withhold funds for Lorca's trip to Barcelona. Lorca was devastated. In a six-page letter defending himself and his goals—yet another plea for parental respect—he promised his father that he would "more than repay" the expense of the trip once he had collected his earnings from *Mariana*. Why begrudge him the money he so desperately needed—especially now, when he had just spent ten months in Granada "with three and a half pesetas to my name (so to speak)"? If his parents refused to pay his way, he would simply go back to Granada and stay there. Xirgu could produce *Mariana* "any way she likes, and with the scenery and the acting as she sees fit. Anything to keep from upsetting you."

Worn down from years of argument, and newly reminded of his son's unyielding determination, his father relented. By mid-May, Lorca was on his way to Barcelona.

In his soldier's uniform Dalí was as dashing as a Hollywood star. Tall, suntanned, slim, he posed coolly beside Lorca not long after the poet reached Barcelona that spring, and the two had their picture taken. Dalí wore his hair brushed neatly back from his porcelain face; he placed his hands in his pockets and extended one uniformed leg gracefully in front of the other. Beside him Lorca looked young and unrefined. He wore a rumpled gray suit and held his hands stiffly together in front of him. An acquaintance who met him during his visit to Catalunya in 1927 recalled that he "exuded 'south' from every pore." Powerless to match Dalí's urban polish, Lorca traded on his rustic Andalusian roots. He cheerfully mocked the ardent Catalan nationalism then rampant in

Barcelona, telling one local reporter, "I'm from the Kingdom of Granada!" He began wearing a red carnation in his lapel.

Throughout the two-month rehearsal period for *Mariana Pineda*, Lorca shuttled back and forth between the Dalí home in nearby Figueres and a hotel room in Barcelona, which he and Dalí sometimes shared when Dalí was able to get leave from the army. The two friends wandered the city together, lost in passionate conversation about art and aesthetics, or about Lorca's play, which Dalí had agreed to design. Lorca deluged the painter with sketches and photographs of typical Andalusian settings. He praised Dalí's "shrewdly intuited" take on the play's design, while Dalí, in turn, gamely applauded Lorca's "sophisticated sentimentality."

On Sunday afternoons they often attended a weekly *tertulia* in the spartan apartment of Rafael Barradas, the bohemian artist who had created designs for Lorca's first play, *The Butterfly's Evil Spell*. Stretched out on the floor, Lorca, Dalí, and their friends discussed music, literature, theater, film, dadaism, and surrealism. As usual, Lorca dominated the conversation. He frequently sat at Barradas's rented piano and belted out popular songs. No one objected, because whatever he said or did was "so terribly interesting," remembered Sebastian Gasch, a rotund Catalan art critic who met Lorca in Barcelona that spring and quickly yielded to the *granadino*'s "fiery, young, impulsive character."

Gasch, like others, was struck not only by Lorca's ebullience but by his abrupt changes of mood. Once, after contentedly listening to a group of Gypsy singers in a local café, Lorca suddenly fell silent. His companions asked what had happened, but he refused to speak. In due course he confessed, with a touch of melodrama, that he had been thinking about death. At times he seemed to Gasch oddly pensive, even devout. One night he told his friends he had to go home early so that he could attend Mass the next morning at the cathedral. Smiling softly, he rolled his dark eyes skyward and murmured something about the "aroma of ancient pomp" he always experienced inside the huge Gothic church. Dalí pointed toward the table where they sat and said, "I'm more interested in this olive."

It was this side of Lorca—contemplative, reverential, nostalgic, even maudlin—that had led him to write *Mariana Pineda*. As he watched his play come to life that spring in Barcelona's Teatro Goya, Lorca must have felt he was recovering some part of his lost childhood. During rehearsals he worked meticulously with the chorus of children who were to sing the ballad of Mariana Pineda at the beginning and end of his play. Seated at a piano, his hands racing "nervously, easily" over the keyboard, Lorca went over the song with his young actors until they understood its essence as clearly as he did. At the final dress rehearsal, a reporter asked him to explain what he had hoped to accomplish with *Mariana.* Lorca answered that he wanted to show his love for "these old things"—for Mariana herself, for the nineteenth-century engravings he and Dalí had attempted to re-create onstage, for the popular ballad about Mariana that he had first heard as a boy. "Perhaps," Lorca mused, "the entire work is nothing more than an example of variations on the theme of the popular ballad."

He was far more comfortable with Xirgu's production of *Mariana Pineda* than he had been with the Madrid premiere of *The Butterfly's Evil Spell.* Dalí's childlike designs for the show delighted him—there was nothing "picturesque" about the artist's use of Andalusian motifs, Lorca told Manuel de Falla—and he thought Xirgu's portrayal of the doomed Mariana "wonderful." He was profoundly indebted to the Catalan actress. She alone, he told a journalist, had dared to produce *Mariana* after "all the companies in Spain that pride themselves on being artistic" had rejected it. She had not only been willing to stage the play, but she had agreed to spend a large sum of money on it—a fact Lorca proudly reported to his family.

He and Xirgu enjoyed an easy rapport. During their first meeting earlier in the year, he had regaled the actress with the story of his woeful debut as a playwright in Madrid in 1920. He told the tale with obvious enjoyment, lingering over the details of his public humiliation. He described how he had cowered in the basement of the theater as the audience above him stomped its disapproval of his play. Xirgu was charmed. She shared Lorca's addiction to the stage, and she loved his robust laugh—a laugh, she said, that seemed to emanate from the vowel O.

Her patrician looks belied Xirgu's working-class origins. She was a statuesque woman with a strong, square face, black eyes, and a dark voice. José Ortega y Gasset, one of her many admirers, wrote that Xirgu's arms formed "curves of harmony." Lorca found her riveting, and later described her as "the actress who breaks the monotony of the footlights with breezes of innovation, who flings handfuls of fire or pitchers of cold water onto the dozing public."

As a child she had given makeshift theatrical performances on her family's dining room table; at ten she appeared in her first amateur production. She made her professional debut on the Catalan stage at eighteen, and by her early thirties she was known to audiences throughout Spain and Latin America as both a formidable actress and a shrewd producer who ran her own theater company with fellow actor Enrique Borrás. The 1922 Nobel laureate, Jacinto Benavente, wrote plays expressly for Xirgu.

The actress was thirty-eight when she premiered *Mariana Pineda*. To capture Lorca's gentle heroine, she softened her usually severe makeup and concealed her dark hair under a mass of shiny blond curls. The audience loved her. On opening night, June 24, 1927—the Feast of Saint John, a day Lorca adored—cheers erupted at the end of each act, and Lorca was called onstage repeatedly to bow beside Xirgu. Flushed with excitement, he gripped the actress's hand and whispered, "Even the old folks are clapping! Even the old folks are clapping!"

Later that evening, as he strolled along the winding gray streets of Barcelona's Gothic Quarter with Xirgu and a handful of friends who had attended the opening, including Salvador and Ana María Dalí, Lorca reenacted the curtain calls he and Xirgu had been asked to take. In a brief, unexpectedly melancholy charade, he bowed solemnly to an imaginary audience. Watching him, Ana María Dalí thought to herself that he was unable to experience or even conceive of joy without acknowledging its antithesis. Eventually the group made its way to a sidewalk café, where Lorca impulsively asked a female street performer to join them. "But without speaking," he instructed the woman. "Like a carnation."

The following day he sent effusive telegrams to friends. "Huge success *Mariana Pineda*. Hugs. Federico-Dalí," read the terse wire Melchor Fernández Almagro received in Madrid. In Granada, Lorca's family waited anxiously for news of the play's reception. Despite a congratulatory cable from Xirgu that morning, Don Federico was unable to relax until he had received confirmation of the play's success from Lorca himself. Late in the afternoon the playwright's telegram arrived, and the family rejoiced.

In their reviews, critics focused more on Lorca's potential than on his achievement. Several reviewers noted the humanity of his characters, and many praised his "luminous" verse. But some questioned whether he belonged in the theater. *La Vanguardia*, one of Barcelona's leading papers, suggested that although Lorca was a "delicate and sentimental poet," he was not a serious playwright. *La Publicitat*'s Doménec Guansi observed that in *Mariana Pineda* Lorca seemed to have been concerned "with nothing more than the creation of atmosphere. Characters? . . . Action?" Critics had raised the same issues with *The Butterfly's Evil Spell*.

A more gratifying appraisal came from the reviewer Francisco Madrid of *La Noche*, another prominent Barcelona paper, who argued that Lorca could "now join the list of Spanish poets who uphold the tradition of poetic theater." In his long and favorable review, Madrid heralded *Mariana Pineda* as a breath of fresh air in an era of mediocre plays, and he praised Lorca and Dalí for their extreme modernity. Lorca clipped the review and sent it to his parents with a note boasting that the article had appeared in "the most important daily in Barcelona, the one with the largest circulation."

Fewer than twenty-four hours after the premiere of *Mariana Pineda*, Lorca opened an exhibition of his drawings in Barcelona's celebrated Dalmau Galleries, the city's leading proponent of avant-garde art. With the exception of two private showings of his sketches at a friend's home in Granada, where the drawings were hung from curtains with pins, he had never publicly shown his work before. Mostly he sketched for pleasure, using whatever was handy—a piece of stationery, a crayon, his sister's colored pencils. He had no desire to be a painter, he joked, because his parents could not tolerate stains in the house. But Dalí admired his visual intuition (which he described as "aphrodisiac") and, together with several other Barcelona friends, persuaded the diminutive, white-haired Josep Dalmau to present an exhibition of Lorca's work in his gallery.

Dalmau had long championed the avant-garde. He introduced Barcelona audiences to the work of Filippo Marinetti and Marcel Duchamp, and he helped launch the careers of Juan Gris, Joan Miró, and Pablo Picasso. Dalí had twice shown his paintings in Dalmau's galleries, and he owed his success in part to the visibility those exhibitions had given him. Lorca's weeklong exhibit drew less attention than Dalí's, but it did receive a few flattering reviews from friends, including Dalí, and to Lorca's astonishment he sold four drawings. He gave the rest away to his Catalan friends.

An eclectic mix of old and new, traditional and avant-garde, the drawings in the exhibition complemented Lorca's poetry collection *Songs*, published one month earlier. Both demonstrated his abiding love of popular Andalusian motifs, his newfound admiration for cubism, and his increasing preoccupation with identity. In a number of his Dalmau sketches Lorca superimposed one dreamlike face on another, as if to offer a graphic interpretation of the ideas he had explored in *Songs*: "Woodcutter. / Sever me from my shadow." Years later he described one of his double-faced images as a self-portrait that shows "man's capacity for crying as well as winning." The works encapsulate the split that characterized Lorca himself: his profound and deeply personal conviction that without sorrow, joy was inconceivable; without death, life incomprehensible.

In a somber drawing called "The Kiss," he sketched a face much like his own, with dense black eyebrows and a wedge of black hair, joined at the lips to a second, featureless face whose oval contour resembles Dalí's. In his own work Dalí, too, had recently begun pairing Lorca's face with his. Each man appeared to covet, or fear, losing himself in the other. Aesthetically they had never been closer. Dalí said later that during this phase of his career, "for the duration of an eclipse," Lorca's shadow "came to darken the virginal originality of my spirit and of my flesh."

Lorca was equally swayed by Dalí. His Barcelona drawings revealed the degree to which he had absorbed the painter's cubist aesthetic and shared Dalí's enthusiasm for surrealism. The exhibition included a formal portrait of Dalí, one of several Lorca made during this period. He had developed his own icon for the artist's face: a Modigliani-like ovoid with almond-shaped eyes, black eyebrows, and full lips. In one of Lorca's portraits of the artist, Dalí appears as a kind of fecund priest wearing a bishop's miter, with fish nibbling at each of the fingers on his right hand. Rife with Freudian overtones, this intensely private work referred to a world only Lorca and Dalí fully understood. Lorca gave the drawing to the painter, who kept it for decades. By way of explaining the image, Dalí said only, "Lorca saw me as an incarnation of life, graced like a dark god."

Days after the closing of both *Mariana Pineda* and his Dalmau exhibition, Lorca boarded a bus with Salvador and Ana María Dalí, and the three took off for Cadaqués. They sat side by side on a rooftop bench. The instant Lorca caught his first glimpse of the village in the distance, he shrieked: "Cadaquééééés! Cadaquééééés!" The Dalís quickly chimed in.

At nineteen, Ana María was leaner and more graceful than she had been during Lorca's first visit to the town, in 1925. Her long, angelic curls were gone, replaced by a stylish 1920s bob. Lorca adored her. At dusk the two took walks together, ambling hand in hand through groves of olive trees while church bells pealed and the sun sank beneath the mountains, casting its pink light on the small white town. Lorca often wore a fisherman's shirt Ana María had made for him. Asked years afterward whether Lorca had been in love with her, Ana María merely blushed. That he loved her was certain—but in ways neither seemed able to articulate.

On Sundays the two attended Mass together. Dalí refused to join them. "I've seen it before," he quipped. But Lorca found the ritual soothing. As he stood beside Ana María in the small sanctuary, immersed in gestures and phrases he had known since boyhood, he seemed "in ecstasy." He continued to identify not with the authoritarian Father of Old Testament doctrine but with the New Testament Christ: symbol of goodness and love, proof that human charity might transcend evil and offset the capriciousness of fate. Only in church, thought Ana María, was Lorca unafraid of death. Elsewhere it obsessed him. Like a frightened child, he insisted on taking their hands whenever he went for a walk with the two Dalís. "He was afraid of dying," Ana María believed, "and it seemed to him that by holding our hands he could remain anchored to life."

At the beach he swam only in shallow water, and even then he clung to Ana María's hand. When she and Dalí ventured farther out to the sea, Lorca remained on shore. He was terrified of drowning.

Even small things alarmed him. At the slightest hint of a sore throat, he insisted that Ana María and Dalí take his temperature and prepare inhalations of eucalyptus leaves. Because they loved him they indulged him. (Later, he apologized to Ana María for his "grave throat illness, which caused you so much trouble.") The three spent whole days playing games together. Dalí and Lorca took turns pretending to be a capricious child, a "*babouet*," who refused to walk or eat. When Lorca played the *babouet* he demanded to be told terrifying stories with unexpectedly comforting endings.

They went sailing together, took part in local festivals, played records all day long, and at night, with the guitarist Regino Sáinz—who was visiting Cadaqués—sat on the beach, while Lorca sang folk songs or recited poems. In dozens of artfully arranged photographs they immortalized their fun: Ana María, holding a phonograph and a stack of records on her lap; Dalí, standing alone in a white terry-cloth robe, bronzed and sultry, his hair damp from the sea; Lorca, clowning on the beach in bathing trunks and a robe, his chunky legs draped in a showgirl's pose, an impish grin on his face. In one snapshot he and Dalí sit across from each other at a table with Lorca's bathrobe cord stretched between their foreheads, as though they are transmitting thoughts back and forth. In another picture, each displays an emblem of his artistic temperament. Dalí, who fancied himself a rational Apollonian, holds a triangle, while Lorca, his hair smoothed back, one hand resting on Salvador's knee, clasps a wine glass.

Lorca's stay in Cadaqués, though brief, was rapturous. He subsequently told a friend that Dalí inspired in him "the same pure emotion" he felt in the presence of the baby Jesus, "abandoned in the Portico of Bethlehem, with the whole germ of the crucifixion already latent beneath the straws of the cradle." Incapable of resisting the painter, he helped Dalí draft and sign a strident "Anti-Artistic Manifesto" exalting the machine age and condemning much of the very literature and art Lorca had once admired. Other friends were alarmed by Dalí's increasingly rigid views on art and his newly "materialistic, irreligious, and objective" behavior. But Lorca maintained that nothing was more dramatic than Dalí's objectivity, and he allowed himself to be swept up in the painter's escalating quest for radical new images and ideas—one of which, paradoxically, was Saint Sebastian, who became for Dalí a paradigm of the emotional control he sought.

The martyred saint had been an intimate point of contact between the two friends for at least a year. In March 1927, Dalí signed a letter to Lorca, "Your Saint Sebastian." Even Ana María was in on the secret. On the back of a postcard to Lorca she wrote, "I'm sending you this card because you might like it; but don't show it to Saint Sebastian. It would be improper." Both men were intrigued by the iconography of the saint: his manly beauty and his passive, at times ecstatic, response to the arrows piercing his flesh. Lorca came to believe that "one of man's most beautiful postures is that of Saint Sebastian." He meant the posture of defeat, willingly accepted.

Dalí persisted in calling Sebastian "Saint Objectivity." In late July he published an exhaustive prose poem on the martyr in the Catalan journal *L'Amic de les Arts*. Dedicated "To F. García Lorca," Dalí's meandering poem extols Sebastian as an exemplar of the modern age. In Sebastian's pose of "exquisite agony," the saint embodies an aesthetic of objectivity that offers a foil to the sentimentality and "putrefaction" Dalí despised. On a more personal level, Sebastian reminded the painter of Lorca. He told Lorca that while at work on the poem, it had often seemed to him that the saint "is you . . . We'll see if Saint Sebastian turns out to be you."

Through the image of Sebastian the two made sly allusions to the intense emotional—and conceivably physical—nature of their involvement. Dalí spoke bluntly of the saint's "*unwounded* ass." Lorca was more oblique. "Saint Sebastian's arrows are made of steel," he wrote to Dalí later that summer, "but the difference between you and me is that you see them as firmly fixed and robust, short arrows that don't come undone, and I see them as long . . . at the moment of the wound. Your Saint Sebastian of ivory contrasts with mine of flesh who is dying all the time, and that's how it must be."

To what degree the martyr reflected Lorca's private relationship with the artist remains unclear. Years later Dalí claimed to have spurned Lorca's sexual advances. But others who knew the artist—Pepín Bello, Luis Buñuel, Rafael Martínez Nadal—suspected Dalí of distorting the truth in order to shock or amuse his admirers, much as he had once feigned love for an adolescent girl because he enjoyed deluding her. Bello and Buñuel both believed Dalí was "asexual," a chaste Apollo to Lorca's earthbound Dionysus.

Dalí's paintings imply otherwise. By 1927 he had replaced the neoclassical lines of his earlier canvases with the stark landscapes of a Freudian world. His sensual portraits of Ana María had given way to cryptic representations of Lorca—often shown as a decapitated head with closed eyes—surrounded by jarring manifestations of Dalí's subconscious: nude female torsos, severed hands, rotting animals, airplanes, fish, phallic gadgets, genitalia. His ambiguous, at times misogynist, depictions of women, together with the prevalence of both homo- and autoerotic images, signal the depth of Dalí's sexual malaise and suggest that in all likelihood he and Lorca engaged in a short-lived physical affair.

Dalí was obsessed by Lorca, and troubled by his obsession. In several paintings he layered Lorca's features over his own or placed one man's face in the other's shadow. At times he simply fused the two faces. Their lives were similarly intertwined. Dalí was beginning to write poetry, while Lorca spent more and more time drawing. In their work, they spoke the same metaphorical language. Each heaped praise on the other. "Federico is better than ever," Dalí wrote to Luis Buñuel in Paris that summer. "He's the great man. His drawings are brilliant."

Buñuel was appalled by the intensity of Dalí's attachment to Lorca. Perhaps because he resented Lorca's refusal to collaborate with him on a film the previous year, or more probably because he detected Lorca's homosexuality and objected to it, Buñuel had come to loathe what he described as Lorca's "extreme narcissism" and "terrible aestheticism." He told Pepín Bello that unless Dalí escaped to Paris, the painter would amount to nothing. Only in Paris, Buñuel said, could Dalí "remake himself, away from García's ill-fated influence."

By early August, Lorca had turned "black" from the Mediterranean sun. He told his brother, now back from his studies abroad, that he had begun writing "a new kind of poetry." But although happy, he missed his family. He asked Paco to kiss everyone for him: "I long more than ever, do you understand me?" He did not explain what he meant by the remark.

Shortly afterward, Lorca abruptly departed from Cadaqués. For reasons left unclear—except to say that his family had urgently called him home—he felt compelled to return to Granada. Something had happened to cloud his relationship with Dalí. From Barcelona, where he stopped overnight on his way home, Lorca sent an impassioned letter to the artist. In it he recalled his distress at leaving Dalí's home. "I was on the verge of throwing myself out of the car in order to stay with you (with little you) in Cadaqués." At a bend in the road leading away from the village he had suddenly experienced a vision of a "tiny" Dalí, "eating a little red hand with oil and using a small plaster fork which you pulled from your eyes. All with the tenderness of a recently hatched chicken."

The heat in Barcelona was oppressive. As he labored to convey his feelings, Lorca thought about Dalí's new paintings, with their logical, keenly proportioned, provocative images. "I get excited thinking of the things you're going to discover about Cadaqués, and I remember a neophyte Salvador Dalí licking the shell of dusk without yet going inside, the palest pink shell of a crab turned on its back." Having now left Cadaqués, Lorca realized what he had lost. In Dalí's absence, Barcelona seemed confused, rushed, "unclear and unhinged"—unlike diaphanous Cadaqués, where Lorca had felt "the blood's circulation" in his shoulders for the first time in his life. Cadaqués was real; in Barcelona, people seemed merely to be "playing and sweating with a concern for forgetting."

He crowded his thoughts onto a sheet of stationery from a Barcelona café. "I want to weep," he wrote. "I've behaved like an indecent donkey's ass with you, you who are the best thing in the world for me. As the minutes go by I see it clearly and I am truly sorry. But this only increases my affection for you and my attachment to your way of thinking and your human quality." Lorca avoided saying more about what had taken place between the two men. He begged Dalí to remember him in his latest work: "Put my name in the painting so that [my name] might amount to something in the world."

Dalí acquiesced. In the foreground of a work he eventually titled *Honey Is Sweeter than Blood,* he placed a likeness of Lorca's head, with its neck severed, eyes wide open, and a trickle of blood seeping from its mouth. Positioned near the head, as though the two had once been attached, Dalí painted the headless torso of a nude woman. Around both he arranged an assortment of rotting carcasses, flies, drops of blood, and sharp geometrical objects that Lorca called "apparatuses." Lorca admired the painting. "The bisected woman is the most beautiful poem one can make from blood," he told Dalí. But he refrained from commenting on the work's more unsettling implications: that his beloved friend seemed to associate him not only with androgyny but with a decaying aesthetic.

Lorca returned to Granada in early August, full of talk about Dalí's genius and their month together in Cadaqués. Virtually everything he saw, did, and thought reminded him of the painter. With its lush trees and aura of "historic melancholy," his family's Huerta de San Vicente recalled the terrace of Dalí's home by the sea.

"I think about you and your little house," he told the artist. "I've never thought more intensely than now. This is the summit. I hope you'll write to me . . . And that you'll tell me if you resent me or if you've erased me from among your friends."

When he and his family traveled to a resort in the Alpujarras later that month, Lorca yearned for his distant friend. He felt isolated in his hotel, where there was "not one decent curvaceous thigh," he told Dalí by letter, ". . . and I

don't like talking to anyone unless it's the waiters who are handsome and I
know what they're going to say to me. I think of you all the time. I think of you
too much. I feel as though I am holding a hot gold coin in my hand and I cannot let go of it. But I don't want to let go of it either, *little son.* I must imagine
that you are hideously ugly in order to love you more."

In the same letter Lorca stressed his esteem for Saint Sebastian and the martyr's "grace in the midst of torture . . . We are all capable of being like Saint Sebastian in the face of rumors and gossip." Inspired by Dalí's prose poem on the
saint, Lorca embarked on his own series of prose poems, the first of which,
"Saint Lucy and Saint Lazarus," he published in November. A fantastic account of a trip to a Spanish city much like Barcelona, the work recalls Louis
Aragon's 1926 surrealist text, *Le Paysan de Paris,* a dreamlike examination of a
modern metropolis. But while Lorca's poem indicates his growing interest in
surrealism, the work stems more immediately from Dalí's "Saint Sebastian,"
with its clipped syntax and circuitous design. In "Saint Lucy" as well as his
other prose poems—"Suicide in Alexandria," "Beheading of the Baptist," and
"Lovers Murdered by a Partridge"—Lorca unveils a cruel, antiseptic, coldly
ironic vision of reality. Motifs from Dalí's paintings—decapitated heads, modern machines, ants, mules, the skeletal remains of fish—fill the poems.

While neither man was ready to associate himself formally with surrealism,
both Lorca and Dalí had begun to experiment with such surrealist techniques
as automatic writing and drawing, and dream images. Of the two men, Dalí,
as usual, was the most radical. Privately he regarded Lorca's "Saint Lucy and
Saint Lazarus" as a "wonderful" piece of work, but the "quintessence of putrefaction." In letters to Lorca he mocked writers whom Lorca had once revered,
and he urged the poet to intensify his quest for the new. "Act of FAITH," he declared. "Lorca, the first truly *future* poet when he is completely purified and
emerges like a motionless, beautiful oil."

Heeding Dalí's call for the creation of stark, inexplicable metaphors, Lorca
turned from words to images and, while at work on his prose poems, began using drawing pencils for inspiration. When the subject of a poem became too
long or "poetically stale," he resolved it by sketching. The act of drawing made
him feel "clean, comforted, happy, childlike," he told the art critic Sebastian
Gasch, whom he had befriended in Barcelona that spring, and who was
quickly becoming one of his most trusted correspondents and greatest fans.
While drawing, Lorca said, "I live moments of an intensity and purity that poetry does not give me." Emboldened by Gasch's lavish praise of his sketches
(the critic compared Lorca's work favorably with Picasso's and predicted that

his "unforgettable drawings" would enjoy a success similar to that of Miró's and Dalí's), Lorca began to talk seriously of publishing his drawings in book form.

His best sketches, he knew, yielded exquisite metaphors. A spare interpretation of Saint Sebastian, for instance, showed only a series of arrows pointing to a series of ink blots, a single eye, and—in what Lorca may have intended as a reference to Sebastian's "unwounded ass"—a single dot surrounded by a small circle. In this and other conceptual drawings, Lorca endeavored "to choose the essential traits of emotion and form, or of super-reality and super-form, to turn them into a symbol that, like a magic key, will lead us to better understand the reality they possess in the world," he explained to Gasch.

And yet he shunned pure abstraction and refused to align himself wholly with surrealism. He insisted that his drawings were grounded in reality, and therefore human. To Gasch's worried observation that he risked slipping into a dangerous state of "perpetual dream" with his visionary sketches, Lorca replied cheerfully that humor and humanity would save him from "the great dark mirrors that poetry and madness wield at the bottom of their chasms." Unlike Dalí, he would not abandon reason, would not sever his bond with the human community. "I am and I feel myself to be treading cautiously in art," he told Gasch. Life itself was another matter. "I fear dreaming and the abyss in the reality of my life, in love, in the daily contact with others. That, yes, is terrible and fantastic."

Publicly he disavowed any link to revolutionary art movements. When Xirgu's production of *Mariana Pineda* opened that fall in Madrid, Lorca told a reporter from the *Heraldo de Madrid* that he was neither an ultraist "nor a member of the avant-garde." His poetic roots lay with Góngora, he said; his theatrical wellspring was Lope de Vega.

By the standards of his recent work, *Mariana Pineda* was hopelessly outdated, but Lorca defended the play on the occasion of its Madrid debut. Asked to explain the drama's many clichés, he answered that he had purposely included these so as to give the work its "romantic, but ironically romantic, character." On opening night, October 12, 1927, Lorca stood confidently backstage and listened to the audience applaud his creation. At the end of each act he strode onstage—"with a vengeance," said one observer—to accept their praise. Outside the theater, Lorca's former grade school teacher, Antonio Rodríguez Espinosa, waited in the dark for news of the play's reception, as he had done seven years earlier at the premiere of *The Butterfly's Evil Spell*. Now, as then, he was too nervous to venture inside the theater. Told at last that *Mariana* had triumphed, Rodríguez Espinosa sighed happily and said, "It had to come."

Once more, triumphant telegrams made their way to Granada. This time Lorca's family packed their bags and set off for Madrid to see the play for themselves. The poet Pedro Salinas met them during their stay in the capital and pronounced them "a most enjoyable family, in whom one finds various, scintillating clues to our friend's personality—almost, almost a study of literary sources."

Reviewers, among them several of Lorca's personal friends, were generous. But dissonant voices and familiar reproofs surfaced. The critic Enrique de Mesa accused Lorca of having loaded his play with every "trick from the old theater . . . the funereal pealing of bells, the flowers that adorn little Mariana as she goes to her death, the long and tedious farewell." Francisco Ayala denounced the work's "intentional ingenuousness. Artificial childishness." During its brief Madrid run, *Mariana* sparked a lively polemic among the city's intellectuals, who debated the play's artistic merits and political bent. As the discussion grew more heated, Pedro Salinas noted that the majority of comments were "adverse." At a banquet in Lorca's honor, guests quibbled about the play until the famed humorist Ramón Gómez de la Serna finally rose, adjusted his monocle, and offered an ironic defense of the work. "It breathes with great freedom, great freedom, great freedom!" he said, and smiled.

Commercially the show was a failure. It ran for only twenty-six performances in Madrid—well short of the hundred that typically signaled a success. On tour in the provinces later that season, it fared even more poorly. Audiences stayed away, and several performances had to be canceled. At a performance in Oviedo, Lorca's self-consciously ornate language led one spectator to surmise, "It must be something written by one of those modern poets." Although he reported to his parents that the play was enjoying a "great success" on tour, Lorca was painfully aware of the truth. To Pepín Bello he described the work as "an embarrassment." To a journalist in Madrid he confessed that if he were to rewrite the play, "I'd do it another way, in one of the thousand ways possible." Perhaps most disappointing, *Mariana* earned little money. Dalí, among others, was dismayed. The painter had hoped to use the profits from Lorca's verse play to underwrite a new project—an "ANTIARTISTIC Magazine."

But despite his disenchantment with *Mariana*, Lorca welcomed the publicity the play generated. Later in the season he published the drama in book form. Theatrical gossip columns speculated about upcoming Lorca productions. The poet Antonio Machado and his brother, Manuel, declared in an interview that Lorca was one of the brightest lights in the contemporary Spanish theater. "Did you see what the Machado brothers said about me?" Lorca asked his parents.

Work by and about him now appeared regularly in the country's prominent literary journals, and there was also talk of him abroad, in both France and Germany. In a front-page article entitled "A Generation and Its Poet," critic Ricardo Baeza of *El Sol* hailed Lorca as "the foremost Spanish lyric poet of our day." Baeza's article embarrassed Lorca even as it pleased him. It "must have produced a great rumpus among certain persons," he told Sebastian Gasch. "I'm truly sorry because I had nothing whatsoever to do with this."

Many of his friends and peers cheered his new celebrity. The poet Gerardo Diego praised him for having finally forsaken his "medieval and random means of self-promotion, and his indolent aversion to proofs and postage stamps." Although he still professed to regard his writing as merely "a game, an amusing diversion," Lorca coveted the attention it brought him. He would sometimes grip one of his friends by the shoulder and exclaim, "Ah, how talented I am! Tell me I'm talented!" "You're so talented," the friend would reply and Lorca would laugh and say, "Yes sir, I am!"

Luis Buñuel, who saw Lorca during his periodic visits to Madrid, found his vanity insufferable. Others thought it charming. Lorca "let himself be adored," an acquaintance remembered. He brazenly courted admirers, promising to dedicate poems to them and then forgetting his promise, or dedicating the same poem to a succession of friends. At *tertulias* he demanded to be the center of attention. If another speaker threatened to upstage him, he often left— only to return moments later with some crucial piece of news that restored him to the spotlight. He loved to ape others' quirks—a friend's blinking eyes or eccentric appearance—but when anyone dared to imitate him, he resented it. If he found himself with someone whose personality seemed capable of outshining his own, he simply walked away.

He grew especially impatient with fellow Andalusian Rafael Alberti, whose career as a poet had taken flight since their first meeting in 1924 (Alberti won the 1925 National Prize for Literature for his verse collection *Marinero en tierra*) and whose passionate recitations of verse rivaled Lorca's. Because both came from the south, comparisons between the two were inevitable, and they began to vie for the role of successor to Juan Ramón Jiménez as the region's reigning poet. Pedro Salinas dubbed them "the little Andalusian boys." Critics spoke of Lorca's influence on Alberti's neopopulist verse, and friends charted their respective development. Pepín Bello complained that Alberti had learned to "copy" images and expressions directly from Lorca's poems. Salinas confided to Jorge Guillén in the fall of 1927 that he thought Alberti's poetry much improved. "He's undoubtedly making more progress than Federico." In time, Lorca became so annoyed by the situation that whenever someone praised Alberti's work in his presence, he feigned a sore throat and left. Aware that Lorca had on occasion spoken ill of him, Alberti implored him to forget their differences. "You don't know how much I'm capable of loving you (this is not a declaration of love). You scarcely know me, cousin." But Alberti, too, engaged in what he later referred to as "minimal battles," and their friendship suffered as a result.

With his elders, Lorca was more forgiving. One evening at a *tertulia* with the irascible Galician playwright Ramón del Valle-Inclán, then in his sixties, Lorca took offense at something Valle-Inclán said or did and made a cutting remark to the older man. Stunned, Valle-Inclán left the gathering early. Lorca instructed his friends to "go with him. Don't leave him alone. I've been cruel." He was childishly content to let others repair his wrong. At another gathering, he deliberately conspired to prevent the humorist Ramón Gómez de la Serna from monopolizing the conversation. But afterward Lorca felt remorseful, and as he left the restaurant he struck up a friendly conversation with Gómez de la Serna. That "was the really charming thing about Federico," recalled his friend Santiago Ontañón, who witnessed the episode.

Friends like Ontañón and Jorge Guillén were willing to overlook the less flattering aspects of Lorca's character—his petulance and immaturity, his incessant and puerile need for adulation. They focused instead on his generosity and basic lack of pretension. Guillén noted that even after Lorca became famous, he remained "Federico"—never "Señor García Lorca," not even to strangers. Among close friends he was easygoing, spontaneous, and ordinary, and yet to Guillén he was plainly the best of their generation. Lorca agreed with this assessment, although he considered Guillén his equal. "We're the captains of the new Spanish poetry," he told the soft-spoken older poet. "Shake on it! You and I have character, personality, something inimitable that comes from within, a unique voice by the grace of God."

In his long treatise "A Generation and Its Poet," Ricardo Baeza had marveled at the magnanimity with which Lorca and his peers spoke of one another. He noted, too, that as poets the group shared certain traits: a veneration for the image, a thirst for purified verse, and a simultaneous regard for tradition and the avant-garde.

In particular, the new generation rallied around the figure of Luis de Góngora, the sixteenth-century Spanish poet about whom Lorca had lectured in early 1926, and whose dispassionate, densely metaphorical verse embodied the aesthetic principles underpinning his and his colleagues' work. Throughout 1927, the tricentennial of Góngora's death, Lorca and his fellow poets rendered elaborate homage to the baroque master. Several literary magazines published special issues devoted to Góngora, and a number of writers delivered lectures on the poet and his work. Both Lorca and Rafael Alberti tried to compose commemorative "solitudes" in honor of Góngora's greatest, most ornate verse collection, *Solitudes*, but only Alberti succeeded. Lorca claimed to have felt irreverent even attempting the feat.

He and his friends persuaded other luminaries to participate in the yearlong tribute to Góngora. Antonio Machado, Manuel de Falla, Pablo Picasso, Salvador Dalí, and even Luis Buñuel (who later dismissed Góngora as "the filthiest beast ever born") all contributed to the anniversary celebrations. But Ramón del Valle-Inclán and a cantankerous Juan Ramón Jiménez—who increasingly sought to distance himself from Lorca's headstrong generation because he could not tolerate their growing aesthetic independence and what he perceived as their "opportunistic" demeanor—both declined to take part.

In Madrid, Góngora's admirers staged a mock auto-da-fe at which they burned effigies of books by the poet's enemies from the baroque era, as well as those from their own period, including Valle-Inclán. After learning that the Spanish Academy had decided to snub Góngora during his anniversary year, they went to the institution at night and urinated on its walls. One evening, Lorca, Alberti, and their friend Concha Méndez, one of the generation's few female poets, rambled through the streets of Madrid wearing enormous broadbrimmed hats while reciting Góngora's lyrics in loud voices.

The year culminated in a three-day homage to Góngora in Seville. Lorca was among a select group of Madrid writers asked to take part in the event as representatives of the "new Spanish literature." On December 15 this "Brilliant Pleiad," as a journalist had dubbed them, boarded a train for the twelve-hour trip south to Seville. "We're like a team of soccer players," Jorge Guillén scribbled to his wife as he sat in the first-class compartment eyeing his companions: Lorca, Alberti, Gerardo Diego, Juan Chabás, and Dámaso Alonso, a short, thickset, balding writer and scholar who was both a Góngora expert and a notorious libertine. Guillén considered himself the only "near-respectable" member of the group, because he was married. Throughout their trip to Seville the six men laughed, talked, and recited poetry. As they rumbled through Córdoba, Góngora's birthplace, they shouted, "Viva Don Luis de Góngora!" Guillén marveled at "these strange animals called poets."

Late that night they pulled into Seville and were met by their host, Ignacio

Sánchez Mejías, a retired bullfighter who was also a connoisseur of literature. During Góngora's tricentennial year, Sánchez Mejías had taken it upon himself to memorize the most difficult of the Cordoban poet's works. Thin, suntanned, and athletic, Sánchez Mejías was, according to a female acquaintance, "seduction itself." He liked to dress ostentatiously in green suits and pink shirts, with ruby cufflinks in the shape of a bull's head. His handsome, scarred face and rugged physique testified to his long years in the bullring. On the night of their arrival in Seville, Sánchez Mejías greeted his illustrious Madrid guests and shepherded them to his ranch on the outskirts of town. They arrived well after midnight. Sánchez Mejías draped his friends in Arab robes and plied them with champagne. He and a Gypsy friend sang *cante jondo*, while Lorca and others recited poetry, and Dámaso Alonso got predictably drunk and began singing in English.

Officially, the three-day Góngora celebration consisted of speeches, lectures, readings, and a photo session with the local press. Unofficially it was a nonstop party. Although it rained daily, nothing quelled the poets' revelry. Each night they caroused with their Seville friends until dawn. At one point Lorca found himself being driven wildly through town by a fat, homely, cattleman-turned-poet named Fernando Villalón, who sped through Seville in his automobile while reciting poetry, oblivious to traffic and to Lorca's face, which was taut with fear. During another outing, Lorca crowded into a boat with a group of friends and endeavored to sail across the swollen Guadalquivir river. As their vessel pitched and turned in the current, Lorca threw himself onto the bottom of the boat. He was the only one of the group to admit his terror.

Far more comfortable onstage, he gave a formal reading of Góngora's *Solitudes* one evening with Rafael Alberti at the Seville Atheneum. The following night Lorca recited his own Gypsy ballads from memory. Although he expected to publish the ballads within a few months, he still thought of them as oral poetry. As he spoke, his olive-skinned face grew tense, and a sliver of black hair fell across his forehead. With one hand he ceremoniously marked out the rhythm of the poems. His audience, enthralled, stood to applaud when he had finished and waved their handkerchiefs in the air, as if at a bullfight. One friend leapt onto his seat and tossed his jacket, collar, and tie at Lorca. Later that night Lorca gave an impromptu piano concert for friends at his hotel.

The poet Luis Cernuda, who met Lorca during the tricentennial celebrations in Seville, never forgot his vitality. Cernuda first glimpsed the Granadan as Lorca was descending the marble staircase in his hotel. Lorca wore black; his dark, cherubic face was sprinkled with moles. Cernuda thought it a face Murillo might have painted. Its light seemed to emanate from the eyes—large, eloquent, melancholy eyes that were somehow at odds with Lorca's short, stocky body. His presence alone was charismatic. Cernuda said later that Lorca needed only to walk into a room for people's faces to brighten and a sudden silence to descend. He was like a river, Cernuda remembered, "always the same and always different, flowing inexhaustibly."

The tricentennial of Luis de Góngora's death marked Lorca's generation from that year forward. Collectively, the young poets who attended the Seville homage—as well as several who did not, including Pedro Salinas, Emilio Prados, Manuel Altolaguirre, and Vicente Aleixandre—became known as the Generation of '27. Although in time their devotion to Góngora waned, and among themselves they sometimes squabbled over ideas and personalities, their respect and affection for one another endured. "We love each other, we adore each other, we're all of us the same person," Lorca declared several years after the Góngora tricentennial. "And they're all such saints!" he said of his fellow poets. "They look after my fame and my glory like a flower, like a flower."

During the tricentennial festivities in Seville, Lorca sketched a set of "astronomical maps of poetry" to show to his colleagues, a tongue-in-cheek visualization of the "Brilliant Pleiad" he and his peers were thought to be. According to a friend who saw the maps, Lorca brashly depicted himself as "the star" of Spain's poetic heavens, "surrounded by an immoderate and by all accounts fabulous number of satellites."

CHAPTER 12

MADNESS OF BREEZE AND TRILL

1928

~

Lorca returned to Granada in time for Christmas. Having been away from home much of the previous year, he could again savor Granada's unique beauty—the runnels of water in the Generalife gardens, the way the sun swept the *vega* clean each afternoon. The wintry town made him feel "at peace with myself."

In the first weeks of 1928, he resolved at last to bring out his "anti-local" magazine, *gallo*, and in doing so to pay ironic tribute to the city he alternately loved and despised. He assembled an editorial staff—including his brother, who agreed to serve as the magazine's official director—and resumed his efforts to sell subscriptions and solicit literary and artistic submissions from friends. Dalí provided a masthead, several drawings, and his long prose poem on Saint Sebastian. Jorge Guillén and Melchor Fernández Almagro also wrote pieces for the magazine's debut issue, and Lorca drafted a facetious "History of this *gallo*," stressing the need to jolt Granada from its lethargy.

The stylish black-and-white magazine premiered on March 9, 1928, and according to Lorca provoked "an absolute scandal" among the local bourgeoisie, who did not know what to make of the irreverent publication. Snide references to Granada appeared throughout the magazine, as did self-consciously avant-garde terms such as "Charleston" and "Kodak." One story was titled "Lucy in Sexquilandia." But *gallo* had its conventional side. To offset the costs of publication, Lorca and his colleagues had sold advertising space to a handful of local businesses—among them a candy shop, a clothing store, and a General

Motors outlet selling Cadillacs—establishments that typified the very bourgeoisie the magazine's creators sought to mock. In a later issue Lorca gamely
noted the distinction between those *granadinos* "who have given us money"
and those he deemed "putrefactions," decaying emblems of the outmoded past.

The magazine's twenty-two pages still smelled of ink when Lorca took *gallo*
in his hands for the first time and cradled it, he said, "the way you hold a baby."
He shrugged off those friends, including Dalí, who criticized the magazine's
parochial focus on Granada. "As I'm its father, I can't judge it. It's dear to me,"
Lorca countered. He was pleased to have joined the ranks of his peers who
were publishing small literary magazines in cities throughout Spain. In
Granada, where the first issue of *gallo* sold out in two days (or so Lorca alleged), the *Defensor de Granada* hailed the arrival of this "hostile new cock" in
the city's staid literary "chicken coop." At a private banquet to celebrate the
magazine's publication, a live rooster strutted through the dining room. Hoping to stoke the fires of controversy, the *Defensor de Granada* published a detailed account of the celebration.

Lorca sparked further debate when, one week after issuing *gallo*, he and his
editorial staff released a second magazine, an "anti-avant-garde" review called
Pavo, or "Turkey." Printed on just one sheet of newsprint, *Pavo* was a genuinely
avant-garde gesture of self-negation, an utter spoof of *gallo* and everything for
which *gallo* stood. Its contents included a parody of Dalí's "Saint Sebastian"
(written by one "Enrique Solí, Swine Slaughterer") as well as a series of mock
avant-garde poems meant to prove the "ease, insipidity, and senselessness" of
the new literature.

Although the *Defensor de Granada* wished the "succulent" review a "long
and prosperous life," *Pavo* vanished after one issue. Weeks later Lorca published a second *gallo*. By *Pavo's* standards, its contents were orthodox: works of
art and literary criticism alternated with local poetry and prose. The magazine's
most radical offering was Dalí's "Anti-Artistic Manifesto," which Lorca had
helped draft the previous summer. But although his name had appeared
among the manifesto's original signatories in Catalunya, Lorca refused to attach his name to the work when it appeared in *gallo*—perhaps because in his
hometown he felt uncomfortable endorsing Dalí's cry for the annihilation of
tradition. (Elsewhere in the magazine, *gallo's* editors called for the preservation
of Granada's oldest buildings.) In Madrid, Pedro Salinas was incensed to learn
that Lorca had published Dalí's manifesto. "To me, these young Andalusians
are becoming more like weathercocks every day," he said.

But Lorca's embrace of the avant-garde was real. The second issue of *gallo*
featured two of his experimental prose dialogues, the first a provocative ac-

count of a young woman's encounter with two men, and the second his droll homage to silent film, "Buster Keaton's Stroll," in which the film star murders his four children and then rides off on a bicycle while the skyline of Philadelphia shimmers in the distance. With its dreamlike structure and pointed references to gramophones and Singer sewing machines, the short script reads like one of Dalí's letters to Lorca. Both men revered Keaton; Dalí thought him the essence of "anti-art."

The second issue of *gallo* also contained a fragment of a novel-in-progress by Francisco García Lorca. To Lorca's delight, his twenty-five-year-old brother had been secretly writing a book for more than a year, and although Paco had begged him not to broadcast news of the project "to the four winds," Lorca could not contain his excitement. He told Jorge Guillén that his brother's novel was

> marvelous. And it's nothing like any of my things. I'm not blinded by the infinite love I have for him . . . My brother was inhibited by my personality, you understand? He couldn't blossom next to me, because my momentum and my art frightened him a bit. He had to get away, travel, meet the world on its own terms. But there it is. The poor thing is studying for a professional position in I don't know what field of law, and he'll succeed so as not to disappoint my parents.

Lorca gently overlooked his brother's shortcomings as a writer. Although the younger man's novel shows touches of originality, it is largely prosaic, and lacks the prodigious vision of Lorca's work. Paco never finished the book, but completed his doctorate in law, as Lorca had predicted, and pursued a diplomatic career. In time he became a perceptive critic of Spanish literature and an ardent spokesman for his older brother's work. Privately, he wrote poetry—simple, deeply felt poems about nature, family, grief, and love. He kept his poems in a desk drawer, hidden from his family. Not wishing to exploit his brother's renown, or perhaps sharing Lorca's aversion to print, he made no effort to publish his verse. Nonetheless, he could not refrain from occasionally echoing his brother. "Yes," wrote Francisco García Lorca in one of his poems, "life is hard and love, impossible."

Lorca continued to miss Dalí. He yearned to go to Barcelona once the painter had finished his year's tour of duty in the army, but Dalí neither encouraged nor invited him. Engrossed in preparations for his first exhibition in Paris, his letters slackened. Dispirited, Lorca told Sebastian Gasch, "If I don't go, it won't be my fault, but the fault of Destiny, or of some contrary wind from which no one is free."

Denied Dalí's company, Lorca became infatuated with another artist, Emilio Aladrén, a slender twenty-one-year-old from Madrid, whose oval face and sultry eyes bore a dramatic resemblance to Dalí's. Aladrén idolized Lorca, with theatrical devotion. After their first meeting in 1925, he begged Lorca to "write to me, write to me every day!" In early 1928, when Lorca chose to remain in Granada rather than return to Madrid, Aladrén sent a peevish note. "I knew you wouldn't come. Granada must have some hold on you that Madrid lacks."

By then the two were regular correspondents. Aladrén thanked Lorca for the many letters, postcards, and telegrams he had received from the poet and confessed that he had twice tried to phone Lorca in Granada. Lorca was flattered by Aladrén's fawning attention and captivated by his good looks, and against his better judgment, he became obsessed with the young artist. Although he refused to name the source of his trouble, Lorca told the poet Gerardo Diego in February that he'd recently had to overcome "ten or twelve conflicts of a literary, amorous, etc., etc., nature" in order to work. To Sebastian Gasch, he talked of the "emotional conflicts" that assaulted him whenever he went to Madrid. In Granada, by contrast, he felt "cleansed."

As in adolescence, he turned to poetry in an effort to resolve, or transcend, the conflict between flesh and spirit that plagued him. In early 1928 he began drafting an immense ode on the topic of Christ's martyrdom. As a teenager he had written compassionately of an eighteen-year-old Christ who longed for love; at twenty-nine, Lorca now wrote of the savior whose death had redeemed humankind. Newly consumed by carnal desire, he empathized with the human Jesus who had experienced temptation and understood its pull. Two months into his poem, Lorca sent Jorge Guillén a photograph of himself taken during a recent excursion to the Alpujarras. "Here I am in Pitres, a village without voice or mountain doves," he jotted on the back of the picture. "Crucified in the Y of the tree."

In the same letter, he promised to send Guillén two new poems, a pair of ten-line *décimas* he had just completed and planned to dedicate to Guillén, a master of the form. Lorca's work on the *décimas* coincided with his work on the ode to Christ; in each he sought the protective constraints of formal metrics and opaque imagery. The previous year he had observed that when Góngora sought to veil his "erotic feeling toward women (which he had to hide because of his clerical habit)," he did so through stylization, so that a given poem's eroticism reached "inviolable heights." The *décima* allowed Lorca to do the same. As brief and rigorous as the sonnet, the ten-line stanza forced him to compress his thinking, and enabled him through metaphor to express his volatile subject: the two ideals of homosexual and heterosexual love.

He titled the *décimas* "Two Norms." In each he outlined a love at once noble and unattainable. Homosexual love—a love the writer has known before and finds again in the person of a radiant adolescent—is fleeting, sterile, cold, and forbidden, but irresistible to the poet, who seeks a sanctuary, an "orchard," where the youth's beauty can flourish:

> Yesterday's norm encountered
> upon my present night.
> Light of adolescence,
> you oppose the snow.
> The stealthy pupils of my eyes
> do not want to take you in:
> two brown girls of floating moon
> and my open heart.
> But my love looks for the orchard
> where your style does not die.

Above his manuscript draft of the poem Lorca sketched a moon, its pale, reflected light suggestive of a nighttime love, a faint embodiment of its daytime counterpart.

Above his draft of the second *décima* Lorca sketched a sun, an emblem of a different kind of love, a fruitful and enduring passion of which the poet longs to partake but cannot. Unable to engage in a relationship with the woman to whom the poem is addressed, the speaker seeks the pure, implicitly sterile "madness" of homosexual love:

> Norm of breast and hip
> under the stretching bough;
> old and newly born,
> virtue of the Spring.
> My naked body yearns to be
> the dahlia of your destiny,
> bee, murmur or wine
> of your number and madness.
> But my love goes on seeking
> pure madness of breeze and trill.

The poems were Lorca's first attempt to articulate his growing acceptance of a love he had for years tried to repudiate. He published "Two Norms" in a small literary journal in May 1928. Among trusted friends, he became more candid about his sexuality. "You don't know what it is to suffer for masculine beauty," he told former Residencia roommate José Antonio Rubio Sacristán.

His understanding of same-sex love—and of love in general—sprang not only from his affair with Aladrén but from his familiarity with Plato's *Symposium*, a work Lorca began rereading in 1928. According to Rafael Martínez Nadal, Lorca became fascinated by Plato's concept of "oneness," of the union, through *eros*, of two disparate halves. "If oneness is the perfect fusion of two halves, he said to me, then we men are jungles of halves eternally in search of the impossible union," Martínez Nadal recalled. At the same time, Lorca came to embrace the Platonic notion that homosexual love is both legitimate and inborn. In the appendix to his copy of the *Symposium*, he underlined the following passage from Pascal's "Discourse on the Passions of Love": "We are born with one type of love in our hearts, which develops accordingly as understanding is perfected, and which leads us to love that which we think is beautiful, without our ever having been told what it consists of."

To Lorca, Emilio Aladrén possessed the exotic looks of a South Sea islander. The artist's dark face was actually a mingling of cultures. He had the high cheekbones and almond-shaped eyes of his Slavic grandmother, and the jet black hair of his Cuban grandfather and Spanish father. Lorca thought him a cross "between Russian and Tahitian." To others, Aladrén resembled a portrait by Gauguin.

He was impulsive, headstrong, and grasping. At Madrid's School of Painting, Sculpture, and Engraving, where he had enrolled as a sculpture student, instructors complained repeatedly about Aladrén's "lack of discipline and frivolous behavior." When he spoke, he gestured effusively; when he wrote, he babbled. In a fatuous, nine-page letter to Lorca he confided, "Federico I'd like to be frank with you I don't know if I can be. At times I think, these days I've thought about it, well not now, but as there's been a moment when I've thought about it and admitted it, like a machine I remember it and write it to you, and the thing is, just imagine, I've thought that I didn't understand how you'd become interested in me." Pages later he added, "I'm beginning to have a lot of ambition. I'm also an idiot and you're really good-natured to put up with me."

Lorca found Aladrén's calculated air of vulnerability bewitching, and when he returned to Madrid for an extended stay in late April 1928, he and the artist became inseparable companions. Lorca took the twenty-one-year-old with him to cafés, introduced him to friends, and paid for his drinks and meals. He professed great faith in Aladrén's meager talents. (He was said to have wooed the sculptor away from a female classmate by praising his "fabulous" gifts and his "Russian temperament.") Aladrén referred demurely to Lorca as "my springtime friend of a recently blooming Residencia garden." In a photograph he can be seen draping one arm possessively over Lorca's shoulder and gazing at the poet with shining eyes. Lorca, unaccustomedly dashing in a double-breasted jacket and pin-striped pants, stares regally into space, shoulders squared, hands folded stiffly in front of him.

They met nearly every night that spring, often in Aladrén's studio, where they listened to *cante jondo* records and drank gin. Later Aladrén sometimes tucked a bottle of gin into his pocket, and the pair wandered off into the streets. One morning shortly before dawn, Martínez Nadal ran into them as they came careening down a street, singing and laughing. "Have you seen the new circus?" Lorca cried out to Nadal. "Emilio! Take off your raincoat and roll on the ground!"

The pavement was damp, and beneath his raincoat Aladrén wore a pearl-gray suit. But to Nadal's astonishment, the young man obediently dropped to the ground, uttered a leonine roar, and began turning somersaults. "Emilio, up!" Lorca barked. Aladrén rose. Lorca helped him on with his coat. Heaving with laughter, they took off arm in arm into the night.

Friends tried to steer Lorca away from the artist. Aladrén was worthless and manipulative, a "tramp," they warned. But Lorca had been so utterly seduced by Emilio's youth and beauty that he allowed the sculptor to use him shamelessly. When Aladrén carved a lifelike plaster bust of him that spring, Lorca spent weeks trying to persuade friends in the press to publish a photograph of the work. "I'd like it to be a surprise for a good friend of mine, a *new artist*," he told a colleague at *ABC*, one of Madrid's most prominent dailies. "This with the utmost discretion. I blush somewhat to ask that it appear in the papers as a photograph of me, but as I said, it's really about someone else, even though I'm the model." In the end, only Madrid's *Gaceta Literaria* and the ever-loyal *Defensor de Granada* agreed to print a picture of the mediocre work. An accompanying caption—very probably supplied by Lorca himself—identified the sculptor as "one of the most brilliant and promising young men in the coming generation of artists."

Aladrén mocked Lorca's efforts at discretion. In letters to friends, he chattered freely about his friendship with Federico, rendering the poet's private life a matter of public gossip. "Isn't it true that it's like a desecration?" he whimpered to Lorca, who subsequently reprimanded Aladrén but forgave him. Lorca's close friends perceived the danger of the situation. Dalí, who had known Aladrén briefly in Madrid and thought poorly of him, urged Lorca to come to his senses: "You're a Christian tempest and you need my paganism. This past season in Madrid you gave yourself to something you should never have given yourself to. I'll come looking for you to give you a sea cure. It will be winter and we'll light a fire. The poor beasts will be stiff with cold. You will remember that you're an inventor of marvels and we'll live together with a camera."

On June 5, 1928, Lorca turned thirty. There was little to celebrate. His childhood was over. Adulthood loomed, with its surfeit of troubles and grief. His dreams of marriage, of a "tranquil and sweet life," had evaporated. His literary career, though flourishing, was an ongoing source of frustration. He remained financially dependent on his parents and emotionally reliant on men like Aladrén, whose careless behavior and talk exposed Lorca to rumor and innuendo. Increasingly, he felt that his life was a sham.

In early July, he traveled north to the Castilian town of Zamora to give a lecture. Afterward he spent several days visiting his former roommate José Antonio Rubio Sacristán. Sacristán saw at once that something was wrong. Lorca seemed more preoccupied than usual. Although he mustered a good show—playing the piano, reciting poetry, inventing nicknames for Sacristán's younger sister—he fell prey to long periods of silence during which he appeared to withdraw, "like a flower that folds its petals when it comes into contact with something sorrowful," Sacristán recalled. This was not the Lorca Sacristán had known at the Residencia, a "volcano of joy and exuberance," a man who liked to exclaim repeatedly as he walked along a street, "Look! Look, what a marvel! Look, what beauty!"

Although Lorca expressed admiration for the Zamoran landscape during automobile excursions into the province, he was obviously distressed. Sometime after his visit he tried to explain his melancholy to Sacristán. "You know that in Zamora I was upset, and with reason. I've been through (I'm going through) one of the most profound crises of my life," he wrote.

> It's my poetic destiny. We cannot gamble with what life and blood give us, because we become enchained when we least desire it. I now realize what it is that the erotic poets mean by the fire of love, and I have come to this realization precisely when I need to cut it from my life in order not to go under. It's stronger than I suspected. If I had continued to nourish it, it would have done away with my heart. You had never seen me so bitter, and it's true. Now I am full of despair, with no wish for anything, crippled. This makes me feel extraordinarily humble. We'll see if I can achieve what I desire with my poetry, we'll see if I can finally cut these terrible bonds and return to my happiness, to my old happiness, a breastplate against bitterness.

Lorca declined to name the source of his despair, but Sacristán had few doubts. He knew of Lorca's involvement with Aladrén. Clearly the sculptor had "reached [Federico's] heart" and threatened to drown him in the turbulent waters of passion. For Lorca, the affair was a bittersweet awakening.

Throughout the spring and early summer of 1928, in the midst of his entanglement with Aladrén, Lorca worked on his Gypsy-ballad collection. The *Revista de Occidente*, under the direction of editor José Ortega y Gasset, had agreed to publish the poems in book form. Lorca found the publication process harrowing, as always. At one point Ortega y Gasset stopped work on the book and demanded that Lorca supply him with three more ballads. Horrified, Lorca convinced him to back down. Only when the book reached the bindery in July did he brighten. "I think it will be beautiful," he told his parents.

Visually, the volume reflected Lorca's dramatic sense of color and pattern. Splashed across the top of the book's white cover, in red ink that reminded one reviewer of "congealed blood," were the words *Romancero Gitano* ("Gypsy Ballads"). Below, a sketch by Lorca showed a vase of sunflowers inked in black against a red map of Spain. The poet's signature, embellished with dainty curlicues, appeared at the bottom of the cover. The whole was a design so guileless a child might have conceived it.

The book came out in July 1928, and to Lorca's bewilderment was an immediate sensation. A second edition appeared within a year; six more followed during the next decade. Ordinary Spaniards so warmed to the collection that they began memorizing and singing Lorca's Gypsy ballads. Friends toasted him at banquets and sent lavish congratulatory notes. "I believe in your authentic poetry, in your inimitable poetry. I believe that you are magnificent," wrote the poet and future Nobel laureate Vicente Aleixandre. Madrid's *El Sol* published not one but two long reviews of the book. Critics hailed Lorca as the greatest Spanish poet since Antonio Machado and Juan Ramón Jiménez. By August 1928, copies of the book had become so scarce that magazines like the *Gaceta Literaria* satirized the phenomenon:

READER: Yes, *Gypsy Ballads*. Do you have *Gypsy Ballads*?

BOOKSELLER: I've sold the only two copies the publisher sent me. But more are on order.

READER: Well, when they get here, save one for me. Put it under your table—underneath a rock.

Lorca trumpeted news of his success to his parents. "Although the book won't earn millions, it will cement my reputation as a poet, and I am nothing if not that," he said. He described the sudden and overwhelming frenzy of his days in Madrid—the banquets and accolades, the press reports, the countless books to inscribe.

But his initial delight in his good fortune quickly gave way to irritation at such an abrupt invasion of his privacy. By late summer Lorca was miserable. The discrepancy between his public and private selves had never been more glaring. Fame had struck him when he least desired it, in the midst of his torment over Aladrén and his concurrent fear of being publicly identified as a homosexual. Celebrity burlesqued his despair. It exposed him to meddlesome eyes and wagging tongues. "I want and rewant my privacy," he wrote mournfully to a friend. "If I'm afraid of stupid fame it's precisely because of this. The famous man has the bitter burden of wearing a cold breast, pierced by deaf spotlights that direct the others to him."

He had published his *Gypsy Ballads* chiefly to please friends who had clamored for its release. But even after agreeing to issue the book he had dawdled over the collection, refusing to type the manuscript because he did not know how to use a typewriter and he trusted no one else with the task. His friend Martínez Nadal had finally extracted the eighteen handwritten ballads from Lorca, typed them, and, with his permission, delivered them to the *Revista de Occidente*.

Once the poems were published, Lorca lost interest in them. After July 1928, he continued to recite his ballads when asked, but with far less zest and spontaneity than before. He even grew to detest one ballad, his melodramatic poem about an adulterous liaison, "The Unfaithful Wife." The poem took on a life of its own after it appeared in print. Eventually Lorca received so many requests to perform the work—most from "well-educated" ladies, he said—that he talked of pulling his *Gypsy Ballads* altogether from bookshops in order to rid himself of the poem. In time, a friend observed, the "greatest proof of friendship" Lorca could give was to recite "The Unfaithful Wife" in one's presence.

Gypsy Ballads embodies the sensual world of the Andalusian Gypsy, a world that permitted Lorca to meld his theatrical and lyrical instincts as never before. In each of the collection's eighteen ballads, he bound dramatic story to lyric form, dialogue to metaphor, and in doing so produced a ballad collection unlike any other. The effort was not without precedent: Andalusian poets— among them Góngora and Jiménez—had for centuries explored and exploited the ballad form, and in the nineteenth century a virtual epidemic of Andalusian ballads had emerged, most of them cliché-ridden portraits of life in the south. But Lorca avoided the mannerisms of his predecessors, combining lyrical and narrative modes in fresh ways to form a tragic "poem" of Andalusia—as he repeatedly described the collection—a poem whose only protagonist, he said, is *pena*, or "sorrow." Reviewing the book for *El Sol*, Ricardo Baeza wrote that each of its poems "is a drama in brief, where everything lives and breathes in harmony, and where even seemingly inanimate things participate in the action."

Lorca's ballads draw on popular superstition and classical myth, Christian symbolism and real-life Gypsy lore, childhood memory and Freudian motifs. Formally, they embrace the conventions of medieval Spanish balladry: a non-stanzaic construction, *in medias res* openings, abrupt endings. But Lorca's reliance on tradition is erratic. He was less interested in presenting a picturesque imitation of existing forms than in forging his own tradition, one whose tone and structure recall the popular Spanish ballad, but whose spirit is sharp, objective, and playful—in short, contemporary.

In many ballads the juxtaposition between old and new is jarring. "Preciosa and the Wind" chronicles the plight of a Gypsy named Preciosa, a figure plucked from a Cervantes novella, as she is chased across the Granadan landscape by a phallus-wielding, pantheistic "wind-man." When Preciosa arrives, at last, at the English consul's home, she is offered "a cup of warm milk, / and a bracer of gin." The "Ballad of the Spanish Civil Guard" features another archetypal character cloaked in contemporary imagery: the Virgin, "dressed / just like a mayor's wife, / in silver chocolate foil / with necklaces of almonds."

Lorca viewed his collection as a single entity, and he insisted that readers do the same. He described *Gypsy Ballads* as an "Andalusian altarpiece" adorned with Gypsies, horses, archangels, rivers, and crimes. Together his ballads constitute an epic Andalusia, born of a landscape he had known, and to some degree worshiped, all his life. Fragments of the region's layered past—allusions to its Roman, Carthaginian, and Arab inhabitants—surface in many of the poems, as do poignant references to twentieth-century Andalusia. Lorca was determined to imbue his vision of the region with historical depth and antecedent, as well as personal anecdote. The book recalls the countryside of his childhood: the olive trees and poplar groves where he first discovered his voice, the ominous Civil Guardsmen he frequently glimpsed on *vega* roads, the desolate Spanish moon.

At the center of the book are three poems dedicated to the "three great Andalusias"—the cities of Granada, Córdoba, and Seville—each personified as an archangel whose masculine beauty is at once ethereal and erotic. Lorca had learned to give voice to his reverence for the male form. Seville's Saint Gabriel is "a beautiful reed of a child, / shoulders wide, slim at the hip, / skin of an apple at night." Granada's lace-covered Saint Michael, the object of a yearly pilgrimage, is "a pretty boy, / fragrant with cologne." Córdoba's Saint Rafael, the city's patron, is a "nude Roman torso" on the shores of the Guadalquivir, where "young boys weave and sing / the truth about the world." Collectively the three archangels—the same figures who rule heaven in Goethe's *Faust*—reign over a pagan Andalusia steeped in Gypsy blood.

In remarks to the press and public, Lorca claimed that the Gypsy was merely a peripheral part of *Gypsy Ballads*, a "refrain" to a much larger "song." But it was primarily this feature of the collection that made the book so novel. Although Andalusian poets such as Salvador Rueda and Manuel María de Santa Ana had previously depicted Gypsy life in ballads, they had done so through stereotypes: the Gypsy as impudent thief, with "wild unruly hair" and "big eyes lost / in immense horizons." Lorca shunned such banalities and sought to ennoble his protagonists. While many, if not most, Spaniards scorned the country's Gypsies, Lorca viewed them romantically. (He once remarked contemptuously that the true Gypsy does not go around villages "ragged and dirty. Those are Hungarians.")

He had grown up near Gypsies and knew their music by heart. His most fundamental interests and instincts found resonance in the Gypsies' ancient and tangled roots, in their sensual embrace of life, in their innately religious existence, and in their status as a persecuted minority. By noting their oppression, yet identifying them as a chosen people, Lorca both verified and amended history. He described the Gypsy as the "truest and purest thing in Andalusia"—in deliberate contrast to the sober Castilian peasants whom his immediate forebears, the Generation of '98, and in particular Antonio Machado, had chosen as emblems of their Spain. Through his ballad collection Lorca hoped, in part, to "harmonize the *mythological Gypsy* with the purely ordinary one of the present day."

He later identified the book's archetypal Gypsy as Antoñito el Camborio, a man whose epic encounter with death is the subject of two ballads. Camborio is the only character "who calls me by name at the moment of his death," Lorca said. The Gypsy's cry, an ironic plea to the author for help, underscores the fundamental artifice of the book:

> "Ay, Federico García,
> call out the Civil Guard!
> My body has been broken
> like a stalk of corn."

As a child, Lorca had known of a real-life Gypsy named Camborio, a hard-drinking horseman from a nearby village in the *vega*, who one day, in an alcohol stupor, fell from his horse onto his knife and died. In his two Camborio ballads, he transforms the clumsy drunk of his youth into a quintessentially elegant Andalusian male, a tragic figure — "brown from green moon, / voice of a virile carnation" — who is mortally stabbed on the road to Seville and dies "in a fine silhouette: / live coin that will never / be matched by another."

Similar acts of metamorphosis occur throughout *Gypsy Ballads*. Time and again Lorca depicts ordinary Gypsy men and women as preternatural gods. The embodiment of pure human instinct, and as such the antithesis of conservative Spanish society, the Gypsies in Lorca's ballads clash repeatedly with the country's rural police force — the blunt, unimaginative Civil Guard, with its black horses, black horseshoes, black tricorns, and skulls "cast in lead." In the "Ballad of the Spanish Civil Guard," the collection's longest work, and one that most approximates the melodrama of nineteenth-century Andalusian ballads, Lorca describes the Guard's brutal assault on a slumbering Gypsy town:

> Rosa, the Camborio,
> sits moaning at her door
> with her severed breasts
> before her on a tray.
> Other girls were running
> chased by their braids,
> in a wind exploding
> with roses of black powder.

Some readers took offense at Lorca's ruthless portrayal of the Civil Guard. But others, who perhaps, like Lorca, had grown up hearing tales of the Guard's cruelty, applauded it. For years Lorca had been haunted by images of the notorious police force, first in childhood, listening to stories of their barbarism, and later in 1919, as a young man in Granada, watching in horror as a regiment of Guardsmen led a band of Gypsy prisoners through the city. The prisoners had been shackled together, their feet torn and bodies bloodied. Lorca could neither forget nor forgive such savagery. He perceived the Guard as an enemy of everything he — and by extension, the Gypsy — stood for: poetry, song, art, life. While writing his ballads Lorca talked frequently about the Civil Guard in letters to friends and family. "The cathedral is pealing and the airplanes dance their afternoon dance," he told the artist Benjamín Palencia in 1925. "The Civil Guard kills one Gypsy a day and adds his name to a list as long and undulating as a Chinese dragon."

Readers of *Gypsy Ballads* were moved by the collection's tragic tales of life and death, by its sensual language and baroque delight in the human body. The book appealed to scholars and poets as well as to untutored field hands. Lorca was not surprised to learn that common people liked his work. Years later he told a journalist, "Molière was right to read his works to his cook."

It dismayed him, though, to find that many readers thought him an untutored, spontaneous, "popular" poet. "How can that be?" he said. "I have as much culture as anyone else, if not more. I spend hours reading and studying." Worse, people believed he was a Gypsy. His dark looks and impassioned recitals of his ballad collection only heightened the misconception. Lorca resented any such classification. "The Gypsies are a theme. And nothing more," he wrote angrily to Jorge Guillén. "I could just as well be a poet of sewing needles and hydraulic landscapes . . . I don't want to be typecast." He vowed never to touch the Gypsy theme again. To a reporter who asked him late in 1928 to explain his background, he said, "I am not a Gypsy."

"What are you?" the reporter asked.

"Andalusian, which isn't the same thing."

Fame not only destroyed Lorca's privacy, it corrupted his work and invited envy. Before the year was out, naysayers had begun predicting his demise. A work like *Gypsy Ballads*, some argued, could only signal the "glory and end of a poet." Others maintained that Lorca was "washed up," "passé," that Rafael Alberti was now the writer to watch—a rising star, a "pure" poet "full of unpublished possibilities." As comparisons of the two mounted, their rivalry intensified. Later in the year, Lorca refused to attend a poetry reading by Alberti.

In an attempt to recover some semblance of peace, Lorca went home to Granada shortly after the publication of his book. He arrived in early August 1928, and for the next three months remained cloistered at his family's Huerta de San Vicente. The place was a sanctuary, "a vision of trees and clear water," he said. By day, Granada had rarely seemed more beautiful. At night, Lorca stood for hours on the balcony outside his bedroom and stared into the black landscape. He was inconsolable. "I am tormented and beaten by passions which I must conquer," he told Sebastian Gasch. To another friend he described himself as "beset by love, by filthiness, by ugly things."

Work became his balm. He wrote "fast and furiously," turning out prose poems, drawings, and poetry. Through "sheer willpower" he believed he could save himself from defeat. He struggled to avoid the confessional mode, which for aesthetic as well as personal reasons he felt he must reject. "I'm going through one of the most painful periods I've experienced in my life," he told Jorge Zalamea, a twenty-three-year-old Colombian poet who had come to

Spain that year with his country's diplomatic corps. Lorca had recently met and come to trust Zalamea. He described to him the difficulty of "trying constantly to keep your state of mind from filtering into your poetry, because it would play on you the dirty trick of exposing the purest part of yourself to the gazes of those who should never see it."

For "reasons of discipline," Lorca returned to the exactitude of the ode form. He renewed work on his ode to Christ and at the same time began work on a new ode, the "Ode and Mockery of Sesostris and Sardanapalus," an allegorical exploration of homosexual love. Each ode, Lorca said, corresponded to a different facet of his personality. The ode to Christ mirrored his soul; the ode to Sesostris reflected his "eroticism."

He was not the first artist to exploit the figure of Sardanapalus as an emblem of erotic love. A legendary Assyrian king known for his luxuriant effeminacy, Sardanapalus had long served as a symbol of bacchanalian excess. Augustine had condemned his debauchery, Verlaine paid tribute to his libertinism, Byron turned him into a bourgeois dandy, and precisely one century before Lorca began work on his ode, the painter Eugène Delacroix made Sardanapalus the subject of one of his greatest canvases, *The Death of Sardanapalus*, a two-fold celebration of sex and death that shocked viewers—both in its time and for decades afterward. Like Lorca, Delacroix had turned to Sardanapalus at a moment when his own impulses and passions threatened to overwhelm him. "I am a slave of my senses," the artist remarked not long before starting the canvas.

Lorca's ode pairs Sardanapalus with the more obscure figure of Sesostris, an Egyptian pharaoh renowned for his military vigor. Collectively the two suggest the opposition between effeminate and manly homosexuality, a topic of growing interest to Lorca. His use of imagery in the "Ode and Mockery of Sesostris and Sardanapalus" also points to Lorca's deepening preoccupation with the sterility of love between men. "Blackberries of light, long needles constrict your ashen waist," he writes of Sardanapalus. "Flowers of mad rock and dark water / cover the fields of your solitudes." He had addressed the same theme in the poem "Two Norms."

As he worked on the ode, the poem seemed to Lorca "full of humor and lament and Dionysiac rhythm." He talked eagerly of publishing an entire book of odes, in part because these stately, dispassionate, erudite poems were "the exact opposite of the *Gypsy Ballads*." But despite his pleasure in the form, he neglected to finish the "Ode and Mockery of Sesostris and Sardanapalus." He may have feared the work's references were too revealing. Or he may simply have lost interest. In any case, he completed just twelve stanzas of the ode.

One moment he was buoyant and the next downcast. He sent terse notes to close friends, pleading for compassion. To plump, generous Sebastian Gasch, the art critic whose affection and admiration had proved such a boon to Lorca's drawings, he wrote, "I'm going through a huge *emotional* crisis (that's right) from which I hope to emerge cured . . . This letter is nothing more than a cry and a tight embrace from Federico." To Melchor Fernández Almagro, who for years had watched over Lorca's career with the devotion of an apostle, he exclaimed, "You'll always be my confessor!" To Rafael Martínez Nadal, his confidant and sometime amanuensis in Madrid, he urged, "Don't get involved with anyone, Rafael. It's better to be cruel with others and not to have to suffer calvary, passion, and death afterward . . . It's a sad fact that the blows a poet receives are the seed of his work, his ladder of light." He begged Nadal not to forsake him. "I'm very isolated and at times still terribly sad. Every day I learn something more about love. The more inflamed I become, the less I understand. Don't stop writing to me."

Lorca's newest correspondent was the Colombian Jorge Zalamea, who revered Lorca's work, and soon after meeting Lorca asked for copies of his poems. "They'll bring me your necessary presence," he said. Because Zalamea was serious and reflective, and because he, too, was in the midst of a dire emotional conflict that summer, Lorca found it easy to confide in him. Their correspondence—of which only fragments remain—was frank, for Zalamea assured Lorca that he would not show his letters to anyone: "I love you and I love myself too much to play games with famous manuscripts." The two communicated by innuendo. "As for E . . . ," wrote Zalamea, in an apparent reference to Emilio Aladrén, "I haven't seen him again." It comforted Lorca to know he was not alone in his unhappiness. "I too have had a very bad time. Very bad," he told Zalamea. "One needs to have the amount of joy God has given me not to succumb before the number of conflicts that have assaulted me lately. But God never abandons me."

He longed in particular to see and talk to Dalí. For the third consecutive summer he implored the painter to visit him in Granada. When it became clear that Dalí could not—or did not want to—visit, Lorca began planning his own trip to Barcelona. "I want to be with all of you," he wrote wistfully to Sebastian Gasch. Meanwhile, he resumed work on a third issue of *gallo*. He intended to dedicate the entire magazine to Dalí.

The artist had changed dramatically in the past year. Ever more enamored of surrealism, the erstwhile Apollonian had begun to espouse anarchic cultural acts: the demolition of Barcelona's Gothic Quarter, the abolition of traditional Catalan dance. The previous year he had informed Lorca that "internal conflicts" were dead. "The soul, complexes, Freud, all of it is shit." Aesthetically he and Lorca were drifting further apart. At times Dalí appeared to resent Lorca's fame and to regret his waning influence on the poet. He seemed jealous of Lorca's success—and jealous, too, of his involvement with Aladrén.

In early September 1928, Dalí sent Lorca a seven-page critique of *Gypsy Ballads*. He scribbled his thoughts on the back of a set of business forms from his father's office and riddled his remarks with arrows, underlined words, corrections, and sketches of human torsos and faces. Although he admitted to admiring one or two poems in Lorca's book (as he told Sebastian Gasch, he also liked the collection's "unconscious erotic inspiration"), he found the writing folkloric and sentimental. "You think perhaps that certain images are arresting or you may find an increased dose of the irrational in your stuff but I can tell you that your poetry does little more than *illustrate* clichés of the most stereotypical and conformist kind."

Dalí believed Lorca's ballads reinforced a traditional view of reality, when instead Lorca should have sought to escape reality. Why must a rider necessarily sit astride a horse? the artist asked. Why must the horse gallop? What if the horse's reins were in fact extensions of the rider's hands? What if "the little hairs on the rider's balls" were faster than the horse?

> One has to allow things to be *free* of the conventional ideas which the intellect forces on them. Then these charming little things will work by themselves in accordance with their real and *consubstantial* manner of being.

Much of Dalí's argument sprang directly from an article he was to publish the following month titled "Reality and Surreality." But while the painter was more favorably disposed toward surrealism than ever before, he was not yet ready to endorse the movement. "Surrealism is *one* of the means of Escape," he advised Lorca. "But it's Escape *itself* that is the important thing."

In the midst of his harangue Dalí abruptly interrupted himself. "Let's let it drop," he urged. He was "less and less" able to express his thoughts in letters. Articles—long diatribes on aesthetic issues—had become his forum of choice. With sudden tenderness he addressed Lorca directly, invoking the ciphered language they alone could decode, gently reminding his old friend of the affection and intimacy that bound them. "Federiquito," he wrote, "in your book which I've taken with me to the mineral places around here to read, I've seen you, little beastie that you are, little erotic beastie, with your sex and the *little eyes of your body*"—here Dalí was alluding to a passage in Lorca's "Ballad of the Marked Man," a poem Lorca had dedicated to Emilio Aladrén—"and your hairs and your terror of death and your wish that if you die *gentlemen will know about it* . . . your thumb in close correspondence with your prick and with the dampness of the lakes of saliva of certain species of *hairy planets* that do exist." The last passage appears verbatim in Dalí's essay "Reality and Surreality."

Dalí knew Lorca as no one else did:

> I love you for what your book reveals you to be, which is quite the opposite of the idea the putrid philistines have put out about you, that is a bronzed Gypsy with black hair, childish heart, etc. etc. . . . . You, little beastie, with your little fingernails, with your body sometimes half possessed by death, in which death wells up from your nails to your shoulders in the most sterile of efforts!

The artist continued to "*believe*" (he underlined the word three times) in Lorca's "inspiration, in your *sweat*, in your astronomical fatality." He assured Lorca that once he had lost his fear of things and learned to "shit" on his fellow poets, to "give up RHYME, in short, Art as understood by the swine—you'll produce witty, horrifying . . . intense, poetic things such as no other poet could."

CHAPTER 13

RAIN FROM THE STARS

1928-29

Lorca made light of Dalí's aesthetic attack. He praised the artist's "intelligence, grace, and acuity" and described his seven-page harangue as "a sharp and arbitrary letter that raises an interesting poetic problem." If anything, the letter, with its blatant homoerotic allusions, heightened his desire to see Dalí. As for *Gypsy Ballads*, Lorca professed to have lost interest in the collection. "It died in my hands in the most tender way," he said.

His new work absorbed him. "All day long I turn out poems like a factory," he told Jorge Zalamea. Heeding Dalí's call for a poetic "escape" from conventional ideas and literary clichés, he began writing what he described as "vein-opening poetry, a poetry that escapes reality with an emotion reflecting all my love of things and my joking about things." In his more private search for an escape from the emotional and sexual conflicts of the preceding year, Lorca looked forward to the arrival of fall, "which gives me life." He longed to restore both meaning and order to the charade his existence had become. He battled against melancholy. There were days when his mood matched the sodden gray skies over Granada, days when he felt as if his life was about to end.

In his letter on *Gypsy Ballads*, Dalí had referred bluntly to Lorca's physical body: his "hairs," "fingernails," "shoulders," "sweat," "thumb," "prick." It was precisely this body, and its intractable demands, that Lorca now sought to escape, much as he had in adolescence. Shortly after hearing from Dalí, he embarked on a set of prose poems, works he claimed were the result of a "new *spiritualistic* manner, pure disembodied emotion, detached from logical control, but—careful! careful!—with a tremendous poetic logic," he explained to Sebastian Gasch. "It's not surrealism—careful!—the clearest consciousness illuminates them."

Despite his disclaimer, Lorca's new poems did verge on surrealism. Dense, depersonalized, full of numbers and jargon, they reflect the movement's scorn for reality and esteem for the unconscious imagery of dreams. Dalí now defined surrealism as not "another ism, but the blossoming of the most intensely spiritual state that ever existed," and by this standard Lorca's "spiritualistic" poems of 1928 were virtually surrealist. In late September Lorca published two of the poems, "Swimmer Submerged" and "Suicide in Alexandria," in the avant-garde journal *L'Amic de les Arts.* Dalí served on the magazine's editorial board.

Since attending the Góngora celebrations the previous year, Lorca had revised his aesthetic thinking, and now distinguished between poetry of the "imagination," as exemplified by Góngora, and the superior poetry of "inspiration." As Lorca saw it, the former reaffirms existing truths by adhering to reality's bounds, while the latter escapes reality by casting off the imagination's chains and yielding to a world of mystery, a world where inspiration falls like a gift from the skies, uncontrolled and inexplicable. It was this second type of poetry that Lorca hoped to create.

He was still trying to clarify his thoughts on the subject when in mid-October he agreed to christen the Granada Atheneum's 1928 season with a lecture, "Imagination, Inspiration, Escape." Most of the city's intellectual set attended the event. Flowers and tapestries trimmed the crowded lecture hall. Many of the women in the audience held bouquets.

At first hesitant to launch into his difficult topic, Lorca warned his audience that he did not want "to outline but to suggest." His own thoughts on the nature of poetic "truth" had shifted so often in recent years that he scarcely knew what to believe. But he understood the poet's mission clearly: "to animate, in the precise sense of the word: to give life to." As a poet he remained committed to the ideal of "pure" poetry. Yet he no longer believed, as Góngora had, that such poetry could be achieved through traditional metaphor. Poetry must free itself from the "puzzle of the image and from the planes of reality." It must ascend to an "ultimate plane of purity and simplicity"—the plane of "escape," poetry's last and purest realm. Although Lorca derived the term from Dalí, both Ortega y Gasset and the Spanish ultraists had also embraced the notion of "escape."

Metaphor, Lorca insisted, must give way to the *hecho poético*—the "poetic event"—a phenomenon at once illogical and incomprehensible, as miraculous as "rain from the stars." In a subsequent version of his lecture, he cited a passage from one of his own Gypsy poems, the "Sleepwalking Ballad," as an example of an *hecho poético*. "If you ask me why I wrote 'A thousand glass tambourines / were wounding the dawn,' I will tell you that I saw them, in the hands of angels and trees, but I won't be able to say more than that, much less explain their meaning. And that's how it should be."

He regarded the *hecho poético* as one of several means of reaching the purest plane of poetry, the "poetry of escape." The surrealists sought to achieve "escape" through dreams and the unconscious, a method Lorca found pure but unclear. "We Latins want sharp profiles and visible mystery. Form and sensuality." As much as he admired Dalí and respected the artist's views on surrealism, Lorca refused to subscribe to any such movement. He preferred to align himself loosely with his peers in the Generation of '27—and even with Juan Ramón Jiménez, whom Dalí reviled—writers who focused exclusively on "reducing poetry to the creation of the poetic event," writers who shunned dogma.

Although the *Defensor de Granada* proclaimed his talk "a complete aesthetic theory," Lorca had only begun to shape his argument. Two weeks later he returned to the topic during a second Atheneum event, "*gallo* Night," an informal gathering aimed at bolstering support for his magazine, which had been foundering since the publication of its second issue in April. Throughout the summer Lorca and his friends had spent long evenings sitting under the sycamore trees at the Alameda Café, outlining the magazine's third issue. Lorca hoped to devote the number exclusively to Dalí. But he had found it impossible, in the midst of the emotional and professional chaos brought on by the publication of his *Gypsy Ballads,* to concentrate on the magazine. One of his fellow editors accused him of no longer loving *gallo*, and there was some truth to the charge. Nonetheless, Lorca mustered a show of enthusiasm for the undertaking on "*gallo* Night."

Each of the magazine's six editors spoke during the course of the evening. They talked about creation and anarchy, the advent of the machine age and their own embrace of a playful, depersonalized art. Lorca was last to take the stage. He titled his short discourse "Sketch de la nueva pintura," or "Sketch of the New Painting." A brief, subjective summary of the state of contemporary art, his talk reiterated the ideas he had expressed two weeks earlier in his lecture on imagination and inspiration. Lorca argued that while Picasso and Braque, like Góngora, had liberated visual art through their creation of startling images, painting had subsequently become sadly cerebral and must evolve. "Where are we headed?" he asked. "We are heading toward instinct, toward chance, toward pure inspiration." In short, visual art was heading toward surrealism, a movement Lorca praised, for it had freed painting from cubism's "disciplined abstractions" and was now steering it toward a "mystical, uncontrolled period of supreme beauty" where the "inexpressible begins to be expressed." Although he refrained from using the term, Lorca was again describing the notion of "escape."

He illustrated his talk with slides of work by Picasso, Gris, de Chirico, Kandinsky, Miró, and, above all, Dalí, whom Lorca now categorized as a "surrealist." Afterward he told Sebastian Gasch that he had paid Dalí "a great tribute" that evening. "I hope to go to Barcelona soon. I really want to see you and to see my friends."

Three weeks after delivering his "Sketch," Lorca went to Madrid, effectively stranding his fellow *gallo* editors in the midst of their work on the third issue of the magazine. Quietly *gallo* folded. Lorca did not care.

In Madrid he settled into a pension with his brother, who was in the midst of studying for his diplomatic exams. Jorge Guillén ran into Lorca shortly after his arrival and found him "more affected, more self-centered" than before, "but terribly charming and vivacious." After his three-month stay in Granada, Lorca was for the moment content to be back in the capital and eager to see his friends. His financial situation had improved as a result of *Gypsy Ballads*, and he sought ways to share the bounty. One day he barged into the offices of the *Revista de Occidente*, announced that he intended to treat a few of his friends to lunch, and demanded a portion of his royalties. The secretary informed him that funds were unavailable. "What do you mean there's no money?" Lorca cried. "Then this isn't the *Revista de Occidente*, it's the *Miseria de Occidente!*" In the end he got his money.

On the evening of December 13, 1928, he gave a lecture at the Residencia. It was his third public talk in as many months, and his first ever in Madrid. Friends packed the institution's small salon and spilled into the adjoining hall. Residencia director Alberto Jiménez Fraud looked on proudly. Lorca's talk was the culmination of an impressive season of Residencia lectures by such distinguished figures as Filippo Marinetti, Le Corbusier, and the famed Egyptologist Howard Carter. But according to Paco García Lorca, who sent home an effusive account of the evening, Jiménez Fraud ranked Lorca's talk among the best of the lot.

Lorca spoke on traditional Spanish lullabies. Given the more radical subject matter of his recent lectures, it was a curious choice of subject—yet it allowed him to probe similar aesthetic territory while at the same time invoking the lost world of his childhood. He sat at the Residencia's grand piano, arms and legs stretched before him, and played, sang, and talked his way through the evening. His listeners were mesmerized. Within three minutes, Paco reported to their parents, Lorca had captured the room.

He had begun drafting his lecture on lullabies nearly a year earlier but had run into difficulties, for although his knowledge of the subject was vast, his aims were complex. He wanted to illustrate and discuss not only the traditional lullabies of Spain's many regions—the distinctive origin and style of the songs, as well as the nature of the women who sing them—but also the world of the child itself, a world steeped in poetic feeling, a world of "pure inspiration." He opened his lecture by placing himself at the heart of the child's peculiarly charged universe. "I have wanted to go down to the rushy shore. Under the yellow tiles. To the outskirts of villages, where the tiger eats little children," he told his audience.

> I am far now from the poet who looks at his watch, who struggles with the statue, with dream, and with anatomy. I have fled all my friends and am going off with the little boy who eats green fruit and watches the ants devour the bird run over by the automobile.

To Lorca, the world of the child embodied the same type of "escape" he sought to achieve as a poet. Filled with gentle descriptions of mother and child, and wistful portraits of childhood itself, his lecture on lullabies offered both a nostalgic look at his own lost youth and a frank appraisal of his current aesthetic. The child, he said, inhabits an "inaccessible poetic world that neither rhetoric nor the pandering imagination nor fantasy can penetrate." The child, like the poet or painter who courts pure inspiration, is capable of discovering mysterious and indecipherable relations between things. "He understands better than we the ineffable key to poetic substance."

As he sat at the Residencia piano, gruffly intoning the lullabies he had heard as a boy, Lorca effected an imaginative return to the simplicity and wonder of his past. The lullaby, he told his audience, is the bridge that links the child's magical world to the adult's more rational one. The mother who croons a song to her son carries him "outside himself into the distance and returns him to her lap tired and ready to sleep. It is a little initiation into poetic adventure, the child's first steps through the world of intellectual representation." As a boy, hearing his parents and servants sing, Lorca had often taken the same journey. As an adult in search of both inspiration and innocence, he now sought to retrace it.

Two days after his lecture on lullabies, *La Gaceta Literaria* published an interview between Lorca and the writer Ernesto Giménez Caballero. In it, Lorca glibly embellished the truth about his past. Asked to reveal the date of his birth, he lied. Instead of 1898, he claimed to have been born "in 1899, June 5th." This would have made him twenty-nine years old at the time of the interview. Asked to recount his family's background, he said gaily, "My family went broke during the last century. Now they're recovering again."

"Thanks to you," said Giménez Caballero.

"Well, all right, thanks to me."

Lorca went on to describe his pastimes as a boy ("saying Masses, making altars, building little theaters"). He listed his friends, who ranged from the sixteenth-century Granadan poet Soto de Rojas to Luis Buñuel. He identified Dalí as a particularly close friend and detailed one of their pranks at the Residencia. It was a flippant, optimistic Lorca who appeared on the pages of the *Gaceta*, a man unfettered by cares or complaints, a poet able to name at least five books he was then "preparing" for publication—not one of which materialized during his lifetime. "What is your present theoretical position?" Giménez Caballero asked.

"To work purely," Lorca answered. "A return to inspiration. Inspiration, pure instinct, the poet's only reason."

The following month, January 1929, Luis Buñuel traveled to Catalunya to collaborate with Salvador Dalí on a script for a surrealist film. To Lorca, the visit signaled a shift in his own friendship with Dalí. Despite his boast to Giménez Caballero, Lorca was not close to Buñuel. Months earlier the filmmaker had come back to Spain from Paris with his head shaved and his mind filled with audacious plans. He had heard rumors of Lorca's homosexuality and was repulsed by them. To their mutual friend Pepín Bello, he announced his dislike of *Gypsy Ballads*, a collection he said was calculated to please "the faggot poets in Seville." To Dalí, Buñuel referred to Lorca as a "son of a bitch" whose "pederastic news" bored him.

Buñuel went swaggering off to Catalunya in January, a walking stick in one hand, a stylish fedora on his head. He and Dalí had their photograph taken one cold day in Figueres. In a show of machismo, Buñuel wore only a single-breasted men's suit; Dalí stood meekly beside him, bundled in an overcoat, scarf, and leather gloves.

During Buñuel's visit, the two men drafted a script for a film they would eventually title *Un Chien Andalou*. The project took them less than a week. They imposed just one guideline on their work: no idea or image could yield a rational explanation. For both men, the collaboration was blissful. They never argued. Buñuel said later that their identification with one another was "complete"—much like the rapport Lorca had enjoyed with Dalí two years earlier in Cadaqués. Culling images from their dreams—including Buñuel's jarring vision of a moon slicing into a cloud as a razor slashes an eyeball—they pieced together a "stupendous screenplay without precedent in the history of the cinema," as Buñuel reported afterward to Pepín Bello. "Dalí and I are closer than ever," he added. In the February 1, 1929, edition of *La Gaceta Literaria*, the two issued a joint announcement of their impending collaboration. To Lorca, the message could hardly have been plainer. Buñuel had usurped his claim on Dalí.

In Madrid, Lorca struggled to surmount his growing depression. The days were icy and short. He found it difficult to muster the energy to work. Dalí's apparent betrayal stunned him. Equally disturbing, his companion of the past year, Emilio Aladrén, had suddenly become involved with a woman. Despite efforts to maintain a friendship, he and Lorca drifted apart. The dissolution of their affair troubled Lorca, who in later years spoke contemptuously of men who veil their true sexual natures in order to feign propriety.

For a time, he distracted himself with a new undertaking. An old acquaintance, the critic, playwright, and stage director Cipriano Rivas Cherif, had recently founded an experimental theater company and wanted to produce one of Lorca's plays. Lorca suggested his one-act tale about a middle-aged man's failed attempt at marriage, *The Love of Don Perlimplín for Belisa in Their Garden*, subtitled "An Erotic *Aleluya* in Four Scenes and A Prologue." He had begun the play shortly after his first visit to Dalí in 1925 and had finished it months later, but he had never attempted to stage the work. Rivas Cherif was delighted to receive the script. He had known and admired Lorca for years and was one of only four people to review *Book of Poems* when it appeared in 1921.

A short, wiry man, possessed by such restless energy that he sometimes seemed to be dancing, Rivas Cherif had devoted much of his life to the creation of a Spanish "art theater," freed from the control of impresarios and devoted to spiritual ideals. He believed that theater should be "an art of imagination," not the tawdry imitation of everyday life usually seen on the Spanish stage. He had studied abroad with theater visionary Gordon Craig and was an ardent fan of Stanislavsky. Like both men, Rivas Cherif hoped to revitalize the theater of his country. In late 1928 he founded an experimental company, El Caracol, housed in a tiny basement in the center of Madrid. Within its first few months of existence, the troupe startled critics and audiences alike by staging a play by Rivas Cherif about lesbianism.

The director planned to offer Lorca's "erotic" fable as his company's second production. A cast of six began rehearsing *Don Perlimplín* in January. Despite his low spirits, Lorca made his way through Madrid's chilly streets to oversee the production and to help design the play's fanciful sets. He felt a particular tenderness toward this script, perhaps because he identified with its loveless protagonist. He later claimed that of all the plays he had written, *Don Perlimplín* was his favorite. As he sat in the dim confines of El Caracol's underground theater and watched the tragic love story of Don Perlimplín unfold, he surely sensed the play's relevance to his own life.

As its subtitle suggests, *Don Perlimplín* is openly erotic. Lorca wrote the brief prose play in the radiant aftermath of his first visit to Cadaqués, during the same period he first began composing what he called "erotic" poetry. The play is short, and its story straightforward. Perlimplín, a timid, bookish bachelor, decides late in life to marry a spirited, beautiful woman named Belisa, who is half his age. Despite his fears about marriage—"Will she be capable of strangling me?"—Perlimplín hears Belisa singing offstage and is unable to resist the pleasures she represents:

> Love, love.
> Between my locked thighs
> the sun swims like a fish.
> Warm water in the rushes;
> love.

The two marry, and on their wedding night—played out on a huge canopy bed topped with plumes—Perlimplín is unable to consummate the marriage. While he sleeps, Belisa betrays him with a procession of men who slip in through the room's six balcony doors. The following day, at dawn, Perlimplín awakes, wearing a set of gilt horns on his head. Although he suspects that his wife has deceived him, he is strangely happy. For the first time in his life, he perceives the world's sensual delights. Sitting on the bed beside his dozing bride, he marvels at the sunrise. "It is a spectacle which . . . it seems untrue . . . , which thrills me! Don't you like it?" he asks. "Yes," Belisa murmurs dreamily. Gently, Perlimplín covers her with a red cape—the red of love, of sex, of death—and as he does so, flocks of paper birds cross the balconies, and light floods the room.

Lorca himself understood that up to this point his play had all the makings of farce. Based on a stock theme in the Spanish theater, the story of a young woman unhappily wed to an impotent old man, *Don Perlimplín* could have ended comically. Lorca described it as a "human puppet play that begins in fun." But he chose to turn his script into something more, into a "grotesque tragedy" with a pathetic, lovesick protagonist—an "anti-hero," he said—who resolves to redeem his deceitful wife by endowing her with a soul. In order to do this, Perlimplín must die. Disguising himself as a mysterious young lover in a red cape, he seduces Belisa. When he is sure of her passion for the caped suitor, he vanishes offstage and returns moments later, bleeding from a dagger wound. Belisa removes the cape and recognizes Perlimplín. "Your husband has just killed me with this emerald dagger," he says. ". . . As he was wounding me, he cried, 'Belisa now has a soul!' "

The girl is at once horrified and confused. She does not realize that the aged Perlimplín and her caped lover are the same man. As Perlimplín dies in her arms, she cries, "Yes . . . but, and the youth? . . . Why have you deceived me?" As Perlimplín's maid begins preparing his body for burial, she tells Belisa, "You are another woman now. You are dressed in the most glorious blood of my master." Like Christ, Perlimplín has sacrificed himself for a greater good. Only with the passage of time will Belisa see that she has murdered her true love, and then she will acquire a soul. Her conversion, according to Lorca, will be the "triumph" of Perlimplín's imagination.

Lorca later claimed to have had "a lot of fun" writing *Don Perlimplín*. He based the play, in part, on the notion of the *aleluya*, a series of brightly tinted vignettes, akin to comic strips, printed on large sheets of colored paper, whose popularity in Spain dates back to the late eighteenth century. The exaggerated style of the cheap broadsides inspired Lorca to give *Don Perlimplín* a vibrant, overstated look, much as his fascination with old engravings had led him to construe *Mariana Pineda* as a nineteenth-century print.

Critics had attacked *Mariana Pineda* for its emphasis on poetry, to the near exclusion of dramatic action. But Lorca's theatrical sensibility had evolved since that play. In *Don Perlimplín* he pushed theatrical spectacle to new heights, setting his play in lavish eighteenth-century splendor and costuming his characters in ornate wigs, headdresses, coats, and bedclothes. He brought to the task a painter's instinct for color and pattern. His stage directions call for Perlimplín's house to have green walls and black furniture, for the perspectives of the dining room to be "deliciously wrong," and for the dining room table itself to resemble a "primitive 'Last Supper.' " In *Don Perlimplín*, more so than in previous plays, Lorca explores the very idea of theater. In the midst of the wedding-night scene, the action of the play is broken by the arrival of two childlike sprites, or *duendes*, who hurriedly draw a gray curtain across the stage and then sit, facing the audience, on the prompter's box. Briefly, the two discuss the nature of theatrical illusion. "It's always nice to cover other people's failings," says one, referring to the curtain that now masks Perlimplín's bed.

"And then the audience can take it upon themselves to uncover them," says the other.

"Because if things are not carefully hidden . . ."

"They will never be revealed." Only through artifice, Lorca suggests, can the truth about human existence be exposed.

On the afternoon of February 6, 1929, Lorca sat in Rivas Cherif's dark little theater watching one of the last rehearsals of *Don Perlimplín*. Things were going poorly. The play had been scheduled to open that evening, but earlier in the day, the Queen Mother of Spain, María Cristina, had died, and the country had gone into mourning. The opening of *Don Perlimplín*, like other events slated to occur that day, was postponed.

Lorca sat in the shadows, fretting over the rehearsal. Onstage, Perlimplín and Belisa were arrayed on their canopied bed on the morning after their wedding night. For some reason the actor playing Perlimplín had removed his headdress. Lorca muttered angrily, "Now you've gone and taken off the horns again!" Absorbed in his play, he failed to realize that the chief of Madrid's police force had quietly entered the theater and was now standing beside him. The police chief announced that he had come to shut down the production. By government order, Lorca's lyrical play about love and death had been deemed unfit for the Spanish public. The ostensible reason for its suppression was that Rivas Cherif had broken the law by holding a rehearsal during the mourning period for the Queen Mother. The real reason appeared to be that a retired army officer was playing the role of Perlimplín, and under the dictatorship of Spanish General Miguel Primo de Rivera, it was not seemly for such a man to appear in public with horns on his head.

Years later, Lorca speculated that his play was shut down because no Spanish citizen, man or woman, wished to be cuckolded. "And this," he cried, "when we're all cuckolded by someone, male or female." He laughed to recall how, on the afternoon of February 6, one of the officers who accompanied the police chief to the theater denounced *Don Perlimplín*, shouting, "This is a mockery! This is an insult to the army!"

But on the actual day his play was suppressed, Lorca was hardly so amused. That afternoon the police chief seized all three copies of his script and took them to the State Security Office in Madrid, where they were stamped with the date of their confiscation and examined by a government censor, who dutifully scratched red pencil lines through such words as "erotic." The scripts were left to molder for years in the Security Office, along with tens of thousands of other such "pornographic" documents confiscated during Primo de Rivera's six-year regime.

Two months after the cancellation of his play, Lorca signed an open letter drafted by José Ortega y Gasset, calling for the formation of a new political party composed of liberal intellectuals and the establishment of a new—and liberal—government. Discontent with Primo de Rivera's dictatorship had reached an all-time high. For years the general had been promising an early end to military rule and a return of government power to civilian hands, but he had repeatedly reneged on his commitment, and instead sought to perpetuate his rule by restructuring the country's political institutions along nationalist, Catholic, and authoritarian lines. His blatant disregard for democratic ideals and his failure to produce a legitimate Spanish constitution angered not only the growing republican opposition—comprised of both the liberal intelligentsia and an organized working class—but many of Spain's liberal monarchists as well. Despite the dictator's claims that his regime represented the interests of all Spaniards, it was clear that his economic policies favored corporate industrialists and, to a lesser extent, large landholding entities, while his social policies appeared to discriminate against employers and landowners. By 1928, increased taxation and mounting deficits and inflation had further eroded support for the general, particularly from Spain's middle class. It was discontent among the army's officer corps, however, many of whom objected to Primo de Rivera's efforts at military reform, that dealt the final blow to his rule. By early 1929, even his closest aides had begun to question the legitimacy and wisdom of Primo de Rivera's government.

In February 1929, Luis Buñuel, who had once called Lorca's *Don Perlimplín* a "piece of shit," went to Paris to begin filming the screenplay he and Dalí had written. Two months later, Dalí joined Buñuel in the French capital. By June they had finished *Un Chien Andalou* (An Andalusian Dog). Although Buñuel denied it, Lorca interpreted the title as a personal affront. "Buñuel's made a shit of a film called *An Andalusian Dog*, and I'm the Andalusian dog," he said. He perceived a cruel allusion to himself in the film's protagonist, a dark-haired young man with an effeminate alter ego who is unable to make love to a woman.

Dalí seemed lost to him. Even before the artist went to Paris, he had snubbed Lorca by revoking his promise to publish one of Lorca's letters in an "anti-art" issue of the Catalan journal *L'Amic de les Arts*. The issue featured a full-page interview between Dalí and Buñuel. Later that spring, in Paris, Dalí grew a threadlike mustache, began wearing fashionable French clothes, and became involved with Gala Eluard, the wife of writer Paul Eluard. The following autumn, Dalí formally joined the surrealists. Across a painting of the Sacred Heart he scribbled the words "Sometimes I spit for pleasure on the portrait of my mother." He then displayed the canvas in a Paris gallery. Informed of the act, Dalí's father demanded that he withdraw the insult. Dalí refused. His father and sister severed all ties with him. "It was as if Salvador had died," Ana María recalled. Dalí's father later wrote to Lorca about the artist's thoughtless act. "He's a disgrace, an ignoramus, and an unrivaled pedant, in addition to being a complete scoundrel. He thinks he knows everything, and yet he doesn't even know how to read and write. In short, you know him better than I . . . You can imagine the grief this nonsense has caused us."

Decades later Dalí admitted that in the late 1920s, a "self-destructive rage" had possessed him. His fury led him to commit a number of indiscretions and to "test my friendship with Lorca," he said. "I suffered honest-to-God fits of jealousy that made me flee him for days on end. I was systematically seeking to isolate myself from everything." In time, the artist became so strident that even Buñuel stopped associating with him.

Lorca tried to salvage something from the wreck his life was threatening to become. The humiliating loss of both Dalí and Aladrén, the suppression of his play, and the ongoing claims of celebrity all contributed to a profound sense of futility. No longer able to work effectively, he all but stopped writing and confined his professional activity to sporadic public appearances. Ten days after the cancellation of *Don Perlimplín*, he delivered his lecture on imagination and inspiration at the Madrid Lyceum Club. Since last giving the talk in November, he had revised its ending and now warned listeners that his current views might change. "As the authentic poet which I am now and will be until my death, I will not stop thrashing myself until one day the inevitable stream of green or yellow blood flows from my body," he announced dramatically. "Anything but sit quietly by the window watching the same landscape."

He began to seek new friends in the capital. Told that he should meet an engaging Chilean diplomat named Carlos Morla Lynch and his wife, Bebé, Lorca made several halfhearted attempts to visit the couple before he finally climbed the stairs to their elegant Madrid apartment and introduced himself. Since coming to Spain, Morla Lynch had read *Gypsy Ballads* and was eager to meet its author. He opened the door to find a young man of average height with a large head, thick black hair, and "somber but dreamy" eyes. The diplomat took Lorca by both hands and pulled him into the apartment. Lorca let out a childlike laugh and began to talk. He stayed with the couple until three the following morning. Before he left, he insisted on singing them a song.

Both Morla and Bebé were French-born Chilean aristocrats, taught from birth to prize art and intelligence. Wherever they went, they moved in elite circles. During Morla's most recent diplomatic posting, to Paris, they had befriended the playwright Jean Cocteau. In Madrid, they quickly opened their home to the city's most distinguished artists and intellectuals. Lorca became a regular guest. He liked the couple enormously. Morla, a bald, blue-eyed, middle-aged man with a bright pink scalp and laugh lines crisscrossing his face, was an exuberant conversationalist with a lively wit. His more reserved wife, Bebé, had ivory skin, black eyes, and ebony hair. Tall and slim, she dressed only in black, white, or gray, often with a strand of pearls around her neck or a single red flower pinned to her dress. When Jorge Guillén met Bebé Morla Lynch he thought her both "very seductive and very worldly."

By March 1929, Lorca had virtually joined the couple's household. "He comes and goes, stays for lunch or supper—or both—naps, sits down at the piano, opens it, sings, closes it, reads us a poem, goes away . . . comes back," wrote Morla Lynch in the diary he had kept since childhood. The diplomat's home became a refuge for the poet. Lorca spent hours sitting beside Morla Lynch on his sunny balcony, talking about art, music, poetry, and theater, while the traffic of Madrid sputtered below them. Sometimes Lorca turned up with no explanation for his presence except that he was feeling despondent. "Even if you say nothing to me, I feel happier with life, and my fear goes away," he told Morla Lynch. The Chilean was struck by Lorca's inexplicable terror of things: "Always that deep obsession . . . lurking beneath his optimism and joy, like a perennial shadow." Lorca seemed most afraid of some unexpected change that might irreparably alter the course of his life. His Andalusian roots, coupled with the often dramatic twists of fate—illness, accident, the indignities of poverty—that he had witnessed as a boy in rural Spain, had made him superstitious.

One morning the two men talked about sorrow. Morla and his wife were still mourning the death, seven months earlier, of their ten-year-old daughter, Colomba, a budding child actress who had died of a congenital disorder. She was the second of two daughters the couple had lost; an older son survived. It was to escape Colomba's memory that Morla and Bebé had left Paris and come to Spain. In Madrid they seldom mentioned their daughter to anyone. Lorca was one of the few people in whom they confided. That morning as he and Morla talked, Lorca patted his chest and confessed that "here, inside," he too had his sorrows, his "*dramones*," as he called them. Morla Lynch feigned surprise. "I live in the anguish of the uncertain 'great beyond,'" Lorca explained. Although he wanted to believe in the immortality of the soul, he was afflicted by doubt. In an ongoing effort to prove the existence of an afterlife, he collected stories of supernatural and near-death experiences: a dying relative who, shortly before his last breath, felt a hand touch his forehead; the simultaneous appearance of a single person in two different locations. Morla suggested that anyone who sought God had already gone halfway toward discovering the "supreme truth." Lorca considered this. After a long pause, he said, "There always remains, even in the greatest skeptics, a very slight, almost imperceptible tremble of doubt, of suspicion and fear. Absolute atheism is not steadfast."

Lorca himself had never wholly abandoned his faith (a friend observed that he "used to get angry at God, to whom he spent his whole life praying"). He attended Mass intermittently, as much for its theatrical splendor as for its meaning. "I'm an aesthetic Catholic," he sometimes said. Or "I'm an anarchic Catholic." Still, he had struggled since adolescence with the paradoxes of Christianity, now and again seeking resolutions in Hinduism and ancient Greek philosophy.

But in the spring of 1929, his belief in himself shaken by the events of the preceding year, he sought a more formal return to Catholicism. The impulse was not without precedent. In an effort to come to grips with their unorthodox sexuality, Oscar Wilde, Jean Cocteau, and Paul Verlaine had each at some time sought the comfort of the Church—in part as a means of reconciling themselves to society. Lorca's rupture with Dalí and degrading affair with Aladrén had similarly revived his desire for spiritual purity, and he turned to the Church in search of both discipline and salvation—concepts pivotal to his ode on Christ, a work he had begun writing in January 1928 and had continued to expand throughout the year.

He called the poem "Ode to the Most Holy Sacrament of the Altar." By the end of 1928, he had completed two sections of the work, "Exposition" and "World." He published these in the December 1928 issue of the *Revista de Occidente*, where they were described as part of a forthcoming book of poems to be published "with photographs." Lorca did not complete the remaining two sections of the ode, "Devil" and "Flesh," until late 1929. At its conclusion, the poem approached two hundred lines.

When he published the first two parts of the ode in the *Revista de Occidente*, Lorca dedicated them to Manuel de Falla, evidently hoping to honor his old friend by linking the composer's name to a poem Lorca viewed as a solemn exaltation of the Eucharist. He failed to consider that his unorthodox approach to his subject might offend Falla. When Jorge Guillén first heard Lorca's ode, he was struck by its "decorative bad taste." But Guillén admired the "grandeur" and inventiveness of the poem.

Identical in form and tone to the "Ode to Salvador Dalí," the "Ode to the Most Holy Sacrament" is both an idiosyncratic interpretation of traditional Catholic theology and a deeply felt tribute to the qualities Christ embodies: purity, compassion, self-sacrifice. Although he admired the rites of Catholicism, Lorca had never embraced the more doctrinaire aspects of his faith; it was the human side of Christ's life and Passion that engaged him. Throughout the poem he couples radical new images—*hechos poéticos*—with authentic details of the Eucharist, drawn, in all likelihood, from his own recollection of Granada's Corpus Christi celebrations, or from even earlier memories of his days as an acolyte in the village church, dressing the altar for Mass. In "Exposition," the opening section of the ode, Lorca presents the Host, the opaque wafer representing Christ's body, as it is seen throughout Spain at Corpus Christi, borne through the streets in a huge golden receptacle by lace-clad priests:

> You, my God, alive inside the monstrance.
> Pierced by your Father's needles of fire.
> Beating like the poor heart of a frog
> kept in a glass container by the doctors.

It was precisely this sort of incongruous imagery—Christ as the impaled heart of a frog—as well as Lorca's implicit condemnation of a father who would willingly murder his son, that prompted Guillén to comment on the poem's "bad taste" and led others, including Falla, to question the author's piety. But Lorca meant to praise, not to mock. He identified keenly with the sacrificed Christ, whom he depicts as the only hope for a dying world. In the poem's three remaining sections, "World," "Devil," and "Flesh," he juxtaposes the innocent Christ with each of the Christian soul's three traditional enemies. In every instance, Christ—"Oh, captive Lamb of three equal voices! / Changeless Sacrament of love and discipline!"—prevails. He calms a bleak urban world threatened by serpents and razors. He vanquishes the Devil, with his "sad beauty" and "shameless faith in no tomorrow," and he redeems original sin.

Within this cosmos, temptations such as greed, materialism, and sexual love fail to satisfy; it is only the pure body of Christ, "your vanquished flesh, broken, trampled / that defeats and dazzles our own flesh."

The poem shares with the "Ode to Salvador Dalí" both a strict alexandrine meter and a thematic preoccupation with purity as a means of transcending fleeting, everyday sensation. In both poems the images are audacious and depersonalized. In a private letter to Pepín Bello, Luis Buñuel accused Lorca of trying to create "surrealistic things" in the "Ode to the Most Holy Sacrament" — "but false ones," he said. Buñuel hated the poem. He told Bello it was "a stinking ode, one that will give Falla's weak member an erection, along with a lot of other artists."

Despite Buñuel's claim, Lorca was not aiming at a surrealist poem, but was instead expressing, in a highly reasoned way, certain deeply held spiritual truths. A friend who read the ode later commented that Lorca was "tormented by God" and hoped to "reap the harvest of his concerns." His dedication to Falla, a man whose life exemplified Christian faith and charity, signaled the seriousness of Lorca's intent. But Lorca misunderstood the nature of Falla's devotion. Stunned to see his name beneath the title of the ode, the composer gently advised Lorca, "Were I to write on the same theme, I would do so with my spirit *on its knees* . . . And then I would make my offering: gold, frankincense, and myrrh. Pure and unalloyed." Although he admitted to being "very honored" by Lorca's tribute, Falla respected the poet too much to hide his disappointment in the ode. "I shall place my hope in the definitive version and in the rest of the poem," he said. Lorca's response to Falla, if he sent one, is lost. But in a later draft of the poem he included an epigraph that reads: "Gold, frankincense, and myrrh."

During the last week of March 1929, Easter week, Lorca quietly left Madrid and went home. Makeshift altars dotted Granada's streets and squares. At night, in the city's dramatic Holy Week processions, long columns of hooded penitents filed through town, carrying polychromed tableaux of the Passion of Christ and bejeweled statues of the Virgin in voluminous robes. Night after night, onlookers lined the streets to watch the mournful parades. Outside the cathedral, *saetas* — austere passages of Gypsy song performed at Easter week — pierced the dark spring air.

Shortly after midnight on Holy Thursday, Lorca took his place at the Alhambra among the men of the Confraternity of Santa María de la Alhambra, a small Catholic church tucked inside the walls of the former Arab stronghold.

The Confraternity was one of several local guilds charged with organizing Granada's Holy Week processions. Earlier, Lorca had approached the leaders of the Confraternity and asked, as a nonmember of the guild, if he might be allowed to march anonymously with the group that night. The Church provides ritual observances for every psychological need, and Lorca's need was extreme. Struck both by the urgency of his request and by his insistence on secrecy, the leaders assented. Only three men in the guild knew of his presence. Gravely, Lorca donned a borrowed tunic and a tall, cone-shaped hood, and knelt before the tableau he would help to parade through the city that night: the weeping figure of Granada's patroness, the Virgin of the Agonies, holding the slain body of Christ on her lap.

At half past midnight a bell tolled. The eerie procession began to move. The Alhambra's gates opened, a *saeta* sounded, and the crowd that had gathered outside the ancient walls of the fortress fell silent. Lorca was among the first marchers to emerge. His face—all but his eyes—was masked. He carried a heavy cross. By choice he had removed his shoes and socks in order to walk barefoot along Granada's cold stone streets. Behind him a squadron of men carried the massive tableau of the Virgin and her Son. Slowly the candlelit parade inched its way down the forested slopes of the Alhambra, onto the streets of the city, past the shadowy facade of the cathedral, and finally back up the steep hill to the Alhambra. The procession lasted four hours. As the marchers returned home to the church of Santa María de la Alhambra, dawn was starting to break. Throughout the night, Lorca held on to his cross.

Afterward, José Martín Campos, one of the few who knew of Lorca's presence in the march, went to thank him for his participation. But the poet had vanished. Martín Campos found only his tunic and hood, heaped at the foot of the cross, with a note: "May God reward you." The next day Lorca returned to Madrid. Two months later, he enrolled officially in the Confraternity.

In Madrid, his gloom deepened. He made vague stabs at work, but his heart was not in it. He was battling a constant cold. In mid-April, he gave a short poetry reading in Madrid and another in Bilbao. He had to get permission from his parents to make the trip. They were worried about him, and Lorca attempted to reassure them. "I'm not to blame for a lot of the things that have happened to me," he said. "The blame lies with life, and with the moral struggles, crises, and conflicts I'm going through. I've always been a child, and I've lived because of you. At the moment I'm quite eager for work, and I'm also eager for spiritual rest." In Bilbao, a photographer snapped his picture. He looked somber, his features uncharacteristically harsh and angular.

He needed a change. Earlier in the year, he had been approached about giving a lecture tour in the United States and Cuba. Although plans for the trip were tentative, Lorca was intrigued. "It could earn me lots of money," he told his parents. His father quickly perceived the utility of the tour. During a business trip to Madrid, Don Federico spoke confidentially to Lorca's friend Rafael Martínez Nadal. Did Nadal think a little time away from Spain might do Lorca some good? he asked. Beneath his dense gray eyebrows, the older man's eyes blazed.

"As a matter of fact, yes, Don Federico," Nadal answered. "I think it wouldn't be at all bad for him."

While his father weighed the potential merits of the journey, Lorca talked glibly about the tour in letters home. He would have to purchase an "elegant lecturer's outfit," he said, and would need to rid himself of his chronic cold, "because if I'm not careful I could lose the very voice that's going to earn me money as a lecturer." By late April, the matter was settled. He would travel to America in June in the company of his former professor and trusted family friend, Fernando de los Ríos, who planned to give a short seminar in New York City that summer. De los Ríos, then forty-nine, had lectured before in the United States and promised to introduce Lorca to friends in Manhattan and to enroll him in classes at Columbia University. Lorca welcomed the news. He later told a friend that in the spring of 1929, before going to New York, he had been on the verge of suicide.

With considerable fanfare, he returned to Granada from Madrid on April 23, 1929. Six days later, Margarita Xirgu brought her production of *Mariana Pineda* to town. To Lorca's chagrin, posters bearing his name festooned the city. He disliked seeing his name displayed so brazenly in his hometown. Although he craved attention, he wanted it on his own terms, and not at the expense of his privacy. Eyeing the posters for his play, he felt as though his childhood had been plucked out by its roots, as though his dearest memories had been desecrated. "I find myself full of responsibility in a place where I never wanted to have it." His quiet trip home the previous month must have seemed a mirage.

During each performance of the play's two-night run in Granada, Lorca obligingly took the stage to accept the applause of the local audience. Even though he now regarded *Mariana Pineda* as "the frail work of a beginner," he was pleased with its reception. At home, he, or someone in his family, clipped a flattering front-page review of the play from the *Defensor de Granada*. Days earlier, the paper had hailed Lorca as the foremost Spanish-speaking poet of his time.

Xirgu remained in Granada for several more days. On May 5, the city held a banquet in honor of the actress and the playwright. Lorca combed his hair neatly back for the occasion and put on a black suit and bow tie; Xirgu wore a dark jacket with a plump fur stole. Friends and family filled the posh Alhambra Palace Hotel. Manuel de Falla was present, as were Fernando de los Ríos, several of Lorca's Rinconcillo colleagues, and his sixty-nine-year-old father, smiling proudly in a three-piece suit. Friends who could not attend the event, including Dalí, sent their congratulations.

With obvious emotion, Lorca addressed the crowd. He thanked Xirgu for her support of his play and thanked his native city for having inspired the work. "If by the grace of God I become famous," he said, "half of that fame will belong to Granada, which formed me and made me what I am: a poet from birth and unable to help it." Then, as though speaking to himself and not to a roomful of faces he had known for most of his life, he said:

> Now, more than ever, I need the silence and spiritual density of Granada's air in order to sustain the duel to death I am fighting with my heart and with poetry. With my heart, to free it from the impossible passion which destroys and from the deceitful shadow of the world which spatters it with sterile salt. With poetry, to construct, despite the fact that she defends herself like a virgin, the wide-awake and true poem where beauty and horror and the ineffable and the repugnant may live and collide in the midst of the most incandescent joy.

On June 5, 1929, his thirty-first birthday, Lorca received his passport. The document erroneously listed the year of his birth as 1900, effectively changing his age to twenty-nine. He sent an extra copy of his passport photograph to Carlos Morla Lynch. The image showed Lorca staring glumly at the camera with pursed lips and one raised eyebrow. Half of his face was in shadow. The ghostly picture reminded Lorca of a murder scene. "Keep it or tear it up," he told Morla. "It's a melancholy Federico I'm sending you and the Federico who writes you now is a Strong Federico."

He claimed to be amused by the prospect of his journey to America. "New York seems horrible to me, but that's exactly why I'm going there. I think I'll have a good time." He planned to remain in America for six or seven months and to spend the remainder of the year in Paris. "Papa is giving me all the money I need." In the United States, de los Ríos would pave his way, "since, as you know, I'm a useless little fool when it comes to practical life."

On June 7, Lorca's friends in Granada held a farewell banquet in his honor.

The following night he caught a train to Madrid. In the capital, friends again toasted him at a private luncheon. On the morning of June 13, Lorca joined Fernando de los Ríos and the professor's niece, Rita María, who was to accompany them for part of the journey, at Madrid's Estación del Norte. The three intended to travel by train to Paris, and from there to England, where Rita María was to remain for the summer. From England, Lorca and de los Ríos would sail to New York.

A handful of friends stood on the platform that morning in Madrid. It was nearly summer. Poppies were blooming in the countryside. Lorca boarded the train with de los Ríos and his niece. As the locomotive pulled away from the station, his friends waved goodbye. Soon they slipped from sight. Soon all of Madrid vanished, and only the windswept fields of Castile remained, filling the windows of his train with their undulating beauty as Lorca slowly made his way north toward France.

Shortly before leaving Madrid, he had told Carlos Morla Lynch that he felt a renewed desire to write and "an unbridled love for poetry, for the verse that fills my soul, still trembling like a tiny antelope from the last brutal arrows." But life was taking him in a new direction, into the cold gray swells of the Atlantic, to America. "Onward!" he wrote. "As insignificant as I may be, I believe I *deserve* to be loved."

CHAPTER 14

NEW WORLD

1929-30

In Paris, Lorca drank hot chocolate and ate croissants. At the Louvre, he instructed de los Ríos's niece to ignore the *Mona Lisa*. "She's a bourgeois!" he laughed. "Don't look at her!"

In London, he admired the lights of Piccadilly Circus but was frightened by the cars. At street crossings he went rigid with fear. After two days in the British capital, Rita María went north to take up a summer teaching position, while Lorca and de los Ríos traveled to Oxford and then to Southampton. In Southampton they boarded the S.S. *Olympic*, and on the morning of June 19 they set sail for America.

The crossing lasted six days. Lorca spent the journey basking in the summer sun until he turned "black as blackest Africa," as he reported in a letter to his parents. "I feel content, full of joy." But to Carlos Morla Lynch he revealed that he was homesick and depressed. "I don't know why I left," he told the Chilean. "I ask myself that question a hundred times a day. I look at myself in the mirror of the narrow cabin and I don't recognize myself. I seem another Federico."

During the long trip he befriended a five-year-old Hungarian boy who was crossing the ocean to be with his father for the first time in his life. The innocence of the boy and the enormity of his quest stunned Lorca. Soon the child would disappear "into the belly of New York, seeking his fortune," Lorca told his parents. "Life will be cruel or kind to him, and I will be but a remote memory, connected with the rhythm of the huge ship and the ocean." When the two parted at the end of their journey, they both wept.

The day was warm and clear on June 26 when the S.S. *Olympic* rounded the tip of Manhattan and steamed upriver, past the gray towers of Wall Street, along the docks and warehouses and apartment buildings of New York City. Lorca had never seen anything like it. The tops of the skyscrapers seemed to him to touch the heavens.

"The two elements the traveler first captures in the big city," he said later, "are extrahuman architecture and furious rhythm. Geometry and anguish." This was the most daring urban landscape of the age, a city Fritz Lang had immortalized in *Metropolis*, a place that dozens of artists and writers, including some of Lorca's Spanish contemporaries, had tried to describe. But nothing Lorca had read, seen, or heard could prepare him for the real-life spectacle of Manhattan. Paris and London were impressive, he told his parents, but New York "has given me the knock-out punch." He searched for some way of conveying to his family the "grandeur" of the place. Finally he hit on an image he thought they might understand. "All Granada," he said, "would fit into three of these buildings."

At the pier, a handful of Spaniards waited to greet the two travelers. Among them were the current chair of the Department of Spanish and Portuguese at Columbia University, Federico de Onís, then sixty-three, and his young colleague Ángel del Río, whom Lorca had known briefly in Madrid in the early 1920s. But Lorca was especially astonished to find Gabriel García Maroto, the genial painter who had published *Book of Poems*, among the group. Maroto had recently come to the United States for an extended visit and was working as a commercial artist in New York City. When he saw Lorca, he threw his arms around the sunburned Granadan and "went crazy hugging and even kissing me," Lorca happily reported to his parents.

His first days in America were a blur of impressions. Through his acquaintances at Columbia, and at de los Ríos's urging, he promptly enrolled as a student at the university and took a dormitory room on the sixth floor of Furnald Hall, overlooking the main campus. From his window he could hear the rumble of traffic on nearby Broadway and the groan of foghorns in the distance. Directly below him lay a field where young men played tennis on warm summer days. He settled quickly into his spartan quarters and told his parents he enjoyed the room's pretty view and constant breezes. But he missed Spain. He asked his family to send photographs of themselves so that he could decorate his new home.

Because he spoke no English, Lorca relied on his Spanish friends to shepherd him through the city. Two days after his arrival, he visited Times Square at night. The sight of so many flashing lights ascending into the sky, "higher than the moon," astounded him. He thought the people on the streets bright "streams" of sweaters and scarves, and the streets themselves "streams" of honking automobiles and radios. Unlike Madrid, where donkeys still drew carts through the city and one could see mountains in the distance, everything in New York was man-made. It was Dalí's machine-age aesthetic come to life. Although Lorca later distanced himself from New York by pronouncing it a rootless world, his initial response was to marvel at the city's technological splendor. He told his parents that the panorama of Broadway by night was "as impressive as a spectacle of nature."

He seized on stereotypes to help him understand the alien city. Times Square was an "army of windows." Wall Street was the "spectacle of the world's money, in all its unbridled splendor and cruelty." New Yorkers themselves reminded him of characters he had seen in American movies: the typist with shapely legs, the gum-chewing office boy, the sidewalk beggar. Lorca was horrified by the number of drunks he saw on the city's streets. He was mystified by Prohibition and spoke scornfully of the "teetotaling" Protestant "idiots" responsible for the nationwide ban on liquor. "Of course, I myself drink nothing without first making sure it is good," he assured his family. The Protestant faith perplexed him. It lacked the ceremonial beauty of the Spanish Church, and he could not, he said, "get it into my head—my Latin head" why anyone would prefer it to Catholicism. Even more bewildering was Judaism. After attending a service in a Jewish synagogue, Lorca pronounced the rite lovely but "meaningless. To me the figure of Christ seems too strong to deny."

Americans in general he found friendly and open, like children. "They are incredibly naive, and extremely helpful." But the American political system disappointed him. In practice, Lorca told his parents, democracy meant "that only the very rich have maids here." For the first time in his life, he had to sew his own buttons onto his clothes.

He believed that having seen New York, he had seen all of America. "Everything is uniformly the same." Americans were tenacious—a trait Lorca admired—but materialistic. Their sexual candor amazed him. In Spain, couples were discreet, but in New York, men and women kissed casually on the streets and in automobiles. American women, he said, possessed tremendous "shishpil" (he meant "sex appeal"). Like many other European visitors, Lorca perceived the modern American woman, with her short hair, revealing skirts, and unorthodox behavior, as a phenomenon unique in the world. To his parents, he talked wearily of the number of beautiful American women who pursued him in New York: "It's a plague I have to endure." What he did not say—but what he surely learned—was that homosexuality was also a more visible phenomenon in New York than in Spain. One of the city's most notorious spots for clandestine homosexual encounters was located on Riverside Drive, not far from Columbia University.

In August, as planned, Fernando de los Ríos left New York. Lorca stayed on, alone except for his new circle of Spanish friends at Columbia. He told his family he was in good spirits—well fed, and surrounded by people who took an interest in him. "I can see now what a good thing it is to have become a man of some fame: all doors are opened to you and everyone treats you with the utmost respect."

He wrote home regularly. His letters were relentlessly buoyant. He explained to his parents that he rose early every morning to study English and then went to English class. In the afternoons he studied or wrote, ate supper in the university dining hall at the unaccustomed hour of seven o'clock (in Spain, supper rarely began before nine-thirty), and then took walks or went to parties. "There are more parties and gatherings here than anyplace else in the world. Americans cannot stand to be alone." To judge by his letters, Manhattan's social and cultural life revolved around Lorca. He was "always turning down invitations." (If one is not careful, he complained, "the old women intellectuals here will devour you.") At parties he played the piano and sang, and he soon began teaching popular songs to Spanish students at Columbia—a task he loved. He described his official title as "Director of the Mixed Choruses of the Spanish Institute of the United States of America."

He pretended to enjoy his studies. He told his parents he carried a dictionary around with him all day long, because the nice Americans were always striking up conversations, and he wanted to participate. "Naturally each question and answer requires fifteen minutes of word hunting in the dictionary. But it is the only way to learn." In truth, Lorca acquired almost no English during his stay in America. He learned to say "ice cream" and "Times Square" (pronouncing it "Tim-es Es-quare," according to a Spanish-speaking acquaintance). He learned how to order ham and eggs in a restaurant, and because it was the only thing he knew how to order, he ate ham and eggs much of the time—or so he claimed. In English class, he spent most of his time mimicking his teacher's gestures and accent. His favorite expression, a friend recalled, was "I don't understand anything." Lorca would shout the phrase while standing in the middle of the street, arms flailing, his face red with laughter.

Contrary to what he told his parents, he spoke Spanish all day long, with anyone. He seemed afraid of English, as if the new language might rob him of the old. At Columbia, he communicated with elevator attendants by extravagant gestures—deep bows and pirouettes. In social situations he sometimes got by in broken French. He later bragged that during his stay in New York, he had made his way around the city by hanging a sign from his neck with his destination printed clearly on it in English.

Troubled by Lorca's inability to grasp the language, Federico de Onís and Ángel del Río arranged for a graduate student named Sofía Megwinoff to tutor him in English. Lorca expressed delight at the idea. He told his parents he hoped the young woman was pretty; if not, he would refuse to work with her. Happily, Sofía was an attractive brunette with big eyes, who charmed Lorca with her spellbinding recitations of works by Edgar Allan Poe. As she spoke, Lorca closed his mouth and hummed along with the poems, tapping out their rhythm with his hands. He understood nothing of their content.

Sofía quickly realized that Lorca had neither the aptitude nor the desire to learn English, and so the two spent their time together exploring the city. Typically Lorca showed up late for their meetings; once, after missing an appointment altogether, he wrote Sofía a note blaming her for having left him "in the lurch." He signed himself, "The betrayed Poet." On another occasion he went on at length about his former girlfriend in Spain, a woman with whom he had been deeply in love, but who had abused him by scratching his face. He had retaliated by grabbing her long hair and dragging her across the floor, he said. Sofía believed the story until Onís and del Río assured her it was a complete fabrication. Lorca had invented the tale, they suggested, in order to make himself seem more interesting.

His true classroom was New York. Dressed in sporty new American attire— an Oxford-cloth shirt and tie, baggy pants, a white tennis sweater—he took to the streets. He visited the aquarium and the zoo ("where I felt like a child") and he made repeated visits to dime stores, where he sometimes sat on the floor and played with toy horses or automobiles. On crowded subway cars he occasionally feigned lameness in order to get a seat. As the underground train clattered along in the dark, he liked to wag his hand beneath his chin like a cowbell and intone, "Talán, talán, talán."

He told his parents he was adapting well to his new environment. "I don't see much of the Spaniards," he lied. "I prefer to live the life of an American."

In truth, he dropped by Ángel del Río's apartment nearly every day and often shared his meals with the young professor and his wife, Amelia. He also befriended a Mexican heiress, María Antonieta Rivas Blair, and took part in weekly gatherings at the offices of the Spanish-language magazine *Alhambra*. He saw both del Río and Gabriel García Maroto at these *tertulias*, as well as the Spanish poet León Felipe and a Puerto Rican intellectual named Ángel Flores. Afterward the group often dined together at a cheap Spanish restaurant near Chinatown.

One night over supper, Flores noticed that Lorca looked glum. He suggested that after the meal they both go to Brooklyn to visit the American poet Hart Crane, whom Flores knew. Lorca agreed, and the two took off by foot across the Brooklyn Bridge to Crane's apartment. The Illinois-born Crane was one year younger than Lorca and had lived in New York since 1923. Earlier in his life he had labored briefly as a factory worker in Cleveland, Ohio; he loved machinery and believed poetry must absorb the aesthetic of the machine age, must "surrender, at least temporarily, to the sensations of urban life." In New York, Crane was at work on a long series of poems inspired by the Brooklyn Bridge, whose "bound cable strands" and "silver terraces" loomed outside his apartment. His first book of poems, *White Buildings*, had appeared in 1926, and he would publish *The Bridge* in 1930. But despite his literary success, Crane was a profoundly tormented man. Poetry sustained him in a life that otherwise teetered on the brink of collapse. When he wasn't writing, he spent much of his time engaged in fleeting homosexual encounters and alcohol binges. In 1932, three years after meeting Lorca, Crane committed suicide by leaping from a ship into the Caribbean.

When Flores and Lorca arrived at Crane's apartment that afternoon in 1929, the American writer answered the door. He was a slight man with big hands, a large face, and dark, melancholy eyes. Behind him, Flores spotted half a dozen inebriated sailors lounging about the room. Crane himself was drunk, but he welcomed the two men into his home, and when Flores introduced him to Lorca, Crane made an attempt to converse with the Spaniard. Neither writer could speak the other's language, but with Flores's help they managed to communicate and eventually got along in pidgin French. Crane asked if Lorca would like to stay on that afternoon, and Lorca indicated that he would. Tactfully, Flores left. On his way out the door, he glanced back and saw Crane in the midst of one group of sailors, telling jokes, and Lorca in the midst of another, drinking whiskey. Flores never learned what happened after his departure.

Although Lorca knew little about Crane when he met him that day, in what was apparently his only encounter with the poet, he almost certainly learned something about Crane's work afterward from Flores and from León Felipe, both of whom admired the American. Lorca came to share Crane's disdain for urban society and his reverence for Walt Whitman, but he could not embrace Crane's faith in the beauty and power of modern technology. Lorca was a poet of the land, not of steel girders and asphalt streets, and the longer he remained in New York, the more he understood this.

By late August, he had begun to shape his own vision of urban America. His sense of the place evolved in part from his growing appreciation of its writers. At the time, his friend Flores was at work on one of the first Spanish translations of Eliot's *The Waste Land* and frequently read portions of the poem to Lorca. Lorca thought Eliot a "terrific poet" and praised his bleak image of the modern city as a wasteland peopled by squalid crowds.

He also admired Whitman. Although *Leaves of Grass* had yet to be translated fully into Spanish, Lorca was familiar with the work, and during his stay in New York enjoyed long talks about the poem with León Felipe, who had come to America in large part to study Whitman. Lorca came away from these conversations with a deeply felt, if not altogether factual, grasp of Whitman's poem. He found the work's long lines and Biblical cadences inspiring, and he was moved by Whitman's effort to celebrate homosexual love. He sympathized with the poet's struggle to forge a noble America. In Whitman's day, Manhattan streets had borne the din of "carts, sluff of boot-soles, talk of the promenaders." But Whitman's nineteenth-century New York was pristine compared to the industrial behemoth Lorca confronted whenever he left his dormitory room. Like Hart Crane, Lorca mourned the loss of Whitman's great democracy, and he came to view the American poet as a symbol of the nation's lost innocence. He later told a group of Spanish writers that the best part of America was Walt Whitman and Abraham Lincoln.

Nearly everywhere he went in New York, Lorca encountered greed, poverty, and filth. Only one place seemed free of depravity—Harlem. Much as Hart Crane viewed the Indian as the epitome of America's flesh and soul, so Lorca came to regard the African American as the country's "spiritual axis."

Late at night he often went with friends to Harlem's jazz clubs and soft-lit cabarets, places whose names—the Cotton Club, Small's Paradise—promised entry to another, more sensual world. Inside, Lorca would sit motionless, his head bowed, eyes lost in reverie, and listen to the sultry beat of drums and the whine of clarinets. From time to time he raised his head abruptly to murmur his approval: "What rhythm! What rhythm! How stupendous!" He learned jazz tunes and spirituals by heart and later sang them among friends, re-creating with astonishing precision the pitch and rhythm of these uniquely American forms. He compared American jazz to Spanish deep song (both had African roots, he said), and he likened the African American to the Gypsy. Each was emblematic of a primitive, carnal, vibrantly human world un-fettered by puritan virtue. Each was a "persecuted" race. Blacks, like Gypsies, bared their suffering through song and dance. "Aside from black art," Lorca would observe, "there is nothing in the United States but mechanics and au-tomatism."

His perception of African Americans, like his response to the Gypsies, was both romantic and naive. Unable to fathom black culture except through mu-sic, Lorca saw what it suited him to see. He made sweeping generalizations. Af-ter briefly meeting the black author Nella Larsen, he described her as an "exquisite" woman possessed by "that deep, moving melancholy which all blacks have." One night in Small's Paradise, he was captivated by the sight of a black woman dancing furiously before a crowd of onlookers who shrieked with pleasure at her performance. Alone among the spectators, Lorca said later, he was able, "for a second," to detect "her reserve, her remoteness, her inner cer-tainty that she had nothing to do with that admiring audience of Americans and foreigners. All Harlem was like her."

He thought Harlem a sanctuary of art and beauty and carnality. Like many white Americans, he was drawn to the neighborhood through his zeal for the primitive, his quest for the avant-garde. Harlem in the 1920s was an African-American Paris, a gathering place for the bohemian periphery of American so-ciety, the setting for a renaissance in black arts and letters, as well as the scene of a burgeoning homosexual subculture. To Lorca, Harlem seemed an oasis of freedom, and he thrilled to it. "The most interesting thing about this city," he told his parents late in the summer of 1929, "is this very mixture of different races and customs. I hope to study them all, and make some sense of this chaos and complexity."

He did not wait long. On August 5, six weeks after arriving in Manhattan, Lorca wrote what appears to have been his first New York poem, a blistering in-dictment of white American civilization and an exaltation of black culture. He titled the work "The King of Harlem." His experience of New York, transitory though it was, had convinced him that beneath the passive gaze of the city's black elevator attendants and janitors throbbed the blood-red pulse of Africa:

Ay, Harlem! Ay, Harlem! Ay, Harlem!
There is no anguish like that of your oppressed reds,
or your blood shuddering with rage inside the dark eclipse,
or your garnet violence, deaf and dumb in the penumbra,
or your grand king a prisoner in the uniform of a doorman.

Appalled by newspaper ads promoting powders to lighten black skin and po-
mades to flatten black hair, Lorca criticized those African Americans who
would deny their race, and he rashly called for black violence to counter the
cruelty of white America. One day, he wrote, black America will crush its op-
pressor, and blood "will flow / on rooftops everywhere, / and burn the blond
women's chlorophyll."

His sympathy for the American black, while patronizing, was genuine. He
deplored bigotry. He had grown up in a city where racist policies had led to the
destruction of a flourishing Arab, Jewish, and Christian civilization. He had
witnessed cruelty against the Gypsies. But nothing in Spain approached the
kind of institutionalized discrimination Lorca saw daily in the United States.
Years later he told a journalist he hoped someday to write a play about the
blacks, but he would remain unable to do so until he understood "a world
shameless and cruel enough to divide its people by color, when color is in fact
the sign of God's artistic genius."

In form as well as subject matter "The King of Harlem" was a departure
from Lorca's previous work. In the poem Lorca adapted the concerns of his earlier verse—social injustice, the dichotomy between instinct and propriety—to
the rhythm and tone of his new environment. He broke from the metrical
forms of his past to forge long, Whitmanesque lines of free verse in which
provocative urban images merge with the staccato cries of *cante jondo*. Referring to himself in the third person, he later said of his trip to New York that it
"enriched and changed the poet's work, since it was the first time he confronted a new world."

Three days after drafting "The King of Harlem," Lorca announced confidently to his parents that he had begun to write, "and I believe what I am writing is good." For the first time in months, inspiration gripped him. Poems and
ideas for poems crowded his mind; he had enough material, he thought, for
two books: "They are typically American poems, and almost all of them deal
with the blacks." He envisioned a cycle of poems not unlike his Gypsy ballads,
about the plight of African Americans in a callous white world. But this concept soon evolved into something much broader. "I am deeply interested in

New York, and think I can strike a new note not only in Spanish poetry but in all that has been written about these things," he explained to his parents. "But don't tell anyone."

His sympathy for black Americans was to a large extent provoked by Lorca's own feeling of rootlessness in white, English-speaking Manhattan. He looked to Spain with growing nostalgia. Although he maintained a cheerful guise during his first months in New York, and indeed informed his parents that he scarcely had "time to feel lonely," he experienced periodic bouts of anguish. While visiting New York that summer, the Spanish novelist Concha Espina ran into Lorca at a dinner party and found him touched with "melancholy." Ángel del Río, who saw Lorca on a more regular basis, drew the same conclusion. From time to time, he recalled, a "shadow of absence" crossed Lorca's dark eyes. There were constant allusions to an emotional crisis, and yet, according to del Río, Lorca never divulged its source.

Late at night, after the rumble of traffic had died down and the summer air had cooled, Lorca often took to the streets by himself. Sometimes he strayed to the waterfront or to the Brooklyn Bridge, where he and Sofía Megwinoff occasionally strolled by day. The site entranced him as it did Hart Crane. Standing alone on the bridge, high above the East river, he could see the formidable gray silhouette of Wall Street to the south, and beyond it—a pinpoint in the inky bay—the Statue of Liberty. Behind him, to the north, the huge granite towers of midtown Manhattan rose into the night. He remained on the bridge, absorbed in his thoughts, a minuscule human figure dwarfed by the huge American metropolis. Returning uptown to Columbia in the dark hours of early morning, he sometimes picked up a pencil or a pen, and in the quiet of his room tried to record his impressions.

As he worked to evoke the reality of New York, the brute city became imaginatively entwined with the lost paradise of Lorca's Spanish childhood. In an elegiac poem he titled "1910 (Intermezzo)," he looked back to a time—his twelfth year—when he had not yet beheld the cruelty of adult life:

> Those eyes of mine in nineteen-ten
> saw no one dead and buried,
> no village fair of ash from the one who weeps at dawn,
> no trembling heart cornered like a sea horse.

The squalor of urban America reinforced the purity of his boyhood memories. In the poem he recalled incidents from childhood—the time he was placed on

a pony that refused to move, the day the family cat ate a frog, the portrait of
Saint Rosa that hung in the maid's bedroom, the rooftops in Granada where
lovers were said to meet:

> Those eyes of mine on the pony's neck,
> on the pierced breast of Santa Rosa as she sleeps,
> on the rooftops of love, with moans and cool hands,
> on a garden where cats devour frogs.

In 1910, Lorca and his brother had seen Halley's comet brighten the sky above
Granada. With the same kind of fury his childhood had blazed and then
evanesced, wrecked in the maelstrom of adolescent passion. Its loss was ir-
reparable: "Don't ask my any questions. I've seen how things / that seek their
way find their void instead."

Viewed through the gray lens of Manhattan, his childhood was nothing now
but a "fable of fountains," a phrase Lorca borrowed from Jorge Guillén to use
as the epigraph and refrain of another New York poem, "Your Childhood in
Menton." Begun, possibly, before Lorca even reached America, the second
poem recalls a broken love affair with a man who has spurned the poet's offer
of love:

> What I gave you, Apollonian man, was the standard of love,
> fits of tears with an estranged nightingale.
> But ruin fed upon you, you whittled yourself to nothing
> for the sake of fleeting, aimless dreams.

With its Mediterranean setting (the town of Menton is located on the French
Riviera) and oblique reference to homosexual love, the poem hints at Lorca's
affairs with both Dalí and Aladrén. Poetically, at least, Lorca appeared to associate both involvements with his lost childhood, for when he first published the
poem in 1932 he titled it *Ribera de 1910* (Shore of 1910).

Despite the distractions of his first weeks in America, Lorca had not forgotten either man. When Ángel Flores published an article about Lorca in the
magazine *Alhambra*, he illustrated it with a set of photographs, several of which
show Lorca cavorting with Dalí in Cadaqués. In one image, Lorca sits across
from the artist at a table beside the sea; the caption reads, "Writing a manifesto
with the painter Dalí." Flores suspected that Lorca gave him the photographs
in order to enhance his reputation as a poet of the avant-garde. Among friends
in New York, Lorca talked enthusiastically about Dalí's revolutionary work. To
Flores, he confessed, "I love him. I love him."

Lorca's memories of Aladrén surfaced more covertly in his poetry. In a work entitled "Fable and Round of the Three Friends," he wrote of a man named Emilio who—like the real-life sculptor Lorca knew in Madrid—moves "in the world of eyes and wounded hands" and "the forgotten shot of gin." In an earlier draft, Lorca included a sly reference to himself in New York, studying English "with one hundred million students who crush the anemones / . . . Oh, Federico!" But in a jarring sequence of images suggesting the brutal loss of identity he had experienced through Aladrén, Lorca removed himself from the final draft of the poem:

> When the pure shapes sank
> under the chirping of daisies,
> I knew they had murdered me.
> They combed the cafés, graveyards, and churches for me,
> pried open casks and cabinets,
> destroyed three skeletons in order to rip out their gold teeth.
> But they couldn't find me anymore.
> They couldn't?
> But they discovered the sixth moon had fled against the torrent,
> and the sea—suddenly!—remembered
> the names of all its drowned.

After six weeks of English class, Lorca knew next to nothing of the new language. Nevertheless, he accepted an invitation to visit a tall blond American student named Philip Cummings in northern Vermont that August. Lorca had met Cummings the previous year in Madrid, and had subsequently taken the American to Granada for a brief visit. He had run into Cummings again, by chance, while traveling from Madrid to Paris earlier in the summer; Cummings had invited him to visit New England during his stay in America—and had offered to pay his train fare. Lorca told his parents the trip would constitute his "moment of truth" in English.

But on the evening of his departure from Grand Central Station Lorca panicked. Convinced that no one would understand him, and that he would therefore be stranded forever in the American wilderness, he shouted and gestured until one of his friends spoke to the train conductor and secured a promise to deposit him safely at his destination. Shortly after leaving New York, Lorca turned out the light in his compartment, opened the window, crawled into bed, and lay there, unable to sleep, he recalled, because "the sight of the moon and the boats on the Hudson river was so wonderful that it filled my head with

ideas." When the sun rose the following morning, he found himself surrounded by the dense green beauty of New England. At the Montpelier station,
Cummings and his father were waiting to greet him. Lorca threw his arms
around both men and cried, "Ay! I've left the dungeon!"

Cummings and his parents were spending the summer in a lakeside cottage
north of Montpelier, not far from the Canadian border, in the village of Eden
Mills. The name delighted Lorca. In the space of a single day, he had exchanged the gritty streets of New York for the clapboard churches and dark
pines of rural Vermont. He welcomed the change, although the bucolic landscape soon made him homesick for Spain. At night, instead of traffic, he was
lulled to sleep by the sound of wind ruffling the leaves outside the sleeping
porch that he and Cummings shared. In the morning, birdsong and the peal of
church bells signaled the start of another day. The two men would lie half-
awake in the cool mountain air, listening.

Philip Cummings was twenty years old in the summer of 1929, eleven years
younger than Lorca. He aspired to be a poet, and during Lorca's ten-day visit
he kept a rhapsodic account of their time together in a diary he later titled "August in Eden. An Hour of Youth." Both Cummings and his parents were tall
and fair-skinned; they reminded Lorca of characters he had seen in Tom Mix
cowboy movies. He was unable to communicate with either parent, except to
say "Thank you" once to Cummings's white-haired mother and to speak to her
in Spanish one morning while she made doughnuts. To his parents, he described the family as a "barcarole of tenderness and bad taste."

He relied on Cummings to translate for him. The young American proudly
took his distinguished Spanish guest around town and introduced him to some
of its more peculiar inhabitants, including two elderly sisters who served Lorca
jasmine tea. Inside their curious house, Lorca spotted birds' nests clinging to
the rafters. He was struck by the fact that the people of Eden Mills cheerfully
accepted such eccentric women. In America, he advised his parents, "everything is tolerated . . . except social scandal. You can have a hundred mistresses
and people know it and nothing happens, but just wait until one of them denounces you and whips up something in public. Then there is no hope for you
socially."

Initially, Lorca delighted in the small town. He likened its outhouses to
priest's confessionals and its rotting tree stumps to castles. One day he tore a
piece of birch bark from a tree and scribbled a note on it to his sisters in
Granada. "The title of this letter is 'Autumn in New England,' " he wrote. He
spent hours sitting by the lake, talking or working intermittently with Cum-

mings on an English translation of *Songs*. When it wasn't raining, the two
hiked through the woods. They came upon a working talc mine, and also an
abandoned village, whose decaying buildings left Lorca sad. "The vanished
people," he murmured. "Where are they?" To his parents, he described the
forested landscape as "acutely romantic."

Although his friendship with Cummings was apparently platonic, Lorca
soon found the American's constant attention cloying. By the end of his
visit, he was desperate to leave. It rained without stop. In the morning, mists
shrouded the lake outside his bedroom, stirring old memories. He was reminded of his childhood, lost, now, in the damp fogs of the *vega*. On the back
of a photograph taken of himself standing beside Lake Eden in a white, V-
necked sweater he wrote: "Me, on the lake, half sportsman and half altar boy."
He was trying to be funny, but there was a melancholy edge to his remark. In
the photograph, Lorca stands by himself on the stony shore of a motionless
lake, a lone figure in an unfamiliar landscape. Beyond him, a range of faint
gray hills folds into an empty sky.

He yearned to recover some recognizable image of himself. He spent hours
writing poetry at Lake Eden. He wrote anywhere, on anything. Sometimes he
sat, hunched, on an overturned boat, scribbling verse on the back of an old envelope, absorbed in the cadences of his native Spanish. The damp woods and
brisk, late summer sky worked their way into poems steeped in loss and longing. The very name of the lake led Lorca to envision himself as a pilgrim in
search of an unattainable Eden, a paradise capable of releasing him from the
earth's pull and providing "love at the end without dawn. Love. Visible love!"
He understood the futility of his quest: "I won't be able to complain / though I
never found what I was looking for."

His surroundings rekindled thoughts of childhood, of a vanished Arcadia
where he did not need to mask his identity with the conceits of language. In
"Double Poem of Lake Eden," one of three poems he completed in Vermont,
Lorca summons "my love's voice from before / . . . voice of my truth." For an
instant it returns to him, a fleeting reminder of his boyhood self, as present but
irredeemable as his own reflected image in the waters of Lake Eden. He begs
his "voice from before" to "burn / this voice of tin and talc!" He dreams of
shedding the lies of adulthood:

> I want to cry saying my name,
> rose, child, and fir on the shore of this lake,
> to speak truly as a man of blood
> killing in myself the mockery and the suggestive power of the word.

But the vision fades, and time presses on. "I was speaking that way when Saturn stopped the trains / and the fog and Dream and Death were looking for me." Years would pass before his poetry spoke with the level of candor Lorca desired.

The leaves were beginning to change color, and he ached to rejoin his Spanish friends. "It doesn't stop raining," he wrote gloomily to Ángel del Río, who was spending the last weeks of summer with his wife and infant son in the Catskill mountains. Lorca hoped to join them shortly. "This family is very nice and full of gentle charm," he said of the Cummingses, "but the woods and the lake plunge me into a state of poetic desperation that is most difficult to bear. I write all day and at night I feel exhausted." There was no liquor in the cottage, and he urgently needed cognac for his "poor heart." He was drowning, he said, in the mists of Eden Mills. Four days later, on the morning of his departure from Vermont, he told Philip Cummings, "You're going to bury me in this fog."

In Bushnellsville, New York, Ángel del Río and his wife waited all day for Lorca to appear. Despite their pleas, he had neglected to tell them what time his train was due to arrive. By nightfall they were distraught. At last, a taxi appeared on the dirt road leading up to their farm. Lorca was leaning out of one of the windows, shouting hysterically. Unable to communicate with each other, he and the driver had been lost for hours. The fare was enormous. Del Río paid the bill and ushered Lorca into his home. Later, Lorca insisted the taxi driver had tried to rob and murder him in a dark corner of the forest.

He relaxed in Bushnellsville. He took walks, sang songs, pretended to study English with Amelia del Río, and fussed over his friends' three-month-old son, Miguel Ángel. When Amelia developed a brief throat infection, the child spent several nights in Lorca's room. Ángel went in to check on his son early one morning and was startled to find Lorca awake, kneeling beside the baby's basket. "Look, the child's dead, he doesn't move," Lorca said, terrified by the sight of the sleeping infant.

He spent nearly three weeks in the Catskills. During his stay he continued to write poems—works whose titles betray his private preoccupations: "Nocturne of Emptied Space," "Landscape with Two Graves and an Assyrian Dog," "Ruin." He befriended the children of the farm's caretaker, a boy and a girl named Stanton and Helen Hogan, and months after leaving Bushnellsville he composed a poem about each child. He portrayed them as emblems of innocence in a menacing world. The cancer that afflicted the children's father in real life became, in Lorca's poem "Little Stanton," an epidemic that beats "like a heart" in the rooms of the boy's house and "wants to go to bed" with the ten-year-old child.

In the poem "Little Girl Drowned in the Well," the abandoned rock quarries that lay just beyond the Hogans' farm became a watery tomb for a virginal child. Years later Lorca claimed that during his visit to Bushnellsville, Stanton Hogan's young sister, "Mary," had fallen into a well and drowned. The shock of her death sent Lorca reeling back to New York City. But in fact no one died during his stay in the Catskills, least of all young Helen Hogan. Lorca's poem was the product of landscape and solitude and of the poet's lifelong obsession with death by water. Lorca himself said the girl's "drowning" in America reminded him of a similar incident in Granada, and it may have been true. Drownings in wells were not uncommon at the time. But Lorca's infatuation with the subject transcended the particular. His image of the chaste child trapped by the "mossy hands" of the well touched on deep-rooted fears that even he could not fully articulate. In his mind, he said, the two drowned girls "became the same child, who cried and cried, unable to leave the circle of the well, in the unmoving water that never reaches the sea."

Lorca had been away from Manhattan for just over a month when he returned to the "frenzied" city on September 21, 1929, and settled into a cell-like cubicle on the twelfth floor of Columbia University's towering John Jay Hall. His new room held little more than a bed and a desk, but the view from its solitary window was magnificent. To the north he could see the dark curve of the Hudson river and, "spanning the horizon," a great bridge "of incredible strength and agility"—the George Washington Bridge, then under construction. To his parents he described the landscape as "prodigiously impressive." And yet his claustrophobic surroundings made him wistful for the gentler panoramas of Granada.

His neighbors in John Jay Hall were mostly loutish American football players, he said, who stretched and yawned and sneezed in public with the nonchalance of animals. "This is a totally savage people, perhaps because there is no class system," he told his parents. He found it all but impossible to communicate with his fellow residents. Most of the time he resorted to sign language. Or he simply kept to himself. According to one resident, Lorca sometimes spent whole days in bed, refusing to emerge even when the buzzer in his room summoned him to a telephone call or a visitor.

He made friends with a pair of Spanish-speaking American students named

John Crow and Francis Hayes, who lived a few doors down the hall. Crow remembered Lorca dropping in at all hours of the day and night to talk about art, artists, American blacks, or the Gypsies and Arabs of Spain. More than once Lorca bragged that he possessed Arab blood himself. He liked to dramatize the most insignificant events of his daily life, and he showed a morbid interest in death—especially violent death. Crow eventually tired of Lorca's spontaneous, late-night visits and his unbearable ego. Lorca was capable, Crow said, of holding forth for hours on his work, his fame, his international success, and his role as the "pinnacle" of achievement within his distinguished family.

Other Americans enjoyed Lorca's bravado. Through friends he met several of New York's most ardent Hispanophiles—people who had lived and worked in Spain and who spoke the language. Among them was a rangy, soft-spoken southerner named Herschel Brickell, an executive at the publishing house Henry Holt & Company. Brickell and his wife, Norma, lived in a lavish apartment on Park Avenue; their living room held a new concert grand piano and enough space for a hundred visitors. On his first visit Lorca gazed longingly at the gleaming piano and confessed that he would like to play. He soon became a regular guest.

Through music he could talk to anyone, even English-speaking New Yorkers. At the Brickells' home he enthralled other guests with his boisterous renditions of popular Spanish songs. "I don't even worry about making a fool of myself," he admitted privately to his family, "for I have never seen kinder, more innocent . . . and more intelligent people." He belted out songs in his coarse, unpolished voice and waited for the inevitable cries of *Olé, más!* before moving on to the next piece. People who knew nothing about Spain crowded around the piano to hear him play. One night in New York the Spanish guitarist Andrés Segovia heard Lorca perform and pronounced him "phenomenal. Phenomenal. He electrified people," Segovia remembered.

To most, his charm was irresistible. Herschel Brickell was mesmerized by Lorca's "lively and eloquent hands," which seemed to flutter as quickly as his mind. Over dinner Lorca told endearing stories about Spain. He explained once how his mother had meticulously taught him American table manners in preparation for his trip to New York. But as a child, he added, he had been allowed to blow bubbles in his water glass. He laughed out loud at the memory. Brickell thought him a genius at conversation. Like so many others, however, he was struck by Lorca's mood swings. One moment he was a capricious child, regaling friends with his antics. Then suddenly he turned into an ageless creature "who had plumbed the depths of evil as often as he had soared to the heights of good."

It was this darker side of himself that Lorca continued to voice in his poetry. Long after midnight, in the solitude of his cramped room high above the city, he wrote. He produced more than a dozen poems during his three-month stay in John Jay Hall, including the final two sections of his "Ode to the Most Holy Sacrament of the Altar," and another pair of works on the subject of Christ. Nostalgia mingled with rage in these poems to yield both a searing critique of urban America and a woeful tribute to his departed youth.

Just two weeks after moving into John Jay Hall, Lorca wrote one of his most disturbing New York poems, "Childhood and Death," a work in which he imagined himself a little boy in a sailor's suit, drowned in a well:

> Drowned, yes, completely drowned, sleep, my child, sleep.
> Child defeated in grade school and in the waltz of the wounded rose,
> amazed by the dark dawning of the thighs' soft hair,
> amazed by his own man chewing tobacco in his left side.

Twice he included his name, "Federico," in the poem, but he later removed it, possibly because he did not wish to identify himself so closely with the dead boy, whose rat-eaten body lies alone at the bottom of the well, among "cold moss and tin lids." But the work's autobiographical references—to Lorca's boyhood failures in school and to his turbulent passage through puberty—are implicit. "Alone, here, I see they have closed the door on me," he writes. His boyhood has become nothing more than a rat scurrying "through a dark, dark garden," a rat that "between its tiny teeth" carries a golden streamer from a child's coffin. Shortly after completing the poem, Lorca sent it to his friend Rafael Martínez Nadal in Spain, "so you can see my state of mind," he wrote. When Nadal reminded Lorca of the poem years later, Lorca swore he never wanted to see it again.

Nadal was among the few correspondents to whom Lorca revealed the bleakness of his situation that fall. To others he painted a joyful picture of himself in New York, surrounded by American friends and making "rapid progress in English." His family, in particular, received detailed narratives of his prosperous life in Manhattan. "I am *more responsible* than ever," he said. He professed to live frugally. At John Jay Hall, he spent fifty-five cents a day on a meal that included "soup, a platter of meat with potatoes, peas, beets, and sauces, a piece of cake or apple pie, a glass of iced tea with lemon, and a cup of coffee with milk or a glass of milk." As a result of the good food, he was putting on weight.

But he found it impossible to live on the monthly allowance his father sent him. He repeatedly asked for more money—additional allowance funds, royalties from his books—so that he could reap every possible benefit from his visit abroad. He especially wanted to see theater in New York. By Spanish standards, the American stage was revolutionary, and Lorca soon realized its potential to influence his own work. "One must think about the theater of the future," he told his parents in October. "Everything that now exists in Spain is dead. Either the theater changes radically or it dies away forever. There is no other solution."

Although Broadway dazzled him, it was the city's fringe companies that most intrigued Lorca. He especially enjoyed black revues, where the actors were the best he had seen anywhere. He attended at least one performance of Chinese theater and came away thinking that Chinese drama was one of the world's great "blocks" of theatrical literature; the sparse settings and broad histrionics of the form confirmed Lorca's sense of the theater as artifice. The fact that he understood neither Chinese nor English scarcely mattered. He was entranced by the sheer spectacle of theater in New York, by the technological wizardry of American scenography and the high quality of American acting and directing. "New York is a unique place for taking the pulse of the new theatrical art," he said. Courageous, noncommercial companies, such as Eva Le Gallienne's Civic Repertory Theatre, thrived. Daring new plays were not only tolerated but honored. One year before Lorca's visit, the Theatre Guild premiered Eugene O'Neill's controversial nine-hour drama about sublimated passion, *Strange Interlude*; the play ran for over four hundred performances and received the 1928 Pulitzer prize. In Spain, such a work would almost certainly have been heavily censored or banned.

Lorca relished the freedom of the American theater. When some of his new acquaintances began talking about staging an English version of his play *Don Perlimplín*, he rejoiced. "Not only would it advance my career," he told his parents, "it would be beautiful to arrive in New York and have them perform what was shamefully banned in Spain or what no one wanted to put on 'because there's no audience for it.' " He also harbored hopes for New York productions of both *The Shoemaker's Prodigious Wife* and *The Billy Club Puppets*. But in the end nothing came of any of these projects.

Meanwhile, he began work on a new script in New York. He declined to elaborate on the nature of the play, except to say that it was linked to his quest for a "theater of the future." He was equally smitten by American movies, especially talking pictures, for which he had a childlike fascination. "In the talkies you hear sighs, the breeze, and even the faintest sounds, all faithfully reproduced," he said. In Spain, Lorca's passion for silent films had led him in 1928 to attempt a short prose piece on Charlie Chaplin, in which he defended the tenderness and sentimentality of the actor's art—his capacity for "unbridled weeping"—and contemplated Chaplin's androgynous nature.

In New York he went further and, with the help of a young Mexican-American artist named Emilio Amero, drafted a film script. One night after viewing a short, abstract film Amero had produced, Lorca chatted excitedly about Spain's vanguard cinema. Although he had not seen the film, he talked with some degree of familiarity about *Un Chien Andalou*; the controversial Dalí-Buñuel collaboration had opened that summer in Paris and been widely discussed in the Spanish press. With his friends' film evidently in mind, Lorca sat down with Amero shortly afterward and began outlining a screenplay. Each time an idea occurred to him, Lorca grabbed a pencil and a piece of paper and jotted it down. The next day he returned with more ideas. The completed script filled twelve small sheets of notebook paper.

As he struggled to transform his ideas into cinematic images, Lorca relied on Amero's superior knowledge of the medium. "Go ahead," he often said. "See what you can do with this. Maybe something will come of it." The finished script consisted of seventy-one separate episodes; Lorca titled it *Trip to the Moon*, possibly in homage to the Jules Verne film that played in Granada in Lorca's youth. But in contrast to Verne's more tangible journey into space, the voyage Lorca outlined in his screenplay is an erotically charged, often violent trip toward death. The script was a visual counterpart to his New York poems, especially those about childhood and death; in both works, sex obliterates childhood and is virtually indistinguishable from death.

Never had Lorca so explicitly detailed his morbid preoccupation with sex, a force he knew to be at once irresistible and deadly. In one frame of *Trip to the Moon*, the words "HELP! HELP!" are superimposed over an image of a woman's genitalia. In another sequence, a moon "fades into a male sex organ and then into a screaming mouth." Throughout the script, female sexuality is a cause for fear, while male sexuality is repressed. Union between male and female is impossible—as is love itself. In the film's closing frames, a cemetery blooms from the mouths of two lovers as they embrace, "and they are seen kissing over a tomb." The script's final, barren image shows a "landscape of a moon with trees swaying in the wind."

Trip to the Moon never made it to the screen. With his usual nonchalance, Lorca left the script with Amero and subsequently lost interest in the idea of producing a film. The medium did not suit him. "I need to be in touch with my audience," he remarked, and went on creating plays. His brief foray into the cinema evidently quelled his need to compete with Dalí and Buñuel. It also showed him provocative new ways of probing his mind.

His introspective existence further led Lorca to create a startling series of visual self-portraits during his stay in New York. Although he tried to dismiss these and other drawings as a simple pastime, they were in fact both a graphic companion to his American poems and a candid subtext to the cheerful letters he routinely sent home to his parents. In sketch after sketch he showed himself dwarfed by the vast American city and pursued by vile beasts. Almost invariably, his face is a featureless ovoid with blank eyes, dense black eyebrows, and a smattering of tiny crescent moons (in Spanish, *lunas*) in place of the moles (or *lunares*) that dotted his face in real life. Embryonic hands curl helplessly in the air; occasionally a cross bisects the composition.

Most of these images contain a chimerical beast that seems emblematic of both death and sexual instinct, and whose effect on Lorca is ambiguous. Sometimes the animal claws at the poet's face as he tries to protect himself. But in at least one self-portrait a weeping Lorca cradles the strange creature in his arms. The beast reappears in a series of large, carefully rendered color sketches. In one image the animal paws at a man's groin; in another, he lies menacingly beside the prone body of a woman who is bleeding from her genitals.

A year or so after leaving New York, Lorca gave one of his American self-portraits to a friend in Spain, who insisted she was unable to identify Lorca's face in the drawing. "What do you mean?" he asked. "You don't recognize the big eyebrows that are joined in the middle or the hair that's parted on both sides?" His friend took another look at the sketch and this time spotted Lorca's wide brow and crescent-shaped eyebrows. But there was little else in the demonic self-portrait to remind her of Lorca.

With the arrival of autumn, a "beautiful light" fell on Manhattan's streets and parks. Lorca began attending football games. The grace and virility of the sport attracted him. "Of course, I could never have been a player," he said to his family.

By late October his life abroad had settled into a familiar pattern. He spent part of his time reading novels and writing poems. Once a week he met with the chorus of the Spanish Institute to rehearse an upcoming program of Spanish folk music. He paid regular visits to his Spanish-speaking friends, and when Spanish celebrities such as the former bullfighter Ignacio Sánchez Mejías, who had played host to Lorca and his peers at the 1927 Góngora tricentennial in Seville, and the guitarist Andrés Segovia toured New York, Lorca helped welcome them. At an appearance by Sánchez Mejías, Lorca introduced the bull-fighter to his New York audience as a "pure hero" of the ring who had recently dedicated himself to literature, and was creating a "valiant, poetic, and highly imaginative" art with a notably Andalusian character. Of Segovia, whom he saw on numerous occasions, Lorca told his parents, "He has taken me to the homes of a couple of millionaires I didn't know, where I have witnessed some hilarious scenes from American life, all of which are very valuable to me."

He now knew his way around the city. Although he occasionally got lost, Lorca had lived in New York for five months and it longer frightened him. He hoped to stay on for at least two more months so that he could earn money on the lecture circuit. He even thought he might tour the western United States.

But on Tuesday, October 29, 1929, the New York Stock Exchange collapsed, and the city Lorca thought he understood plunged into chaos. Distraught crowds flocked to Wall Street, together with newsreel cameramen, reporters, mounted policemen, couriers, and hundreds of taxicabs. The roar of traders on the floor inside the Stock Exchange was audible a block away; a journalist compared the sound of the shouting to the cry of a dying animal. Between ten o'-clock and three in the afternoon that day, eight billion dollars vanished. Spectators absorbed the news with stunned disbelief. "There were no smiles," *The New York Times* reported. "There were no tears either. Just the camaraderie of fellow-sufferers."

At the height of the pandemonium, Lorca went to Wall Street with Ángel del Río. For once, the reality of New York outstripped his imagination. "I see it," he cried. "I understand it now." The sight of so many desperate human beings dazed him. He spent seven hours milling around in the crowd. "I just couldn't leave," he told his parents. "Everywhere one looked, there were men shouting and arguing like animals and women crying. Groups of Jews were screaming and wailing on the stairways and on every corner." People fainted, cars honked, telephones screamed. At one point Lorca encountered a friend who tearfully told him she had just lost her life savings. Lorca tried to console her.

On his way home, he came across a suicide victim. The man had leapt to his death from the upper floors of a midtown Manhattan hotel, and as Lorca approached the scene, "they were removing the cadaver. He was a very tall red-haired man, and all I can remember is his huge, floury white hands against the gray cement street," he reported matter-of-factly to his family. "This sight gave me a new vision of American civilization, and I found it all very logical. I don't mean that I liked it. But I watched it all in cold blood, and I am happy I witnessed it." Years later Lorca boasted that he had seen not one but six suicides on Black Tuesday.

Shortly after the Crash, Lorca told his parents that the collapse of the American stock market would have no bearing on the international economy. The reality of the situation interested him far less than its metaphorical implications. The spectacle of Black Tuesday confirmed his perception of the United States as a spiritless nation controlled by "two or three bankers." He later said he was "lucky" to have witnessed the Crash. No other event so shaped and focused his poetic concept of American civilization. Shocked by the economic crisis and the confusion it spawned, he began a new series of poems, works whose force and intensity startled his friends. By the end of 1929 he had completed at least five new poems. He was confident he would return to Spain with "two good books of poetry." He regarded his American verse as the best he had ever written. "I think everything of mine pales alongside these latest poems, which are, so to speak, *symphonic*, like the noise and complexity of New York."

As Lorca worked on his poetry, he carried battered copies of individual poems around with him in his pockets. Whenever possible, he read them to friends. Most listeners found the impromptu recitals electrifying. "His voice would rise to a shout and then fall to a whisper, like a sea which carried you along on its tide," Emilio Amero recalled. To Herschel Brickell, Lorca's fiery readings showed the degree to which America had "troubled his soul."

Eventually, what Lorca thought would be two books of American poems became a single collection entitled *Poet in New York*. Although the book remained unpublished until 1940, he devoted considerable time and energy to it in the 1930s, organizing and reorganizing its components and envisioning the collection in a number of different permutations. To audiences who heard him recite parts of the work in America and later in Spain, Lorca revealed a new self, a poet whose bitter account of urban America recalls "The moon! The police. The foghorns of the ocean liners! / Facades of rust, of smoke, anemones, rubber gloves."

In choosing the city as the essential theme and setting of his poems, he was knowingly heeding the example of Baudelaire, Poe, Eliot, Crane, and even his own compatriot Juan Ramón Jiménez, whose impressionistic 1917 evocation of New York City, *Diary of a Newly Wed Poet*, recounts the author's response to such sights as Broadway and the Manhattan skyline. But Lorca's take on American life is far more profound. He later spoke of his New York poems as representing an encounter between two poetic worlds—his own and New York's. He had no interest in writing a conventional narrative of his trip to America. "What I will give is my lyrical reaction," he said. His perspective was not that of a tourist but of a "man who looks up at the great mechanical workings of the elevated train and feels the sparks of burning coal fall into his eyes." He approached the task with the fury Rubén Darío had displayed in his 1903 diatribe against the United States, "To Roosevelt," a poem Lorca clearly had in mind as he labored over his New York collection, especially his odes.

In a departure from his previous work, Lorca wrote nearly all of his New York poetry in free verse. The poems' dense, at times hallucinatory imagery led many critics to suggest that with this collection he was trying to imitate Rafael Alberti's most recent book, *Upon the Angels,* an avant-garde work that differed markedly from Alberti's earlier, neopopular verse. Although Lorca refused to acknowledge any debt to Alberti, he was in all likelihood influenced by *Upon the Angels,* which appeared in Spain a few months before his departure for New York and sparked considerable interest among the country's literary elite. *Poet in New York* shares with Alberti's collection a certain dreamlike quality that justifiably prompted many readers to label both works surrealist.

But although influenced by surrealism, Lorca's New York poems owe more to Góngoran metaphor and cubist techniques of collage than to André Breton's radical ethos. Lorca was not one to subscribe to movements—especially one so dogmatic as surrealism. His American poems are their own creation. Each, he said, is a self-sufficient entity, an "escape" from reality, a poetic *hecho* or "event." While at times impenetrable, even to him, these poetic "events," Lorca explained, "respond to an exclusively poetic logic and follow the dense constructs of human emotion and the poem's architecture."

In the collection's best poems fact blends with fiction, and language with emotion, to yield both a public indictment of urban society and a private cry of despair. With his American poems, Lorca returned for the first time in nearly ten years to a first-person, confessional voice. The solitude of his experience abroad, coupled with his linguistic isolation, had forced him to look inward: "I, poet without arms, lost / in the vomiting multitude." The aloof, dispassionate voice of *Songs, Poem of the Deep Song,* and *Gypsy Ballads* no longer sufficed. If he was to decry an inhuman world, Lorca must acknowledge his own humanity. And yet, though grounded in reality, the embittered "I" of his New York poems is just as much an invention as the carefree "I" of the letters Lorca sent to his family from America.

His sense of rootlessness in New York fueled a poetic vision of an alien metropolis where life has no value: "What matters is this: emptied space. Lonely world. / River's mouth." Love exists merely in brief, unhappy encounters—often with sailors. Death is everywhere. (For a time, Lorca considered titling the collection *Introduction to Death.*) In a civilization numbed by cruelty, only pain "keeps everything awake." There is no possibility of redemption in Lorca's city, "only a crowd of laments / unbuttoning their clothes, waiting for the bullets."

Stripped of faith by his confrontation with America, robbed of identity, the protagonist of *Poet in New York* alludes no fewer than nine times to his own murder. Not since his earliest work—*Impressions and Landscapes* and his juvenilia—had Lorca painted so dire a portrait of the human race. Nor had he railed so furiously against the Catholic Church. In the Whitmanesque "Cry to Rome (From the Tower of the Chrysler Building)," a poem originally called "Ode to Injustice," Lorca scorns the Church—"the great dome / that military tongues anoint with oil"—and denounces its leader:

> But the man dressed in white
> knows nothing of the mystery of the wheat ear,
> or the moans of a woman giving birth,
> or the fact that Christ can still give water . . .

At the center of this punishing world is the innocent child Lorca yearned both to be and to engender. Lost, abandoned, drowned—the image of the child surfaces throughout the collection, a symbol of purity in a corrupt adult world. In an early draft of one poem, "Abandoned Church (Ballad of the Great War)," Lorca recalled the child he had literally helped to bury when he was four years old, his baby brother Luis, dead at the age of twenty months from some childhood malady and here transformed into the poet's son, a victim of the First World War, "lost in the arches, one Friday, Day of the Dead."

From the start of his American odyssey, Lorca had seized on childhood as a primary motif of his journey. The five-year-old Hungarian boy whom he had met while crossing the Atlantic—the "rose of Hungary who disappears into the belly of New York, seeking his fortune"—foreshadowed Lorca's own overseas quest, both real and metaphorical, for the self he had once been. Away from Spain, he wrestled not only with the loss of his boyhood innocence but with the implied sterility of his existence as a homosexual. In a sonnet entitled "Adam"—a poem Lorca wrote in Manhattan but ultimately chose to exclude from *Poet in New York*—he postulates the viability of two types of offspring: the blood-red, mortal child of flesh and veins, and the imagined, eternal child of art. The first is the product of a heterosexual "Adam" who "dreams in the fever of the clay / of a child who comes galloping / through the double pulse of his cheek." The second, and implicitly superior, child is the creation of a "dark, other Adam" who dreams "a neuter moon of seedless stone / where the child of light will burn."

Gradually, Lorca was coming to terms with the idea of himself as an "other Adam." Freed from the influence of family life and from the constraints of Spanish society, he became more outspoken in the United States, more willing to reveal himself through his work. It was above all the example of Whitman that showed him how to proceed. From conversations with his friend León Felipe, Lorca learned of Whitman's love for "comrades" and of his attempt to articulate that love in *Leaves of Grass*. Whitman complained that his "insolent poems" did not reflect the "real Me [who] still stands / untouched, untold, altogether unreached." But to Lorca, the American succeeded in forging a poetic language through which to convey the beauty of love between men. He grew to idolize Whitman, and in one of the longest, most explicit poems of his New York cycle, the "Ode to Walt Whitman," he voiced his admiration:

> Enemy of the satyr,
> enemy of the vine,
> and lover of bodies beneath rough cloth . . .

Begun in Manhattan and completed some three months after he left New York, Lorca's "Ode to Walt Whitman" expands on themes he had addressed more tentatively in such poems as "Song of the Little Pansy," his ode to Sesostris, and "Two Norms." The poem frankly confronts the issue of homosexual love, positing Whitman himself as an exemplar of such passion at its most sublime:

> . . . virile beauty,
> who among mountains of coal, billboards, and railroads,
> dreamed of becoming a river and sleeping like a river
> with that comrade who would place in your breast
> the small ache of an ignorant leopard.

But Whitman's dream is sullied by the "gray rats" of twentieth-century America, by the "machinery and lament" of urban New York, and most of all by the "faggots of the world, murderers of doves," who point their "stained fingers" at Whitman and cry, "He's one, too! That's right!"

Against the corrupt love of the "faggot" who flaunts his "tumescent flesh and unclean thoughts" in bordellos and bars, Lorca pits the virile example of Whitman, whose passion for his own sex is both honorable and good. Lorca hated the effeminate homosexual—perhaps because he feared such traits in himself.

Speaking in general of this type of man, he once said, "He amuses me with his womanish urge to wash, to iron and sew, to put on makeup, to wear skirts, to speak with effeminate gestures and movements. But I don't like it." Whitman allowed Lorca to suggest another ideal: "Adam of blood, Macho, / man alone at sea, Walt Whitman, lovely old man." If homosexual passion does not lead to the procreation of children, so be it; in a world where life is rounded by death, all types of love are noble:

> Man is able, if he wishes, to guide his desire
> through a vein of coral or a nude as blue as the sky.
> Tomorrow, loves will become stones, and Time
> a breeze that drowses in the branches.

On December 7, Lorca's sister Concha married Manuel Fernández-Montesinos in Granada. From New York, Lorca wrote to say that he hoped the newlyweds would not wait long to start a family, "since Paco and I are such drones and haven't married and had children."

He was determined to remain in the United States until his lecture tour materialized and he earned some money from it. The Christmas season arrived, and with it the odd spectacle of pine trees in storefronts, private homes, and even Times Square. Privately, Lorca thought the holiday simply an excuse for American Christians to flaunt their "scorn for the Jews . . . who bear the brunt of business." But he enjoyed the festivities. He spent Christmas Eve with friends at the Brickells' lavish apartment. At midnight the group attended Mass at Saint Paul the Apostle Catholic Church. "What a beautiful Mass!" Lorca cried afterward. Later, over hotcakes and maple syrup at a Childs restaurant, he regaled his friends with stories of Christmas in Spain. In a subsequent letter home he commented on the high incidence of alcohol poisoning in New York City on Christmas Day; as usual, he inflated the facts to make his point.

Shortly after the holidays, Lorca announced to his family that in March he planned to go to Cuba to give a series of lectures. On January 21, at Vassar College, he delivered the first of his long-postponed American lectures. He wrangled with Vassar over his fee. Citing the current economic crisis, the college had dropped its original offer of $100 to $75. Lorca was furious. He told Professor Margarita de Mayo of the Spanish Department that he had expected to be "treated with the proper consideration, but I see that I was wrong." Nevertheless, he agreed to go through with the lecture. "I'll make the sacrifice," he told de Mayo. Afterward, he informed his parents that "three hundred" girls, some of them "very pretty," had attended his lecture. He dismissed the talk itself, on Spanish folk songs, as "a joke." But as he explained later, "In America you can say anything you want to, since, with a few exceptions, they're a little slow." He intended to use the money he'd earned to buy a pair of shoes and a suit, "because I'm now *stark naked. Naked!*"

In February, at Columbia University, he gave his second and final American lecture, a revised version of his talk "Imagination, Inspiration, and Escape." New York's Spanish-speaking *La Prensa* published a glowing account of the occasion. Lorca clipped the review and sent it home to his parents, with an apology for the accompanying photograph. It made him look uglier than he was, he said—when in fact he had recently been told by an elderly New York woman that he was handsome. "And in the picture I'm sending you I look horribly ugly . . . and I'm not so ugly . . . perhaps a little . . . but not that much."

Lorca admitted to his parents that he lacked the character to be a professional lecturer. It was "too serious" a business for him, he said, "and it seems useless." Still, if he was to earn his keep in Cuba by going on the lecture circuit, he must learn to adapt.

On March 4, 1930, he boarded a train for Florida. To a friend he confessed that he wanted to make this part of the trip by train because the ocean frightened him.

In Miami, where he spent a day, Lorca basked in the summerlike air and marveled at the number of "umbrellas and cars and naked women" to be found on the beach. By the time he boarded his ship for Cuba, Manhattan was already a distant memory. He later spoke of his trip to Cuba as a journey from night into day, from darkness into sun. As his ship sailed toward the Antilles, New York's "edges and rhythm, form and anguish" seemed to vanish into a welter of blue sky. "The Chrysler Building defends itself from the sun with its huge silver beak, and bridges, ships, railways, and men seem deafened and chained: chained by a cruel economic system whose throat must soon be cut."

And yet New York had given him what he later described as "the most useful experience of my life." The harsh American city had delivered him from an abyss. He had arrived in Manhattan nine months earlier, unable to write, fearful of love, still shuddering from the effects of fame, and now, in the spring of 1930, he was writing prolifically and dreaming of writing more. He was even able to imagine himself in love. Three weeks before leaving New York, on February 13, the day before Valentine's Day, he composed a love poem, "Little Viennese Waltz," his most intensely homoerotic work to date. To the lilting pulse

of a waltzlike meter, the poet offers himself—his beautiful self—in the act of
love:

> In Vienna I will dance with you
> in a costume with
> a river's head.
> See how the hyacinths line my banks!
> I will leave my mouth between your legs,
> my soul in photographs and lilies,
> and in the dark wake of your footsteps,
> my love, my love, I will have to leave
> violin and grave, the ribbons of the waltz.

His friend Ángel del Río later said he thought Lorca discovered "new layers of
his most private personality" during his stay in New York. Del Río refrained
from elaborating on his statement, except to note, with discretion, that Lorca's
"emotional crisis" the previous year had touched on "delicate fibers of his personality, problems which cannot be hastily appraised or dismissed."

Lorca's self-enforced withdrawal from the world as he knew it—from Spain,
from the Spanish language, from family and friends—had ultimately led him
back to himself, and from there to others. He left the United States with renewed faith in his work, a more compassionate understanding of his sexuality,
and a newfound enthusiasm for life. He told his parents he was already planning his next trip abroad—"to Russia." This time he intended to pay for the
journey himself.

As his ship sailed into Havana's bottle-shaped bay, the colors of the warm
Caribbean island gradually came into view: yellows, pinks, phosphorescent
greens, and the relentless blue of the sky. Lorca was reminded of his native Andalusia. Palm trees were dancing in the wind. Rising like a mirage from the
azure water of the bay, Havana itself stood before him: white, sun-struck, shim-
mering.

CHAPTER 15

SPANISH AMERICA

1930

Lorca's first impulse on arriving in Cuba was to fling his coat and gloves to the ground in joy. Suddenly the world was familiar. Cries of *Oye, chico!* rang out from the quayside. On Havana's cobblestoned streets, the smell of cigars mingled with the aroma of coffee and magnolias. There were cafés and fountains, tiled patios and tall windows with balconies.

Nearly everything reminded him of home. The sky was the blue of the sky over Málaga; the sea was as beautiful as the Mediterranean—except that its hues seemed more "violent." In downtown Havana, Lorca heard people singing the same slow, sad habaneras that his aunt Isabel and cousin Aurelia used to sing in Fuente Vaqueros. Cuba was much as Lorca had imagined it as a boy, peering into the pungent cigar boxes his father received regularly from the faraway island. Inside, each cigar box had contained a vibrant picture of palm-lined roads and dark tobacco leaves, a profusion of gold medallions, and a portrait of Romeo and Juliet locked in an embrace. Somehow this incongruous assortment of images struck Lorca as apt, and in one of his first letters home to his family, he described Cuba as "caressing, smooth, terribly sensual."

A small gathering of Cuban writers and journalists greeted Lorca's ship when it docked in Havana on March 7, 1930. The city's leading newspaper, the *Diario de Marina*, published a front-page article heralding the arrival of Spain's "most prestigious" contemporary poet. Lorca attributed such attention to the "exaggerated" nature of Havanans. But he welcomed the fuss. In Cuba, adoration burned as brightly as the sun. Lorca shed the solitude of his New York days as eagerly as he shed his winter coat. He donned a white linen suit, turned his face toward the light, and settled into the relaxed rhythms of island existence.

What was to have been a brief visit to Cuba—a short lecture tour sponsored by the Hispanic-Cuban Institute of Culture—quickly turned into a three-month stay. Even then, Lorca found it difficult to leave. "I've spent the happiest days of my life here," he said gratefully. Within five days of his arrival he gave two lectures in Havana's Teatro Principal de la Comedia. He promptly became the toast of the town. Unlike other lecturers, who wore sober suits and stood stiffly behind podiums, Lorca strode onstage in brightly colored sweaters and ties, and struck up a jovial rapport with his listeners. During his first talk, he announced that as a student in Madrid he had often parodied the boring speakers he had been forced to hear at the Residencia. In Cuba, he said, "I'll parody myself." Audiences loved him. At the ticket booth, long lines formed for his next lectures.

He had boundless energy. On the night before his third Havana lecture, he stayed up until dawn, drinking rum and reciting poetry with several Cuban acquaintances. In the morning Lorca briskly took the stage at the Teatro Principal, sat down at a piano, and with "lightness and ease" launched into his musical lecture on Spanish lullabies. His exhausted companions from the previous evening looked on with amazement.

Lorca "doesn't lend himself, he gives himself," wrote the author of a long tribute in the monthly avant-garde journal *Revista de Avance*, one of Cuba's more prominent literary publications. "He is bursting with answers as well as questions. He knows everything and knows nothing. He has a hollow in the palm of each hand for the golden orb of his beliefs, and his curiosity is like that of Adam." During his stay in Cuba, the *Revista* published a number of Lorca's works, including two New York poems, and issued flattering accounts of his lectures. Other magazines followed suit. Lorca could not have gone unnoticed if he had tried.

Through the auspices of the *Revista*, he met most of the country's young poets, essayists, and journalists, men who shared his enthusiasm for the avant-garde and his passion for verse. During their first encounter, over lunch, Lorca lifted a glass of rum to his eyes and after a long pause said to poet Nicolás Guillén, "This is called seeing life rum-colored." Guillén was entranced. Everything about Lorca, he thought, inspired one to love life and to revere art.

Lorca carried scraps of paper in his pockets for jotting down ideas and observations, the seeds of poems. He seized any opportunity to recite his verse to new friends. He was especially eager to present his American poems. Listeners in Cuba responded much as they had in New York, with astonishment and awe. One month after his arrival, word of the startling new collection appeared in Havana's *Diario de Marina*. The paper reported that Lorca had worked "like a Benedictine" on the poems, revising key words four and five times until the ensemble achieved its quality of "naked and solitary beauty." Each manuscript erasure represented a "long, internal struggle."

Midway through his stay in Havana, Lorca's old friend Adolfo Salazar, the musician and critic, arrived in Cuba from Spain to give a lecture series. Salazar immediately went in search of Lorca and found him in his room at the Union Hotel, reclining on the bed in a yellow bathrobe while reciting verse to a dozen or so young men. "What in the hell are you reading?" Salazar asked.

"They're my New York poems," Lorca said. "Sit down. Listen."

Salazar was stunned. The radical nature of the new poems took him utterly by surprise. And yet Lorca himself appeared unchanged. He was a bit older perhaps (his hairline had begun to recede), but, to Salazar, he seemed "more Andalusian" than ever. He obviously felt at home in Cuba.

Lorca's room at the Union Hotel, like his rooms at the Residencia in Madrid, fast became one of the most popular spots in Havana. Often by the time Lorca woke late in the morning, visitors—most, if not all, of them young male writers—were waiting for him in the hallway outside his door. If the guests were to his liking, Lorca invited them in to talk while he washed and dressed. He welcomed their attention and clearly enjoyed the promiscuous nature of the setting; Havana had rid him of the inhibitions that constrained his behavior in Spain. One observer described the ritual as a "scene from an Athenian gymnasium."

Lorca relished his sudden status as an international celebrity. To a young man from rural Cuba who introduced himself as a "poet," Lorca smiled indulgently and said, "Local, I take it?" He flirted openly with the young women who begged him to sign their autograph books. "If you write to me in Spain, your mother won't find out," he told one girl. His social invitations were so numerous he could not keep track of them. Once, on his way home from an event, someone asked him where he had just been. Lorca shrugged and replied, "I've forgotten." He told his parents it would take "three or four hours" simply to clip all the newspaper articles that had been written about him. "I am going to give more lectures than I thought," he added, "and that is the proof of my success here." Ultimately he gave seven talks in Cuba, all of them versions of lectures he had first delivered in Spain.

But even he grew tired of the incessant attention. Scarcely able to take a walk without attracting a crowd, he sometimes simply disappeared. Rumor had it he occasionally slipped off to the black *barrios* near the docks. He was fascinated by black life in Havana and later declared that Cuban blacks, unlike those he had seen in New York, were "without tragedy." He attached little importance to the island's existing racial tensions and depicted himself as a hero for having insisted on one occasion that blacks be allowed to attend one of his lectures—a privilege normally denied them. Whether or not he was telling the truth, Lorca seemed eager to impress others with the degree of his racial tolerance. He sent his family a photograph of himself with his arms draped affectionately around three black children, and in letters home he talked avidly about black culture.

But he could be condescending. He told his parents that Cuban women were the most beautiful women in the world because they all bore a "drop of Negro blood," and the "blacker" they were, the "better." In a gesture more revealing of his ambivalence toward women, he sent Rafael Martínez Nadal a crude sketch of a black woman with coiled hair, thick lips, and hoop earrings. Beneath the drawing he wrote, "Oh, Cuba! Oh rhythm of dry seeds! / Oh, hot waist and drop of wood! / The blacks are coming to adore this goddess, this Saint Barbara of the tremulous cunt. That's why I am sending her to you. Perhaps she'll serve as an amulet."

By the end of his stay, at least one local newspaper reported that Lorca had "gone native" for Cuban culture, and Lorca agreed. He regarded the island as a paradise. He loved its orchids and sugarcane stalks, the tropical-fruit flavors of its ice cream and the exotic names of its desserts. In a restaurant he once wrapped a napkin around his head like a turban and clapped his hands to summon a waiter. He then slowly intoned the name of a dish he wished to order: "Cham-po-la de gua-ná-ba-ná!" He had never heard of a more euphonic refreshment, he said.

During his three-month visit, Lorca took part in Havana's Easter week celebrations and went on a crocodile hunt in the countryside, a spectacle he described as "a bit scary and very dangerous." But he claimed to have acquitted himself with "cold-bloodedness." He sought opportunities to meet ordinary Cuban citizens: fishermen, busboys, poverty-stricken villagers struggling to survive under dictator Gerardo Machado's corrupt regime. While in Havana, Lorca voiced his support for members of the Cuban opposition and proclaimed his hatred of all dictatorships. In a token show of childlike enthusiasm for the cause of social reform, he took part in a local telephone strike.

His remarks on dictatorships had as much, if not more, to do with Spain than with Cuba. In the wake of the international economic crisis triggered by the Crash of 1929, disgruntled Spaniards had taken to the streets of Madrid the previous fall—while Lorca was still in New York—demanding an end to General Primo de Rivera's six-year dictatorship. "What will become of Spain?" Lorca had asked his parents in December. In January, Primo de Rivera had stepped down and fled to Paris. He died two months later of diabetic complications, during Lorca's first weeks in Havana. Spain itself remained in a state of unrest, and Lorca worried about his country's future. Although the king, Alfonso XIII, retained control of the government, there were renewed calls for an end to the monarchy and growing appeals for the establishment of a Spanish republic. "What's happening over there is a volcano!" Lorca told his family.

He ended most of his days in Havana in a café or bar, listening to Cuban music. He especially liked the Cuban *son*, a sinuous, rumbalike dance accompanied by marimbas, bongo drums, and maracas. At once African and Spanish, the *son* possessed a lush, tropical sound that Lorca found mesmerizing. Occasionally he sat down at a piano and tried to replicate the music.

The *son* inspired the only poem Lorca is known to have written in Cuba, "Son de negros en Cuba," or "Blacks Dancing to Cuban Rhythms." Fusing childhood impressions of Cuba and contemporary images of the island, he produced a songlike poem in which figures from his father's cigar boxes combine with tobacco plants, crocodiles, palm trees, and rum to create a moving tribute to a country Lorca had come to love. With its incantatory refrain—"I'm going to Santiago"—the work evokes the hypnotic throb of the *son*. Lorca evidently carried a copy of the poem with him in his pocket when he visited the city of Santiago, on Cuba's southeastern coast, to give a reading in early April.

He published the work that spring in the Cuban journal *Musicalia*, whose editors, Antonio and María Muñoz de Quevedo, befriended Lorca during his stay in Havana. He spent long hours in the Quevedo home, playing the couple's piano and socializing with their musical and artistic friends and acquaintances. Although residents of Cuba, the Quevedos were Spanish by birth, and counted Manuel de Falla among their close friends. Like others entranced by Lorca's talent and charm, Antonio Quevedo kept a diary in which he recorded Lorca's activities and moods. Later, Quevedo published an account of Lorca's stay in Cuba—much as Philip Cummings and Herschel Brickell would each publish their recollections of Lorca's visit to America. The older and more famous he became, the more Lorca resented this sort of scrutiny. In Havana,

Quevedo's devotion to him became so suffocating that on occasion Lorca fled the man's presence.

Late at night, as moonlit figures strolled the waterfront in linen suits and satin pumps, and sea breezes washed the city, an air of what one visitor described as "invitation and surrender" gripped Havana. With twenty-six-year-old Luis Cardoza y Aragón, a Guatemalan diplomat whom Lorca had met in Havana, and with whom he appeared to enjoy a platonic friendship, Lorca frequently shared a late dinner over wine, followed by a tour of the city's exuberant night life. According to Cardoza y Aragón, Lorca reveled in Havana's "magnificent sensuality."

More than once, the two men attended a raucous cabaret at the Teatro Alhambra, where performers ridiculed the Cuban government and staged pornographic vignettes before a bellowing, all-male audience. Lorca relished the place. It typified the kind of raw theatrical fare he longed to see in Spain. With Cardoza y Aragón, he began planning his own cabaret sketch, an adaptation of the Book of Genesis for music hall. But the project, like so many others, came to nothing.

Knowing Lorca's penchant for the city's libertine night life, Cardoza y Aragón took him one night to a gaudy Havana brothel. As they stood together in the brothel's huge salon, with its mirrored walls and assortment of naked and scantily clad prostitutes, Lorca asked, "Why aren't there any boys?" To Cardoza y Aragón, his homosexuality was "patent." At one point, Lorca revealed to Luis that he had gone swimming in Cuba with a group of naked black men who later invited him to a baptism and wedding. That he should have done so was not surprising, but that he should relate the story with such candor—even to a close friend—startled Cardoza y Aragón.

If New York had nudged Lorca toward an acceptance of his sexuality, Cuba allowed him to celebrate it. During his visit to the island, he was rumored to have had numerous liaisons, and even to have been briefly detained in jail for a sexual indiscretion. He was indisputably involved with a handsome twenty-year-old man of mixed racial origin named Lamadrid, and his friendship with another young man, Juan Ernesto Pérez de la Riva, raised many eyebrows, including those of the young man's parents, who forbade their son to see Lorca once they realized Lorca's sexual orientation. In a series of Cuban photographs, Lorca poses happily beside an unidentified young man whose thin, polished face and provocative gaze are reminiscent of Salvador Dalí's. Another snapshot shows a radiant Lorca at the Havana Yacht Club, wearing a dark pin-striped jacket and light-colored slacks, surrounded by five men in skimpy bathing trunks.

While in Cuba, Lorca began writing the most audacious play of his career, a complex, multifaceted work that boldly explores the nature of homosexual passion. He told Cardoza y Aragón that he intended to create the sort of theater no one had yet had the courage to create, to write a play that would make Oscar Wilde look insignificant, like "some sort of obese, pusillanimous queen." In his room in downtown Havana, Lorca filled seven pages of hotel letterhead with the play's opening moments. Although he did not finish the script in Cuba, the play was clearly a result of his visit to the New World, a response to the personal as well as aesthetic discoveries Lorca made overseas. In New York, he had witnessed a revolutionary new kind of theater. In Cuba, he learned not only to accept his homosexuality but to rejoice in it. His new play *El Público*—literally, *The Audience*—was "unproduceable," he said later, because it spoke a truth no one wanted to hear. Even in Havana, friends to whom he read fragments of the script found it disturbing.

Among those to hear parts of the play were members of Havana's eccentric Loynaz family, two brothers and two sisters who lived in one of the city's more opulent neighborhoods. Their extravagant home, which Lorca nicknamed "my haunted house," was crammed with costumes and curios dating back to the sixteenth century. Lorca spent many afternoons there, writing, playing the piano, drinking whiskey and soda, and reciting his work to the Loynaz siblings, who like the Quevedos were a vital part of Cuba's intellectual and artistic world. To the bewilderment of young Flor Loynaz, Lorca sometimes plucked a manuscript from his pocket after eating a greasy slice of mortadella, then proceeded to read aloud from the page. He didn't mind soiling his work.

During his visits to the Loynaz family, Lorca worked on *The Audience*. The house and its unorthodox inhabitants seem to have inspired parts of his script. He set one scene among Roman ruins reminiscent of the statuary that stood in the Loynaz garden. Throughout the play, actors don masks and disguises, blurring the line between truth and fiction much as the Loynaz siblings did whenever they pulled out their trunks of costumes and masqueraded as Indians or peasants. But when Lorca read segments of the play to the family, they were perplexed by the work and laughed at parts of it. Unperturbed, he went on reading.

Both Flor Loynaz and her sister, Dulce María, a writer, remembered Lorca as a charming but unattractive man whose dark, beautiful eyes were his best feature. "He was very open and always very happy," Loynaz recalled. "I think that for him it was a sin to be sad." Nevertheless, Lorca fell prey to strange fears in Cuba. For the first and only time in his life, he became obsessed by the possibility that he might have cancer, and he underwent surgery to have several moles removed. When Dulce María Loynaz visited him in the hospital, she discovered Lorca lying in bed with tiny burns and incisions scattered across his skin. Brightly, he told Dulce María that he had "plugged up all the cracks where the dreaded disease could sneak in." He entertained other visitors by singing Cuban songs. To Adolfo Salazar he revealed that he had been told he might someday contract stomach cancer. "But just think! To die of cancer!" he exclaimed. "It must be such a beautiful disease. Cancer is an astronomical name. So it would be rather like suffering from a lovely constellation."

Lorca spent his final day in Cuba, June 12, with Adolfo Salazar and Flor Loynaz. Over lunch in his hotel, he talked calmly and read poems to his friends. He seemed content to linger for hours. After a while, Salazar, who was to accompany Lorca on the long journey home to Spain, began to fret about missing their ship. Finally he spoke up. "Federico, it's getting late. You'll miss the boat. Send someone to bring down your luggage."

"I haven't packed yet," Lorca said. Dumbfounded, Salazar and Loynaz rushed upstairs to his room, filled what little luggage Lorca had, tossed it into Loynaz's car, and hurried to the pier.

From the deck of his ship, the *Manuel Arnus*, Lorca posed for a photograph. His suit was rumpled, and he held a pipe in his hand as he gazed soberly at the camera. A week earlier he had turned thirty-two. He had been away from Spain for one year. As his ship pulled slowly away from its berth, he remained on deck, waving to Flor Loynaz. She watched until he vanished.

At sea, Lorca resumed work on his "Ode to Walt Whitman." He finished the poem on June 15. Together with *The Audience*, the ode would stand as a testament to the emotional and sexual metamorphosis he had undergone in America. He remained deeply protective of both works, reading each only to trusted friends. He never published his ode to Whitman in Spain. He knew the sort of climate to which he was returning.

On June 19, the *Manuel Arnus* docked briefly in New York City before crossing the Atlantic to Spain. While his fellow passengers went sightseeing in New York, Lorca stayed onboard, having neglected to secure the proper documents for entering the United States. Instead, he sent a telegram to his friends in the city, begging them to "come see me." When the other passengers returned to the *Manuel Arnus* later that afternoon, they found the ship's salon packed with Lorca's friends, including a number of Columbia University students who had known the poet through his work as director of the Mixed Choruses of the Spanish Institute. Lorca sat at the piano, singing.

At least one friend who came to see him that day was horrified by the change she perceived since his visit to Cuba. "It's just as well you couldn't come," Norma Brickell wrote afterward to another of Lorca's New York acquaintances. "He's not our Federico any more, but a very different person. Wholly male, and very vulgar."

CHAPTER 16

AUDIENCE

1930-31

The moment he returned to Granada, Lorca began plotting his next visit to America. He found it all but impossible to describe the "long and splendid trip" he had just concluded. "*Ay Ay Ay Ay Ay!!* I'm dying!" he complained by letter to Rafael Martínez Nadal as he sat one day beneath a fig tree in the *vega*, struggling to find words to express himself. "My flesh is shattered from the beauty of America and above all the beauty of Havana."

Abroad, he told Nadal, he had written a number of "scandalous poems and scandalous theater, too," and he intended to return to the United States in January. "That will tell you everything. It's easy to get produced in New York." In the meantime he desperately wanted to read his new drama, which possessed a "frankly homosexual theme," to certain friends in Madrid. "I think it's my best poem," he said, adding mischievously, "Here in Granada I'm having fun with some delicious things as well. There's a little bullfighter . . ."

A Granadan priest who had known Lorca in his university days spotted him on the street one day after his return from America, and was surprised by the change in Lorca's appearance. Instead of the simple ties and slim black suits he had worn in the 1920s, Lorca sported a brightly colored shirt and baggy jacket and pants. The priest asked if New York had wrought the same change to his personality. "No," Lorca answered happily. "I'm still the same. New York's asphalt and petroleum weren't able to change me."

But he was mistaken to believe the experience had left him unmarked. Lorca returned to Spain a brasher, more sardonic man. Shortly after his arrival he wrote to Salvador Dalí—their first correspondence in nearly two years—urging the artist to join him in New York the following January. "You could stay there for six months and then return to Paris or you could travel to Moscow with me," Lorca suggested. "I am going to have an exhibition in New York as I already have a gallery and an enormous quantity of idiot friends, millionaire pansies and ladies who buy new paintings and will make our winter a pleasant one. You know how I can turn on the charm."

His family rejoiced to have Lorca home again. He settled easily back into the routines of country life at the Huerta de San Vicente: the daily trek into town to retrieve his mail, the late nights reading or writing in his room, the timeworn methods of preserving food and laundering clothes (no more "terrible washing machines" to destroy his socks, as in New York). He padded about the house in his pajamas, content to play the piano or indulge in childlike games, even at thirty-two, while the rest of his family went about their business. Neighbors later recalled the time Lorca substituted cornflowers for roses in his mother's table arrangement, and the day he delivered an impromptu sermon from the balcony of his room.

From America, Lorca had followed his family's activities closely during the previous year. He had gently encouraged his brother to "keep up his spirits" while preparing to take a set of qualifying exams, and he had sent effusive congratulations to his sister Concha upon her marriage to Manolo Montesinos. The couple were now expecting their first child. But it was his mother he had missed the most. Jubilant at being back in her presence, he told a friend that summer that he loved to put his arms around his gray-haired mother, hoist her in the air, and rock her like a little girl. She was so tiny, he said, that lifting her was easy. "Federico, by God, you're killing me!" Vicenta Lorca would squeal as her son whirled her about in his arms. When his mother lay down to take a nap, Lorca would softly wave a fan over her until she fell asleep, so that the flies didn't bother her.

Throughout the summer the entire family kept a close watch on the country's unfolding political crisis. In the wake of Primo de Rivera's resignation and death earlier in the year, King Alfonso XIII had clung to power despite cries for his removal. Recently the king had appointed a new military dictator, but neither man enjoyed the support of the Spanish people. Even the Church and the army opposed the arrangement. Daily the situation grew more unstable. At the Huerta de San Vicente, the Lorca family pored over each edition of the liberal *Defensor de Granada*, whose editor, Constantino Ruiz Carnero, a former member of the Rinconcillo, had been one of Lorca's good friends in adolescence. The paper consistently expressed its disapproval of the monarchy and its support for a Spanish republic—a position that Lorca's family, and in particular his seventy-one-year-old father, embraced. Close family friend Fernando de los Ríos was a leading advocate of the republican cause.

Lorca himself remained more absorbed by work than by politics. Within weeks of arriving home he resumed work on his play *The Audience.* By August 22 he had finished a first draft of the script. In early October he returned to Madrid, glowing with enthusiasm, and announced to journalist Miguel Pérez Ferrero of the *Heraldo de Madrid* that he had written a new drama. "It consists," he said, "of six acts and a murder."

"For whom is it intended—not the murder, but the work itself?" Pérez Ferrero inquired.

"I don't know if it can actually be produced. The main characters in the play are horses."

"Marvelous, Federico," said the journalist.

In Madrid, friends noticed a change in Lorca. The poet Luis Cernuda met him by chance at the home of a mutual acquaintance and thought he perceived a "greater decisiveness" in Lorca's manner. "It was as if something once intimate and secret in him had been affirmed." As always, Lorca played the piano that afternoon, but to Cernuda he seemed more sensual, less melancholy, than before. His thick face and plain features somehow "ennobled themselves" as he performed. When he finished, he folded his hands as if in prayer. "The rite had ended," Cernuda wrote eight years later, recalling the magic of Lorca's presence.

Even Lorca's former roommate José Antonio Rubio Sacristán, whose own journey to New York earlier in the year had coincided with Lorca's, thought him altered since his return. Sacristán became convinced that Lorca's flight to America was precipitated by a need "to recognize his nature and accept it." Following the trip, Lorca seemed less secretive about his sexuality. To Sacristán, the difference could be summarized in one word. Lorca was more "cynical."

Equally unsettling was the change in his writing. As soon as he returned to Madrid, he began pulling copies of his New York poems from his pockets and reading them to friends. He bragged about his achievement abroad. To an acquaintance who asked what he had accomplished overseas, Lorca responded, "I've done the most difficult thing. I've been a poet in New York."

With earlier works, he had relied primarily on his voice to convey the essence of a given poem. With his American poetry Lorca furrowed his brow, lifted his head, and gestured vigorously with one hand. When he finished, he sat back quietly and took a sip of whiskey or cognac, as if the effort of reciting his work had completely fatigued him. One evening a listener commented on the enormous physical effort the readings seemed to require. "I have to defend these poems against incomprehension, dilettantism, and benevolent smiles," Lorca explained.

Late one night he read *The Audience* to Carlos and Bebé Morla Lynch and a group of friends who were gathered in their elegant Madrid apartment. When Lorca finished, the room fell silent. One man confessed that he had understood nothing of the play. Bebé Morla Lynch cried out in dismay, "Federico! You don't honestly intend for that to be staged! It's impossible! Aside from the scandal it would provoke, it can't be staged!" Her husband said nothing. The play so disturbed Carlos Morla Lynch that when he eventually published a revised version of the diary he had kept during these years, he eliminated any mention of *The Audience*.

Later that evening, Lorca strolled along Madrid's darkened streets with his friend Rafael Martínez Nadal. "They haven't understood anything, or else they were shocked, and I can understand it," Lorca said. "The work is very difficult and at the moment unproduceable, they're right. But in ten or twenty years it will be a great success. You'll see." In fact, more than fifty years passed before *The Audience* premiered in Madrid—and even then, many who saw the play found it baffling.

Because *The Audience* remained unproduced in his lifetime, Lorca was unable to revise the script in rehearsal, as he did with other plays. Nor did he leave precise instructions as to the arrangement of the drama's various parts. The existing manuscript, which remained for years in Martínez Nadal's possession, lacks at least one scene, and the placement of another scene—the short, masquelike "Song of the Idiot Shepherd"—is uncertain. Lorca may have meant this interlude to serve as a Shakespearean prologue to the play itself, a witty summation of the work's central preoccupation: the role of artifice in both theater and society.

At first glance, *The Audience* appears to be scarcely more than a miscellany of loosely connected images and ideas. The dialogue often seems arbitrary, and the play's visual elements incongruous. In one stage direction, Lorca calls for an office to have "a great hand printed on the wall" and X rays for windows. The play's coherence and meaning come not from its narrative structure but from a quasi-expressionistic accumulation of concepts and symbols. Throughout the script Lorca repeats lines, actions, and images, so that characters echo one another in voice and appearance. The sense of metamorphosis, of one thing mystically becoming another, is continual.

Spectacle outweighs dialogue to such an extent that at times *The Audience* is more like cinema than theater. Characters change costume instantly by passing behind screens; empty masks bleat like lambs; a "slow shower of rigid white gloves" falls from the sky. For years Lorca had been moving in the direction of a more spectacle-based theater, but only *Don Perlimplín* had approached the level of visual splendor called for in *The Audience*. How Lorca intended for some of the play's more preposterous stage effects to be carried out is unclear. Even he declared the script to be unproduceable.

But by placing such emphasis on scenic illusion, he was able to question the very nature of theater. The issue had obsessed him for years. In a brief dramatic sketch undertaken in adolescence, he had explored the inherent conflict between stage and audience. "The drama," he wrote in a stage direction to the earlier sketch, "ought to take place within the audience, not the characters."

In *The Audience* he expands on this idea. It is Lorca's most radical play, his most daring departure from conventional dramaturgy. Born, in part, of his exposure to New York's dynamic theater scene, *The Audience* constitutes Lorca's fiercest challenge to the bourgeois crowds who filled Spain's theaters with their hidebound taste and polite expectations. "One must destroy the theater or live in the theater!" cries a character in the play. The line echoes what Lorca himself said to his parents from New York: "Either the theater changes radically, or it dies away forever."

With this play, Lorca called for nothing less than the abolition of the theater as he knew it—the "open air theater" of lies and appearances. In its place he proposes a revolutionary new "theater beneath the sand," a theater capable of unmasking society's most repellant truths. Heeding the example of authors he had admired since childhood—Goethe, Shakespeare, Calderón—he envisions the theater as a metaphor for the world. In doing so, his appeal for theatrical truth becomes a broader cry for human truth.

The Audience opens with a straightforward premise: a theater company has decided to stage an experimental production of *Romeo and Juliet*, in which the two protagonists are to be played, respectively, by a man of thirty and a boy of fifteen, who in "real life" are genuinely in love. From this simple foundation Lorca constructs a maze of images and actions through which the play's characters are led to investigate the nature of desire, and in particular homosexual desire. The play's two protagonists, Enrique and Gonzalo, occupy the work's moral center. Although their appearances and even identities shift throughout the drama, they remain essentially the same two men.

Alone among a cast of role-playing cowards, Gonzalo speaks the truth. He is virile and brave, a Whitmanesque homosexual who boasts of being "more of a man than Adam." Publicly Gonzalo declares his passion for Enrique and demands that they display their love onstage, thereby inaugurating the "true theater, the theater beneath the sand." But Enrique, whose several guises include that of a stage director, resists him. Timid and duplicitous, he denies any attachment to Gonzalo and announces that his theater "will always be in the open air!" To prove his heterosexual vigor, Enrique calls out for Helen—the quintessential woman of ancient mythology, Faust's feminine ideal. "She loved me greatly when my theater was in the open air," he insists.

Intent on exposing Enrique's hypocrisy, Gonzalo retaliates. "I've got to put you on the stage whether you like it or not. You've made me suffer too much." He calls for a folding screen to be brought out. The play's most commanding image, the screen functions throughout the drama as a kind of lie detector; no one can pass behind it without having the truth about himself revealed. When Enrique is pushed behind the screen, he emerges as a young boy dressed in a white satin outfit with a white ruff. According to Lorca's stage direction, the boy should be played by an actress. Others who cross behind the screen—men who have attempted to hide their true sexuality—metamorphose into effeminate pederasts carrying lorgnettes and whips. Only the Director's manservant, the one true heterosexual in the play, remains unchanged by the device.

That Lorca admired Gonzalo, and yearned to undertake his same crusade for the truth, is plain. From one scene to the next, one identity to another, Gonzalo challenges Enrique to bare the truth—much as Lorca sought, in part through this play, to confront disingenuous men such as Emilio Aladrén. Gonzalo vows to struggle "with the mask" until he succeeds in seeing Enrique naked. "I love you in front of the others because I abhor the mask, and because now I've succeeded in ripping it off you," he says. But conventional society will not tolerate truthsayers like Gonzalo. Ultimately he is crucified for his deeds. Suspended nude on an upright bed, with a crown of blue thorns on his head, he is attended by a sadistic male nurse who periodically extracts blood from his moribund body.

Never again would Lorca bare the truth about himself so explicitly. The language of *The Audience* is blunt and often scatalogical. There is a frank discussion of the anus; the character of Juliet is costumed so that her "pink celluloid breasts" are exposed. The world of the play, like that of the New York poems, is harsh, cold, menacing. In one of Lorca's more startling moments, several horses break into Juliet's tomb, order her to strip, then proceed to lash her naked buttocks with their tails, and to "urinate" on her by releasing jets of water from the black lacquer canes they carry. "Now we've inaugurated the true theater. The theater beneath the sand," one of them proclaims.

Lorca's aim was not merely to shock but to reveal the unpleasant truth about human existence, to transcend the bounds of social convention by showing how much of life takes place behind masks. "In the bedroom, when we stick our fingers in our noses, or delicately explore our rear," the Director observes, "the plaster of the mask pushes down so heavily on our flesh that we can scarcely lie down on the bed." Toward the end of this dizzying play-within-a-play, the audience attending the Director's experimental production of *Romeo and Juliet* riots upon discovering that the two protagonists are actually men. They murder the actors, seek to kill both the author and the Director, and in a sequence reminiscent of Pirandello's *Six Characters in Search of an Author*, a group of bourgeois ladies stumbles about the darkened theater, madly hunting for an exit to reality.

Several students in the audience defend the unorthodox production. "In the final analysis," one asks, "do Romeo and Juliet necessarily have to be a man and a woman for the tomb scene to come off in a heartrending and lifelike way?"

"No," says another. "It's not necessary, and that's what the Stage Director set out so brilliantly to demonstrate."

Lorca maintained that *The Audience* was impossible to stage. And yet the following year, when an actress named Irene López Heredia expressed interest in producing the play, he triumphantly told his parents that if a production of *The Audience* were to take place, it "would be sensational and one of the greatest literary battles of its time." For the moment, at least, he seemed open to parental knowledge of the work, although there is no further indication that Lorca's parents read the play. López Heredia eventually rejected the idea of a production, as did Cipriano Rivas Cherif, the man who had boldly premiered his own drama about homosexual love in 1928, and who had tried to produce Lorca's *Don Perlimplín* in early 1929. Apparently even Rivas Cherif lacked either the courage or the means to take on *The Audience*.

Much as he cherished his play, Lorca knew the danger it posed. In 1933 he told a journalist he had no intention of producing *The Audience*. "I don't think any company would dare to present it onstage, and no audience would tolerate it without becoming indignant," he said. "Because it's a mirror image of the audience. Onstage it displays the private dramas that are going on inside each and every spectator as he watches the performance. And since people's private dramas are often quite bitter and generally dishonorable, the spectators would immediately rise up and demand that the performance be stopped."

He repeatedly called the play "a poem to be hissed." Nevertheless, he openly discussed the work with reporters, and in 1933 published two scenes from *The*

Audience in a Spanish literary journal. Among friends and acquaintances he continued to read the play. One spring afternoon he invited several friends to join him in his Madrid apartment to hear the work. It was hot, and, according to at least one of the four men who attended the reading, Lorca insisted on taking off his clothes. Naked, he proceeded to read his play.

By the time Lorca returned to Madrid in October 1930, Margarita Xirgu and her theater company had opened a new season at the Teatro Español, one of the oldest and most important theaters in the capital. Ever since her production of *Mariana Pineda* three years earlier, the statuesque Catalan actress had hoped to premiere another Lorca work. For some time, she had had her eye on *The Shoemaker's Prodigious Wife*, the lively two-act farce Lorca first began writing in 1924 and finished revising in 1929 during his stay in New York.

Lorca was untroubled by the seeming discrepancy between a lighthearted work such as *The Shoemaker's Prodigious Wife* and the radical new theater he was trying to achieve with *The Audience*. He regarded both plays as cures for the ailing Spanish stage—the first, because it embraced the country's vital popular tradition, and the second, because it shattered nearly every convention of the bourgeois theater. But Lorca was shrewd enough to realize that if he intended to succeed on the stage, let alone make money, *The Shoemaker's Prodigious Wife* was the play to produce. Besides, Xirgu clearly preferred it to the experimental work.

In early December, Lorca read the farce to the actress and her company. Delighted by the work, Xirgu announced to the press that she intended to produce a "chamber" version of the play within the next few weeks. Rehearsals began at once under the direction of her close friend and literary adviser, Cipriano Rivas Cherif. Lorca agreed to design *The Shoemaker's Prodigious Wife* and to assist Rivas Cherif with its staging. As a director, Lorca proved resourceful. He brought to the task a painter's sense of composition and a musician's understanding of timing. Rhythm—the tempo of the performance—was crucial. "An actor can't be one second late on an entrance," he stated. Xirgu learned to trust him implicitly. She reportedly told Vicenta Lorca, "If Federico wants us to roll on the floor, we'll do it."

They planned to open the play on Christmas Eve. In the meantime, the Society of Courses and Lectures in Madrid announced that it intended to premiere Lorca's puppet play, *The Tragicomedy of Don Cristóbal*, early the following year. The writer and columnist Ramón Gómez de la Serna published a glowing analysis of the play in *El Sol*, and praised Lorca as a "miraculous poet."

"As you can see," Lorca informed his parents, "I've become a fashionable little boy after my useful and advantageous trip to America."

He was also in demand on the lecture circuit. In early December he made a quick trip north to give a pair of talks in the coastal cities of San Sebastián and Gijón. In San Sebastián he delivered his lecture on deep song. The local press hailed his gifts "as both a poet and a scholar." While in the Basque resort, Lorca met up with Emilio Aladrén, in what was apparently their first encounter in more than a year. Penniless but dapper, Aladrén evidently charmed Lorca into paying his way "for everything" during their short time together. One observer who saw the two men in San Sebastián remembered Lorca's plump legs and flat-footed gait, in contrast to the tall, slender Aladrén, who though disheveled wore an elegant raincoat.

Earlier in the year Aladrén had sent Lorca an effusive note welcoming him home from America: "Emilio Aladrén Perojo K.[isses] T.[he] H.[and] of Federico García Lorca, is delighted to hear of his return to Spain, and takes this opportunity to tell him that he cannot imagine how pleased he would be to receive word of him." It is not known whether Lorca responded to the invitation, but he saved Aladrén's note. Less than a year after his reunion with Lorca in San Sebastián, Aladrén married an Englishwoman.

Lorca repeated his lecture on deep song in Gijón on December 14. But the event went unreported, as recent political events had abruptly shut down the press. Two days earlier, on December 12, a band of pro-Republican army officers in Jaca, a tiny garrison town in the Spanish Pyrenees, had attempted a coup d'état. Loyalist troops immediately quashed the uprising and arrested its two chief conspirators, Captains Fermín Galán Rodríguez and Ángel García Hernández. On December 14, the day of Lorca's talk, the two men were executed. The following day, Republican sympathizers staged demonstrations across the country, and Spanish workers declared a general strike. The government quickly took control of the situation and jailed Spain's six principal Republican leaders—among them Lorca's friend Fernando de los Ríos.

Despite the failure of the December rising, the Republican cause flourished. Citizens throughout Spain condemned the government for its savage response to the attempted coup, and Fermín Galán Rodríguez and Ángel García Hernández became martyrs. From prison, de los Ríos and his fellow Republican leaders resumed their struggle for a democratically elected Spanish government. In Madrid, clandestine pamphlets and pro-Republican broadsheets began to circulate. According to poet Pedro Salinas, the atmosphere in the capital became "absolutely pre-revolutionary."

Lorca remained detached from the situation. Although he worried about de los Ríos, as did the rest of the Lorca family, he was preoccupied with the impending premiere of his play at the Teatro Español. On the evening of December 24, 1930, *The Shoemaker's Prodigious Wife* opened as scheduled. Due to the Christmas holiday, nearly every other commercial theater in the city was dark that night, a fact that only reinforced the unconventional nature of the performance at the Español. Vicenta Lorca wrote from Granada to say she hoped the production would be a success, for that alone would "compensate" for the play's having disrupted a family holiday.

Lorca was mildly apprehensive about the play. In an interview published that morning, he took pains to distinguish between *The Shoemaker's Prodigious Wife* and what he called his "real work. My real work is yet to come," he told a reporter. ". . . Do you know what I call it? *The Audience*. That's the one . . . that's the one . . . Profound drama, very profound."

As Paco García Lorca sat in the plush interior of the Teatro Español on Christmas Eve and watched his brother's play unfold, he recalled the puppet show Federico had staged eight years earlier in the family's living room in Granada. Then, as now, Lorca had exercised control over nearly every aspect of the production. In addition to writing the script and assisting Rivas Cherif with its direction, Lorca had transcribed songs and music for *The Shoemaker's Prodigious Wife*, designed the play's brightly colored costumes and sets, and on opening night even performed the work's prologue. He did so, he said, in order to "share the anxiety of opening night as both author and actor." Dressed—like the allegorical author who opens Calderón's *Grand Theater of the World*—in a top hat and a huge cape sprinkled with stars, Lorca took to the stage of the Español and bluntly commanded his audience to pay attention and his actors to be quiet. Watching his brother, Paco was reminded of the Federico who had crouched behind a handmade puppet stage in the family's living room in 1923, and in the role of the irascible Don Cristóbal had badgered and bantered with his audience until gales of high-pitched laughter filled the room.

When he first began writing *The Shoemaker's Prodigious Wife* in 1924, Lorca had envisioned the play as a bawdy, fast-paced puppet farce. Later versions of the work, though obviously intended for human actors, retained elements of the puppet theater. Critics who reviewed Xirgu's 1930 production commented on the toylike quality of its costumes, sets, and characters. The production itself, some said, resembled a carnival. Lorca described his farce as "violent" and "vulgar," and drew attention to its popular roots. In at least one stage direction to the 1930 script, he demanded that an actor speak "in an exaggerated way" and move his head "like a wire puppet."

An amalgam of styles, *The Shoemaker's Prodigious Wife* blends the ferocity of the puppet stage with the antics of Roman comedy and Italian commedia dell'arte and the humanity of Spanish Golden Age drama. Its title deliberately recalls Calderón's *The Prodigious Magician*, whose protagonist, like Lorca's Shoemaker's Wife, performs "prodigious" deeds. But the play's most palpable Golden Age source is Cervantes. Thematically Lorca's farce draws on the stock situation of a young woman married to an old man, a motif Cervantes often employed. Stylistically the work shares the wit, speed, and comic excess of a Cervantes interlude or *entremés*, a one-act farcical skit with deep roots in the Spanish tradition, of which Cervantes was an acknowledged master.

The text of *The Shoemaker's Prodigious Wife* is only a small part of its overall conception. Equally important are the color and pattern of its sets and costumes, the rhythm of its music and dance. Through his emphasis on spectacle, Lorca was able to stress the links between his play and other, less sophisticated forms of entertainment, such as the circus, cabaret, vaudeville, and the *sainete*, a type of lyrical, one-act sketch especially popular in eighteenth-century Spain. He viewed the farce as another episode in his ongoing struggle to combat the stale realism of the contemporary Spanish stage by restoring the theater to its popular origins.

Laden with traditional Andalusian idioms, songs, and superstitions, *The Shoemaker's Prodigious Wife* is the most thoroughly popular of Lorca's plays. He began writing it in 1924, at the height of his friendship with Manuel de Falla, whose comic operas spring directly from the popular tradition. Like Falla, Lorca was an inveterate collector of village sayings and songs. Whenever he heard a striking utterance he almost always repeated it to friends, and eventually incorporated it into his work. For *The Shoemaker's Prodigious Wife*, he derived whole passages of dialogue from the conversational idiosyncrasies of a friend's maid. "Ask a duchess to tell you the names of the lovers of Teruel," he said once, referring to a popular Spanish folktale, "and she won't know. But the cook, the cook, yes! And she'll know hundreds of lines by heart from *El Cid* and Zorrilla's *Don Juan*."

Lorca subtitled his play "A Violent Farce in Two Acts and A Prologue." The word "violent," he said, denotes the nature of the protagonist's fight against reality—a fight that by implication Lorca shared. Elsewhere he described his play as "a simple farce, with a pure classical tone." In his choice of genre, Lorca was acknowledging both historical precedent and contemporary taste, for by the mid-1920s, a number of writers, most conspicuously the playwrights Ramón del Valle-Inclán and Jacinto Grau, both of whom Lorca knew personally, were experimenting with comedy as an antidote to the realism and sentimentality of mainstream Spanish literature.

The Shoemaker's Prodigious Wife is one of Lorca's few comedies, and the only one of his plays not to end in the death, real or metaphorical, of a leading character. Lorca himself said that although he could have channeled the play's "dramatic material" into a more serious form, he preferred to handle it "in a fresh, joyful way, leaving other possible treatments for later." But while *The Shoemaker's Prodigious Wife* follows the traditional plot line of farce and embraces many of the genre's conventions, it is more deeply and subtly drawn. The play's two protagonists, although based on stock comic characters, possess a poignant humanity, and their story, also drawn from comic convention, is enriched by Lorca's complex poetic vision.

Lorca had previously explored the motif of an old man married to a young woman in his brief and lyrical play *Don Perlimplín*, a work he described as a "grotesque" tragedy. With *The Shoemaker's Prodigious Wife* he returned to the theme, this time focusing chiefly on its comic ramifications. His play takes place in an Andalusian village, where a spirited eighteen-year-old bride, trapped in an arranged marriage to a fifty-three-year-old shoemaker, struggles to escape her misery. Given no choice as a woman but to be "either a nun or a dishrag," as she tartly phrases it, and painfully aware that she is unlikely to have children, the Shoemaker's Wife resorts to fantasy as her only means of escape from a reality she finds unbearable. She taunts her aging husband with extravagant accounts of her former suitors and gleefully informs him that as a wife, she will do just as she pleases. "Fantasizer! Fantasizer! Fantasizer!" he cries in retaliation, as two of his neighbors eavesdrop through a prominent upstage window.

Lorca had not forgotten the claustrophobic nature of rural life in Andalusia, where village gossips pass judgment on those who flout convention, and "malice and bad will" (as Lorca once expressed it in a letter) permeate everyday life. In *The Shoemaker's Prodigious Wife* he re-creates the cloying atmosphere he had experienced as a boy growing up in small *vega* towns. Gossiping villagers scrutinize and deride the Shoemaker and his unruly wife throughout the play. According to Lorca, they represent "the voice of conscience, of religion, of remorse." They are also a quintessential device of the stage, an archetypal chorus whose function is so "indispensable . . . so profoundly theatrical, that I cannot conceive of its exclusion," he observed.

Ultimately, his neighbors' mockery and his wife's abuse so torment the Shoemaker that he leaves home. Only then does his young wife discover how deeply she loves him. Her sole source of comfort is a small village boy, whom she calls "my little shepherd of Bethlehem." An emblem of both the child and the freedom she will never possess, the boy alone elicits true affection from the Shoe-

maker's Wife. Christ-like in his innocence, the child is a visual and poetic reminder of the boy Lorca himself once was. When the child offers to give the
Shoemaker's Wife "the great sword of my grandfather, the one who went off to
war," Lorca is most likely remembering his own great-grandfather who fought
in Spain's Carlist wars during the late nineteenth century. When the boy reacts
ecstatically to the arrival of an itinerant puppeteer, it is his own childhood response to such events that Lorca evokes.

True to the conventions of its genre, *The Shoemaker's Prodigious Wife* culminates in a recognition scene. Unaware that she is talking to the Shoemaker in
disguise, the Shoemaker's Wife tells a wandering puppeteer how deeply she
loves her husband. Moved by her confession, he reveals his identity, and for an
instant the pair enjoy a blissful reunion. But it does not last. Within moments
the Shoemaker's Wife begins berating her husband, and as their neighbors take
up their accustomed post at the window, the couple's turbulent marriage resumes. Even in this most comic of plays, Lorca could not bring himself to present an unambiguously happy ending. His understanding of human behavior
would not warrant it. True love, he knew, is a chimera. There is no escaping
the solitude of human existence.

The original script for *The Shoemaker's Prodigious Wife* did not include a
prologue. Lorca added the speech during rehearsals for the play in 1930, perhaps intending it as a defense of the qualities for which his first produced play,
The Butterfly's Evil Spell, had been lampooned: poetry, fantasy, symbolism. Or
perhaps, having resigned himself to the impossibility of producing *The Audience*, he hoped to commence his theatrical revolution in a more acceptable
way. In any case, he made his stand. "Esteemed audience," he began, then
hastily changed his approach. "No, not 'esteemed audience,' just 'audience.'"
In an effort to eradicate the false wall of fear and cowardice that traditionally
separates an author from his audience, he explained, he would dispense with
outmoded words such as "esteemed."

Lorca was in fact mocking the urbane crowds who typically filled the stalls at
opening night performances in Madrid. He preferred a less sophisticated audience for his work. The theater, he argued in his prologue, is too often "a financial operation." As a result, "poetry retreats from the stage in search of other
environments where people are not shocked when a tree, for example, turns
into a puff of smoke, or when three fishes, through the love of a hand and a
word, become three million fishes to feed the hunger of a multitude."

The Shoemaker's Prodigious Wife—like so much else that he wrote—is
Lorca's response to the need for a genuinely poetic theater in Spain. At the end
of the play's prologue, the Author bids farewell to his audience and doffs his

hat. As he does so, a ray of green light emerges from the depths of his hat, followed by a jet of water. "Pardon me," says the Author, with a touch of irony to his voice. The curtain rises, the lights brighten, and the Shoemaker's Wife comes raging onto the stage.

Because *The Shoemaker's Prodigious Wife* had been advertised as an "experimental" production, many critics chose to ignore the play's debut in 1930. Of those who did review the Christmas Eve premiere, several pointed out that it was far less experimental than Lorca's previous plays. But they admitted that in its simplicity, brevity, and mirth, the farce was nevertheless unconventional.

The critic Enrique Díez-Canedo of *El Sol*, one of Lorca's most ardent fans, gave *The Shoemaker's Prodigious Wife* its most generous review. Hailing Lorca as "a true poet," Díez-Canedo praised the work's charm, vigor, and humanity, and noted its popular tone. He was particularly struck by the play's unsentimental denouement, which he described as "more purely definitive" than the "happy-ever-after" endings usually given to comedies.

A number of reviewers focused on the play's simplicity and lack of pretension. Some used words such as "ingenuous" and "childlike." Others were more severe. Luis Paris, of *El Imparcial*, attacked the play as "a banal, insubstantial . . . little work." Juan Olmedilla, of the *Heraldo de Madrid*, dismissed it as a "torpid and clumsy parody" of Ramón del Valle-Inclán's more probing experiments with comedy and the puppet tradition. Lorca's farce lacked "charm, interest, and depth of character," wrote Olmedilla. This was all the more disappointing, he added, because Lorca showed such promise as an author. Even his good friend Pedro Salinas took exception to Lorca's play. Privately, Salinas called it a "simple, entertaining little thing, with lots of local color, charming bits, etc. But without stature. A childish prank."

Few who saw the farce seemed willing or able to acknowledge its more serious implications. As Lorca later took pains to emphasize, the character of the Shoemaker's Wife, in her persistent, sometimes violent confrontation with reality, embodies a fundamental human longing. She epitomizes "the struggle between reality and fantasy (and by fantasy I mean all that is unattainable) which exists deep within every human being." In her quest for the impossible—a quest that surfaces time and again in Lorca's poetic cosmos—the Shoemaker's Wife has a single ally: a little boy. He is "a compendium of tenderness," Lorca explained, "and a symbol of things that are still just seedlings." Only children, Lorca believed, are oblivious to the pain of empty, unmitigated desire.

Xirgu and her company performed *The Shoemaker's Prodigious Wife* thirty-three times in Madrid before closing the farce on April 17, 1931. The play's modest success in the capital earned Lorca favorable notices from as far away as Barcelona, where Salvador Dalí's father one day spotted an enthusiastic review. He clipped the article and sent it to Lorca with a note of congratulations.

"I don't know if you're aware that I had to evict my son from the house," the older man wrote. Not only had Dalí defiled his mother's memory by spitting on her portrait, he had recently taken up with a married woman, Gala Eluard, and was now living openly and shamelessly with her. More shocking still, the woman's husband approved of the affair. Upon hearing this last bit of news, Lorca burst out laughing.

CHAPTER 17

REPUBLIC

1931

From jail, Fernando de los Ríos and his colleagues in the Republican movement continued to agitate for a new government. Shortly after their imprisonment in December 1930, they issued a manifesto to the people of Spain, demanding a "republic based on national sovereignty and represented by a Constituent Assembly."

In Madrid rumors swirled and revolutionary tracts littered the sidewalks. The country's leading intellectuals held secret meetings in bars, took covert trips, and issued pro-Republican pamphlets. At the Café Granja del Henar, playwright Ramón del Valle-Inclán's nightly *tertulia* became a political forum. In early February 1931, writer José Ortega y Gasset and two pro-Republican colleagues published a manifesto in the Spanish press. The document called for "writers and artists, doctors, engineers, architects," and especially the young, to form an association "in support of the Republic."

Few could ignore the turmoil. Pedro Salinas wrote of the "rumors, the passionate conversations, the retorts, the obligatory hell" that enveloped Madrid during the first months of 1931. Virtually everyone Salinas knew had joined the fray. "Only the *children*, only Alberti and Lorca, go on worrying exclusively about themselves and about each other," he told Jorge Guillén. But Salinas was wrong to deem Rafael Alberti apolitical. In early March, at the final performance of his new play, *The Uninhabited Man*, Alberti had the names of the jailed Republican leaders read aloud from the stage. A telegram from Unamuno, declaring his support for the Republican movement, followed. Alberti's liberal audience applauded the readings, then poured into the streets of Madrid in a boisterous show of enthusiasm for a new government. By the time the police arrived, the theater was empty, and no arrests could be made.

Lorca undoubtedly knew about—and almost certainly envied—the attention Alberti received for his defiant act. The two men continued to be wary of one another. The previous year, Alberti had married the young writer María Teresa Léon, and the couple seemed destined for a productive life devoted to their shared passions: politics and literature. Since 1929, Alberti's work had become increasingly strident. He aligned himself with the working classes—an affiliation he, unlike Lorca, claimed as a legitimate birthright—and sought, through writing, to be both politically effective and artistically pure, a goal not easily achieved. Lorca objected to Alberti's partisan verse, which he thought a corruption of true art. Their mutual friend, the diplomat Carlos Morla Lynch, observed in his diary at about this time: "They're preoccupied, those two—the one with the other—and they keep an eye on each other."

But aside from an obvious and unavoidable interest in the outcome of the current political situation, Lorca himself kept aloof from politics. At Morla Lynch's home, where he now spent most of his evenings, guests seldom discussed political developments. They argued instead about literature or gossiped about everyday events. The ambience inside the apartment, unlike the "volcano" brewing on the streets outside, was calm. Visitors arranged themselves on velvet chairs surrounded by Persian rugs, lacquer tables, and reproductions of French and Asian paintings. In the dining room, where Bebé Morla Lynch served informal suppers, guests drank from green and white crystal glasses. Over dinner Lorca performed his usual antics. "Your mother must be very interesting, for she managed to give you such a talented imagination," Morla Lynch taunted Lorca later that year. "But, my God, she's brought you up badly! . . . The hours you keep . . . or don't keep. Your habit of sitting down at the table and then going off to have a pee when the second course has already started."

Morla was especially struck by the difference between Lorca and his younger brother, Paco. Earlier in the year the two siblings had taken a studio apartment together in Madrid. The small flat, which overlooked a garage and a convent school, was Lorca's first permanent residence in the capital and was to remain his home in Madrid for the next two years. Inside the sunny apartment, Lorca spent hours playing the piano and singing for friends while his brother sat in the adjoining room, trying to study for his diplomatic exams.

Morla Lynch thought both brothers intelligent and charming. But while Lorca exuded vigor and energy, Paco, leaner and more conventionally handsome than his brother, was all "serenity and balance." Lorca's black eyes sparkled, and his laughter was as "turbulent" as a geyser. Paco possessed a "limpid, tranquil" gaze, and laughed with the "freshness" of a breeze. Sensible and studious, he avoided the "fits of ecstasy" and the "imaginative impertinence" to which his older brother was prone.

To some, the brothers seemed more distant this year than previously. A number of friends believed this was due to Lorca's growing sexual candor. In the wake of his visit to the United States and Cuba, he had become far less circumspect. A theater colleague who arranged to meet him in his apartment in Madrid one day showed up at the appointed time and was met at the door by Lorca, who was dressed in nothing but a pair of underpants. Inside the apartment stood fellow poet Luis Cernuda, who was naked. "We were doing tumbling exercises," Lorca remarked dryly. Without dressing, he and Cernuda sat down and began to converse with their visitor.

In early 1931, in a letter to Jorge Guillén, Pedro Salinas mentioned that Lorca was "always off somewhere, among those friends *du côté de Charlus*"—a play on Proust's *Du côté de chez Swann*. Salinas was probably referring to Carlos Morla Lynch and his circle. A few years later, when Guillén himself finally met Morla Lynch, he pronounced the diplomat "an absurd Charlus," who, though enjoyable, had a "pederastic" demeanor. "Might he not be a corruptor of minors?" Guillén worried.

There is no proof that Guillén's allegations were correct. But it was clear that Morla Lynch enjoyed the company of homosexual men, and that he encouraged the frank discussion of sex and sexuality at his nightly soirees. When Lorca teased him by suggesting that their mutual friend Adolfo Salazar, a homosexual, was infatuated with Morla, the diplomat gleefully went along with the joke. Spotting Salazar in a room one day, Morla poked his head in the door and said, "I'm just crazy about you!" Salazar reacted with a gesture of disgust.

Lorca himself came and went as he pleased from Morla's apartment. He had his customary seat on the corner sofa, and he kept his guitar stored behind a living room door. He helped himself to food and drink from the refrigerator, played the piano, worked in Morla's office, and occasionally soaked in the diplomat's bathtub while Morla and his son combed their hair. "I . . . have a great affection for your bathroom," Lorca told the Chilean. After coming down with a sore throat, Lorca once spent an entire day lying on the sofa while Morla and his wife nursed him. Whenever they sought to paint his throat with medication, Lorca stuck his tongue out as far as he could, grabbed it with both hands, and, with his eyes bulging, allowed the couple to perform the procedure.

He felt free to bring friends to the diplomat's home at any hour of the day or night, without telephoning ahead of time. One night, on impulse, he dragged Pedro Salinas and several others to Morla's apartment. The moment they arrived, Lorca introduced his friends to Bebé Morla Lynch and started to ransack the couple's closets and kitchen. Within minutes he was improvising a vaudeville routine. He costumed his friends in Bebé's fur coats, put kitchen pots on their heads, and gave them silver trays to hold as shields.

Salinas witnessed this sort of behavior more than once. Lorca loved to stage impromptu performances and to lead friends through poetic charades. On Morla's saint's day in 1931, he presented an improvised show at midnight. Wrapped in a bedsheet, with curtain rings on his wrists, he performed a snake dance, then delivered a "Holy Week sermon," and finally, holding two teacups to his chest as breasts, offered an original interpretation of the legendary Mata Hari's "latest dance."

Like the prodigious shoemaker's wife of his imagination, Lorca waged a constant battle against the poverty of reality. Since childhood he had been unable to resist the impulse to embellish his surroundings, to transform ordinary existence into theatrical spectacle. More often than not, he viewed life as an empty stage in need of costumes, props, actors, and poetry. He could bring anything to life, a friend recalled: "a glass, a pencil holder, a newspaper, a napkin, a hat, an umbrella." He loved to invent words and had a complete vocabulary of made-up sayings. At restaurants he liked to order imaginary items—a "*chorpatélico*," some "*pimpavonillas*"—then watch to see if the waiter could deduce what it was he wanted. Salinas was present during one such outing. "We dined as usual," he remembered, "but the meal was surrounded with that fantastic, ingenuous, poetic humor typical of Federico."

Morla Lynch kept a running account in his diary of the poet's habits, actions, and sayings. Every night he jotted down the events of the preceding day. His entries on Lorca alone were sufficient to fill a book. Lorca knew about the diary and approved of it. Morla sometimes left the volume out for friends and family members to read and respond to. "Federico lives the truth of my home," he wrote one day after reading parts of the diary to Lorca.

Occasionally Morla tried to analyze Lorca's character. Whenever an argument arose, the diplomat observed, Lorca usually wandered off to play the piano, thumb through a magazine, or telephone a friend. He is "not a man of polemics," Morla concluded. But on those few occasions when Lorca did engage in a dispute, he rarely conceded defeat. He was "conscious of his superior talent." Keenly aware of Lorca's mood swings, the diplomat noticed that during his periodic bouts of "misanthropy," Lorca would decline invitations and refuse to see people. In the spring of 1931, Morla tried to introduce him to the pianist Artur Rubinstein, but Lorca chose to stay home in his pajamas rather than meet the famed performer.

His principal source of fear, "the great anxiety that oppresses him," Morla saw, was "the idea of death." Lorca spoke of death as a "fixed, terrible, dreadful obsession" that dwells within every human being. "At all hours. Always! Whenever we undertake a journey or say 'good night' to a loved one, we are haunted by death," he said to Morla one day. "It would be different if we knew with certainty the limits involved." The unalterable yet cruelly random nature of the event plagued him: he was doomed to die, but on what date, where, and how? And after death, what would become of him? Was there an afterlife? Lorca rubbed his hand across his forehead and asked Morla to read something from his diary. Morla chose a passage he had written about his dead daughter, Colomba. Lorca's spirits lifted. The passage, he said, proved that even in death the essence of one's being can go on living somewhere, "perennially."

By early April 1931, the government of Spain was in disarray. "These months have been awful," Salinas wrote to Guillén on April 2. "The reason: P O L I - T I C S. Written just like that, with as many capital letters and spaces as possible."

In February 1931, Dámaso Berenguer, the army general who had governed Spain for a year at the king's behest, resigned. In March, Alfonso XIII called for municipal elections throughout the nation. Although not a general election, the results of this vote for local candidates would provide a reliable reading of the country's mood. Election day was set for Sunday, April 12.

The polls opened at eight in the morning. Later that day Lorca ran into Carlos Morla Lynch in Madrid's congested Puerta del Sol, and the two sat down to coffee in a café. To Morla, Lorca seemed more "curious" about the election than "ardent." As they sat talking, taxis streamed past, many with Republican posters prominently displayed. Onlookers roared their approval. At one point a brief disturbance broke out, and the police arrived with "sabers in hand" to end the fracas. No one was hurt, but Morla found the spectacle unnerving.

By nightfall, rumors of a Republican victory were rampant. Lorca made his way across town to another café to meet a group of friends. While crossing the vast Plaza de Cibeles near the post office, he suddenly found himself in the midst of a huge, peaceful demonstration in support of the Republic. Just as he joined the marchers, a squadron of Civil Guardsmen appeared and abruptly blocked the path of the crowd. Shouts rang out, followed by gunshots. The marchers fled. Caught in the melee, Lorca fell to the ground and injured his finger. Eventually he reached the café where his friends awaited him. He arrived breathless, his face damp with perspiration and his clothing spattered with dust. Gesturing frantically and sucking on his wounded finger, he explained in a shrill voice what had happened to him. Meanwhile, people rushed in and out of the café with fresh rumors. At one point, someone reported that the government was about to declare a state of war. Under the circumstances, many who heard the announcement believed it.

Contrary to expectations, the Spanish monarchy won the popular vote on April 12, 1931, in large part because the country's powerful landowners ensured a monarchist victory in the countryside. But in the cities, pro-monarchy candidates lost heavily. The final figures for the election were never published and probably never counted. It scarcely mattered. Despite the monarchy's statistical victory, it was clear to most that the people of Spain wanted a new government.

One day after the election, in demonstrations across the country, exultant crowds proclaimed the birth of a Spanish republic. In Madrid, the king consulted his advisers and was told that if he did not renounce the throne immediately, civil war was likely to erupt. Alfonso XIII promptly commenced negotiations for the transfer of power to a prime minister.

On Tuesday, April 14, two days after the election, dawn broke quietly in Madrid. The streets were all but empty. Morning newspapers carried reports of a new government, but nothing was confirmed. As the day wore on, crowds assembled outside the Royal Palace. Inside the huge white building, the king and his family were packing their bags. At approximately four o'clock that afternoon, a Republican flag rose slowly above the main post office building in the Plaza de Cibeles—the spot where two days earlier Lorca had been shoved to the ground. News of the flag's appearance spread through the city. People poured into the streets, chanting the "Marseillaise" and the "Internationale." They sang derogatory tunes about the king and toppled a statue of his grandmother, Isabel II, the controversial nineteenth-century queen whose inept rule had led to the establishment of a short-lived First Spanish Republic. Members of the Civil Guard watched, motionless.

By nightfall, the news was official: King Alfonso XIII had elected to leave Spain. "I no longer enjoy the love of my people," he announced in a terse statement that appeared that evening in newspapers throughout the country. Earlier in the day, officials had released the jailed leaders of the Republican movement. Among them was Lorca's friend Fernando de los Ríos, who was quickly named minister of justice in a new Republican cabinet.

Like many of his compatriots, Lorca rejoiced in the advent of the Second

Spanish Republic. He took part in street demonstrations celebrating the new government and voiced his support for its liberal policies. Later in the month he autographed a copy of his *Gypsy Ballads* for a friend. Inside the cover he wrote, "Federico—1931—Republican April."

The leaders of the Republic wasted no time in implementing their radical agenda. They promptly changed the Spanish flag, revised the national anthem, and christened a number of streets with new, Republican-inspired names. They scheduled elections for a constituent parliament, introduced agrarian reforms, and, in an effort to diminish the Church's grip on public life, secularized hospitals, cemeteries, and schools. Most significantly, the Republican prime minister and his cabinet launched an ambitious series of cultural and educational programs aimed at reducing the nation's alarming rate of illiteracy. Lorca spoke out in favor of these initiatives and announced that he would volunteer his own services as a music teacher. He intended to form a youth orchestra, he said, using musical instruments especially designed to be played by small hands.

Journalists called the Republican government *la niña bonita*: the beautiful child. But the new regime's honeymoon was fleeting. In early May, the Archbishop of Toledo and Primate of the Spanish Church, Cardinal Segura, issued a stinging pastoral letter in which he praised Alfonso XIII and urged believers to "fight like intrepid warriors" against those who wished to "destroy religion." The Republican leaders countered by demanding that Segura be exiled from Spain.

By mid-May, members of the Spanish military had begun plotting to overthrow the new government. On May 10, monarchists clashed openly with Republican sympathizers in downtown Madrid. Someone set fire to the offices of the pro-monarchist newspaper *ABC*. The following day, churches and convents throughout the country were burned, most likely by members of the extreme-left anarchist movement. In Madrid alone, six convents went up in flames. Lorca spotted two nuns fleeing the site of one of the fires, carrying a portable typewriter case between them. According to the story he told a journalist—a tale he almost certainly embellished—he took pity on the women and put them in a taxi. "Sir, you seem like a good Christian," the nuns said to him, "so we're going to tell you what we're carrying in this case. We're carrying the Holy Sacrament." Lorca fell to his knees in awe.

In the wake of the burnings, the Republican government reluctantly declared martial law and authorized the use of the Civil Guard to prevent further violence. A tenuous peace returned to the country. But the episode tarnished the new government's image. Lorca noticed that in the convent school across the street from his apartment, the girls changed the words to one of their favorite songs. Where previously they had sung, "What the king commands, the mayor commands," they now intoned, "What the president commands, the mayor commands." Fearful of government scrutiny, the nuns in charge of the convent had changed the lyrics in deference to the nation's new, anti-monarchy regime.

Lorca's newfound interest in politics soon subsided. Although a passionate believer in the Republic and its ideals, he lacked the zealotry of his colleague Rafael Alberti, who shortly after the proclamation of the Second Republic premiered a blatantly political new play, *Fermín Galán*, a heroic account of the failed Republican uprising in Jaca in 1930. Margarita Xirgu opened Alberti's play in Madrid's Teatro Español on June 1, 1931, less than two months after the declaration of the Second Republic. On opening night the play sparked a fight between Republican and monarchist sympathizers in the audience.

Lorca had other concerns. His improved "economic position" had given him an unaccustomed serenity, and he had resolved to publish his work—"all my things, absolutely all of them"—despite his lifelong distaste for publication. He was especially eager to bring out his American poems, which had sparked considerable interest among both journalists and publishers. "All the publishers" were after him, he told his parents. Although he did not yet know how to organize the collections, he expected his American poems to fill two books.

Meanwhile, he embarked on a musical collaboration with his friend Encarnación López, the singer and dancer known as La Argentinita, who had appeared in *The Butterfly's Evil Spell* in 1920, and whom Lorca often saw socially in the company of her lover, the former bullfighter Ignacio Sánchez Mejías. La Argentinita's limpid soprano voice and graceful dancing had helped salvage *The Butterfly's Evil Spell* at its disastrous opening, and the two had remained close friends. In the spring of 1931 she and Lorca recorded a series of Spanish folk songs, works Lorca had known since childhood. La Argentinita sang and played the castanets while Lorca accompanied her on the piano—the first and only time he allowed his exuberant playing to be recorded. The songs came out that summer in a set of five 78-rpm records. Critics applauded the set, and copies sold briskly. In Granada, Concha and Isabel García Lorca played the records "at all hours." Lorca was pleased with the project. He thought it showcased his musical skills "quite well," and he expected the records to yield "a lot of money very quickly." But royalty payments failed to materialize as swiftly as he had hoped, and in time he had to ask his parents for some "emergency relief."

He also resumed work on the deep-song poems he had begun in 1921. He had published several of the poems in magazines, and had talked repeatedly of issuing the series in book form. But it was not until 1931, when Rafael Martínez Nadal urged him to do something with the poems, that Lorca at last made up his mind to publish the collection. Nadal saw the project through to completion. He introduced Lorca to publisher Julio Gómez de la Serna of Ediciones Ulises, a small new publishing house in Madrid, and he helped arrange and type the manuscript.

Lorca relied on Nadal's advice. The two spent so much time together that when Vicenta Lorca needed to get in touch with her son from Granada, she sometimes sent a letter to Nadal's house in Madrid. Handsome and vigorous, with curly blond hair and mischievous eyes, Nadal understood Lorca as few did. Lorca described their friendship as "a marble pillar that grows more beautiful with time." He looked to Martínez Nadal for insights into his writing, and he valued the "violent sincerity" with which the younger man criticized his work. Privately, Nadal teased Lorca about his sexuality, calling him "Federicón" in letters—a play on the Spanish term *maricón,* or "queer"—and sending rapturous descriptions of the beautiful male bodies to be seen at local swimming pools. "Such distended muscles! They made me weep. You'd weep too."

The two friends labored over *Poem of the Deep Song.* Although he worried about the brevity of the collection, Lorca was ruthless in selecting poems for the book. "And this one?" Nadal once asked after Lorca had cut a poem from the ensemble. "Rhetorical," Lorca replied, and drew a huge X through the piece. When Nadal typed up the final manuscript, it contained only fifty short poems—scarcely enough to fill a book. Lorca laughed and suggested the poems be printed exclusively on one side of each page. In the end, he lengthened the volume by adding a handful of thematically linked dialogues and poems. Written several years later than his original deep-song poems, the new works bore little stylistic resemblance to their predecessors. Nevertheless, Lorca was happy with the volume. On the day he and Nadal finished the manuscript, they dined at the Martínez Nadal home. Too excited to eat, Lorca picked at his food and toyed absentmindedly with his silverware. He told Nadal's mother that *Poem of the Deep Song* would be a wonderful book, and he promised to give her the first copy.

The 171-page volume came out in late May 1931, shortly before Lorca's thirty-third birthday. The book went on sale in June, accompanied by an advertising campaign promoting the collection as "the great poet's muse in its purest, most brilliant form." Most of the poems in the book were distributed among four sections devoted to four types of Gypsy deep song. A prefatory note warned that the collection, composed largely in 1921, was written "with all the exaltation and valor of the most obvious youth." As such, it represented a "first stage" in the author's career.

Critics responded favorably to *Poem of the Deep Song*. The essayist Azorín called it a "book of mystical poetry [that] carries us to the Infinite." In Barcelona, Lorca's friend Sebastian Gasch contributed a highly personal review to the magazine *Mirador*. Gasch hailed the reemergence of what he called the "true Lorca," the "pure-blooded Andalusian Lorca"—as opposed to the "cosmopolitan Lorca" who had recently flirted with "pseudo-surrealism." In Madrid, the critic Agustín Espinosa sounded a rare negative note. In his review for *La Gaceta Literaria*, Espinosa dismissed *Poem of the Deep Song* as a kind of "Spanish Maeterlinck." One only needed to translate Lorca's deep-song poems into French, Espinosa suggested, substitute a Belgian landscape for an Andalusian one, and think "north" wherever Lorca writes "south," in order to perfect the analogy.

Lorca went home to Granada in July. This year, more so than others, he missed his friends in Madrid keenly, especially Carlos and Bebé Morla Lynch. He kept a portrait of Bebé on his desk at the Huerta de San Vicente. As he worked, he gazed at it repeatedly, sometimes falling prey to "intense attacks of affection," which he "cured" by drinking local wine in one of Granada's garden cafés and remembering his absent friends "amidst the fragrance of the myrtles." He stayed in touch with both Bebé and her husband, although at heart he professed to find letters "frozen." The very notepaper on which he wrote felt cold to him, he said, "despite the fact that my hands are resting sweetly on its surface." The spoken word alone retained the vigor of life.

At his father's Huerta de San Vicente, roses bloomed in the garden, and the sound of lullabies wafted through the house. The previous December, Concha García Lorca had given birth to her first child, a daughter, and family life now revolved around the little girl. Lorca doted on his niece and godchild. At her birth he had insisted she be named Vicenta, after her grandmother, and she was. He had offered to pay for her baptism, and promised that his distinguished friends, the Chilean ambassadors, would attend the event. He welcomed the infant's disruptive presence in his home. He loved the lullabies with which she was sung to sleep, and when she spoke her first words that summer he sent a long, poetic account of the event to Carlos Morla Lynch: "A day of jubilation at home. For the first time the baby has said *ma-ma-ma-ma*. And then she got excited and said *ma-ta-pa-la-ca-ti-pa*. It's the text of an angelic telephone call, without doubt, where the child sheds her innocence in order to pass through the terrible and theological gate of human reason."

orca with Dalí in Barcelona, spring 927. Earlier in the year Dalí had told orca that despite the impediments of s obligatory military service, "We ve to spend three months together Cadaqués, it's fated. No, not fated, it certain."

ELOW With Dalí in Cadaqués, 1927.

Clown with Double Face, 1927, ink and colored pencil. Lorca sketched numerous double-faced drawings. He later described one such image as a "self-portrait" that shows "man's capacity for crying as well as winning."

Although he feared drowning, Lorca loved the sea. "For me there is no greater pleasure in life than the contemplation and enjoyment of this happy mystery," he said in 1927. The town of Cadaqués is visible behind him.

ABOVE With Ana María Dalí, Cadaqués, 1927. "García Lorca had a great simplicity about him," Ana María would write. "He lacked my brother's pretension."

LEFT Cadaqués, 1927. Photograph by Ana María Dalí.

With his companion Emilio Aladrén, whom Lorca described as "a good friend of mine, a novel artist," *c.* 1928.

ABOVE Lorca's own design for the first edition of *Gypsy Ballads* (1928)

RIGHT For Lorca, this "extremely spiritual" 1929 passport photograph possessed the "light of a murder scene."

In New York, 1929. Beside Lorca is the Mexican heiress María Antonieta Rivas Mercado, who after meeting Lorca in America described him to a friend as "a strange young man with a somewhat clumsy, ambling walk, as though his legs were too heavy from the knee down. . . . Simple and open in his relations with others. Deep and full of life . . . He is a child, but a clumsy one, as though his body were about to escape from him, or weighed too much."

The first edition of *Poet in New York*, published posthumously in New York, in a bilingual volume, in 1940. Approximately one month after its publication, Lorca's friend José Bergamín brought out a Spanish edition in Mexico.

Self-Portrait in New York, c. 1929–31, ink. One of several New York–era drawings showing Lorca's face (with *lunas*, or "moons," instead of *lunares*, or "moles") in juxtaposition with a phantasmagorical beast. In "Moon and Panorama of the Insects (Love Poem)," in *Poet in New York*, Lorca writes, "Watch out for your hands and feet, my love, / since I must give up my face, / my face, my face, yes, my half-eaten face!"

While in Bushnellsville, New York, 1929, Lorca wrote poems whose titles betrayed his private preoccupations: "Nocturne of Emptied Space," "Landscape with Two Graves and an Assyrian Dog," "Ruin."

In Havana, June 8, 1930, four days before his departure. "I've spent the happiest days of my life here," Lorca said.

With swimmers from the Havana Yacht Club, 1930.

Federico and Francisco García Lorca, 1930. Lorca once indicated to a friend that his brother was "inhibited by my personality, do you understand?"

federico garcía lorca
POEMA
del CANTE JONDO

1 baladilla de los tres ríos.
2 poema de la siguiriya gitana.
3 poema de la soleá.
4 poema de la saeta.
5 gráfico de la petenera.
6 dos muchachas: la lola. amparo.
7 viñetas flamencas.
8 tres ciudades.
9 seis caprichos.
10 escena del teniente coronel de la guardia civil.
11 diálogo del amargo.

ediciones ulises

ABOVE The first edition of *Poem of the Deep Song* (1931).

LEFT With his niece Tica, 1931. Two years later Lorca remarked that without the presence of children in their house, he and his family would go "crazy."

With the Chilean diplomat Carlos Morla Lynch (*left*), one of Lorca's closest friends in Madrid in the 1930s.

Bebé Morla Lynch, 1933. Lorca kept a picture of her on his desk in Granada.

BELOW Lorca's good friend and sometime amanuensis Rafael Martínez Nadal (*right*), who criticized the poet's work with a "violent sincerity" that Lorca welcomed.

ABOVE With the music critic Adolfo Salazar (*left*), at a Madrid fair, *c.* 1930. In 1921, Salazar gave Lorca his first favorable review in the national press.

The bullfighter Ignacio Sánchez Mejías, 1934. His return to the ring that year prompted Lorca to comment, "Ignacio has just announced his own death to me."

But in the midst of so much life, death hovered. Earlier in the summer one of Morla Lynch's close friends, a bullfighter named Gitanillo, had been wounded in the bullring. The man lingered for weeks in a Madrid hospital. Throughout the ordeal Lorca sent Morla tender letters of condolence. "I can imagine how you must have suffered, and I am with you because I understand you and because I too am accustomed to suffering from things people neither understand nor suspect," Lorca wrote in August, after Gitanillo had finally died. "Between one person and another there are tiny spider threads that eventually turn into wires and even bars of steel. When death separates us we are left with a bloody wound in the place of each thread."

By mid-August Lorca claimed to have finished a new book of poetry, "one of the most intense works to leave my hands." He called it *Poems for the Dead*. "I've been like a fountain," he told an acquaintance. "Writing day and night. At times I've had a fever like the old romantics, but without losing this immense conscious joy of creating." While *Poems for the Dead* never appeared as a book, Lorca seems to have drafted at least six new poems that summer, works whose stark imagery and opaque language are reminiscent of his New York poems. Earlier in the year he told a journalist he had come to view poetry "with a new eye." As a result, he intended to invest his verse with greater lyricism and pathos. "But a cold, precise, purely objective pathos."

In August, Lorca completed a new play, *Once Five Years Pass*. Like *The Audience*, which he continued to read to select friends, the new drama was an attempt to shatter the bounds of the mainstream theater. Lorca had conceived of the play before going home to Granada that summer and had talked about it with Carlos and Bebé Morla Lynch. Bebé had expressed such enthusiasm for the work that Lorca looked to her portrait for encouragement as he labored over the script. He appears to have written the play in its entirety that summer, working rapidly in both pencil and ink. He finished and dated the manuscript on August 19, 1931.

He subtitled the drama "a legend of time," a notion derived largely from Victor Hugo's "Legend of the Handsome Pécopin and the Beautiful Baldour." In Hugo's story, two lovers are separated for one hundred years; when at last they are reunited, one is a young man and the other an old woman. In Lorca's play, two lovers agree to wait five years before marrying. But when five years have passed, the young woman has abandoned her fiancé for a virile soccer player. The bereft Young Man—as he is called throughout the play—is left to mourn his "purposeless love." In desperation he pursues a second woman, a typist who has loved him for years, but she too now scorns him. "I'll marry you," she taunts, "once five years pass!"

Written with the freedom and unity of a poem and the fluidity of film, *Once Five Years Pass* is both a dreamlike meditation on the phenomenon of time and a deliberate obfuscation of conventional theatrical time. The play begins at six in the evening and ends at midnight, but its events span the course of five years. The concept of past and future does not exist; things are merely "now" or "never." Lorca's distortion of time reflects both his own fascination with the subject and that of his contemporaries Luigi Pirandello, Jean Cocteau, and even Salvador Dalí, who in 1931 completed *The Persistence of Memory*.

As a child Lorca had experienced time "as an elemental, shaping force" his brother recalled. "To [Federico], the living mystery of a perishable individual flower or the rock beside the water were more vital manifestations of time than the flux of great events." As an adolescent, Lorca wrote obsessively of decay and decline in the natural world, and of time's incessant pull on the fabric of human love and life. He was sharply aware of time's passage—especially so in the summer of 1931, with the birth of his niece and the consequent start of a new generation in his family.

Images of children and of childhood surface throughout the play. According to Isabel García Lorca, *Once Five Years Pass* consists "entirely of my brother's childhood recollections." The play is in many ways a private elegy, scattered with figures and events from Lorca's past: a child's funeral, a dead cat, a boy who used to wear a clown's costume whenever he came to play with Lorca and his siblings. A sense of loss pervades the play. In act 1, a Dead Boy, "dressed in white, as though for his First Communion, with a crown of white roses on his head," comes onstage with a Dead Cat. Both long to be restored to life. "We'll go from house to house until we reach the place the seahorses call home," the Boy tells the Cat.

> It isn't heaven. It's solid ground,
> with the grass swaying to and fro,
> and a lot of crickets chirping,
> and slingshots for shooting stones,
> and the wind just like a sword,
> and the clouds all floating over.
> I want to be a boy! A boy!

But Death, in the form of a hand, reaches out and seizes both the Boy and the Cat, and although neither is seen again in the play, each is repeatedly mentioned by other characters, in different contexts, so that together they metamorphose into a poignant emblem of lost innocence.

Also lost are the offspring of failed attempts at love. Here, as in a number of

other works, most conspicuously *Suites* and his New York poems, Lorca summons the motif of the unborn child. In the second act, after learning that his fiancée has broken their engagement, the Young Man is visited by a Mannequin
dressed in a bridal gown. Brandishing a child's pink suit, the Mannequin tor-
ments the Young Man with thoughts of the child he will never beget: "Two
streams of white milk flow from me / with a sorrow that soaks my silk robes / . . .
My son! I want to have my son! / . . . And he is your son!" For the Young Man,
the unborn child is both a literal embodiment of the love he has lost and a figurative reminder of the sterility to which his cerebral existence has condemned
him.

A melancholy figure with a pale face and a faintly androgynous nature, the
Young Man inhabits a world of books and dreams. He prefers fantasizing about
the future, or recalling the past, to living in the present. The noise and vitality
of everyday existence frighten him. When Death, in the guise of three Cardplayers, confronts him at the end of the play, he seeks refuge in his memories
of childhood. But these cannot save him; he has run out of time. One of the
Cardplayers fires a silent arrow from a pistol, and the Young Man's hands fly to
his heart. "One must live!" cries the Cardplayer. "One mustn't wait!" shouts his
companion. Dying, the Young Man murmurs, "I have lost everything."

Lorca constructed his play using expressionist techniques, so that each of the
drama's various components reflects some aspect of the protagonist's state of
mind. The play's settings—a library, a turn-of-the-century bedroom, a forest—
underscore the Young Man's emotional and intellectual turmoil. Secondary
characters—an Old Man, a Boy, a Harlequin, a Mask—serve as refracted images of the Young Man's mind and memory. Lighting and sound suggest
changes in his mood. In essence, the play takes place inside its protagonist's
mind. Years earlier Lorca had attempted a similar effect in a brief allegorical
play entitled *Theater of Souls*, a work written in 1919 when Lorca was just
twenty-one. He subtitled that play "Landscapes of a Spiritual Life" and noted
that its action "occurs in the marvelous theater of our interior world." With
Once Five Years Pass he returned to the idea, this time bringing to it the full
weight of his theatrical experience and imagination.

He made few public remarks about his new play, except to observe somewhat offhandedly that it is "a mystery play, written in prose and verse, whose
theme is the passage of time." But the work obviously meant a great deal to
him. His brother said later that *Once Five Years Pass* contains a "personal vision
and personal emotions, objectified by art." Lorca undoubtedly saw parts of himself in the play's protagonist, a man whose fear of death and tendency to dwell
in the past lead him to shun the visceral life of the present. For the Young Man,

as for most Lorca protagonists, desire remains unsatisfied. He can experience neither the joy of love nor the consolation of children. His past is lost to him; his future is cut short by death.

Throughout the play Lorca invokes the fifteenth-century poet Jorge Manrique's classic image of life as a river flowing into the sea of death—an image to which Lorca had been drawn for years. "Who'll wear my wedding dress?" the Mannequin asks, after the Young Man's fiancée has left him and it becomes clear that her bridal gown will go unused. The Mannequin answers her own question: "The river's mouth will wear it, to marry the sea."

By late summer, Republican fervor gripped the *vega*. Shortly after the proclamation of the Republic in April, residents of Fuente Vaqueros had called for the abolition of the death penalty and the creation of a public library. In the spirit of a new and secular Spain, they had also renamed one of the village's streets. The former Calle Iglesias (Church Street) became Calle Federico García Lorca, in honor of the town's most famous son.

Lorca did not comment publicly on the street's new name. But he did agree to speak at the dedication of the new village library late that summer. For the occasion he drafted one of the longest, most explicitly political talks of his career—although his politics were in the service of what he perceived to be a greater good, culture. Scribbled in pencil, with ink corrections, the talk filled thirty small sheets of paper.

On a hot, sunny day in early September 1931, he stood beneath an awning in the center of Fuente Vaqueros and gave the speech to a throng of listeners who pressed close to hear him. He talked about books, libraries, and the significance of "culture" in the Spanish Republic. Without culture or books, Lorca said, the people of Spain could not begin to claim their basic rights and liberties. Nor could they grasp the meaning of life. "If I were hungry and destitute on the street, I wouldn't ask for a loaf of bread, I would ask for half a loaf of bread and one book," he said. He gave an extended history of the book, beginning with its origins in cave inscriptions and ending in his own day, with newspapers, "the great book of the daily press." He hailed the power of books to change governments, and he decried those governments that dared to censor books. Books, Lorca declared, are the seeds of political revolution. "The French Revolution comes from the *Encyclopedia* and all of Rousseau's books, and every socialist and communist movement today springs from one great book, Karl Marx's *Das Kapital*."

Lorca praised the people of Fuente Vaqueros for their progressive instincts and their love of art. As he gazed out into the sunlit village square, with its crowd of familiar faces, he thanked the town for the formative role it had played in his life. He promised his audience that wherever he went he would acknowledge his birthplace, "so that whatever glory or fame I might achieve will also belong to this friendly, this modern, this tantalizing liberal village, Fuente Vaqueros."

From his spot on the speaker's platform, he could see the small white house where he had been born thirty-three years earlier, and also the street that now bore his name. He must have been tempted that day "to escape into lost corners of his childhood"—or so his brother later surmised, recalling the event. "But what a sense of duty and of loyalty kept him at his post as an orator!" The past, as Lorca knew from the play he had just completed, was irretrievable. He had no choice but to leap into the tumult of the present, into the whirling river of time.

CHAPTER 18

A PEOPLE'S THEATER

1931-32

At the end of September Lorca returned to Madrid, radiant after his long summer holiday in the *vega*. To Carlos Morla Lynch he seemed "more *granadino* than ever." After supper one night in Morla's apartment, Lorca spontaneously pulled a sheaf of papers from his pocket and began reading *Once Five Years Pass* to Morla, Bebé, and their friends. Morla sat beside Lorca on the floor; Bebé reclined on the couch. Some in the room sipped whiskey. One man smoked a cigar.

Lorca read—impetuously, and with a sustained rhythm—until three in the morning. Morla thought the play "magnificent, lavish, opulent . . . audacious and daring." But he did not understand it. His wife found the work "quite explicit and clear . . . [It] concentrates the past in a fixed and static present that doesn't progress," she said. Morla disagreed. "It's madness, come on!" he jotted in his diary.

Not far from Morla's apartment, in an imposing nineteenth-century building flanked by two sculpted lions, Spain's newly elected Constituent Cortes had begun drafting a constitution. Debate raged throughout the fall of 1931. Liberal representatives sparred with conservatives over almost every article in the document. In the end, the Left prevailed. The new constitution declared Spain "a democratic republic of workers of all classes." It granted the vote to both men and women, legalized divorce, abolished the death penalty, nullified all titles of nobility, and renounced war as an instrument of national policy. Most controversial were the document's restrictions on the Catholic Church. The constitution effectively abolished religious education and imposed formidable constraints on clerical activities and organizations.

Passage of the constitution came at a price. In the midst of the debates, moderate Catholic Republicans split from the government, and the leader of the party's left wing, Manuel Azaña, became the new prime minister. Azaña quickly forged a coalition with the party's socialist constituency. To men such as José Ortega y Gasset and Miguel de Unamuno, both of whom participated in the fractious constitutional debates, these were alarming developments. Ortega y Gasset and Unamuno had each envisioned a tolerant republic run by enlightened intellectuals—not the small-minded, anticlerical regime that emerged on the floor of the parliament building. Both men came away from the debates deeply disillusioned with the government they had helped elect.

In early October, Lorca attended a session of the Cortes. Packed into a gallery with dozens of other spectators, he watched as his old friend and teacher Fernando de los Ríos, now Republican minister of justice, gave an inflammatory speech calling for the complete separation of church and state. De los Ríos assailed the Catholic Church for its stranglehold on the country's intellectual life, and spoke with regret of the Jews who had been expelled from Spain by the Catholic monarchs in 1492. Liberals applauded the speech; conservatives blasted it. Lorca left the Cortes overcome by emotion.

To friends, he expressed intense enthusiasm for the young Republic and its leaders, particularly de los Ríos, whom he had known for nearly twenty years. He was also acquainted with the new prime minister, Manuel Azaña, who was married to the sister of Lorca's friend and theater colleague Cipriano Rivas Cherif. A writer, translator, and critic as well as a politician, Azaña had helped publish some of Lorca's earliest poems in the early 1920s and had attended the Madrid premiere of *Mariana Pineda* in 1927. A dramatist in his own right, Azaña maintained a close friendship with the actress Margarita Xirgu. Several months after he became prime minister, Xirgu premiered one of Azaña's plays in Madrid.

Lorca had never known any Spanish government to be so integrally linked to the nation's cultural life. Nor, for that matter, had he known any government he could admire. The regime espoused the same liberal ideals his parents had always championed, and its leaders shared Lorca's belief that art was a viable means of promoting social justice. Lorca became swept up in the reforming spirit of the Second Republic. Late one November night he burst into Morla Lynch's apartment, brimming with news. In collaboration with a group of university students, he said, he intended to help found and direct a national stage company aimed at "saving the Spanish theater and bringing it within reach of the people." They planned to call their company "La Barraca"—the name of the makeshift wooden stalls that typically housed puppet shows and other performances at village fairs. "We'll take La Barraca to every region in Spain. We'll go to Paris, to America . . . to Japan . . ."

Morla interrupted him. "How do you plan to fund this fascinating project?"

"We'll worry about that later," Lorca replied. "Those are just details."

On November 25, Fernando de los Ríos publicly declared his support of La Barraca. Five days later, the Spanish Students' Union formally requested government funding for the company. On December 2, 1931, Lorca spoke to the press about the project. With evangelical zeal, he outlined La Barraca's mission: "To give back to the people what is rightfully theirs." By this he meant the theater itself, for he believed the roots of the art lay with ordinary Spanish citizens. With La Barraca, as with his deep-song poems, puppet plays, and Gypsy ballads, Lorca sought to revive the popular Spanish tradition and reestablish his childhood bond with "the people." He later rephrased his objective: "We will remove plays from the libraries, take them away from scholars, and restore them to the sunlight and fresh air of the village square." He told a journalist, "It has to be us, the 'istas,' the 'snobs,' who dust off the old gold buried in the sepulchers."

On December 15, in a reshuffling of the Republican cabinet, Fernando de los Ríos was made minister of education. His appointment virtually assured funding for La Barraca. De los Ríos had visited Russia in 1920 and had seen firsthand the work of Stanislavsky's Moscow Art Theater. He believed wholeheartedly in the power of theater to strengthen national unity by reminding citizens of their shared heritage. He also believed in Lorca's talent, as he had from the moment he first heard him play the piano in the Granada Arts Center in 1916.

Official confirmation of funding came through early the following year. Although he claimed the title did not suit him, Lorca was named artistic director of La Barraca. By that time he had already begun organizing the company and planning its repertoire. The project enthralled him. La Barraca, his brother said later, "was like a dazzling toy that a generous government had placed in his hands."

Political controversy dogged the company from the outset. In January 1932, the satirical right-wing newspaper *Gracia y Justicia* published a "Ballad of Federico" ridiculing the troupe and its director. The long poem mocked both Lorca and his chief government patron, calling Lorca a "Gypsy" and de los Ríos "Sephardic." In a pointed reference to Lorca's "Ballad of the Spanish Civil Guard," the poem's anonymous author suggested that the Civil Guard be warned of the two men's theatrical activities. In March, *Gracia y Justicia* again lampooned La Barraca. This time the paper attacked the "leftist," "socialist," "heterodox" politics of the company. Neither Lorca nor de los Ríos acknowledged the affront. Two weeks later, de los Ríos told members of the Cortes that La Barraca signaled the start of a "new spiritual world" in Spain, a world of "collaboration between the classes, of fraternity among men." Lorca went on running the company as if nothing had happened.

His chief assistant in the endeavor was Eduardo Ugarte, a balding, bespectacled playwright and producer in his mid-twenties, who had recently returned to Spain from a short stint as a Hollywood screenwriter. Shy and soft-spoken, he shared Lorca's contempt for the commercial stage, which Ugarte called "recipe theater." He was both awkward and absentminded—he sometimes went out onto the street with a dinner napkin still tucked into his shirt—and Lorca laughed at his eccentricities. But he admired Ugarte's gentle manner, and came to depend on his acute theatrical sensibility. At auditions and rehearsals the two sat side by side. "I do everything the way I see fit," Lorca told a reporter. "[Ugarte] watches it and tells me if it's good or bad. I always follow his advice, because it's always sound. He's the critic every artist needs." When Ugarte remarked that one of Lorca's costume designs was "a piece of shit," Lorca merely agreed with him.

They auditioned dozens of candidates, most of them university students, for La Barraca's acting company. Applicants were asked to read passages of poetry or prose and sometimes to sing a song. Lorca took notes. "Small—nervous—will do," he scribbled beside the name of one candidate. "Cold but will do," he jotted beside another. In time he amassed a file of more than one hundred actors classified according to type: "Male lead," "Seducer," "Unhappy man," "Traitor," and so on.

He and Ugarte selected approximately two dozen students for their company. Lorca wanted the troupe to be egalitarian, and he insisted that "a democratic and cordial camaraderie governs all of us." No one in the ensemble received a salary; most joined the company for idealistic reasons. One actor later recalled that he signed up for La Barraca so that he could do something "effective," something "positive" with his life by helping to revitalize Spain.

Rehearsals began in early 1932. As artistic director, Lorca drove his young cast relentlessly. He knew precisely how he wanted to interpret each work, and he pushed his actors until he achieved his goal. He first read a given script to the cast, interpreting each role himself, much as he did when he read his own plays to friends. His voice was "incredibly malleable," a friend remembered. "He was practically a ventriloquist." He then staged the work, meticulously blocking his actors' movements. He told cast members where to stand onstage and what to do at specific moments. "Not that way, no," he would call out in the midst of a line reading. "Say it with amazement, not fear." He often illustrated what he wanted by acting it out himself. He fretted over the rhythm of his productions. Rhythm, he said repeatedly, is the most important aspect of any theatrical performance. He also paid close attention to music, and frequently embellished nonmusical texts by adding popular songs and melodies to the original script.

Lorca worked hard to distinguish his brand of popular theater from the conventional fare seen on the mainstream Spanish stage. He eliminated the prompter's box from his productions and demanded that actors learn the entire play, not just their individual roles, as performers typically did in the commercial theater. He talked of establishing a seminar so that his student actors could further hone their craft and study the plays in the company's repertory. During rehearsals he sometimes referred to Stanislavsky, whose theater, like Lorca's, was born of frustration with the conventions of nineteenth-century dramaturgy.

Demanding though he was as a director, Lorca neither intimidated nor patronized his actors. He rarely lost his temper, and when he gave orders he did so graciously. Offstage he fostered a spirit of friendship. After rehearsals he sometimes treated his company to tapas and drinks. "And to hell with my tiny income!" he would cry. But at the same time he maintained a certain distance from his actors, most of whom were at least fifteen years his junior. On one occasion he lost his temper with a company member who presumed to be on equal footing with him. When eighteen-year-old Álvaro Custodio, who joined La Barraca in its first season, suggested to Lorca that he include the work of playwright Eugene O'Neill in La Barraca's repertory, Lorca replied angrily that this was not the purpose of the company, nor did Custodio have any right to make such a proposal. He fired the actor on the spot. In subsequent years the two men occasionally ran into each other, and although Lorca was unfailingly polite, neither man spoke of the incident, and Lorca never invited Custodio to rejoin the company.

He chose La Barraca's repertoire with scrupulous care. He did not allow the company to produce his own work (he did not want the troupe to be a vehicle for self-promotion), but instead set out to present the work of other authors: contemporary as well as classical, foreign as well as Spanish. He spoke ambitiously of producing "German, Russian, Jewish theater. The best of the old and the new. Works with the sap of the people, that can reach the people." He even hoped to stage what he called "the great social works of Russia—but without any trace of propaganda, of course."

Primarily he aimed to revive and exalt the great plays of the Spanish Golden Age. He detested the blatantly romantic treatment these works customarily received. He described the divide between the theater of his own day and that of his Golden Age predecessors as a "river of meringue and hypocrisy." He and Ugarte both believed, along with a number of their contemporaries, that by restaging the Spanish classics they could modernize the Spanish theater. Lorca insisted that Spain's Golden Age playwrights—Lope de Vega, Calderón, Tirso de Molina, Cervantes—had given the country a "true national theater" and were "our most representative poets."

Accordingly, for La Barraca's first season, Lorca chose to present three Cervantes interludes together with Calderón's most famous play, *Life Is a Dream.* Lorca had long revered both authors. He had included an interlude attributed to Cervantes in the holiday puppet festival he staged with Manuel de Falla in 1923, and he had drawn inspiration from Calderón while writing both *The Shoemaker's Prodigious Wife* and *The Audience.* He once described the origin of his own theater as "Calderonian. A theater of magic." In 1932 Lorca told Barraca audiences that through Calderón's mystical theater one could arrive at "the great drama, the best drama, which is performed thousands of times every day, the best theatrical tragedy in the world. I am referring to the Holy Sacrifice of the Mass." To skeptics who wondered why a theater troupe subsidized by a Republican government should present a miracle play, Lorca explained that Calderón and Cervantes together embodied the two extremes of the Spanish theater. Cervantes was "Earth"—human, sensual, and popular—while Calderón was "Heaven"—divine, symbolic, rational. Between them lay the "whole compass of the stage and all theatrical possibilities, past, present, and future."

When it came to staging *Life Is a Dream,* Lorca himself played the role of "Shadow." It was the second time in his life he had deigned to appear onstage in a play; two years earlier he had performed in his own *The Shoemaker's Prodigious Wife.* For *Life Is a Dream* he draped himself from head to toe in black tulle, concealed his hands with black gloves, and veiled his face with a huge, hornlike black headdress. With fluttering arms and a voice "as dark as his costume" he took the stage, and under a ghostly blue light pretended to reign over the creation of the world. He looked, a friend recalled, like "a Tibetan widow."

Lorca had rarely been happier. "La Barraca keeps him in a state of euphoria," Morla Lynch noted in his diary that spring.

In March, in addition to his theater work, Lorca embarked on an extensive lecture series. He gave his first talk, a new lecture-recital entitled "Poet in New York," in Madrid on March 16. Morla Lynch was in the audience, as were many of the city's most prominent writers. The crowd burst into applause as Lorca calmly took his place at the front of the room, sat down beside a small table, sniffed a bouquet of carnations, shuffled his lecture notes, adjusted his water pitcher, and began to speak. "He couldn't be more serene if he were in his own home," Morla thought.

"Whenever I speak before a large group, I always think I must have opened the wrong door," Lorca began.

> Some friendly hands have given me a shove, and here I am. Half of us wander around completely lost amid drop curtains, painted trees, and tin fountains, and just when we think we have found our room, or our circle of lukewarm sun, we meet an alligator who swallows us alive, or . . . an audience, as I have. And today the only show I can offer you is some bitter, living poetry. Perhaps I can lash its eyes open for you.

The talk that followed was not "a lecture but a poetry reading," not an objective account of a trip to New York but a "lyrical reaction" to the city, Lorca explained. A more accurate title for the presentation might be "New York in a Poet," he continued. "The poet is me, purely and simply: a poet who has neither talent nor genius, but who can sometimes escape through the murky edge of the looking glass of day more quickly than most children."

Since returning from America two years earlier, he had read his New York poems to countless friends. Many were dazzled by the unorthodox works; others found them bewildering or even repugnant. By drafting a lecture-recital on the subject of the trip, Lorca sought both to contextualize the poems for listeners and to make sense of the collection himself, to find a cohesive arrangement for its eventual publication. "I'll publish it later," he said of the series in 1933.

> But first I want to make it known in lecture form. I'll read my poems and explain how they came to be . . . But not all of them . . . All of them would be too much. It's a huge book. Enormous. A killer book.

More fiction than fact, Lorca's lecture on New York presents a dramatic portrait of the poet's encounter with the New World. Passages of prose alternate with poems to suggest an archetypal confrontation between innocence and evil, darkness and light, childhood and death. In his earliest drafts of the talk (which he continued to revise over a period of several years) Lorca dwells on the dichotomy between black Americans and their moneyed white oppressors. Later versions of the work are less strident. But the essence of the talk remains the same: America, Lorca asserts, is a cold, racist, grasping civilization that murders its pure and betrays its poets.

Audiences received "Poet in New York" with enthusiasm. Reviewing Lorca's debut recital of the talk, critic Victor de la Serna wrote that the New York poem cycle constituted the "greatest achievement of contemporary Spanish poetry, both now and for some time to come." Lorca gave his talk twice more that spring. It became a permanent part of his lecture repertoire and, as such, a valuable means of honing his New York poems before he consigned them to the printed page.

Between March 16 and May 29, 1932, Lorca delivered a total of six lectures in cities throughout Spain. Several talks were commissioned by "Committees for Intellectual Cooperation," a new, pro-Republican organization designed to foster the intellectual enlightenment of the Spanish people. In addition to "Poet in New York," Lorca gave a revised version of the deep-song lecture he had written ten years earlier. He spoke in Valladolid, Seville, San Sebastián, Salamanca, and various locations in Galicia.

At each stop the routine was much the same. A group of admiring young intellectuals and writers would greet the celebrated poet at the train station and whisk him off to lunch. In the evening Lorca would give his lecture, followed by dinner and a nocturnal stroll through town in the company of a half-dozen or so devotees. To everyone's delight, he invariably oohed and aahed over the city's monuments. The following morning a glowing review of his visit would appear in the local newspaper, and Lorca would depart for his next destination.

As a speaker he was casual, if not careless. He usually sat to give his talks, one leg crossed over the other. He read from notes scribbled on odd-sized sheets of paper. At one lecture a reporter noticed that parts of Lorca's talk were written on hotel letterhead. He clearly reworked his talks as he traveled, jotting phrases whenever and wherever inspiration struck.

He savored the attention he received on the lecture circuit. Journalists fawned over him. He is as "bronze" as his Gypsy characters, one reporter observed after attending a talk. Audiences, too, idolized him. In Salamanca, his listeners clapped so strenuously at the end of Lorca's lecture on deep song that he was compelled to take an encore bow. Afterward he turned to Morla Lynch, who had accompanied him to Salamanca, and with childlike joy asked repeatedly, "Carlos, what did you think of the ovation they gave me?"

Of all the stops on his itinerary, the place that most intrigued Lorca was

Galicia, a corner of northwestern Spain known as much for its poverty as for its
rain-soaked beauty. Lorca had first visited Galicia in 1917 while touring Spain
with Professor Berrueta. He had been struck then by the region's "eternal rain"
and the "sweet green of the land." On his return in 1932 he told a reporter he
hoped to "write a poem on Galician themes."

He spent several days in the region, traveling first to the city of Vigo, then
north to Santiago de Compostela. He arrived in Santiago wearing a heavy
beige suit with "quite an American cut" and a red silk tie. To the poets and university students who clustered around him, he seemed the embodiment of urban sophistication. His young admirers followed him everywhere. Dazed by
their proximity to fame, they hesitated to speak directly to Lorca, and instead
talked among themselves in hushed tones while waiting for the poet to ex-
pound on the mysteries of his craft and the wonders of their city. Lorca did not
disappoint. As he ambled along the town's gray stone streets he talked on and
on. In the Plaza de Quintana, behind the city's majestic cathedral, he announced that because this particular square was "so closed-off, so intimate and
complete," he would like to remain there for the rest of his life.

In groups Lorca invariably monopolized the conversation, a habit annoying
to some but to others endearing. He loved to soliloquize, vaulting with ease
from one topic to another, one extravagant theory to the next. He punctuated
his talk with anecdotes and proverbs. He was always poetic and funny, always
"daring," a friend remembered. He knew how to please a crowd. In Santiago he
indulged in one of his favorite tricks—pretending to compose a sonnet spontaneously while sitting in a restaurant, when in fact he had written the poem
long ago and was merely copying it from memory to impress his admirers.

One young man who met Lorca during his visit to Santiago was so taken by
the poet that when Lorca placed a spray of flowers on the tomb of a local author, the young man, Carlos Martínez Barbeito, an aspiring poet, plucked a
camellia from Lorca's bouquet and took it home with him to dry. Before Lorca
left Santiago, Martínez Barbeito dedicated a poem to him as a farewell present.
Shortly afterward Lorca sent the work back; as a gesture of thanks to a reverent
young fan, he'd had the poem privately printed in Madrid.

The two became good friends. For a period of several months they exchanged richly detailed letters in which Lorca reflected on his own calling as a
writer and encouraged the young Galician to pursue a literary career. "You
mustn't abandon poetry," he told Martínez Barbeito in May. Later he asked,
"Are you still writing? Don't give it up, because you've got *the stuff*, and you
must shape and polish it." He sent books to the younger poet—"for your poetic
formation"—and reminded him that poetry "is a hard discipline, but it offers

the highest reward. It distances us from reality so that we are able to love reality passionately from a more tolerant and generous plane."

Martínez Barbeito relished Lorca's flattery. Although few of his letters to Lorca survive, those that do suggest the depth and intimacy of his attachment to the poet. Sometime in 1932 he scrawled on a postcard to Lorca, "Do you realize that my father was standing beside me while I was writing that second letter to you yesterday?" The postcard, Martínez Barbeito added, was meant to be shared with others. "To you I won't say anything. Why should I? You already know everything."

Lorca actively courted such attention from adoring young men. Besides Martínez Barbeito, he became infatuated that year with a twenty-two-year-old writer named Ernesto Pérez Guerra. Tall, thin, handsome, and intelligent, Pérez Guerra charmed Lorca from the moment they met. Although born in Galicia, Pérez Guerra had left the region as a child and moved to Madrid with his family. But he remained an ardent Galician, and when he discovered Lorca's fondness for the region he immediately began regaling him with descriptions of Galician customs and superstitions. Lorca was enchanted.

A profound, and apparently passionate, friendship developed between the two. Pérez Guerra later admitted to having been captivated by Lorca, not so much by his physical appearance, which except for his extraordinarily expressive black eyes was plain, but by his "presence." Wherever he went, Lorca took command of the space around him, "and everything else became audience," said Pérez Guerra. Lorca's "presence" transcended his art. He was somehow "phosphorescent. He glowed from within."

For a brief period, Pérez Guerra became Lorca's closest, most trusted friend and primary audience—much as Dalí had been in the mid-1920s. A sometime critic, editor, and poet, Pérez Guerra was clever, vibrant, and, according to one friend, "as beautiful as a god." He engaged in long, solemn conversations with Lorca about books and poetry. Inspired by their friendship and by his own rekindled interest in Galicia, Lorca announced in 1932 that he wanted to write a series of poems about the region. He intended to write them in Galician, though, not Spanish. He knew the language "passively," having heard it during his travels and in conversation with Galician friends. Occasionally, when he perceived an intriguing word in Galician, he would jot it down in a notebook, together with his observations about the region's dramatic landscape.

Of his urge to evoke Galicia in Galician, Lorca said later that in 1932 the region gripped his imagination "in such a way that I felt myself to be a poet of the high grass and of the lofty, slow rains. I felt myself to be a Galician poet, and I sensed an imperious need to write poetry." Except for a few poems composed

the previous summer, he had largely stopped writing verse since his return
from America. The theater interested him more. But he could not resist attempting a series of six brief, intensely lyrical poems that paid homage to
Ernesto Pérez Guerra's birthplace.

Lorca was familiar with modern Galician literature, and in particular with
the elegiac work of the nineteenth-century poet Rosalía de Castro, whose tomb
he visited in Santiago in the spring of 1932. He was also acquainted with medieval Galician-Portuguese lyric verse, and he loved to play and sing Galician
folk songs on the piano. In drafting his own Galician poetry, he drew heavily
on these disparate sources. His six poems include a "Lullaby in Death for Rosalía de Castro," two works dedicated to the city of Santiago, and a ballad in
which Lorca recounts a popular Galician pilgrimage. Together the poems depict an archetypal Galicia washed by melancholy rains and bounded by the
sea.

In the most personal work of the series, and also the least specifically Galician, Lorca mourns a youth who has drowned in one of the region's many
rivers. The short poem, "Nocturne of the Drowned Youth," opens with a bleak
summons whose final image recalls Jorge Manrique's famed lyric:

> Let us go down, silent, to the bank of the ford
> to look at the youth who drowned there, in the water.
>
> Let us go down, silent, to the shore of the air
> before this river takes him down to the sea.

While Lorca may have witnessed the aftermath of a drowning in Galicia during
one of his visits, his poem is less about the literal death of a young man than
about the figurative loss of childhood innocence in the waters of erotic love:

> His soul was weeping, wounded and small,
> under needles of pine and of grasses.
>
> Water descended, flung down from the moon,
> and covered the naked mountain with violets.

In the "Nocturne" Lorca mentions Galicia's Sil river as the site of the young
man's drowning. As it happened, Ernesto Pérez Guerra had been born near the
shores of the Sil river, and during their first encounter Lorca told him, "Someday I'll write a poem with the Sil in it."

The two men worked together to draft Lorca's "Six Galician Poems." Pérez

Guerra later characterized his role in the process as that of a "living dictionary
. . . a poetic and discriminating dictionary." It appears that Lorca first drafted
each poem in Spanish or a defective Galician, then read or showed it to Pérez
Guerra, who in turn translated the work into a sophisticated Galician. The extent to which the younger man was responsible for the syntax of the final poems is unclear. Lorca responded "intuitively" to his suggestions for Galician
vocabulary, Pérez Guerra said later, selecting from a range of possibilities the
one word that "sprang from his lyrical balls." Afterward the two friends took
turns copying out Lorca's poems in Galician on scraps of paper from Lorca's
desk. Drafts of the six poems found their way onto an invitation to tea, a royalties statement, and the back of an envelope.

Lorca finished the last of his lectures in late May. By then rehearsals for La Barraca's debut performance were in high gear. According to Lorca, the company
went through "eighty rehearsals" for *Life Is a Dream*. Friends and invited guests
sometimes sat in on the sessions. The poet Vicente Aleixandre attended one
Barraca rehearsal, as did the actress Margarita Xirgu. Even Prime Minister
Manuel Azaña found time to drop in on the company. Observers were struck
by Lorca's tenacity as a director. After watching a rehearsal one guest exclaimed, "What a slave driver García Lorca is! What a slave driver!"

He had seldom been busier. In late May, he accompanied Fernando de los
Ríos and several other government officials on a trip to select the site of La Barraca's premiere performance; they chose the tiny Castilian village of Burgo de
Osma. On May 29 Lorca gave his final lecture in Salamanca. On June 1, in
Madrid, he delivered a brief eulogy for a painter who had recently died. On
June 5, 1932, his thirty-fourth birthday, Lorca attended the Madrid wedding of
his childhood friend Manolo Altolaguirre and the poet Concha Méndez. Méndez had wanted the ceremony to be unconventional. Altolaguirre planned to
wear a green suit, and Méndez to carry a bouquet of parsley. After the ceremony, as the wedding guests filed out of the church, Juan Ramón Jiménez began tossing coins at a crowd of street urchins and shouting, "Repeat after me:
Long live poetry! Long live art!" Vividly aware of his own new status as a
celebrity, Lorca made his way from one group of wedding guests to another,
chatting expansively with friends and acquaintances. To Carlos Morla Lynch,
he seemed to possess "the elegance of a revolutionary genius."

But as much as he enjoyed this sort of occasion, Lorca generally disliked
what passed for social life in Madrid. He particularly loathed the idle chitchat
of the city's literati. He became so bored by the conversation inside the editor-

ial offices of Ortega y Gasset's *Revista de Occidente* that on one occasion he
fled the building. "The impression I get from these 'men of letters' is that they
live outside nature," he wrote afterward to Carlos Martínez Barbeito.

> I imagine them in some long, airtight corridor, banging their heads against the walls in
> an effort to discover something, while I . . . dear Carlos, want only to breakfast on the
> sound of the sea, and like the good poet I am, to take communion with a great mill-
> wheel every morning of my life.

He found Ortega y Gasset himself especially grating. The two frequently ran
into each other at the *Revista de Occidente*. To Lorca's annoyance, the philosopher invariably tried to talk to him about politics and to ask his opinion of current affairs. "I have no opinion other than to give them all a good drubbing,"
Lorca told Martínez Barbeito. Privately he spoofed Ortega y Gasset. At dinners
he would point to the oil and vinegar cruets and ask to be passed "the Ortega"
and then "the Gasset." He told a friend once that he had seen Ortega "peeling
off layers of intelligence." To demonstrate what he meant, Lorca put his hand
to his forehead and with a "fffuazz!" sound pretended to tear bark from a tree.

On July 6, La Barraca held its final dress rehearsal for *Life Is a Dream*. Morla
Lynch noted the vigor and authority with which Lorca strode from one end of
the room to the other, barking orders and waving his hands. At home, Morla's
apartment was festooned with posters bearing the company's new logo: an actor's mask superimposed over a blue carriage wheel, with the words "La Barraca, University Theater, Federal Union of Hispanic Students" printed in red
above and below it.

The company was scheduled to make its debut performance on July 10, 1932,
in Burgo de Osma. The twenty-nine-member troupe set out from Madrid in
two government vans and a Chevrolet truck. The few women in La Barraca
wore blue skirts and blouses; the men wore one-piece blue workmen's coveralls
chosen to show the company's solidarity with "the people," as Lorca phrased it.
Both outfits featured the troupe's colorful logo. But because the uniforms were
unorthodox, misunderstandings sometimes arose. The residents of one town
mistook La Barraca for a band of communists and refused to sell them food.
More frequently, Lorca and his young actors were assumed to be ordinary la-
borers. "You look like a mechanic, sir," a reporter said to Lorca one day.

"Well, at the moment I'm just a stage director," Lorca replied brightly.

At Burgo de Osma, local dignitaries ceremoniously greeted the company. As
the troupe began unpacking costumes and setting up scenery in the main
square, a town crier marched through the village, spreading word of La Ba-

rraca's presence. At ten o'clock that evening the company gave its first public performance. People crowded into the square to watch. Lorca gave a brief speech outlining La Barraca's goals ("to bring poetry and art to the Spanish people") and describing the company's aesthetic principles (freedom from "sentimentality"; "noble purity"). Then the performance—in this case, three Cervantes interludes—began. The crowd was thrilled, reviewers were laudatory, and Lorca's friend Jorge Guillén, who had traveled from Madrid to witness the premiere, thought the production full of "charm," "levity," and "radiance."

During the next two days La Barraca gave two additional performances in neighboring towns, where the response was much the same. But on Wednesday, July 13, during an appearance in the provincial capital of Soria, local authorities inadvertently charged admission for La Barraca's performance, and the public protested. Although not the company's fault, the error sullied the young troupe's image.

Matters worsened on July 15, when poor weather forced a planned outdoor performance in the village of San Juan de Duero to be moved inside a church. The last-minute change rankled La Barraca's actors, who proceeded to give a distracted and unintentionally comic rendition of *Life Is a Dream*. Midway through the performance a group of right-wing hecklers, who had apparently come from Madrid expressly for this purpose, surrounded the small stage and threatened to attack the performers. The lights went out, the production came to an abrupt halt, and in the ensuing confusion members of the audience began hurling insults and even pebbles at the stage. Draped in the voluminous black folds of his Shadow costume, Lorca appeared before the crowd to plead for calm and to warn them against the danger of trampling on electrical cables. People mistook him for a priest and obeyed him. Eventually the police arrived and escorted the actors safely back to their hotel, although they had to follow a circuitous route to avoid being ambushed by their detractors.

Both right- and left-wing newspapers published copious accounts of the melee in San Juan de Duero. The conservative *Voz de Soria* blamed La Barraca for the disturbances and accused its thirty-four-year-old director of allowing himself to be guided by political fantasy. Although distraught, Lorca took comfort a few days later from a Barraca performance in the small town of Almazán. There, the audience was so mesmerized by the production that when a sudden downpour took place in the midst of the play, no one so much as opened an umbrella. By the end of the evening cast and audience alike were soaked, but few minded. In years to come Lorca loved to tell the story of this performance, when the only thing audible was "the murmur of rain falling on the stage, Calderón's lines, and the music that accompanied them." He was perhaps especially gratified because Fernando de los Ríos was in the audience that evening, catching his first glimpse of La Barraca in action.

On the way back to Madrid later that week, one of the company's trucks skidded on a curb and overturned. Several students received minor injuries, and at least one was seriously hurt. Though shaken by the accident, Lorca's actors managed to give an outdoor performance in Madrid a few days later. On July 23, *Gracia y Justicia* published another of its attacks on the company. Noting the mishaps that had plagued La Barraca on its first outing—the admission fiasco in Soria, the disturbances in San Juan de Duero, and even the truck accident on the way home—the newspaper's editorial staff denounced the troupe and questioned the sanity of its director, whom they called Federico García "Loca" (Crazy). There were deliberate references to Lorca's sexuality. His actors were described as *"niños simpaticones"*—a snide reference to *maricón* (queer)—and Lorca himself was described as the "flower of the Andalusian ballad." Lorca had not been hurt in the truck accident, the paper reported, because at the time he was traveling in another van, the one "carrying all the girls."

Lorca undoubtedly saw the article in *Gracia y Justicia* but chose to ignore it. In an interview with the *Heraldo de Madrid* a few days later, he announced that La Barraca would embark on its second excursion in late August. He had been pleased by their first outing. People had responded enthusiastically to the company, despite the "daring" nature of its stagecraft. As for those who chose to view La Barraca in a "political light," they were "wrong! The University Theater has no political bent of any sort. It is simply theater."

But he was tilting at windmills. As his colleague Eduardo Ugarte had observed earlier in the year, these were "fundamentally political" times, and no art—even one that aspired to a "noble purity"—could long remain outside the fray.

CHAPTER 19

APPLAUSE AND GLORY

1932-33

Before setting out on a second Barraca expedition, Lorca returned home to Granada for a short rest. Lullabies again drifted through the Huerta de San Vicente. Earlier in the year, Concha García Lorca had given birth to a son, Manolo. Lorca lavished so much attention on the infant and his sister that a friend accused him of spending all of his time playing with the children. Soon the older of the two, Tica, was big enough for Lorca to sit her on top of the piano and teach her to sing folk songs.

To the strains of lullabies he added the sounds of two records, which he played incessantly on the gramophone that August: a Bach cantata and a collection of songs by the *cante jondo* singer Tomás Pavón. Lorca played the recordings so often that his family became "profoundly" fed up with the monotony of the sound. But he persisted. He needed the music as inspiration for a new play he wished to complete that month. As a writer he had found that music delivers "what you're hoping to capture. It brings it to you. There are voices that say: come here, write this, say that . . . Wherever I work there must be music."

His new play was a departure from the two scripts Lorca had most recently finished. Unlike *The Audience* and *Once Five Years Pass*, the new work, *Blood Wedding*, a three-act tragedy, had strong ties to both the classical and popular traditions. He had first conceived of the play in 1928, but it was only in 1932, in the flush of his achievement with La Barraca and his renewed exposure to the classics of the Spanish Golden Age, that he brought himself to compose the work. The experience of producing theater had taught him, as it did Shake-speare and Molière, how to write plays. He drafted *Blood Wedding* in less than a month.

The work stemmed from an incident Lorca had read about in the newspaper four years earlier. The moment he'd seen the story he had exclaimed to a friend, "It's amazing! Read this. It's a drama you'd be hard-pressed to invent." A bride in the southern Spanish province of Almería had disappeared with her cousin on the morning of her wedding, and her bridegroom had gone in search of the couple. Some time later the cousin's dead body had been found, and near it the bride, in disarray. She told authorities she had been in love with her cousin and had planned to run away with him. The bridegroom was arrested for the cousin's murder; it later turned out the bridegroom's brother had com-mitted the crime.

The press gave the incident sensational coverage. For days the *Heraldo de Madrid* issued up-to-the-minute reports on the story. At one point the paper even printed a fictional dialogue between the bride and her lover. *ABC* titled its account of the case "Tragic Conclusion to a Wedding." In Almería province, a popular ballad chronicling the affair quickly materialized. By 1931, at least one Spanish writer had used the incident as the basis for a novel.

Lorca talked off and on to friends about the story. It touched on themes cen-tral to his work: illicit love, death, revenge, the force of human instinct. The facts of the murder mingled with his memories of Almería province, where he had briefly gone to school at the age of eight or nine. He could remember the region's moonlike aura, the pale sweep of its unwatered land and the ferocity of its light. As a playwright he generally allowed such details to percolate in his imagination, sometimes for years, before they fused into a solid theatrical vi-sion. He described his approach as "a long, constant, exhaustive thought process. And then, finally, the definitive move from the mind to the stage." Of-ten he began with "notes, observations taken from life itself, or sometimes from the newspaper." Even his most stylized plays—*Don Perlimplín*, *Mariana Pineda*—sprang from reality, if only from the aesthetic reality of a cartoon or a ballad. The act of writing itself went briskly: "I spend three or four years think-ing about a play, and then I write it in fifteen days."

With *Blood Wedding* Lorca sought both to reimagine the events that had taken place in Almería in 1928 and to revive the classical theater. He later boasted that *Blood Wedding* was the first tragedy "to be written in Spain for many, many decades." He had long viewed rural Spanish life, with its stark blend of Catholic dogma and pagan superstition, as innately tragic. Noting the quantity of macabre crucifixions to be found in Spanish villages, he had argued in *Impressions and Landscapes* that "the tragic, the *real*, is what speaks to people's hearts, and that's why artists who seek popular success always create Christ figures full of purple sores." Lorca's experience with La Barraca had reinforced his belief in the theater's ancient ties to the people. More than ever he was convinced that if the twentieth-century Spanish theater was to be saved it must return both to the people and to its earliest forms. "Without a tragic sense there is no theater," he insisted. The Spanish theater "must return to tragedy." Lorca also knew that a more traditional work such as *Blood Wedding* would be far easier to sell than the experimental plays he had recently been writing.

There were contemporary precedents for the undertaking. As a young man Lorca had read in translation John Millington Synge's one-act tragedy of rural Irish life, *Riders to the Sea*, and been impressed by the work and by Synge's achievement. Although he never publicly acknowledged his debt to Synge's play, it clearly served as a model for *Blood Wedding*, for it showed Lorca how effectively one could translate into tragedy the harsh circumstances of contemporary life in an isolated, agrarian community—where men work the fields or fish the seas, and women remain at home, awaiting the inevitable deaths of their husbands and sons. In Synge's Maurya, whose lamentation for her dead sons provides a welcome coda to the harrowing events of *Riders to the Sea*, Lorca found a prototype for the Bride's Mother in *Blood Wedding*. In the play's final scene, she, like Maurya, keens the dead.

Lorca may also have been familiar with Gabriele D'Annunzio's turn-of-the-century "pastoral tragedy," *The Daughter of Jorio*, which had been translated into Spanish and produced in Madrid in the mid-1920s. In Spain, Lorca's colleague Eduardo Marquina had written a series of rural dramas, and these too may have served as inspiration. But Lorca was equally influenced by older sources: Shakespeare, Lope de Vega, and the Greek tragedians. Within two years of completing *Blood Wedding* he remarked that because he had grown up with both the land and the sea (perhaps he was thinking of Almería), he was at once Iberian and Hellenic. And yet as always, he refused to adhere strictly to the rules. In drafting his first tragedy, he aimed to invoke the classical forms "with freedom," he said. He wanted to meld the past and the present, to create a theater that like the great dramas of antiquity "breathes with titanic force and seeks its soul, its action, its vigor in what is popular, in the people."

Blood Wedding preserves a number of elements from the original story Lorca read about in the newspaper. The play takes place in an arid, inhospitable landscape much like Almería province. The drama itself tells of a bride who elopes with her cousin on her wedding day. Her bridegroom pursues them, and his hunt ends in death.

To this fact-based framework Lorca added details meant to darken the story's Freudian undertones and to heighten its power as myth. His bride and her lover flee not into desert terrain—as their real-life counterparts did—but into a dank forest where death waits. It is not the bride's cousin alone who dies in Lorca's play, but both the cousin and the bridegroom who kill one another with knives. (The actual bride's cousin was shot—a far more prosaic death.) The cousin in *Blood Wedding* is married and has an infant son, unlike his real-life source, who was a bachelor.

To readers of *Gypsy Ballads* and *Poem of the Deep Song*, this was familiar ground. *Blood Wedding* re-creates the archetypal Spain of those collections—a region steeped in passion and blood, in popular Andalusian imagery and song, a world where nature reigns. "The fault is not mine," the bride's adulterous lover states. "The fault belongs to the land." Nature itself is a protagonist, most provocatively in the forest scene, where the Moon—a "young woodcutter with a white face"—appears, seeking blood to warm his icy flesh. Characters throughout the play recall the cycles of nature: the planting and harvesting of crops, the earth's rotation from day to night, and from birth to death. Had his most distant childhood memories not borne the "flavor of the earth," Lorca reflected, "I could not have written *Blood Wedding*." The play allowed him to capture the details of the Andalusian countryside "with the same spirit I felt in my boyhood years."

If the allegory in *Blood Wedding* is at times excessive, as some of Lorca's critics and friends charged, it is nonetheless striking. The play, in essence, is a long poem, in which passages of verse and prose combine to produce a lyrical portrait of Spain and its people. Lorca's productions of Golden Age drama earlier in the year had reinforced his appreciation for the power of spectacle. To his brother, he described the Golden Age theater as a visual and musical "holiday" for the senses—an effect to which he clearly aspired in *Blood Wedding*. The bride's home is rendered in "gray whites and cold blues," while the bride herself wears a black wedding dress. The play's final scene, a requiem for the dead, takes place in a brilliant white room without "a single gray, or a single shadow, or the barest trace of perspective." Against this backdrop two girls in dark blue dresses wind a skein of red yarn.

Critical moments of the play are set to music. In both a lullaby and a wedding song, Lorca blends traditional verbal motifs and lyrics with metaphors of his own invention to suggest the impending tragedy. Structurally, *Blood Wed-*

ding reveals traces of the Bach cantata to which he listened so assiduously while working. Parts of the drama correspond to arias, recitatives, and chorales. In at least one production of *Blood Wedding*, Lorca underscored the play's affinity with Bach by introducing the forest scene with a passage from the Second Brandenburg Concerto.

In its shape, tone, and subject, its compression of detail and dense verbal imagery, the play recalls its Renaissance and baroque forebears—Shakespeare, Lope de Vega, Calderón—as well as the tragedies of classical Greece. But Lorca's work is also contemporary. Techniques from the expressionist theater inform much of the play. Only one character in *Blood Wedding*, the bride's cousin, Leonardo, is called by name; others are referred to by type: Bride, Mother-in-Law, Wife. The climactic forest scene, which Lorca later cited as his favorite part of the play, marks an abrupt stylistic shift from the more conventional passages that precede it. With its "great, moist tree trunks," "murky atmosphere," and fantastical Woodcutters, it is reminiscent of the jungle in Eugene O'Neill's *The Emperor Jones*, a play Lorca very probably knew. When the Moon and Death, in the guise of a Beggar Woman, appear, he said, "the realism that dominates the tragedy until that moment is ruptured and gives way to poetic fantasy, where naturally I find myself most at home, like a fish in water."

Visual and musical symbols suggest the actual moment of death. Seconds before the two male protagonists kill one another, the stage turns blue, the Moon emerges, and a violin duet sounds. Suddenly two screams shatter the air, and the music stops. In silence, the Beggar Woman, draped in a shroud, steps onstage. With her back turned to the audience she spreads her cloak, like a prehistoric bird, and the curtain falls.

In a sense Lorca had been rehearsing this scene for years. Components of the forest sequence—the Woodcutters, the Moon, Death, the forest itself—appear, variously, in *The Butterfly's Evil Spell*, *Once Five Years Pass*, and *Gypsy Ballads*. The moon, in particular, had obsessed Lorca at least since adolescence. At twenty he described the moon's light as "sacred, sacred, sacred," in spite of the fact that it "wounds you too much." In *Impressions and Landscapes* he called the moon a "comforter of the sad. Poets' aide. Refuge of the passionate. Perverse and chaste rose. Ark of sensuality and mysticism. Infinite artist of the minor key." He viewed the moon as the richest of the celestial bodies, a force linked to fertility, water, time, and death, a substance whose reflected light suggests reflected things—recollections of childhood, of lost loves. The moon had cast its pale light on Lorca's work from the start. "I am a poet of the night," observes the Poet in Lorca's *The Billy Club Puppets.* "Pay me in silver. Silver coins look like they're lit by the moon."

Lorca had no sooner finished *Blood Wedding* than he set off on his second expedition with La Barraca. The group left Madrid on August 21 for a tour of northern Spain, including Galicia, where they received flattering press coverage. One reviewer hailed the company as an emblem of "freedom" and "revolution."

The tour went smoothly. In cities and villages along the country's verdant northern coast, audiences welcomed the young troupe. According to Lorca, La Barraca typically attracted two types of people: writers and intellectuals, and those Lorca simplistically described as "rustic *campesinos*," poorly educated men and women who worked in fields and factories. The single group that did not warm to the company, he said, was the "frivolous and material-minded" bourgeoisie. Despite the fact that he and his family belonged to it, Lorca despised Spain's middle class. He accused it of having "killed" the theater, of having "perverted it." His remarks seemed not to affect his affluent parents, who over the years had grown accustomed to their son's hyperbole.

In interviews and conversation Lorca insisted time and again that La Barraca's best audiences were ordinary Spaniards. They "know what the theater is. They gave birth to it." Although they might not grasp the intellectual or theological ramifications of a play such as Calderón's *Life Is a Dream*, he noted with condescension, they could nevertheless "feel it." Lorca loved to study the crowds who came to watch La Barraca, to scrutinize their response to the company's work. He relished their slightest gesture of approval. The purity of people's reactions to the troupe reaffirmed his faith in the power and magic of the theater. On the day after a performance, villagers would often spot Barraca actors on the street, and in their excitement cry out, "She was so and so! He was that one!" An elderly man once murmured wistfully to several company members, "How I'd love to travel around with you to God's little villages, playing the fool."

On reaching a new town, Lorca often struck out by himself to explore the sights while his crew unpacked costumes and set up the stage. Dressed in his blue mechanic's coveralls, with the Barraca emblem boldly displayed on his breast pocket, he visited churches and monuments and chatted with townspeople. He often gave coins to the curious children who inevitably clustered around him. He loved playing the star. Occasionally he made a clumsy attempt at helping with preparations for the evening performance, but for the most part he left his colleagues to attend to the more mundane tasks of their enterprise. Despite his affection for the working-class uniform he wore with such pride, Lorca disdained manual labor and used his childhood limp as an excuse to avoid it. "Federico was not made for physical work," one company member recalled kindly.

In most towns the routine was the same. The troupe arrived by truck and selected a performance site—often in a square backed by a picturesque church or civic building. As they unpacked, a town crier would roam the streets, announcing their presence. At curtain time residents brought chairs and cushions into the square and settled down to watch Lorca's young actors perform. After the production, which generally lasted ninety minutes, company members dismantled the stage and stored their equipment. The following day, enthusiastic reviews usually appeared in the local press. The actors always bought copies to take home.

Lorca staged his Barraca productions with an eye to authenticity and innovation. He used traditional musical instruments—lutes, guitars, *vihuelas*—to accompany his shows. He carefully selected the company's designers and sketched many of La Barraca's costumes himself. Visually his productions were novel. Instead of conventional footlights, actors were lit by overhead spotlights. And yet there was nothing fussy about his work. "This is not art theater," Lorca cautioned. For financial as well as logistical reasons, productions remained simple.

Lorca's pioneering work nonetheless helped spark the rejuvenation of Spanish stagecraft in the 1930s, and as such was the realization of a lifelong dream. "For me La Barraca is my entire work, the work that interests me, that excites me even more than my literary work," he said. During his years with La Barraca he wrote almost no poetry. It didn't matter. The theater gratified him in ways that verse could not. It was alive, and therefore always in flux. No performance was immutable—hence Lorca's constant impulse to tinker with both productions and scripts. Late in 1932 he was asked if he had neglected poetry for La Barraca. "No," he replied. "I haven't set it aside. At the moment we're immersed in the poetry of Calderón, Cervantes, and Lope de Rueda."

Watching Lorca at work with La Barraca, barking orders, singing, stepping over sets and properties as he got ready for a performance, his friend Pedro Salinas was reminded of the boy Federico who "set up a theater in the living room of his home in Granada." La Barraca was Lorca's "big toy, his childhood dream come to life." To the student actors and designers in his troupe he was an inspiration, a teacher, an irrepressible comic with a bagful of tricks, a virtuoso— albeit one whose relentless antics sometimes tested their patience. On the road,

Lorca sang with the group. The company even had a special song for truck breakdowns. In every town he visited he unearthed a piano, often untuned, and with his actors at his side he played popular melodies and belted out songs. He talked nonstop; he always had a topic. He read his work to the group. One night in the small medieval town of Santillana del Mar, after rain had forced the company to cancel its performance, Lorca assembled the entourage by a fireplace in their hotel and read *Once Five Years Pass*. Many found the play perplexing, but few forgot the reading.

He was somehow larger than life. Dressed in the shapeless blue coveralls he had grown to love, he would run his fingers dramatically through his black hair, and as he did so his massive head seemed larger and more imposing than ever, one Barraca actress remembered. There was an air of exaggeration and mischief to almost everything he did. At dinners he sometimes urged his actors to rub their fingernails together so that they could hear the "song of the little lice," and he taught them to unfurl their napkins over their faces, like stage curtains. It was one of his favorite tricks.

Inevitably, his constant need for attention, persistent chatter, and histrionics became irritating. Before every Barraca performance Lorca spoke to the audience, explaining the company's goals and introducing the play they were about to see. He stood onstage, reading from tiny sheets of paper on which he had scribbled his remarks. Some actors thought the talks "excessively pompous," and to an extent they were right. At times Lorca expounded at length, with considerable bombast, on the history of the Spanish theater. During one such session a backstage technician managed to attach a chain to Lorca. In the midst of Lorca's long delivery, the technician suddenly yanked on the chain and dragged him offstage.

In September Lorca returned to Madrid, brandishing his draft of *Blood Wedding*. "I've got a drama you're going to love," he crowed to a colleague shortly after his arrival.

He immediately began reading the play to friends. At a small gathering in Rafael Martínez Nadal's apartment, people drank wine and argued for hours about the work's forest scene. Was it a "grotesque" disruption of an otherwise authentic tragedy? Lorca maintained that it was not.

When he read his play late one night to a small gathering in Morla Lynch's apartment, the group was spellbound. It didn't matter that Lorca at first lost his script and as a result did not begin the reading until one-thirty in the morning, or that Morla himself insisted the play's title was too melodramatic. When the reading ended, no one spoke. Their silence, Morla thought, was "more eloquent" than any applause.

Lorca continued to read the play, and to his delight, people liked it. Virtually no one had appreciated *Once Five Years Pass* or *The Audience*, and for the most part he had consigned those scripts to a desk drawer. But listeners were riveted by *Blood Wedding*. Lorca read simply, interpreting each character through word as well as gesture, but without overt histrionics. By the sheer force of his delivery he was able to suggest both the setting and the ambience of the play. At the end of one reading, a friend broke down in tears. Encouraged by such reactions, Lorca began circulating the play among prospective producers. He first sent the script to the celebrated Argentine actress Lola Membrives, then touring in Madrid, whom he envisioned in the role of the Bride's Mother. But Membrives turned him down, citing prior commitments. In truth, she wanted to play the Bride. Lorca was annoyed. When they met for the first time a few days later, Membrives said, "Lorca, you've got to write a play for me in which I sing, dance, play the guitar, die, and do everything."

"Why?" he shrugged. "It's already been written. Do *Carmen*."

Late one night he telephoned another actress, the beautiful, fine-featured Josefina Díaz de Artigas, to ask if he could read his new play to her. "Come whenever you want," the actress said.

"Would you mind if I came over right now?" Lorca asked.

Shortly afterward Lorca turned up at Díaz's home with his friends Ignacio Sánchez Mejías and La Argentinita. Lorca plunged into a recital of *Blood Wedding*. The actress was captivated. Despite the fact that she and her ensemble were known chiefly for their productions of light comedies, she agreed that night to stage Lorca's tragedy later in the season. She too wanted to play the role of the Bride.

In October, Lorca accompanied La Barraca to Granada, where they took part in a four-hundredth anniversary tribute to the University of Granada. The troupe gave two performances. During their visit Lorca took members of the company around the city and introduced them to his friends and family. He persuaded one of his young actors, a wealthy student with a showy convertible, to drive him through town in his car while Lorca waved ostentatiously to pedestrians. It was his way of poking fun at the city's bourgeoisie.

Later in the month La Barraca gave two performances in Madrid. Critic Miguel Pérez Ferrero of the *Heraldo de Madrid* published a laudatory review of the company's work, acknowledging, in particular, Lorca's remarkable gifts as a director, actor, and poet. The conservative magazine *Blanco y Negro* also took note of La Barraca. In its November 6 issue it published a two-page photo spread showing the group in full dress for *Life Is a Dream*. Their costumes were boldly patterned and their makeup exaggerated. Lorca wore his gauzy black "shadow" headdress. At thirty-four, he still had a cherubic face. His eyes, their almond contours defined by thick black lines, stared gravely off to one side.

He had seldom been more celebrated or lived a more public existence. And yet he longed for companionship. Autumn arrived in Madrid, and with it crystalline days that recalled his youth in Granada. He grew wistful. To Eduardo Rodríguez Valdivieso, a young Granadan poet whom he had met the previous winter and with whom he was enamored, Lorca sketched the doleful city of his teens. "I remember with distant melancholy the huge yellow goblets on the old trees of the Campillo, and the acacia leaves that fill the solitary Plaza of the Lobos, and the divine first cold wind that ripples the water in the Plaza Nueva. Everything that is the Granada of my dreams and of my solitude, when I was an adolescent and no one had yet loved me." He told Valdivieso he hoped their friendship would blossom, and he pleaded with the young man not to divulge the contents of their correspondence. "Because a letter that is shared is a bond that is broken."

A brief lecture trip took Lorca to Galicia in late November. On his return he told Valdivieso that he felt "tired and rather alone." In mid-December he made a hasty trip to Barcelona to give his lecture-recital "Poet in New York." It was his first visit to the city since 1927, and the press showered him with attention. "García Lorca has traveled through all of Spain. He knows France, England, Cuba, the United States, Canada," one paper reported. Presumably Lorca himself had supplied this inflated information. Another paper described him as "*modernísimo.*" At the recital itself, women in feathers and tulles sighed and murmured approvingly as he read. Later, during a private reception, several ladies begged Lorca to recite his famous Gypsy ballad "The Unfaithful Wife." He refused. "No, not 'The Unfaithful Wife.' No . . . It's the one poem that dissatisfied women always ask me to read," he said. The mawkish poem embarrassed him.

Reviewers praised his Barcelona recital. Critic Guillermo Díaz-Plaja declared that with his New York poetry, Lorca had transformed himself from a "minor poet" into one with an "epic voice." He had become a national celebrity. Sixteen of his poems appeared in Gerardo Diego's 1932 anthology, *Contemporary Spanish Poetry*, the first major compilation of work by members of the Generation of '27 and their immediate predecessors. Lorca confessed to being pleased with the poems Diego had selected for the collection—a sampling of works, all of them elegiac in tone, dating back to *Book of Poems*. "You've captured me just as I am," he said. "Because contrary to what people think, I'm not a happy poet but a sad one." In a biographical note to the anthology, he admitted that his aesthetic stance was in a constant state of change. "I will burn down the Parthenon at night so that I can begin building it again in the morning and never finish."

By late December 1932, he was back in Madrid. Earlier that month his parents had vacated their apartment in Granada and moved to the Spanish capital in order to be closer to their children. Their two sons were by then more or less permanent residents of Madrid, and their twenty-three-year-old daughter, Isabel, had recently begun to attend university there. Only Concha remained in Granada with her husband and two children. Although they would continue to spend their summers at the Huerta de San Vicente in Granada, Lorca's family had decided to make Madrid their winter home.

They settled into a spacious flat on the seventh floor of an apartment house on Calle Alcalá, one of the city's busiest thoroughfares. Soon after their arrival, Lorca abandoned the studio apartment he and Paco had shared since 1931 and moved in with his parents and sister. Although thirty-four, he still coveted the financial and emotional security of family life. His parents' airy apartment had tall ceilings and polished wood floors, and its windows looked out on a distant panorama of hills and fields. "No house is more joyful than this one," Lorca told a journalist. "Everywhere you look there is light, lots of light . . . So much wonderful light!"

He furnished his small bedroom with a studio couch and a work table whose cluttered surface held, among other belongings, colored pencils and India ink for sketching. On the walls he hung copies of paintings by Zurburán and Picasso. Because his room stood near the apartment's main entrance, Lorca was able to hear who came and went through the front door. When unwanted guests arrived to see him, he ordered the maid to send them away. Once, in mid-February, he instructed her to tell a pair of visitors that he was in Toledo celebrating Corpus Christi—a summer holiday. His callers were incensed. As they left, Lorca heard one mutter to the other, "No one treats me like that. No one."

On December 19, 1932, La Barraca gave a special performance at Madrid's opulent Teatro Español. Members of the invited audience that night included the president of the Spanish Republic, several cabinet ministers, various repre-

sentatives from the Cortes, and other prominent politicians and government officials.

Keen to impress such an august crowd, Lorca revised his usual introductory
remarks. Reading, as always, from a sheaf of handwritten notes, he spoke of the
novelty of La Barraca's work and stressed the as yet imperfect state of the company's productions. He reminded his listeners, many of whom were directly responsible for funding La Barraca, that in carrying out their modest work, he
and the other members of his company were acting not from self-interest but
for the "joy of being able to collaborate, as best we can, in this beautiful hour of
a new Spain."

The following day, in his review of the performance, critic Enrique Díez-
Canedo of *El Sol* noted the uneven quality of the ensemble's work—a fact he
attributed both to scant rehearsal time and to the amateur status of its student
actors. But he urged theater professionals to pay attention to the young group,
for La Barraca's unorthodox choice of repertoire and novel staging indicated a
genuine quest for a new theatrical style. Similar praise came from *La Libertad*,
where it was suggested that La Barraca might pave the way for a national Spanish theater company. Meanwhile the right-wing press renewed its assault on
Lorca's troupe. One week after La Barraca's appearance at the Teatro Español,
Gracia y Justicia published a derisive account of the event, noting that the
house that evening had been filled with "socialist tuxedos that seemed cut to
order."

Lorca ignored such attacks. He was proud of his company's achievement
and optimistic about its future. In its first year of existence, La Barraca had
given over sixty performances to nearly 125,000 Spaniards. Lorca had begun
speaking openly to the press about taking his company abroad—to Paris, London, even Mexico—so that foreign audiences could appreciate the "spirit of the
youth" in the "new Spain." There was talk, as well, of tours to Berlin and possibly Moscow. In the meantime, Lorca was offered the directorship of the National Lyric Theater, a post he ultimately declined.

Over the Christmas holidays he traveled with La Barraca to the southern
coast of Spain for a brief series of performances. On the beach at Alicante, he
had his picture taken. Beneath his baggy coveralls he wore a white shirt and a
pullover sweater. Except for the Barraca emblem on his chest, with its theatrical masks, he looked like an ordinary laborer. His hair was combed straight
back from his face, revealing a tiny widow's peak; deep lines had begun to
crease his jowls. He was stout, and, as one acquaintance observed, while not
handsome, he glowed. His stocky frame cast a long, thin shadow onto the

ground. Behind him the glistening waters of the Mediterranean lapped at the sand.

Rehearsals for *Blood Wedding* began early in the new year. Eduardo Marquina, the director of Josefina Díaz's company and a longtime admirer of Lorca's work, assumed responsibility for staging the play, with Lorca's assistance. Marquina told reporters he hoped this would be the first García Lorca production to strike the theatergoing public with "full force and efficacy."

Lorca showed up for every rehearsal and relentlessly pushed the cast to adapt their performances to the play's unconventional style. Actor Manuel Collado, who played the Bridegroom, later contended that "no play in the Spanish theater has ever been rehearsed so thoroughly." Lorca treated his script like a musical score. He staged the play's massive wedding scene as if it were a concert. "You, no!" he would sometimes cry out while rehearsing the scene. "Your voice is too sharp! You over there—you try it! I need a heavier voice . . . I need a fresh voice." He continuously interrupted the action of another scene to shout, "It has to be mathematical!"

For the most part he reveled in his combined role of author and director. "Tell me I'm great. Tell me!" he cried with childlike joy to one actress. But occasionally his contentment gave way to rage. One day he exploded at Josefina Díaz. When the pretty brunette persistently failed to achieve the result he desired in a particular scene, he screamed, "No!! Any one of my actresses in La Barraca could do it better!" Díaz burst into tears. "Crying is easy," Lorca snarled. "Any woman could do it better than you."

He was frustrated by the shortcomings of his cast, whom he later described as "secondhand artists." Neither Díaz nor the other members of her company knew how to cope with the poetic and dramatic complexities of Lorca's tragedy, a play whose heightened language and broad theatricality could easily, in the wrong hands, slip into melodrama. Díaz and her colleagues were comic actors. Their work in the play's critical and difficult final scene, where a chorus of women keens for the dead, so disappointed Lorca that he eventually silenced the chorus and ordered the Bride alone to speak. He grew exasperated with the actress who played the Moon because she insisted on reciting her speech with excessive histrionics. "Don't pull that Lorca business on me!" he cried, referring to the way his own imitators often tried to replicate his recitals of poetry—with a broad Andalusian accent and the singsong chant of a Gypsy. He lumbered onto the stage and commanded the young actress to pronounce her speech with a correct Castilian accent. "The work is written in pure Castilian," he reminded her.

By March, Madrid buzzed with talk of Lorca's play. *El Imparcial* observed on March 3 that it would be nice "if *Blood Wedding* were to open at last." Earlier, in response to a survey in which leading playwrights were asked their opinion of the contemporary Spanish stage, Lorca had bluntly told the same newspaper, "The Spanish theater of the day doesn't interest me." The gossip column wondered aloud if with *Blood Wedding* Lorca might not "launch the theatrical revolution he so desires."

The play opened on March 8, 1933, in Madrid's Teatro Beatriz, seven months after Lorca had finished writing the work. Luminaries packed the opening night house, among them Miguel de Unamuno. Jacinto Benavente and the Quintero brothers—pillars of the bourgeois stage Lorca loathed—were also present, as were a number of Lorca's friends and fellow poets.

The curtain rose on a simple room painted in yellow hues. Lorca's friend and sometime Barraca colleague, the artist Santiago Ontañón, had designed the sets and costumes in collaboration with another designer and with the close involvement of Lorca himself. Listeners found the play instantly riveting. By the time the wedding scene took place in act 2, the audience could not suppress its enthusiasm. In the midst of the scene, as actors poured onstage singing "Awaken, Bride, awaken!" the opening night crowd erupted in applause, and Lorca was forced to come onstage, interrupting the action of the play, to acknowledge his admirers. He emerged trembling, pale, and disheveled, and took his place beside his actors. With a dazed look on his face, he bowed to the house.

The action resumed. At the end of each act Lorca was called onstage to salute the crowd. When the final curtain fell on the churchlike white enclosure Ontañón had designed for the play's last scene, no one moved. Seconds later the theater burst into applause. Carlos Morla Lynch, who had fretted about the play all evening, hurried backstage to congratulate Lorca. He found the playwright looking "radiant and newly calm."

Reviews were ecstatic. Critic after critic wrote that with *Blood Wedding* Lorca had finally proven himself as good a playwright as he was a poet. They lauded his keen dramatic sense, his "balance" and "eclecticism" as a writer. They praised the manner in which he had fused the lyrical with the dramatic. The play's "sensuality" and "rural perfume" earned high marks, as did its unique blend of classical, popular, and contemporary elements. Several critics remarked on the similarity between *Blood Wedding* and *Gypsy Ballads*.

The play's spectacle drew the most attention. Arturo Morí of *El Liberal* observed that while the story of *Blood Wedding* was familiar, the play's form, style, and overt poetic symbolism were not, and these made the play "new." To many viewers, *Blood Wedding* represented a leap forward in the evolution of the Spanish theater. But a number of critics quibbled about the forest scene. *ABC* called it "inferior" to the rest of the play, claiming that in this instance Lorca had carried the "device of the poetic symbol" too far. The politically conservative *El Debate* and *Informaciones* both charged that Lorca's personification of the Moon and Death diminished the mounting tension of the drama and was "unjustified" and "puerile." Some critics insisted that in this scene alone, the playwright in Lorca had yielded to the poet, with unfortunate consequences.

Lorca defended his choice. A few months after the play's premiere, he explained in an interview that although he'd been accused—by "a member of the bourgeoisie"—of having exceeded the bounds of reality with his forest scene, "I could say to him: 'You, good sir, are going to die and you'll be carried out in a coffin with your hands crossed on your chest. And you, too, will transcend reality. *That* is reality.'" In at least one subsequent production of *Blood Wedding*, Lorca resisted pressure from the play's director to eliminate the character of the Moon from the text. He was convinced that if he could succeed in making his human Moon work, the device would triumph.

Josefina Díaz gave thirty-eight additional performances of *Blood Wedding* before closing her 1933 season in Madrid. She then took the work on tour in the Spanish provinces. Throughout the country critics responded favorably to the play. In a personal letter to Lorca, the poet Antonio Machado called *Blood Wedding* a "magnificent tragedy." Lola Membrives, the famed Argentine actress who had brusquely rejected the script the previous fall, asked if she could produce the play in Buenos Aires. Lorca said yes.

"I feel calm and content, because I've had the first great triumph of my life," he remarked to Eduardo Valdivieso shortly after the play's premiere. *Blood Wedding* had confirmed Lorca's potential as a playwright and proved to him that his work could attract an audience. It had also made him money. For the first time in his life he approached true financial independence.

But eventually the incessant flow of congratulatory visits, reviews, and letters fatigued him. Sometime that spring Lorca confessed to Valdivieso that his only preoccupation "these days" was Valdivieso himself, "my distant friend, whom I love and have not been able to write to." Lorca brooded about the young man. "Why haven't you written me?" he asked shortly after the opening of *Blood Wedding*. "Everyone but you has written to congratulate me. Are you annoyed with me?"

The trappings of celebrity—the adulation and applause—merely intensified his isolation and made Lorca yearn for a genuine companion, someone in whom he could trust, someone to love. "I'm hemmed in by people who *pretend* to love me, and I know what they say can't be half true," he told Valdivieso. "And that's why I look back to Granada, where you are and where I know you'll remember me tenderly and faithfully." He dreamt of spending summer afternoons with Valdivieso in Granada, reading books together, making new discoveries, strengthening their friendship. Although surrounded by "applause and glory," he felt bitterly alone. As it had in 1928 with the publication of *Gypsy Ballads*, fame rang hollow.

CHAPTER 20

VOICE OF LOVE

1933

At home with his parents in Madrid, Lorca came and went as he pleased. He ate when it suited him, entertained friends at random, and shut himself away in his room whenever he wished to be undisturbed. He sometimes wrote late at night or in the early hours of the morning. He slept until lunchtime. To a reporter he admitted, "I sleep a lot . . . That way my nerves are calm." Often he was just getting up, still dressed in his bathrobe, when people arrived to see him. Late morning was practically the only time friends could count on finding him at home.

He generally ate lunch with his parents, then left the apartment for the day. He spent his afternoons and evenings meandering through Madrid with friends. He toured the café circuit, dropped in on Morla Lynch's salon, and late at night could often be found strolling along the streets, "like an island surrounded by friends," recalled the stage designer and artist Santiago Ontañón. "From a distance you could hear his frank, luminous laughter." A cousin of Lorca's once accused him of being a "true noctambulist," and suggested that Lorca would adore the festival of Ramadan, because he could sleep all day and stay up all night.

His parents indulged his cavalier existence. They welcomed his friends at meals and did not object when Lorca turned their home into a base of operations for his theatrical projects. Paco García Lorca once came home to find the apartment strewn with metallic wigs for a Barraca production. Lorca knew that he owed his privileged existence to his parents, and was unashamed of it.

When asked during an interview whether he was able to support himself with his writing, he replied blithely, "No, fortunately I don't have to make a living from my pen. If I did, I wouldn't be so happy. Thank heavens I have parents—parents who sometimes scold me, but who are very good and who always pay in the end."

His mother's hair was now fully gray, and her pretty face gently etched by the passage of time. When Lorca talked about her to others, "it was as if he was talking about his daughter, a very young daughter whom he must watch over with great care," a friend observed. "She formed me poetically," Lorca had said of Vicenta Lorca in 1932. "I owe her everything I am and everything I become."

His father had also aged. At seventy-three, Don Federico García's body was thick and his face deeply scored, but beneath burly gray eyebrows his dark eyes sparkled. He wore three-piece suits with a gold watch chain pulled across his abdomen, and he sucked on cigars. "One feels that he is the 'boss,' that he's the one who gives the orders," Morla Lynch jotted in his diary after meeting Lorca's father. Don Federico looked like what he was: a rich property owner from the countryside. He exuded "Andalusian eloquence," Morla thought. Lorca described him in print as "a gentleman from Granada," adding, "My father is delightful."

Blood Wedding was still in rehearsal in early 1933 when Lorca agreed to let the newly established Women's Civic Culture Club of Madrid produce two of his plays, Don Perlimplín and The Shoemaker's Prodigious Wife. The club—whose cumbersome name Lorca insisted on shortening to "Theatrical Culture Club," and eventually to "Anfistora Club," a made-up name—was an amateur group dedicated to the intellectual betterment of women. Its founder, Pura Ucelay, a tall, stylish woman in her fifties, had, like many Spanish women, been denied a university education, and was determined to give females a chance to participate in the nation's cultural life. She was part of a growing cadre of Spanish women who in the 1920s and early '30s endured contempt and often ridicule in their efforts to promote female independence and education. Married, with four daughters, Ucelay insisted that her children's dowries be spent on education, not husbands. Her daughter Margarita, who took part in Ucelay's Theatrical Culture Club, described her mother as a "bourgeois feminist."

Although she lacked formal stage training, Ucelay was a self-professed "devotee of the theater" whose refined sense of the art derived, in part, from years of travel abroad with both her uncle and her husband. With her Theatrical Culture Club, Ucelay hoped to combat what she saw as the "decadence" of the Spanish stage. She aimed to present one meticulously prepared show a year, and she wanted the club's first production to be Lorca's *The Shoemaker's Prodigious Wife*. She had seen the play at its premiere in 1930 and admired the work, and although she had never met Lorca, she sought him out one day in a Madrid café and boldly asked if she might be allowed to produce his play.

"For a charity event?" he inquired.

"Yes, absolutely! We're a dramatic arts club."

Lorca was charmed. When Ucelay offered to pay him to direct the work, he laughed and named a preposterously high price. He then suggested that since the play was short, Ucelay should combine it with a second offering, *Don Perlimplín*. He could foresee just one problem: he had lost his only copy of the work. But if Ucelay could locate a script for *Don Perlimplín*, he would direct both plays.

The next day, an elegantly attired Pura Ucelay turned up at the State Security Office in Madrid, where the manuscript for *Don Perlimplín* had been deposited in 1929 after its confiscation by government authorities. With the advent of the Spanish Republic, Ucelay assumed she could retrieve the document without any problem. When officials located the work, however, and spotted its subtitle—"Erotic *Aleluya*"—they balked. Ucelay was forced to return several times before the authorities would relinquish the script. Each time she appeared, she heard someone mutter, "That crazy woman is here again, the one who's looking for pornography."

Lorca began rehearsing the two plays in February 1933, in the midst of preparations for the premiere of *Blood Wedding*. He was especially enthusiastic about *Don Perlimplín*, whose only previous production had been blocked by the government. The script still bore the censor's red pencil marks.

Because of his busy schedule, he relied on Ucelay to do much of the directorial work for both plays. He generally showed up at the club's rehearsal space at sundown, often with his brother or a friend. The moment he appeared he took charge. "There was no more discussion or argument," Ucelay's daughter Margarita recalled. "He was a hurricane." As usual, he focused on rhythm, timing, and sound. He treated his plays like operas, making certain that each word received the proper intonation, that each character achieved its unique rhythm. He found his amateur cast less jaded than many professional actors, and he savored the enthusiasm they brought to their work.

He tinkered compulsively with the script for *Don Perlimplín*. During rehearsals he dictated cuts and revisions to Pura Ucelay and to his friend Santiago Ontañón, who in addition to designing the production was playing the lead role. Cast members were astounded by the intensity of Lorca's work on the text. They did not realize that many of the changes he made to the script were modifications he had decided upon years earlier, and that he was feigning spontaneity to impress them. One day, to their amazement, he interrupted a rehearsal of the play's final scene and crept off by himself to a corner, where he sat with one foot propped on a chair and a piece of paper spread across his knee, hurriedly composing a "new" speech for Don Perlimplín. In fact, he had written the speech three years before.

On April 5, 1933, one month after the premiere of *Blood Wedding*, Pura Ucelay's Theatrical Culture Club gave a single performance of Lorca's two plays in Madrid's Teatro Español. Earlier in the day, *El Sol* had published an interview with Lorca in which the playwright and director talked excitedly about his desire to establish a number of theatrical clubs aimed at combating the "kitsch" theater of the contemporary Spanish stage. He believed that amateur theater clubs could and should present works "that the commercial theaters won't allow," and during the next three years he remained committed to helping Ucelay and her club do so.

Lorca himself played the Author in Ucelay's April 5 production of *The Shoemaker's Prodigious Wife*. Although he made minor changes to the text, he staged the production much as Margarita Xirgu had at its premiere in 1930. He even used the same costumes. He devoted far more time and energy to *Don Perlimplín*, which he likened to a "chamber opera." "The work is built over music," he explained. Accordingly, he filled the brief production with musical interludes and background melodies by Scarlatti, one of his favorite composers. To further the effect of eighteenth-century splendor, he called for opulent costumes and sets: pale green curtains, painted backdrops, pastel frock coats and gowns, and powdered wigs.

Responses to the two productions were mixed. Many reviewers had seen and liked *The Shoemaker's Prodigious Wife* in 1930. But *Don Perlimplín* was new to them. Because politics determined much of what they thought and wrote, the liberal press by and large praised the work, while right-wing papers attacked it. More than one critic noted that in the role of Perlimplín, the corpulent Santiago Ontañón was all but inaudible. In the future, one reviewer suggested, Ontañón should stick to set design, not acting. The critic M. Núñez de Arenas of *La Voz* applauded the "admirable discoveries" of Lorca's witty play, its "maliciously sexual humor . . . and truly youthful, clever, amusing agility." But he termed Lorca a "terrible misogynist" for the reductive way he portrayed women in his work. In his three most recent productions—*Don Perlimplín, The Shoe-*

maker's *Prodigious Wife*, and *Blood Wedding*—Lorca had presented "three different women, three, and not one of them is good," argued Núñez de Arenas, mindless of his own misogyny. "We men are poor things in their hands."

Among a handful of negative reviews, the conservative *Hoja Literaria* labeled *Don Perlimplín* "anachronistic" and suggested that Lorca refrain from producing his old work. *La Época* dismissed the play as "an unjustified and unjustifiable caprice by its author." Right-wing opposition to the work stemmed in part from the play's notoriety as "pornography." Even someone so open-minded as Dr. Gregorio Marañón, a physician who had written profusely on human sexuality, and a personal friend of both Lorca and Carlos Morla Lynch, took offense at the play's eroticism. When Santiago Ontañón came onstage wearing a cuckold's horns during the Theatrical Culture Club's single performance of *Don Perlimplín*, Marañón abruptly rose from his box seat and left the theater. Asked two years later why *Don Perlimplín* was never again produced, Lorca said, "In Spain no one wants to be cuckolded . . . Even in the theater, actors don't want to be cuckolded!"

Sometime after the debut of *Don Perlimplín*, Lorca composed a long letter to Eduardo Rodríguez Valdivieso in Granada. He wrote the letter at two in the morning, in bed, shortly before slipping into what the called "the divine, boatless sea of Dreaming." Silence enveloped him, and in the stillness of the moment his mind turned to Valdivieso. "I want to tell you how much I love you and how much I think about you."

Recently Valdivieso had confessed to Lorca that he was alone and unhappy, and grateful for the friendship of so exalted a man as Lorca. "Your letter moved me immensely and made me love you more," Lorca wrote.

> I see you alone, filled with love and spirit and beauty, and I feel your solitude like a beautiful landscape where I could sleep forever. I too am alone, even though you think I'm not because I'm successful and receive crowns of glory. But I lack the divine crown of love.

He begged Valdivieso to send him at least two letters. "Will you do that? Now we must stay together always." He ached to be with his young friend in Granada, to bask in the region's warm spring air, to take in "the pagan smell of the temples, the tender green shoots the *vega* sends up when she's dressed like a bride." But he was plagued by the thought that Valdivieso did not share the intensity of his devotion, "that you don't love me as I love you. I don't know. In any case tell me. My friendship soars like an eagle and you are capable of killing it with one rifle shot."

He asked Valdivieso to treat his letter kindly, for it contained the "truth" of his feelings. "If you reject them, they will come like frightened little ducks to find the bitter waters of my reality." Lorca waited for a reply, but Valdivieso did not write back. Decades later he said that Lorca was mistaken to have thought him capable of reciprocating such passion.

In April, municipal elections took place throughout Spain. Citizens voted overwhelmingly for right-wing candidates. The opposition called for the resignation of Prime Minister Manuel Azaña. But the Republican leader clung to power, his popularity in decline, his credibility strained. At last, in September 1933, Azaña stepped down from office. New elections were scheduled for November.

Prior to Azaña's resignation, controversy had continued to plague the Republic. The previous year, army rebels had attempted a coup d'état in both Seville and Madrid; from his window at the Ministry of War, Azaña had witnessed fighting in the streets of the nation's capital. The government had survived the coup attempt and gone on to enjoy a short-lived period of prestige. But in early 1933 new trouble erupted. On January 11, extreme-left anarchists in Cádiz province briefly took control of the village of Casas Viejas and proclaimed communist rule. The following day, the government dispatched both Civil and Assault Guard troops to quash the rebellion. In their effort to flush out the rebels, guards set fire to a shack where several anarchists had taken refuge. The only two anarchists who managed to escape the flames were shot as they fled the building. The next day, troops executed another dozen suspected anarchists. Spaniards everywhere decried the incident. Right-wing leaders accused Azaña and his administration of "murdering the people," and although a parliamentary investigation failed to prove the charges, the public remained convinced of the government's complicity in the deaths. José Ortega y Gasset openly proclaimed his disappointment in Azaña's regime.

On January 30, 1933, two weeks after the Casas Viejas debacle, Adolf Hitler became chancellor of Germany. In Spain, interest in the fascist movement grew. By mid-March the country had its first fascist magazine, *El Fascio.* Its editor was the same man who edited *Gracia y Justicia,* the satirical review that regularly mocked Lorca and La Barraca. Alarmed by the appearance of *El Fascio,* the government quickly confiscated the magazine's inaugural issue and banned further publication. But enthusiasm for the movement spread. In a March 22 letter to *ABC,* José Antonio Primo de Rivera, the thirty-year-old son of the dictator who had ruled Spain in the 1920s, voiced his support for fascism.

He spoke of the movement's potential to restore unity to Spain, to the "Father-land."

Reports from Germany told of growing Nazi persecution of Jews. In Madrid, Carlos Morla Lynch noticed an influx of German Jewish refugees. On May 1— May Day—the poet Rafael Alberti and his wife, María Teresa León, launched a pro-communist, antifascist magazine called *Octubre. Escritores y Artistas Revolucionarios.* A few months earlier Alberti and León had visited Berlin and experienced firsthand the "climate of violence" in Germany. On February 27, they witnessed the burning of the Reichstag. They returned to Spain determined to expose the evils of fascism. The first issue of their magazine contained a manifesto condemning Hitler's regime and its savage disregard for the "principles of humanity." Lorca's name topped the list of signatories.

But although he believed in the social mission of art, and from time to time allowed himself to be swept up in the issues of the day, Lorca remained ambivalent about organized politics. Neither its language nor its routines held much appeal for him. An artist, not an activist, he clung to the belief that literature could, and should, contribute to the betterment of society, but must be stripped of political rhetoric in order to do so effectively. Unlike Alberti, he was at best a selective, at times naive, participant in his country's political life—a follower, not a leader. In 1932 he told a group of students, "Politics is the ugliest, most disagreeable thing I know." In April 1933 he signed a manifesto endorsing the Bolshevik Revolution—he was one of a hundred or so prominent Spaniards to do so—but he never joined the Communist Party, and in interviews he showed little understanding of its aims and activities. Once, after being asked his opinion on the possibility of a communist revolution in Chile, he remarked that such an event would mark a "pathetic end to civilization and aristocracy!" Ordinary Chileans, he predicted, would end up "like the Russian nobility, ruined and forced to work in order to eat."

While he sympathized with Alberti's political views, he scorned the poet's activism, which he felt diminished his power as a writer. Alberti had become a card-carrying Communist in the early 1930s, and as the decade progressed, both he and his verse grew increasingly more politicized. He regularly declaimed his revolutionary poems at political meetings in workers' libraries and in town squares. In his most radical writings, notably the 1933 volume *Un fantasma recorre Europa* (A Specter Is Haunting Europe), Alberti espoused a Marxist transformation of the social system. Lorca felt the intensity of Alberti's political commitment weakened the aesthetic quality of his work, and he made no effort to veil his disapproval. It was yet another means of jousting with his

fellow Andalusian in their ongoing contest to supplant Juan Ramón Jiménez as
"the" poet from the south. Alberti "has turned communist and is no longer
writing poetry, even though he thinks he is," Lorca told a journalist in the summer of 1933.

> He's writing bad journalism. Proletarian art, proletarian theater! What is *that*? The
> artist, and particularly the poet, is always an anarchist in the best sense of the word. He
> must heed only the call that arises within him from three strong voices: the voice of
> death, with all its foreboding, the voice of love, and the voice of art.

Despite his quarrel with Alberti's politics Lorca agreed in early May to collaborate with his friend in an evening of Andalusian song and dance. In Germany, Alberti had given a lecture on "Popular Poetry in the Spanish Lyric." He
was asked to repeat the talk in Madrid at the Teatro Español, and he invited
Lorca to accompany him on the piano. They were joined by Lorca's close
friend Encarnación López, La Argentinita.

The evening was a success. Alberti spoke; Lorca played the piano and—at
Alberti's insistence—recited a poem from his collection *Songs*. La Argentinita
dazzled the crowd with her swirling skirts and clattering castanets. At the curtain call, Lorca delayed joining his colleagues onstage until someone in the
audience shouted, "Federico, Federico, Federico!" Hesitantly, he stepped forward. Although some of his friends claimed that he had demeaned himself by
accepting a "secondary role" to Alberti, Lorca seemed pleased with the collaboration. He and Rafael were both Andalusians, he reminded a reporter. "We've
each scoured Spain inch by inch in search of her immortal popular essences."

He saw much of La Argentinita in the months that followed, often in the
company of her companion, Ignacio Sánchez Mejías. The vivacious brunette
danced at a lecture on Granada that Lorca gave at the Residencia de Estudiantes that spring, and, in June, when she and her company presented Manuel de
Falla's *El amor brujo* in Cádiz and Madrid, Lorca was in the audience. To
many Spaniards, the poet and the dancer were inextricably linked because of
the five-disc, 78-rpm recording of folk songs they had made the previous year.
Sometime later they collaborated on a pair of theatrical spectacles blending
dance, music, and story drawn from the popular Spanish tradition. The second
of these, a ballet entitled *The Cuckolds' Pilgrimage*, was partially inspired by a
yearly pilgrimage in the Andalusian village of Moclín, located some twenty
miles from Lorca's birthplace. For years Lorca had toyed with the notion of a
theatrical spectacle based on the pilgrimage. In the mid-1920s he had worked
with the director Cipriano Rivas Cherif and the composer Gustavo Pittaluga to

create a rudimentary version of the ballet. The work was performed in a concert version in 1930, but it did not receive a full-scale theatrical production until 1933, when La Argentinita and her Spanish Dance Company presented it in Madrid.

To what extent Lorca contributed to the spectacle is uncertain. But his familiarity with the Moclín pilgrimage helped provide the impetus for the work. Although neither he nor his family had ever witnessed the annual rite, they were well aware of it each October as dozens of pilgrims wound their way through the *vega* toward the sun-bleached town of Moclín. From there the pilgrims ascended a spiral path to the Sanctuary of Moclín, where they petitioned Christ to cure them of their woes. Chief among the supplicants were childless women, who made the long journey in the hope of achieving fertility. Lorca was fascinated by the ritual. Its mix of pagan cult and Christian belief reaffirmed his sense of the primitive nature of faith.

He empathized above all with the women who sought release from their childless state. He had never forgotten the fact that his father's first wife, Matilde Palacios, had remained childless throughout her fourteen-year marriage to Don Federico. As Lorca grew older he made repeated allusions to childlessness in his poems and plays: "My unborn children pursue me" (*Suites*); "The Shoemaker's Wife will never have children" (*The Shoemaker's Prodigious Wife*); "My child. I want my child!" (*Once Five Years Pass*). Imaginatively the concept of infertility fueled his vision of human love as an innately bleak enterprise. Desire yields only a void; passion leads to nothing but the ghostly cry of an unborn infant.

He was acutely conscious of his own inability to engender a child. The topic was both a poetic conceit and a private preoccupation. Lorca worshiped his niece and nephew and lavished attention on his friends' children, and while his own childless condition freed him to live and work impulsively, indeed sometimes carelessly, it also removed him from the most basic of human cycles, and this was a fact to which he never entirely reconciled himself.

The issue became especially poignant to him in the spring of 1933, when his friend Concha Méndez, who had married Manolo Altolaguirre the previous year, went into labor. Friends streamed into the couple's tiny Madrid apartment throughout the afternoon and evening as Méndez struggled to give birth. When Lorca approached her bedside, his friend murmured, "I'm dying."

"Nonsense," he told her. "You're creating life."

Méndez's labor went on for hours, while friends bided their time in the room next door. Once, after she let out a scream, Lorca interrupted a story to cry, "Shout more, Conchita, shout hard . . . it will help!" Eventually Méndez had to be taken by ambulance to the hospital, where she lost her child. To Lorca, the infant's death was a shock.

A few months later, he began writing a new play, one he described as a "drama of barrenness." As he explained it to Morla Lynch, the work was about childless women whose frustrated maternal instincts ultimately lead to tragedy. Central to the play would be a theatrical reenactment of the annual Moclín rite which had also inspired *The Cuckolds' Pilgrimage*. Lorca had apparently been thinking about the work for years and needed only to write it. "It's finished in here," he told Morla, tapping his forehead. He seems to have begun drafting the play in June 1933, perhaps during a hasty visit home to Granada. ("Get my room ready, thoroughly whitewashed," he instructed his parents before leaving Madrid.) By mid-July he was able to tell the *Heraldo de Madrid* that he was at work on the second play of a "dramatic trilogy of the Spanish land." *Blood Wedding* was the first component of the trilogy, and part three was "taking shape in my heart right now. It will be called *The Destruction of Sodom.*" Part two, the tragedy he was currently writing, was as yet untitled. But its theme was "the sterile woman." By early August Lorca had settled on a title for the work: *Yerma*. The word, in Spanish, means "barren."

Preparations for La Barraca's 1933 touring season forced him to interrupt his work on *Yerma* that summer. The company premiered a new production of Lope de Vega's *Fuenteovejuna* in Valencia on June 28, and rehearsals for the play consumed Lorca's time and attention.

To Lope's drama about political upheaval in a fifteenth-century Spanish village Lorca added popular songs, music, and dance. He put so much energy into staging the play's wedding scene—as he had done with similar scenes in Tirso de Molina's *Burlador de Sevilla* and his own *Blood Wedding*—that his actors nicknamed him "Federico, wedding specialist." He demanded that real wine, dried figs, and almonds be used during the scene in *Fuenteovejuna*, and that schoolchildren be drafted as extras in each of the towns La Barraca visited.

His production of *Fuenteovejuna* was transparently pro-Republican. Lorca condensed Lope's script so that its focus became not the king and queen of Spain but the country's rural population. Instead of period costumes, actors wore clothes from the 1930s. The evil Knight Commander who terrorizes the villagers of *Fuenteovejuna* appeared in a black business suit, underscoring his ties with the formidable *caciques* of Lorca's day, local power holders who by their wealth and affiliations controlled much of everyday life in the Spanish countryside. It was typical of Lorca to toy so boldly with an existing script. He was fond of reading the Spanish classics to friends, cutting lines as he went whenever he thought a passage too long. He shunned the notion of a definitive production. Given enough money, he remarked to a journalist that summer, he would stage "several versions of the same work: one old, another modern. One lavish, another highly simplified."

His updated staging of Lope's work earned Lorca the wrath of the right-wing press. Lorca was unapologetic. At the play's debut in Valencia, invitations were sent to local labor organizations. Workers, keenly attuned to its political implications, greeted the drama with tumultuous applause.

La Barraca followed its Valencia appearance with trips to both southern and northern Spain. Anti-Republican hecklers booed the company in Navarra, but otherwise the group was well received. Lorca dismissed any hint of political controversy. The troupe had enjoyed a magnificent reception throughout its journey, he insisted. As for the "nasty imputations of those who would see in our theater a political objective," he and his actors were innocent. "There is nothing political about La Barraca. It is theater, just theater."

The company concluded its summer season with an extended stay in the city of Santander, on the Cantabrian coast. Cold, wet skies enveloped the mountains that flanked the town; Lorca had to wear a raincoat and scarf. La Barraca gave three performances in as many days at Santander's International Summer University, a non-degree school established the previous year by the Republican government. Most of Spain's leading intellectuals were involved with the university. Lorca's friend and fellow poet Pedro Salinas, the secretary of the board of trustees, was present during La Barraca's visit, as were a number of his other friends, including Carlos and Bebé Morla Lynch, who were spending the August holiday in a nearby village.

The university was housed in a massive stone palace built on a spur of land jutting into the Cantabrian sea. Shortly after his arrival, Lorca roamed the site on foot, testing different locations acoustically and visually before selecting a particular spot for La Barraca's three outdoor performances. Some two thousand people, many of them foreign students, attended the opening presentation of three Cervantes interludes. Critics praised the ensemble. One reviewer noted the extremely intelligent direction that characterized the troupe's work. Lorca revealed in a subsequent interview that he was attempting to train some of La Barraca's young actors to be directors. "A theater, first and foremost, is a good director," he said smugly. He was increasingly brash in his pronouncements. A week before coming to Santander he had told a newspaper that the contemporary Spanish stage was, generally speaking, "a theater by and for swine. That's right, a theater created by swine for swine."

Shocked by the bluntness of Lorca's statement, his interviewer asked, "What kind of theater are you trying to create?"

"Popular," Lorca answered. "Always popular. While it may have aristocratic roots in spirit and style, it must always be nourished by 'popular' sap. And if I continue working, I hope to influence the European theater."

He exuded confidence. Jorge Guillén, who was in Santander to take part in the city's summer university, had lunch with him one afternoon and came away convinced that Lorca was "better than ever." Herschel Brickell, the publishing executive who had befriended Lorca in New York, also visited Santander that August and attended one of La Barraca's productions. Afterward he and Lorca sat up late, talking. The early morning sky was streaked with pink when they parted. *"Vaya con Dios, amigo,"* Lorca called out as Brickell left him. The American continued on his way, thinking as he went that, like Browning, he had "seen Shelley plain."

Lorca was happier than he had been in years. The cause, in part, was a young man who had joined La Barraca earlier that season, a twenty-one-year-old student from Madrid named Rafael Rodríguez Rapún. Muscular and debonair, with curly brown hair, dark eyes, and a lopsided grin, Rapún signed on as the company's secretary in early 1933 and within months became Lorca's closest companion. By autumn, as he confessed by letter to Lorca, Rapún was accustomed to spending "every hour of the day" in Lorca's company.

Although he was officially an engineering student at the University of Madrid, Rapún's true love was literature. He occasionally wrote poetry, and through Lorca came to know and befriend many of the writers of the Generation of '27. His fellow Barraca members admired his scrupulous and efficient management of the company's accounts. A gifted mathematician, Rapún generally carried a thick blue notebook with him on Barraca outings, in which he made copious notes on the troupe's expenses.

To most he was affable and modest, a "decent" young man whose devotion to Lorca was genuine, not self-serving. But to some he seemed peculiar. Barraca member Luis Sáenz de la Calzada remembered Rapún as "violent and elemental." According to Sáenz, Rapún became sexually aroused whenever the van in which they were traveling overtook another vehicle on the road. He was prone, as well, to angry outbursts, a trait Sáenz attributed to the fact that Rapún was "at a crossroads" in his life. The struggle between mathematics and poetry, between engineering and theater at times overwhelmed him, as did his deepening attachment to Lorca, which, while exhilarating, was fraught with danger of both a private and a public kind.

Rapún was handsome in a classical sense, with the long, straight nose of a

Greek statue. He had a robust physique, and he walked with a sure stride. He often wore black, which set off his bright white teeth and made his smile "more luminous." Women found him seductive, and Rapún was responsive to them. But once he met Lorca he succumbed irretrievably to the poet's charm. Rapún became "immersed" in Lorca, recalled Barraca member Modesto Higueras. "It was something tremendous." To another friend who witnessed their affair, Rapún was clearly "the passion" for whom Lorca, then thirty-five, had been waiting much of his life.

On Barraca outings, they were inseparable. They shared sleeping quarters, sometimes with other company members. In the spring of 1933, Rapún attended Lorca's performance with Rafael Alberti and La Argentinita in Madrid and evidently accompanied Lorca to La Argentinita's presentation of *El amor brujo* in Cádiz. The two men were photographed together among the palm trees and flower beds of the Hotel Reina Cristina in Algeciras. In one picture they sit side by side in wicker lawn chairs. Lorca, squinting into the sun, holds a filter-tipped cigarette in his hand. Reclining casually in his chair, one leg draped over the other, hair brushed back from his forehead, he is the image of cool sophistication. Rapún, younger than Lorca and less accustomed to the camera's scrutiny, slouches in his seat. He is heavyset, and although not an athlete, he projects a sportive, vaguely raffish air. Each man seems utterly at home with the other.

Lorca liked to call Rapún *tres erres* — "three Rs" — a reference to Rapún's initials. In Madrid the pair made the rounds of the café circuit together. They exchanged letters and books. Over time Lorca gave Rapún several elaborately inscribed editions of his books. Inside a copy of *Songs* he wrote, "With a hug from your old, old friend Federico." In August 1933, Lorca brought out a private, limited edition of his *Ode to Walt Whitman*. Published in Mexico, the slim volume was intended for close friends only. Lorca illustrated his copy for Rapún with an intricate sketch of Whitman's face, half-bearded, half-framed by flowing locks of hair. "To my dear friend Rafael," Lorca wrote beside the drawing, "from his companion Federico." Emboldened, perhaps, by his friendship with Rapún and his growing theatrical celebrity, Lorca also published two scenes from *The Audience* in a Spanish literary journal in 1933. He told the *Heraldo de Madrid* that he intended to publish the entire play in the near future, and although he failed to do so, he did give a copy of the manuscript to Rapún, together with a draft of his unfinished play *The Destruction of Sodom*.

Eventually Rapún came to function as Lorca's private secretary, handling the poet's business matters and shielding him from the public. He was evasive about the nature of his relationship with Lorca. Early one morning, after impulsively going with Lorca to see the sun rise in Toledo, he returned home to find his father waiting for him. The elder Rapún, a modest employee of a gasoline distribution firm, was perplexed by his son's eccentric behavior. In time he confronted Rapún directly about Lorca's reported homosexuality. Rapún assured his father that, although as an artist Lorca was sensitive, perhaps even feminine, and although he had homosexual friends, Lorca was not himself a homosexual.

Among their colleagues in La Barraca the two were similarly discreet. Many in the company believed the pair's friendship, while close, was platonic. One member recalled Lorca declaring repeatedly that the essential thing in life was to have a friend with whom one could forget one's worries, as Achilles had with Patroclus. "Having a good friend is better than having a good marriage," Lorca said with a smile. He knew better than to defy convention among those who were fundamentally conventional. The conservative press had already given him a taste of Spanish morality and the sort of ridicule it could spawn.

The young artist and set designer José Caballero, one of Lorca's closest friends in La Barraca, insisted years later that Lorca's friendship with Rafael Rodríguez Rapún was so private that it was impossible for any outsider to know with certainty the extent of their devotion to one another. "Federico was so open, so very open," Caballero remembered. "And yet at the same time he was so closed."

CHAPTER 21

OUR AMERICA

1933-34

Six thousand miles away, in the city of Buenos Aires, Lola Membrives, the Argentine actress who had turned down the chance to premiere *Blood Wedding* in Madrid, opened a new production of the play on July 29, 1933, to unanimously rave reviews—a rare feat in the sophisticated and discriminating Argentine capital. Membrives gave twenty additional performances of the play, all to packed houses, before closing her season on August 7.

Lorca was at first unaware of his overseas success. On the night of July 29, he later recalled, he lay in bed with a fever in a tiny village where he had gone to perform with La Barraca. When he awoke that night, he found his blanket covered with bugs. "That's how it goes," he shrugged. While crowds were applauding him in Buenos Aires, he was fighting off insects in a remote Spanish town.

Soon he began receiving letters from Membrives and Juan Reforzo, the actress's husband and business partner, imploring him to visit Argentina. "Your name," wrote Reforzo, "is on everyone's lips . . . You've conquered Buenos Aires in a matter of hours." The couple encouraged Lorca to come in mid-September, in time for the reopening of *Blood Wedding* at the start of Membrives's next season. They offered to pay his expenses and to arrange a lecture series for him.

Lorca demurred. He did not particularly like Membrives, despite her status as the most famous actress in Argentina, and he resented her curt dismissal of *Blood Wedding* the previous year. It annoyed him that she only deigned to produce his work after other performers had proven its box-office merit.

He told Reforzo he would make the trip on one condition: that he be given passage on a "very large ship." Reforzo promptly agreed. But Lorca continued to vacillate. "As soon as I've consulted my parents, I'll send you my acceptance," he promised. In the end, the offer was too tantalizing to resist. In late August Lorca decided to make the trip. Sometime later he told a journalist that upon receiving Membrives's invitation, he had accepted her offer "immediately."

He left Madrid by train for Barcelona on September 28. Rapún accompanied him to the station in a taxi. On their way there, Lorca scribbled a letter petitioning the Spanish government to exempt his friend from obligatory military service in Africa. Ultimately the entreaty worked, and Rapún was excused from domestic as well as foreign service.

Lorca reached Barcelona the following day and dropped in briefly on the actress Margarita Xirgu. "I have a new work for you," he announced, waving the first two acts of *Yerma*. Xirgu refused to look at the play. In Buenos Aires, she told Lorca, a local company would undoubtedly ask to premiere the work, and he would feel obliged to let them. "No, Margarita," he insisted, "*Yerma* is for you and only for you."

The script remained in Lorca's possession later that afternoon as he boarded the Italian liner *Conte Grande*. With him was Manuel Fontanals, an artist and set designer who was married to an actress in Membrives's company. Membrives had asked Fontanals to help redesign *Blood Wedding*. Slender and deeply tanned, with golden hair and bright white teeth, Fontanals looked and behaved like a matinee idol. He often sported a white cravat and bowler hat, and carried a walking stick, which he never used. On board the *Conte Grande*, he and Lorca wore tuxedos each time they visited the ship's elegant dining room.

The trip took two weeks. According to Lorca, the *Conte Grande* scarcely moved "a hair" throughout the journey. He managed to write a new lecture and otherwise spent his time reading, or talking to Fontanals, whom he found far more entertaining than the rest of the ship's "mummylike" passengers. Inside his cabin Lorca brightened the walls with photographs of his family, and in a letter to his parents confessed that whenever he saw an older passenger on the ship he thought of his mother and father. He also missed his young niece and nephew, who "sparkle so brightly and bring us such joy." During a brief stop at the Canary Islands he mailed home a long letter to his family as well as a postcard to Rafael Rapún.

As the *Conte Grande* crossed the equator, each passenger received a diploma from the ship's crew. Days later, near the Brazilian coast, Lorca spotted flying fish in the sea and, above the water, "tiny white butterflies borne by the wind from the land." He was thrilled to be returning to "American soil." But this time, he told his parents, he was coming to "our America, Spanish America."

The *Conte Grande* sailed into the harbor of Montevideo, Uruguay, on the morning of October 13. Dozens of reporters, photographers, dignitaries, and fans were waiting to greet the celebrated Spanish playwright. Lola Membrives had presented *Blood Wedding* in the city two months earlier, and the play's triumphant run had sparked enormous interest in its author. Journalists and admirers swarmed around Lorca. They asked questions, held out autograph books and slips of paper, and snapped pictures. Lorca smiled, bewildered by the commotion. "What can I tell you?" he said repeatedly. He asked that photographs not be taken, but few heeded his request. One reporter scrutinized his appearance and later informed readers that the writer was

> of medium height, dark, with a rather coppery face, black hair, thick eyebrows, a wide forehead, a tiny mouth, a penetrating gaze, a small nose, and an almost round face . . . He seems extremely young, younger than he really is, for as we understand it, he's about twenty-six years old.

In fact, Lorca was thirty-five.

Eventually the ship sounded its horn, and Lorca embarked on the final leg of his journey to Buenos Aires. As the *Conte Grande* sailed upstream along the enormous Plata river toward Argentina, he was joined by Membrives's husband, Juan Reforzo, and the critic Pablo Suero, both of whom had boarded in Montevideo. Suero took an immediate liking to Lorca. He was struck by the playwright's "handsome" forehead and "plum-colored gaze," by his rapid-fire speech and pronounced Andalusian accent. Suero found it difficult to believe that someone so "boylike" had written as profound a tragedy as *Blood Wedding*.

During their daylong journey to Buenos Aires, Suero deluged Lorca with questions. ("They killed me with interviews," Lorca said afterward, recounting the trip to his parents.) Topics ranged from New York, to Salvador Dalí, to Manuel de Falla, to La Barraca, and Lorca's parents. "My father is charming," Lorca declared. In the midst of having his photograph taken, he turned gravely to Suero and asked, "Do you know what will happen as a result of your generosity? My mother will be happy when she sees a copy of *Noticias Gráficas* with my picture in it."

"And that's enough for you?" Suero asked.

"Ah, that's more than enough . . ."

Lorca talked about his recent publications, including the limited edition of

Ode to Walt Whitman that he had just issued, and a series of waltz poems he hoped to publish in the near future. "I detest what's fashionable," he said, by way of explaining his interest in something so quaint as a waltz. He spoke briefly about *Blood Wedding*, but, as Suero observed, he was far more interested in discussing "the theater he wants to do." Lorca talked of *The Audience* and apparently read *Once Five Years Pass* and the first half of *Yerma* to Suero, who thought Lorca's experimental work epitomized "the theater of the future."

"You know something else?" Lorca mused, as he and Suero sailed slowly along the muddy Plata river.

> In art, you must never let yourself remain quiet or complacent . . . You must have the courage to hammer your head against things and against life . . . and then we'll see what happens . . . Another thing that's essential is to respect your instincts. The day you stop fighting your instincts — that's the day you've learned to live.

They reached Buenos Aires that evening. "How grand it is!" Lorca exclaimed as he beheld the constellation of lights girding the city's busy shoreline. It was spring, and the air was mild. A crowd of admirers stood waiting on the pier as he stepped onto the gangplank, suntanned and smiling. He carried a briefcase and wore a dark, double-breasted coat with a velvet collar. His hair was unkempt. As he made his way down the stairs to the pier, the crowd burst into applause, and he heard someone shout, "Federico! Federico! Ay! Ay!" To his amazement he spotted a group of former neighbors from Fuente Vaqueros, men and women who had emigrated to Buenos Aires from Spain in the early 1920s. "He's from our village! He's from our village!" they cried, as a photographer snapped their picture. A woman who had known Lorca as an infant threw her arms around the husky poet and wept. Lorca's eyes welled with tears.

Reporters surrounded him. Speechless, he fumbled with his bags and at last muttered to one member of the press:

> Please forgive me. It's just that when I travel, I don't know who I am. It's what I call the "discomfort of traveling," the discomfort of arrival and departure, when people drag you from one side to the other, and in a daze you respond mechanically and let yourself be pushed and pulled, oblivious to everything around you.

He then gave an impromptu interview in which he discussed his plays — with emphasis on *The Audience* and *Once Five Years Pass* — his poetry, and his writing habits. "I never deliberately set out to create literature," he said. "It's just that during certain times I have an irresistible urge to write. Then I write, feverishly, for a few months, so that I can get back to living as soon as possible." He confessed that in Buenos Aires he was anxious to "have fun, enjoy life, live!" He wanted to get to know the city, "to make friends and meet girls."

Nearly three million people inhabited Buenos Aires in 1933. By and large a cosmopolitan lot, of European descent, they were accustomed to elegant dining in cafés and clubs, to leisurely strolls along the city's boulevards, and late-night displays of tango dancing. They were immensely proud of their sprawling riverfront city, whose grandeur rivaled that of Paris. Mansard roofs, cupolas, domes, and fanciful figures of winged women punctuated the low skyline. Palm trees, shrubs, cactuses, and fountains filled the squares.

Lorca settled into a small room at the Castelar Hotel on the Avenida de Mayo, in the heart of Buenos Aires. Chocolate shops and theaters lined the fashionable street outside his hotel. Inside, Lorca pinned photographs of his niece Tica to the wall above his bed. He also hung a snapshot of himself, in his Barraca uniform, standing in the midst of a cabbage field with his arms outstretched in an eerie, Christ-like pose.

"I don't stop for a minute," he told his parents by letter five days after his arrival. He sent home a mass of newspaper clippings—"just a small part of what's been published and what . . . I've been able to collect." Someone had retained a clipping service to track press coverage of his visit. "I've had to hire a secretary to answer the phone and receive visitors," he marveled. "Just like a government minister!" Although he found being a celebrity "an awful nuisance," he also courted attention by visiting the offices of local newspapers and introducing himself to journalists. On his first night in Buenos Aires Lorca attended Pablo Suero's translation of an audacious new play about contemporary German society, Ferdinand Bruckner's *Sickness of Youth*, a work whose sexual candor, in particular, astonished him. In Madrid, he told reporters, such a play could never be produced. During the course of the evening, the audience discovered Lorca's presence in their midst and applauded him. From his box seat he thanked the crowd. "Here in this enormous city I'm as famous as a bullfighter," he told his family.

On October 20, one week after his arrival, he gave the first of four lectures for the Buenos Aires Friends of Art Society. His talk, "Play and Theory of the *Duende*," was new. Lorca had drafted it on the *Conte Grande* and further revised it on reaching Buenos Aires. A reporter for the *Correo de Galicia* went to Lorca's hotel room on the evening of the lecture and found a typist hunched over Lorca's manuscript, straining to decipher the poet's handwriting. The desk was strewn with cigarettes, books, pencils, papers, and loose change in a variety of currencies. Lorca was in the shower, singing. "What's this word?" cried the typist.

"Which one?" Lorca shouted, and went on singing.

"Elvira . . . Elvira . . . What?"

"Hot Elvira, lad," Lorca cried. "She's called 'Hot Elvira.' It's the sacred and aristocratic name of a whore from Seville."

A moment later he emerged from the shower, embraced the reporter, posed briefly for a photograph in his bathrobe, and hurriedly answered questions while he dressed. He then tossed a tie around his neck, gave a farewell hug to his interviewer, and raced out the door on his way to the lecture hall.

In his new talk, "Play and Theory of the *Duende*," Lorca returned to the subject of poetic creation, this time focusing on a phenomenon peculiar to Spain—the irrational, demonic, death-seeking spirit known as *duende*, without which deep inspiration is impossible. "That's the secret of art: to have *duende*," he remarked to an Argentine journalist a few days before the lecture. In Andalusia, dancers, bullfighters, and singers were said to possess *duende*. Alternately a visible presence and an ineffable quality, *duende*, Lorca said, is "the hidden spirit of disconsolate Spain." It alone gives artists the power to move audiences in profound ways, baptizing them "in dark water." Lorca claimed to have been visited by a *duende* early one morning in Buenos Aires. Dressed in a red-and-gold costume with a pointed green hood, the tiny sprite had flown through his hotel room on wings. Lorca believed he had brought the spirit to life and could subsequently order it about. "Do you understand the consequences?" he said later to a reporter. "Can you dare to imagine them . . . my *duende* perched on my shoulder as I give my lectures?"

Difficult though it was to describe, Lorca knew what it meant to "have" *duende*. " 'All that has black sounds has *duende*,' " he said in his lecture, quoting a Gypsy singer he had once met in Seville. "And there is no greater truth. These black sounds are the mystery, the roots fastened in the mire that we all know and ignore, the mire that gives us the very substance of art." Neither "angel" nor "muse"—both of which may grace an artist from without—the *duende* emanates from "the remotest mansions of the blood." It "wounds" an artist. "And in the healing of that wound, which never closes, lies the invented, strange qualities of a man's work."

Ultimately the *duende* is linked with death, and dependent on an artist's acknowledgment of his or her mortality. The *duende* "does not come at all unless he sees that death is possible," Lorca told his Argentine audience. Inasmuch as Spain is a nation preoccupied with death—where the national sport, bullfighting, is a sport of death, and where a dead man, Lorca argued, is "more alive as a dead man than any place else in the world"—the *duende* is a uniquely Spanish phenomenon, deeply rooted in popular thought and superstition. While creators in other countries may at times possess it, the *duende* most commonly visits the artists of Spain, men and women such as Goya, Quevedo, Zurburán, Jorge Manrique, Saint Teresa, the bullfighter Joselito, and the Andalusian singer Pastora Pavón, whose "scorched" voice, Lorca said, conveys "not forms but the marrow of forms." Although he refrained from saying so, he obviously counted himself among this elite group, for death was his muse, and the *duende* its most palpable incarnation.

The Buenos Aires audience loved his talk. Even if his subject was obscure and his jargon dense, they warmed to the histrionics of his delivery. To his parents, Lorca characterized his inaugural lecture as "extraordinarily successful. You have no idea!" He continued to be amazed by the degree of his celebrity in Argentina. He'd had his picture taken "more than two hundred" times. "Photographs in bed, in a bathing suit, on the street looking out of a window. It's too much!" He was both exhausted and happy.

Later in the week he gave his second lecture, "How a City Sings from November to November," a lyrical account of one year in the life of Granada. Accompanying himself on the piano, he sang and spoke his way through the seasonal fluctuations of his hometown, regaling listeners with the sounds of Arab folk tunes and Christian ballads. He bellowed songs with what one reviewer described as a sailor's voice. At the close of his elegiac talk he told his audience that year in, year out, Granada would "always be like this. Before and now. We must leave, but Granada remains. Eternal in time, but fleeting in these poor hands—these hands of mine, the smallest of her children."

The demand for tickets to his final two lectures, "Poet in New York" and a revised version of his 1923 talk on Andalusian deep song, was so great that officials considered moving the events to a larger hall. All four of Lorca's Buenos Aires talks were broadcast by radio, vastly expanding his audience and prompting a barrage of requests for photographs of the poet, especially from women. "It's expensive attending to every female admirer," Lorca complained to his parents. When, in response to audience demand, he gave a repeat performance of his *Duende* lecture on November 14, women "invaded" the auditorium, a reporter observed.

In late October, Lola Membrives reopened *Blood Wedding* with a gala performance in the cavernous Teatro Avenida. Resplendent in a black tuxedo and starched white shirt, Lorca surveyed the huge crowd that packed the theater that evening. Twice the audience applauded him, at the start and close of his play. To his delight, he heard someone cry "Marvelous!" in the midst of the forest scene. The sophistication and acuity of the Argentine audience astounded him. "As I was sailing up the Plata river, with waves as ruddy and rough as a lion's mane," he told the crowd afterward, standing on the stage of the Avenida to address them, "I never dreamt I would receive the trembling white dove of faith that this enormous city has placed in my hands. For I don't deserve it." Later he described the evening to his parents: "In Madrid, nothing happened. But here I've had an apotheosis fit for the bullring."

The stream of interviews and photographs flowed on. Autograph seekers hounded him. Admirers made their way, like pilgrims, to his hotel room. Prominent society women invited Lorca to meals, and he rarely refused. Afterward, among friends, he made fun of his hostesses, imitating their mannerisms. To his parents, he deliberately dramatized his popularity among women. "Not a day goes by that I don't receive declarations of love from young ladies (they must be out of their minds!), telling me the most remarkable things!" he wrote. One night, Victoria Ocampo, a wealthy Argentine writer, ask Lorca to her home for a candlelit dinner. During the course of the evening she began flirting with him. When he realized what she intended, he left. Later, he told friends that in Buenos Aires a beautiful woman had come to his hotel room and, in an effort to seduce him, removed her clothes. Lorca ordered her to leave.

He soon grew weary of the incessant attention. Because his photograph appeared so frequently in the newspapers, people recognized him on the street. Despite exhaustion, he had trouble sleeping. He craved solitude, but was "always being invited out and taken or brought somewhere." Sometimes he fled engagements. "I'm an Andalusian, don't forget," he would say afterward with a chuckle, and glance at his wristwatch. In photographs he began to sport what he called a "false smile." Although he claimed to hate interviews, he submitted to them, "because it means I've conquered an immense public for my theater." He professed dismay at seeing his name plastered about the city on posters. "I feel as if I'm standing naked before crowds of curious onlookers . . . But I must tolerate it because that's what the theater demands."

He was not without his detractors. Arturo Cambours, a Buenos Aires resident who spent an afternoon touring the city with Lorca, expressed disgust at Lorca's vanity. "Spanish poetry began and ended with him. The Spanish theater began and ended with him. *Yerma*, whose third act he had yet to finish, would be the consummation of Greek tragedy," Cambours remembered. He described Lorca as a "conceited fool, a fat and petulant little charlatan." The writer Jorge Luis Borges was similarly disappointed by the Spaniard. When the two met briefly, Lorca seemed to Borges to be acting a part, performing the role of "a professional Andalusian." Lorca apparently sensed Borges's dislike and subtly mocked the Argentine by speaking gravely about the "tragedy" of the United States of America, and the one figure who embodied it.

"Who is that?" asked Borges.

"Mickey Mouse," Lorca replied. Borges, thinking the comment infantile, walked off in a huff. Years later he claimed that Lorca had always struck him as a "minor poet," an exclusively "picturesque" author whose verses revealed "a certain intimate coldness." Borges deemed him a writer "incapable of passion."

Lorca recoiled from snobs and social climbers who merely wanted to rub shoulders with a famous author. He preferred to spend his time with friends, many of them writers, drinking wine or vodka in taverns and cafés, or wandering the streets. Sometimes at dawn, after a night of roaming the city with friends, Lorca would slip into a church to hear Mass.

Among his closest friends in Argentina was the celebrated Chilean poet Pablo Neruda, who had recently been appointed Santiago's consul in Buenos Aires. Twenty-nine years old, tall, big-boned, and pale, Neruda was both physically and imaginatively imposing. He had large, vigilant eyes, "rather like those of a bemused lizard," a friend was to write. Earlier in the year Neruda had published the first volume of his third collection of poetry, *Residence on Earth*, a startling series of poems written between 1927 and 1932 during the poet's service as a member of his country's diplomatic corps in Asia. Dense and hallucinatory, the poems in *Residence on Earth* pushed the Spanish language to new heights. Young Argentine writers were riveted by the collection.

Lorca met Neruda in Buenos Aires that fall. As usual, Lorca seized the floor within minutes of his arrival and launched into a vigorous discussion of poets and playwrights. Neruda was mesmerized. Physically, Lorca struck him as dark, "darker than the darkest of Spaniards, as dark as a Mexican or a Gypsy." Years later, in a poignant memoir, Neruda remembered Lorca as a torrent of motion and joy,

> an effervescent child, the young channel of a powerful river. He squandered his imagination, he spoke with enlightenment . . . he cracked walls with his laughter, he improvised the impossible, and in his hands a prank became a work of art. I have never seen such magnetism and such constructiveness in a human being.

The two became immediate friends. Unlike the more cerebral and aristocratic Borges, Neruda relished Lorca's exuberance and shared his robust appetite for life. Both men came from rural backgrounds, and both felt an affinity with the working class. Born and raised in the remote wine country of southern Chile, Neruda had spent his student days in Santiago as an impoverished bohemian who wore black clothes and wrote melancholy verse. His father opposed his desire to be a poet. When Neruda showed him his first poem, his father glanced at it and asked, "Where did you copy this from?" Neruda never fully recovered from the insult. At sixteen he renounced the name his parents had given him at birth—Ricardo Eliecer Neftalí Reyes—and took a new name, Pablo Neruda, after the Czech poet Jan Neruda.

He published his first book of poems at nineteen, and a second collection, *Twenty Poems of Love and a Song of Despair,* at twenty. The direct, intensely sensual poems in this volume resonated with readers, and Neruda became famous. As a result of his celebrity, he was appointed to the Chilean consular service, and between the ages of twenty-eight served in Rangoon, Ceylon, Java, and Singapore. In Java he met and married his first wife, Maruca. But the marriage was unhappy, and Neruda increasingly sought the company of other women.

Lorca admired the Chilean immensely. He inscribed a copy of his *Gypsy Ballads,* "For my dear Pablo, one of the few great poets I've had the good fortune to love and know." During the course of their friendship, which lasted well beyond Lorca's stay in Buenos Aires, he often asked Neruda what he was writing or what he had just completed. Lorca so revered the Chilean's work that whenever he heard Neruda begin to recite his poems, he would raise his arms, cover his ears, shake his head and cry, "Stop! Stop! That's enough, don't read any more—you'll influence me!"

On November 20, he and Neruda attended a banquet organized in their honor by the Buenos Aires PEN Club. When it came time to thank their hosts, both poets rose simultaneously from their seats. "Ladies . . . ," said Neruda, ". . . and gentlemen," continued Lorca. Speaking antiphonally, they delivered a short, impassioned speech about a man who had inspired them both, "the poet of America and of Spain," said Lorca. "Rubén . . ." ". . . Darío," cried Neruda. In unison they raised their glasses to toast the fabled Nicaraguan, whose "lexical fiesta, . . . crashing consonants, lights and forms" had forever enriched the Spanish language. It had been Lorca's idea to present the talk jointly—like two bullfighters, he explained, battling the same animal with a single cape.

By late November, reporters were hailing Lorca's "gastronomic" endurance. The banquets and homages continued. With the president of the Argentine republic in attendance, fans marked the one hundredth performance of *Blood Wedding* with food and dancing until dawn. Lorca, sprucely attired in a black tuxedo, read excerpts from his work and dutifully posed for photographers. On another occasion, at a luncheon, he wolfed down food "like a decadent Roman," intoning Andalusian *coplas* with every course. Afterward, over brandy, he played the piano and sang.

Newspapers churned out stories about the poet. One journalist described him lounging in bed in his hotel room in a pair of striped pajamas, conversing with visitors. Another reporter found him standing in front of the mirror in his room, his face lathered in soap. "Come on in," Lorca cried. "I'm shaving. I'll be dressed in a minute in my blue coveralls, a cheap and very comfortable piece of clothing." The reporter carefully noted Lorca's appearance: his "full moon face," vibrant eyes, ample mouth, and athletic chest.

By December, Buenos Aires bookstores had been picked clean of copies of *Gypsy Ballads* and *Poem of the Deep Song*. Fans clamored for more books, but Lorca had brought none with him. When asked if he might reissue some of his poetry in Argentina, he politely refused. He would only publish when he no longer had to attend to "reporters, authors, actors, poets, writers," and others, he said. To the suggestion that he write a series of poems inspired by Buenos Aires, as he had done in New York, he said, "I don't want to force anything . . . because then everything comes out wrong."

Victoria Ocampo succeeded in bringing out two new editions of *Gypsy Ballads* during Lorca's visit. Despite his aversion to publication, Lorca was delighted. "This is a triumph by any measure . . . because it proves my existence here in South America and my influence over an entire Spanish-speaking continent," he told his parents. "I don't think people at home realize just what this means."

With fame came money. In addition to lecture fees, Lorca received a percentage of Membrives's box-office take. He told his parents he intended to put his theater royalties into savings and to use the rest of his earnings for living expenses. He talked incessantly of money in his letters home and on several occasions transferred large sums to his parents. Once, after wiring 10,000 pesetas to his father, he turned to a friend and announced that he had done so in order to needle Don Federico. "And to make him see that writing poems can be more lucrative than selling grain and land," he laughed. Another friend remembered Lorca's insisting that he was sending money home so that his father would realize that "the puppeteer, too, is capable of earning money."

The scheme worked. In Granada, Don Federico ordered his driver to take him to the post office one day, because "the boy who never earned a cent, who was always coming to me for help—now he's the one who's sending me money." To Lorca himself, the older man was more restrained. In a letter that November, Don Federico thanked his son for the money he had sent home, adding, "Frankly, we don't need it. But what you send is safer here than it is in your pockets, and since it's yours, it will always be at your disposal."

In a further attempt to please his father, Lorca devoted a portion of his time overseas to looking after a family relative who had left Spain a few years earlier and fallen on hard times. Máximo Delgado, one of Don Federico Garciá Rodríguez's many cousins, lived nearly two hundred miles north of Buenos Aires, in the town of Rosario. Although he worked whenever he could, he had no stable income. Lorca sent him money shortly after reaching Argentina, and eventually visited the young immigrant in Rosario. He found Máximo selling prints on the streets. Lorca assured his father that he would not leave Argentina until he had helped their cousin find steady employment, and he apparently tried to keep his word.

He squandered even more money on his mother. His hotel room filled with trinkets purchased expressly for Vicenta Lorca. According to an Argentine acquaintance, Lorca once spent hours prowling the city in search of a cactus to take to his mother. During an interview he confessed that because of Doña Vicenta, he had no plans to marry. "My brother and sisters, yes, they can marry. But I belong to my mother." He bought Vicenta a costly fox fur in Buenos Aires. "Now don't go telling me it's expensive," he warned her, "because I'm thrilled to have bought it and I'd be terribly upset if you were to object!"

Delighted with her son's success, his mother assured Lorca that "no woman will wear a fur around her shoulders with more pride and satisfaction than I'll feel wearing yours, for it's a souvenir you've purchased with the fruits of your labors." She cautioned Lorca to be prudent, however, and to earn as much money as he could, for the economic situation in Spain was not promising. She also urged him to be careful. "Watch what you eat, don't stay up too late, and keep an eye on your health, because we're awfully far away, and it terrifies me to think that something might happen to you." Vicenta Lorca was sixty-three years old when she wrote this letter. Her son was thirty-five.

In interviews Lorca mentioned his family regularly, "because you are the only thing I really care about in the world," he told his parents. He spoke often about Spain as well. The country's political situation had again worsened, and reports of trouble appeared almost daily in the Argentine press. Lorca followed the news intently.

National elections were scheduled to take place in Spain on November 19, 1933. At least two new political parties were grappling for power: CEDA (Confederación Española de Derechas Autónomas, or Spanish Confederation of Autonomous Right-Wing Groups), a right-wing Catholic alliance, and the Spanish Falange, founded by José Antonio Primo de Rivera, the son of the former dictator. Although "not a fascist movement," according to its leader, the Falange nevertheless shared goals similar to those of Hitler's Nazis and Mussolini's Fascists. At the party's inaugural meeting in Madrid in late October, José Antonio vowed that if the Spanish fatherland were to be maligned, "no dialect but the dialect of fists and pistols would suffice."

Argentine reporters questioned Lorca repeatedly about the situation in Spain. Although he tried to appear impartial, he occasionally voiced an opinion. A month before the Spanish elections he told a writer for *Crítica* that although Spain had a powerful right-wing faction, those "who love and enjoy freedom are on the Left." Privately he fretted about his country. During the weeks leading up to the Spanish election, violent confrontations took place throughout the nation. In late October, his friend Pura Ucelay informed Lorca that Assault Guards were stationed throughout Madrid, and people spoke of nothing but politics. "There is great anticipation for the female vote," she added. For the first time in history, Spanish women had been granted the right to cast a ballot.

Lorca urged his family, and in particular his brother, "not to get involved in political arguments." He grew so visibly upset about the situation that his Argentine friends refrained from discussing the subject in his presence. One night at a party in his honor, Lorca heard someone praise the Spanish monarchy, and by implication the right wing. The remark so incensed Lorca that he left the gathering. As election day drew near, his worries deepened. "God willing, things will turn out well," he told his parents. But they did not. Incidents of violence marred the balloting in several Spanish cities, including Seville, where left-wing activists murdered a member of the right wing. At the end of the day, right-wing Catholic and centrist candidates had won a majority of seats in parliament. Republican nominees lagged far behind.

During the next weeks, a new coalition government, led by the centrist Alejandro Lerroux, promptly began dismantling the more progressive programs implemented by former prime minister Manuel Azaña and his left-wing colleagues. The political situation in Spain deteriorated. Vicenta Lorca informed Lorca that matters were "more shameful" than ever. In early December a series of anarchist strikes rocked the nation. Sporadic gunfire rattled the streets of Zaragoza, and soldiers with machine guns patrolled the city. In both

Madrid and Barcelona bombs exploded. Bombs also went off in Granada, where leftist extremists tried to set fire to a convent. Six thousand miles away, Lorca feared for his family's safety. A few weeks after the election he declared that Spain was "a volcano that could erupt" at any minute.

To his mother's dismay, Lorca decided to remain in Argentina through Christmas. Lola Membrives planned to present *The Shoemaker's Prodigious Wife* and *Mariana Pineda* during the holiday season, and he wanted to be on hand for those productions. From Spain, Pura Ucelay wrote to express her disappointment. She had been counting on Lorca to help her with the Anfistora Club's next theatrical presentation. Eduardo Ugarte, co-director of La Barraca, also wanted him to return. Under the country's new government, he warned Lorca, the company was in danger of losing its funding. Meanwhile, the troupe had recently added a production of Tirso de Molina's *The Trickster of Seville* to its repertory. Cast in the minor role of Corydon, a fisherman, was Rafael Rodríguez Rapún.

Rapún, then twenty-one, wrote to Lorca at least once that fall, the only surviving fragment of correspondence between the two men. In a long, affectionate letter, he talked about friends, activities, and La Barraca, and thanked Lorca for the postcard he had sent during his journey to Argentina. Rapún alluded slyly to the nature of his relationship with Lorca. "Of course I'm playing the role of Corydon fairly well," he teased, "even though, as Ugarte says, I may be a 'corydon' in the real sense of the word." The term, a traditional name for an Arcadian shepherd, had long been used to signify homosexual love. In 1924, André Gide had published a Socratic dialogue in defense of same-sex love, which he called *Corydon*. Subtitled "A Novel about the Love That Cannot Speak Its Name," Gide's book appeared in Spanish translation in 1929, and by 1931 had gone through two subsequent editions.

Rapún closed his letter to Lorca with a declaration of love:

> I remember you constantly. It's impossible to forget someone with whom you've spent every hour of the day for months. Especially if you feel as powerfully drawn to that person as I do to you. But I console myself with the fact that when you return, we can repeat those hours. And it's a consolation to know that you've gone off to fulfill a mission . . . Now that I've written you a little something, I'll stop, although you deserve more. I'll continue to write to you often. A huge embrace from one who never stops thinking of you, Rafael.

In Buenos Aires, Lorca reportedly became infatuated with at least two young men, one of whom is said to have spurned his advances. For decades after his visit, rumors about his supposed liaisons in Argentina persisted. In a book inscription for fellow poet Ricardo Molinari, Lorca hinted at some sort of passionate involvement in the Argentine capital. "LOVE BUENOS AIRES GRANADA CADAQUÉS MADRID," he wrote. Molinari asked him what he meant. "They are the places where I have loved the most," Lorca said, without further explanation.

Publicly, he sought to remain discreet during his stay in Buenos Aires. Evidently he turned down an invitation to meet Alberto Nin Frías, an Argentine author whose chief area of interest was the link between homosexuality and creativity. Lorca was nevertheless intrigued to know that Nin Frías had cited him in his recent study of homosexuality and literature, *Alexis, or the Significance of the Uranian Temperament.* When he returned to Spain the following year, he told a friend to be sure to read the work, "because among other things it mentions me."

As the Argentine spring blossomed into summer, Lorca began wearing a white linen suit, and frequently a white cotton sailor's shirt with a V-shaped neck and a dark sash. He took childlike delight in donning the shirt and going to the beach to "awaken" the seashells by calling out to them. He sent his parents a photograph of himself dressed head to toe in a sailor's uniform—including bell-bottomed trousers. Beside him were three unidentified men in similar attire. "I'm a little drunk here," Lorca scrawled on the back of the picture. "But that's as far as I went." Imaginatively, he became captivated by the image of the sailor and began sketching sailors compulsively, occasionally depicting them in a composition with a bottle of rum or the word "beer" or "wine." Sometimes he showed flowers sprouting from their eyes. Frequently he wrote the word "love" on the brim of their caps.

For nearly a decade he had been fascinated by the figure of the sailor. In the mid-1920s he had sketched a sailor holding a red rose in his hand, with the word "love" printed on his hatband. He was drawn to the archetype of the sailor as a man who has forsworn conventional life, and the companionship of women, in order to roam the seas in the company of other men. The erotic connotations are clear. But Lorca's interest in the sailor motif transcended the merely sexual. Because he regarded the sea itself as the embodiment of love, life, and ultimately death—Jorge Manrique's fathomless tomb—he viewed the sailor as an emblem of human striving. "We're all like the sailor," he once said to a friend. "From the ports come the murmur of accordions and the turbid, soapy noise of the piers, from the mountains comes the plate of silence that shepherds eat, but we hear only our distances." At the bottom of one of the sailor sketches he produced in Buenos Aires, Lorca wrote, "Only mystery keeps us alive, only mystery."

In late December, in a public address from the stage of the Teatro Avenida, he welcomed the crew of a Spanish frigate to Argentina. "People use a white handkerchief to say goodbye and a warm hand to say hello," he told the sailors.

> Hands and handkerchiefs form a trembling garland along the shore of every port in the world . . . Between the handkerchief that sends him off and the hand that welcomes him home lies the sailor's true greeting: arrival and departure, happiness and sadness, in the dark, dead waves that push against the stone of the pier.

He made dozens of drawings in Buenos Aires. Lacking the time and inclination to write, Lorca poured himself into art. He had not sketched so prolifically since New York. On loose sheets of paper, inside books, as an embellishment to his autograph, he drew trailing vines, lemons, flowers, arrows, faces, and harlequins. He turned his signature into a work of art, elongating the letters of his name, twining them around one another, embroidering them with images.

He illustrated poems by his Argentine friends. He produced four drawings of sailors to accompany the Mexican writer Salvador Novo's bilingual *Seamen Rhymes*. Lorca made the sketches as a surprise and presented them to Novo, who was in the hospital at the time. During his visit, Lorca insisted that he could relieve the symptoms of Novo's ailment through Gypsy remedies, one of which entailed tossing water out of the window. Moments later, a hospital administrator appeared and briskly informed the two that a pedestrian had just been splashed by water from Novo's room.

In collaboration with Neruda, Lorca created ten pen-and-ink drawings to illustrate a short series of poems and phrases by the Chilean. The two men produced a single handmade copy of the work, which they later gave to a friend. Lorca's illustrations recall the disturbing drawings generated by his visit to New York four years earlier. Coupled with such phrases as "Only Death," "Nuptial Material," and "Severity," individual sketches show skeletons, drops of blood, and abstracted features of the human anatomy. In a drawing called "Sexual Water," Lorca depicts a nude female torso, with blood and handlike tentacles spilling from her vagina, and the words "Moon" and "Love" trailing from her mouth.

The final sketch of the series shows two decapitated, eyeless, bleeding heads—one of which is clearly Lorca's, the other Neruda's—displayed side by side on a table beneath a crescent moon with a single eye. Like the mock deaths Lorca had staged at the Residencia, the drawing seems an attempt to stare death in the face and, by so doing, to diminish the terrible power of its grip. Underneath the image Lorca wrote, "Severed heads of Federico García

Lorca and Pablo Neruda, authors of this book of poems. This pathetic drawing was made on the afternoon of Tuesday the 13th of [March,] 1934 in the city of Santa María de los Buenos Aires, as were all the other drawings."

Neruda attended the opening night performance of Lola Membrives's new production of *The Shoemaker's Prodigious Wife* on December 1, 1933. According to one audience member, "all of Buenos Aires" was present that evening, and sat waving to one another in the theater before the curtain rose.

Lorca revised his farce substantially for Membrives, who was older, plumper, and more brunette than the lithe young blonde called for in the original script. Membrives was also a gifted singer and dancer, and Lorca accordingly added five music and dance sequences to his play, so that it now resembled a comic opera more than a conventional farce. He told a reporter that he preferred the newer, more musical rendition of his play. Margarita Xirgu's 1930 performance of the work had been merely a "chamber version," he said. "Its true premiere is in Buenos Aires."

Lorca spent the afternoon of December 1 vigorously rehearsing the cast of *The Shoemaker's Prodigious Wife*. He praised those actors who had done well and reprimanded those who had strayed from his concept of the play. He seemed apprehensive about the production, and in interviews tried repeatedly to prepare Argentine audiences for the play by reminding them that with its "light and lively rhythm" it differed vastly from *Blood Wedding*. "I'd be tempted to call the work a 'pantocomedy,' if the word didn't sound so pharmaceutical to me," he said. ". . . The work is almost a ballet. It's both a pantomime and a play."

He performed the opening night prologue himself. Dressed in a tuxedo and carrying a top hat in his hand, he spoke to the huge crowd about the magic of the theater. He then released a live dove from his hat. As the bird flew through the house, the audience clapped. Critics and theatergoers were charmed by the vibrancy of the production's music, dance, and scenery, but less enthusiastic about the script, which many thought too brief. Well-wishers crowded into Lorca's flower-filled dressing room after the performance. Beaming, he hugged them. "Membrives is crazy about me!" he gushed afterward in a letter to his parents.

> Of course! I'm a lottery that she's just won! . . . I get the impression that I can produce anything here, no matter how daring it is, because the public has tremendous respect for its authors, unlike the uncouth Madrid crowds that *stomp their feet* the moment you give them something they don't understand.

Two weeks later he premiered another work, a half-hour review of popular Spanish songs called *Fin de Fiesta*, performed by Membrives and several actresses from her company. The short spectacle was designed to supplement *The Shoemaker's Prodigious Wife*, and included many of Lorca's favorite songs. "One certainly sees the spirit of García Lorca in it," a reviewer said of the show. A reporter who stopped in to watch a rehearsal found Lorca striding energetically through an empty theater as Membrives and her colleagues rehearsed. "Don't lose the rhythm!" Lorca cried, and waved his arms to mark the beat. "Just a minute. Those rhythms are like this," he said, and sat down at a piano to illustrate his point. "Girls, hold your arms up! Very good. That's better." Lorca turned to his visitor and said, "I could go on staging these 'fin de fiestas' for years."

In Buenos Aires he spoke at length about music. "Songs are creatures," he explained, "delicate creatures that must be carefully tended so that no part of their rhythm is altered." He talked of staging an evening of Christmas carols in Argentina, and arranged to meet the tango king, Carlos Gardel. Whenever possible, Lorca played the piano for friends, dazzling them with his effortless control of the instrument. "After a while he no longer watched the keys," an acquaintance recalled. "He would lift his head, sharpen his expression, lean back at the waist, smile his radiant smile, and sing." When a friend suggested to him that he seemed destined to resume the musical career he had abandoned in his teens, Lorca grabbed him by the shoulder, grinned, and said, "It's possible you're right." In an interview with Pablo Suero, he confessed, "I am primarily a musician."

He received so many invitations for Christmas that he did not know which to accept. Because summer was at its height, and the Argentine beaches lovely, he decided to spend the holiday swimming with friends.

On Christmas day, a local Jewish magazine published an interview in which Lorca proclaimed himself a "good friend" of the city's large Jewish population and defended himself against charges of anti-Semitism. A number of Jews had taken offense at *The Shoemaker's Prodigious Wife*, where the Shoemaker and his wife denounce their gossiping Andalusian neighbors as "Jewish executioners" and "rude Jews." In the interview, Lorca struggled to explain that while the word "Jew" was a traditional term of insult in rural Andalusia, it was not anti-Semitic. "One says 'Jew' contemptuously, yes, but without thinking of actual Jews," he said clumsily, adding that the moment he had realized his play was offensive, he had revised the script to read "hag" instead of "Jew."

He did not mention the rise of anti-Semitism in Germany—reports of which appeared regularly in the Buenos Aires press—nor did he acknowledge that, under the circumstances, his choice of vocabulary in *The Shoemaker's Prodigious Wife* might be justifiably viewed as injurious to the Jewish people. Despite his lifelong protestations of sympathy for the oppressed, Lorca seemed oblivious to the impact of racist language. He professed genuine surprise and "distress" at the fact that his play had offended the Jewish community. His own surname, he volunteered, was Jewish. "So you can see that, having a Semitic name, I could not possibly hate you." As for the Jews' status in Spain, he said, "I consider them to be a very expressive part of our heritage."

The Shoemaker's Prodigious Wife ran for fifty performances in Buenos Aires, closing on January 4, 1934. A week later, Membrives opened a new production of Lorca's decade-old *Mariana Pineda*. Lorca was even more jittery about this play than about *The Shoemaker's Prodigious Wife*. Although to his parents he predicted that *Mariana* would enjoy the same overseas success as his other plays, to the Argentine public he was almost apologetic about the work. While not his first play, he explained in an interview in *La Nación*, *Mariana Pineda* "is nevertheless one of my earliest works, and I feel about her the way a bridegroom feels about a bride." He told readers of *Crítica* that he had written the play at the age of twenty; in fact, he was twenty-five when he began *Mariana Pineda*. Speaking to the opening night audience from the stage of the Teatro Avenida, he described *Mariana Pineda* as a "youthful work," which still bore the "scent of jasmine that filled my parents' garden as I was writing the play."

The audience responded enthusiastically to the work. Lorca was called onstage at the end of the play, and in a brief statement confessed that he did not know what to say to such a large crowd. With so many faces staring up at him, he felt "small, with the shyness of a man who is too closely watched." Reviews of the production were, at best, lukewarm. *La Prensa* called *Mariana Pineda* monotonous and suggested the play should never have been produced—not in 1927 and not in 1934. *El Diario Español* issued a stinging critique, not only of the work but of its author. According to the paper, Lorca had "progressed little, either theatrically or literarily," since the age of ten. Had he gone into "experimental choreography" rather than literature, he would be world-famous. The tone of the paper's remarks suggests the degree of envy Lorca's celebrity had begun to provoke. Two weeks later, *El Diario Español* again attacked Lorca, this time insisting that *Blood Wedding* was overrated, and the city of Buenos Aires foolish for having placed Lorca on a "false pedestal."

In letters home, Lorca maintained an air of confidence. *Mariana Pineda* was

a "resounding success," he told his family. By the end of the opening night performance, the "whole theater was crying. It was an apotheosis, and Lola kissed
me onstage in front of everyone, and the theater was on its feet." He promised
his parents that he would soon return to Spain, although he would miss "this
delightful country, which loves me so much, and where everything I do has
repercussions."

Shortly afterward, Membrives announced to the press that she intended to
open her company's fall season on March 10 with the premiere of Lorca's
newest play, *Yerma*. Although Lorca had assured Margarita Xirgu that the
play belonged to her, he had evidently changed his mind, as Xirgu had
predicted, and now wanted both Membrives and Xirgu to premiere the
work simultaneously in Buenos Aires and Madrid. "It will be tremendous,"
he wrote to his family, "and people will see the difference between the two
audiences."

But first he had to finish the play. In November he told a journalist he
needed to go "to the country, to some quiet and green corner," in order to complete *Yerma*. By late January 1934, newspapers were speculating that Lorca intended to write the last act of his play either "in the country or in some resort."
The "resort" turned out to be the city of Montevideo, Uruguay, where Lola
Membrives and her husband planned to spend several weeks so that the actress
could recuperate from her strenuous Buenos Aires season. The couple booked
a hotel room for Lorca immediately next door to theirs, in downtown Montevideo.

He arrived in Montevideo by ship, with Membrives's husband, Juan Reforzo,
on the morning of January 30. Dressed in a white linen suit and wing-tip shoes,
his face bronzed by the sun, Lorca stood at the rail of the ship to greet the
crush of journalists, friends, and dignitaries who had come to meet him. In the
stifling heat, he spoke briefly to reporters about *Yerma*. Yes, he intended to work
on the play in Montevideo, he said. "Is it possible you'll give the work to another company?" someone asked.

"I couldn't tell you," Lorca replied. "In the theater you can never be sure of
anything."

After checking into his hotel room, he changed into his sailor's shirt and
joined two Uruguayan writers for lunch. He knew one of the two, Enrique
Amorím, from Buenos Aires. It was Amorím, in fact, who had given him the
very shirt he was wearing. Over lunch, Lorca continued to talk about *Yerma*.
"Two acts. I've got two acts, and you know what? I like them. I like them!" The
third act would be "magnificent," he said. "People know the Lorca of *Gypsy*

Ballads, of *Deep Song*, of *Blood Wedding*. But they haven't seen anything! Now I'm in full García Lorca mode." He tossed his head back, waved his hands, closed his eyes, and grinned. "Now I'm writing what I've always wanted to write. You'll see."

After lunch, the writers climbed into Amorím's automobile for a tour of the city. Lorca chattered on. When he glimpsed the countryside outside Montevideo, he shrieked with pleasure. "The greens! Did you see the greens?" Sometime later, near the beach, they encountered two horses walking along a road, followed by two children. Lorca grew suddenly gloomy. "I am surrounded by death! Death, physical death," he announced. "My death. Yours. And yours. Do you understand? . . . Tell me: why does death stalk me?" Out loud, he imagined what would happen if the horses abruptly kicked the two children. He envisioned a child's face, "covered in blood and shattered, right here in front of me." Then he fell silent.

Not far away, the ocean washed rhythmically against the land. The three men walked down to the beach. While the Uruguayans sat on a rock, Lorca recited his New York poems. He now called the collection *Introduction to Death*. His impromptu performance lasted two hours. By the time he finished, the sky was dark. Afterward, as they walked toward Amorím's car, Lorca again spoke about death. "That's what I sing," he said. ". . . I do it so that people will love me." Moments later he launched into a recital of poems by Machado and Jiménez. It was ten o'clock in the evening. He had been going strong since noon.

He told Amorím that he needed the sea in order to write. "Just as I need music. I don't know. It's the magic circle." But despite the ocean's calming presence, Lorca was unable to work in Montevideo. From the instant he arrived until his departure fifteen days later, the press tracked nearly everything he did and said. People recognized him on the streets. During Carnival, he rode through Montevideo in a parade. "It's Lorca! It's Lorca!" the crowd chanted. "He's hot!" A woman stepped forward, holding a baby. "Kiss him on the forehead, Federico!" she begged, and Lorca did.

He had agreed to give two lectures in the Uruguayan capital, but because the demand for tickets was so great, he quickly added two more talks to his schedule. The president of Uruguay attended Lorca's first lecture. Uruguayan poets, politicians, and actors sought him out during his stay in Montevideo. There were banquets, cocktail parties, and luncheons. Lorca spent time with the Spanish ambassador, Enrique Díez-Canedo, a short, jovial man who had followed his career for years and, in his capacity as a literary critic, had published numerous reviews of Lorca's work in both Spain and South America. Lorca stayed briefly with Díez-Canedo and his family in Montevideo, and later boasted that the ambassador had treated him "like a father."

He found time, as well, to visit his old friend and former Rinconcillo companion José Mora Guarnido, who had left Granada in 1923 and moved to Montevideo. For years Mora had used his influence as a journalist to promote Lorca's name and work in the Uruguayan capital. The day after Lorca reached Montevideo, the two men met in a café and, sitting at a table piled high with bottles of orangeade, reminisced about the past. "The first article ever written about me—you wrote it," Lorca recalled.

"I'd forgotten!" said Mora. "Do you still have it?"

"I do. And everything that's been said about me since, you said first in that article."

But Mora saw disappointingly little of his friend during his visit to Uruguay, because Lorca became distracted by new friends and acquaintances. He spent hours with Amorím and his wife, Esther, who pampered Lorca by preparing eucalyptus infusions for his throat, just as Salvador and Ana María Dalí had done years earlier in Spain. Lorca also befriended the Uruguayan poet Juana de Ibarbourou, who later remembered his "large, noble head" and "chestnut-brown eyes, which, despite his general euphoria, were quite sad." One morning the two attended Mass together. Ibarbourou was struck by the way Lorca clutched his rosary—so stiffly that it resembled a piece of wire. Afterward, over lunch, he stuffed himself with olives and appetizers while telling stories. Ibarbourou thought him as boylike as her young son, who that day watched Lorca with amazement.

He still found it impossible to write. Fans besieged him. A reporter turned up at his hotel one day for an interview and discovered Lorca hiding in a tunnel in the basement. Evidently, a crowd of young women seeking autographs had planted themselves at the entrances to the hotel, and, much as he enjoyed such adulation, Lorca wanted to avoid them. "Don't ask me to sing," he cautioned the reporter.

"No, sir."

"Don't ask me to recite poetry."

"No, sir."

"Don't ask me to play the piano."

"No, sir."

"Don't ask me to read you the two acts of *Yerma* which I think I've completed."

"No, sir."

"Don't ask me for an autographed photograph."

"No, sir."

"Or for a tiny piece of my sailor's shirt."

"No, sir."

"And above all, for God's sake, don't ask me to write something clever for you!"

Lorca then explained that he had come to Montevideo with the aim of completing *Yerma*. "Or rather, I didn't come, I was brought here. Membrives, who wants my play, abducted me and brought me here." But in Montevideo, his admirers had prevented him from working on the script. "Membrives tells me to shut myself away under lock and key," he continued. "And I say to her, yes, I've got no choice but to lock myself away, because if I don't, I'll end up being locked away by doctor's orders. But where? Would you mind telling me where?"

In time, Lorca also grew tired of Membrives, who became so desperate for a finished script that she conspired to isolate him from his friends and fans. She ordered the hotel to inform guests that he was away from his room when, in fact, he was inside, working. Lorca was at first amused by her tactics, then angry. He had never completely liked or trusted Membrives, in part because her ego rivaled his own. Toward the end of his visit to Uruguay, he behaved like "a fugitive," a friend remembered, practically fleeing from the actress and taking refuge in private homes.

He made no progress on *Yerma* in Montevideo. But he did manage to complete an adaptation of Lope de Vega's *La dama boba*, which he had agreed to do for the Argentine actress Eva Franco, and he made revisions to his 1923 puppet play about Don Cristóbal. Lorca planned to produce both works when he returned to Buenos Aires. He spent his last day in Montevideo visiting the grave of an old Spanish friend, Rafael Barradas, the artist who had designed the costumes for his first play, *The Butterfly's Evil Spell*, and whose spartan Barcelona apartment Lorca had visited in the mid-1920s. A native Uruguayan, Barradas had returned to Montevideo in 1928 and died there shortly afterward from tuberculosis.

Dressed in a white linen suit, Lorca stood beside his friend's grave on the morning of February 16 and scattered a handful of tiny flowers one by one onto the earth. Attached to each flower was a card bearing the name of one of Barradas's friends in Spain. It was raining. Several of Lorca's Uruguayan friends stood with him. No one spoke. Later that day, Lorca left Montevideo. José

Mora Guarnido and Enrique Díez-Canedo found him on board his ship one hour before setting sail for Buenos Aires. Lorca made no reference to his departure. When the moment came for his friends to leave, he embraced them and murmured, "See you later." "Every time we say / goodbye," he had written ten years earlier, "we leave something of ourselves / in the cold current of the wind."

Lorca returned to Buenos Aires on the morning of February 17, and that afternoon read his adaptation of *La dama boba* to Eva Franco and her company. He also wrote to inform his family that he planned to wire them the earnings from his Montevideo lectures. "You can do whatever you want with this money, because it's yours. Mama and Papa can spend it all if they like. You've certainly spent enough on me." He announced that he had booked his return passage to Spain on March 6. He knew his mother would be pleased. In a recent letter she had beseeched Lorca to come home: "Wrap up your affairs, pack your suitcases as best you can, and get on with it." The entire Lorca family, she reminded him, had moved to Madrid "principally for you, and as it turns out, you're not even here."

Membrives opened her fall season on March 1 with a tribute to Lorca. Although he claimed it was difficult to recite a theatrical work in the one place "where an author's dreams come true," Lorca read the first two scenes of *Yerma* to the audience that night. They eagerly applauded the work. He told the crowd he intended to leave Buenos Aires on March 6, but he suggested he might change his mind and stay. "Days go by, nights go by, a month and a half, but . . . as the old ballad says, 'I remain . . .' I leap from the sixth to the twentieth to the thirtieth and then to the first of the month. Nothing! I'm still here, as you can see."

Two nights later he attended the premiere of Eva Franco's production of *La dama boba*, now retitled *La niña boba*, "The Simple-Minded Girl." Chiefly as a lark, Lorca had agreed to adapt Lope's play for the actress, and since returning to Buenos Aires, had devoted much of his time to helping Eva polish the rhythm and diction of her company's performance. To Lope's script he added music and songs, but, as he admonished the critic Octavio Ramírez of *La Nación*, he did not rewrite the work. "I've cut it, which is a very different matter. You can't rewrite a masterpiece. That's a sin I'd never dare commit." Franco's production was a hit, commercially as well as critically; ultimately it ran for nearly two hundred performances.

Lorca thanked the audience from the stage on opening night, and with profound emotion invoked the memory of Lope de Vega, "marvel of nature and father of the theater." Eva Franco was astonished to realize that Lorca was nervous when speaking to the public. He told the actress he was shy about being watched, that he felt "spied upon." Because of his timidity, he rarely improvised his remarks to audiences. Instead, he always carried a small piece of paper with him.

As he had anticipated, Lorca extended his stay in Buenos Aires. On March 10, *La Nación* announced that, because he had been unable to complete the script, Lorca had withdrawn *Yerma* from Membrives's forthcoming season and had suggested that the actress produce *Once Five Years Pass* in its place. Membrives and Lorca were rumored to have come to physical blows over the issue. According to one witness, Lorca interrupted a reading of *Yerma* at Membrives's house and curtly informed the actress that he had no intention of letting her premiere the work, because he had written it for Margarita Xirgu. He was fed up with Membrives's imperious treatment of him. His decision so infuriated the actress that she threatened retaliation. Her actors nicknamed her "Lola balls." But in the end, she did nothing.

In public, Lorca maintained a pretense of well-being. On March 15, at a special performance of *La niña boba* given for the actors of Buenos Aires, he praised Membrives, calling her a "distinguished actress . . . a *maja* with a fan of fire, a somber woman or crazy girl, a true glory of the theater." That night he also spoke out against the purely commercial theater. He reminded Argentina's actors that the theater is

> an art, a great art, an art born with man, one that he carries in the noblest part of his soul. When man wants to express what is most profound about his history and his being, he does so through performance, through the repetition of physical attitudes.

Ten days later, on March 25, he was still in Buenos Aires. At one-thirty that morning he and designer Manuel Fontanals presented a once-only performance of Lorca's newly revised puppet play, *Don Cristóbal's Puppet Show*, at the Teatro Avenida. The production was intended as a farewell gift to the people of Buenos Aires.

Lorca stood behind a small, brightly colored stage in the lobby of the theater, and together with actors from Membrives's company presented three puppet plays: a portion of the *Eumenides*, by Aeschylus; a Cervantes interlude;

and his own *Don Cristóbal's Puppet Show*. The performance lasted until dawn. He opened the presentation with a quick exchange between two puppets—an autobiographical "Poet," with a receding hairline and thick black eyebrows, and Don Cristóbal. The two puppets reminisced about the show they had staged together eleven years earlier, with Manuel de Falla, in Lorca's living room in Granada.

"I'm sad," Cristóbal confessed.

"What's this?" the Poet asked.

"Nothing. I'm going away with Lorca and Fontanals. They've told me to say goodbye, because in the end I can't shed tears, and they can . . . and they don't want to become sad." Cristóbal thanked the audience and praised Lola Membrives. "May she always remember us, and may she remember Federico, who will always love her."

In addition to a Poet, Lorca's new version of *Don Cristóbal's Puppet Show* featured a Director, who periodically interrupts the action to rebuke cast members whenever they deviate from the written text, and who at the close of the play pleads for an end to the "boredom and vulgarity to which we have condemned the stage." Fast-paced, loosely structured, and filled with bawdy language, the new show was both an exploration and a defense of creative freedom. Several women and at least one man in the audience took offense at the play's salacious dialogue and blatant sexual allusions, and walked out on Lorca's early-morning performance.

"If bad words are capable of frightening people, what effect will good words have?" a reporter quipped afterward. Others howled at the ribald exchanges between Cristóbal and Rosita. "What are you going to do to me?" Rosita asks her new husband shortly after their marriage.

"I'm going to make you moooooo!"

"And at midnight, what will you do?"

"I'll make you aaaaaaah!"

"And at three in the morning?"

"I'll make you piiiiii!"

Funnier still were Lorca's deliberate jibes at those who sat in the Avenida that night watching his play: theater reviewers, writers, artists, and actors whom he had come to know during his six-month stay in Argentina, including Pablo Neruda. Early in the play, Don Cristóbal lists several of these people by name and describes the sounds they make while snoring. Lorca also made a fleeting reference to himself. "If you don't keep quiet, I'll go up there and split that big cornbread face of yours!" the Director commands the Poet in the play's opening scene. Scrutinizing his brother's play years later, Paco García Lorca recognized in the Poet's "cornbread" looks Lorca's own "brown face, with its salient cheekbones, a face made fuller by the passage of time."

His success in Buenos Aires and Montevideo had proved to Lorca that his work could attract an international audience. He regarded his experience as a "triumph for the Spanish theater." As he prepared to leave South America, his mind reeled with ideas for new projects. "You can't imagine how many ideas," he said later.

On the eve of his departure from Buenos Aires, he visited Pablo Neruda. Even then, Lorca remained captive to his celebrity. A journalist recorded and subsequently published the poets' conversation that night. "It's hard for me to leave Buenos Aires!" Lorca exclaimed, deliberately tailoring his remarks to a wider public. "I spent months roaming New York, and when I left, I did so almost happily . . . But now, although I'm anxious to join my loved ones, I feel as if I'm leaving a part of myself behind in this magical city." He praised Neruda. Then he began to weep. After a moment, Neruda broke the silence and talked about something else. Later, Lorca confessed that he detested goodbyes. "They break my heart. Please, tomorrow at the ship, be happy, all of you," he urged. "Let's pretend that I'm going to the Tigris, and that we'll see each other again someday."

The following day, March 27, Lorca boarded a transatlantic liner bound for Spain. With him were the designer Manuel Fontanals and his daughter, Rosa María. Friends assembled on the pier to see them off. "This is so that the party can continue," Lorca told the group, and he handed them a small package. When they later opened the box, his friends found a "fabulous wad" of money inside. They spent the sum on one exuberant party after another.

Laden with memories and gifts—more than a dozen autographed books and an assortment of colonial silver pieces, including an ornate soup tureen from Uruguay—Lorca set sail. Weeks earlier he had told a reporter, "To myself, I still feel like a child. The emotions of childhood are still with me." An immigrant woman from Fuente Vaqueros had approached him during his last weeks in Buenos Aires and shown him an old, yellowing photograph of a baby. "Do you know him, Federico?" she had asked.

"No."

"It's you, when you were a year old. I was present at your birth." She pointed to a spot on the photograph where the cardboard was torn. "Your little hands did that when the picture was new. You ripped it . . . the rip in this photograph is such a wonderful souvenir for me." Lorca wanted to hug the woman, to kiss the photograph. But instead he simply stared at it. "There it was, my first work," he told the reporter. "I don't know whether it was good or bad. But it was mine."

His ship, the *Conte Biancamano*, docked briefly in Río de Janeiro on March 30, the day before Easter. Alfonso Reyes, the Mexican ambassador to Brazil and a writer whom Lorca knew casually, presented Lorca with a glass case containing the preserved remains of half a dozen brightly colored Brazilian butterflies.

Five days later, in the midst of the Atlantic, Lorca drafted a series of five new poems. He later included the works in a larger collection based loosely on traditional Arabic and Persian verse forms. In each of the five poems, he alludes to his circumstances at the moment of composition. "As I am lost in the heart of certain children," he writes in "Ghazal of the Flight,"

> I have often been lost on the sea.
> Not knowing water, I keep looking
> to be consumed in luminous death.

In "Ghazal of Dark Death," he longs to "sleep the sleep of that child / who wanted to cut his heart out on the sea." He speaks of a drowned child in "Qasida of One Wounded by Water," and of the wind in "Qasida of the Weeping" and "Qasida of the Impossible Hand." The boundaries between childhood, love, and death blur in all five of the poems Lorca wrote during his journey home, but nowhere is the distinction between life and death more obscure than in "Ghazal of the Flight":

> There is no one who can kiss
> without feeling the smile of those without faces;
> there is no one who can touch
> an infant and forget the immobile skulls of horses.

From the start of his career, Lorca had grounded his work in the belief that life, death, and beauty are intertwined, that neither love nor children can deliver human beings from the fundamental sorrow of existence. As he sailed east toward Spain, toward those he loved most in the world, he pondered the evanescence of life and imagined both the comfort and the anguish of oblivion:

> I want to sleep just a moment,
> a moment, a minute, a century.
> But let it be known that I have not died:

> that there is a stable of gold in my lips,
> that I am the West Wind's little friend,
> that I am the enormous shadow of my tears.

During his last weeks in Buenos Aires, Lorca had talked at length to journalist José Luna about death. "Death begins when we are resting," Lorca had said.

Next time you're at a party, talking serenely, take a look at everyone's shoes. You'll see them resting, horribly resting. You'll see that they are dumb, somber, expressionless things, utterly useless and already about to die. Boots and feet, when they are resting, obsess me with their deathliness. I look at a pair of resting feet—resting in that tragic way that only feet can learn—and I think, "Ten, twenty, forty years more and their repose will be absolute. Or maybe in a few minutes. Maybe in an hour. Death is already in them."

For that reason, Lorca explained, he never took naps with his shoes on. If he so much as glanced at his feet while lying in bed, he was reminded of the corpses he had seen as a boy in the *vega*. "Their feet were always like that, close together, resting, in their new shoes . . . And that," he told his interviewer, "is death."

CHAPTER 22

SAD BREEZE IN THE OLIVE GROVES

1934

$\rightleftharpoons$

After a journey of sixteen days, the *Conte Biancamano* docked in Barcelona on April 11, 1934. Lorca immediately caught the train for Madrid, and arrived in the capital grinning "with satisfaction," remembered Pedro Salinas, and giddy with pride at the enormous amount of money he had made overseas. Pulling handfuls of pesetas from his pockets, he treated friends to drinks and dinner. When members of La Barraca tried to give him a banquet, Lorca surreptitiously contrived to pay the bill.

Dressed in a white linen suit, suntanned, jubilant, he looked and behaved like the celebrity he had become. At home and abroad, people proclaimed him an "ambassador" of Spanish literature. There was talk of sending him to the Philippines as a representative of the "new Spanish poetry." Schools in Spain now taught his poems; theater companies vied for his work. The *Defensor de Granada* noted that overseas Lorca had been "definitively consecrated the Man of the Stage." During a brief visit to Granada later that month, Lorca told a friend, "The sky is weighing me down. What success! You can't ask for more." He said that in Argentina he had been paid "for the nonsense I used to do over here. Lots of money. The theater was full every day. They want me to go back." He boasted that the experience had made him believe in God. "I have no choice but to believe!"

Under the heading "Our Embassy Returns," the *Heraldo de Madrid* published an interview with him on April 14. In it, a beaming Lorca ushered journalist Miguel Pérez Ferrero into his parents' apartment in Madrid, pointed to a table, and said, "Look." Pérez Ferrero beheld an "astonishing" display of clip-pings from Lorca's Argentine visit: editorials, reviews, stories, photographs. Of the trip itself, Lorca said briskly:

> I'll give you a few facts. One hundred and seventy performances of *Blood Wedding*, a hundred of *The Shoemaker's Prodigious Wife*, and most recently *Mariana Pineda*, which is heading toward its fortieth performance . . . As for the Buenos Aires public, they're extremely respectful. If they like a work, they go to see it. If not, the company stops offering it after the third performance. Fortunately, that hasn't happened in my case.

He discussed the state of the contemporary Spanish stage: "In Spain, the bour-geoisie and the middle class, who have prostituted our theater, will soon learn how to fix it." He reviewed his accomplishments as a lecturer in both Buenos Aires and Montevideo, and he talked of the quantity of his work that had been published in South America. Pérez Ferrero asked his thoughts on the current political situation in Spain. "But isn't this politics?" Lorca cried. "I believe it is. Great politics, effective politics, marvelous politics!"

The Second Spanish Republic marked its third anniversary on April 14, 1934. Despite celebrations throughout Madrid, the mood on the streets was somber. At one point, authorities discovered a Republican flag, fringed in black, flying over the post office building. It was quickly removed.

Since the November 1933 elections, the Spanish government had undergone a number of drastic changes. In the first months of 1934, the coalition govern-ment of Prime Minister Alejandro Lerroux had repealed a variety of legislative acts imposed by earlier Republican leaders. Lerroux's administration had restored religious education and government payment of priests' salaries, granted clemency to all political prisoners, and abandoned efforts to reform the country's corrupt agrarian system. His right-wing cabinet had also tried, unsuc-cessfully, to restore capital punishment.

In early April, Lerroux abruptly resigned in protest after the Spanish presi-dent, Niceto Alcalá Zamora, delayed ratifying the new act granting clemency to political prisoners. Months of ineffective rule by a new prime minister, Ri-cardo Samper, followed. Violent confrontations took place in villages through-out the Spanish countryside. In several places, military drills by both right- and left-wing groups became a regular Sunday afternoon event. For many citizens, the specter of Hitler's Germany—where a legally elected, constitutional government was being systematically dismantled—loomed large. Spaniards worried in particular about the role the Catholic Church had played in Hitler's rise to power. In 1933 the Vatican had signed a Concordat with the German Führer. During the week that Lorca returned to Spain, speakers at a gathering of right-wing Catholic youths in Granada openly voiced their admiration for both Hitler and Mussolini.

Blissfully immersed in the commotion surrounding his triumphant return, Lorca overlooked the more troubling implications of his country's political turmoil and settled comfortably into his old routines: nightly soirees at Morla Lynch's home, daily rehearsals with La Barraca. The company had just returned from an excursion to Morocco. Lorca hoped to take them to Argentina, and talked excitedly about the prospect. During his absence the troupe had come under attack by right-wing journalists, who accused the company of taking jobs away from Madrid's unemployed professional actors. The left-wing press had defended the company, noting that it consisted exclusively of student actors who received no salary. For a time, members of the troupe feared they might lose their government subsidy. Although the debate eventually slackened, the company's status remained tenuous.

In mid-May, the troupe staged the first of several private shows using a set of puppets Lorca had brought back with him from his Buenos Aires production of *Don Cristóbal's Puppet Show*. Lorca himself took part in the spectacle, playing the role of the Poet in a sanitized version of the bawdy *Cristóbal* he had presented in Argentina. (For the Barraca performance, he instructed one of his student actresses to cut a sequence of lines in which Rosita applies rice powder so that Don Cristóbal's "cock hurts her better.") That month Lorca also helped direct a production of Ferenc Molnár's *Liliom* for Pura Ucelay's Anfistora Club; the show opened at Madrid's Teatro Español in late spring.

On June 1, Pablo Neruda arrived in Madrid with his wife, Maruca. The two were on their way to the Chilean consulate in Barcelona, where the thirty-year-old Neruda had been assigned a diplomatic post. Lorca went to the train station with his companion Rafael Rodríguez Rapún and others to greet the couple. Neruda emerged tall and pale from the car, his pockets stuffed with newspapers. The group immediately took off for a tavern, where they drank wine, talked, and recited poetry.

It soon became clear that Neruda had no intention of settling in Barcelona. For the first several months of his appointment, he shuttled back and forth between the Catalan capital and Madrid; early the following year he transferred permanently to the Chilean consulate in Madrid. His home became the site of boisterous gatherings that lasted for days, fueled by Neruda's lethal "punch concoctions" and his indifference to time. Guests would pack crosswise into beds so that everyone had room to sleep; people often woke to find the party still in full swing. The festivities frequently culminated in the "inauguration" of a public monument, a rite invented by Lorca and Neruda. Posing as civic authorities, the two poets would stand beside some monument in the capital and deliver grandiloquent speeches while their friends imitated a ceremonial band. At a formal presentation later in the year, Lorca introduced Neruda as one of the great Latin American poets of his day, a writer "closer to death than to philosophy, closer to pain than to intelligence, closer to blood than to ink." Neruda "lacks the two elements with which so many false poets have lived: hatred and irony," he said. For his part, Neruda thought Lorca "the guiding spirit of this moment in our language."

The Chilean dropped in regularly on Lorca's Barraca rehearsals. Lorca devoted much of June and July 1934 to the troupe, preparing his actors for their weeklong residency that August at the International University in Santander. Controversy continued to plague the company. On July 5, the Falangist paper *FE* accused La Barraca of moving "in the turbid waters of Jewish Marxism." The paper addressed Lorca's student performers directly: "Your duty to this hungry nation . . . is to present an example of sacrifice. An example of sacrifice, students, not of licentiousness. Nor should you be wasting money that doesn't belong to you."

Lorca defended the company in interviews. He told journalist Juan Chabás that no professional troupe could rival La Barraca. He praised the intelligence and enthusiasm of his young actors. "What's more," he said, "by dint of all these rehearsals and experiences, I feel I'm turning into a stage director. It's a long and difficult process." Chabás asked if Lorca's directorial work kept him from writing. "Not at all," Lorca said. "I'm working a great deal. Right now I'm about to finish *Yerma*, my second tragedy." He intended to give the Spanish theater "tragedies," he said, because "our theatrical tradition demands it." He insisted that directing did not distract him from writing. "It's all the same! Everything becomes the joy of creating, of making things."

In late July, Lorca went home to the Huerta de San Vicente in Granada to celebrate his saint's day. He remained in Granada for a couple of weeks, basking in the silence of the *vega* and the scent of jasmine that enveloped his family's summer home. During his stay he put the finishing touches to *Yerma*, his tragedy about a childless woman. He told a friend he had already begun planning his next drama, *Doña Rosita the Spinster*. He hoped to finish the second play after La Barraca's visit to Santander. "Since I've got it all thought out, it will only take me a few days' work," he said.

On July 17, the day before his saint's day, one of Lorca's oldest friends, Paquito Soriano Lapresa, died from a sudden illness. He was thirty-nine. Lorca had known Soriano since adolescence, when both were members of the Rinconcillo. The eccentric only son of a wealthy Granada family, Soriano had shared Lorca's impish sense of fun (he once wore a green pepper on his nose during Carnival) and his fondness for romantic music and the poetry of Juan Ramón Jiménez. Lorca had dedicated a chapter of *Impressions and Landscapes* to "Paquito Soriano, exotic and admirable spirit." At thirty-six, he was devastated to learn of Soriano's death. "You can well imagine the grief we, his friends, have endured," he told Rafael Martínez Nadal that August. "One of the most wonderful men I've ever known has died."

Three days after Soriano's death, the *Defensor de Granada* announced the birth of Concha García Lorca's third child, a daughter, Lorca's second niece. Although he had long viewed birth and death as inextricable halves of a single whole, Lorca had seldom witnessed so dramatic a confluence of the two. As he rejoiced in his niece's birth, he mourned his friend's death, and vice versa. Sometime that summer—very probably in the last week of July and first two weeks of August—he composed a number of new poems in which he explored the bonds between birth, death, and love. By fall, Lorca had begun to think of these individual poems—together with a sprinkling of works written in 1931, and the poems he had composed in April 1934 during his voyage home from Argentina—as a unified collection, one loosely based, he said, on traditional Arab verse forms.

He called the collection *The Divan at Tamarit*—"divan" from the Persian *diwan*, meaning an anthology of verse, and "Tamarit" from the proper Arab name his uncle Francisco had given to his country home, the Huerta de Tamarit, located a few hundred yards from the Huerta de San Vicente. Lorca so loved his uncle's whitewashed house that he described it as "a collection of postcard pictures," and told a cousin who lived there, "You must never, never sell it. I want it for myself." He thought its address "the prettiest" in the world: "Huerta del Tamarit, Término de Fargui, Granada."

By choosing to associate *The Divan at Tamarit* with Arab verse forms, Lorca was giving voice to ideas and images that had absorbed him since childhood. He had read Arab poetry in his teens, and in his twenties had talked of dedicating an issue of *gallo* to "the Arabic poets of the Alhambra." "When our *coplas* reach the very extremes of Pain and Love," he had said in his lecture on Gypsy deep song, "they become linked expressively with the magnificent verses of Arab and Persian poets." He particularly admired the sensuality of Arab verse.

His interest in the form was part of a widespread revival of interest in Arab culture in the early 1930s in Spain. By 1934 the University of Granada had inaugurated a School of Arab Studies aimed at promoting the study of the region's Arab heritage. Lorca knew at least one member of the school's faculty, Emilio García Gómez, a scholar of Arab literature whose influential anthology of Arab-Andalusian poetry, *Poemas arábigos-andaluces*, published in 1930, had introduced many Spaniards to the extravagant metaphors and exotic language of Arab verse. In the summer of 1934, García Gómez told Lorca that he intended to devote his next book to Ibn Zamrak, the poet whose work adorned the walls of the Alhambra. Lorca countered by announcing that he intended to publish his own homage to the poets who once inhabited Arab Granada, *The Divan at Tamarit*.

Although he failed to issue the collection in 1934, Lorca did deliver a manuscript of the work to his friend Antonio Gallego Burín, who promised to publish the book through the auspices of the University of Granada. García Gómez agreed to contribute an introduction to the volume. The finished collection numbered twenty poems. Lorca divided these into two roughly equal sections of "ghazals" and "qasidas," poems dimly based on traditional Middle Eastern verse forms. Like their ancient Persian counterparts, Lorca's "ghazals" dwell principally on love and sex, while his "qasidas"—historically a longer, metrically more complex form—focus chiefly on death. Throughout the collection love and death intermingle. The volume as a whole, one of the most intricate and fully realized of Lorca's poetic endeavors, offers a profound meditation on the constant exchange between the living and the dead, between earth and the cosmos.

Set in Granada, and written mostly in conventional metrical forms, the *Divan* differs markedly from the free verse and urban imagery of its most immediate predecessor, the verse collection he eventually titled *Poet in New York*, although both works stress Lorca's morbid awareness of death, pain, and the futility of human desire. *Poet in New York* had revived his earlier conviction that place is inseparable from personal dilemmas. In the *Divan*, the poet's affection for Granada—a trait he shares with his Arab forebears—is central. Lorca writes of the city's gardens, sky, and omnipresent water, of its pale ruins, and of the sensual abandon that distinguishes Granada from its more earthbound Andalusian neighbors, Córdoba and Seville.

Some poems are short and songlike; others are densely phrased and heavily symbolic; still others employ an erratic free verse. Together they trace the course of an archetypal love affair, from its first pulse to its eventual consummation, dissolution, and aftermath. Through his unnamed protagonist, Lorca hints at his own experience of love, and gives voice to his most enduring preoccupations, while at the same time rendering homage to the city of his youth and its glorious Arab past.

The *Divan* is both more personal and more erotic than any collection Lorca had written to date. Many poems bear veiled allusions to homosexual love, and suggest Lorca's growing desire both to acknowledge and to celebrate his sexuality. The book's opening work, "Ghazal of Love Unforeseen," is emblematic of the whole. The four-stanza poem, one of the most explicitly carnal in the *Divan*, boldly envisions a sudden passionate encounter between the poet and his beloved, drawing links between their contemporary night of "unforeseen" love, with its "thousand Persian ponies," and the tales in *A Thousand and One Nights*, where nights of new love are threatened by death:

> No one understood the perfume, ever:
> the dark magnolia of your belly.
> No one ever knew you martyred
> love's hummingbird between your teeth.
>
> A thousand Persian ponies fell asleep
> in the moonlit plaza of your brow,
> while four nights through I bound
> your waist, the enemy of snow.

The poet dreams of a lasting emotional commitment ("I searched my breast to give you / the ivory letters saying: Ever"), but it is not to be, and in the aftermath of his failed affair, he suffers with Biblical grandeur:

> Ever, ever, my agony's garden,
> your elusive form forever:
> blood of your veins in my mouth,
> your mouth now lightless for my death.

In much of the *Divan*, the protagonist meets a similar fate. Love seems always to evaporate; only suffering endures. The pattern is circular: the agony of existence and certainty of death lead the poet to seek both comfort and oblivion in the act of love; and yet love invariably disappoints, or fails, thereby reminding him of death and of the agony of existence. In "Ghazal of the Love That Hides from Sight," Lorca's protagonist engages in an affair with a lover whose name he does not even bother to learn: "I burned in your body / without knowing whose it was." In "Ghazal of the Memory of Love," he seeks to retain his painful memories of a doomed relationship—memories that, paradoxically, assure him he is alive:

> Don't take your memory with you.
> Leave it alone in my breast,
>
> a shudder of cherry trees
> in white January martyrdom.
>
> A wall of bad dreams
> divides me from the dead.

Everywhere, love and sex—especially heterosexual, procreative sex—lead to death. The male speaker of "Qasida of the Woman Prone" envisions a pregnant woman whose "womb is a struggle of roots. / Your lips are a dawn without contour. / Under the lukewarm roses of the bed / the dead men moan, awaiting their turn." The familiar motif of a drowned child returns in "Ghazal of the Dead Child," where the literal death of a child becomes the figurative death of childhood, and drowning and lovemaking are indistinguishable. Both lead to death:

> No crumb of cloud remained on the land
> when you were drowning in the river.
>
> A giant of water fell down the mountains
> and the valley rolled by with irises and dogs.
> Your body, shadowed violet by my hands,
> dead on the bank, was an archangel of cold.

In one poem after another, human existence—birth, life, love, sex, time, death—dissolves into nothingness. Faced with the void, the poet resigns himself to extinction and asks only for what he cannot have: a helping hand to ease him through the last hours of life. "I want nothing else, only a hand," Lorca writes in "Qasida of the Impossible Hand":

> a wounded hand, if possible.
> I want nothing else, only a hand,
> though I spend a thousand nights without a bed.
>
> It would be a pale lily of lime,
> a dove tethered fast to my heart.

It would be the guard who, on the night of my death,
would block entrance absolutely to the moon.

I want nothing else, only that hand,
for the daily unctions and my agony's white sheet.
I want nothing else, only that hand,
to carry a wing of my own death.

Everything else all passes away.
Now blush without name. Perpetual star.
Everything else is something else: sad wind,
while the leaves flee, whirling in flocks.

Lorca returned to Madrid in early August. He planned to leave the capital on Saturday evening, August 11, and travel with La Barraca to Santander, on the north coast of Spain, for a weeklong series of performances at the International University. Several of Lorca's colleagues, including the poet Jorge Guillén, were already in Santander for the summer university term.

That Saturday afternoon, in a bullring in the small town of Manzanares, south of Madrid, Lorca's friend Ignacio Sánchez Mejías, who had recently returned to the ring, was gored by a bull named Granadino. Sánchez Mejías received superficial treatment in a local infirmary and was transported by ambulance to Madrid. He arrived in the capital early Sunday morning, August 12, bleeding profusely. Despite transfusions and surgery, gangrene set in, and the bullfighter fell into a delirium. He died at 9:45 a.m. on Monday, August 13. He was forty-three.

The instant he heard about his friend's injury, Lorca canceled his travel plans and remained in Madrid to monitor his condition. Because of the gravity of his injuries, friends were not allowed to visit the bullfighter in the hospital but had to rely instead on periodic reports from his doctors. By phone, Lorca conveyed the details to his colleagues in Santander. "Operation." "Transfusion." "They're doing everything they can," he told Jorge Guillén.

And then, in a hoarse, barely audible voice: "They say he's lost. Gangrene."

Shortly before 10 a.m. on August 13, Lorca telephoned Guillén a last time. "It's over. Ignacio died at a quarter to ten. I'm leaving for Santander. I refuse to see it!"

Lorca arrived in Santander that evening and shut himself away with friends—Guillén, Pedro Salinas, Gerardo Diego, and others—to mourn the bullfighter they had all known and loved. Most, like Lorca, had met Sánchez Mejías for the first time in 1927, during the Góngora Tricentennial in Seville.

Then, and subsequently, Sánchez Mejías had endeared himself to them by his exuberant embrace of their work, his love of popular music, and his own "valiant" (as Lorca phrased it) attempts at playwriting. He had retired from bullfighting in 1927 in order to devote himself to a fledgling literary career. Seven years later he announced his return to the ring. Friends tried to dissuade him. But Sánchez Mejías persisted, impelled in part by financial necessity. Older, heavier, and in generally poor shape, he squeezed back into his gaudy uniforms, and in the summer of 1934 made five successful appearances in the ring before going to Manzanares on August 11.

Lorca worshiped him. He had followed his friend's literary career with interest and admiration, and in recent years had spent a great deal of time with the bullfighter and his companion, La Argentinita, in Madrid. Lorca regarded Sánchez Mejías as a hero, both in and out of the bullring. Told of his friend's intent to return to bullfighting in 1934, Lorca remarked soberly to a mutual acquaintance, "Ignacio has just announced his own death to me." On the day after the bullfighter's funeral, Lorca strolled quietly through a park in Santander with the French writer and Hispanist Marcelle Auclair. He wondered out loud "through what minuscule chink" Sánchez Mejías had now slipped. After a long pause, he turned to Auclair and said:

> Ignacio's death is like my own death, an apprenticeship for my own death. I feel an astonishing sense of calm. Is it, perhaps, because I intuitively expected it to happen? There are moments when I see the dead Ignacio so vividly that I can imagine his body, destroyed, pulled apart by worms and brambles, and I find only a silence which is not nothingness, but mystery.

By the end of October 1934, Lorca had written a poem—his longest ever—in memory of the bullfighter; his colleague Rafael Alberti had also composed a poetic homage to Sánchez Mejías. Lorca described his own effort as an "elegy I never wanted to write." He drafted parts of the poem in both Granada and Madrid, and revised the complete work in Pablo Neruda's home in Madrid. He said later that in writing *Lament for Ignacio Sánchez Mejías*, as he called the work, he hoped both to honor his friend and to reveal the "heroic, pagan, popular, and mystic beauty that exists in the fight between man and bull." He viewed the bullfight as a sacred, inherently erotic rite, the "public representation of the victory of human virtue over bestial instinct." At once clear and hermetic, disciplined and free, *Lament for Ignacio Sánchez Mejías* is the work of a writer at the peak of his technical and imaginative maturity. It is the culmination of Lorca's trajectory as an elegiac poet—a keenly felt homage to a close friend as well as a formal lamentation for a tragic hero, an everyman whose epic death demands a Homeric response.

Each of the work's four sections strikes a distinctive tone and tempo; the work as a whole functions both as a single entity and as a suite of interconnected poems reflecting the poet's complex response to his friend's death, and his thoughts on death in general. It offers little in the way of celebration or consolation, and as such is more properly a lament, with roots in ancient Greek and Roman texts, than an elegy. The bullfighter's sacrificial death leads to extinction, not salvation. And yet because he has chosen to confront, rather than flee, his inevitable end, Sánchez Mejías is a hero.

Lorca relished the ceremony of the bullfight, its "sacred rhythm." "In it," he said, "everything is measured, even anguish and death itself." Although he understood little about actual bullfights ("What are they doing now?" he typically asked friends whenever he attended one), he had on several occasions mentioned his desire to write about bullfighting. He had hoped to devote a section of *gallo* to the art, and in the late 1920s had drafted portions of an "Ode to the Fighting Bull" as well as a brief prose sketch on the two antagonistic "halves" of the bullring. The sketch, "Sun and Shadow," belonged to a projected *Tauromaquia*, which Lorca never completed.

He was keenly interested in bullfighting as myth, as a "dark religion" practiced by a nation whose outward contours resemble the hide of a bull, of a "sacrificed animal." He was familiar with early Iberian and Dionysian bull cults, with the Cretan Minotaur, and with the notion, by then commonplace, of Andalusia as ancient Tartessus, the site of Hercules' tenth labor: the retrieval of the mythical red bulls of Geryon. Bullfighting's pagan roots underpin much of the *Lament for Ignacio Sánchez Mejías,* as do its Christian overtones. The bullfight, Lorca believed, is an "authentic religious drama where, as in the Mass, a god is adored and sacrificed."

The opening section of the poem, "The Goring and the Death," is in effect a protracted litany, whose incantatory refrain builds in urgency as the clinical details of the bullfighter's wounding and death unfold:

> At five in the afternoon.
> It was exactly five in the afternoon.
> A boy brought the white sheet
> *at five in the afternoon.*
> A basketful of lime in readiness
> *at five in the afternoon.*
> Beyond that, death and death alone
> *at five in the afternoon.*

Although Sánchez Mejías had died at 9:45 in the morning, Lorca chose the more resonant "five in the afternoon" as his friend's metaphorical hour of death. On the day of the bullfighter's funeral, the Madrid newspaper *ABC* had announced in bold type that the burial procession would begin "at five o'clock in the afternoon"; the day after the funeral the same paper reported that the dead man's coffin had left the chapel "at exactly five o'clock." Lorca seized on the hour—the "hour of truth," according to a Castilian proverb—and transformed it into a repetitive sound whose cumulative effect is that of a thudding drum summoning mourners to a funeral. "When I was composing the *Lament*," he said later, "the line with the fateful 'five in the afternoon' filled my head like the tolling of a bell, and I broke into a cold sweat thinking that such an hour was waiting for me, too. Sharp and precise like a knife. The hour was the awful thing."

The poem's second section, "The Spilled Blood," continues the saga of the bullfighter's death. Written in a ballad meter that recalls the dead or dying Andalusian heroes of Lorca's *Gypsy Ballads*, "The Spilled Blood" recounts the great quantity of blood that filled the sand of the bullring where Sánchez Mejías was gored. Confronted by the awful sight, the poet cries recurrently, "I refuse to see it!"—the precise words Lorca had used when informing Jorge Guillén of Sánchez Mejías's death. Allusions to early Andalusian bull cults and to a set of weathered Iberian sculptures—the so-called "bulls of Guisando"— outside Madrid elevate the bullfighter's prosaic death in a twentieth-century hospital room to an event of mythical stature:

> The cow of this ancient world
> was running her dreary tongue
> over snoutfuls of blood
> spilled across the sand,
> and the bulls of Guisando,
> almost death and nearly stone,
> lowed like two centuries
> tired of treading earth.
> No.
> I refuse to see it!

The man Lorca knew and loved in life becomes an epic hero, a "prince," a "marble torso," a vestige of "Rome's Andalusia":

> What a great fighter in the ring!
> What a good mountaineer on the heights!

How gentle toward ears of grain!
How harsh applying the spurs!
How tender toward the dew!
How dazzling at the fair!
How magnificent when he wielded
the last banderillas of the dark.

In section three, "Presence of the Body," the heroic bullfighter—"Ignacio the wellborn"—metamorphoses into a rotting cadaver surrounded by "fetid silence" and "wet to the bone with tears of snow." As he contemplates his friend's body, Lorca moves from anguish toward acceptance, from a private refusal to see Sánchez Mejías's blood to a public acknowledgment of the inevitability of death:

I don't want them covering his face with kerchiefs
to break him in to the wearing of death.
Go now, Ignacio. Feel no more the hot bellows.
Sleep, soar, repose. The sea dies too!

"Presence of the Body" leads to "Absence of the Soul," the last of the *Lament*'s four sections, a six-stanza reckoning of the ways that death has rendered Sánchez Mejías obsolete. The opening stanza sets the tone for the section and introduces its blunt refrain:

The bull does not know you, nor the fig tree,
nor horses, nor the ants on your floors.
The child does not know you, nor the evening,
because your death is forever.

Only the final two stanzas of the section offer a semblance of consolation:

No one knows you. No one. But I sing you—
sing your profile and your grace, for later on.
The signal ripeness of your mastery.
The way you sought death out, savored its taste.
The sadness just beneath your gay valor.

Not soon, if ever, will Andalusia see
so towering a man, so venturesome.
I sing his elegance with words that moan
and remember a sad breeze in the olive groves.

Years earlier, Sánchez Mejías had told Lorca that as a sixteen-year-old, he had once sneaked out of his father's house and gone to a nearby farm in order to fight bulls from his neighbor's herd. "I was proud of my passes," the bullfighter remembered, "but it made me sad that there was no one there to applaud me. So when a breeze rustled the olive trees, I lifted my hand and waved."

Lorca dedicated *Lament for Ignacio Sánchez Mejías* to his "dear friend Encarnación López Júlvez," La Argentinita, the dancer who had been the married bullfighter's lover for the past several years. He published the poem in its entirety in the spring of 1935, in a twenty-two-page edition illustrated by José Caballero. The volume included a formal obituary portrait of Sánchez Mejías—a traditional taurine image, with a border, a crown, a list of the places where the bullfighter had enjoyed his greatest successes, and the name of the bull that had killed him. Lorca refused, however, to let Caballero print the bull's real name, Granadino. Its linguistic proximity to "Granada" unnerved him. He told the painter to put instead, "A bull from the stable of Ayala killed him."

Both friends and reviewers praised the poem. Miguel Pérez Ferrero of the *Heraldo de Madrid* observed that for "those who want to know him in the future," Sánchez Mejías, "and what he implied," is alive in the *Lament*. In the southern town of Huelva, a reviewer for *La Provincia* hailed Lorca's "clear and strong" silhouette of the bullfighter, but questioned the poet's decision to dedicate the work to Sánchez Mejías's lover. "It's unpleasant, this sort of bad taste."

Lorca ignored all commentary. "What I've written will never rival four lines sung by a weeping Gypsy woman in Seville," he told friends. "Little night stars," the Gypsy had intoned,

> let me cross over the bridge,
> for I want to see my Ignacio
> whose body lives on the other shore.

CHAPTER 23

REVOLUTION

1934-35

More than ever, Lorca wanted to create theater. He relished the impermanence of the stage. Plays "last as long as the performance lasts, and nothing more," he said. The beauty of the theater is that, "scarcely created, it vanishes. It is the art of the moment. It is built upon sand." He felt an "enormous sense of laziness and dismay" at the thought of selecting and preparing his poetry for publication. The theater, on the other hand, posed no such threat. "I go on with my life, and with my life, my theater," he announced in late 1934, "to which I intend from this day on to dedicate the most deeply felt of my poetic urges."

His work with La Barraca, in particular, had led Lorca to see himself as a man of the stage: a playwright, a director, a designer, a participant in the renovation of the Spanish theater. Miguel de Unamuno attended a performance by La Barraca at the International University in Santander in the summer of 1934, and afterward published an article about the group's inspired educational work. La Barraca, he stressed, is a "profound movement, one that is not only pedagogical, but in the strictest sense of the word is demagogic—that is, political."

Frenchman Jean Prévost also saw the company perform in Santander in 1934 and told Lorca he had not seen a better university theater anywhere in Europe. "Come to Paris," he urged. The Spanish poet Dámaso Alonso talked of founding a similar troupe in Barcelona. The Italian journalist Ezio Levi published an account of La Barraca's work in a 1934 issue of the Milan journal *Scenario*. Levi tried to arrange for the company to visit Italy, and he persuaded Luigi Pirandello to invite Lorca to attend an international theater congress in Rome as a representative of Spain. Lorca asked Levi if he could bring Rafael Rapún with him. "The Congress invites me to bring along my wife, but since I don't have one, could I bring along the secretary of La Barraca, who is also my private secretary?" Lorca confessed his ambivalence about the congress. "You know that I'm intense and not very sociable, and I'm a little frightened by all official things. I have a childish character, and it will be good to be with so many brilliant people."

Ultimately he declined Pirandello's invitation. By late September the producers of *Yerma* had decided to stage the work during the fall theater season, and Lorca did not want to miss any rehearsals. He told Pirandello that domestic obligations prevented him from leaving Spain.

The Spanish Cortes reconvened in Madrid on October 1, 1934. At the opening session of the parliamentary body, José María Gil Robles, the Catholic spokesman for the Spanish Right and leader of the right-wing Catholic alliance, CEDA—the largest single party in the Cortes—withdrew both his and CEDA's support from the foundering government of Prime Minister Ricardo Samper. Samper's cabinet dissolved, as did the tenuous coalition between the country's right- and left-wing parties.

The Spanish president, Niceto Alcalá Zamora, promptly asked former prime minister Alejandro Lerroux to form a new coalition government. Lerroux did so, and for the first time included three members of CEDA in the nation's cabinet. Many Spaniards—even some conservative Republicans—were appalled. Because of its strict pro-Catholic stance, the party had never sworn allegiance to the Republic. Leftists, in particular, feared that Lerroux's endorsement of CEDA marked the country's first step toward a fascist regime. While not officially a fascist, the party's power-hungry leader, Gil Robles, had visited Germany in 1933 to meet with Hitler and study Nazi propaganda. In Spain, he encouraged his followers to greet him as Jefe, as though he were the Führer or Duce, and to mouth anti-Semitic slogans. He and his right-wing CEDA colleagues mounted rallies similar to the one Hitler had staged at Nuremberg. In April 1934, Gil Robles had braved a cold rain in El Escorial—the site of Philip II's imposing sixteenth-century monastery, and the burial ground for all of Spain's kings—to tell some thirty thousand Catholic youths from Madrid that if the Republican revolution "descended into the streets," they would be there to meet it heroically. The crowd cheered. In early September 1934, Gil Robles had staged a similar youth rally at Covadonga, in Asturias, the site of an eighth-

century battle traditionally considered the start of the long Christian reconquest of Arab Spain. Through his shrewdly symbolic act, the Catholic leader
tapped into the central epic of Spanish history and, to those willing to see it, established a clear link between the Muslim invaders of medieval Spain and the
left-wing working classes of the twentieth century.

In protest against CEDA's presence in the Spanish cabinet, several Republican leaders, among them former prime minister Manuel Azaña, resigned. The
country's leading trade union called for a nationwide general strike; workers in
Madrid, Barcelona, and the northern province of Asturias complied. Strikes in
Madrid and Barcelona, where Catalan nationalists proclaimed a short-lived, independent Catalan state, were quickly put down; in Barcelona, approximately
twenty citizens died in skirmishes with the Spanish military. At a rally in
Madrid, José Antonio Primo de Rivera, head of the Spanish Falange and the de
facto leader of the country's fascist movement, spoke out against the Moscow-
based "Marxist-Jewish" conspiracy that threatened to destroy Spain.

In Asturias, a stretch of rugged green land along the country's northern coast,
Spanish miners launched a full-scale working-class revolution in opposition to
what they regarded as the "fascist conquest of power in Madrid." The Asturian
revolt began on the morning of October 5. Within three days, striking miners
controlled much of the region. Revolutionary committees dedicated to a "new
society" run by "comrades" took over the administration of towns and villages.
Makeshift recruitment offices summoned workers between the ages of eighteen
and forty to join the "Red Army." By mid-October, thirty thousand workers
were mobilized for battle, and the Spanish military had imposed martial law.
The miners' strike had become an undeclared civil war.

Francisco Franco, a short, pallid, forty-two-year-old general in the Spanish
army known for his right-wing views and icy demeanor, was put in charge of all
military operations in Asturias. As a young cadet in the Toledo Infantry Academy, and later as a twenty-eight-year-old major stationed in Spanish Morocco,
Franco had honed his combat skills and earned a reputation for brutality. His
troops routinely decapitated Moroccan prisoners and displayed their severed
heads as trophies; Franco himself condoned the killing and mutilation of prisoners, and once ordered one of his own men shot by a firing squad after the soldier refused to eat his rations.

A vehement nationalist who in time saw himself as a contemporary El Cid
come to vanquish the heathen communist hordes, Franco reveled in his powerful new role as military and, by virtue of martial law, political commander of
Asturias. From his command room in the Ministry of War in Madrid, he directed the movement of troops, ships, and trains to be used in crushing the

miners' revolution. He shipped Arab mercenaries from Morocco to Asturias, ordered the bombing and shelling of working-class districts in Asturian mining towns, and instructed army units to fire on civilians. "This is a frontier war against socialism, communism, and whatever attacks civilization in order to replace it with barbarism," he told a reporter.

By October 10, Franco's campaign of repression had quelled the revolution in the region's two largest cities, Oviedo and Gijón. Summary executions of workers took place in both towns. Terrorized by the ferocity of Franco's tactics and the cruelty of his troops—particularly his Moroccan units, who committed untold atrocities—and demoralized by the high number of civilian losses, especially among women and children, the remaining Asturian rebels surrendered by October 20. Right-wing Spaniards proclaimed Franco the "savior of the country." Prime Minister Lerroux subsequently awarded him the Gran Cruz de Mérito Militar and appointed him Commander-in-Chief of the Spanish Armed Forces in Morocco, a post Franco considered "the most important military command."

The Republican government promptly violated the terms of the workers' surrender. Inside temporary jails, soldiers committed rape, torture, and murder. All told, more than a thousand Asturian civilians, most of them miners, died as a result of the three-week revolution. Another three thousand citizens were injured. Between thirty thousand and forty thousand people were arrested.

In a blatant propaganda campaign, the far-right press circulated false stories of atrocities carried out by striking workers against their military opponents, and against children and nuns; at least one left-wing reporter who tried to set the record straight was shot dead. Until 1935, the government censored all accounts of the Asturian revolution; consequently, Spanish citizens knew little about what had actually happened. A parliamentary committee eventually investigated the rebellion and its aftermath, and disclosed evidence of torture inside Asturian jails. But many Spaniards so feared a recurrence of the violence that shook Asturias in 1934 that they began to favor a military dictatorship over the chaos of the current Republican administration. Despite efforts to steer his government toward a more moderate path, Prime Minister Lerroux was unable to contain the quarreling factions of his coalition administration. By March 1935, Lerroux had formed a new cabinet. Five of its members belonged to CEDA.

Lorca remained in Madrid throughout the Asturian crisis. The episode horrified him. "My God," he said to a friend, "why are these things happening?" Like others, he became accustomed to the sight of soldiers patrolling the capital's streets and rooftops with rifles. One day he heard gunfire outside his family's apartment; he was certain it was machine-gun fire. Suddenly a random bullet struck near, or in, the apartment, and Lorca panicked. He telephoned Rafael Rapún in hysterics. Rapún reminded Lorca that it was just a stray bullet and, urging him to remain calm, hurried to the apartment to console him.

To members of Lorca's generation, the Asturian rebellion was a "culminating moment," in the words of poet Juan Gil-Albert, a call to action, an urgent signal, wrote Manolo Altolaguirre, "to adapt our work, our lives, to the liberation of Spain." The battle lines were clear: Spain had plunged into a bitter struggle between Republican and Nationalist, Left and Right, communist and fascist. In the wake of the Asturian revolt, new left-wing literary reviews and journals appeared, as did proletarian books and poems, ranging from autobiographical works such as *Blood of October*, by an Asturian miner, to political verse by Rafael Alberti and Emilio Prados. In a newspaper article, poet José Moreno Villa warned that a "cruel poison is pulsing through our blood, a mad toxin."

Seventeen years earlier, in his adolescent essay "Patriotism," written in October 1917, at the height of the First World War, Lorca had railed against war and the attitudes that provoked it. He had decried Spain's bellicose past, its legacy of inquisition and extermination, its "political crimes." He had mourned the kindhearted men—"Martyrs! Christs! Quixotes!"—who sacrificed their lives to the cause of peace. "Where are the poets so that they can weep?" he asked. The Asturian revolt and its savage aftermath refueled his indignation. Although he neither belonged to nor backed any political party, Lorca voluntarily spoke out against the bloodshed that had occurred in northern Spain. Asked in the fall of 1934 why La Barraca did not plan to give any performances that season, he answered dramatically, "How are we going to perform when there are so many widows in Spain!" He knew at least two people who were imprisoned as a result of the Asturian revolution; one was Manuel Azaña, the former Republican prime minister, who, despite having played no role in the rebellion, was arrested by government authorities in Barcelona on October 7, subjected to a vicious smear campaign, and imprisoned for three months. Azaña became a vivid symbol for all victims of the repression. In November, Lorca signed a collective letter of protest demanding Azaña's release from jail. In late December, Azaña was freed. Lorca told a journalist that at times he wondered why, given what was happening in the world, he continued to write. "But one must work," he said. "Work and help those who deserve it. Work even though sometimes you think the effort is useless. Work as a form of protest."

He feared for Spain's future. He regretted the factions that divided his country; their existence countered his notion of what it meant to be part of the hu-

man community. He found Spain's newly contentious political atmosphere suffocating. The previous summer, while touring with La Barraca, he had run
into José Antonio Primo de Rivera, the young leader of the Spanish Falange.
Lorca was sitting in a restaurant with several members of his company—all of
them dressed in their blue Barraca coveralls—when Primo de Rivera walked in
with three of his colleagues, each wearing the blue shirt of the Falange. "Look,
there's José Antonio," actor Modesto Higueras whispered to Lorca.

"Yes, I've seen him," Lorca said nervously. Primo de Rivera recognized Lorca
and scribbled something onto a napkin, which he then handed to a waiter to
give to the poet. Lorca glanced at the note and hastily slipped it into his pocket.
Higueras asked what it said.

"Shhh," Lorca muttered. "Don't say anything to me. Don't say anything."
Later Higueras found the napkin and read it. "Federico," the Falangist leader
had written. "Don't you think that with your blue coveralls and our blue shirts
we could between us forge a better Spain?"

Daily life went on. In Madrid, Lorca presided over a nightly *tertulia* in a café
across from the city's main post office building. Writers and Barraca actors
drifted in and out of the gatherings; Lorca and other poets—Neruda, Alberti—
frequently read their work. Neruda was at the time preoccupied with the health
of his first child, a daughter born prematurely with hydrocephalus in August
1934 and subsequently diagnosed with Down's syndrome. Lorca marked the infant's sad arrival with a poem, "Lines on the Birth of Malva Marina Neruda," in
which he mourned his inability to "shatter the dark feet / of the night that
howls through the stones," to "halt the immense awful wind / that takes away
dahlias and leaves shadows behind." He did his best to console Neruda.

After their *tertulia*, Lorca and his friends often went out to supper, or to another café, or to someone's house. Lorca rarely went to bed before two in the
morning. Sometimes he returned home after midnight and wrote until dawn.
He told a reporter he worked "at all hours. If I pushed myself, I could write all
day long, but I don't want to chain myself down." To another journalist he confessed that he worked only when he felt "an irresistible urge to write. Then I
write, feverishly, for a few months, so that I can get back to living as soon as
possible." Living, he said, "is most important to me . . . I spend the day in the
street: in cafés, chatting."

By the fall of 1934, Lorca was, according to Pedro Salinas, an "institution" in
Madrid. He welcomed friends to *tertulias* with hugs and laughter and friendly
banter, and was "more than a person, he was a climate," Salinas recalled. At

night he wandered through the city with friends, talking at the top of his voice and laughing. One could hear his forthright, luminous laughter far in the distance. Friends trailed after him as fans would a celebrated bullfighter. His mother talked fondly of Lorca's "celestial court"—by which she meant the talented, "handsome . . . intelligent . . . amusing" young men who invariably surrounded her son.

He was no longer slender, as he had been in his twenties. At thirty-six, his face and body had widened. He had what one friend described as a "big, square, majestic head. Federico was a man crowned by his head." He wore his black hair combed back from his face; stray locks often fell onto his forehead, and he was forever brushing them away with a mechanical sweep of his hand. Moles dotted his face. Whenever he had a formal portrait taken, studio photographers retouched his hair and skin to make both seem flawless.

He tried to dress stylishly but more often than not looked slightly disheveled. The knot in his tie was almost always too big and loose, and never centered. His clothes were sometimes rumpled. He walked with an uneven gait. He smoked sporadically, at times puffing fretfully on one cigarette after another while telling a story. He drank when it pleased him. He had an enormous capacity for whiskey and brandy, a friend remembered, but was also capable of going for days without alcohol.

To many, Lorca was a "synonym for joy." He continued to have moments of gloom, however, brief lapses during which he fell silent, the light in his eyes dimmed, and he became vague and distant. During such "absent" spells he would often fix his eyes on some remote object and move his lips as though speaking; when friends called his name, he refused to respond. Afterward he would return to the reality around him with what Ernesto Pérez Guerra described as "a renewed impetus toward extroversion," a renewed desire to "yield to the joy of the moment." Pérez Guerra believed that Lorca was "sociable by will and solitary by nature. But he was a solitary being for whom solitude was intolerable." At Morla Lynch's home, when asked to play the piano and sing, Lorca sometimes said, "No, I've got a cold, and I'm tormented by at least six personal tragedies." Then he would sing.

He lived a compartmentalized life. With close friends he was open about his sexuality; with others—particularly his family—he was evasive. He enjoyed numerous liaisons. "He'd get excited about a boy, and sometimes they'd travel, go to the provinces," remembered the artist and amateur actor Santiago Ontañón, who had known Lorca for years. "He needed lots of sexual adventures," recalled the painter Gregorio Prieto. "But he was discreet. He knew whom to approach, when and where." His "erotic stamina," said a friend from Granada, was "formidable." He delighted in ogling handsome young men. Manolo Alto-laguirre later sketched an evocative portrait of Lorca "at dawn, as he returned home from love and from wine. From music and perfumes, Federico, sensual poet, lost, carried away in the labyrinth of blood." Luis Cernuda recalled "the radiant young men / who loved you so."

Lorca accepted the contradictory nature of his existence. In 1934 he told a reporter that "the majority of men have a special life that they use like a calling card. It's the life by which they are publicly known, by which they introduce themselves . . . But those same men also have another life, a gray life that is hidden, torturous, diabolical, and that they try to hide like an ugly sin." He knew that despite the more tolerant atmosphere of the Second Spanish Republic, hatred of homosexuals ran deep in Spain. In 1933, the right-wing newspaper *El Duende* had published a diatribe against *"los ambiguos"*—"the ambiguous ones"—homosexual men who, since 1930 and the onset of the Republic, had "corrupted" Madrid by inflicting their "vice" on "innocent young men." The article called for the arrest of such reprobates.

Lorca himself had encountered similar attitudes. Certain of his detractors, particularly the newspaper *Gracia y Justicia*, routinely alluded to his sexuality; some right-wing opponents of La Barraca referred to the company as "Sodom on the road." In the summer of 1934 in Granada, Lorca had briefly visited the town casino with a friend. While there, an older man had turned to him and remarked, "They say you poets are queers."

Lorca feigned indifference. "What do you mean, poets?" he asked. But he knew that among certain circles he was disliked. In Buenos Aires he had admitted to a reporter that not all Spaniards appreciated his work. "They say it's good, but I don't really know. I don't really know if they like my poems. The priests in Granada, for instance, don't find them amusing."

In mid-November, *Yerma* began rehearsals in Madrid with Margarita Xirgu in the title role. The play was scheduled to open in late December at the Teatro Español. Although he had toyed with giving the work to Lola Membrives to premiere in Buenos Aires, Lorca had ultimately settled on the more regal, less temperamental Xirgu. He told an acquaintance, "We must all stick by Margarita, because Margarita loves the theater more than anyone else."

He often took friends with him to rehearsals. He would telephone the young painter José Caballero, whom he had commissioned to design the poster for the production, and identify himself as the nonsensical "Don Críspulo Tentor, de Onteniente"—a sure sign, Caballero recalled, "that Lorca wanted something from me." The two inevitably arrived late at the theater. Each time, Lorca would invent some preposterous excuse for his tardiness. His motto, said Caballero, was "late, but on time." Xirgu called him "the impossible Federico," and bemoaned his improvisatory approach to life. Whenever he showed up late for a rehearsal the actress had to start the session from the top so that he would not—as he insisted—miss a single detail. One day Xirgu lost her patience. "Federico," she told him, "I love you a lot, but rehearsals start at a given time, and we make actors who arrive late pay a five-peseta fine. Since you always come late, you'll have to pay just like everyone else." Lorca paused, then kissed Xirgu effusively and began rummaging in his pockets. "You're completely and absolutely right," he said, and handed her fifty pesetas. "If you don't mind, I'll just give you this in advance."

By mid-December, talk of *Yerma* permeated the Madrid press. Public curiosity about the work reached such heights that the play's producers had to restrict the final dress rehearsal to invited guests only. Annoyed at being shut out of the rehearsal, one journalist took his revenge in print and informed readers of the Madrid daily *La Voz* that the only people to attend the event were "pale little boys who don't drink wine." The piece—with its implied slur against homosexuals—distressed Lorca, who complained about it to the play's director, Cipriano Rivas Cherif. Rivas Cherif banned the journalist from entering the theater during the run of the production.

On December 28, the day before opening night, *El Sol* reported that according to those who had seen the tragedy, *Yerma* was Lorca's best work to date. Among the luminaries to attend the final dress rehearsal were the celebrated Galician dramatist Ramón del Valle-Inclán, who praised the work, and Miguel de Unamuno, who told reporters that *Yerma* was an "auspicious" drama by a playwright at the "top of his form." Jacinto Benavente, the 1922 Nobel laureate, also attended, and sought out Lorca after the first act to congratulate him. Lorca listened, pleased, but confessed that the play seemed "hopelessly bad" to him that evening. "Everything weighs me down . . . Everything seems hollow."

"No, friend," Benavente assured him. "Don't worry."

The story of an unhappily married woman who yearns in vain to have a child, *Yerma* was the second in Lorca's proposed trilogy of Spanish tragedies. He described it as a play with a classical theme but a contemporary treatment and "modern" intentions. "We must return to tragedy," he said. "Our theatrical tradition demands that we do so."

He subtitled *Yerma* a "Tragic Poem"—the only one of his plays to be designated as such. Unlike its more complex predecessor, *Blood Wedding*, whose drama springs primarily from its plot, *Yerma* dwells on a single character,

Yerma, and her intensely private struggle to transcend her situation. The work is a long, intricate poem written in prose and punctuated with passages of verse, a solitary cry from a protagonist of mythic proportion. The cast, as in Greek drama, is minimal, and formal choruses intensify and comment on the action. In its profound and persistent reliance on nature as an accomplice to human emotion, the play is fully Andalusian.

The name Yerma, the feminine of the adjective *yermo*, means barren land. Throughout the play Lorca contrasts dry, arid elements of nature with such wet, life-giving entities as rivers, wombs, and rain. Bound to the natural world, Yerma goes out in her bare feet "to walk the earth, I don't know why," and carries jugs of water to her table to quench her thirst. By contrast, her pale, passionless husband, Juan, spends entire days pruning fruit trees and whole nights watering his crops—to no avail. He cannot make nature flourish. "There's very little water," he complains.

From one scene to the next, words and phrases echo one another, forming an elaborate web of imagery that points repeatedly to the play's title and principal concern: the barren woman, or, more broadly, the sterility of desire. As the drama unfolds, time passes. In act 1, Yerma has been married two years; by the end of act 2, it is five. Clocks strike, the years drag on, and Yerma continues to seek the impossible. "Juan, do you hear me? Juan. It is time," she says to her husband at the opening of the play.

Unlike other women in the village, Yerma refuses to stay inside her house, despite her husband's efforts to confine her. She roams the countryside, talking to a man named Victor whose presence, she claims, is "like a jet of water that fills your whole mouth." Town gossips describe her as "mannish"; her husband accuses her of not being a "real woman" and orders his two spinster sisters to keep her captive at home. Yerma herself acknowledges her sexual ambiguity. During nightly forays to the shed to feed the oxen—something "no woman does," she admits—her footsteps sound to her "like those of a man."

Like all of Lorca's tragic protagonists, in poems as well as plays, Yerma is powerless to halt the historical current that pulls her along. Much of her life passes in a state of reverie during which she croons lullabies to make-believe children. Alone and desolate, she vents her passion in brief soliloquies whose rhymed and metered lines underscore the classic stature of her grief. Once, with Victor, she believes she hears a child weeping. Lorca compares her suffering to Christ's. "What a hard time you're having, what a hard time, but remember the wounds of Our Lord!" a neighbor advises. But Yerma shuns the consolations of conventional faith. Trapped in a loveless union and determined to preserve her honor, despite her infatuation with Victor, she turns for help to an old pagan woman and conjurer, Dolores, who is reputed to know ways of achieving fertility. "God help me," Yerma implores the woman.

"Not God. I've never cared for God," Dolores insists. "When will you people realize he doesn't exist? It's men who'll have to help you."

The tragedy culminates in a bacchanalian pilgrimage to a mountain hermitage, where childless women pray for the miracle of pregnancy. The scene is drawn from the real-life pilgrimage in the town of Moclín, near Fuente Vaqueros, which had long fascinated Lorca. He later maintained that in *Blood Wedding* he had written choral passages "with the timidity of a beginner." By the time he drafted *Yerma* he had mastered the device of the chorus, and in both the pilgrimage scene and a second, earlier passage, where a group of village women launder clothes beside a stream, he created choral moments of such intense lyricism that at least two reviewers pronounced them "poems." The effect was deliberate. At rehearsals, Lorca drove his cast to achieve a precise rhythm in each scene so that it would achieve a poetic unity. In the clothes-washing scene he instructed his actresses to move their hands and garments rhythmically, and to talk and sing in a rising crescendo of sound.

At the center of the climactic pilgrimage scene he staged a lurid dance whose pagan celebration of lust recalls the frenzied action of Walpurgis Night in Goethe's *Faust*. At times Lorca's extravagant spectacle unintentionally verges on comedy. During the dance in *Yerma*, a horn-wielding "Male" and a "Female" clutching a strap of harness bells mime the impregnation of a childless woman, while onlookers cheer them on to ever more ecstatic heights. "Seven times she moaned, and / nine times she rose, and / fifteen times the jasmine / fused with the orange," the crowd shrieks.

"Now use the horn!" they shout.

"Oh, how the wife is throbbing!" someone cries. Children refer to the pair as "the devil and his wife."

In the midst of the scene, Dolores reveals to Yerma that her husband, Juan, is infertile. She counsels Yerma to find another man. But Yerma cannot defy fate. She confronts Juan, who confesses that he has never wanted children, only a wife and a home; he begs Yerma to embrace him. She does so. Her grief quickly turns to rage, and in a fury she strangles him. "What do you want to know?" she cries out to the stunned villagers who suddenly gather around her. "Don't come near me, because I have killed my child. I myself have murdered my own child!" The play ends on this maudlin note. As the final curtain falls, the sounds of the pilgrimage go on in the distance.

For years Lorca had been appalled by the plight of women in Spanish society, particularly in rural Spain. As an adolescent he had written compulsively—

in prose, poetry, and theater—of the constraints imposed on women in Andalusian villages. In their tightly circumscribed lives he saw a reflection of his
own struggle to transcend hidebound social and religious convention; he saw
what happens when instinct is suppressed and nature denied. "Girls like me,
who grow up in the country, have all doors closed to them," Yerma observes at
the start of the drama. "Everything becomes half-words and gestures, because
we're not supposed to know these things." Elsewhere she says, "Men have another life: the flocks, the trees, conversation; we women have nothing but children and caring for our children."

   With *Yerma*, Lorca created both a portrait and an indictment of traditional
Andalusian society and its treatment of women. Local superstitions and turns of
phrase combine with elements of popular song and dance to evoke the flavor of
the region, while characters such as Juan and his two spinster sisters embody
recognizable Andalusian types. In the work's female characters, especially
Yerma, Lorca revived his lifelong fascination with Andalusian spinsters, widows, nuns, and childless wives—women for whom love is at best a matter of dep-
rivation, at worst a rebuke. As he wrote the work he doubtless recalled his
father's childless first wife, Matilde Palacios, whose portrait stood for years in
the Lorca family home.

   The extent to which *Yerma* reflects Lorca's own yearning for a child is a matter of speculation—as it was among his friends at the time of *Yerma's* premiere.
He had grown up in a pair of villages like the one Yerma inhabits. He knew the
attitudes that governed village life. He knew that as the oldest son of a wealthy
Andalusian landowner he was expected to engender offspring to perpetuate his
family's name. That he loved children was clear. He lavished attention on his
nieces and nephew. When his oldest niece, Tica, fell gravely ill, he spent hours
sitting with the girl in her bedroom, singing songs and trying to make her
laugh. Children—lost, unborn, drowned, longed for—permeate Lorca's work,
nowhere more poignantly than in *Yerma*. At the play's opening in December of
1934, his close friend Encarnación López, who had known him for fifteen
years, remarked, "The work is Federico's own tragedy. What he'd like most in
this world is to get pregnant and give birth . . . It's what he truly longs for: to be
pregnant, to give birth to a little boy or little girl . . . Yerma is Federico, the
tragedy of Federico."

Two weeks before opening night, Lorca gave an interview in which he talked
about *Yerma*, his work in general, and his desire to write socially relevant plays.
"I want to take topics and problems that people are afraid of confronting and

put them onstage," he said. He declared his allegiance to the poor and disen-
franchised, to the working classes. "In this world I am, and will always remain,
on the side of the poor. I will always be on the side of those who have nothing,
those to whom even the peace of having nothing is denied. We—and I'm referring to those of us who matter intellectually, who were educated in well-off,
middle-class surroundings—have been called to the sacrifice. We must accept
it." In the wake of the Asturian rebellion, some construed his remarks—which
appeared in the December 15 edition of *El Sol* and a week later in the *Defensor
de Granada*—as inflammatory.

By opening night, December 29, 1934, it was widely rumored that members
of the far Right planned to disrupt the premiere of *Yerma*. The play's opponents
had two aims: to protest against Lorca and to denounce his leading actress,
Margarita Xirgu, whose friendship with the Republican leader and sometime
playwright Manuel Azaña was widely known. After Azaña's release from prison
on December 28, Xirgu had offered him asylum in her home near Barcelona—
a gesture the right wing could not tolerate. Xirgu later defended her actions by
pointing out that Azaña was married to one of her closest friends, the sister of
the stage director Cipriano Rivas Cherif. She rejected charges that by siding
with Azaña and by producing his plays, she was creating political theater: "The
only thing I cared about was continuing my work as an actress."

Tickets for opening night sold out almost the moment the box office at the
Teatro Español opened to the public. Lorca feared that his adversaries—right-
wing extremists who opposed his liberal views and unconventional lifestyle and
who envied his fame—had bought out the house in order to humiliate him by
deliberately refusing to fill the seats. As curtain time approached on the night
of the twenty-ninth he stood backstage, dressed in a black tuxedo, and asked
José Caballero if anyone was in the audience. "Nobody's going to come," he
muttered.

"The theater is full," Caballero told him.

"That doesn't mean anything!" Lorca snapped.

Carlos Morla Lynch arrived at the Español to find scalpers doing a brisk
trade outside the massive stone building, and a line of taxis and automobiles
depositing theatergoers at the doors. Inside, the auditorium was packed. Many
of the city's intelligentsia were present, including Miguel de Unamuno, who
had so admired the play at its dress rehearsal that he chose to see it a second
time. Lorca waited backstage, wringing his hands and trying to smile. At one
point he quipped to Caballero, "If it doesn't go well and things don't turn out
the way they should, it's your fault."

At approximately ten o'clock the curtain rose on artist Manuel Fontanals's stylized rendering of a hillside Andalusian village with tall white houses under a brilliant blue sky. Xirgu, as Yerma, sat motionless, her eyes closed, on a stool in front of one of the houses. Offstage, a voice began to sing a lullaby. Then, from one of the theater's upper balconies, several members of the Spanish Falange began to hiss. Shouts followed. For a moment, Xirgu had to suspend her performance. But she remained serene. Audience members cried out for silence. Backstage, Lorca could hear shouts of protest and the sound of stomping feet.

The episode did not last long. The protesters were quickly evicted, and the play went on without incident. The audience doubled its applause during the work's two choral scenes, and as the final curtain fell on Yerma's desperate cry—"I have killed my child!"—the crowd burst into a long and tumultuous ovation. People from the upper seats streamed into the orchestra section. Overcome by emotion, Lorca made his way onto the stage. When Xirgu broke down and hid her face in her hands, Lorca put his arm around her and motioned to the crowd to applaud the actress. As the curtain fell for the final time, he kissed Xirgu's hands, one after the other, and said, "Your hand took me to the stage for the first time . . . You gave me your hand then, and you continue giving it to me now."

"Today I give it to you," the actress replied. "When I'm old, you'll give it to me. But until then, you'll write me many plays."

Reviews were mixed. In general, right-wing newspapers attacked the play, while left-wing publications praised it. Adjectives used to describe the work ranged from "brilliant" and "irreverent" to "crude" and "immoral." (Curiously, the official government censor had found nothing objectionable, "either morally or politically," in the work.) The sheer volume of reviews was so great that Lorca's family hired a clipping service to track the press coverage. Several critics commented on the unusual prevalence of young people and intellectuals among the opening night crowd—a phenomenon unique to playwrights like Lorca and Alberti, whose innovative work attracted audiences weary of the country's more traditional theatrical fare. At least two reviewers suggested that it was only because of its youthful and "indiscriminate" audience that Yerma received such a warm ovation at its premiere. One right-wing critic called attention to the number of homosexuals present on opening night, and suggested that until the public prosecutor shut down the production, Yerma would continue to be a "shameful affront" both to the Spanish theater and to all "honorable and decent people."

Reviewers on both sides of the political spectrum remarked on the lack of a conventional plot in Yerma. Some felt this detracted from the play, while others regarded it as a surprising stylistic choice that heightened the work's tension and theatricality. Many noted the drama's highly poetic nature, and the familiar debate as to whether Lorca was a better poet than playwright resurfaced. A handful of critics concluded that with *Yerma*, Lorca had proven himself superior as a poet. *La Nación* charged that the subject of *Yerma* was not substantial enough to warrant a three-act play. Lorca "should have looked for problems that are more accessible and better suited to the stage, and should stay away from topics like this, which are virtually obstetrical in origin." *ABC* lamented the work's "slow and repetitive development," and advised "Señor García Lorca" to eliminate the script's many vulgarities, in accordance with the "laws of culture and elegance—if not other, more powerful laws." *El Debate* contended that in his "hallucinatory desire for originality," Lorca had followed "paths of extravagance." The paper called *Yerma* a "miserable production" filled with "blasphemies."

Others heralded the play's novelty. In his review for the democratic *El Pueblo*, Ceferino Avecilla declared that with *Yerma*, Spain had at last joined the mainstream of contemporary European theater. Avecilla hailed the work's "revolutionary theatricality" and defended the politics and artistry of its leading actress. The Madrid daily *La Tierra* termed *Yerma* the salvation of a theatrical season that had otherwise been dominated by tasteless bourgeois melodrama. In Alicante, the critic Isaac Pacheco proclaimed *Yerma* "the start of a revolution in the theater."

Drawn, in large part, by its provocative treatment of taboo subjects—sex, adultery, maternal instinct, murder—audiences flocked to the play. By mid-March, *Yerma* had exceeded a hundred consecutive performances—the first of Lorca's plays to do so in Spain. It was his biggest domestic hit to date. But controversy continued to boil. Opponents of the work objected to *Yerma* for two primary reasons: Xirgu's friendship with Manuel Azaña, and the play's purported immorality, specifically its anti-Catholicism, as epitomized by the character of the old pagan woman. In early January, *Gracia y Justicia* published a snide account of the drama, noting its "many blasphemies, artistic and otherwise," which "García's friends applauded furiously." The following day, in a front-page article for the *Diario de Madrid*, the critic Corpus Barga analyzed *Yerma* in social and political as well as artistic terms, suggesting that Lorca had posed "the deepest political problem—why is the Spanish woman as she is?" Barga criticized those who viewed the play as exclusively political, forgetting "that it is tragedy," and that "all tragedy is politics." Lorca's play, he submitted, "is the tragedy of sexuality in Spain . . . Before the social revolution in Russia wasn't there a sexual revolution?"

By late January, word of the furor surrounding *Yerma* had reached France. To Lorca's delight, a prominent Italian theater journal compared the uproar to that provoked by Ibsen's *A Doll's House* at its premiere. Throughout the first months of 1935, Lorca followed the debate with interest. At home, he accumulated a stack of clippings and correspondence, including a letter from a woman who wrote to condemn his depiction of motherhood in the play. "May it please you to know, Señor Idiot, that there are many, many women who are so honorable and good that they have become mothers without once experiencing any sensual sensation with the male (vulgar husband)," she wrote.

For the most part Lorca dismissed such attacks, yet he regretted the political overtones his play had acquired as a result of its contentious premiere. "As you know," he told a friend on opening night, "I'm liberal and antifascist, but I don't like extremists." Although he supported Azaña, whom he saw with some frequency in Madrid, he was not on close terms with the man, as Xirgu was. His dealings with the Republican leadership in general always occurred in either a social or theatrical context: encounters in Morla Lynch's salon or in the Teatro Español or appearances with La Barraca. Lorca repeatedly sought to distance himself and his art from political motives. When a reporter asked if some of the attitudes expressed in *Yerma*—in particular the protagonist's insistence on honor—weren't, in fact, "conservative" rather than "politically insurgent," as many claimed, Lorca resisted both terms. "I'm a Christian," he said. "My protagonist's free will is limited . . . by the Spanish concept of honor."

In early 1935, the conservative Catholic daily *El Siglo Futuro* included *Yerma* on a list of spectacles that readers should refrain from seeing. The paper pronounced the drama crude, disrespectful, and overly sensual. Months later, officials in Granada banned the presentation of *Yerma* during the city's 1935 Corpus Christi celebrations. They argued that the play's moral content would be particularly offensive to the local population during a high Christian holiday.

CHAPTER 24

THEATER OF POETS

1935

Emboldened by the public's response to *Yerma*, Lorca announced shortly after the start of the new year that he was about to complete the third installment in his trilogy of Spanish tragedies. He described his new play, *The Destruction of Sodom*, as an "audacious" work with a "grave and compromising title." "I think those who have liked my latest works will not be disappointed." He had in fact drafted only fragments of the play; he never finished *The Destruction of Sodom*.

To members of the press he talked about other projects: *Doña Rosita the Spinster*, a play into which he had poured his "greatest feelings"; his adaptation of Lope de Vega's *La dama boba*, which Margarita Xirgu intended to produce in 1935. On his own he made a list of further plays he hoped to write: *Chimera* ("Hallucination"); *The Flavor of Blood* ("Drama of Desire"); *The Fear of the Sea* ("Drama of the Cantabrian Coast"); *The Man and the Pony* ("Andalusian Myth"); *The Beautiful Woman* ("Poem of the Desired Woman"); *The Dark Stone* ("Epéntico Drama"); *House of Maternity*; *Flesh of the Cannon* ("Anti-War Drama"); *The Dark Corners* ("Flamenco Work"); *The Nuns of Granada* ("Poetic Chronicle"). Of these, Lorca evidently began work on only two: *Chimera* and *House of Maternity*. He later claimed to have embarked on an additional drama, *Blood Has No Voice*, a work about incest, whose "crudeness and passionate violence" would make *Yerma*, by contrast, seem to possess "a language of archangels."

"I have no interest in being ancient or modern, only in being myself, in being natural," he said of his work as a dramatist. "I know very well how to do semi-intellectual theater, but that's not what counts. In our day, the poet must open his veins for the people. That's why . . . I've devoted myself to the theater, because it permits a more direct contact with the masses." His remarks appeared in the February 18, 1935, edition of *La Voz*, one of several Madrid newspapers then participating in a subscription drive to benefit children orphaned by the previous year's Asturian revolt.

In a subsequent interview, Lorca argued that the theater "must capture the drama of real life. An antiquated theater, nourished only by fantasy, is not theater."

The year 1935 marked the tricentennial of Lope de Vega's death, an event widely celebrated by the Spanish theater community. Spain's greatest, most prolific playwright, Lope was born in 1562, just seventeen months before Shakespeare, and died in August 1635. He wrote more than 1,500 plays during his career, nearly a third of which survive. Most are comedies rich in traditional Spanish folklore, song, and dance. Lope also wrote a handful of novels and thousands of poems, chiefly ballads, sonnets, and songs. He is widely considered the progenitor of a national Spanish theater. By drawing attention to him in his anniversary year, his twentieth-century heirs sought to establish a firm link between their own theatrical renaissance and the one Lope had engendered in the sixteenth and seventeenth centuries. No intervening generation had approached Lope's achievement. Common to both Lope and his twentieth-century proponents was a spirit of freedom and innovation sparked in part by tumultuous political change.

Cervantes had called Lope a "Marvel of Nature." Lorca spoke of him with veneration as "a man of national tradition" and praised his "theater of love, adventure, and grief." He particularly admired, and sought to emulate, Lope's method of integrating popular song—lullabies, serenades, threshing and wedding songs—into his plays, in such a way that these become not simply ornamental but vital to the action. Lorca saw himself as a spiritual and aesthetic heir to Lope, writing plays exalting Spain's historical and cultural patrimony, and in the process participating in the creation of a second Spanish Golden Age.

To help launch the country's yearlong observation of Lope's tricentennial, Lorca collaborated with Pura Ucelay, founder of the amateur Anfistora Club, on a production of Lope's *Peribáñez and the Knight Commander of Ocaña*. The production opened on January 25, 1935, in Madrid's Capitol Theater.

Dozens of prominent Spanish critics and writers attended. In a speech to the opening-night audience, Lorca called for nothing less than "the whole climate of the Spanish theater arts" to change, for renewed contact to be made with the deepest traditions of the Spanish theater. He urged his listeners to restore Spain's Golden Age authors—Lope de Vega, whose theater he described as "so very human"; Calderón; Tirso de Molina; Cervantes—to their rightful place, to rescue "our living, shining, immortal classical theater" from oblivion, to repair the "incredible estrangement" that marked the breach between contemporary Spaniards and "our most representative poets."

His own efforts at breaching the divide had led Lorca to help direct *Peribáñez*, a seventeenth-century play about a fifteenth-century figure, which he and Ucelay had chosen to perform in twentieth-century dress—a "necessary anachronism" if the production was to engage a contemporary audience. "A historic re-creation of the period would get lost, without substance, in our hands," Lorca argued. By costuming their cast in authentic peasant clothing from the Spanish countryside of 1935, he and Ucelay hoped to bring the atmosphere of Lope's play "nobly and peacefully" to life. They had spent days scouring the province of Castile for both old clothes and old songs with which to "animate" their production. They had stopped at inns and asked to hear local songs, "the most ancient tunes, the ones the old folks know." They had asked people to haul stored clothing from trunks. In order to procure one piece of attire, they had even fought with a priest. "How we had to plead in order to convince him!"

Lorca did not mention that during his costume-finding expedition with Ucelay, he witnessed a scene so gruesome that it continued to prey on him long after its occurrence. While traveling one day through an area filled with evergreens and low hills, the car in which he and Ucelay were riding had broken down. As the automobile was being repaired, a herd of swine suddenly appeared and within minutes attacked a flock of lambs grazing nearby. By the time the assault ended the lambs were dead, and blood and trampled wool littered the landscape. Wild-eyed, Lorca drew his hand across his eyes, then took a piece of paper and scribbled a few lines of what appeared to be verse. Ucelay later asked to see what he had written, but Lorca claimed to have lost the paper. In writing the poem, Ucelay surmised, he had tried to free himself "from the horror" of the event.

That evening the two stopped to eat in a small town where death bells were tolling. "It's for a local girl who threw herself into a well. A love affair," a villager explained. Lorca abruptly stood up. "Let's go back to Madrid," he said.

Sometime later he described the episode in even more mythical terms to Pablo Neruda, transforming the "flock of lambs" in Ucelay's version of the story into a "single lamb" of archetypal dimension. His voice quivering, Lorca told how one morning while traveling with Ucelay he had awakened at dawn and gone outside to watch the sunrise. A thick mist shrouded the landscape. As he sat waiting for the sky to brighten, a tiny lamb appeared. The animal had apparently strayed from its flock. Moments later a half-dozen black swine emerged from the gloom, crossed the road, and to Lorca's horror fell on the lamb. "Federico, prey to an inexpressible fear, immobilized by horror, watched as the black swine killed and devoured the lamb," Neruda would remember. "When he told me about it on his return to Madrid, his voice still trembled. Because of his childlike sensitivity, the tragedy of the death obsessed him to the point of delirium."

At the end of January, the actors and actresses of Madrid petitioned Margarita Xirgu to present a special after-hours performance of *Yerma* so that they could see the celebrated show. Xirgu agreed, and gave an "actors-only" performance of the production at one-thirty in the morning on February 1. Thunderous applause erupted the moment the curtain rose, and Xirgu had to wait for the noise to die down before starting the play. The crowd clapped strenuously at the end of each act and gave the cast a standing ovation at the final curtain. Xirgu wept with gratitude as bouquets of flowers from her colleagues fell at her feet.

Moments later Lorca spoke to the audience from the stage. He wore a double-breasted, pin-striped suit with a white shirt and black bow tie. His hair was slicked back, and his face showed deepening lines. He told the crowd that for some time he had rejected homages, tributes, and testimonial dinners in his honor, for each such event signaled "another brick on our literary tomb," and brought bad luck to its recipient. But he had agreed to accept this tribute because it came from his peers.

He stated his case for a "theater of social action." "I'm not talking tonight as an author, or as a poet, or as a simple student of the rich panorama of human life, but as an ardent, impassioned devotee of the theater and its social action. The theater is one of the most expressive and useful instruments for the edification of a country, and the barometer that measures its greatness or decline." His speech was a further refinement of his lifelong attempt to articulate a theatrical aesthetic. He had always regarded the stage as a temple of art,

not of commerce; as a place where spectator and performer confront one another with sometimes violent consequences. In his prologue to *The Shoemaker's Prodigious Wife,* in the opening exchange of his *Cristóbal* plays,
throughout *The Audience,* he had denounced the bourgeois theater of the day
and called for a theater of magic, one that shocks viewers by revealing the unexpected.

A decadent theater, he told his listeners that evening,

> can cheapen and lull to sleep an entire nation. A people that does not cherish and sup-
> port its theater is either dead or dying, just as a theater that does not use laughter and
> tears to take the social and historical pulse, the drama of its people and the genuine
> color of its landscape and spirit, has no right to call itself a theater, but should be
> thought of instead as a game hall or a place for doing that dreadful thing known as
> "killing time."

Lorca vowed to continue fighting for artistic freedom as long as he lived—"if I
live." He promised that his "burning love for the theater" would not wane. He
swore that he would go on seeking the truth, working to replace the worn-out
conventions of the commercial stage with the nobility of genuine art. "I know,"
he said in closing,

> that it is not those people who say, "Now, now, now," with their eyes fixed on the
> small jaws of the box office, who are right, but rather those who say, "Tomorrow,
> tomorrow, tomorrow," and feel the approach of the new life which is hovering over the
> world.

Yerma continued to enthrall the public and to prompt debate. In late February, the controversial Republican leader Manuel Azaña attended a performance of the play. Released from jail just two months earlier, Azaña was newly
determined to revive both his reputation and the Republican left wing. The
former prime minister sat prominently in a box seat, and at intermission formally presented Xirgu with a diamond-studded insignia of the left wing of the
Republican Party. Others from the Republican Left gave her flowers. During
the final curtain call, audience members showered the stage with bouquets,
and cries of "*Viva la República!*" rang out.

On March 12, Xirgu and her company celebrated the hundredth performance of *Yerma*. Ultimately the play ran for an impressive 150 performances
before closing on April 20, 1935. Asked if he was satisfied with the success of his
drama, Lorca remarked:

Success never satisfies me. Success is almost always a momentary stroke of luck that
has nothing to do with a given work's intrinsic value. Many glorious men who left behind great works for humanity never knew the flatteries of success during their lifetime. On the other hand, there are plenty of people who have gone through life
leaping and dancing from one triumph to the next, and whose works have sunk into
the grave with them—or sometimes before. Believe me, I'd prefer to belong to the first
category.

He survived his own bout with failure in February 1935, when Irene
Lewisohn, co-founder and director of the Neighborhood Playhouse in New
York City, premiered the first English version of *Blood Wedding*. Lewisohn had
approached Lorca two years earlier for permission to produce the tragedy. The
playwright had worked closely with translator José Weissberger to create a plau-
sible rendering of his play in English, and he had sung songs to Lewisohn so
that she could set her American production of the work to appropriate music.

Under the title *Bitter Oleander*, the play opened in New York on February 11.
Reviews were caustic. In a city whose theater scene was dominated by such
works of political and social realism as Clifford Odets's *Waiting for Lefty*, which
opened in a Group Theater production one month before *Bitter Oleander*,
Lorca's lyrical Andalusian drama fell on uncomprehending ears. Both audiences and critics found Weissberger's stilted translation laughable. Robert
Benchley of *The New Yorker*, a critic known for his plainspoken wit, ridiculed
the play, despite what he conceded were "moments of considerable poetic virtuosity." Benchley described the stage set as a theatrical interpretation "of an
old Spanish intestinal tract" and suggested that any discussion of *Bitter Oleander* be turned over to "our Better Relations with Spain Department."

A handful of American critics perceived the work's merits. The *New York
Sun*'s Richard Lockridge called it an "intense and moving drama." Stark Young
of *The New Republic* hailed Lorca's "bold and poetic mind" and his "deceiving
simplicity," but warned that "racially the play is hopelessly far from us." It was a
complaint English-speaking audiences of Lorca's plays would continue to regis-
ter. In Spain, newspapers noted the play's poor reception overseas. Lorca acknowledged the "beastly things" the New York press had said about his play,
but insisted his work had not failed totally with the public. "I've already said I
don't pay any attention to critics."

In early 1935 the Argentine actress Lola Membrives came to Spain to present
a Madrid season with her company. She immediately announced plans to premiere Lorca's newest play, *Doña Rosita the Spinster*. A reporter for *La Voz* advised her to be careful. "You're going to find yourself up against a mass of

people worn out by politics. For a lot of them, the name 'Lorca' is equivalent to
'the devil.' " The journalist then explained that this was due primarily to
Lorca's affiliation with Xirgu, whose friendship with Manuel Azaña continued
to irritate conservatives. The reporter suggested that because Membrives herself possessed no such "political tarnish," the country's right-wing "cretins"
might leave her alone.

Membrives was undaunted. Although Lorca did not offer her *Doña Rosita*,
as she had hoped, the actress did present revivals of *The Shoemaker's Prodigious
Wife* and *Blood Wedding*. Audiences responded exuberantly to both productions, and reviews were good. For a period of approximately one month, Lorca
had three plays running simultaneously in the Spanish capital. Critics traced
his evolution as a playwright from one work to the next. Following her Madrid
run, Membrives took both *The Shoemaker's Prodigious Wife* and *Blood Wedding* on the road to Zaragoza and then to Barcelona. In Madrid, Lorca's name
remained in the news. He issued a fifth edition of his *Gypsy Ballads*. He also
attended a public reading by Margarita Xirgu of *Lament for Ignacio Sánchez
Mejías*, oversaw two amateur productions of *Don Cristóbal's Puppet Show*, and
delivered the first in a series of three radio broadcasts to Argentina, in which he
reminisced about his stay in Buenos Aires and described the unique cultural
and topographical traits of Spain. His broadcasts the previous year in Buenos
Aires had shown him the power of radio, and he embraced the medium as a
new means of disseminating his vision.

He was earning more money than ever. Reporters speculated, correctly, that
he was one of the season's most financially prosperous playwrights. To friends,
Lorca talked fancifully of building a seaside home on the Mediterranean. "Because now it's *my* turn to be earning money," he joked. He did not know what
to do with his wealth—only how to spend it. He was careless about his funds,
leaving coins and peseta notes heaped on his desk, giving large amounts of
cash to the household servants so that they could go shopping, but neglecting
to ask for change. Old friends such as Morla Lynch began turning to him for
loans. "I realize you must be giving money to half the world, and that I'm not
the only one who's pestering you," Morla wrote in a letter asking to borrow a
thousand pesetas. Jorge Guillén ran into Lorca's father one day and asked the
older man if he had finally stopped worrying about his son's fortunes. Don Federico grinned. "Now, yes."

Lorca himself was indifferent to his earnings, and insisted that success would
not "shackle" him. After all, he had grown up wealthy. "I'll always work as I
have up until now, disinterestedly, with no aim but that of my own satisfaction.
One should remember Saint Francis: 'Don't work for the love of money; distill

sensuality into sensitivity; be obedient'—in other words, be true to yourself."
He claimed that each morning he forgot what he had written the day before.
"That's the secret of being modest and working courageously." He wrote plays
not for money or glory, he said, but because "if I don't, I'll rot inside. If glory
and money come, welcome! And if not, fine. Money is sometimes useful, but
not always. Glory, here on earth, is a vague thing that a lot of deluded people
dream of having, and it usually brings nothing but bitterness and sorrow."

Despite his new riches, Lorca continued to work, live, and dress much as he
always had. Morla Lynch noticed at a cocktail party in the late spring of 1935
that Lorca was still wearing the same unfashionable pair of shoes he had worn
for years. The shoes buckled clumsily on one side and were so unsightly his
friends nicknamed them "Juana La Loca's slippers," because they resembled
the shoes worn in a painting by the "mad" daughter of Ferdinand and Isabella.
Lorca found the epithet amusing and went on wearing the shoes.

On May 23, *El Sol* announced that Lorca had completed a new play, *Doña
Rosita the Spinster*, and intended to give a private reading of the work to
friends. Morla Lynch heard the play in June and was enchanted; it reminded
him of a waltz he had known in childhood, one that invariably filled him with
"romantic tenderness." Lorca also read the work to Margarita Xirgu, and told
the actress the play was hers to premiere.

Although he had begun work on *Doña Rosita* in the summer of 1934, he had
first conceived the play in 1924, when he sketched a yellow arch spanning a garden, and beneath the arch wrote "Doña Rosita the Spinster," followed by a list
of characters. He returned to the play in the mid-1930s in order to "rest" from
his tragedies *Blood Wedding* and *Yerma*. "I wanted to create a simple, friendly
comedy," he explained. "But that's not what emerged. What emerged is a poem
that seems to me to have more tears than my two previous productions. As far
as I can tell, fortune has tapped me for the serious side of the theater, chiefly
because of my poetic temperament."

The play's full title is *Doña Rosita the Spinster, or The Language of the Flowers*. Its subtitle—"Poem of Granada, at the Turn of the Century, Divided into
Various Gardens, with Scenes of Song and Dance"—is one of the rare instances when Lorca specified the locale and time period of a given play. The
work is intensely of and about Granada, with abundant references to local
streets, buildings, and foods, as well as local phrases and songs and even the
proper names of real-life *granadinos*. Rosita herself, a woman who ages thirty
years during the course of the action, and who never marries, despite her en-

gagement to a beloved cousin, is emblematic of the city she inhabits, a city Lorca had long regarded as a forgotten backwater, beautiful and passionate but doomed to neglect.

He based much of the play on the notion of a rose that blossoms, withers, and dies in a single day. In the mid-1920s, the poet José Moreno Villa, whom Lorca knew from the Residencia, had introduced Lorca to a nineteenth-century French book listing all known varieties of the rose, together with their Latin and modern names. Among the varieties was the *rosa mutabilis*, or "mutable rose," a flower whose color fades as it ages. Lorca immediately seized on the image and began drafting a short play, *Mutable Rose*, which he subsequently abandoned. Years later he returned to the idea in *Doña Rosita*. The play is steeped in floral motifs and lore, from its opening line ("And my seeds?" asks Rosita's uncle, an amateur gardener) to its final passage, a poetic account of the last moments in the life of the *rosa mutabilis*: "And when the night arrives / her petals begin to fall."

While drafting *Doña Rosita* Lorca consulted turn-of-the-century almanacs, magazines, and books in an effort to verify the historical and horticultural details of his play. He tore out pages of particular interest, including a glossary of the "language of flowers," and kept these on his desk for reference as he worked. From a list of thirty-one flowers and their meanings, he incorporated fourteen into his script, adding five more of his own invention. Rosita herself, whose name means "little rose," identifies powerfully with the *rosa mutabilis*, which "opens in the morning / red as blood," and in the afternoon "turns white, with the pallor / of a cheek of salt," before succumbing at nightfall to death. In act 1, Rosita dresses in rose pink; by the start of act 3, thirty years later, she has taken to wearing pale pink; in the play's final moments she dons a floor-length white gown. Each of her costumes reflects the prevailing fashion of its day—proof of the extent to which Rosita is a prisoner of taste and time.

The play traces her demise from an optimistic twenty-year-old girl, betrothed to a cousin she adores, to a mournful fifty-year-old spinster, abandoned by her fiancé and resigned to an existence without the companionship of either husband or children. "I am as I am. And I cannot change. The only thing left to me now is my dignity," Rosita tells her aunt. Tormented by the realization that the hope which sustained her for decades has died, she confides, "I want to run away, not to be able to see, to be calm, empty . . . (Doesn't a poor woman have the right to breathe freely?) And yet hope pursues me, stalks me, gnaws at me, like a dying wolf trying to sink his teeth in for the last time."

Lorca described *Doña Rosita* as a "profound drama of the Andalusian spin-

ster, and of the Spanish spinster in general." He believed that in Spain unmarried women were routinely sacrificed on the altar of social convention, and
went from being "maidens" like Rosita, "meek on the outside and scorched
within," to "that grotesque and disturbing thing known as a Spanish spinster,"
whose traits he described with clinical detachment: "flaccid breasts, spreading
thighs, pupils with a distant gleam." "How long will the Doña Rositas in Spain
go on like this?" he asked. He had confronted the same issue in some of his earliest work, most pointedly in the 1918 poem "Elegy," where he compares an unmarried woman to a "magnolia" fated to "wither." At one point Lorca labeled
Rosita an "elegy" for spinsters and a sorrowful drama "for families." Most Spanish families, he observed, possess one spinster, and "where there isn't one, there
are two. It has always grieved me to see that in Spain, in order for one girl to get
married, twenty virgins must be sacrificed." Rosita herself acknowledges the
poignancy of her condition: "I know my eyes will always be young, and that my
back will become more bent with every passing day. After all, what's happened
to me has happened to thousands of women." She refers to herself as an "old
maid."

In writing the play Lorca drew on a variety of memories and figures from his
youth, among them a first cousin, Clotilde García Picossi, whose fiancé had
abandoned her in order to go to Argentina, where he eventually married another woman and fell into destitution. One of Lorca's more eccentric grade
school teachers in Granada, Don Martín Sheroff y Aví, a failed poet with red
hair and unkempt clothes, served as a model for the fictive Don Martín, a
teacher and failed poet with red hair and a disheveled appearance, who tries
unsuccessfully to woo Rosita in the play's final act. Among the neglected works
the fictional Martín has written is a drama, *The Daughter of Jefté*, whose title is
that of the opera Lorca's boyhood piano teacher, Antonio Segura Mesa, wrote
but never produced. Lorca also drew inspiration from his childhood maid Dolores, whose earthy humor and unstinting generosity are replicated in the character of the Housekeeper who cares for Rosita and her aunt and uncle.

Other characters are quintessential *granadino* "types." There is Señor X, a
pompous professor of political economy who is loosely based on an economics
professor Lorca knew, and detested, at the University of Granada; there are
three *cursilonas*—"pretentious old maids"—whose tasteless saint's day gift to
Rosita is a figurine of a "little girl dressed in pink who's also a barometer"; there
are also three "Manolas," pretty coquettes of the sort that Goya once painted,
who heighten their charms through the skillful use of fans, mantillas, and tall
tortoiseshell combs.

Lorca said later that *Doña Rosita* depicts the "vulgar" and "ordinary" of urban life; he called attention to the play's turn-of-the-century setting, terming it
an era of black cancan stockings, big-breasted women, lights, and jewels. He
praised the work's "magnificent bad taste." "Because it's a drama of the sadness
of bad taste. The desolate and terrible tragedy of vulgarity," he said. Through
Rosita—particularly through its peripheral characters, who are more accurately
caricatures than three-dimensional characters—Lorca mocked the bourgeois
pretensions of his middle-class Granadan neighbors, and showed them to be
captives of unyielding mores. The play embodies "the tragic history of our social life," he said. It embraces "the whole tragedy of Spanish and provincial pretentiousness."

A reviewer later asked Lorca if *Doña Rosita* was a satire. "Perhaps," he
mused. "Maybe it's an elegy," he added. He told his brother while writing the
play that "if in certain scenes the audience doesn't know what to do, whether to
laugh or to cry, that will be a success for me." The most Chekhovian of his
plays, *Rosita* is a fusion of pathos and farce that culminates in a scene of near-
tragic dimension, one whose structure and tone recall the final act of *The
Cherry Orchard*, a play Lorca undoubtedly knew. He had read and admired
Chekhov's short stories as an adolescent and very likely saw one or both of Eva
Le Gallienne's productions of *The Cherry Orchard* and *The Seagull* during his
visit to New York; Le Gallienne modeled her version of *The Cherry Orchard* on
the Moscow Art Theater's innovative production of the work in the early 1920s.
The last act of Lorca's *Doña Rosita* suggests the structure and tone of
Chekhov's play. Forced by financial need to vacate the home they have lived in
for decades, Rosita and her aunt remove the last of the flowerpots from the
greenhouse that belonged to Rosita's late uncle. As dusk arrives, the women depart the house. Moments later, a loose door to the greenhouse begins banging
offstage. The rear balcony opens, and white curtains flutter in the wind. The final curtain falls.

The action of the play is sparse: Rosita becomes engaged; she waits for her fiancé to return from Argentina; she reconciles herself to spinsterhood and
leaves her childhood home. Act 1 takes place in 1885, act 2 in 1900, and act 3 in
1911—a year Lorca characterized as "tight-fitting skirts, the airplane. One step
further, the war." The play, like *Once Five Years Pass*, is a "legend of time" re-
plete with reminders of time: striking clocks, tolling bells, changing dress styles,
the daily arrival of the postman, the physical aging of its protagonists. There is
much talk of the twentieth century and its inventions. Rosita herself is obsessed
with time. "She wants everything in a hurry," the Housekeeper complains. "It's
today and already she'd like it to be the day after tomorrow." As the play un-

folds, Rosita evolves from a young woman preoccupied with the future into an aging spinster haunted by the past. Her progress is mirrored by the changes that befall her uncle's prize rose, the celebrated *rosa mutabilis*, which blooms in act 1, is accidentally clipped in act 2 ("It was still red," her uncle laments), and ultimately dies.

Toward the end of the play, Rosita speaks of the suffering she has endured. Her speech—one of the most beautiful in Lorca's theater—is at once a heartbreaking meditation on the destructive power of time and a tribute to the dignity of the human spirit. During the course of the play, Rosita has seen childhood friends marry, give birth, and die; all the while, she has waited for her own life to begin. The symbolic and social death she endures at the close of the play is more terrible than many of the real deaths Lorca gave to other protagonists. "Each year that passed was like an intimate piece of clothing torn from my body," Rosita tells her aunt.

> And today one friend gets married, and another and another, and tomorrow she has a son, and he grows up and comes to show me his examination marks, and they build new houses and make new songs, and I stay the same, with the same trembling as always; there I am, the same as before, cutting the same carnation, watching the same clouds; and one day I'm out walking, and I realize I don't know anyone. Girls and boys leave me behind because I can't keep up, and one says, "There's the old maid." And another one, a handsome boy with curly hair, says, "No one would cast an eye at her anymore." And I hear it, and I can't cry out, but go on, with a mouth full of poison and an overpowering desire to flee, to take off my shoes, to rest and never, never move from my corner again.

In late June 1935, Lorca went home for the summer to his family's flower-filled Huerta de San Vicente. A Galician-born journalist and friend, Eduardo Blanco-Amor, joined him in Granada for an extended visit. Blanco-Amor had lived in Argentina since 1919, where he worked as a correspondent for *La Nación*; he had returned to Spain in 1934 for a year's stay, and during that time had met Lorca through fellow Galician Ernesto Pérez Guerra. Swarthy and stout, with black hair, dark eyes, and a foppish air, Blanco-Amor was one year older than Lorca and viewed himself as Lorca's "spiritual representative." He told Federico he intended to defend and exalt his career as if it were his own. "In the end," he said, "if my life had no other aim than to serve you, it would be well justified."

He was rumored to have tried seducing Lorca. Lorca referred to him, privately, as "artificial, with the vulgar qualities of an Argentine tango." Nevertheless, he found Blanco-Amor sufficiently useful and entertaining that he welcomed him into his home that summer and even turned to the journalist for help in revising the six Galician poems he had begun a few years earlier. During his stay in Granada, Blanco-Amor published three articles detailing his visit with Lorca; decades later he issued an additional series of articles recalling the 1935 visit. He told of touring the Huerta de San Vicente with Lorca's father, who caressed tufts of wheat as he strode through his fields. He described Vicenta Lorca as she sat sewing, "tiny, gracious, harmonious." He mentioned Concha García Lorca's daily visits to the Huerta with her three young children.

Acutely conscious of his host's fame, Blanco-Amor toyed with writing a biography of Lorca called "Excursion to Federico García Lorca." He took photographs of the poet in various settings around the Huerta. One picture shows Lorca with his mother, a petite, sober-faced woman in her mid-sixties, with gray hair swept back in a loose bun. Lorca inscribed the image for Blanco-Amor: "For Eduardo, with the woman I love most in the world. Lorca, 1935." In another photograph, Lorca stands at the desk in his bedroom, dressed in his Barraca coveralls, grinning. Behind him, a Barraca poster hangs on the wall.

Violence briefly disrupted their holiday. In early July, Lorca's old friend Constantino Ruiz Carnero, editor in chief of the *Defensor de Granada* and a former member of the Rinconcillo, was assaulted in his home by the local president of Acción Popular, a political group affiliated with CEDA, the right-wing Catholic alliance. For months the *Defensor* had issued stinging attacks against CEDA; Ruiz Carnero's beating was clearly an act of retribution. Within a day of its occurrence, Blanco-Amor published an account of the incident. He claimed that he and Lorca had been visiting a friend when suddenly they heard "terrible blows" in the apartment below them. They went downstairs and found Ruiz Carnero on the floor, his glasses shattered. Whether or not Blanco-Amor was telling the truth in insisting that he and Lorca witnessed the aftermath of the assault—he was sometimes prone to exaggeration—it is plain that Lorca was aware of the incident and shared his fellow citizens' indignation at its occurrence.

In early May 1935, Prime Minister Lerroux formed a new cabinet that included five members of CEDA, among them the party's fanatical leader, Gil Robles, el Jefe, whom Lerroux designated minister of war. Gil Robles promptly recalled General Francisco Franco from his post in Morocco, and appointed him chief of the general staff. Lerroux's CEDA-dominated government worked to further dismantle the reforms Manuel Azaña and his administration had set into place, and to purge loyal Republican officers from the ranks of the Spanish army. By the summer of 1935 conservative government forces had prevailed in their long-standing efforts to cut government spending for La Barraca, and the troupe had lost much of its funding. *El Liberal* reported in June that La Barraca faced both economic and political difficulties. Company members were told they could no longer rehearse in the auditorium at the Residencia. Earlier in the year a new Falangist newspaper, *Haz*, had criticized the company's pro-Republican production of Lope de Vega's *Fuenteovejuna*. The paper accused the troupe of having transformed "an authentically Spanish drama" into a "petty Russophile drama," and suggested that in staging the production Lorca had been swayed by "undesirable elements of the most repugnant communist type."

Lorca defended his company. He said he intended to do only one thing about La Barraca's dire financial situation: "Go on performing. Somebody will pay." La Barraca, he vowed, "will not die because I don't intend for it to die." When his actors ran out of costumes, they would perform in their blue cover-alls. If authorities refused to let them perform in the streets, "We'll perform in caves and create a secret theater."

Lorca accompanied the group on its last tour to Santander in late August 1935. The local press welcomed the company's arrival but noted the sadness of the occasion, given the "miserable subsidy" to which the troupe had been re-duced. Rain fell throughout their weeklong residency. Lorca stayed long enough to attend the final dress rehearsal of the troupe's new production of Lope's *The Knight of Olmedo*, but the play was underrehearsed, and even Lorca lacked enthusiasm for it. He left Santander immediately afterward and returned to Madrid without waiting for the opening night. The rest of the com-pany departed a few days later. "Will we ever hear them again?" a journalist asked after they had left.

In late August, Lorca attended Margarita Xirgu's new production of Lope de Vega's *Fuenteovejuna* in the town of Fuenteovejuna in southern Spain. He had seen the same production earlier in the summer in Granada. The play, about political repression and upheaval in a fifteenth-century Spanish village, sparked controversy, as it had when La Barraca first premiered a version of the work in 1933—although any such controversy was now heightened as a result of the As-turian uprising.

When Xirgu and her company reached Fuenteovejuna, they discovered that village authorities had imprisoned a local anarchist so that he could not hear the performance and be inspired by it. Lorca joined Xirgu in announcing to the town that she would not present the play unless the anarchist was freed.

The mayor yielded, and the man was released. During the final curtain call for the play, audience members were so moved by the work and its call for liberty that they rushed the stage crying, "Fuenteovejuna, all for one!" They pushed aside local officials, who in turn tried to fight off the villagers. Lorca was terrified. He thought the crowd wanted to lynch the actors who had played the villains. To his relief, he eventually realized the audience was simply trying to express its gratitude, both for the play and for the release of the anarchist.

Days later Xirgu presented Lorca's adaptation of Lope's *La dama boba* in Madrid. The performance took place in the midst of a poplar grove in the city's elegant Retiro Park; some five thousand people attended. Afterward, the poet and playwright Manuel Machado read lines of verse in honor of Lope de Vega. Lorca told reporters that in adapting Lope's script—which he had first done in Buenos Aires for the actress Eva Franco—he had sought to achieve the rhythm of a Molière farce. To that end, he had cut a number of "unnecessary" and "bad" lines from the play. Some reviewers questioned his choice; they complained that by "meddling" with the text, Lorca had "betrayed" one of Spain's classical authors. Lorca countered that his actions were no different than those of a musician who interprets a Chopin piano piece. The interpretation might change, he said, but the work remained the same. The Spanish classics could likewise be interpreted and reinterpreted in dozens of ways, "so long as it's always done by a poet who lives them in his heart and soul." He had merely eliminated the "dead spots" in *La dama boba*. "The classical Spanish theater is full of such dead spots."

Since 1931, and the advent of the Republic, the Spanish theater had undergone a small but profound renaissance. Plays such as Lorca's *Yerma*, and productions like Xirgu's *Fuenteovejuna* and *La dama boba*, signaled a new direction in stagecraft and dramatic technique, as well as a greater awareness of the nation's Golden Age roots. Xirgu herself had all but stopped producing mainstream commercial plays during the Republic. Except for a handful of works by Jacinto Benavente, she concentrated solely on revivals of classical authors (Sophocles, Goethe, Lope de Vega, Calderón) and new work by innovative modern playwrights, primarily Unamuno, Valle-Inclán, and Lorca, about whom she said, "Each of his plays is more beautiful, more transcendent than the last."

Xirgu's productions were straightforward and clean; she removed the prompter's shell from the stage, and in her interpretations of the classics strove for a rare accuracy of detail. Toward that end, she, like her idol, Eleonora

Duse, spent hours studying old paintings in the Prado and other museums. Xirgu was vocal in her praise of the Republican government's role in helping to promote and sustain a theatrical revolution in Spain. She noted that previous administrations had granted not "one peseta" to protect and guarantee theatrical activity. Her own 1933 production of *Medea*, directed by Cipriano Rivas Cherif and performed at the ancient Roman amphitheater in Mérida, Spain, drew three thousand people, among them the president of the Republic and several high-ranking Republican officials. The quality of Xirgu's work in that performance moved one observer to credit the actress with the inauguration of "a grand new era in theatrical culture."

Mediocre performances of trite plays performed by overworked, underpaid actors nevertheless continued to dominate Spain's main stages during the 1930s. Lorca steadily voiced his contempt for such work. Asked in 1933 to give his opinion of the Spanish theater of his day, he replied, "The contemporary Spanish theater doesn't interest me."

In 1934, shortly before *Yerma*'s premiere, he again attacked the commercial stage, decrying the fact that "because some man has a few million at his disposal he can establish himself as a censor of works and a definer of the theater. This is intolerable and shameful. It's a tyranny, which like other tyrannies, only leads to disaster." He praised theatrical managers like Xirgu, who in selecting her company's mostly classical repertoire bravely ignored both prevailing tastes and financial concerns. Her innovative work at the Teatro Español with director Rivas Cherif had helped achieve Lorca's dream of a classless theater, one where "blue-blooded ladies" sit side by side with their maids. "The moment the people in the top balconies come down into the orchestra seats," he said, "everything will be resolved."

In the spring of 1935 Lorca remarked in an interview that "the contemporary Spanish theater is unquestionably poor and lacks any sort of poetic virtue." He affirmed that the only theater capable of enduring "is the theater of poets . . . And the greater the poet, the better the theater." But he drew a distinction between "lyric" and "dramatic," or theatrical, poetry: "In the theater, the presence of verse does not signify poetry." He described his own theater as "poetic, and always poetic."

In May 1935 a journalist asked Lorca if he was optimistic about the rehabilitation of the contemporary Spanish stage. "I believe in and fervently hope for the reblossoming of our theatrical art," he said. "We have more than enough intelligence and artistic ability." Neither the continued popularity of bourgeois melodrama nor the imminent demise of his cherished Barraca had entirely dampened his spirits. The theater's "true mission," he said, is "to educate the multitudes," a concept he described as "Nietzschean. That's why Nietzsche wounds my heart."

In another interview later that summer, he told a reporter, "If I've momentarily reduced my poetic output, it's because I now consider my dramatic output to be sufficiently beneficial that I am modestly putting it to educational use. I'm always an optimist, but now even more so."

CHAPTER 25

TO ENTER INTO THE SOUL OF THE PEOPLE

1935

O n September 8, Margarita Xirgu gave a final performance of *La dama boba* in Madrid. Four days later she and her company opened the fall season in Barcelona with a production of the same play. Audiences loved the work, and critics praised Lorca's "delicate and careful" adaptation of Lope de Vega's text. Lorca joined Xirgu in Catalunya and settled into the actress's seaside home in Badalona, a fishing village forty-five minutes from Barcelona. It was his first protracted stay in the region since 1927. From the balconies of Xirgu's house he could see fishing boats and nets scattered on the shores of the Mediterranean, a body of water, he had once said, which made him forget "my sex, my status, my soul, my gift of tears . . . everything! My heart alone is pierced by a keen desire to imitate it and to remain like it, bitter, phosphoric, and eternally awake."

He planned to stay with Xirgu throughout the fall while the actress presented first *La dama boba*, then *Yerma*, and eventually *Doña Rosita the Spinster*. Lorca quickly became the talk of Barcelona and a regular at cafés in the city's theater district. Journalists fought for the chance to profile him. One reporter noted that he possessed "the eyes and the feet and spontaneous grace of a legitimate Andalusian." Lorca capitalized on the exotic nature of his southern origins by talking insistently about bullfights, Gypsies, and deep song. To the theater critic Ignacio Agustí, who befriended the playwright during his stay in Barcelona, Lorca showed a more "ordinary" side. Judging from his appearance (turtleneck sweaters, rumpled shirts), "he could have been a mechanic, a carpenter, or a bricklayer—not a poet," Agustí recalled.

On September 17, Xirgu opened her season's second offering, *Yerma*; for a time the play ran in repertory with *La dama boba*. Immediately prior to the opening of *Yerma* the Catalan press questioned the work's morality. Lorca conceded that his play might be censored. "And if it is, then clearly I'm responsible," he said, and smiled. Curiosity about the work reached such heights that on opening night the theater became "dangerously" crowded. Shouts erupted in ticket lines outside the box office as people forced their way into the building. Eventually the police intervened. Lorca looked on with satisfaction. "This is the way it should be," he said. "People should be passionate about the theater. It's good to see them fighting and arguing like this, as though they were at a rugby match."

That evening he and Xirgu were called onstage repeatedly to accept the crowd's applause. At the final curtain, Lorca acknowledged his debt, both to Barcelona—where in 1927, with *Mariana Pineda*, he had experienced his "baptism of blood in the theater"—and to Xirgu. "I give all this applause to Margarita Xirgu," he said. Reviews of the production were mixed. Although some critics hailed *Yerma* as a "song to motherhood," a "profound monologue by a wounded woman who shrieks her pain," others predictably attacked the play's "crudeness, degeneration, and sensuality." The controversy heightened public interest in the work. During its five-week run in Barcelona Lorca was called onstage nightly. "We authors must pay tribute to success, must go out to 'bathe in the waves' of applause," he said. Wherever he went people surrounded him. Strangers gave him gifts. Two separate literary journals held homages in his honor. Journalists demanded interviews; local organizations requested poetry readings. Lorca relished the attention and sought to inflate his fame. He told *La Humanitat* that his *Gypsy Ballads*, now in its sixth edition, had sold "more than sixty thousand copies"—a modest exaggeration. When the Catalan art critic Sebastian Gasch, who had known Lorca since 1927, met with him in Barcelona that fall, he found Lorca so preoccupied with his own fame that Gasch refused to do more than exchange a few "trivial words" with him.

"*Yerma*'s success in Barcelona is unique," Lorca wrote to his parents, still eager for their approval. "I can't recall such enthusiasm, not even in Buenos Aires. The theater is jammed, and tickets cost six pesetas, an unheard-of price these days." His mother congratulated him on his success and reminded him "to be careful and not throw your money away foolishly. Save what you can for yourself, because financial success isn't always certain."

On October 6 Lorca gave a public reading to commemorate the first anniversary of the Asturian revolution. Sponsored by the Barcelona Atheneum and held in a crowded theater, the event was broadcast over radio and aimed specifically at the "workers" of Catalunya. Lorca sat onstage for the reading, behind a table with a huge Radio Barcelona microphone. He wore a light-colored suit with a dark bow tie. Xirgu sat beside him, dressed in a floor-length gown in shades of white, pale yellow, and pink.

The moment Lorca began to speak, the packed auditorium fell silent. He read two of his more stridently antiauthoritarian works, "The King of Harlem" and the "Ballad of the Spanish Civil Guard." "Oh city of the gypsies! / Corners hung with banners. / Put your green lights out: / the Civil Guard is coming," he intoned. ". . . They are riding two abreast / to the celebrating city. / The murmur of everlastings / invades their cartridge belts." The poem's graphic indictment of the country's rural police force sparked sympathetic murmurs in the audience. When he finished, the crowd jumped up and shouted, "Long live the poet of the people!"

Afterward, fans stood in line for more than an hour and a half to shake Lorca's hand. He was so moved he felt a lump in his throat and could scarcely speak. For years he had felt estranged from the working classes who had been his neighbors and friends in childhood, but whose lives differed so dramatically from the bourgeois existence he had come to enjoy as a "rich man's son." The recital restored him to his roots. He told his parents, "It seemed so true, this contact with the real people."

He marveled at those who had come to hear him: "artisans, old workers, mechanics, children, students. It was the loveliest act I have experienced in my life." The event was bound to provoke his opponents, but he didn't care. In a nation so torn by political, religious, and social discord as Spain was in 1935, no public figure could escape accusations of partisanship. Besides, Lorca was proud of his liberal ideals. "No doubt the Right will seize upon all this in its campaign against Margarita and me, but it doesn't matter," he said to his parents. "It is almost better that way—the way we stand will be out in the open once and for all. Anyway, in Spain it is no longer possible to be *neutral*."

Earlier in the week, he had insisted that mere popularity did not interest him. "It's too frivolous." The most beautiful thing a poet could hope to achieve was "to enter into the soul of the people—this is poetry!" When asked to define the role he thought poets should play in the struggle for social justice, he replied that poets cannot remain impassive; they must absorb and understand the "frightening tragedy of the oppressed," must do everything in their power to fight "for a more just, more humane world." He spoke briefly about war, calling it "monstrous, criminal." He found it incomprehensible that after the "bitter proof" of World War I, people still believed in fighting. "It is a disgrace for our civilization."

Lorca's reading to commemorate the Asturian revolt coincided with news of the Italian army's invasion of the independent African empire of Abyssinia, the first step by Mussolini toward creating a "new Roman empire" to free Italy from the "prison of the Mediterranean." Headlines in Barcelona announced the "Advance of Fascist Troops on Ethiopia." Subsequent reports told of futile efforts by the League of Nations to check the dictator's aggression. Two months earlier, the government of Italy had invited Lorca and Xirgu to participate in a tricentennial homage to Lope de Vega. Xirgu had accepted and planned to visit Italy that fall on a four-city tour of the country; while there she intended to present *Yerma* and to star in a new production of Lorca's adaptation of *La dama boba*, directed by the 1934 Nobel laureate, Luigi Pirandello. But because of the Abyssinian invasion, the actress canceled her Italian tour and announced that she would extend her company's season in Barcelona to include a new production of *Blood Wedding*.

Lorca condemned what he described as the "tyranny" of the fascist regimes in Italy as well as Germany, and declared his solidarity with artists in both countries. In early November he signed an open letter calling for an end to the fighting in Ethiopia. Other signatories included Antonio Machado and Fernando de los Ríos. "Spaniards!" the letter began. "To put your moral weight behind Abyssinia today is to defend our own future, which must not be linked to anything but reason, law, and peace." The document appeared in newspapers throughout Spain; in Madrid, *Gracia y Justicia* ridiculed both Lorca and Machado for having signed the letter. Meanwhile, Lorca announced his desire to write a "work of peace," a play entitled *Soldiers Who Don't Want to Go to War*, in which various women—mothers, sisters, daughters, girlfriends, wives—decry the governments who instigate war.

Within weeks of the cancellation of her Italian tour, the citizens of Barcelona staged a tribute in Xirgu's honor. Proceeds from the event were to benefit Spain's political prisoners. Approximately eight thousand people crowded into Barcelona's Olympia Theater to render homage to the handsome actress, then forty-seven, whose political courage and artistic daring were to her fans a source of both pride and inspiration. Former prime minister Manuel Azaña sent his regards, as did the cellist Pablo Casals. Bouquets of flowers, many bearing the symbol of Catalunya, a region long known for its liberal politics, showered the actress at the end of the evening. As he watched the colorful spectacle, Lorca applauded the spirited Catalan audience. "What a people!" he cried.

In the midst of *Yerma*'s five-week Barcelona run, Ana María Dalí came to Barcelona to see Lorca. It was the first time in nearly a decade they had met. Then twenty-seven, the painter's sister was more beautiful than ever, with limpid brown eyes and a beatific smile. She found Lorca at the theater, and the two went off to a café. They talked at length about Ana María's brother, who had recently returned to Cadaqués with his wife, Gala Eluard, after being expelled by the French surrealists for "counterrevolutionary activities," which included outspoken praise of Hitler and fascism. Although Lorca had not seen Dalí since 1928, neither man had forgotten the other. In 1930, Lorca had written to Dalí to suggest that they go to New York and Moscow together. In 1934, Dalí had invited Lorca to visit him in Cadaqués. "If you came we could understand each other better now about many things. Gala is terribly curious to meet you." The artist had proposed that he and Lorca collaborate on an opera. He signed his letter "your *Budo*," a probable reference to *Buda*, or "Buddha."

Soon after his visit with Ana María, Lorca saw Dalí for the first time in seven years. On the day of their reunion, September 28, Lorca had been expected to attend a concert in his honor. When he failed to appear, his absence sparked a crisis until someone discovered his whereabouts and announced to the gathering that the playwright had gone off to the nearby town of Tarragona with the celebrated Catalan artist Salvador Dalí. A local newspaper observed wryly that while Lorca "may hold the record for receiving the most invitations, he also holds the record for not attending parties to which he's been invited."

Lorca and Dalí saw each other frequently that fall. Lorca seized every occasion to demonstrate his affection for his old friend. During a recital at a Barcelona bookstore, he read his 1926 "Ode to Salvador Dalí," a work not ordinarily part of his repertoire. Asked his thoughts on contemporary Catalan art, he said, "For me, Dalí is the purest of all contemporary painters." On the subject of his own work—specifically, whether the characters in his plays were "real or symbolic"—Lorca said in an interview that while each of his characters was real, each also embodied a symbol. "They're an aesthetic reality. That's why Salvador Dalí and the surrealists like them so much."

Dalí praised the "*extremely dark* and surrealist ideas" that filled Lorca's *Yerma*. He proposed to Lorca that they "do things together again," and the two made plans to collaborate on a project that both would write and design. "We're twin spirits," Lorca told a reporter, overlooking Dalí's right-wing political views. "Here's the proof: seven years without seeing each other, and we agree on everything as if we'd been talking daily. Genius, genius: Salvador Dalí." But the project never transpired, and after a few months their friendship again slackened. Dalí was preoccupied with his wife and with his growing international fame, Lorca with his new work and the demands of a high-profile theater career. Neither could turn back the clock.

Yerma ended its Barcelona run on October 20. Five days later Xirgu presented the play in Tarragona; the following day she and her company traveled south to Valencia to open a three-week run featuring performances of Lorca's Yerma, Lope de Vega's La dama boba and Fuenteovejuna, and Zorrilla's Don Juan Tenorio. Lorca arrived in Valencia on November 9 after a hurried trip home to Madrid, where he gave a poetry reading to a group of schoolchildren. He traveled to Valencia from Madrid by plane. He had been fascinated by air travel ever since Lindbergh's celebrated Atlantic crossing. He talked of the "fragility" and "uncertainty" of the airplane's wings, and described the pilot's art as that of being "suspended between two abysses, face-to-face with death."

Critics in Valencia raved about Yerma, and audiences praised the work. Lorca told El Mercantil Valenciano that only two types of problems were currently of interest in art: "social and sexual. Works that don't address one of these are destined to fail, even when they're good. I choose to deal with the sexual, because it appeals to me more." In Valencia, as in Barcelona, politics colored audience attitudes toward Yerma. On the play's closing night, a wildly enthusiastic crowd filled the theater, and Xirgu received floral bouquets from two local Republican associations. The previous day, young Valencian Republicans had staged a huge outdoor protest against fascism and war. A speaker at the event warned the crowd that Spain had reached a political turning point, and citizens must "influence the historic destiny of our country."

Lorca refrained from political activity in Valencia. During his brief stay in the city he responded dutifully to reporters' questions about his work, and he obliged local theatergoers by going onstage during performances of Yerma to accept their accolades. But to friends and colleagues he seemed distracted. His sometime secretary and close companion, Rafael Rodríguez Rapún, had promised to visit him in Valencia. On the appointed day Lorca went to the train station to meet him. But although he waited impatiently for Rapún to arrive, the handsome engineering student, then twenty-three, never showed up. The two men did not see each other until a week or so later, when Rapún traveled to Barcelona. Their friendship of nearly three years had become an increasing source of distress to Lorca; among trusted friends, he complained of Rapún's growing need to engage in heterosexual liaisons.

While in Valencia, or shortly afterward, Lorca drafted a series of sonnets chronicling a love affair between two unnamed persons. He worked impulsively, scribbling the poems on stationery from Valencia's Hotel Victoria. The sonnets range in subject from the mundane ("The Poet Speaks with His Beloved on the Telephone"; "The Poet Asks His Love to Write Him") to the exalted ("Sonnet of the Rose Garland"; "Sonnet of the Sweet Complaint"). Collectively the poems speak of a troubled, at times cruel relationship between two partners, one of whom—the first-person "Poet"—is more blindly devoted than the other, and consequently suffers more.

In writing the sonnets Lorca was careful not to disclose the gender of his protagonists, a considerable feat given the gender-specific nature of the Spanish language. But in one poem, "Love Sleeps in the Poet's Breast," the narrator uses a masculine past participle to describe his beloved, thus indicating that their affair is homosexual. In an earlier draft of another sonnet, Lorca was even more candid. He titled the poem "Soneto gongorino en que Federico manda a su amigo una paloma": "Sonnet in the Manner of Góngora in Which Federico Sends His [Male] Friend a Dove." Ultimately, Lorca rejected the title in favor of the more oblique "Sonnet in the Manner of Góngora in Which the Poet Sends His Beloved a Dove."

To the poet Vicente Aleixandre, Lorca later referred to the cycle as "Sonnets of Dark Love." In public, however, he spoke only of his "sonnets" or "book of sonnets." Aleixandre believed that to Lorca "dark love" meant simply "the love of difficult passion . . . of dark and painful, unrequited, or badly experienced passion." It did not specifically mean homosexual love, but rather "love without destination, without a future." After hearing the eleven poems for the first time, Aleixandre turned to Lorca and exclaimed, "How much you've had to love, how much you've had to suffer!" Lorca gazed at his friend and smiled.

His decision to undertake the series in late 1935 sprang in part from a chance encounter in Valencia with the poet Juan Gil-Albert, who was about to publish his own first sonnet collection, *Mysterious Presence*, a series of poems openly addressed to another male. Gil-Albert read passages of the book to Lorca, who was both moved by the collection and challenged by its existence to attempt a similar sequence. Gil-Albert also gave Lorca a curious gift during his visit to Valencia, a live dove in a cage. The gesture subsequently formed the anecdotal basis for Lorca's "Sonnet in the Manner of Góngora in Which the Poet Sends His Beloved a Dove."

By 1935, love poetry had again become fashionable in Spain, as the impersonal, dehumanized verse of the mid-1920s gave way to a "new romanticism," a "rehumanization" of literature, prompted to some degree by a greater concern for politics and the pressing realities of contemporary Spanish life. Classical forms were also newly in vogue. In 1933, Lorca's friend Pedro Salinas had published *La voz a ti debida*, a collection of love poems whose title, "My Voice Because of You," recalls the second eclogue of the Golden Age poet Garcilaso. Younger writers such as Miguel Hernández, Germán Bleiberg, and the Granadan poet Luis Rosales were likewise writing love poems and experimenting with classical forms. Lorca spoke of their efforts as a "crusade," and characterized his own sonnet cycle as a similar "return to prescribed forms after a wide-ranging and sunny stroll through the freedom of meter and rhyme."

For years he had admired the sonnet's "apparently cold" form, its ability to preserve "an eternal feeling," and he sought to master its stringent requirements. "You can't be a poet until you make sonnets," he said. "You must dominate the sonnet, and not allow it to dominate you." In his periodic attempts at the form, he had followed Golden Age convention by linking the sonnet with such topics as death, love, and the enduring nature of art. He aspired to a command of the genre as powerful as Shakespeare's. "One hundred sonnets . . . just like the ones Shakespeare wrote!" he remarked to a friend in 1935. He believed that Shakespeare's sonnets "could not have been written except by a man who had homosexual tendencies." He also admired Whitman's twelve-sonnet series dramatizing a homosexual attachment.

He confessed to a friend in the summer of 1935 that he had "never stopped being a romantic poet," despite the decadelong popularity of cerebral, "pure" verse. In the early 1930s he had talked of issuing a book of love poems written in "waltz time": *Because I Love Only You (Tanda of Waltzes)*; he wrote two intensely personal "waltz" poems before setting aside the series to focus on *The Divan at Tamarit*, a collection preoccupied with love, although always in the context of death. His sonnets of dark love are a further product of a romantic imagination. They describe a flawed but vital love affair, one so necessary that all aspects of it, even suffering, are to be cherished. The author of the sonnets speaks of his beloved in Christ-like terms as "my hidden treasure . . . my cross, my dampened pain"; he refers to himself as "a dog, and you alone my master." A gulf of misunderstanding separates the two protagonists of the series, even at their most intimate:

> We two, the night ahead, the full moon looming:
> I began to weep while you laughed.
> Your scorn became a god, and my complaints
> were little doves and moments in a chain.

> We two, the night behind, crystal of pain,
> and you wept over deep and distant things.
> My sorrow was a clump of agony
> resting on your fragile heart of sand.
>
> The dawn drew us together on the bed.
> Our mouths were waiting near the frozen spout
> of blood that spilled forth in an endless flow.
>
> The sun came through the shuttered balcony
> and the coral of life opened its branch,
> and settled here upon my shrouded heart.

The wound of love is always preferable to nothing at all. "Never let me lose the marvel / of your statue-like eyes, or the accent / the solitary rose of your breath / places on my cheek at night," Lorca writes in "Sonnet of the Sweet Complaint." In "The Poet Tells the Truth," a work whose title, subject, and syntax recall the autobiographical "Double Poem of Lake Eden" of 1929, the poet demands to "cry his grief" so that his beloved will come to him "in a dusk of nightingales / with a dagger, with kisses, and with you." The poet seeks "no end . . . to the unwinding / of 'I love you, you love me.' "

The phrase "dark love" appears in just one sonnet, the only untitled poem in the sequence, a work in which Lorca addresses both his beloved and the invisible "voice" that stalks them:

> O secret voice of dark love!
> O bleating without fleece! O wound!
> O needle of gall, sunken camellia!
> O current without sea, city without walls!

Lorca's "voice of dark love" is sterile, secretive, tragic, and by implication illicit—a "dog in the heart," a voice "persecuted" or "beleaguered," a "borderless silence" the poet yearns to escape:

> Away from me, simmering voice of ice,
> and lose me not among the weeds
> where flesh and heaven moan, leaving no fruit.
>
> Forsake the hard ivory of my head,
> take pity on me, break my pain!
> For I am love, for I am nature!

In each of his eleven sonnets Lorca combines literary traditions and styles. Pe-
trarchan attitudes, form, and idioms ("sweet complaint," "simmering voice of
ice," "wound of love") alternate with contemporary images. Profane love
blends with divine in sometimes bewildering ways; the poet repeatedly compares his suffering to the Passion of Christ. Strains of courtly love mingle with
echoes of the sixteenth-century Spanish mystics, Golden Age sonneteers, and
Shakespeare, whose sonnets, like Lorca's, recount the author's painful attachment to a mysterious, "dark" other. At times Lorca's compulsive use of cultural
and literary allusions obscures the emotional content of his poems; some images are so densely encoded they are impossible to decipher. Others are unexpectedly simple. In "The Poet Speaks with His Beloved on the Telephone," the
author invokes an everyday icon to describe an encounter with his lover:

> Your voice watered the dune of my breast
> in the sweet wooden booth.
> South of my feet, it was spring,
> and north of my brow, a fern blossomed.
>
> Within that narrow space a pine of light
> sang out, but with no dawn, no seed to sow;
> and my lament for the first time
> hung coronets of hope upon the roof.

Although other events—his recent reunion with Dalí, his introduction to
Gil-Albert's sonnet collection—helped to inspire the series, Lorca seems to
have written his sonnets of dark love with one person in mind: Rafael Rodríguez Rapún. In the poem "The Poet Asks His Love for the Enchanted City
of Cuenca," Lorca alludes to a trip the two made together to the city of Cuenca
in 1935. He and Rapún had been close friends, and by all appearances lovers,
since 1933. Their involvement, like the affair chronicled in the sonnets, was to
Lorca both gratifying and fraught with disappointment. And yet he could not
imagine forsaking it. More so than any other poetry sequence or play, his sonnets of dark love reveal Lorca in the grip of passion: greedy, blind, obsessive, a
man so consumed by desire that he will forgive his companion anything, even
pain, so long as their love endures.

Lorca returned to Barcelona in mid-November to help Margarita Xirgu stage a
revival of *Blood Wedding*. He composed new music for several scenes, and accompanied the production himself on the piano. He promised Barcelona audi-

ences that in contrast to Josefina Díaz's lackluster premiere of the work in Madrid in 1933, Xirgu's 1935 production would constitute the "true premiere" of *Blood Wedding*. Spanish theatergoers would at last see the "tragedy" he had intended, not the mere "drama" Díaz had staged.

Midway through rehearsals, Rapún joined Lorca in Barcelona. The younger man's presence quickly proved a source of frustration. One night, while out with Lorca and a group of friends, Rapún disappeared with a Gypsy woman. By the next day, when he had not returned to the hotel room he and Lorca shared, Lorca was so distraught he skipped that afternoon's *Blood Wedding* rehearsal. The play's director, Cipriano Rivas Cherif, a gaunt man in his mid-forties, went off in search of the playwright and found him sitting by himself in a café, his head resting gloomily in his hands. Lorca scarcely recognized the director. Rivas Cherif asked what had happened. Lorca hesitated, then burst out, "He hasn't been home all morning. He's left me. It's not possible!"

Rivas Cherif pressed for details. Lorca mentioned the Gypsy woman. He then produced a packet of letters Rapún had sent him during the course of their two-and-a-half-year involvement. Lorca leafed through the pile, pulling out letter after letter in an attempt to prove to Rivas Cherif the depth of Rapún's feelings for him. The first note, written before the two men had even met, expressed admiration for Lorca's *Gypsy Ballads*. Subsequent letters indicated Rapún's surprise at Lorca's interest in him; at one point Rafael wondered if Lorca was playing a joke on him by professing such intense devotion. Rapún's final letters bore witness to a full-fledged love affair.

"I'm not sad. I'm heartbroken," Lorca told Rivas Cherif, adding dramatically, "My flesh, my blood, my entire body and soul have been betrayed." Although he had known the director since the early 1920s, and at one point had hoped Rivas Cherif would premiere *The Audience*, it was the first time Lorca had spoken so frankly to the older man about his homosexuality. He explained that he had been attracted to men since childhood. "I have never known a woman." He attributed his sexual preference to the deep respect he had for his mother, a notion Rivas Cherif dismissed as second-rate Freudianism. Lorca managed to laugh.

The director demanded to know how anyone so intrigued by the world as Lorca was could cut himself off from half the human race. "Haven't *you* deprived yourself of the other half?" Lorca asked. "Normality is neither your way of knowing only women, nor mine. What's normal is love without limits." Although he acknowledged his contempt for "the effeminate homosexual, the pansy," Lorca defended same-sex love as emblematic of a "new morality, a morality of complete freedom." Love, he argued, transcends the morality of

Catholic dogma; it is not simply about having children, or about hierarchical family roles. "With my way, there is no misrepresentation. Both partners remain as they are, without bartering. No one gives orders; no one dominates; there is no submission. There is no assigning of roles . . . There is only abandon and mutual enjoyment."

He had rarely been more candid. The events of his own life had in recent months combined so strikingly with world events—the Asturian revolution, the invasion of Abyssinia, the rise of fascism—that Lorca had little choice but to view the two as linked, and to speak out in defense of both social and sexual freedom. His recent work bore testament to his claim a few weeks earlier that only two kinds of problems were of interest in art: "social and sexual." Both *Blood Wedding* and *Yerma* directly challenge the sexual politics of traditional Spanish society. Even a play so apparently genteel as *Doña Rosita the Spinster* questions the value of conventional gender roles and mocks the tyranny of bourgeois taste. Though more personal and therefore subtle, Lorca's sonnets likewise proclaim the legitimacy of a new kind of love, one unfettered by orthodox notions of courtship and marriage. His statements to Rivas Cherif merely underscored such thinking.

Rivas Cherif waited a discreet twenty-two years before publicly disclosing the content of his conversation with Lorca that November afternoon. He recalled just one other time when Lorca touched on the topic. While discussing his work one day, Lorca told the director he intended to write a "realist drama" about homosexuality, in which a straitlaced older man—not unlike Lorca's father—demands to know why his son has been refused membership in the town casino. "Because I'm homosexual," the son replies.

"What do you think of that for an opening?" Lorca asked.

"Don't write it," Rivas Cherif advised.

Blood Wedding opened in Barcelona on November 22. The production, starring Margarita Xirgu as the Bride's Mother, received both critical and public acclaim and played to full houses. Three weeks later, on December 12, Xirgu premiered *Doña Rosita the Spinster* in Barcelona's Principal Palace Theater. Lorca missed several rehearsals in order to go to Madrid in mid-December to attend the opening of a new Barraca production of his own version of Lope de Vega's *The Knight of Olmedo*; the work was the final installment in the company's yearlong tribute to the Golden Age playwright. Lorca returned to Barcelona in time to direct the last rehearsals for *Doña Rosita*. Posters advertised the play as a "poem for families."

Spectators jammed the entrances to the theater and formed long lines at the box office windows shortly before the ten o'clock curtain on December 12. Red and white lights—colors emblematic of Rosita—bathed the outside of the theater; inside, the packed auditorium hummed with anticipation. Earlier that month, a Madrid reporter had noted the unprecedented air of "expectation" surrounding the premiere of Lorca's newest play. Lorca's brother, Paco, and sister Isabel flew in from Madrid for the opening.

As the curtain rose on the gauche interior of Rosita's bourgeois Granada home, Lorca, watching from offstage, muttered, "What magnificent bad taste!" At the end of the second act, the audience gave the cast a standing ovation. Lorca and his actors had to go onstage eight times before the crowd quieted down. At the interval a theater critic remarked that even the appearance of a stagehand who stumbled while crossing the set struck him as "marvelous." During the play's third and final act, the mood in the theater shifted abruptly as Xirgu, in the role of Rosita, changed from a lovesick young woman, dressed gaily in pink clothes and blond ringlets, into an aging spinster in a plain white gown. "An intense emotion invades us," wrote one reviewer, describing the effect of the transformation.

Nearly a dozen critics had flown to Barcelona from Madrid for the play's premiere, and within a week *Doña Rosita* had received more than twenty-five reviews. Although some critics questioned the work's genre (was it a comedy, a tragedy, or both?) and style (were its characters "realistic" or not?), nearly everyone praised the originality and power of Lorca's script. "No one can say that García Lorca repeats himself," wrote Antonio de Obregón of the *Diario de Madrid*. Barcelona's *La Noche* termed *Rosita* a "Christmas present, a beautiful romantic miniature" from Lorca to the people of Barcelona. Critic Antonio Espina ranked *Doña Rosita* among "the greatest works of both the modern Spanish theater and theaters beyond Spain." *La Vanguardia*'s María Luz Morales, one of the few female critics in Spain, wrote that *Rosita* "equals" the finest productions of the contemporary European stage. In contrast to the "tragic rawness" of *Blood Wedding* and the "profound humanity" of *Yerma*, said Morales, *Rosita* was all "delicacy and shading," and as such epitomized the era it sought to represent.

A number of reviewers called attention to Lorca's constant experimentation as a playwright. "He is faithful to only one thing: his poetic temperament," one said. Another noted the "Franciscan" compassion toward "small things" that permeated *Rosita*. Others mentioned the resemblance between Lorca's play and Chekhov's *The Cherry Orchard*. The play's only negative review came from Ignacio Agustí of *L'Instant*, who felt that Lorca had not effectively resolved the dichotomy between the drama's picturesque exterior and its tragic interior. Agustí called *Rosita* a "disoriented work" that was neither a drama nor a caricature but an uncomfortable hybrid of the two. Lorca later told Agustí he agreed with the critic's appraisal of his script and was revising it accordingly. "I don't do anything well except tragedy," he confided. Despite his celebrity, he considered himself "a real novice. I'm learning how to handle my craft," he told another acquaintance. "One must climb the ladder step by step . . . My work has scarcely begun. I see it off in the future, like a dense orb."

By Christmas Eve, *Doña Rosita* was the most successful play in Barcelona. The drama's first act was broadcast over Radio Barcelona. Thrilled by the play's floral theme, the city's florists sent daily bouquets to Xirgu. Lorca talked giddily of his achievement, which he thought the most well-deserved triumph of his career. He called *Rosita* his "youngest and dearest daughter."

Once more he became the toast of Barcelona. He attended banquets, gave poetry readings, took part in a homage to the late composer Isaac Albéniz, for which he composed a sonnet. Later in the month he wrote a second commemorative sonnet for a special issue of Pablo Neruda's new literary magazine, *Caballo Verde para la Poesía*; the new sonnet paid tribute to a little-known Uruguayan poet and translator, Julio Herrera y Reissig, who had died in 1910. Despite his more visible life as a celebrated man of the theater, and his oft-stated desire to write plays, Lorca continued to view poetry as a critical part of his being, both private and public. In the weeks after *Rosita*'s premiere he resumed work on his sonnets of dark love, revising and expanding the series for publication in 1936. That the collection dealt with material of an extraordinarily personal nature did not frighten him; he was determined to publish the sequence. He believed that poetry was above all indispensable in times of political and social stress, for it restored a sense of order and proportion to the world. "I'm now writing a book of sonnets," he told a friend. "We must return to this."

On December 22, Margarita Xirgu gave a special performance of *Rosita* for the local florists' union. At the end of the evening Lorca thanked the florists for the support they had shown his play by sending floral arrangements to its star. "This is the revolution," he remarked afterward. "The florists' unions bring bouquets of flowers to me, to the poet. Do you realize what this means?"

The following day, December 23, the city of Barcelona honored Lorca at a banquet in a central hotel. Distinguished Catalan personalities and Lorca's close friends toasted the playwright with champagne. Lorca gave an extemporaneous speech—one of the few times in his career he did not read from a prepared text. He thanked his hosts and, intent on proving his ties to ordinary, working-class people, recalled the childhood maids and housekeepers who had proved such an inspiration to him as a writer. He told journalist Luis Góngora of *La Noche* that the mayor of Granada ought to see his remarks, so that the latter could know "how I feel about my home. And I'll say to him: I'm more mayor of Granada than you are." He was confident that he had done more for his hometown than many of the city's elected officials and upstanding middle-class citizens.

Góngora asked Lorca if he was happy. "Happy isn't the word. I'd like to premiere all my theater work here," Lorca replied.

The journalist then asked if the people of Granada were as supportive of his work as the Barcelona public. "Granada is a closed city," Lorca answered carefully. "Wonderful, but closed. And it should be that way." He had long regarded his hometown as a provincial backwater, concealed from the sea by mountains, cut off from the world by hidebound attitudes, and yet, because of its isolation, uniquely beautiful. "Ángel Ganivet, the most illustrious *granadino* of the nineteenth century, used to say, 'When I go to Granada, only the air greets me.' But it doesn't matter," Lorca went on. "Granada is Granada, and it's fine as it is."

CHAPTER 26

THE DREAM OF LIFE

1936

The town of Fuente Vaqueros sent New Year's greetings to Lorca on January 1, 1936. Nearly fifty residents of the village, including the mayor, signed the short note applauding his achievements and acknowledging him as "the true poet of the people. You, better than anyone, know how to fill your profoundly beautiful dramas with all of the pain, the immense tragedy of those who suffer, who endure lives saturated with injustice."

Lorca returned to Madrid in January, "gushing" with talk of his recent triumphs in Catalunya and future plans for both travel and work. He had promised to accompany Margarita Xirgu on an extended tour to Cuba, Mexico, and South America that year. The actress intended to leave Spain on January 30 and head first to Cuba, where she would present both *Yerma* and Lorca's version of *La dama boba*. Lorca planned to meet up with her overseas. Meanwhile he immersed himself in work. In late December he brought out his *Six Galician Poems*. In January he issued *Blood Wedding* and *First Songs*, a small compilation of early suites. He inscribed a copy of *First Songs* for Rafael Rodríguez Rapún; near his signature he sketched two weeping faces—one with heavy eyebrows much like his own—whose lips almost meet in a kiss.

Within the next few months Lorca hoped to bring out his volume of sonnets as well as a collection of "Old Spanish Songs (For Piano and Voice)"; *The Divan at Tamarit* was slated for publication later that spring. The previous year he had published both the *Lament for Ignacio Sánchez Mejías* and a French translation of his *Gypsy Ballads*. There was growing foreign interest in his work. In

Spain, publishers were competing for the rights to *Yerma*. Lorca kept them at bay. "I'm so lazy I keep forgetting about it from one day to the next," he said. His mother told journalist Pablo Suero that the only way to get her son's work into print was to "take all his papers away from him and give them to the press."

At heart Lorca remained hesitant to publish. "I don't believe a poet should produce too much," he had said in 1935. "One should be demanding. Scrutinize what you've written, take a close look at a book before hurling it out into the market." By early 1936 he was still wrestling with his projected collection of New York poems. He intended to call the collection *Poet in New York*, and to dedicate its third section, "Streets and Dreams," to "Rafael R. Rapún," with an epigraph by Vicente Aleixandre: "A paper bird inside the breast / says the time for kisses has not arrived." He predicted that his volume of New York poems would exceed three hundred pages and "will be so heavy you can kill someone with it."

In late 1934 or early 1935, in the immediate wake of the Asturian revolution, he had begun work on a new play. The *Heraldo de Madrid*, which published an ample account of Lorca's "feverish" theatrical activity in the "Rumors" section of its February 12, 1936, edition, described the new drama as an "ultramodern work" about an acute social problem, a play in which stage and audience are indistinguishable, and theatergoers participate directly in the action. Lorca had not yet chosen a title for the play, although he admired Calderón's phrase "life is a dream." Eventually the *Heraldo* revealed that Lorca planned to call it *The Dream of Life*.

He referred to the work variously as a "comedy," a "drama," and, on at least one occasion, as a "political tragedy." Its links to the Asturian rebellion were striking. During the course of the action a revolution erupts, gunshots are fired, soldiers take over the streets, bombs fall, a worker is killed, and a panicked public tries to force its way into the theater for safety. From the outset the play is confrontational. It opens with a long prologue by its Author, who informs viewers that he has no intention of entertaining them but will instead show them "a tiny corner of reality," will shout "simple truths you do not wish to hear." "If you believe in death, why this cruelty, this indifference to the terrible pain of your fellow beings?" he demands. ". . . Why must we always go to the theater to see what is happening and not what is happening to us?"

In early 1935, during Margarita Xirgu's special, after-hours performance of *Yerma* for the actors of Madrid, Lorca had called for a "theater of social action," one that "takes the social and historical pulse" of its nation. He had begun work on *The Dream of Life* at approximately the same time he was drafting the talk. In the prologue to his play he reiterates key points of the speech: that the commercial stage is both decadent and deadly, that true theater must shock, that acting forces an encounter between life and dream. The same ideas emerge in the prologues to Lorca's puppet plays and *The Shoemaker's Prodigious Wife*, and in a theater piece called *Dragon*, begun sometime between 1928 and 1930 and never finished, in which a stage director attempts to startle his bourgeois audience by insisting they scrutinize the duplicity of their lives and relationships.

The Dream of Life is the most blatant of Lorca's efforts to shape a confrontation between stage and audience. The Author warns spectators that nothing they see onstage will be invented, that its angels and shadows are "just as real as lust, the coins you carry in your pocket, or the latent cancer in a woman's breast or on a merchant's weary lip." The play itself recapitulates the ideas set forth in the prologue. A theater company is rehearsing a production of *A Midsummer Night's Dream* when a revolution occurs outside the theater; in the ensuing tumult, spectators crowd onstage together with actors costumed in Shakespearean dress. A woman audience member cries out for her children and is coached by an actress to alter the inflection of her scream. "Her voice has a false air about it that will never succeed in moving anyone," the actress explains. The line between dream and reality blurs. Actors fear for their props, spectators for their offspring. The Author demands that the doors of the theater be opened so that people on the streets can take refuge inside: "I don't want real blood to be shed next to the walls of deception."

Although he did not elaborate on its technical innovations, Lorca proudly described the first act of the play—the only extant act—as a "completely subversive act which assumes a veritable technical revolution, an enormous advance." In drafting the script he appears to have been influenced by the German director Erwin Piscator, whose militant productions of the 1920s used film, cartoons, treadmills, and other devices to show the bonds between dramatic situations and real-life events. Lorca admired Piscator's achievement in having established a "true theater of the masses, a theater of revolutionary education," but he faulted the director for having failed to adapt his efforts to a broader public. With *The Dream of Life*, Lorca hoped to create a bona fide people's theater, one stripped of artifice ("the silver goblets . . . the ermine costumes") and devoted to truth.

He described his play as a blend of social and religious themes, which together reveal "my constant anguish about the great beyond." According to Margarita Xirgu, who heard parts of the script in 1935, the play's second act was to take place in a mortuary, and its final act in a heaven filled with "Andalusian

ABOVE The professor and socialist leader Fernando de los Ríos, who as republican Minister of Education funded La Barraca in the early 1930s.

LEFT Co-director Eduardo Ugarte (*left*) and Lorca, in their Barraca uniforms, during a tour with the company, *c.* 1932.

Ernesto Pérez Guerra (*left*), who collaborated with Lorca on *Six Galician Poems*. Pérez Guerra later characterized Lorca as "a solitary being for whom solitude was intolerable."

With Rafael Rodríguez Rapún, in the gardens of the Hotel Reina Cristina, Algeciras, 1933.

RIGHT Ticket, *Blood Wedding*, 1933. Despite the "crowns of glory" he received as a result of the play's resounding success, Lorca complained that he still lacked "the divine crown of love."

BELOW In Madrid, 1934, with the actress Lola Membrives and the playwright Eduardo Marquina.

EMPRESA: DIAZ-ARGÜELLES
EMPRESA: DIAZ-ARGÜELLES

TEATRO AVENIDA

Gran Compañía de Alta Comedia LOLA MEMBRIVES · PRIMER ACTOR: RICARDO PUGA

MARTES 21 DE NOVIEMBRE · A LAS 22 EN PUNTO

Función Extraordinaria en Honor de FEDERICO GARCIA LORCA
CON MOTIVO DE LA

REPRESENTACIONES
DE SU GRANDIOSO POEMA DRAMATICO

100 BODAS DE SANGRE 100

CREACION GENIAL de LOLA MEMBRIVES

RECITACION DE POESIAS POR SU AUTOR FEDERICO GARCIA LORCA

ABOVE Reading the script for *Doña Rosita the Spinster* to Margarita Xirgu's company, Barcelona, October 1935.

LEFT With Margarita Xirgu and Cipriano Rivas Cherif, Barcelona, 1935.

Poster by José Caballero and Juan Antonio Morales, 1934.

ABOVE Montevideo, 1934.

RIGHT Severed hands, *c.* 1935–36.
In "The Martyrdom of St. Eulalia" (1928), Lorca
described St. Eulalia's "severed hands, / able still to
join / in sweet, decapitated prayer." The motif of
severed hands appears repeatedly in his poems
and drawings.

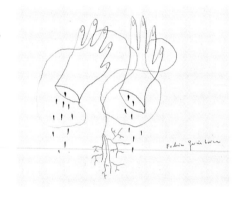

BELOW "I'm always being taken or brought
somewhere so that I have no time for anything,"
Lorca told his parents shortly after reaching
Buenos Aires in 1933.

RIGHT Lorca, at the reopening of *Blood Wedding* in Buenos Aires, September 1933. On the back of the photograph he wrote that he disliked this picture "because I was extremely nervous from so much kissing and handshaking. . . . That's why I've got a false smile here, because what I really wanted was to be left alone."

BELOW In Buenos Aires, Lorca inscribed copies of his books for friends. He liked to play with the letters in his name and to embellish his signature with drawings.

ABOVE Sailor from the *Moreno*, 1934. "We're all like the sailor", Lorca once said. ". . . we hear only our distances."

LEFT Pablo Neruda (*standing, far left*), with Lorca and friends, at a party in Buenos Aires, 1934.

GONZALO MENÉNDEZ PIDAL

A Rafael Rrrrrrrr.

PRIMER ROMANCERO GITANO
(1924-1927)

Federico

LEFT With friends at a Madrid fair,
1936. Lorca's hand touches Rafael
Rodríguez Rapún's forehead.

ABOVE Dedication to Rafael
Rodriguez Rapún, 1930s. Lorca
called Rapún "three Rs," a reference
to his initials.

BELOW Lorca, at a banquet given in
his honor by Catalan writers and
artists, Barcelona, December 1935.
A friend observed that when Lorca
talked, he moved his hands as if
playing an accordion.

ABOVE Lorca at a dinner honoring
Argentine journalists, Madrid, 1936.
To his right is Rafael Alberti's wife,
María Teresa León; to his left is the
poet Vicente Aleixandre. That spring,
Lorca was "richer than ever with life
and with projects," said a friend.

RIGHT In his parents' home in
Granada, 1935. "I am primarily a
musician," Lorca told a reporter
in 1933.

Madrid, c. 1935:
(standing, left to right)
Rafael Alberti, Luis
Buñuel, Lorca; (seated,
left to right) Eduardo
Ugarte, Pepe Díaz,
María Teresa León, and
Miguel González.

With Rafael Rodríguez Rapún, Madrid, 1935. As one friend remembered, for Lorca "Rapún wa
the passion."

angels." The actress recalled that Lorca intended for the play's Author to die on the streets in the midst of the revolution. The fictive transformation the Author undergoes during the course of the play—from a man once exclusively interested in art to an activist who fights for the workers—points to the real-life challenges Lorca and the members of his generation faced as a result of the Asturian revolt.

The Dream of Life is both poetic and confrontational, fantastic and real. It is closest in style and content to *The Audience*, a work that likewise explores the contradictions between truth and fiction, actor and audience, and that takes as its fundamental premise the production of a play by Shakespeare. In *The Audience*, the play-within-a-play is *Romeo and Juliet*, a work Lorca once confessed he wished he had written. In *The Dream of Life* it is *A Midsummer Night's Dream*, a text incidental to *The Audience* and critical to Lorca's first produced play, *The Butterfly's Evil Spell*. As a teenager Lorca had been so struck by Shakespeare's comedy that he said it "poisoned" his soul, for it taught him to view love as fickle, if not cruel. He admired Shakespeare's phantasmagoric plot, and in his own effort to create a full-length, theatrical "dream" he so adroitly mixed the improbable with the quotidian that the two are indistinguishable.

His use of Shakespeare's comedy of love to underpin a play in which revolution erupts and workers are murdered underscores Lorca's growing conviction that the sexual is ultimately political. The Author in *The Dream of Life* describes Shakespeare's play as a "somber plot" whose various parts together "demonstrate that love, whatever kind of love it might be, is an accident and doesn't depend on us at all." This, he acknowledges, is a "terrible" but useful truth, one vital to a society rent by hatred and intolerance. "A destructive truth can lead to suicide," he advises. "What the world needs now more than ever are comforting truths, truths that are constructive."

By the start of 1936, the Second Spanish Republic was in the midst of its twenty-sixth governmental crisis. Internal squabbling and two massive financial scandals had discredited the administration of Prime Minister Alejandro Lerroux, forcing Lerroux from office in the fall of 1935. Gil Robles, leader of CEDA, had prepared to assume power. But President Niceto Alcalá Zamora refused to sanction the move, in part to avoid alienating the Left and in part because he rightly suspected Gil Robles of having helped foment government instability in order to usurp control of the country. To settle the crisis Zamora dissolved the Spanish parliament in early January 1936 and called for national elections to take place the following month. Chastened by their defeat three years earlier in the last national elections, and newly invigorated by a series of mass, pro-Left meetings conducted by Manuel Azaña in the latter half of 1935, the country's left-wing parties briefly, and with difficulty, set aside their differences to forge a Popular Front. Despite right-wing propaganda to the contrary, the Spanish Popular Front was not a creation of the Comintern but a socialist-republican coalition harking back to the first days of the Republic. Its existence nonetheless convinced members of the extreme Right that a Moscow-based Spanish revolution was imminent. Within days of the Front's establishment, the right-wing leader Calvo Sotelo, head of Spain's Monarchist Party, called for military force to combat the "red hordes of communism" threatening the nation. Sotelo warned that if Spaniards did not elect a conservative government in the upcoming elections, a "Red Flag" would fly over Spain.

On several occasions Lorca had lent his support to Russian and communist causes. Together with a hundred or so others, his name appeared on a 1933 registry of the "Association of Friends of the Soviet Union," a Madrid-based organization. Although leery of endorsing all facets of the Russian Revolution, and unwilling to join the Communist Party, he had from time to time expressed his admiration for Soviet literature, art, and film; he especially liked *The Battleship Potemkin*, with its wealth of "revolutionary feelings" and impressive "armies" of workers. In late 1935 he admitted that he was "eager to know Russia personally."

He was not alone. Most of his friends—writers, artists, actors, students in La Barraca—were caught up in the pro-communist, antifascist dialectic of the moment, and openly took sides in the struggle. On Sunday, February 9, 1936, one week before the national elections, Lorca joined fellow writers, trade unionists, and members of the working class at a banquet to honor the communist poet Rafael Alberti and his wife, María Teresa León. The couple had left Spain in 1934 to visit Russia, but after learning in February 1935 that their apartment in Madrid had been searched—in all likelihood by Gil Robles's right-wing adherents—they had postponed their return until late 1935, shortly after the collapse of Lerroux's coalition government and Gil Robles's consequent loss of authority.

At the banquet, Lorca read a manifesto in support of the Popular Front and the Republic; the document was subsequently published, with some three hundred signatories, under the title "Intellectuals with the Popular Front." *Mundo Obrero*, the official newspaper of the Spanish Communist Party, mentioned Lorca's reading in its account of the Alberti-León banquet. The mainstream press also noted Lorca's presence at the event, together with other prominent liberal writers and the outspoken Communist Dolores Ibarrurí. After the banquet, Lorca posed for a photograph with Alberti, León, and the filmmaker Luis Buñuel, who now lived in Madrid with his wife and child. Buñuel and Lorca had reconciled their differences in the early 1930s, and for some time had been comfortable, if not close, friends. The four stood together in the cold, arms and hands interlocked, smiling at the camera, their faces bright with optimism.

Five days later—two days before the elections—Lorca took part in a second politically charged tribute, this one in honor of the Galician playwright Ramón del Valle-Inclán, who had died in early January, at the age of sixty-nine, after a long illness. An inveterate liberal and vocal proponent of the Republic, Valle-Inclán had at one point waged an unsuccessful campaign for election to parliament. On his deathbed he had voiced his hope for a left-wing victory in the February elections. His posthumous homage was deliberately timed to coincide with those elections. Lorca read poems by Rubén Darío at the tribute. In their coverage of the event both *Mundo Obrero* and *El Socialista* noted Lorca's participation.

On Sunday, February 16, election day, Lorca, his parents, his friend José Fernández-Montesinos, and the Argentine journalist Pablo Suero posed for a portrait as they sat inside the family apartment, at a table set for lunch. At thirty-seven, Lorca's face resembled his father's: round and thick, with heavy jowls and vibrant eyes. He wore his black hair plastered against his head. Don Federico himself had aged markedly. Then seventy-six, his hair and mustache were completely white; the skin on his face hung in loose folds. He stared at the camera with apparent exhaustion. Beside him, his sixty-five-year-old wife looked as she always had, serene and shy. Vicenta Lorca's gray hair rose in waves from her plump, finely featured face; a hint of melancholy filled her eyes. A day earlier she had told Suero, "If we don't win [the elections], then we can say goodbye to Spain! . . . They'll throw us out—that is, if they don't kill us!"

On election day voters throughout Spain remained calm, except in Granada province, where scattered violence and death threats prevented some citizens from voting. Elsewhere, tens of thousands of Assault and Civil Guards ensured the safety of the country's polling sites. By the end of the day, the left-wing Popular Front had won both the popular vote and a majority of seats in parliament. But their victory was fragile. Had the right-wing National Front merged with the Center, the two parties combined would have possessed a slight numerical majority. As the election results became known, jubilant crowds at first poured into the streets of Madrid, sowing panic among right-wing circles. Later the city fell unaccustomedly silent. Under pressure from conservative factions, the government issued a State of Alarm. Dance halls and nightclubs closed their doors. The usually hectic Puerta del Sol sat empty. There was little sign of the young men and women who days earlier had surged through the capital, sporting red armbands and leftist slogans.

The conservative press wasted no time in denouncing the vote. *ABC* declared the newly re-elected Republic "essentially revolutionary" and noted the radical bias of its constituents. On February 17, the day after the elections, rumors of a possible military coup spread through Madrid. Army generals Manuel Goded, Angel Rodríguez del Barrio, and Francisco Franco were in actuality then conspiring to overthrow the new government; only their suspicion that the army was not yet ready for a coup prevented them from taking action.

On February 19, Manuel Azaña assumed power as the new prime minister of Spain. Azaña maintained an official State of Alarm throughout the country, with strict press censorship. He signed a general amnesty for all political prisoners, an act intended primarily to liberate Republicans jailed as a result of the Asturian rising. On February 21, Azaña's new minister of war, General Carlos Masquelet, issued a series of military postings. These included orders that Francisco Franco be removed from his government post as Chief of the General Staff and sent to Las Palmas to serve as Commandant General of the Canary Islands. Franco viewed the posting as "banishment," and his resentment of the Republic blossomed into aggression. In the Canaries, where he was kept under government surveillance, Franco talked openly of his admiration for Mussolini, and resumed plotting a military coup.

In the weeks immediately following the elections, members of the Left staged parades in Madrid and other large cities. In Granada, where the election results and charges of electoral corruption had split the public into opposing factions, massive demonstrations—some of them violent—by both right- and left-wing groups took place. Proponents of the radical Left set fire to Catholic and right-wing institutions. In early March, the liberal *Defensor de Granada* called for the February elections to be annulled. On March 9, members of the Falange attacked Granada; they disrupted classes in the university medical school, skirmished with antifascist protesters, and fired on a crowd of workers. Several citizens were wounded. The local trade union retaliated by calling a general strike. Citizens burned the Falange headquarters, the offices of the conservative daily *Ideal*, the headquarters of the local Catholic party, a theater, and two cafés. Three weeks later the Spanish Cortes annulled the Granada elections.

Throughout the country, tensions deepened. The brittle left-wing coalition began to splinter, while right-wing groups banded together, fueled by their mutual dread of a communist revolution. Unwilling to make even a show of backing a government in which they no longer believed, mainstream conservative leaders looked for the first time with interest to José Antonio Primo de Rivera's extreme-right Falange party. Droves of young Catholics who had supported Gil Robles the previous year shifted their allegiance to the Falange, with its promise of a swift and violent resolution to the current crisis. In Madrid, poet Pedro Salinas noted that Spain was becoming "more poisoned and more hate-filled every day."

As always, Lorca sided with the Left. He backed Manuel Azaña, whom he had known for years, and he subscribed to traditionally liberal views on most issues. One week after the elections he joined several dozen writers and intellectuals in declaring their support for a manifesto by the Universal Union for Peace, calling for a resolution of the Italian-Ethiopian conflict, a revitalization of the Geneva peace efforts, and an end to violence in general. Azaña was one of the manifesto's principal signatories.

"As an observer of life," Lorca believed, "the artist cannot remain insensitive to the social question." Accordingly, he lent his celebrity and his work to causes he deemed worthy. He read excerpts from his *Gypsy Ballads* at a benefit for the Children's Aid Association, a library for poor children that he had helped to found in Madrid; at the benefit he allowed a copy of his book to be auctioned on behalf of the association. He also read his ballads at a left-wing gathering in support of Brazilian antifascists; he signed documents protesting against repression in Latin America and Portugal; and he signed a public letter protesting the arrest, in January, of Spanish poet Miguel Hernández, who was accused of conspiracy against the government.

Pedro Salinas worried that Lorca was trying to emulate Rafael Alberti, and that by doing so he risked falling into "the social trap" and compromising his art. Salinas criticized Lorca's unfinished play *The Dream of Life* as a "scorchingly communist drama." But Lorca was no Alberti, and his play, although set in the midst of a political revolution and sensitive to the social ramifications of political strife, was primarily concerned with more basic aspects of the human condition, and with aesthetic questions that had perplexed Lorca throughout his career: the nature of reality and artifice, the role of dreams, the artist's responsibility to society. The Asturian revolution weighed heavily on Lorca, but he was not so naive as to think he could redress such problems through literature. He did not write activist poems or theater, as Alberti did. He did not subscribe to dogma. He refused to join a political party, and he was selective in signing petitions.

In 1935 he had laughingly told Rafael Martínez Nadal that he was not politi-

cal, but rather "an anarchist-communist-libertarian, a pagan-Catholic, a tradi-
tionalist and monarchist who supports Don Duarte of Portugal." His chief
concern was human rights, not political rhetoric. He believed in the fundamental purity of art, and in his own free will. He continued to fraternize with
right-wing acquaintances, and was rumored to have spoken to José Antonio
Primo de Rivera more than once that year. When his friend Pura Ucelay asked
him where he stood politically, Lorca answered, "Look, I greet some people
like this"—he raised his hand in a Nazi salute—"and others like this"—he
raised a clenched communist fist. "But to my friends, *this*," he cried, and held
out his hand for Ucelay to shake.

By 1936, though, even Lorca was forced to acknowledge that his work had
political implications. In January a lieutenant colonel of the Civil Guard in
Tarragona, near Barcelona, filed an official complaint against his "Ballad of the
Spanish Civil Guard." Lorca received a court citation. According to an account
he later gave the press, he spoke to the prosecuting attorney and explained to
him "in minute detail what the purpose of my ballad was, my concept of the
Civil Guard, of poetry, of images, of surrealism, of literature, and of I don't
know how many other things." The government dropped the charges. The attorney general of the Republic said afterward that in reviewing the case he had
been reminded of the sixteenth-century Spanish judge who sent Cervantes to
jail.

In both action and words, Lorca continued to demand justice for people of all
races and origins. During a hasty trip to San Sebastián in early March to give
his lecture-recital on *Gypsy Ballads*, the same talk he had delivered in
Barcelona the previous fall, he pointedly attacked the rich, proclaiming the
true Gypsy "incapable of wrong, like many people who are dying of hunger
right now because they won't sell their age-old voice to the men who possess
nothing but money, which is such a puny thing." The packed auditorium gave
Lorca a lengthy ovation.

In April he attended a concert in Madrid by the African-American singer
Marian Anderson and spoke at a tribute to the poet Luis Cernuda on the occa-
sion of the publication of Cernuda's new book, *Reality and Desire*. Most of the
Generation of '27 were present. The celebration lasted until dawn. Months ear-
lier Lorca had praised the spirit of friendship that marked his generation:
"Envy and petty grievances are unheard of, and one poet will defend another."
At least two writers who attended Cernuda's publication party, Concha Mén-
dez and the Valencian Juan Gil-Albert, found the gathering touched with a

sense of doom. Most of the participants were silent, tranquil, "as if in a dream," Méndez recalled. By the end of the evening even Cernuda, who had tucked a sprightly white carnation into the lapel of his gray suit, seemed unwilling or unable to talk. The gathering dissolved into small groups, and these eventually vanished into the early-morning air. Later that night Méndez dreamt that someone had stabbed Lorca to death.

The violence in Madrid and elsewhere in Spain continued to escalate. The country was in a state of undeclared war. In March, members of the Falange had begun ostentatiously riding through the capital in squads of motorcars, wielding machine guns. As they drove through working-class neighborhoods they fired sporadically at alleged "Reds." On March 13, they tried to murder a socialist member of parliament. The congressman survived, but his bodyguard died. A day later Prime Minister Azaña outlawed the Falange and jailed much of its leadership, including José Antonio Primo de Rivera. But the violence persisted. Both extreme-right and extreme-left groups roamed Madrid, firing at random targets. José Ortega y Gasset's brother escaped a Falangist bomb attack on his home in early April. Days later a Republican judge was shot dead, apparently in retribution for having sentenced a member of the Falange to life in prison. The following week, April 13, a member of the Civil Guard was shot and killed during a military parade in Madrid. At his funeral two days later, right-wing extremists retaliated by killing twelve people. In early May, Falangists murdered a prominent Republican official.

At *tertulias* in his home, the Chilean diplomat Carlos Morla Lynch observed a deepening sense of fear and weariness. Guests rarely talked of anything but politics. Lorca turned up from time to time, but his visits were less frequent, and when he came, he tended to read from his New York poems, which he hoped to publish soon. Dark lines rimmed his eyes and underscored his jowls. In photographs he looked subdued, even grim. But according to poet and critic Guillermo de Torre, who ran into him that spring, Lorca remained buoyant, upbeat, "richer than ever with life and with projects." His *Gypsy Ballads* were about to go into a seventh edition; the print version of *Blood Wedding* had sold out within a matter of months; *The Divan at Tamarit* was scheduled for imminent publication. The poet and publisher José Bergamín planned to issue a multivolume edition of Lorca's complete works for the theater, as well as *Poet in New York*. There was talk of a French production of *The Shoemaker's Prodigious Wife*, and Lorca's name had been sent to Manuel Azaña as a possible candidate to head a National Theater of Spain.

Lorca used his renown to further the cause of human rights. In a long interview in the Madrid daily *La Voz* in early April, he noted that his latest play, *The*

Dream of Life, addressed a pervasive "religious and socioeconomic problem." Invoking strains of communist rhetoric he launched into a brief diatribe against the inequities of the world economy:

> I see it clearly. Two men are walking along a riverbank. One is rich, the other poor. One has a full belly, the other pollutes the air with his yawns. The rich man says, "Oh, what a pretty boat I see on the water! Look, look sir, at the iris flowering on the shore." And the poor man grumbles, "I'm hungry, I don't see anything. I'm hungry, very hungry." The day hunger disappears the world will see the greatest spiritual explosion humanity has ever known. Men will never ever be able to imagine the happiness that will erupt on the day of the Great Revolution.

As if aware that he had suddenly gone too far, Lorca interrupted himself. "I'm speaking to you like a pure socialist, aren't I?" But although he meant the statement as a disclaimer, it did little to blunt the radical nature of his remarks, which received widespread publicity. In addition to *La Voz,* three major Spanish dailies published excerpts from the interview.

Lorca edged ever closer to active political engagement. But true to his contradictory nature, he remained on the periphery of his country's political life, an observer sometimes roused to the level of a participant. During the city's May Day celebrations, he was spotted in Madrid, waving a red tie and shouting his support for the working classes. Crowds of socialist and communist youths paraded through the capital that day, carrying portraits of Lenin and Stalin, and singing the "Internationale." In a short piece for the May 1 edition of the Communist paper *¡Ayuda!,* Lorca expressed his "great affection" for the workers of Spain and praised their quest "for a more just, more humane society." A caption in *¡Ayuda!* described Lorca as "always on the side of anything that represents social justice." Later in the month he attended a massive banquet honoring three antifascist French writers who were visiting Spain. He declined to speak at the event, however. "I've come here as a friend of my friends, not to make speeches on topics that don't pertain to me," he said.

In early April, La Barraca traveled to Barcelona. Lorca did not go with them. During the past year he had grown increasingly more distant from the company, until his absence had at last been made "definitive" in late 1935, and a film director, Antonio Román, had been appointed to replace him. In its four years under Lorca's leadership, La Barraca had presented nearly two hundred free performances of classic Spanish plays in towns, villages, and cities throughout the country. It grieved Lorca to part from the troupe. He asked the

Barcelona paper *La Noche* to announce that, as he was no longer affiliated with the company, he could not be held accountable for the quality of its performances in Barcelona that April.

He plunged into his own theater work. Under the auspices of the Anfistora Club, Pura Ucelay wanted to premiere his so-called "legend of time," *Once Five Years Pass*, in Madrid in July 1936. By coincidence, Lorca had completed the script almost five years earlier to the day, on August 19, 1931. Although he considered the play one of his "unproduceable" texts, along with *The Audience* and *The Dream of Life*, he consented to let Ucelay stage the work, and he took an active role in rehearsals. He told the amateur cast not to stress the melancholy quality of their lines, but instead to give them more life, "more ardor." He sat in the rehearsal hall, his script on his knees, deleting lines that didn't work. When he realized the protagonist's death at the end of the play was lasting longer than it should, he rapidly crossed out the last eight lines of the script. He joked and bantered with actors as he worked, and generally enjoyed himself. But in June he abruptly canceled the production and told Ucelay he preferred to wait until fall to premiere his theatrical legend of time. He gave vague reasons for his decision: a trip to Granada, his planned visit to North and South America. Some thought he feared premiering the potentially controversial work in such politically troubled times.

But he also knew that audiences were not ready for the play. *Once Five Years Pass* belonged to what Lorca described as his "impossible theater," a term he had used publicly for the first time in 1933. By "impossible" he meant plays that were deliberately experimental and avant-garde, plays not likely to be embraced by the public, plays whose unorthodox nature and technical difficulties made them inherently "unperformable." He regarded his "impossible theater"—*Once Five Years Pass, The Audience, The Dream of Life*—as his real work, his "true aim. In order to demonstrate a personality and earn respect I've written other things," he conceded in the midst of rehearsals for *Once Five Years Pass*. By postponing the play, he explained to Ucelay, he was merely waiting for a more propitious time. When he had become a genuinely popular playwright, when his works were presented "simultaneously in three Madrid theaters," as he hoped would happen in the fall of 1936, "then audiences will stick by me no matter what I do, and we can produce unproduceable works."

In the meantime he had started another play, a more commercially viable tragedy in the same vein as *Blood Wedding* and *Yerma*. In its May 29 "Rumors" section, the *Heraldo de Madrid* described Lorca's new work as a "drama of Andalusian sexuality," and noted that the playwright was on the verge of completing the script. He carried the text with him in his pocket throughout the spring and read it to friends as often as two or three times a day. When he finished a scene he sometimes rushed across the street from his family's apartment to his friend Adolfo Salazar's home, crying, "Not one drop of poetry! Reality! Pure realism!" When he completed a first draft he told Salazar that he was finally beginning his "true career as a dramatic poet."

He called the play *The House of Bernarda Alba*, with the subtitle "Drama of Women in the Villages of Spain." He noted that the work should resemble "a photographic document." In an effort to simulate the effect of photography he set the play in black and white, with the exception of one costume, a green dress worn briefly, and to great theatrical effect, in the third act. He had been interested in photography for more than a decade; in the 1920s he had attempted a short series of "photographic plays" in which characters are frozen in time, as if by a camera's lens. In *The House of Bernarda Alba* he called for subtle gradations of hue—the action begins in an "extremely white room," then moves to a "white room" and finally to the "four slightly bluish white walls" of an interior patio—gradations that create a quasi-cinematic effect. From the outset of his career, Lorca had striven to think of literature in terms of other media (engravings, ballads, legends, photography), and to write in one genre in terms of another, a way of challenging as well as reshaping the experience of poetry and theater. He found that the restrictions of one genre allowed for greater freedom in others. Because he was himself so accomplished an artist in a variety of disciplines, he was able to transcend aesthetic boundaries with credibility.

He hoped to produce *The House of Bernarda Alba* in the fall of 1936, with Margarita Xirgu in the title role. He told Carlos Morla Lynch that he had based the drama on real-life characters and incidents in a village where he had lived as a child. The village was Asquerosa; his principal source of inspiration was a woman who had lived next door to his cousins, a widow whom he said was named "Doña Bernarda" and who ruled tyrannically over her five unmarried daughters. Lorca regarded her as a "mute and cold hell." As a boy, he claimed, he had often seen Bernarda's daughters pass through the village "like shadows, always silent and always dressed in black." He had never spoken to the girls, but because his cousins shared a well with the family, he had sometimes spied on them.

As always, he was embroidering reality. The widow's actual name was Frasquita—not Bernarda—Alba, and in addition to her five daughters she had one son. The family lived across the street from the church, next door to Lorca's first cousins, with whom they did share a well. In 1907 Lorca, his brother, Paco, and sister Concha had been confirmed in the village church together with Frasquita Alba's six offspring and nearly two hundred other village children. Frasquita herself had died in 1924, but Lorca had no qualms about using her surname, Alba ("dawn"), in his play, despite pleas from his mother that he "change her last name, too, change it!" He borrowed additional village names, including those of three of Frasquita's daughters, for most of the remaining characters in his all-female cast, and he fleshed out his "drama of women" with the homely details of everyday village life.

Although he finished a draft of *The House of Bernarda Alba* on June 19, 1936, he told a friend that he intended to rewrite, or at least modify, the second and third acts. By way of defending his script, he repeated what he had said the previous fall: "The only topics that interest me for the theater are social and sexual ones." *The House of Bernarda Alba* addresses both. Set in an arid Spanish village at the height of summer, the drama takes place entirely inside the house of Bernarda Alba, whose second husband has just been buried as the play begins. Bernarda's first—and last—word onstage is "Silence!" A despot enslaved by the cruel conventions and petty gossip of village life, she informs her five unmarried daughters that for the next eight years they will remain in mourning for their father, dressed in black, confined to their home like nuns in a cloister. "In the meantime, you can begin embroidering your trousseaux," she instructs.

Her daughters Martirio and Adela both pine after a village bachelor, Pepe el Romano, who though never seen onstage fills the claustrophobic air of Bernarda's house with his implicit masculine presence. By village tradition, Pepe is reduced to seeking the hand of Bernarda's oldest daughter, Angustias, an ungainly spinster of thirty-nine who has inherited her late father's wealth. As they embroider sheets for her trousseau, her sisters gossip about Angustias and discuss the charms of her twenty-five-year-old fiancé. In time it becomes clear that Adela has had secret nighttime liaisons with Pepe—has in fact made love to him. When word arrives, in act 2, that a village girl who has had an illegitimate child is about to be stoned by her neighbors, it is Adela who cries for the young woman's life to be spared, while Bernarda declares, "Yes, let them bring olive sticks and hoe handles, let them all come and kill her."

In the play's final act Adela decides to flee her mother's prison and run off with Pepe. "With the whole village against me, burning me with their fiery fingers, persecuted by people who say they are decent, and in front of all of them I'll put on the crown of thorns worn by every mistress of a married man." Her escape is short-lived. Her sister Martirio alerts Bernarda to Adela's plans; Bernarda goes off with a shotgun to kill Pepe. Thinking her lover dead, Adela hangs herself. Bernarda returns, having failed to murder Pepe ("It was my fault.

A woman can't aim"), and learns of her daughter's suicide. She briefly loses control—her only lapse in the drama—then quickly regains her composure and orders Adela's body cut down from the rafters and carried to her room and dressed "as if she were a maiden." Propriety must reign; appearances are to be preserved. "I want no weeping," Bernarda tells her four remaining daughters. "Death must be looked at face-to-face. Silence! (*To one daughter.*) Be quiet, I said! (*To another daughter.*) Tears, when you're alone. We will all drown ourselves in a sea of mourning! She, the youngest daughter of Bernarda Alba, has died a virgin. Do you hear me? Silence, silence I said. Silence!"

Despite Lorca's claims to have achieved a state of "pure realism" with *The House of Bernarda Alba* ("Not one drop of poetry!"), the play is in fact a profoundly poetic instance of stylized realism. "I've eliminated a lot of things in this tragedy, a lot of easy songs, a lot of little ballads and lyrics," Lorca told a group of friends who attended a private reading of the script that spring. "I want my theatrical work to have severity and simplicity." Throughout his twenty years as a playwright he had gradually learned to strip his work of lyrical excess until at last, with *The House of Bernarda Alba*, he created a play steeped in poetic language and imagery but grounded in physical and emotional fact. Theater, he said, "is poetry that rises from the page and becomes human . . . Theater demands that the characters who appear onstage wear costumes of poetry and at the same time that their bones and blood be visible."

Ostensibly less radical than Lorca's other plays, *The House of Bernarda Alba* takes place indoors, is written in prose, and employs such timeworn theatrical conventions as household servants and offstage deaths. But within its apparent orthodoxy it is revolutionary. Silence punctuates the dialogue in highly developed, rhythmic ways; poetry infuses the prose; characters move and speak with the exaggerated gestures of the puppet theater. The story is conceived on an epic scale. Lorca calls for "two hundred women" dressed in black to appear onstage in the opening scene; he wanted the rafters of Bernarda's ceiling to be completely covered with hanging melons. The paintings on Bernarda's walls show legendary kings and nymphs. Bernarda's mother, the Biblically named María Josefa, a madwoman consumed by erotic desire and obsessed with children, periodically escapes from her locked offstage room to interrupt and comment on the action with the clairvoyance of a Tieresias or a Fool. Lorca modeled María Josefa on a woman he had known in his youth, the deranged grandmother of distant relatives.

Although he had long been appalled by the brutality of female existence in rural Spain, no play of Lorca's more directly depicts the austerity and sorrow of women's lives in the south than *The House of Bernarda Alba*. "In church, women should look at no man but the priest, and at him only because he's wearing skirts," Bernarda reminds her daughters. In Bernarda's world, a woman's lot is marriage, followed by confinement inside the home. "To be born a woman is the worst punishment," says her daughter Amelia. Within the constraints of Lorca's black-and-white "photograph" of village life, men assume a near-mythical—if stereotypical—status; faithless and sensual, they roam the outdoors, taming horses, plowing and cultivating the earth, marrying only because they want "a submissive dog to cook for them."

Lorca had been asked in 1934 why he wrote so many plays for and about women. He gave two answers—one poetic, one practical. "It's because women are more passionate, they rationalize less, they're more human, more vegetal," he said, adding, "Moreover, an author would find himself in great difficulties if his heroes were men. There's an appalling lack of actors, of good actors, you understand." He was right: the number of Spanish companies run by female actresses far outweighed those run by men. Lorca wondered nevertheless if it wasn't "too daring" to exclude males entirely from the cast of *The House of Bernarda Alba*, but it was a risk he was willing to take in order to heighten the play's impact. With *The House of Bernarda Alba* he aimed to jolt Spain as Ibsen had shocked northern Europe a half-century earlier with *A Doll's House*. As late as 1919, when Ibsen's drama played Granada, a critic wrote that Nora "cannot be a Spanish wife, nor Torvald a husband born in Spain." *The House of Bernarda Alba* suggests otherwise. It shows the ancient Spanish caste system and code of honor at their deadliest and, like *Yerma* and *Blood Wedding*, demonstrates that women are equally as passionate as men. It also reveals the fatal consequences of repression—social, sexual, and by implication political.

With *The House of Bernarda Alba*, Lorca completed the "trilogy of the Spanish land" he had begun in 1933 with *Blood Wedding* and continued in 1934 with *Yerma*. For some time he had claimed the last play in the trio would be *The Destruction of Sodom* (a play he sometimes referred to as *The Daughters of Lot*). But he settled on *The House of Bernarda Alba*, a work whose thematic similarity to its predecessors guaranteed some degree of critical and commercial parity. With Xirgu in the title role of Bernarda, Lorca was further assured of another theatrical triumph.

He tended to think of his plays in sequence. The creation of one work often impelled him toward another; later that summer he would begin writing a sequel to *Doña Rosita the Spinster*. He talked as well of creating a Biblical trilogy based on Old Testament figures; among those under consideration were Samson and Delilah, Judith, David, Thamar and Amnon, and Cain and Abel. According to Rafael Martínez Nadal, Lorca began making serious plans to write an antiwar drama about Cain and Abel during the late spring and early summer of 1936. He intended the drama as a parable.

By June, members of the Communist, Socialist, and Anarchist parties were openly promoting a left-wing revolution in Spain. Through its incendiary coverage of leftist rallies and demonstrations, the right-wing press fanned middle-class fears of a communist state, and convinced many that only a military coup could save Spain. Army conspirators moved rapidly forward with their plans to overthrow the government. Rumors of an attempt to establish a dictatorship swept through Madrid. Warned of a probable military plot, the Republican government failed to act decisively, and the army conspiracy flourished.

With the onset of warm weather, the violence on the city's streets worsened. By mid-June, members of parliament were frankly asking, "Will it be war?" Gil Robles argued that Spaniards were witnessing the "funeral service of democracy." His fellow conservative Calvo Sotelo, head of the Monarchist Party, decreed that the Spanish army must be prepared to rise "against anarchy—if that should be necessary."

On June 5 Lorca turned thirty-eight. He had never particularly wanted to grow old. He continued to look back with rapture on his childhood. "My laughter today," he told a journalist in 1935, "is the same laughter I had yesterday, the laughter of childhood, of the countryside, my rustic laughter, which I will always, always defend, until the day I die." He joked that he was afraid to publish his New York poems, for doing so would make him old, and he disliked old age. At nineteen he had pondered the "withered eyes of the old / treasures of life that evaporate / enamel cavities that recapitulate / distant laments." At thirty-six he had confessed,

> At a gathering of elderly men I wouldn't be able to say one word. Those squinty, tearful gray eyes, those sneering lips, those paternal smiles terrify me, and their affection is as undesirable as a rope pulling us toward an abyss. That's what old people are—the rope, the ligature between youth and the abyss of death.

When it came to his own life, he said he hoped to "grow old" in the Andalusian seaport of Cádiz. He envisioned himself at eighty, "with a white beard, supported by a cane, enormously popular and loved by the people of Cádiz . . . a Spanish Walt Whitman."

Five days after his birthday, on June 10, *El Sol* published a long and expansive conversation between Lorca and the celebrated Spanish cartoonist Luis

Bagaría, known for his irreverent caricatures of the country's leading political and cultural figures. The two men touched on a variety of topics, from poetry to politics, from bullfighting to *cante jondo*. Lorca restated his belief that under the present circumstances the artist must fight for social justice, "must set aside his bouquet of white lilies and sink to his waist in the mud to help those who are looking for lilies." He denounced nationalism ("I am a brother to everyone, and I loathe the man who sacrifices himself for an abstract nationalist ideal") and rashly condemned the Catholic reconquest of Arab Granada in 1492 as

> a terrible moment, even though they say just the opposite in the schools. An admirable civilization was lost, and a poetry, astronomy, architecture, and delicacy unique in the world, in order to give way to a poor, cowardly, narrow-minded city inhabited at present by the worst bourgeoisie in Spain.

That his remarks were bound to offend conservative Granadans did not seem to bother Lorca. He did request, however, that an exchange about communism and fascism be deleted from the interview before its publication. "It strikes me as imprudent at this precise moment," he said, "and besides, it's already been answered."

Turning to issues of a more metaphysical bent—and to a subject that Lorca had earlier in the year described as a source of "constant anguish" to him—he and Bagaría debated whether the "indecipherable mystery" of poetic creation led one toward the afterlife or away from it. "Neither the poet nor anyone possesses the secret to the world," Lorca suggested. "Being good," he added, "together with the ass and the philosopher," he hoped someday to have the "agreeable surprise" of finding himself in the great beyond. In the meantime, the pressures and sorrows of corporeal existence kept him grounded on earth. He asked Bagaría where the cartoonist derived his obvious "thirst for the great beyond. Do you really want to outlive yourself? Don't you think that everything has already been decided, and that with or without faith, man can do nothing?"

"You're right, unfortunately you're right," Bagaría said.

> At heart I'm a nonbeliever hungry to believe. It's so tragically sad to disappear forever. Health, the lips of women, the glass of good wine that made you forget the tragic truth; landscape, the light that made you forget the shadows! In the tragic end, I would only wish for one thing: that my body be buried in a garden, that at the very least my "great beyond" be a fruitful one.

Lorca did not respond to Bagaría's comments—or, if he did, his remarks were not published. With his next question he abruptly changed the subject.

"Would you mind telling me why every politician you caricature has the face of a frog?" he inquired.

"Because," said Bagaría, "most of them live in ponds."

Friends continued to urge Lorca to join the Communist Party. Lorca resisted. He did not want to support the party directly, he said. He turned down an invitation to attend a pro-Soviet tribute to the late Russian playwright and novelist Maxim Gorky on June 30, saying, "I don't want that. I'm a friend to all. The only thing I want is for everyone to be able to work and eat." He complained about the "abusive" treatment he received from those communist friends and acquaintances, among them Rafael Alberti, who persisted in trying to make him join their cause. To José Antonio Rubio Sacristán he remarked, "Those of us who have mothers like you and I do—how are we going to become communists?"

By late June he was still toying with the possibility of a trip to Mexico, where Margarita Xirgu was enjoying a triumphant tour. The dancer La Argentinita also happened to be on tour in Mexico, and she implored Lorca to visit. In April he had sent word to Xirgu that his departure was "imminent." He planned to sail first to New York, then travel by train to Mexico. "Five days on the train! Such joy!" he told friends. Evidently he purchased tickets for the journey. By July, though, he had decided to postpone the trip until after a summer visit with his family in Granada. He appears to have had a second reason for changing his mind. He wanted Rafael Rapún to travel with him. Xirgu had apparently made preliminary arrangements for the young man to do so, but Rapún's father refused to let him go before he had completed his university exams. Accordingly, Lorca delayed his trip. He informed friends and reporters that before going to Mexico he intended to complete *The House of Bernarda Alba*, so that Xirgu could premiere the play in the fall. As soon as he had finished the script, he would leave Spain.

The last weeks of June and first week of July brought strikes by trade union members, elevator attendants, waiters, even bullfighters. Political murders took place almost daily. On July 2 two Falangists sitting at a Madrid café were shot and killed by a gunman in a passing motorcar. Later that day, right-wing extremists sought revenge by murdering two presumed members of the Left.

Lorca grew more and more fearful. By July his parents had left Madrid for Granada; his sister Isabel was living at Madrid's Residencia de Señoritas, studying for a teaching degree in Spanish literature and language; his brother was stationed in Egypt as a member of the Spanish diplomatic corps. Left alone in his family's spacious, seventh-floor Madrid apartment, Lorca yielded to old fears and superstitions. He had always been afraid of everyday things—water, automobiles, traffic, street crossings. He often pleaded with taxi drivers to slow down, shouting, "We're going to crash!" Morbidly afraid of crossing city streets, he would latch on to a friend's arm and sometimes leap back to the curb in a panic after setting out into traffic. Earlier that spring, during rehearsals for *Once Five Years Pass*, he had thrown himself beneath a piano after hearing a car suddenly backfire on a street outside the theater.

But with the exception of a two-week period in Granada in 1919, when members of the Left and Right had clashed in bloody street demonstrations, he had never experienced the kind of violence that gripped Madrid in early July 1936. He became so petrified that he rarely went out except in the company of close friends, men like Rafael Martínez Nadal, Adolfo Salazar, Rapún, the artist José Caballero, Carlos Morla Lynch, Pablo Neruda. He and Neruda sometimes talked about politics. Both were upset by the situation in Spain, although Neruda was not then the political activist he would later become. "I'm a diplomat," he told Rafael Alberti. "I don't understand politics at all, and I'm not interested in it."

In late June Lorca accompanied a small group of friends to an outdoor fair; before a painted carnival backdrop they had their picture taken together. Lorca stood in the top row, grinning. With one hand he reached around to touch Rapún on the forehead. But such outings were increasingly rare. José Caballero visited Lorca one day and found him cowering inside his family's apartment with the blinds drawn. He confessed that he hated sleeping alone in the vacant flat. Martínez Nadal noticed that Lorca seemed more and more lost, hesitant, alone. Although he gave several readings of *The House of Bernarda Alba* to friends, and continued to work on his sonnets of dark love, he was distracted. On July 4 he signed a manifesto in protest against the government of Portuguese dictator Antonio de Oliveiro Salazar. On July 11, at a gathering in Pablo Neruda's home, he told a member of the Spanish parliament that he intended to join his parents as soon as possible in Granada, because he could no longer bear the anxiety of remaining in Madrid, waiting for "I don't know what." Besides, his saint's day was approaching on July 18, and he wanted to be with his family.

At approximately nine in the evening on Sunday, July 12, four Falangists murdered a leftist member of the Assault Guard in Madrid. The dead man's colleagues immediately set out to reap revenge by killing the two most prominent leaders of the right wing, Gil Robles and Calvo Sotelo. They were unable to locate Robles. At three the following morning they found Sotelo in his

Madrid apartment, kidnapped him, shot him twice in the head, and dumped his body in a cemetery on the outskirts of the city. His identity was not discovered until noon that day, Monday, July 13. Ordinary Spaniards were horrified. The murder proved that the Republican government could no longer control its own forces. Members of the right wing demanded vengeance. Wealthy citizens fled Madrid, and the roads to France and Portugal became clogged with refugees.

On Tuesday, July 14, Sotelo was buried in Madrid. As his casket was lowered into the ground, mourners raised their arms in a fascist salute. That same day, during funeral services for the slain member of the Assault Guard, Republican, Communist, and Socialist sympathizers lifted clenched fists into the air.

The moment he learned of Sotelo's death on July 13, Lorca resolved to leave Madrid at once. The killing terrified him. "What's going to happen?" he asked poet Juan Gil-Albert, whom he encountered in a café. Lorca was "extremely nervous," Gil-Albert remembered.

Lorca spent much of the day with Rafael Martínez Nadal. Over brandy they talked about the country's political situation. "Rafael," Lorca said, puffing agitatedly on a cigarette, "these fields are going to be strewn with corpses." "My mind is made up," he said moments later. "I'm going to Granada, come what may."

He dropped in on his friends Concha Méndez and Manolo Altolaguirre, and gave Altolaguirre a sheaf of poems to print. "I'm scared," he told the couple. Méndez thought he seemed pensive and sad. As he left, he said simply, "Goodbye, goodbye!" He did not disclose his travel plans. The pair learned later that evening that Lorca had gone to Granada. Others did not hear of his departure until days afterward. Rafael Rodríguez Rapún was out of town on July 13 and missed Lorca entirely.

With Nadal's help Lorca purchased a train ticket for the evening of July 13, then went home to his apartment and listlessly began tossing belongings into his suitcases. Nadal rearranged the bags and shut them. On their way to the train station that evening they stopped at the Residencia de Señoritas to say goodbye to Lorca's sister Isabel and to Fernando de los Ríos's daughter, Laura, who was also living at the Residencia that summer. Nadal waited in the taxi while Lorca hugged both women.

It was still light outside at 9 p.m., when Lorca rang the doorbell at the home of his old friend and former elementary-school teacher, Antonio Rodríguez Espinosa. Espinosa's maid answered the door. Lorca announced himself. "Don Homobono Picadillo."

"What's this rogue Don Homobono up to now?" Espinosa said as he came to the door. He was a bald, heavyset man in his late sixties.

"Nothing except to borrow two hundred pesetas from you, because I'm leaving at ten-thirty tonight for Granada," Lorca told him. "There's a thunderstorm brewing and I'm going home. I'll be safe from the lightning there."

CHAPTER 27

FOUNTAIN

1936

Lorca arrived home on the morning of July 14, relieved to be out of Madrid and surrounded by family. Bright red blooms flowered on the pomegranate bushes at his parents' Huerta de San Vicente. The scent of roses and jasmine laced the air. He talked exuberantly of his sister Isabel's achievements at school in the capital, where she had just passed her teaching exams, and caught up on his brother's news. Rumors of an attempt against the secretary of the Spanish delegation in Cairo, where Paco was stationed, had reached the family a few days earlier and sent his parents into a panic. A subsequent cable dispelled their fears. "The soul went back into our body," Vicenta Lorca said.

That afternoon, the Huerta's newly installed telephone rang for Lorca. It was his old friend Constantino Ruiz Carnero, editor of the *Defensor de Granada*, calling to welcome him home. The next day, July 15, the *Defensor* announced Lorca's arrival in a front-page article headlined "García Lorca in Granada." The piece noted that Lorca's stay in the city would be intentionally brief. On July 16, the conservative *Ideal* followed suit with a line in its Travelers section informing readers that "the poet Don Federico García Lorca is in Granada." *Ideal* had recently resumed publication after a four-month absence caused by damage to its offices during the political demonstrations that followed the February elections. The city's remaining daily, *El Noticiero Granadino*, announced Lorca's presence on July 17.

Lorca tried to settle into old routines, but Granada, like Madrid, though to a lesser extent, was in the grip of political upheaval, and the atmosphere was tense. Since the February elections, nearly six hundred *granadinos* had joined the local Falange party. Transit workers had gone on strike in late June. On July 1, its first day back in print, the unabashedly right-wing *Ideal* had declared that Granada was "in a state of unrest which stems from the total absence of public Power." The paper went on to note that the road ahead, toward "God and Spain," would entail sacrifices, "to be certain, but sacrifice has never been futile when carried out in defense of a just cause."

During his first days in Granada, Lorca read *The House of Bernarda Alba* to friends and endeavored to work on a new play, *The Dreams of My Cousin Aurelia*, which he hoped to complete that summer. He had begun the script earlier in the year and planned to premiere it in the fall, perhaps simultaneously with *The House of Bernarda Alba*. Both works take place in villages Lorca had lived in as a child—*The House of Bernarda Alba* in Asquerosa, *Aurelia* in his birthplace, Fuente Vaqueros. He described *Aurelia* as an "elegy of provincial life," a homage to the days when human existence still yielded to fantasy and dreams, before the advent of the machine age with its factories and engines.

Set in 1910, the year of Lorca's twelfth birthday, a time Lorca had long associated with a loss of innocence, both personal and cultural, *Aurelia* belonged to a sequence of so-called Granadan chronicles that began with *Doña Rosita the Spinster* and was to continue with a play called *The Nuns of Granada*. Lorca based the work's protagonist, Aurelia, on a cousin he had known and loved as a child, a young woman, Aurelia, much celebrated for her "mad and feverish dreams." As a boy, Lorca used to race to Aurelia's home in Fuente Vaqueros whenever thunder struck, to watch her collapse into a rocking chair in a faint and shriek, "Just look at me, I'm dying!" He relished the girl's impromptu theatrics.

Aurelia knew Lorca wanted to write a play about her in 1936 and was charmed by the idea. He completed a single act of the work, much of which is a long and comic exchange between Aurelia and three older women, who read and discuss a novel as if its characters were close personal friends. For Aurelia, fiction is a more compelling reality than everyday life. "Do you think one can live without reading novels and putting on plays?" she asks. "Especially in this village, which has a pack of men I've never once seen laugh." She scorns her suitors and dotes on her young cousin, Federico García Lorca, a small boy whose face is sprinkled with beauty spots. Fact and fantasy blur as Venetian gondoliers serenade Aurelia and the child during the town's Carnival festivities; the boy is entranced by the spectacle of masked figures in his village. He adores Aurelia. Nestled in her lap, he murmurs, "Cousin, how beautiful you are."

"You are handsomer."

"You have a waist and breasts and curly hair with flowers. I don't have any of that."

"But it's because I'm a woman."

"That must be why."

"You, in turn, have moles, like tiny little moons of tender moss. Why don't you give them to me?"

"Take them!"

Lorca had rendered the figure of the boy before—in his suites, in *Songs*, in the New York poems, in lectures, and most compellingly in his plays: *The Shoemaker's Prodigious Wife, Once Five Years Pass, Doña Rosita*, and now *Aurelia*, written on the cusp of middle age, in Lorca's thirty-ninth year, in the midst of cataclysmic social and political change. As always the child is an emblem of the purity and evanescence of youth, but in *Aurelia* he is more: a wistful self-portrait sketched with the same naive strokes that mark Lorca's drawings, a precocious reminder of the last generation born before the advent of modern war and technology.

Much as he longed to recover the past, Lorca had learned to live in the present, something his heroine Aurelia has failed to do. Had he completed the play, he intended to end *Aurelia* with what he described as a "therapeutic slap in the face to its protagonist," an incident so startling that it would transform *Aurelia's* dream-filled stage into "the four real and true walls of her house." Lorca did not finish his script, however. Instead of a "slap in the face," the play's sole surviving act ends with a bittersweet song about love, performed in unison by Aurelia, a band of gondoliers, and her young cousin Federico García Lorca:

> Lovestruck gondolier,
> with your matchless face,
> row, row without rest,
> for love will never come
> Never, never come
> never, never come
> Never, never will love come
> Love, love (Ah, what a beautiful thing!)
> yes yes yes, gondolier, no.
> Farewell, beautiful girl, farewell.
> Farewell, beautiful girl, farewell.

Toward nightfall on Friday, July 17, the day before Lorca's saint's day, word reached Granada that army officers in garrisons throughout Spanish Morocco had risen in arms against the Republican government. The news was sketchy and confusing. Radio Granada, in conjunction with Madrid's Union Radio, broadcast optimistic reports suggesting that the rising had failed. But households able to receive broadcasts from Tetuán, in Spanish Morocco, heard otherwise. According to the Tetuán Civil Guard, the rising was a triumph. The jailed leader of the Falange, José Antonio Prima de Rivera, issued a manifesto that night announcing his party's endorsement of the military rebellion.

By dawn the following day, July 18, Nationalist troops under the command of Generals Francisco Franco and Luis Orgaz had taken control of Las Palmas, the capital city of the Canary Islands, and declared martial law throughout the archipelago. At 5 a.m., Franco released a manifesto denouncing foreign influences in Spain and threatening "war without quarter against the exploiters of politics." This manifesto was immediately broadcast in both the Canary Islands and Spanish Morocco. For its part Radio Madrid announced later that morning that "absolutely no one" on the Spanish mainland had taken part in "this absurd plot," and that the rising would quickly be quelled. It was the Republican government's first official acknowledgment of the insurrection. Few listeners were reassured. Even as the broadcast was being read, army garrisons throughout Andalusia—in Seville, Cádiz, Jerez, Córdoba, and a number of smaller towns—were rising against the government. In Granada, left-wing sympathizers marched in the streets.

Friends and family members dropped by the Huerta de San Vicente all day long on the eighteenth to pay their respects to Lorca and his father on their saint's day. They brought liquors and sweets. But fewer people than usual showed up, and the atmosphere was strained. Lorca was clearly preoccupied. He talked to his cousin Vicente López about Sotelo's murder earlier in the week and admitted that he was worried. To Eduardo Valdivieso, he seemed uncharacteristically silent, as if unable to think. "He was frightened, he had doubts, uncertainties," Valdivieso saw. That morning, apparently in honor of his saint's day, the *Heraldo de Madrid* had published a striking black-and-white cartoon showing Lorca in profile, with an enormous black eyebrow, wearing little-boy shorts and a white shirt with a cravat. A tongue-in-cheek caption read:

García Lorca. "Precious child, Mama's pride." He's a delight. You'll see: he's only seven and a half years old. He hasn't had appendicitis, and they claim he has the brain of an adult . . . And yet, Federico García Lorca isn't badly educated, and he's now over thirty.

By dusk Seville had fallen to the Nationalists. General Gonzalo Queipo de Llano seized control of the city and captured its radio station. At eight o'clock he made the first in a series of inflammatory broadcasts. Listeners in Granada heard Queipo announce the "victorious advance" of the Nationalist movement throughout Spain. He told of military columns advancing on Córdoba, Madrid, and Granada, and warned that the "rabble" who resisted the rising would be shot "like dogs." Radio Madrid meanwhile declared that the Nationalist insurrection had been crushed across the nation, even in Seville, and that several rebel officers, including Generals Franco and Queipo de Llano, had been dismissed. It was the first indication from the government that anything unusual had occurred on the Spanish mainland. Strident patriotic music followed the Madrid broadcast, punctuated by exhortations to the "people of Spain" to "stay tuned in. Do not turn off your radios. Rumors are being circulated by traitors. Stay tuned in."

At 10 p.m. the Communist leader Dolores Ibarruri came on the air from Madrid and urged citizens to resist the rebellion. Women, she said, must prepare to fight the insurgents with knives and boiling oil. Ibarruri's closing words became the rallying cry of the Left: "They shall not pass! ¡No pasarán!" Later that night both the president of the Republic and the prime minister resigned and appointed party stalwart and master of compromise Diego Martínez Barrio in their stead, with the expectation that he would strike a deal with the rebels rather than fight them. Cries of "treason" and "traitor" greeted the news of his appointment. Workers poured into Madrid's Puerta del Sol, demanding "arms, arms, arms."

Granada's *Ideal* announced the following morning, July 19, that a state of war had been declared in Seville, but that the rest of Spain remained loyal to the government. According to the civil governor of the province, "absolute" order reigned in Granada, and security measures had been taken to prevent a military insurrection. Radio broadcasts from Madrid informed Spaniards that the country's new government had accepted "fascism's declaration of war upon the Spanish people" and would begin distributing arms to the working classes.

The Spanish Civil War had begun. Before the sun rose on the capital, trucks sped through Madrid carrying rifles to trade union headquarters. Civil governors throughout the country were ordered to do the same. But in many cities it was too late; a second wave of military risings had already begun. By the end of the day Nationalists had seized Burgos, Zaragoza, Pamplona, Valladolid, and Segovia. In the south, troops from Africa began arriving in Algeciras and Cádiz to shore up existing Nationalist strongholds in Seville and Cádiz. Republicans held on to Madrid, Valencia, and Barcelona. In the countryside, zones alternated from town to town. In Granada, Republican supporters marched on the city hall, demanding arms. The civil governor responded by sending troops into the streets to disperse the crowds. Opposing factions clashed throughout the night.

Dawn broke the next day, Monday, July 20, on a city braced for war. Military squads patrolled the streets of Granada. As sunlight burned off the last vestiges of night air, shots rang out in the center of town. Two bodies were found, victims of a confrontation between Republican and Falangist youths. By noon, downtown Granada was jammed with people calling for arms. The civil governor refused to distribute weapons, despite orders that he do so from the city's military general Miguel Campins Aura, a Republican loyalist. At 5 p.m. soldiers in the Granada garrison rose against Campins. Within an hour rebels had forced the general to sign a declaration of war and had seized the airport, city hall, Republican outposts throughout the city, and Radio Granada. They arrested the civil governor and his staff as well as the city's newly elected mayor, Manuel Fernández-Montesinos, husband to Concha García Lorca. A socialist physician, Montesinos had been voted into office just ten days earlier by Granada's city council. He was herded into prison along with dozens of other detainees. Jail cells meant to hold one prisoner quickly filled with as many as twenty men.

Sometime before 6 p.m. Nationalist rebels made their first radio broadcast. "*Granadinos!*" a voice declared. "At this moment Granada joins the National rising for the salvation of Spain. The army is now on the streets." Stores abruptly closed, taxis vanished, all public transportation ceased — including bus and rail services out of the city. Residents shut themselves inside their homes and listened intently to both Radio Granada and Radio Seville, desperate to glean some truth from the vague and often contradictory broadcasts they heard.

Republican resistance fighters took to the Albaicín, the tangled white Gypsy quarter sprawled across the city's northern edge, below the Alhambra. At entrance points to the neighborhood they dug trenches and skirmished with rebels. From covert positions on the Alhambra, Nationalist soldiers fired down onto the quarter. Gunfire and grenades sounded through the night.

In huge black letters, the July 21st edition of *Ideal* announced a declaration of war throughout Granada province. Citizens possessing weapons were ordered to surrender them immediately to the nearest member of the military or to the Civil Guard. Anyone caught using or manufacturing firearms would receive the "maximum punishment." Assemblies of more than three persons were prohibited. Left-wing publications and political parties were banned. Labor strikes became punishable by death. Throughout Granada, members of the Civil and Assault Guards stationed themselves in squares and on street corners. Right-wing crowds cheered as Nationalist troops made their way through the city. Non-soldiers incurred ridicule. "Those who don't wear uniforms should wear skirts," people jeered.

The fighting in the Albaicín worsened. Artillery fire from six cannons positioned in the Alhambra punctuated the clatter of machine guns as rebels continued their siege on the neighborhood. Workers shot back from terraces and balconies. Early the following morning, July 22, Radio Granada broadcast an ultimatum ordering female residents of the Albaicín to surrender. Shortly afterward a column of women and children filed out of the quarter. They were searched and taken to a camp on the outskirts of town. Rebel planes attacked the men who remained with bullets and hand grenades. Cannonfire jolted the neighborhood. By the morning of Thursday, July 23, white flags hung limply throughout the Albaicín. A full surrender followed. Soldiers entered the quarter and went methodically from house to whitewashed house in search of Republican partisans. The Nationalist victory in Granada was complete. For the first time in three days the city fell silent.

Within two days General Franco had sent an envoy from Africa, General Orgaz, to reinforce the Nationalist hold on Granada. Cheering citizens lined the general's route from the airfield to the center of town. Orgaz promptly ordered the formation of local Nationalist militias and began recruiting troops. Some five thousand *granadinos* enlisted. Nine hundred civilians also joined the Falange. Soldiers took charge of the city and its administration. On August 3, further reinforcements from Africa flew into Granada. That evening troops marched through the city to the sound of military bands and shrieking crowds. More troops from Africa followed. The city's cafés and bars filled with men in uniform: Falangists, Civil Guardsmen, legionnaires.

So-called "undesirables"—former members of the Civil Government, Republican partisans, prominent members of trade unions—were arrested and jailed by the hundreds. Officials drew up lists; neighbors denounced neighbors. The city's first execution took place July 21, one day after the Nationalists seized Granada. From then on, each day before sunrise, truckloads of condemned prisoners were driven to the town cemetery above the Alhambra and shot, or taken to more remote locations on the outskirts of town. From his *carmen* not far below the city cemetery, Manuel de Falla could hear vehicles straining uphill every morning with their human freight. By August *Ideal* had begun publishing official announcements of executions. The paper noted twenty deaths on August 8; three days later the number rose to twenty-nine. Because the city was surrounded by Republican territory—at some points the Republican zone lay as close as ten miles—the repression in Granada was severe.

The civilian population yielded in terror to the caprices of the Nationalist regime.

Eduardo Valdivieso went to visit Lorca several times during the first days of the insurrection. He arrived one afternoon to find Lorca just waking up from a nap; the poet had dreamt that a group of women clad in black dresses and veils had threatened him with black crucifixes. As Lorca described the nightmare to Valdivieso and his mother, Eduardo watched Vicenta Lorca. Her face, he recalled, was "beset with anguish."

Like most of Granada, the family was petrified. Concha's husband, Manuel, was in prison. Isabel García Lorca remained in Madrid, cut off from her parents and siblings; Paco was in Cairo, serving a government now at war. Although the Huerta de San Vicente lay roughly a mile from the center of town, in the midst of the *vega*, Lorca and his parents could occasionally hear gunfire, especially at night, and they were aware of the arrests taking place daily throughout the province.

At 11 a.m., Wednesday, July 29, Republican planes bombarded Granada for the first time. Residents of the city heard the purr of war planes, then the blast of explosives hitting the earth. Citizens panicked. The Republican air campaign lasted two weeks. Several civilians perished during the assault. Granada's single warning siren was so ineffective it sounded only after bombs had fallen. At the Huerta de San Vicente, Concha García Lorca and her children's nursemaid, Angelina Cordobilla, hid under the family's grand piano whenever bombs fell. Lorca invariably came downstairs in his bathrobe and crawled under the instrument with them, murmuring, "Angelina, I'm terrified. Let me in beside you, I'm frightened." He always remained with the women until the barrage ended.

On Thursday, August 6, a Falange squad drove up to the Huerta de San Vicente. Without explanation they searched the Lorca home. They appeared to be seeking a secret radio which Lorca was said to be using to contact Russia. The squad found nothing and left. Both Lorca and his family now realized they were themselves at risk.

A day later, at lunchtime, the architect Alfredo Rodríguez Orgaz, an old friend of Lorca's, showed up at the Huerta. A radical socialist, Rodríguez Orgaz had been inside Granada's city hall on the afternoon of July 20 when Nationalist troops seized the building and arrested most of its occupants. He had fled for his life and spent the ensuing two weeks in hiding. He told Lorca and his family about the executions that were occurring daily in Granada. Despite the grim news, Lorca seemed optimistic. He was convinced that the situation was temporary, and talked about a recent radio broadcast from the Socialist leader Indalecio Prieto, who had predicted a quick end to the Granada siege. "Granada is surrounded by Republicans, and the revolt will soon fail," Lorca said.

Rodríguez Orgaz was less confident. He asked Lorca's father to help him escape that night to Republican territory. In the midst of their conversation, a neighbor informed the family that cars were approaching the Huerta. Rodríguez Orgaz bolted out the back door and hid under a clump of bushes. A squad of Falangists pulled up at the front door, in pursuit of the architect. For the second time in two days, uniformed men searched the Lorca house, but found nothing and left. That night Rodríguez Orgaz escaped to the Republican town of Santa Fe, halfway between Granada and Fuente Vaqueros. From there he went to Málaga, also in Republican hands. Lorca turned down the chance to go with him.

A third Falange squad turned up at the Huerta de San Vicente three days later, on August 9. This time they came to interrogate the Huerta's caretaker, Gabriel Perea Ruiz, whose brothers had been accused of murder. Perea Ruiz and his sister, Carmen, had worked for the Lorca family since the mid-1920s, and lived in a guesthouse adjoining the Huerta. The squad searched the Perea home, and with the butts of their rifles assaulted both Gabriel and his mother, Isabel. The victims fell to their knees. From his bedroom window next door, Concha García Lorca's four-year-old son, Manolo, woke from a nap to see Gabriel Perea strapped to a tree in the front yard. Falangists in blue shirts were beating him.

The squad then entered the Huerta. They threw Lorca down the stairs and hit him. "Queer!" they taunted. "Here we have the friend of Fernando de los Ríos," one officer cried. Lorca replied that he was indeed a friend to the Socialist leader, but that he was also a friend to many others, and that political allegiances meant nothing to him. The Falangists ignored him. They forced everyone inside the Huerta to line up on the front terrace, as if to be shot. Isabel Perea begged the men not to harm anyone. Moments later a second Falange squad pulled into the driveway and ordered the first squad to cease its inquest; evidently they lacked a proper search warrant. Both squads eventually left, taking Gabriel Perea Ruiz with them. Later that night Perea Ruiz returned to the Huerta, visibly undone. He had been brutally interrogated by officials in the Civil Government building. The following day, *Ideal* noted Perea's "detention" on the charge that he had deliberately concealed information concerning his brothers' whereabouts.

Within hours of the episode, Lorca telephoned his friend Luis Rosales in downtown Granada. Rosales was a poet and philosophy student whose three brothers were ardent members of the Falange. At their insistence, Luis too had joined the party on July 20, although he considered himself apolitical. He now worked as a secretary in a Falange barracks. Twelve years younger than Lorca, slender and blond, he had admired the poet for years and thought of himself as his disciple. The two had often met at cafés in Granada, or on the terrace of the Huerta, to read and discuss poetry. In 1935 Rosales had published his first volume of poems.

The moment Lorca told Rosales about the Falange visit, Rosales hurried out to the Huerta. He talked at length with Lorca and his family about the situation and its implications. No one, not even Rosales, thought matters so dire as to be a question of life and death. But Lorca's family feared for his safety. He was famous and rich, and his liberal views were well known to *granadinos*. He had offended the city's more conservative residents in 1934 with *Yerma*, and in April 1936 had risked further insult to the city's Catholic constituents with his outspoken comments on the Reconquest of 1492. Many Granadans assumed he was a communist. Others hated him for his homosexuality. Behind his back they called him "the queer with the bow tie."

Rosales outlined three options available to Lorca. He could escape to the Republican zone, an idea Lorca's father embraced but Lorca rejected. "He was terrified at the thought of being all alone in a no-man's-land between the two zones," Rosales recalled. He could move in temporarily with Manuel de Falla, whose fervent Catholicism was well known to the Falange, and would by association guarantee Lorca some measure of protection. Or he could stay with the Rosales family at their home in the center of Granada, assuming Rosales's father perceived no danger in the arrangement. It was a quiet house, loyal to the Falange, where Lorca would be able to live and work undisturbed until the immediate crisis had passed. Lorca and his family agreed that, under the circumstances, the last choice seemed wisest, and they accepted the invitation. Lorca would remain within easy distance of home, in the company of a good friend and fellow writer, whose family affiliations would protect him from danger.

Don Federico asked his chauffeur, Francisco Murillo, to come to the Huerta on the evening of August 10 to pick up "the young man." Lorca was waiting when Murillo arrived shortly after 11 p.m. He wore a navy suit with a white shirt and black tie, and he held a bundle of clothes in his hand with a pair of blue-

and-white striped pajamas wrapped around them. He climbed into the car, a
seven-seat blue Nash, and Murillo drove him the short distance through town
to the Rosales home. The streets were empty. They pulled up at a three-story
townhouse on Calle Angulo, a few blocks from the Civil Government building
where Perea Ruiz had been interrogated the previous evening. Murillo opened
the door for Lorca. "Goodbye, Paco, goodbye!" Lorca said to the chauffeur and
stepped out of the car. Murillo drove off quickly. He did not wait to see who let
Lorca in.

Not long after his departure, another unit of the Falange went to the Huerta
and found that Lorca had gone. They searched the house in pursuit of items
that might implicate the poet in the "red" cause. They even dismantled his piano to see if it held the clandestine radio with which he was rumored to have
been in communication with Russia. They continued their hunt a few hundred
yards down the road, at his cousin's Huerta del Tamarit. There, they looked inside a large earthenware jug, hoping to find Lorca hidden in its shadows.

The Rosales home was a typical Granadan townhouse with an interior patio
and a marble staircase leading to its upper floors. Lorca was given a bedroom
on the third floor of the house, in what was essentially a private apartment
where the family's Aunt Luisa, then sixty-one, lived. Additional family members—Luis, one brother, their mother, father, and a sister, Esperanza—lived
downstairs.

At first Lorca seemed apprehensive about the family. But after a day or two
he relaxed and slipped into a routine of reading, piano playing, writing, and
conversation. He talked to his family by phone, and he smoked incessantly. Because the Rosales men were seldom home, he spent most of his time alone or
with the women in the household. He played popular songs on Aunt Luisa's piano and listened compulsively to her radio. "What false reports have you heard
today?" he sometimes teased Esperanza Rosales, then twenty-seven. Every
morning Esperanza brought him the paper. Lorca read reports of bomb damage in Granada and executions of alleged "communists" and "reds." On the
morning after his arrival, *Ideal* announced that thirty people had been shot in
the previous twenty-four hours, many because they had promoted "Marxist propaganda." Two days later the paper published a tribute to the late Monarchist
leader Calvo Sotelo, "Martyr of Spain," one month after his death.

Temperatures reached the nineties each day. Late in the afternoon, Lorca
would join the Rosales women in the shade of the patio downstairs for coffee
and conversation. They talked about the weather, the progress of the war, news

of the day. Lorca told stories about his travels and discussed the work he planned to do when he returned to Madrid. He was filled with ideas for the theater. He told Esperanza Rosales, who worried about her boyfriend in Madrid, that once the fighting had ended "the three of us will go together to the opening of my next play." He nicknamed Esperanza "my divine jailer."

When Luis Rosales returned home late at night, still clad in his blue Falange uniform, he and Lorca often talked about poetry, with particular emphasis on Lorca's forthcoming collection of sonnets. Lorca wanted the volume to include his eleven sonnets of dark love and at least four elegiac sonnets composed at various points in his career. He planned to call the book *The Garden of Sonnets.* He sometimes read poems to Rosales. The two also talked of composing an anthem to the Spaniards who had perished in the fighting that summer. Lorca volunteered to write the music if Rosales would draft the lyrics.

He did not think of himself as "in hiding," nor did the family attempt to conceal his presence. Lorca assured Esperanza Rosales that he had "never been involved with politics. I'm too afraid . . . To take sides you need a level of courage that I lack . . . What a shame that wasn't the case with my brother-in-law!" He said repeatedly that politics did not interest him. Despite the extraordinary nature of his situation he remained buoyant. He called the family's wine cellar "*el bombario,*" because he and the Rosales women used it as a bomb shelter whenever Republican planes attacked the city. As they crouched among the family's earthenware jugs of wine, Lorca joked that no bomb could possibly fall on such a "hospitable house."

The Republican air raids ended on August 15. That day a unit of the Falange appeared at the Huerta de San Vicente with a warrant for Lorca's arrest. After a hasty search of the house, they threatened to seize the poet's father if his family did not disclose Lorca's whereabouts. Concha García Lorca broke down and told them where to find her brother.

At dawn on Sunday, August 16, Manuel Fernández-Montesinos was shot by a firing squad. The priest who took his final confession went in person to the Lorca family to inform them of his death. Concha, who had turned thirty-three two days earlier, was sitting in a corner of her parents' home when Vicenta Lorca came to tell her the news. The instant she saw her mother's face Concha knew what had happened.

Lorca learned by telephone of his brother-in-law's death. He was devastated, and feared for his sister and her three children. The Rosales family had begun to worry about Lorca himself. A Falangist friend had warned them that a number of new arrests were taking place, and that Lorca might be in danger. The family talked of moving him to a safer location, perhaps to Manuel de Falla's *carmen*.

At approximately one o'clock that afternoon, a car with three uniformed officers in it pulled up to the Rosales house. Soldiers armed with machine guns stationed themselves along the street and on neighboring rooftops. Additional troops cordoned off the surrounding streets. The three officers presented themselves at the front door of the Rosales home and announced that they had come to arrest Lorca. Of the three, one was obviously in charge: Ramón Ruiz Alonso, a loud, belligerent man dressed in blue coveralls emblazoned with the Falangist insignia. A former parliament member from CEDA, and recent convert to the Falange, Ruiz Alonso detested the Left and hated Lorca, whom he had referred to earlier in the year as "the one with the swollen head." Despite his membership in the organization, Ruiz Alonso was also contemptuous of the Falange leadership, who had apparently refused his request for financial compensation upon joining the party. His complex and strained relationship with the Falange may have led to Ruiz Alonso's critical role in Lorca's arrest, for by removing a presumed "red" from the home of loyal Falangists in broad daylight, he could embarrass the organization, and thus reap his petty revenge.

The Rosales men were not home that afternoon. Alone, Mrs. Rosales bravely confronted Ruiz Alonso and his two companions. She refused to let the men take Lorca from her house and demanded to know the reason for his arrest.

"His works," one of them answered.

Mrs. Rosales persisted. She reminded the officers of her family's allegiance to the Falange, and insisted that she be allowed to telephone her husband and sons. Ruiz Alonso consented. For the next half-hour, Mrs. Rosales tried frantically to reach one of the men in her family. Finally she located her son Miguel at the Falange barracks. Ruiz Alonso drove off to get him. The two returned to the house shortly afterward, accompanied by several additional men.

Miguel Rosales had been unable to dissuade Ruiz Alonso from his mission. When asked what crime Lorca had committed, Ruiz Alonso said, "He's done more damage with a pen than others have with a pistol."

Lorca was upstairs and heard the commotion below him. When it became clear that he was to be arrested, he knelt with Aunt Luisa before an image of the Sacred Heart and prayed. He was in a state of near collapse, trembling and weeping. As he left the house he said goodbye to Aunt Luisa and Mrs. Rosales. To Esperanza he murmured, "I won't give you my hand because I don't want you to think we're not going to see each other again." He wore dark gray pants and a white shirt with a tie hung loosely around its collar. Ruiz Alonso led him out the door and around the corner to the waiting car.

Minutes after his departure Mrs. Rosales telephoned the Lorca family. Later in the day her husband went in person to see Lorca's father. The two men paid a hurried visit to the Lorca family lawyer, hoping to prepare a legal defense of Lorca's case in the event that the rebels granted him a trial.

Lorca was driven to the Civil Government building on Calle Duquesa, directly next door to the University of Granada's botanical gardens, a few blocks from the Rosales home. He was searched and confined to an office. Miguel Rosales, who had accompanied him on the brief journey, assured him that he would not be harmed.

Later that day, Luis Rosales and his brother José, a long-standing member of the Falange, went to the Civil Government building to demand an explanation for Lorca's arrest. They were told to leave. Luis subsequently filed an official document clarifying his decision to allow Lorca to stay at his house and emphasizing that at no point had he or anyone else considered Lorca "in hiding," that the poet's presence had in fact been known to several members of the Falange. Rosales defended his actions and swore his devotion to "the defense of my Religion, my Flag, and my Fatherland." He and his family were clearly at risk for their role in the episode. Within two days of Lorca's arrest, Luis Rosales donated a ring to the Falange, and his father made a sizable gift of gold jewelry and coins "for the Fatherland."

José Rosales was allowed to see Lorca on the evening of August 16. He gave him a carton of Camel cigarettes. Lorca asked José to donate money to the Falange in his name. A neighbor of the Rosales family was also permitted to see Lorca and apparently gave him some blankets from Mrs. Rosales. A third witness who saw Lorca during his confinement in the Civil Government building remembered him as silent and plainly dismayed.

On the morning of Monday, August 17, Concha García Lorca's nursemaid, Angelina Cordobilla, entered the long, sparsely furnished room where Lorca was kept under armed guard. "Angelina, Angelina, why have you come?" Lorca said.

"Your mother sends me." She gave Lorca a basket containing an egg-and-potato omelette, a thermos of coffee, and tobacco. A guard checked the food to see that it concealed nothing. But Lorca had no appetite, and Angelina quickly left.

Temperatures climbed high into the nineties that afternoon. Lorca remained locked inside the Civil Government building.

According to a neighbor who happened to be on the street early the following morning, Lorca was taken from the building at around 3 a.m., Tuesday, August 18, handcuffed to another man, Dióscoro Galindo González, a lame schoolteacher who had been arrested one hour earlier. The two prisoners were placed in a car, with a driver, two guards, and two members of the Falange.

The seven men drove through Granada in the dark, to the northwest edge of the city, and turned onto a pitted road that snaked sharply up into the parched foothills of the Sierra Nevada. There was no moonlight. Six miles from Granada, three thousand feet above sea level, in the tiny whitewashed village of Víznar, the car stopped before an eighteenth-century palace that had been turned into a Nationalist command post. After a short wait—apparently for the exchange of papers—Lorca and his companion were driven to a red stone building just below Víznar, at the edge of a sudden ravine. Until that month the building, La Colonia, had been used as a summer play space for children. Since August 1 it had served as a holding cell for condemned prisoners.

Soldiers, guards, grave diggers, and a pair of housekeepers occupied the upper floor of La Colonia. Lorca was held downstairs. With him were the schoolteacher Galindo González, and two bullfighters known for their left-wing politics. A young guard, José Jover Tripaldi, was on duty that night. In an effort to calm his prisoners, Tripaldi at first told them they would be sent out the following day to help build a road. Lorca offered him a cigarette and tried to make conversation. He asked if he might have a newspaper and more tobacco the next morning. Tripaldi said yes. Sometime later, Tripaldi revealed the truth to the four men. A devout Catholic, he believed it his Christian duty to tell them they were about to be killed, and to offer them the chance to make a final confession. Lorca was dazed. "I haven't done anything!" he cried. He tried to recite a prayer. "My mother taught it all to me, you know? And now I've forgotten it," he said, weeping. "Will I be damned?" Tripaldi told him he would not.

Shortly before dawn the four prisoners were removed from La Colonia and driven by truck along the ravine to an empty stretch of hillside flecked with olive trees. Miles below them in the distance lay the *vega*. A few hundred feet beyond them, near the village of Alfacar, stood an eleventh-century Arab reservoir, Fuente Grande—in Arabic, *Ainadamar*, "The Fountain of Tears." For centuries its waters had supplied the city of Granada.

The sun had not yet risen when Lorca and his three companions heard the click of rifles. They were shot beside a stand of olive trees. As daylight broke, grave diggers sunk their shovels into the earth and began their morning's work.

EPILOGUE

On August 18 or 19—the precise date is uncertain—Angelina Cordobilla went again to the Civil Government building in Granada to deliver food to Lorca. Guards told her Lorca was gone, and sent her home. On or about the same day Manuel de Falla went to the Civil Government building to plead for his friend's release. He was curtly informed that his petition was useless, for Lorca had died that morning. Falla immediately took the news to Lorca's family.

Concha García Lorca was sitting in her room, still in shock over her husband's death, when her father appeared in the doorway, white as chalk. "Federico?" she asked.

"Federico," he said.

Don Federico clung to hope for the next three months. But Concha knew at once that her brother was gone. Within days of Lorca's death, his father received a note written in Lorca's hand. "Dear Father, please give the bearer of this letter 2,000 pesetas," it read. Don Federico carried the note with him for years. It was Lorca's last manuscript.

Margarita Xirgu was in Havana, performing in *Yerma*, when she learned of Lorca's death. That night she changed the ending of his play so that Yerma's final cry—"I myself have murdered my own child"—became a heart-stricken wail: "They have murdered my child."

"If one had searched diligently, scouring every corner of the land for someone to sacrifice, to sacrifice as a symbol," Pablo Neruda wrote one year after

Lorca's death, "one could not have found in anyone or in anything, to the degree it existed in this man who was chosen, the essence of Spain, its vitality and its profundity." Lorca's murder pushed Neruda into a political activism he had long resisted. "We will never be able to forget this crime nor forgive it," he told a Paris audience in early 1937. "We will never put it out of our minds, never will we excuse it. Never."

Pedro Salinas mourned Lorca's sudden disappearance, "in the full flush of his youth, leaving in our hands a sheaf of marvelous poems." Juan Ramón Jiménez spoke of "this unwanted death." Antonio Machado urged those who knew Lorca to

> carve a monument
> out of dream stone
> for the poet in the Alhambra,
> over a fountain where the grieving water
> shall say forever:
> The crime was in Granada, his Granada.

Machado died in 1939, during the last months of the Spanish Civil War, having succumbed to pneumonia while attempting to flee Spain. Miguel de Unamuno died in the fifth month of the war, in 1936, in Salamanca, his heart shattered by the "stupid regime of terror" that had split his country. "There is nothing worse than the marriage of the barracks mentality with that of the sacristy," he wrote bitterly to a friend shortly after the war began. "And then, the spiritual leprosy of Spain: resentment, envy, hatred for intelligence."

The Spanish Civil War lasted nearly three years, from July 1936 until the end of March 1939, and claimed more than 500,000 lives, 130,000 of those by execution. In Granada alone, as many as five thousand people were killed by firing squads.

Impassioned volunteers from some fifty-four countries—including three thousand American partisans with the Abraham Lincoln Brigade, their passports stamped "Not Valid for Travel in Spain"—"presented their lives," in W. H. Auden's eloquent phrase, for the Republican cause. Stalin contributed a thousand pilots, planes, tanks, and over two thousand "advisers." To Franco's Nationalist *movimiento*, Hitler sent a complete air force, with nearly ten thousand pilots and weapons specialists. Mussolini volunteered 75,000 Italian troops so that fascism might prevail.

Ernest Hemingway, George Orwell, André Malraux each fought in and wrote about the war. Picasso immortalized its savagery in his immense gray-and-white canvas *Guernica*. For an entire generation, the conflict in Spain became a crusade of good against evil, a prelude to World War II, the concentration camps, air raids against defenseless civilians. "We left our hearts there," said Herbert L. Matthews of *The New York Times*, recalling the brutal war. "Treacherous generals: look at my dead house, look at my Broken Spain," wrote Neruda.

Among those who perished in battle was Lorca's companion Rafael Rodríguez Rapún, who died near Santander on August 18, 1937, the first anniversary of Lorca's death, from wounds suffered while fighting for the Republic.

Franco's triumphant Nationalist soldiers marched into Madrid on the morning of March 27, 1939. The capital had remained in Republican hands until then. For the first time, red-and-yellow Nationalist flags hung from windows and balconies; men and women in makeshift fascist uniforms—black shirts and trousers—raced through the streets, hands lifted in the fascist salute, shouting "Franco, Franco!" Three days later the last remaining Republican strongholds—Cartagena, Albacete, Guadalajara—fell to the Nationalists. On March 31, Franco wrote his final communiqué: "Having captured and disarmed the red army, Nationalist troops today took their last objectives. The war is finished."

Four decades of dictatorship followed. The arrest and execution of alleged Republican sympathizers continued. In July 1939, four months after the cease-fire, a visitor to Spain reported between 200 and 250 shootings a day in Madrid, 150 in Barcelona.

Franco's government never accepted responsibility for Lorca's murder. But officials in the Nationalist movement—specifically General Queipo de Llano of Seville—had clearly sanctioned the killing. Within two days of Lorca's death in 1936, Queipo announced by radio that the 1922 Nobel laureate, Jacinto Benavente, "who never meddled in politics," had been murdered by "Marxist mobs" in Madrid. Queipo also claimed that Marxist assassins had killed at least five additional Spanish playwrights. The reports were patently false. Authorities had concocted them in an attempt to diminish the impact of Lorca's disappearance.

The government's lone acknowledgment of Lorca's death was a certificate, issued in 1940, stating that Lorca "died in the month of August 1936 from war wounds, his body having been found on the 20th day of the same month on the road from Víznar to Alfacar."

Lorca's body has in fact never been found. For decades the precise spot near

Víznar, where he and hundreds of others were shot and buried in shallow graves, remained an official secret, a pockmarked landscape few dared to visit, much less inspect, for fear of arrest by the Civil Guard.

In 1986, eleven years after Franco's death and the restitution of democracy to Spain, the socialist government of Prime Minister Felipe González constructed a monument on the site of Lorca's execution, "in memory of Federico García Lorca and all the victims of the Civil War."

The surviving members of Lorca's immediate family—his parents, brother, two sisters, nephew, and two nieces—left Spain at various points during and shortly after the war, and were reunited in 1940 in New York City. Francisco García Lorca married the daughter of Fernando de los Ríos, Laura, in 1942. He taught Spanish literature at Columbia University and Queens College, and gave classes at Hunter College, Harvard University, and New York University. For nine years he directed the Spanish program at Middlebury Summer School in Vermont, where his colleagues included fellow exiles Fernando de los Ríos, Pedro Salinas, and Jorge Guillén.

Lorca's brother longed for an early end to Franco's dictatorship, and a prompt return to Spain. It was not to be. His mother and sisters went back to Madrid in 1951. Paco remained in America until his retirement from Columbia in 1966.

Don Federico García Rodríguez never returned home. Lorca's father died in America in 1945, nine years after his oldest son's death in Granada. The landowner had abandoned all hope of seeing Spain again. He never learned English; his young grandson, Manolo, translated the daily paper into Spanish for him.

All but a handful of writers in Lorca's generation left Spain after the war, condemned by politics and their abhorrence of Franco's regime to "rot in accursed exile," as Pedro Salinas put it. "Are we reaching the end of the end or is something new beginning?" Rafael Alberti wondered as the Civil War drew to a close. Alberti viewed the future as "frozen"; in poetry and prose he mourned Lorca's death.

Jiménez, Machado, Guillén, Salinas, Alberti, Cernuda, Altolaguirre, Prados, Méndez: "They all left," wrote Vicente Aleixandre, one of the few poets of the Generation of '27 to stay behind, "all together at one moment, on very different paths."

Manuel de Falla went to Argentina, Luis Buñuel to the United States and eventually Mexico. Salvador Dalí spent the first ten years after the war in the United States, then he returned to Cadaqués with his wife. Ever the sensationalist, he embraced *franquismo* and brashly applauded Lorca's murder. "The moment I learned of his death . . . I cried '*Olé!*' That's what a Spaniard says in the presence of a bullfighter who has just executed a particularly successful move before a bleeding beast. I thought that for Federico García Lorca, it was the most beautiful way of dying: killed by the Civil War." In a more sober moment Dalí spoke of Lorca's death as "ignoble . . . Lorca was in essence the most apolitical person on earth."

At his death, Lorca left behind at least three unproduced, full-length plays—*The Audience, Once Five Years Pass,* and *The House of Bernarda Alba.* He left several unpublished poetry collections—*Suites, The Divan at Tamarit, Poet in New York, The Garden of Sonnets*—and nearly four hundred unpublished drawings, as well as letters, fragments of plays and poems, and lists of projected works.

The state of his manuscripts demonstrates the extent to which the act and art of creation were a part of his everyday life. He wrote poems on invitations to tea, royalty statements, envelopes, and drawings. He sketched drawings in the margins of letters and plays, and wrote plays on the backs of poems. He was "an extraordinary creature," said Jorge Guillén, "a creature of Creation, the crossroads of Creation, a man immersed in Creation who partook of deep creative currents."

Lorca drew no distinction between art and life. The piano was as much a part of his existence as food and drink. He could turn an ordinary party into a performance, a restaurant outing into a one-man recital. His letters—some of them festooned with sketches, most of them intimate revelations of himself—were works of art, cherished by their recipients. His very conversation was cause for awe.

He was a poet—more precisely a "poet of the people"—who viewed poetry as "something that walks along the streets," that exists everywhere: in men, in women, in the "unpredictable path of a dog." "Poetry has no limits," he said four months before his death.

It can be waiting for us in the doorway in the cold early hours before dawn when you come home with tired feet and the collar of your coat turned up. It can be waiting for us in the water of a fountain, perched on the flower of an olive tree, set out to dry on a piece of white fabric on a terrace roof. What you cannot do is set out to write poetry with the mathematical rigor of one who goes out to buy a liter-and-a-half of oil.

In a career that spanned only nineteen years, Lorca exhausted the origins of Spanish poetry and theater, and in nine books of verse and thirteen plays resurrected and renewed its most basic strains: ballad, song, sonnet, puppet show, tragedy, farce. He sought, and found, provocative new ways of melding poetry and stagecraft, and in doing so anticipated the plays of Tennessee Williams, Harold Pinter, Samuel Beckett. Through his work with La Barraca, and his collaborations with Xirgu and Cipriano Rivas Cherif, he helped inaugurate a second Golden Age of the Spanish theater. Through his poems he continues to speak to readers worldwide of all that is most central to the human condition: the capriciousness of time, the impossibility of love, the phantoms of identity, art, childhood, sex, and death.

In life, Lorca was best known for his Andalusian works: *Gypsy Ballads, Poem of the Deep Song, Blood Wedding, Yerma, Doña Rosita the Spinster,* and *Lament for Ignacio Sánchez Mejías,* his epic portrait of a beloved friend and towering Andalusian "prince," who "sought death out, savored its taste." Lorca never entirely shook the image he had earned as a result of *Gypsy Ballads*—the poet as bronzed Gypsy with black hair and soulful eyes, whose work depicts a tragic south steeped in dark sounds and blood. His friends knew otherwise and, in memoirs, essays, poems, letters, and interviews, have recalled a more genuine Lorca—a playful, irreverent, opinionated, exasperating, utterly contemporary man and artist, who in the last years of his life wrote such provocative works as *Poet in New York, The Audience, Once Five Years Pass, Sonnets of Dark Love,* and the first act of *The Dream of Life.*

That none of these plays or poetry collections was published or produced during Lorca's life is testament both to his abiding belief in the vitality of the living word, and to the audacity of the works themselves. As a writer, Lorca craved confrontation. When his 1930 play *The Audience* at last made its Spanish stage debut in the late 1980s, the work's volatile content and radical form still sparked debate. The discovery and publication of additional manuscripts left behind at Lorca's death—*The Divan at Tamarit, Suites, Trip to the Moon, The House of Bernarda Alba,* the unfinished "Ode and Mockery of Sesostris and Sardanapalus," the first act of *The Dreams of My Cousin Aurelia,* incidental poems to and about friends, lectures, essays, interviews, hundreds of drawings, reams of juvenilia, and a heartbreakingly beautiful collection of letters to family and friends—have further defined the range and depth of a man who in the spring of 1936 told Adolfo Salazar that he was just embarking on his "true career as a dramatic poet."

Lorca viewed himself in grandiose terms, like the "Marvel of Nature" that

Cervantes saw in Lope de Vega. He dreamt of being as prolific as Lope, and as influential.

A year or two before his death, Lorca told a reporter that he was then at work on approximately "four thousand five hundred and fifty-nine" projects. "Now of those," he teased, "I'll write only four at the most."

In 1935 a journalist asked him which of his plays he liked best. "Among the works I've already produced I don't have any favorites," Lorca answered. "I'm in love with the ones I haven't written yet."

NOTES

BIBLIOGRAPHY

ACKNOWLEDGMENTS

INDEX

NOTES

The following abbreviations are used throughout:

AFFGL   Archivo de la Fundación Federico García Lorca, Madrid

BFFGL   *Boletín de la Fundación Federico García Lorca*

C   Federico García Lorca. *Conferencias.* Ed. Christopher Maurer. 2 vols. Madrid: Alianza, 1984.

EC   ———. *Epistolario completo.* 1 vol. Bk. I (1910–26), ed. Christopher Maurer. Bk. II (1927–36), ed. Andrew A. Anderson. Madrid: Cátedra, 1997.

FGL   Federico García Lorca

FM   Francisco García Lorca. *Federico y su mundo.* Ed. Mario Hernández. 3rd ed. Madrid: Alianza, 1981.

G, I   Ian Gibson. *Federico García Lorca I. De Fuente Vaqueros a Nueva York, 1898–1929.* Barcelona: Grijalbo, 1985.

G, II   ———. *Federico García Lorca II. De Nueva York a Fuente Grande, 1929–1936.* Barcelona: Grijalbo, 1987.

GM   Francisco García Lorca. *In the Green Morning: Memories of Federico.* Trans. Christopher Maurer. Prologue by Mario Hernández. New York: New Directions, 1986.

OC   Federico García Lorca. *Obras completas.* Ed. Miguel García-Posada. 4 vols. Barcelona: Galaxia Gutenberg / Círculo de Lectores, 1996.

Other works cited are listed in the Bibliography.

EPIGRAPH

"I remember a certain": *FM,* 18, translated in *GM,* 9–10.

PROLOGUE: 1918

3 **FGL gives reading:** *Defensor de Granada*, March 18, 1918, 1; Eloy Escobar de la Riva, "Centro Artístico," *El Noticiero Granadino*, March 18, 1918.
3 **"just one more flower":** Unless otherwise specified, all passages from *Impressions and Landscapes* are taken from FGL, *Impresiones y paisajes*, in *OC*, IV, 50–65.
4 **"hits the streets . . . everyone":** *EC*, 50.
4 **"What will become . . . of my book":** FGL, "Visión," in *OC*, IV, 318–22; see also FGL, *Poesía inédita*, 199.
4 **"In a century of zeppelins . . . Pan"** and **"Why fight against":** *EC*, 48–49.
4 **Lorca family supports Allies:** Author interview with Isabel García Lorca.
4 **"shell shock" and "barbarous":** *Defensor de Granada*, June 5, 1918, 3.
4 **FGL denounces patriotism:** "El patriotismo" (October 29, 1917), in *OC*, IV, 731–36.
5 **FGL writes at night:** *FM*, 160. See also "The Night," a 1917 poem in which Lorca describes the "silence of night"; he signed this poem at dawn (*OC*, IV, 234–36, and FGL, *Poesía inédita*, 62).
5 **"toward the good":** FGL, *Prosa inédita*, 152.
5 **passionate "romantic":** *EC*, 46; see also FGL, *Místicas*, in *OC*, IV, 537–631.
5 **"There is within me":** "Apunte," in *OC*, IV, 663.
5 **"who filled the world":** "Mística que se trata de una angustia suprema que no se borra nunca," in *OC*, IV, 558–61.
6 **"a desert . . . the Christs":** "El patriotismo," in *OC*, IV, 735.
6 **FGL sees himself as Don Quixote:** "Breves meditaciones. De mi diario," in *OC*, IV, 662.

I. FOUNTAINS: 1898-1905

7 **"My Village":** "Mi pueblo," in *OC*, IV, 843–67.
8 **"kissed":** *FM*, 26–27; *GM*, 16–17.
8 **Poverty of FGL friend:** FGL, "Mi pueblo," in *OC*, IV, 854–58.
8 **Federico García Rodríguez:** Fuente Vaqueros, Church Archive, Baptisms, bk. 3, no. 148; author interview with Carmen Perea and Manuel Padilla; Mora Guarnido, 18; Couffon, 20; *FM*, 27–28; *GM*, 17; Salobreña, 74; author interview with Evaristo Correal and Pepe Toledano.
8 **"intelligence," "passion," and "farmer, a rich man":** Giménez Caballero.
9 **Federico García Rodríguez's marriage to Matilde Palacios Ríos:** Fuente Vaqueros, Church Archive, Marriages, bk. 2, nos. 175–76; *G, I*, 38; Cabrolié, 35–36, 47; Couffon, 20. For Matilde's death and will see Fuente Vaqueros, Juzgado, Deaths, vol. 9, bk. 5, no. 328; Cabrolié, 37; Archivo de Protócolos Notariales del Colegio de Granada, Protócolo, Santa Fe, 1894, Notaría de Cristóbal Pacheco y Rosales, vol. II, no. 1.748.878. For Enrique García's death see Fuente Vaqueros, Juzgado, Deaths, vol. 4, 1888, bk. 14, no. 117. I am grateful to Ian Gibson for allowing me to consult Martine Cabrolié's excellent study of the socio-economic background of the Lorca family.
9 **Matilde Palacios dictates will:** Archivo de Protócolos Notariales del Colegio de Granada, Protócolo, Santa Fe, 1894, Notaría de Cristóbal Pacheco y Rosales, vol. II, no. 1.748.878.
9 **Federico García Rodríguez purchases properties:** Registro de Propiedad, Santa Fe, vol. 439, fol. 29; Cabrolié 41, 99.
9 **Federico García Rodríguez proposes to Vicenta Lorca:** Auclair, 51; Higuera Rojas,

164; Fernández-Montesinos García, "Descripción," ix; author interview with Manuel Fernández-Montesinos García; author interview with Amelia Agostini del Río.

10   **Vicenta Lorca:** Granada, Ayuntamiento Archive, Baptisms, 1870, no. 560, Parroquia de Sta. Escolástica, no. 126; Cabrolié, 44–47, 75, 83; G, I, 42–43; Molina Fajardo, 20; Granada, Huerta de San Vicente Archive. For Vicenta Lorca's death see Granada, Ayuntamiento Archive, Deaths, no. 673, Parroquia de Sta. Escolástica, no. 62. For the death of Vicenta Lorca's mother, Concepción Romero, see Cabrolié, 83; Fuente Vaqueros, Deaths, Partido Judicial de Santa Fe, Registro Civil, bk. 15.

10   **"After all that struggle":** Cabrolié, 83; G, I, 43.

10   **Federico García Rodríguez and Vicenta Lorca marry:** Juzgado Municipal de Fuente Vaqueros, 1889, Marriages, bks. 6, 7, and 8.

11   **FGL's birth and baptism:** Fuente Vaqueros, Juzgado, Births, 1897–1901, vol. 8, bk. 20, no. 549; Cabrolié, 86; Antonio Gallego Morell, "Treinta partidas de bautismo de escritores granadinos," *Boletín de la Real Academia Española* (January–April 1954).

10–11 **Luis García Lorca's death and FGL's response:** Fuente Vaqueros, Juzgado Municipal, Deaths, bk. 16, no. 680; FGL, "Tentación" (December 17, 1917), AFFGL; FGL, *Suites*, 267; FGL, *Poeta en Nueva York*, 152n; Walsh, 115.

12   **"streams of black blood" and "look of terror":** FGL, "Fray Antonio (Poema raro)," in *OC*, IV, 764.

12   **Francisco García Lorca's birth:** Fuente Vaqueros, Juzgado, Births, bk. 21, vol. 9, 1902, no. 48.

12   **Concha García Lorca's birth:** Fuente Vaqueros, Juzgado, Births, bk. 22, vol. 10, 1903, no. 61.

12   **Family moves to new house in Fuente Vaqueros:** G, I, 40; Cabrolié, 99.

12–13 **FGL attends church and school:** FGL, "Mi pueblo," in *OC*, IV, 846–64; Martín, *Federico García Lorca, heterodoxo*, 187; G, I, 60. On the distinction between male and female in twentieth-century Spanish society see Julian A. Pitt-Rivers, *The People of the Sierra*, 2nd ed. (Chicago: University of Chicago Press, 1971), 84–109.

13   **Childhood games and "greatest emotions":** FM, 61; FGL, "Mi pueblo," in *OC*, IV, 858–61.

13   **"clumsy gait":** FM, 61; GM, 45.

13   **FGL on horseback:** FM, 54.

13–14 **FGL and childhood theatrics:** "Cuando Carmen jugaba con Federico a los Títeres de Cachiporra," *Ideal* (Granada), June 4, 1978, 31–32; Couffon, 23–24; Francisco García Lorca, introduction to FGL, *Five Plays*, 9; Francisco García Lorca, prologue to FGL, *Three Tragedies*, 9; Molina Fajardo, 82.

14   **Vicenta Lorca encourages FGL:** See, for example, letters from Vicenta Lorca to FGL (November 9, 1920; November 18, 1920; March 29, 1921), AFFGL.

14   **"I was shocked":** EC, 736.

14   **Family's admiration for Victor Hugo:** FM, 47–50; Martín, *Federico García Lorca, heterodoxo*, 131–32, 143; Cano, 20, as told to Cano by Isabel García Rodríguez.

14   **Storytelling:** FGL, "Mi pueblo," in *OC*, IV, 845–46; Mora Guarnido, 24–25, 26, 30; Luis Lacasa, "Recuerdo y trayectoria de Federico García Lorca," *Literatura soviética* (Moscow), 1946, 38–46.

14   **Music in the García Lorca household:** FM, 55, 61; Martínez Nadal, in FGL, *Autógrafos I*, xvi; Couffon, 24–25; Molina Fajardo, 85; G, I, 38; Higuera Rojas, 166.

15   **"the fandango . . . ardor":** OC, IV, 251.

15   **"The rich child listens":** OC, III, 117, trans. in FGL, *Deep Song*, 10.

15   "a rich little boy": Giménez Caballero.

15   García family and annual gatherings: FM, 52–53, 56; Molina Fajardo, 20, 85.

15   "Such a delicate child!": FGL, "Retablo del dolor gigante. Quico," in OC, IV, 808–11; trans. Maurer, introduction to FGL, Collected Poems, x.

15–16   "all poor women" and "misery and neglect": FGL, "Mi amiguita rubia," in OC, IV, 854–58; FM, 406–7.

16   "without thinking": FGL, "Retablo de dolor ingenuo. Adelaida," in OC, IV, 812–15.

16   FGL's love of the landscape: FM, 54; GM, 40; FGL, Suites, 220; Cano, 13; Mora Guarnido, 21; Luna, "La vida," in OC, III, 523–27. See also Proel; FM, 22–23; GM, 12.

16   History of the vega: FM, 11; GM, 3; Salobreña, 14; J.N.P. Watson, "In Honour of Sala-manca. The Duke of Wellington's Andalusian Estate, I," Country Life (London), September 4, 1980, 779–81, and "Some 'Near Run Things.' The Duke of Wellington's Andalusian Es-tate, II," Country Life (London), September 12, 1980, 886–88.

17   FGL sees Roman mosaic unearthed: Luna, "La vida," in OC, III, 523–27; FM, 35; GM, 23.

2. NEW WORLDS: 1905-15

18   Lorca family moves to Asquerosa: Cabrolié, 99; Mora Guarnido, 19; "Cuando Carmen ju-gaba con Federico a los Títeres de Cachiporra," Ideal (Granada), June 4, 1978.

18   "repulsive": In 1941 the town's name was officially changed to Valderrubio, a reference to the local cultivation of blond, or "rubio," tobacco (Hernández, "Francisco y Federico Gar-cía Lorca," xi); FGL, Cartas, postales, poemas y dibujos, ed. Antonio Gallego Morell (Madrid: Edición Moneda y Crédito, 1968), 43f.

18   "one of the prettiest": EC, 119.

18   Don Federico's land holdings in Asquerosa: Cabrolié, 41, 99; Registro de Propiedad, Santa Fe, vol. 499, bks. 71, 81, 111, and vol. 439, fol. 29.

18–19   lack of privacy in Asquerosa: FM, 54.

19   "It's full of stupid etiquette": EC, 355.

19   FGL sent to school in Almería: In all likelihood FGL spent two years in Almería, from 1906 to 1908, possibly even staying until the spring of 1909. His name appears only in the book for the academic year 1907–08, however, and in a list of students who were examined on September 21, 1908.

19   Antonio Rodríguez Espinosa: FM, 65–66; GM, 49–50; AFFGL (photograph collection); Antonio Gallego Morell, "D. Antonio Rodriguez Espinosa, maestro de García Lorca, tam-bién era poeta," in Lecturas del 27, 67–80; Pascual González Guzmán, "Federico in Almería. Nuevos datos para la biografía de García Lorca," PSA XXXV (November 1964), 206–7; Gabriel Nuñez-Ruiz, "Lorca, escolarillo almeriense," Revista de Literatura XLVI, 91 (January–June 1984), 135–36.

19   "to embark on another life" and "the boss's kid": FGL, "Mi escuela," in OC, IV, 848.

19   "most turbulent": Couffon, 37n.

19   FGL attends school in Almería: Gabriel Nuñez-Ruiz, "Lorca, escolarillo almeriense," Re-vista de Literatura XLVI, 91 (January–June 1984), 140–41; Martín Martín, 37.

19   FGL falls ill: Giménez Caballero; Couffon, 37n.; FM, 67; Martín Martín, 37, 60; Emilio Orozco Díaz, "Federico García Lorca se gradúa de bachiller. (Notas en torno a unos años de la vida del poeta)," in Lecturas del 27, 12–13; G, I, 70.

20   "I asked for a mirror": FGL, "Nota autobiográfica," OC, III, 306. The poem, if it existed, has not survived.

20   FGL recuperates in Asquerosa: FM, 67.

20 **Lorca family moves to Granada:** Martín Martín, 60; *FM*, 49, 67; Emilio Orozco Díaz, "Federico García Lorca se gradúa de bachiller. (Notas en torno a unos años de la vida del poeta)," in *Lecturas del* 27, 12–13. According to Isabel García Lorca, the house at Acera del Darro was filled with the constant sound of murmuring water (Isabel García Lorca, 11).

20 **"blood of the wounded earth":** FGL, "Canción oriental," in *OC*, I, 143.

20 **"has two rivers":** *OC*, III, 138; FGL, *How a City Sings from November to November.*

20 **"everything reduced and concentrated":** Morla Lynch, 317; *OC*, III, 79–80.

21 **"great crime of the Inquisition":** FGL, "El patriotismo" (October 27, 1917), in *OC*, IV, 733.

21 **"tensed Federico's soul":** *FM*, 118; *GM*, 96.

21 **"fatal duel":** FGL, "Semana Santa en Granada," *OC*, III, 271–74.

21 **FGL's affinity with Arab culture:** Crow, 54; Rodrigo, *Memoria*, 189; Isabel García Lorca, 15–16.

22 **"suffers and weeps":** *OC*, III, 138.

22 **Vicenta Lorca decorates home:** *FM*, 70; Mora Guarnido, 18–19, 47–48.

22 **Isabel García Lorca's birth and Vicenta Lorca's illness:** Registro Civil de Granada, Births, 1909, no. 92, 232; *FM*, 45, 79, 80.

22 **"Mama I want to see you":** *EC*, 25.

22 **FGL begins school in Granada:** When FGL first took the exam in June 1909, he passed only the Spanish language segment of the test; he was reexamined in September 1909 and in June and September 1910, and passed (Martín Martín, 38, 41–42, 55–56, 72).

22 **FGL attends private Granada academy:** Martín Martín, 73; *FM*, 76–77; Rodrigo, *Memoria*, 19–20; Emilio Orozco Díaz, "Federico García Lorca se gradúa de bachiller. (Notas en torno a unos años de la vida del poeta)," in *Lecturas del* 27, 34, 38.

22–23 **Classmates tease FGL:** *G*, *I*, 95; Higuera Rojas, 14; author interview with Joaquín Alemán Marín.

23 **"like a sailor" and "normal":** Author interview with Joaquín Alemán Marín.

23 **FGL struggles in school:** Martín Martín, 56, 80–81; *FM*, 88; *GM*, 68. On Don Federico's response to FGL's negligence, see *FM*, 82; also author interview with Joaquín Alemán Marín.

23 **"schoolboy pride":** *FM*, 82.

23 **"vile":** *EC*, 51.

23 **"Federico, study!":** *FM*, 82.

23 **FGL's curriculum:** Martín Martín, 80, 144. On FGL's inability to learn French, see *FM*, 73; *GM*, 56.

23 **FGL receives *bachillerato*:** Martín Martín, 126–27, 131; University of Granada Archive, undergraduate records, 614–63; Huerta de San Vicente Archive, Granada.

23 **FGL's adolescent reading:** *FM*, 99–100, 143–44, 161; Rafael Martínez Nadal, "Guía al lector," in FGL, *El público y Comedia sin título*, 247. For underlined passages in FGL library, see Fernández-Montesinos García, "Descripción." On FGL's preoccupation with Omar Khayyám, see Ian Gibson, "Un probable artículo de Lorca sobre Omar Jayyam," *Cuadernos Hispanoamericanos* 433–36, vol. I (July–August 1986), 37–42.

23 **"It has everything":** Rodrigo, *García Lorca*, 196.

24 **"not a set of rules":** "Rubén Darío," in *Benét's Reader's Encyclopedia*, ed. Bruce Murphy, 4th ed. (New York: HarperCollins, 1996), 251.

24 **"Rubén Darío, 'The Magnificent' ":** FGL, "Las reglas en la música," *El Diario de Burgos*, August 18, 1917, in *OC*, IV, 42.

25 **FGL and his brother recite Hugo dialogue:** *FM*, 49–50; trans. *GM*, 35.

25 **FGL drafts siblings into performances:** *FM*, 70; Francisco García Lorca, introduction to

FGL, *Three Tragedies*, 10; Isabel García Lorca, 15–16; Auclair, 56; author interview with Joaquín Alemán Marín.

25   **FGL creates altars:** *FM*, 70; Francisco García Lorca, introduction to FGL, *Three Tragedies*, 10.

25   **FGL's love of disguise:** Rodrigo, *Memoria*, 87–88; *G, I*, 186; *FM*, 124–25.

25   **Religion in the Lorca home:** Isabel García Lorca, 17–19; author interview with Isabel García Lorca.

25   **"We're not going to that church":** Isabel García Lorca, 17.

26   **"Only stay a little while":** Author interview with Isabel García Lorca.

26   **FGL studies piano:** *FM*, 55–56, 424; Mora Guarnido, 77.

26   **"took the Holy Orders . . . passion":** *EC*, 49.

26   **"No one":** FGL, "Las reglas en la música," *El Diario de Burgos*, August 18, 1917, in *OC, IV*, 42.

26   **"like a madman":** Quevedo, *El poeta*, 10.

26   **"It wouldn't be proper":** *G, I*, 101.

26   **"*I love you*":** FGL, "Mi piano," in *OC, IV*, 666–67.

26   **"a woman who is always asleep" and "she is unpredictable":** FGL, "Fray Antonio (Poema raro)," in *OC, IV*, 756–57.

26   **"painful song":** FGL, "Elogio. Beethoven" (December 20, 1917), in *OC, IV*, 242.

26   **FGL begins composing:** Auclair, 59; *OC, IV*, 1051–52; Christopher Maurer, "Lorca y las formas de la música," in Soria Olmedo, 248–50.

26–27   **Antonio Segura Mesa:** Ian Gibson, "Federico García Lorca, su maestro de música y un artículo olvidado," *Insula* XXI (1966); Auclair, 58–59; Mora Guarnido, 75–77; Giménez Caballero; *FM*, 424.

27   **"Just because I haven't reached":** Mora Guarnido, 75.

27   **"a saint":** FGL, *Impresiones y paisajes* (author's dedication).

27   **FGL plays piano at Granada Arts Center:** Rodrigo, *Memoria*, 80–81; FGL, "Nota autobiográfica," *OC, III*, 306.

27   **FGL enrolls in University of Granada:** The Spanish university system at that time allowed students to take preparatory courses in certain disciplines, such as Philosophy and Letters, before completing their secondary school degree. University of Granada Archive, School of Philosophy and Letters records, 201–20, and Schools of Law and Philosophy and Arts records, 138–13; *FM*, 93–94.

28   **FGL expelled from class:** *FM*, 89.

28   **Paco García Lorca receives university degree:** University of Granada, General Library, academic record of Francisco García Lorca, nos. 565–67.

28   **FGL befriends university librarian:** Mora Guarnido, 145–46.

28   **FGL meets de los Ríos:** Fernando de los Ríos, "Fusilaron a F. García Lorca porque él representaba el pensamiento español . . . ," *La Prensa* (New York), October 11, 1937, 3.

28   **"eloquence, wisdom, and honesty":** Rodrigo, *Memoria*, 102.

28   **"spiritual grandson":** Virgilio Zapatero, "Estudio preliminar," in Fernando de los Ríos, *Escritos sobre democracia y socialismo*, ed. Virgilio Zapatero (Madrid: Taurus, 1975), 10–46.

29   **Fernando de los Ríos:** University of Granada, General Library, personal records of Fernando de los Ríos, 0169–1; *FM*, 96; Virgilio Zapatero, "Estudio preliminar," in Fernando de los Ríos, *Escritos sobre democracia y socialismo*, ed. Virgilio Zapatero (Madrid: Taurus, 1975), 10–46; Hernández, introduction to *FM*, xvii; Rodrigo, *Memoria*, 100; author interview with Álvaro Custodio.

29   **"listen" and "inner voice":** Hernández, introduction to *FM*, xvii.

29 **De los Ríos encourages FGL:** Hernández, introduction to *FM*, xviii; *FM*, 96; Mora Guarnido, 103–4.

29 **Paco García Lorca begins writing:** *FM*, 166.

29 **"I don't know":** Higuera Rojas, 186–87. On Don Federico's frustrations, see also *FM*, 94–95.

30 **"The children who were in my grade school":** FGL, "Mi escuela," in *OC*, IV, 848–49. Christopher Maurer presents an insightful discussion of this issue in his introduction to FGL, *Collected Poems*, x–xi.

30 **"the enormous mustachioed face," "life of fun," and "a true but charitable":** *OC*, III, 178; trans. FGL, *Deep Song*, 104.

3. YOUNG SPANIARD: 1915-16

32 **Father blames FGL's friends and "Why can't you just":** Mora Guarnido, 102–3.

32 **El Rinconcillo:** Other members of the group were Constantino Ruiz Carnero, Ramón Pérez de Roda, Juan Cristóbal, and Luis Mariscal.

32 **Friends send letter:** *FM*, 93–94. The letter was apparently published in *El Noticiero Granadino*, but because copies of the newspaper from the relevant years are missing, the specific contents of the letter remain unknown.

32 **FGL meets José Mora Guarnido:** Mora Guarnido, 47–48.

32 **José Mora Guarnido:** *FM*, 92; Rodrigo, *Memoria*, 80.

32 **"Granadan spirit":** José Mora Guarnido and Constantino Ruiz Carnero, *Libro de Granada* (1915), 18.

32 **"distant murmur":** Mora Guarnido, 48.

32 **"To my friend Federico García Lorca":** Fernández-Montesinos García, "Descripción," 97.

32 **"living archive":** José A. Muñoz Rojas, "Melchor y Federico en su correspondencia," *Ideal* (Granada), May 29, 1986, 19.

33 **Ángel Ganivet and *Granada the Beautiful*:** *FM*, 126–27; Ángel Ganivet, *Granada la bella* (Helsinki: 1896), 5, 33.

33 **"the most illustrious *granadino*":** Luis Góngora, "Apostillas a una cena de artistas," *La Noche* (Barcelona), December, 24, 1935, in *OC*, III, 623.

33 **Generation of '98:** Donald L. Shaw, *The Generation of 1898 in Spain* (London and Ton-bridge: Ernest Benn, 1975); Brenan, *Literature*, 373–75; Ward, 238–39; Auclair, 40–42; *FM*, 126.

33 **Rinconcillo's campaign to reform Granada:** See, for example, Rodrigo, *Memoria*, 141, citing correspondence from José Mora Guarnido to Melchor Fernández Almagro, Casa de los Tiros Archive, Granada. On the group's activities, see *FM*, 145–46; *EC*, 128, 148–49, 130–31.

34 **FGL resigns from Arts Center and "direction":** Together with Paquito Soriano, Melchor Fernández Almagro, and Antonio Gallego Burín, FGL signed a letter of resignation dated September 19, 1918 (Centro Artístico Archive, Granada).

34 **FGL meets Berrueta:** *FM*, 90–92.

34 **"lazy atmosphere":** *El Diario de Burgos*, November 4, 1916, 1.

34 **Martín Domínguez Berrueta:** University of Granada Archive, personal records of Martín Domínguez Berrueta, 673–6; *FM*, 90; María Cruz Ebro, *Memoria de una burgalesa*, *1885–1931* (Burgos: Diputación Provincial, 1952), 227–28; *G, I*, 104–5; *Lucidarium* 1 (Granada), June 1916, 3–4.

34 **"cheap histrionics":** Mora Guarnido, 83.

35   Berrueta's semi-annual expeditions: Cano, 25; *G, I*, 114.

35   "know and love Spain": *El Diario de Burgos*, November 4, 1916, 1.

35   Berrueta's selection of travelers: Mora Guarnido, 85–86.

35   "For the first time": Martínez Nadal, introduction to FGL, *Poems*, ix.

35   Berrueta expedition, June 1916: "Para los anales"; *G, I*, 114.

35   FGL keeps notes: FGL, "Fres-del-val" and other juvenilia (1916–17), in FGL, *Prosa inédita*, 463–88.

35   "Here among these golden stones" and "solemn black chord": FGL, *Impresiones y paisajes*, 136, and *OC*, IV, 110–15.

35   FGL reads impressions to Rinconcillo: Camilo José Cela, *La rueda de los ocios* (Barcelona: Editorial Mateu [Colección La Pluma. Autores españoles], 1957), 243, citing Melchor Fernández Almagro.

35   Segura Mesa's death: *La Gaceta del Sur* (Granada), May 27, 1916; *Defensor de Granada*, May 31, 1916.

35   Don Federico refuses to let FGL study in Paris: Auclair, 59; *G, I*, 112; Arciniegas.

35   "Since his parents": FGL, "Nota autobiográfica," *OC*, III, 306. In this 1930 document, FGL remarks, "The poet's life in Granada, until the year 1917, was dedicated exclusively to music."

36   "Never in poetry": Arciniegas.

36   FGL meets Machado: "Para los anales"; *G, I*, 115–16; *Noticiero Granadino*, June 15, 1916, 1; *FM*, 91; Rafael Laínez Alcalá, "Recuerdo de Antonio Machado en Baeza (1914–1918)," in Antonio Chicharro Chamorro, ed., *Antonio Machado y Baeza a través de la crítica* (Baeza: Universidad de verano de Baeza [Cursos internacionales de la Universidad de Granada], 1983), 56; Miguel Ángel Baamonde, "Antonio Machado y Domínguez Berrueta. Ensayo a torno a un trabajo desconocido de Antonio Machado," *Insula* 269 (April 1969), 1, 12.

36   Antonio Machado: Ward, 348–49; Antonio Chicharro Chamorro, ed., *Antonio Machado y Baeza a través de la crítica* (Baeza: Universidad de verano de Baeza [Cursos internationales de la Universidad de Granada], 1983), 11–93; Moreno Villa, 89; Alberti, *La arboleda perdida*, 220; Antonio Machado, *Selected Poems*, trans. Alan S. Trueblood (Cambridge, Mass.: Harvard University Press, 1982), 88–91.

37   FGL inscribes poem: FGL, *Collected Poems*, 776–81. FGL signed his name "Federico García Lorca, 7 August 1918"; the book in question belonged to Antonio Gallego Burín (Antonio Gallego Morell, "Cuando Federico leyó a Machado," *La Estafeta Literaria* [November 15, 1944], 25.

37   Second Berrueta expedition, October 1916: University of Granada Archive, personal records of Martín Domínguez Berrueta, 673–76; trip itinerary, AFFGL; "Para los anales."

38   "all red, all kneaded," "full of melancholy," and "There were few": FGL, *Impresiones y paisajes*, 18–23, in *OC*, IV, 54–57.

38   FGL describes visit to cloister, "took photographs," and "everything the Saint": *EC*, 29–30.

38   Mariscal and FGL appear before Ávila public and "young musician": "En el Instituto," *El Diario de Ávila*, October 20, 1916, 1.

38   Article copied and sent: FGL to parents (October 20, 1916), AFFGL.

38   FGL receives similar notices: In Santiago, FGL was hailed as a "disciple" of the composer Enrique Granados (*Diario de Galicia* [Santiago de Compostela], October 27, 1916); *G, I*, 121.

38   "But I'm stronger": *EC*, 31.

38   FGL asks father for money: *EC*, 31, 35.

38   "I'm in Salamanca": *EC*, 32.

38 "an eighteen-year-old boy": *EC*, 31.

39 FGL meets Unamuno: "Para los anales."

39 "not only of Salamanca": Antonio Machado, *Cartas a Miguel de Unamuno*, ed. José Ramón Arana (Mexico: Ediciones Monegros, 1957), 21.

39 FGL recommends Unamuno's work: *EC*, 52–53.

39 FGL inscribes poem in *Essays*: Manuel Fernández-Montesinos, "Lorca y Unamuno: Nuevos datos," *Ideal* (Granada), May 29, 1987, 11.

39 Miguel de Unamuno: Martin Nozick, *Miguel de Unamuno* (New York: Twayne, 1971), 32; Ward, 583; Donald L. Shaw, *The Generation of 1898 in Spain* (London and Tonbridge: Ernest Benn, 1975), 41–74.

39 "serene intuition": Donald L. Shaw, *The Generation of 1898 in Spain* (London and Tonbridge: Ernest Benn, 1975), 42–47.

39 "One year since": Martín, *Federico García Lorca, heterodoxo y mártir*, 150; see also *FM*, 160.

40 "Think of it": Antonio Machado, *Selected Poems*, trans. Alan S. Trueblood (Cambridge, Mass.: Harvard University Press, 1982), 145.

4. CRUCIBLE: 1917-18

41 FGL writes at night: *FM*, 160. See also "The Night," a 1917 poem in which FGL describes the "silence of night" (*OC*, IV, 234); he signed this poem at dawn (FGL, *Poesía inédita*, 62).

41 "Another day . . . growing light": FGL, "Mística que se trata de una angustia suprema que no se borra nunca," in *OC*, IV, 564.

41 "Am I to blame": FGL, "Meditación apasionada y sentimental," *OC*, IV, 656, trans. Maurer, introduction to FGL, *Collected Poems*, xxv.

41 "strange opinions": Higuera Rojas, 38. On FGL's unkempt appearance see Mora Guarnido, 105; also author interview with Vicente López.

41 FGL's use of music in early writing: Maurer, "Sobre la prosa temprana," 14–18; *FM*, 158; Maurer, introduction to FGL, *Prosa inédita*.

42 Influence of Darío: Many scholars have written about Darío's influence on FGL; see, for instance, Umbral, 43; J. B. Trend, *Lorca and the Spanish Poetic Tradition*, 4; *G, I*, 210, 214; *FM*, 162; Río, "El poeta Federico García Lorca," 178.

42 "delightful bad taste": *OC*, III, 230.

42 "When will my carnal Calvary" and "my spirit . . . sacrifice of semen": FGL, "[¿Qué hay detrás de mí . . . ?]," in *OC*, IV, 649.

42 "lips that burn": FGL, "Canciones de besos al estilo de Oriente," in *OC*, IV, 674.

42 FGL writes dialogue between Sappho and Plato: FGL, "El poema de la carne. Nostalgia olorosa y ensoñadora," in *OC*, IV, 693–95.

42 "to be a flower": FGL, "Mística que trata de la melancolía," in *OC*, IV, 547, trans. Maurer, introduction to FGL, *Collected Poems*, xxviii.

42–43 "An exotic and distant virgin" and "most of the time": FGL, "Pierrot. Poema íntimo," in *OC*, IV, 833.

43 "My Village": FGL, "Mi pueblo," in *OC*, IV, 843–64. On the significance of Compadre Pastor's death see Maurer, introduction to FGL, *Prosa inédita*, 40–41.

43 "things," "beautiful," and "If all this is": Vicenta Lorca to FGL (November 18, 1920), AFFGL, excerpted in *EC*, 87n.

44 "Good God!": Mora Guarnido, 108.

44 "You're just going to turn" and "If only I could!": Auclair, 49.

44   FGL publishes piece on Zorrilla: FGL, "Fantasía simbólica," in *OC*, IV, 39–41.

44   FGL's love of poetry and "a young olive tree": Miguel Pérez Ferrero, *Vida de Antonio Machado y Manuel* (Madrid: Espasa-Calpe [Colección Austral], 1960), 185–88.

44   FGL in Baeza, summer 1917: *G*, *I*, 162–64.

44   "I want a friendship": Lorenzo Martínez Fuset to FGL (n.d.), AFFGL.

44–45   "woman. She is lovely": Lorenzo Martínez Fuset to FGL (May 1, 1918), AFFGL.

45   "her dramas and stories": Lorenzo Martínez Fuset to FGL (February 14, 1918), AFFGL. The girl's full name was Amelia Agustina González Blanco.

45   "And I, like the saints": FGL, "Oración" (May 15, 1918), in *OC*, IV, 367.

45   "*Don Juan!*": Lorenzo Martínez Fuset to FGL (November 24, 1916; February 14, 1918), AFFGL.

45   "schoolboy scruples" and "without timidity": *EC*, 49n.

45   "Let the goblet . . . speaking with God": FGL, "Oración," in *OC*, IV, 368–69, trans. Maurer, introduction to FGL, *Collected Poems*, xxvii.

46   "under preparation": FGL, "San Pedro de Cardeña," *El Diario de Burgos*, August 3, 1917, 1.

46   FGL visit to the monastery of Silos: FGL, *Impresiones y paisajes*, 82–100, and *OC*, IV, 79–102. Friends who accompanied FGL on this visit have confirmed his account of the story (*G*, *I*, 169).

46   FGL stays on in Burgos: *G*, *I*, 172.

46   "Father says for you": Vicenta Lorca to FGL (August 9, 1917), AFFGL.

46   FGL publishes two articles in Burgos, 1917: *El Diario de Burgos*, August 18 and 22, 1917, 1.

46–47   "How are you going to lock": *OC*, IV, 43.

47   "For the cathedral's gray towers": *EC*, 237–38.

47   FGL falls in love with girl in Burgos: *G*, *I*, 176.

47   "I suppose all this": Rodrigo, *Memoria*, 139.

47   "Are you grieving": Lorenzo Martínez Fuset to FGL (September 7, 1917), AFFGL.

47   Lorca home on Acera del Casino: For dates of residence see University of Granada Archive, School of Law records, 138–13, and School of Philosophy and Letters records, 201–20; also author interview with Vicente López. Description of the home's interior is taken from Mora Guarnido, 18–19; *FM*, 266; and author interview with Vicente López.

47   "Friar Antonio": FGL, *Fray Antonio*, in *OC*, IV, 738–70. FGL left behind a series of notes on San Juan Clímaco's *La escala espiritual* (*OC*, IV, 868); the poet himself refers to *La escala espiritual* in his lecture on the *duende* (*OC*, III, 155).

48   FGL writes first poem: *FM*, 162; AFFGL.

48   "the *poet*": Fernández-Montesinos García, "Descripción," 21.

48   "I am a poet": Higuera Rojas, 104.

48   "with a word as if it were an accordion": As told to Francisco García Lorca by the writer and humorist Ramón Gómez de la Serna (*FM*, 64).

48   "mysteries of prosody": Auclair, 67.

48   FGL, on kingdoms of "poetry" and "melancholy": *EC*, 48.

48   "tragic weddings": FGL, "Romanzas con palabras" (March 1918), in *OC*, IV, 317.

48   "the roses that smell": FGL, "Carnaval. Visión interior" (1918), in *OC*, IV, 288.

48   "sensualized" and "amorous ravings": Lorenzo Martínez Fuset to FGL (n.d.), AFFGL.

48   "My life / wants to sink": FGL, "Crepúsculo," in *OC*, IV, 361.

48–49   "The spring of my life" and "What a huge sorrow": FGL, "Aria de primavera que es casi una elegía del mes de octubre" (April 30, 1918), in *OC*, IV, 340–45.

49   FGL's friends respond to his plans to publish book: Mora Guarnido, 86; Rodrigo, *Memoria*, 94–95; *FM*, 93; *G*, *I*, 177.

49 **Encounter between Mora Guarnido and Federico García Rodríguez**: Mora Guarnido, 92–93.

49 **FGL prepares manuscript**: Rafael Lozano Miralles, introduction to FGL, *Impresiones y paisajes*, ed. Rafael Lozano Miralles (Madrid: Cátedra, 1994), 33–38.

49 **"To my great friend Antonio"**: Rodrigo, *Memoria*, 97–98.

50 **"unnecessary trivialities"**: Aureliano del Castillo, "Libros. *Impresiones y paisajes* de Federico García Lorca," *Defensor de Granada*, April 19, 1918, 1.

50 **"portrait of the artist . . . knot his tie"**: Luis de Luna, "Comentarios. *Impresiones y paisajes*," *El Éxito* (Granada), May 10, 1918, 3.

50 *Impressions and Landscapes*: Unless otherwise specified, all passages are taken from FGL, *Impresiones y paisajes*, in *OC*, IV, 50–166.

51 **"tiny blemishes . . . the artist's formation"**: Aureliano del Castillo, "Libros. *Impresiones y paisajes* de Federico García Lorca," *Defensor de Granada*, April 19, 1918, 1.

51 **FGL and elegy**: See, for example, Maurer, introduction to FGL, *Collected Poems*, xxiii–xxxvii, and Maurer, introduction to FGL, *Prosa inédita*, 34–38.

52 **Berrueta's response to *Impressions and Landscapes***: Emilio Orozco Díaz, "Federico García Lorca se gradúa de bachiller. (Notas en torno a unos años de la vida del poeta)," in *Lecturas del 27*, 51.

52 **"violence"**: AFFGL in G, I, 185.

52 **"the venerable memory" and "dear teacher D. Martín"**: FGL, *Impresiones y paisajes*, in *OC*, IV, 165.

52 **"domestic flatteries"**: Berrueta evidently took offense to parts of an article in an issue of *La Publicidad* which appeared sometime before May 3, 1918, the date of Berrueta's letter to FGL. The offending issue has subsequently been lost, and it is therefore impossible to know what was said about Berrueta, and what role FGL may have played in such remarks.

52 **Berrueta's death**: University of Granada, General Library, personal record of Martín Domínguez Berrueta, nos. 673–76.

53 **"I'll never forgive myself"**: FGL said this to Berrueta's son in 1932 (G, II, 182–83).

53 **"abandon his law studies . . . harder to triumph"**: Lorenzo Martínez Fuset to FGL (April 9, 1918), AFFGL.

53 **FGL drops out of school**: In 1920, one month after Berrueta's death, FGL told Antonio Gallego Burín that he could now resume his studies at the University of Granada, because until then it had been "uncomfortable having [Berrueta] give me my exams" (*EC*, 78).

53 **"No one has taught me as much"**: Arciniegas.

53 **"Whenever he found himself"**: Manolo Altolaguirre said this of FGL (Morales, 207).

5. DEBUT 1918-20

54 **Childhood friend dies**: FGL, "Paz," in *OC*, IV, 378–80. The friend was Vicente Mercado.

54 **FGL broods about death**: Among the poems FGL wrote during the summer of 1918 was a work called "The Death of Ophelia" (*OC*, IV, 463–66). In 1918, FGL also joined a group of Rinconcillo friends in a makeshift performance of a tale about a secret treasure. Decked in a turban, cape, and robe, FGL played the part of an Arab guard who is murdered. He allowed himself to be photographed both in the act of being stabbed and in death itself (Rodrigo, *Memoria*, 189–90).

54 **Progress of World War I**: Jay Winter and Blaine Baggett, *The Great War and the Shaping of the 20th Century* (New York: Penguin Studio, 1996). For Duhamel quote, see 165.

54 **"failure of the soul"**: FGL, "Aurora del siglo XX," in *OC*, IV, 459–63.

55   **FGL attends Armistice celebration:** Rodrigo, *Memoria*, 104.

55   **De los Ríos gives speech:** Rodrigo, *Memoria*, 103.

55   **FGL hates militarism:** *EC*, 49.

55   **FGL avoids military service:** *FM*, 61; *GM*, 46; Ayuntamiento de Granada Archive.

55   **Political disturbances in Spain, early 1919:** Mora Guarnido, 151; Rodrigo, *Memoria*, 148–51; Payne, 2; Thomas, 34; Jackson, 6.

55   **"Viva Lenin":** Payne, 5. The years 1918–20 were commonly referred to in Andalusia as the "Bolshevik Years" (Carr, *Modern Spain*, 90–91).

55   **FGL and Rinconcillo denounce *caciquismo*:** Rodrigo, *Memoria*, 157, 177, quoting from *La Gaceta del Sur* (Granada), February 15, 1919.

55   **Labor crisis in Granada, February, 1919:** Rodrigo, *Memoria*, 153–56, 163–64; José Acosta Medina, *La Granada de ayer* (Granada: Imprenta Márquez, 1973), 107–9; "El caciquismo en Granada. La indignación no decrece. La persecución contra Don Fernando de los Ríos," *El Sol* (Madrid), February 9, 1919, 1.

55–56   **FGL's response to crisis:** Rodrigo, *Memoria*, 157.

56   **"giant skeleton":** *OC*, IV, 37–38.

56   **"Tell your father":** José Mora Guarnido to FGL (n.d.), AFFGL. Years later FGL gave the same advice to another local artist. "Throw your paintbrushes to the wind and get out of Granada," he told aspiring painter José Guerrero, and Guerrero did ("Yo le debo todo a Granada," *Ideal* [Granada], June 17, 1985, 11).

56   **FGL decides to move to Madrid:** *FM*, 175–76; Lorenzo Martínez Fuset to FGL (April 9, 1918), AFFGL; Giménez Caballero; *G, I*, 182. At twenty FGL had already published a book, two poems, and several articles in the Granada press (on FGL's early publications see *Boletín del Centro Artístico*, Zorrilla issue [1917]; *G, I*, 137; *FM*, 159; Gallego Morell, *Antonio Gallego Burín*, 28).

57   **"whatever he feels like doing":** *FM*, 95; *GM*, 74.

57   **FGL travels to Madrid, spring 1919:** Fernández Almagro; *G, I*, 229; Río, "Federico García Lorca," 193, 198; Mora Guarnido, 118; *FM*, 195.

57   **FGL's new clothes:** Mora Guarnido later described the "funny wardrobe" FGL initially wore in Madrid (118).

57   **"I feel as if":** *EC*, 57.

57   **Vicenta Lorca correspondence to Mora Guarnido and FGL:** José Mora Guarnido, "Doña Vicenta Lorca. Dolor y ventura de las madres de España," unidentified newspaper clipping (n.d.), Eduardo Blanco-Amor Archive, Orense; Vicenta Lorca to FGL, AFFGL.

57   **Granada friends pave FGL's way:** Mora Guarnido, 117–18.

57   **"like a wedge":** José Mora Guarnido, "El primer libro de Federico García Lorca," *El Noticiero Granadino*, July 3, 1921, 1.

57   **Marquina's response to FGL:** *EC*, 57.

57   **"so we can read":** *EC*, 60.

58   **"stupendous":** *EC*, 60.

58   **"great poet of mist":** FGL, *Impresiones y paisajes*, 187.

58   **"snub-nosed":** Juan Ramón Jiménez, "Federico García Lorca, el cárdeno granadí," in *Españoles de tres mundos*, ed. Ricardo Gullón (Madrid: Aguilar, 1969), 344.

58   **"young little poets":** *EC*, 60.

59   **"Your poet came":** Jiménez, *Selección de cartas*, 105.

59   **"My father is just rich":** [Residencia de Estudiantes], 120.

59   **"dreamy-eyed":** Alberto Jiménez Fraud, "Lorca y otros poetas," *El Nacional* (Caracas), September 19, 1957.

59   **FGL gives reading at Residencia:** *EC*, 59; Fernández Almagro.

59 **"improved enormously"**: Fernández Almagro and Gallego Burín, 39.

59 **"This business" and "If I don't"**: *EC*, 60–61.

59 **FGL attends tribute for de los Ríos**: Rodrigo, *Memoria*, 165; "Homenaje a don Fernando," *Defensor de Granada*, June 16, 1919, 1.

60 **De los Ríos elected to Parliament**: Rodrigo, *Memoria*, 162–63, 165; *El Sol* (Madrid), June 4, 1919.

60 **A Doll's House**: *La Alhambra* (Granada), June 15 and 30, 1919, 358.

60 **"destined to die young"**: A. Goldsborough Serrat, *Imagen humana y literaria de Gregorio Martínez Sierra* (Madrid: The author, 1965), 16.

60 **"This poem is pure theater!"**: Gibson offers a full description of this encounter, based upon his interview with Miguel Cerón Rubio, a friend of FGL's who was also present at the reading (*G, I*, 254–55).

61 **Martínez Sierra sends letters to FGL**: *G, I*, 255–56.

61 **FGL returns to Madrid, November 1919**: See Rodrigo, *Memoria*, 201–4; Auclair, 75; *EC*, 63n.

61 **"unendurable" and "with my silent little room"**: *EC*, 63.

61 **"the truth" and "please pick them up . . . indolent temperament"**: Francisco García Lorca to FGL (November 29, 1919), AFFGL, excerpted in *EC*, 63n.

61 **"a firm date"**: Gregorio Martínez Sierra to FGL (January 1920), AFFGL.

62 **"so much literary deadwood . . . richly primed"; Eduardo Marquina's interest in FGL's plays and poetry; and "hurry to 'arrive' . . . good work"**: *EC*, 63.

62 **"spiritual home"**: Auclair, 74–75; Alberto Jiménez Fraud, "Cincuentenario de la Residencia," in *La Residencia de Estudiantes. Visita a Maquiavelo* (Barcelona: Ariel, 1972), 63.

62 **The Residencia de Estudiantes**: [Residencia de Estudiantes]; John Crispin, *Oxford y Cambridge en Madrid. La Residencia de Estudiantes (1910–36) y su entorno cultural* (Santander: La Isla de los Ratones, 1981); José Bello, "Retrato del artista en la Residencia," *ABC* (Madrid), January 24, 1989, xxii–xxiii; Moreno Villa, 106; José Moreno Villa, "La Residencia," *Residencia* I, 1 (Madrid, 1926), 26; Alberto Jiménez Fraud, "Cincuentenario de la Residencia," in *La Residencia de Estudiantes*, 62–85; Auclair, 73; *FM*, 174; *EC*, 101n; author interviews with Arturo Sáenz de la Calzada, José Antonio Rubio Sacristán, and H. C. Rickard.

62 **"Oxford and Cambridge"**: In 1925, on visiting the Residencia for the first time, the British Hispanist John B. Trend dubbed it "Oxford and Cambridge in Madrid" (Auclair, 73).

62 **"bathed in sunlight" and "because I have to get up"**: *EC*, 66.

63 **"happy . . . I'm handsome"**: FGL, "El poema de mi cuarto" (April 8, 1920), AFFGL.

63 **"Resi"**: Alberti, "Imagen primera," 107; Cano, 46.

63 **"whales frying"**: Sáenz de la Calzada, 209.

63 **"You get absorbed"**: *EC*, 66.

63 **FGL's room free of academic tomes**: Guillermo de Torre, "Presencia de Federico García Lorca," in *La aventura estética de nuestra edad* (Barcelona: Seix Barral, 1962), 265–88.

63 **"did practically . . . always on vacation"**: Alberti, "Imagen primera," 117.

63 **Lectures at the Residencia**: Moreno Villa, 105–6; [Residencia de Estudiantes], 66–93.

63 **"nearly one thousand . . . air and sunshine"**: *OC*, III, 150.

63 **"literary accent . . . pedantry"**: *Diario de la Marina* (Havana), March 10, 1930, 12. Decades later, FGL's sister Isabel would recall that her brother disliked, above all, "pedantic and stupid people; he couldn't stand pedantry" ("Next Spring Federico García Lorca's Unpublished Works Will Come Out. Isabel García Lorca Talks About Her Brother the Writer," *España* 90, November, 1990, 16).

63 **FGL's popularity in Madrid**: Belamich, 27; Salinas; Alberti, *La arboleda*, 219; Martínez

Nadal, introduction to FGL, *Poems*, xii–xiii; Ángel del Río, "Federico García Lorca, Artista y poeta realmente prodigioso," *La Prensa* (New York), October 13, 1937, 4.

63 **"strength and weakness"**: Río, "Federico García Lorca," 199.

64 **FGL plays piano at Residencia**: Ontañón; "Memorias del doctor Carlos Martínez. I. La Residencia de Estudiantes," *El Comercio* (Gijón), October 29, 1990; Juan Chabás, "Federico García Lorca," in *Literatura española contemporanea 1898–1950* (Havana: Cultural, 1952), 435; Alberti, "Imagen primera," 115–16; Aub, 99; Alberto Jiménez Fraud, "Lorca y otros poetas," *El Nacional* (Caracas), September 19, 1957; Moreno Villa, *Vida en claro*, 108–10.

64 **"electric"**: Modesto Laza Palacios, "Recuerdo de cuatro amigos," *Sur* (Málaga), April 14, 1971, 7.

64 **"gave the impression . . . secret"**: Moreno Villa, *Vida en claro*, 110.

64 **"Play Schumann!"**: Aub, 99.

64 **"farmboy sings"**: OC, III, 137.

64 **Luis Buñuel**: Aub, 50, 267; Buñuel, *Mi último suspiro*; Moreno Villa, *Vida en claro*, 112–13; Modesto Laza Palacios, "Recuerdo de cuatro amigos," *Sur* (Málaga), April 14, 1971, 7.

64 **"uncouth, provincial athlete"**: Buñuel, *Mi último suspiro*, 65, 155.

64 **"dark, shining gaze"**: Buñuel, *Mi último suspiro*, 64.

64 **"made me know"**: Buñuel, *Mi último suspiro*, 65.

64 **FGL and Buñuel roam Madrid**: Buñuel, *Mi último suspiro*, 220; Aub, 103; José de la Colina y Tomás Pérez Turrent, "Aragón, Madrid, Paris . . . Entrevista con Luis Buñuel," *Contracampo* 16 (Madrid, October–November, 1980), 26–39.

64 **"My one great joy"**: Prados, 29–30.

64 **Emilio Prados**: Prados was in the midst of a three-year struggle to come to grips with his homosexuality (Patricio Hernández, "Presentación del epistolario de Emilio Prados a Federico García Lorca," *BFFGL*, 21–22 [December 1997], 11–12).

65 **"with whom I can discuss . . . all the more"**: Prados, 29–30.

65 **Prados contracts tuberculosis**: José María Amado, "[Conversación con Darío Carmona]," *Litoral* 29–30 (June–August 1972), n.p.

65 **"farewell . . . Will I be left alone"**: Emilio Prados to FGL (*c*. March 20, 1921), AFFGL, in Roger Tinnell, "Epistolario de Emilio Prados a Federico García Lorca," *BFFGL* 21–22 (December 1997), 31–33.

65 **"ridding ourselves"**: Emilio Prados to FGL (1922), AFFGL, in Roger Tinnell, "Epistolario de Emilio Prados a Federico García Lorca," *BFFGL* 21–22 (December 1997), 40.

65 **"a poor, impassioned"**: *EC*, 47. It is difficult to know if FGL is making a veiled allusion to Verlaine's homosexuality, and thus hinting at his own sexual ambiguity, or merely stating his kinship with the bohemian poet. That FGL felt an enduring bond with Verlaine is clear from references to the French writer in *Impressions and Landscapes*, *Songs*, and the lecture on Luis de Góngora, among other works.

66 **"although it never amounted"**: Aub, 104–5.

66 **Dr. Marañón lectures at Residencia**: [Residencia de Estudiantes], 84, 115.

66 **"freed us forever"**: Author interview with Arturo Sáenz de la Calzada.

66 **"strange and modern"**: FGL, "El poema de mi cuarto" (April 8, 1920), AFFGL.

66 **Café life in Madrid, c. 1920**: Josep Pla, *Madrid, 1921. Un dietario* (Madrid: Alianza, 1986), 73–74; Buñuel, *Mi último suspiro*, 62; Torre, 58–59; Guardia, 106; Ernesto Giménez Caballero, "Literatura española, 1918–30," in *Los vanguardistas españoles* (1925–35), 48; Moreno Villa, *Vida en claro*, 141; *FM*, 192–93; Maurer, introduction to FGL, *Collected Poems*, lii–liii; Javier Pérez Bazo, *La poesía en el siglo XX: Hasta 1939* (Madrid: Playor, 1984), 20–24; Río, "Federico García Lorca," 198; Andrew A. Anderson, "The Cultural Perspective" (unpublished Ph.D. diss. chapter), 7–9; author interview with Arturo Sáenz de la Calzada.

66 **FGL frequents Madrid *tertulias***: *FM*, 146; Mora Guarnido, 117–18; Ontañón and Moreiro, 149–50; Cano, 40; José Mora Guarnido, "El primer libro de Federico García Lorca," *El Noticiero Granadino*, July 3, 1921, 1; author interview with Santiago Ontañón.

67 **FGL works infrequently in Madrid**: Sánchez Vidal, 52; Auclair, 78; author interview with José Antonio Rubio Sacristán.

67 **FGL loses manuscripts**: Auclair, 78.

67 **"According to Martínez Sierra's"**: *EC*, 68.

67 **FGL takes part in rehearsals**: Mora Guarnido, 124; Fernández Almagro.

67 **"the greatest success"**: *EC*, 67.

67 **"I have to do theater"**: Author interview with José Antonio Rubio Sacristán.

68 **Hugo's fondness for small animals and plants**: Martín, *Federico García Lorca, heterodoxo*, 131–32, 143.

68 **"poisoned"**: The poem, dated October 23, 1917, reads in part: "That devil Shakespeare! / What poison he's poured into my soul! / Love is a terrible accident! / We sleep, and on waking / A fairy makes us adore / The first thing we see. / Such a deep tragedy! And what does God think?" (*OC*, IV, 217–19; see also María Clementa Millán, introduction to FGL, *El público*, 39–42n). FGL returned to *A Midsummer Night's Dream* in both *The Audience* and *The Dream of Life* (*G*, II, 111; Anderson, "Some Shakespearean Reminiscences," 189).

68 ***The Butterfly's Evil Spell***: All passages from *The Butterfly's Evil Spell* are taken from *OC*, IV, 167–211.

68 **Maeterlinck's preoccupation with death**: In his 1891 play *The Intruder*, Maeterlinck personifies death in much the same way FGL does in *The Butterfly's Evil Spell* (Maurice Maeterlinck, *The Intruder*, in Haskell M. Block and Robert G. Shedd, ed., *Masters of Modern Drama* [New York: Random House, 1962]). For Maeterlinck's influence on *The Butterfly's Evil Spell*, see Fernández Cifuentes, 35.

69 **FGL struggles to find title for play**: Mora Guarnido, 125; *FM*, 262; Francisco García Lorca, prologue to FGL, *Three Tragedies*, 12.

69 **Difficulties with set designs**: Mora Guarnido, 124; *FM*, 263; Carlos Reyero Hermosilla, *Gregorio Martínez Sierra y el Teatro de Arte* (Madrid: Fundación Juan March, 1980), 10.

69 **Martínez Sierra's impatience**: According to Mora Guarnido, Martínez Sierra worked with a "strange impatience" on this production (124).

69 **"mute anguish"**: Morales, 188.

69 **FGL attempts to withdraw play**: Mora Guarnido, 126; Morales, 188; *FM*, 265.

69 **FGL declines to contribute self-critique**: *G*, I, 261, citing correspondence from *La Tribuna* to FGL, AFFGL.

69 **Confusion surrounds premiere**: *Heraldo de Madrid*, March 11, 12, 13, and 16, 1920; *El Sol* (Madrid), March 11, 16, and 17, 1920.

69 **"anything you like"**: Mora Guarnido, 125.

70 **"Any comedy . . . at home"**: Joaquín Belda, *En el país del bluff; veinte días en Nueva York* (Madrid: Biblioteca Hispania, 1925), 75.

70 **"The public today"**: R. Martínez de la Riva, "Vida nacional. El teatro de Martínez Sierra," *Blanco y Negro*, November 20, 1921.

70 **FGL's friends attend opening night**: Fernández Almagro; Guardia, 274–75; "Memorias del doctor Carlos Martínez. I. La Residencia de Estudiantes," *El Comercio* (Gijón), October 29, 1990; *FM*, 263. According to Isabel García Lorca, María Luisa Egea had left Granada sometime in the late teens or early 1920s; she later married a German businessman (*G*, I, 192).

70 **FGL waits backstage**: Rodrigo, *García Lorca*, 60.

70 **Madrid critics attend opening**: Fernández Almagro.

70   **"Ladies and Gentlemen"**: *OC*, IV, 168.

70   **"little horns"**: Mora Guarnido, 128.

70–71   **"This is for Atheneumites!"**: Ángel del Río, "El *'Romancero gitano'* fue la consagración de García Lorca," *La Prensa* (New York), October 14, 1937, 4.

71   **"We can't hear"**: Guardia, 274.

71   **Description of opening night**: Fernández Almagro; Guardia, 274–75; Rodrigo, *Memoria*, 203; *FM*, 263; Ángel del Río, "El *'Romancero gitano,'* fue la consagracíon de García Lorca," *La Prensa* (New York), October 14, 1937, 4; *G*, I, 262.

71   **"I'm visibly moved . . . about the audience"**: Fernández Almagro.

71   **"stomping on my head"**: Rodrigo, *García Lorca*, 60.

71   **"awful time"**: Rodrigo, *Memoria*, 203.

71   **FGL credits La Argentinita**: Morla Lynch, 29.

71   **FGL prevented from going onstage and Rodríguez Espinosa awaits news**: Fernández Almagro.

71   **"The work was not a success"**: *FM*, 266.

71   **"In order to create"**: F. Aznar Navarro, *La Correspondencia* (Madrid), March 23, 1920, 4. For an overview of critical reactions to the play see Fernández Cifuentes, 44, and Dougherty and Vilches, 131.

71   **"Señor García Lorca"**: Manuel Machado, *La Libertad* (Madrid), March 23, 1920.

72   **"conventional" and night at the zoo**: Don Pablos, "Teatro Eslava: Dos estrenos," *Heraldo de Madrid*, March 23, 1920, 6.

72   **"the highly esteemed"**: F. Aznar Navarro, *La Correspondencia* (Madrid), March 23, 1920, 4.

72   **"extremely noble"**: J. A., *El Sol* (Madrid), March 23, 1920, 11.

72   **FGL's response to *The Butterfly's Evil Spell* debacle**: *G*, I, 265; Alberti, "Imagen," 128; Ontañón; "El poeta español García Lorca, en el Avenida," *El Diario Español* (Buenos Aires), October 25, 1933, 3.

72   **"the classic debut"**: Morla Lynch, 29.

72   **"one consecutive performance"**: Eduardo Blanco-Amor, "Federico, otra vez; la misma vez," *El País* (Madrid), October 1, 1978, VI.

6. PORTRAIT OF YOUTH: 1920-21

73   **FGL sends angry letter to father**: *EC*, 72–75. That FGL remained in Madrid well into April 1920 is clear from Fernández-Montesinos, "Federico García Lorca en la Residencia de Estudiantes," 6; and José María Barrera López, "Amistad y evocaciones: Pedro Garfías y Federico García Lorca," *BFFGL* 9 (June 1991), 169.

74   **FGL's father apparently relents**: Although the guitarist Regino Sáinz de la Maza recalled meeting FGL in Granada in late May 1920 (Paloma Sáinz de la Maza, *Regino Sáinz de la Maza. Semblanza de mi padre* [Burgos: Excmo. Ayuntamiento, 1982], 141), evidence from FGL's letters home suggests he remained in Madrid until late June 1920, and probably mailed his review of Sáinz's appearance to Granada's *Gaceta del Sur* (Andrew A. Anderson, "¿Entre prodigio y protegido? El joven Lorca en Madrid [1919–20]," *BFFGL* 17 [June 1995], 97).

74   **"I can have the pleasure"**: *EC*, 77.

74   **"You must force"**: Agustí, 293.

74   **FGL writes play about Jehovah**: According to the manuscript of the work, FGL began this untitled play on May 6, 1920 (AFFGL).

74   **"like all of us"**: FGL, "Notas de arte: Sáinz de la Maza," *Gaceta del Sur* (Granada), May 27, 1920, 1, in *OC*, III, 277.

74   "If you'd pass": All quotations in this passage are taken from FGL to Antonio Gallego Burín (*EC*, 77–80).

74–75 "Little by little," "It pains my father," and "Must I, Antonio": *EC*, 77–78. For background material on Antonio Gallego Burín see Gallego Morell, *Antonio Gallego Burín*, 13–37.

75   **FGL writes verse, summer 1920:** Hernández, introduction to FGL, *Libro de poemas*.

75   "there'd be hell": José Fernandez-Montesinos went along with FGL's scheme mostly "in order to get a laugh, because we've all been laughing about that confounded Faculty of Letters" (Rodrigo, *Memoria*, 137–38).

75   **FGL passes exams:** University of Granada Archive, School of Philosophy and Letters records, 201–20.

75   "memorable place": Mora Guarnido, 82.

75   "I am utterly engrossed": *G, I*, 287, citing a letter in a private archive.

75   "everything I do": *EC*, 81.

75   "My father is extraordinary": Aub, 99.

75   "*mi niña Isabelita*": *EC*, 118.

76   "great news": *EC*, 85.

76   "my child": *EC*, 100. On FGL's gift of bonbons, see *EC*, 107n.

76   "is more important": Vicenta Lorca to FGL (October 28, 1920), AFFGL, excerpted in *EC*, 84n.

76   **Vicenta Lorca correspondence to FGL:** AFFGL.

76   **Don Federico waits for mail:** Correspondence from Vicenta Lorca to FGL (March 29, 1921; April 26, 1921).

76   "forgetting that it could kill me": Vicenta Lorca to FGL (spring 1921), AFFGL.

76   **FGL friendship with Emilia Llanos:** Higuera Rojas, 76–88; Gallego Morell, *Sobre García Lorca*, 75.

76   "as one should remember . . . telltale sign remains forever!": *EC*, 92.

76   **Birth and baptism of Isabel Clara Ángeles Ortiz:** Rodrigo, *Memoria*, 204–6. Shortly after Isabel Clara's birth, FGL wrote a poem in which he expressed his desire that her parents' home be a "meadow of flowers" of unparalleled beauty, and that the "nightingale" of their love continue to flourish (AFFGL).

77   "look at pretty things": Rodrigo, *Memoria*, 202.

77   "and I love them": Higuera, 104.

77   "He is so timid": Jiménez, *Selección de cartas*, 141.

77   "true": *EC*, 184n.

77   **Marquina and Martínez Sierra express interest in FGL's work:** *EC*, 63.

77   "You mustn't content yourself": Vicenta Lorca to FGL (spring 1921), AFFGL.

77   "the precarious publicity": José Mora Guarnido, "Dos poetas andaluces: Federico García Lorca y Rafael Alberti," *Pluma* IV (Montevideo, 1928), 51–57.

77   "irresponsibility and impetuosity": *EC*, 117.

77   "To defend them": Guillén, "Federico en persona," xlviii.

77   "with a sense of rupture": Mora Guarnido, 121.

77   "I publish only": Auclair, 84.

77   "almost by force": Mora Guarnido, 121.

77   **Gabriel García Maroto:** Mora Guarnido, 121–22; Hernández, introduction to FGL, *Libro de poemas*, 33; Gabriel García Maroto, *La nueva Espaná 1930. Resumen de la vida artística española desde el año 1927 hasta hoy* (Madrid: Biblos, [1931]), 21 and frontispiece.

78   "ugly": *EC*, 115–16. He added that in the fall of 1921 he intended to bring out a second book with Martínez Sierra—a collection of newer poems.

78   FGL selects poems for inclusion in poetry collection: *FM*, 190; Martín, *Federico García Lorca, heterodoxo*, 98–100; Hernández, "Francisco y Federico García Lorca," ii–iii.

78   "you're confronting": *EC*, 115.

78   "a pure poet . . . hackneyed ideas": *EC*, 105.

78   "As far as the public": Vicenta Lorca to FGL (spring 1921), AFFGL.

78   "to help you": Hernández, "Francisco y Federico García Lorca," xii; trans. *GM*, xvi.

78   FGL helps plan Tagore visit: FGL correspondence to parents (spring 1921), *EC*, 103–14. See also "Rabindranath Tagore, en Madrid," *El Sol* (Madrid), April 6, 1921, 1; "Teatros. Escuela Nueva. El rey y la reina," *El Sol* (Madrid), April 11, 1921, 3; "Viaje suspendido Rabindranath Tagore," *El Sol* (Madrid), April 27, 1921.

78   "Federico, don't waste time": Vicenta Lorca to FGL ([1921]), AFFGL.

78   "if he's happy": Vicenta Lorca to FGL (May 2, 1921), AFFGL.

78   "I'm turning blacker": *EC*, 113.

79   FGL shares room with Pepín Bello: Sánchez Vidal, 52.

79   "dissection and putrefaction": María Asunción Mateo, "Entrevista. José Bello. 'Las relaciones de Lorca y Dalí han sido falseadas,'" *Blanco y Negro* (Madrid), May 26, 1991, 74–79.

79   "a mischievous genius": Martínez Nadal, *Cuatro lecciones*, 22.

79   Pepín Bello: Buñuel, *Mi último suspiro*, 63–64, 71; Aub, 287; Sánchez Vidal, 35; *G, I*, 358–59; Rafael Santos Torroella, "Pepín Bello, o la amistad."

79   "special aura": José Bello to FGL (December 2, 1926), AFFGL. In this letter Bello also expressed his thoughts on the temperamental traits he and FGL shared.

79   "cherry": José Bello to FGL (August 27, 1924), AFFGL; *G, I*, 360.

79   FGL reads Lope de Vega plays: Sánchez Vidal, 56. Bello. later claimed to know more than one hundred plays by Lope, without having read a single text himself. He knew them solely through FGL's readings, he said.

79   "labor pains": Consuelo Lluva, "José Bello. El cuarto amigo," *Heraldo de Aragón* (Zaragoza), January 5, 1990, 7.

79   "the most perfect thing" and "I'm very happy": *EC*, 114, 117.

79   *Book of Poems* published: Hernández, introduction to FGL, *Libro de poemas*, 39.

79   Bello signs copies of *Book of Poems*: Sánchez Vidal, 52.

80   Relationship between FGL and brother: Hernández, "Francisco y Federico García Lorca," i; *GM*, viii; Manuel Fernández-Montesinos, "Federico García Lorca en su entorno humano," *Problemas de edición de la obra de Federico García Lorca* (University of Granada, 1984).

80   Paco García Lorca advises FGL to include early work in book: This was not the first time Paco helped to organize his brother's writing. Working together, the two Lorca brothers first attempted to select and organize Federico's juvenilia in March 1918. On his own, Paco continued this work until November 1918, when he reached a round number of one hundred poems. After December 1918, neither brother attempted to select or organize the poems. Paco's initial selection of one hundred poems was never printed as a book (*Catálogo general de los fondos documentales de la Fundación Federico García Lorca. Vol. II. Manuscritos de la obra poética juvenil [1917–19]*, ed. Christian de Paepe [Madrid: Ministerio de Cultura, Fundación Banesto, Fundación Federico García Lorca, 1993]).

80   "I offer, in this book": *OC, I*, 59. José Mora Guarnido would later suggest that the book's publisher, Gabriel García Maroto, wrote the prologue to *Book of Poems* rather than FGL himself. Mora Guarnido believed FGL might have given the task to Maroto, much as he allowed Gregorio Martínez Sierra to take responsibility for the title of *The Butterfly's Evil Spell*. Some critics agree with Mora's theory; others do not. The tone of the prologue to *Book of Poems* is reminiscent of the tone of FGL's prologue to *Impressions and Land-*

scapes, and it therefore seems probable the poet had some hand in its composition (Mora Guarnido, 122, 179; see also Hernández, introduction to FGL, *Libro de poemas*, 33–34).

80 **Presence of *vega* in *Book of Poems***: FM, 58; José Mora Guarnido, "El primer libro de Federico García Lorca," *El Noticiero Granadino*, July 3, 1921, 1; Morris, *Son of Andalusia*, 146–76.

81 **FGL's gift for images**: Maurer, introduction to FGL, *Collected Poems*, liii; José Hierro, "El primer Lorca," *Cuadernos Hispanoamericanos* 224–25 (August–September 1968), 437–62; Hernández, introduction to FGL, *Libro de poemas*.

81 **Influence of Darío and Jiménez on *Book of Poems***: FM, 194; Río, "El poeta Federico García Lorca," 178; Umbral, 43; Miguel García-Posada, introduction to FGL, *Poesía I*, 2nd. ed. (Madrid: Akal, 1982), 127; Morris, *Son of Andalusia*, 167–68. There are hints, too, of the early Spanish poet Salvador Rueda in this collection (see Carlos Edmundo de Ory, "Salvador Rueda y García Lorca," *Cuadernos Hispanoamericanos* 255 [March 1971], 417–44).

81 **Machado's influence on *Book of Poems***: FM, 194; José Manuel González Herrán, "Resonancias de Machado en el *Libro de poemas* de García Lorca," *Pena Labra* 24–25 (summer 1977), n.p.; Donald L. Shaw, *The Generation of 1898 in Spain* (London and Tonbridge: Ernest Benn, 1975), 133–36; Morris, *A Generation*, 6–7.

81 **FGL's use of popular song in *Book of Poems***: Hernández, introduction to FGL, *Libro de poemas*, 26; Devoto, "Notas sobre el elemento tradicional"; FGL, *Autógrafos III*, 240f. See also Ian Gibson's fine study of Lorca's "Sad Ballad" ("Lorca's 'Balada triste': Children's Songs and the Theme of Sexual Disharmony in *Libro de poemas*," *Bulletin of Hispanic Studies* [Liverpool], XLVI [1969], 21–38).

82 **"I'm very happy . . . herd of panthers"**: EC, 119.

83 **Maroto neglects to promote *Book of Poems***: Adolfo Salazar to FGL (August 13, 1921), AFFGL. According to a letter from an employee at Maroto's press, FGL failed to tell anyone where to send the books, and copies of *Book of Poems* were accordingly not shipped to the Ganivet Bookstore in Granada until July 15, one month after the book's publication. Copies were not sent to Madrid bookstores until July 21 (EC, 122n, and Maurer, "De la correspondencia," 61). For FGL's requests for help from friends see, for example, EC, 119.

83 **"a singer of stars"**: José Mora Guarnido, "El primer libro de Federico García Lorca," *El Noticiero Granadino*, July 3, 1921, 1.

83 **Adolfo Salazar**: Salazar's first article on literature was a review of a book on Spain by the British musicologist John B. Trend. It appeared on July 15, 1921, just two weeks before his review of *Book of Poems* (Adolfo Salazar, "Los amigos de España. Como ve nuestro país un escritor inglés," *El Sol* [Madrid], July 15, 1921, 3; Adolfo Salazar to FGL [November 9, 1921], AFFGL; Adolfo Salazar to FGL [August 13, 1921], AFFGL; Adolfo Salazar to FGL [July 31, 1921], AFFGL).

83 **"A New Poet"**: This and all subsequent passages from this review are taken from Adolfo Salazar, "Un poeta nuevo. Federico García Lorca," *El Sol* (Madrid), July 30, 1921, 3.

83 **Salazar writes to Federico García Lorca**: Adolfo Salazar to FGL (July 31, 1921), AFFGL; see also EC, 121n.

83–84 **"The only way to repay . . . find myself in my book" and "If you could only see"**: EC, 121–22, trans. FGL, *Selected Letters*, 17–18.

84 **"are oblivious . . . your spirit"**: Adolfo Salazar to FGL (August 13, 1921), AFFGL.

84 ***Book of Poems* receives three additional reviews**: Hernández, introduction to FGL, *Libro de poemas*, 27, 40. See also Cipriano Rivas Cherif, "Federico García Lorca," *La Pluma* II, 15 (Madrid, August 1921), 126–27; and Guillermo de Torre, "Libro de poemas por Federico García Lorca," *Cosmópolis* 35 (Madrid, November 1921), 528.

84 "less reminiscent": Trend, 2–3. The original review appeared on January 14, 1922, in *The Nation and the Athenaeum.*

84 "languished in silence": EC, 756.

84 "a failure": EC, 121–22, trans. FGL, *Selected Letters*, 17–18.

84 "our local poet": Salvador de Madariaga, "Tres estampas de Federico García Lorca," in *De Galdós a Lorca* (Buenos Aires: Sudamericana, 1960), 219.

84 FGL experiments with haiku: Hernández, "Francisco y Federico García Lorca," xiii. In a note to his family in 1921 he explained that haiku was the "utmost Japanese song, which the new French poets have brought to Europe and which, because of my particular love for everything that's new, I am attempting as a mere pastime" (FGL, "Hai-Kais de felicitación a Mama" [1921], AFFGL).

85 "render in words": EC, 124; trans. FGL, *Selected Letters*, 18.

85 "Especially at nightfall": EC, 123.

85 "The night sky": FGL, "Fin," in *OC*, I, 217, trans. FGL, *Collected Poems*, 245. All subsequent translations from *Suites* are taken from FGL, *Collected Poems.*

85 FGL composes some seventy-five poems: André Belamich, introduction to FGL, *Suites*, 9–14; EC, 136; Hernández, introduction to FGL, *Primeras canciones*, 24.

86 FGL publishes suites in *Índice*: Comincioli, 61–62; *Índice* 2–3 (1921).

86 FGL receives letter soliciting financial help: Juan Guerrero to FGL (December 26, 1922), AFFGL.

86 FGL studies guitar: EC, 123.

86–87 *"hammering* away," *"old people . . . with laughter,"* and *"I'm very much loved"*: EC, 124–25; see also Morris, *Son of Andalusia*, 34.

87 "I see life is now casting": EC, 125; trans. FGL, *Selected Letters*, 19.

87 "I'm coming back": FGL, *Collected Poems*, 249.

7. FALLA: 1921-23

88 FGL resumes law studies: University of Granada Archive, School of Law records, 138–13. See also *FM*, 98. To an economics professor who took pity on him and rallied others to his cause, FGL later dedicated a poem (*G, I*, 302; *OC*, I, 414.)

88 "neither sad nor happy": EC, 131.

88 "You're not doing anything": Melchor Fernández Almagro to FGL (October 13, 1921), AFFGL.

88 "I don't like to think of you": Adolfo Salazar to FGL (November 9, 1921), AFFGL.

88 "architects and junk dealers . . . color or ambiance": Letter from FGL and others to Centro Artístico de Granada, Centro Artístico Archive.

88 *"granadinos* of pure stock": EC, 149. Granadans had recently begun to shed their age-old bias against the Moors who once occupied the city. In the 1920s, the University of Granada began to offer courses in Arabic languages, and a Center for Arabic Studies opened (see Emilio García Gómez, *La Silla del Moro y nuevas escenas andaluzas* [Madrid: Austral Espasa Calpe, n.d.], 77).

89 Gypsy song: For examples of *cante jondo* see Brenan, *The Literature*, 330–34, and OC, III, 40–50.

89 Falla urges FGL and friends to stage festival: In fact, it was Miguel Cerón, a friend of Falla's in Granada, who apparently first suggested the idea of a *cante jondo* competition to the composer. On the origins and organization of the festival see Hernández, introduction

to FGL, *Poema del cante jondo*, 22–23; Rodrigo, *Memoria*, 214; Eduardo Molinda Fajardo, *Manuel de Falla y el "cante jondo"* (Granada: University of Granada, 1962), 49; and Granada press reports (January–June 1922).

89   **Manuel de Falla:** *FM*, 148; Manuel Orozco, *Falla. Biografía ilustrada* (Barcelona: Destino, 1968); Adams, 78–79; Rodrigo, *Memoria*, 184; María Martínez Sierra, *Gregorio y yo. Medio siglo de colaboración* (México: Biografías Gandesa, 1953), 120–21. For Falla's thoughts on the term "Maestro," see *EC*, 210n.

89–90 **"When you're dead" and "a saint":** Suero, "Crónica."

90   **"my dear son":** Brickell, 389.

90   **"the most beautiful panorama":** Sopeña, 65.

90   **"silence, above all silence":** Rodrigo, *Memoria*, 198, citing an interview in *La Voz* (Madrid), July 12, 1920. On Falla's mania for silence see also *FM*, 149–52.

90   **"new ideas and new projects":** *Casa Museo Manuel de Falla*, 66, citing article by Adolfo Salazar in *El Sol* (Madrid), October 25, 1921.

90   **"frugal":** *FM*, 157. See also Mora Guarnido, 156–58; Emilio García Gómez, *La Silla del Moro y neuvas escenas andaluzas* (Madrid: Austral Espasa Calpe, n.d.), 84–85; Auclair, 110.

91   **"to become better each day":** Suero, "Crónica."

91   **"truth without authenticity":** Maurer, introduction to FGL, *Collected Poems*, xlv.

91   *coplas:* Brenan, *The Literature*, 330; FGL, *Deep Song*, 31.

91–92 **"naked," "all the passions," and "consult the wind":** *C*, I, 51–71, trans. FGL, *Deep Song*, 24–33; see also *OC*, III, 33–52.

92   **FGL helps circulate petition:** *EC*, 136.

92   **FGL serenades Falla:** *EC*, 137–38; Juan Viniegra, "Charla con Miguel Cerón," in Juan de Loxa, ed., *Federico del Sagrado Corazón de Jesús–Manuel María de Dolores Falla Matheu* (Fuentevaqueros, Granada: Comisión Organizadora del Hermanamiento Falla-Lorca, 1982), 25.

92   **"Manuelito":** *EC*, 136.

92   **FGL relates story of festival organization:** *OC*, III, 33–34.

92   **"than a musician":** *C*, I, 55–56.

93   **FGL and Manolo Ángeles Ortiz seek singers:** Rodrigo, *Memoria*, 218–19; Auclair, 116–18. On the death of Ángeles Ortiz's wife, Paquita, see Rodrigo, *Memoria*, 206–16, 275.

93   **"bloodcurdling":** Auclair, 116.

93   **FGL's knowledge of popular song:** Ontañón; Marcelle Schveitzer, "Souvenir sur Federico García Lorca," in Louis Parrot, *Federico García Lorca*, with Marcelle Schveitzer and Armand Guibert (Paris: Seghers, 1947), 193; Federico de Onís, "García Lorca, folklorista," *Revista Hispánica Moderna* VI (1940), 3–4, Auclair, 170. See also FGL's lectures on lullabies and *cante jondo* in *OC*, III.

93   **"book of hours":** Rodolfo Halffter, "Manuel de Falla y los compositores del Grupo de Madrid de la Generación del 27," in *La Música en la Generación del 27. Homenaje a Lorca. 1915 / 1936* exhibition catalog (Madrid: Ministry of Culture, 1986), 39.

93   **"While a cathedral":** *OC*, III, 113, trans. FGL, *Deep Song*, 8.

94   **"magnificent poetry":** "García Lorca presenta hoy tres canciones populares escenificadas," *Crítica* (Buenos Aires), December 15, 1933, in FGL, *La zapatera prodigiosa*, 188.

94   **"much calmer . . . all memories":** *EC*, 143.

94   **Silverio Franconetti anecdote:** Luis Rosales, "Evocación de Federico," *Cuadernos Hispanoamericanos* 475 (January 1990), 32.

94   **"festival full of dirty":** Antonio Gallego Morell, "El concurso de Cante Jondo en la Granada de 1922," *ABC* (Madrid), November 5, 1960.

95   **"poor, badly constructed lecture"**: This and all subsequent quotations from FGL's deep-song lecture are taken from *OC*, III, 33–52; trans. FGL, *Deep Song*, 23–41. In the 1930s FGL shortened the title of this talk to "Architecture of the Deep Song."

95   **"grand success"**: "Centro Artístico: Conferencia sobre el 'cante jondo,'" *Noticiero Granadino*, February 21, 1922, 4.

95   **"some family storms" and "so much beauty"**: FGL to Adolfo Salazar (February 2, 1922), in María Teresa Babín, *Federico García Lorca. Cincuenta años de gloria (1936–1986)* (San Juan, P.R.: Biblioteca de Autores Puertorriqueños, 1986), 41–43. On Buñuel's telegram, see *EC*, 142.

96   **"Andalusian character . . . master of my soul"**: *EC*, 141.

96   **FGL begins *Poem of the Deep Song***: In fact, FGL wrote the first of his deep-song poems, the six "Viñetas flamencas," in August 1921. During this same period he composed the six-part suite "Remansos." It is difficult to know whether he originally intended to include "Viñetas" in his *Suites* or in the later *Poem of the Deep Song*. He does not seem to have fully conceived of the idea of a deep-song collection until November of 1921 (Mario Hernández, "Ocho cartas inéditas [Comentario]," *Trece de Nieve* 1–2, 2nd series, 2nd ed. [Madrid, December 1976], 45; Belamich, 29; FGL, *Poema del cante jondo*, 193; Morris, *Son of Andalusia*, 185–250.

96   **"the little golden roof tiles," "distinct from . . . sublime songs," and *"another orientation . . . never touched this theme"***: *EC*, 136–37.

97   **"*Malagueñas, soleares*"**: Morris, *Son of Andalusia*, 193–94.

97   **"we can do nothing"**: C, I, 71–72, trans. FGL, *Poem of the Deep Song*, 33–34. See also Maurer, introduction to FGL, *Collected Poems*, xliii–xliv.

97   **"a terrible cry . . . measured silence"**: *OC*, III, 36.

97   **"The Silence"**: This and all subsequent passages from *Poem of the Deep Song* are taken from *OC*, I, 305–43, trans. FGL, *Collected Poems*.

98   **"The olive trees"**: G, I, 306. For FGL's use of anecdotal material in this collection see *FM*, 40–41.

98–99   **FGL and Andalusia**: Many critics have written extensively on this topic; see, for example, Morris, *Son of Andalusia*; Miguel García-Posada, introduction to FGL, *Poesía I*, 2nd ed. (Madrid: Akal, 1982), 83–87; Allen Josephs, *White Wall of Spain: The Mysteries of Andalusian Culture* (Ames, Iowa: Iowa State University Press, 1983); Umbral, 13.

100   **FGL reads poems to Gypsies**: Hernández, introduction to FGL, *Poema del cante jondo*, 23–27.

100   **"distinguished and aristocratic" and "Granada has a poet . . . glory"**: "En el Palace Hotel," *Defensor de Granada*, June 8, 1922.

100   **"all of its detractors"**: FGL, "Cuartilla García Lorca," *Noticiero Granadino*, June 18, 1922, in *OC*, III, 357.

100   **Deep Song Competition of 1922**: Auclair, 121; "De Granada: El 'cante jondo,'" *Defensor de Granada*, June 21, 1922; "'El cante jondo,'" *Defensor de Granada*, June 9, 1922, 1; "'El cante jondo,'" *Noticiero Granadino*, June 8, 1922.

100   **"knows nothing"**: *OC*, III, 45.

100   **"wound from a traitor's"**: Bernardo Morales Pareja, "La fiesta de la raza," *Defensor de Granada*, June 23, 1922, 1.

101   **"festival of great Truth"**: Antonio Gallego Burín, "El concurso de 'cante jondo,'" *Noticiero Granadino*, June 15, 1922.

101   **"I told you . . . bullfight"**: FGL, "Cuartilla García Lorca," *Noticiero Granadino*, June 18, 1922, in *OC*, III, 357.

101   **"very happy . . . 'pianissimo of gold'"**: *EC*, 147.

101 "little plaintive . . . unhappy heart" and "You have no idea . . . pregnant": EC, 155, trans. FGL, Selected Letters, 35.

101 "calm and serene": EC, 148.

101–2 "admirable book . . . water obsession I suffer!": EC, 155–56, trans. FGL, Selected Letters, 35–36.

102 "Enough of Castile!": EC, 148.

102 Falla's enthusiasm for puppet theater: EC, 138; Casa Museo Manuel de Falla, 50; G, I, 281; Rodrigo, Memoria, 120–21.

103 "our own invention . . . faultless art": EC, 153, trans. FGL, Selected Letters, 29.

103 "backbone": FGL, "Diálogo del poeta y don Cristóbal," Crítica (Buenos Aires), March 26, 1934.

103 "the dream of my youth": EC, 138.

103 "represents the joy of free living": This and all subsequent quotations from The Billy Club Puppets are taken from OC, II, 40–79.

105 "Then my Señor Papá": EC, 162.

105 "that dandyish": EC, 150, trans. FGL, Selected Letters, 21.

105 "My father's so funny!": Altolaguirre, Obras completas I, 282.

105 "terribly happy . . . with a child's enthusiasm": EC, 165.

105 Lanz's enthusiasm for puppet show: Hermenegildo Lanz Archive, Granada.

106 "curls and ribbons": FGL, "Diálogo del poeta y don Cristóbal," Crítica (Buenos Aires), March 26, 1934.

106 "upon that roomful": FM, 275, trans. GM, 147.

106 1923 puppet play: For descriptions of this event see Francisco García Lorca, introduction to FGL, Five Plays, 10–12; Hernández, "Retablo de las maravillas"; FM, 270–75; José Mora Guarnido, "Crónicas granadinas. El teatro 'Cachiporra' de Andalucía," La Voz (Madrid), January 19, 1923; author interviews with Enrique Lanz and Manuel Fernández-Montesinos; and Hermenegildo Lanz Archive, Granada.

106 Press coverage of puppet show: Hernández, "Retablo de las maravillas"; José Mora Guarnido, "Crónicas granadinas. El teatro 'Cachiporra' de Andalucía," La Voz (Madrid), January 19, 1923; José Francés, "Los bellos ejemplos. En Granada resucita el Guignol," La Esfera (Madrid), X, 475, February 10, 1923.

106 "six, eight, or ten": Hermenegildo Lanz Archive, Granada.

106 "the State . . . spider": Altolaguirre, Obras completas I, 280–82; Manuel Altolaguirre, "Recuerdos de Federico García Lorca," Previsión y Seguridad (Monterey, 1944), 601; Auclair, 73.

107 FGL completes university degree: FM, 93–102; Torre, 58–63.

8. GARDEN OF POSSIBILITIES: 1923-24

108 FGL and Francisco García Lorca travel to Madrid: EC, 171–72. See also Vicenta Lorca to Federico García Rodríguez (March 19, 1923), AFFGL, and GM, xvi and xviii.

108 "feted and pursued": EC, 176.

108 "little poet . . . torpor": Andrew A. Anderson, "Adolfo Salazar, El poeta forastero: Una evocación olvidada de Federico García Lorca," BFFGL 4 (December 1988), 114–19.

109 "unbelievably kind": GM, xvii.

109 "Paco" and "Pico": Mario Hernández, "García Lorca y Vicente Aleixandre: Papeles perdidos, líneas halladas," in Soria Olmedo, 229.

109 "lively, fresh, and spontaneous": Salinas and Guillén, 40.

109 "Czechoslovak painter": Buñuel, Mi último suspiro, 66.

109 "savior": Dalí, *Vida secreta*, 4.

110 "like mad . . . I am sure of it": Gibson et al., 21; Gibson, "Salvador Dalí," 61.

110 "In a short time . . . with myself": Gibson, "Salvador Dalí," 61.

110 **FGL meets Dalí:** Buñuel, *Mi último suspiro*, 66; Santos Torroella, *Dalí residente*, 23; Dalí, *Vida secreta*, 188–89; G, I, 334, 370; Vázquez Ocaña, *García Lorca: Vida*, 103.

111 "Should I be liking this?": José María Moreiro, "Dalí, en el centro de los recuerdos," *El País Semanal* (Madrid), October 23, 1983, 17.

111 "almost mute": Moreno Villa, *Vida en claro*, 111.

111 "I'll say . . . very interesting painter": José María Moreiro, "Dalí, en el centro de los recuerdos," *El País Semanal* (Madrid), October 23, 1983, 19.

111 "nothing more than Lorca's echo": [Residencia de Estudiantes], 120.

111 "We drank lousy local champagne": Dalí, *Vida secreta*, 212.

112 *"that plays . . . fifteen days"*: EC, 188.

112 *Master Peter's Puppet Show: Master Peter's Puppet Show* premiered on a puppet stage in the home of the Princesse de Polignac, an American heiress who had underwritten the cost of the production. In the audience were Paul Valéry, Igor Stravinsky, and Pablo Picasso (Juan Bustos, "Hermenegildo Lanz, el gran desconocido," *Diario de Granada*, June 24, 1983, 16–17). See also Falla correspondence to FGL and Francisco García Lorca, AFFGL.

112 "Even if you don't": Vicenta Lorca to FGL (*c.* March 1923), AFFGL, excerpted in *EC*, 180n.

112 "in love": *EC*, 250.

112 "put his hands": *EC*, 239.

112 "control . . . real artist": *EC*, 192n.

112 "My fear": Gregorio Martínez Sierra to FGL (August 31, 1923), AFFGL.

113 **Vicenta Lorca tries to hide guitar:** *EC*, 206.

113 "I'm going through a feverish": *EC*, 198.

113 "feverishly," "pin it down," and "fugitive and *alive*": *EC*, 196.

113 "penetrated . . . not Lorca": *EC*, 193–94.

113 "I feel a real panic": *EC*, 198–200.

113 "Garden of the Lunar Grapefruits": All passages from this poem are taken from OC, I, 270–71, trans. FGL, *Collected Poems*, 352–90.

113 "garden of possibilities": *EC*, 196–97.

113 "My unborn children": *EC*, 202.

113–14 "Now I've discovered," "none of the dead hours . . . going to be born": *EC*, 158. The dating of this letter is problematic: Marie Laffranque suggests FGL wrote it in 1925 (introduction to FGL, *Teatro inconcluso*, 20); Christopher Maurer suggests September 1922 (*EC*, 157–58n). Thematically, the letter reflects many of the concerns that were preoccupying FGL in the fall of 1923.

114 "and what great pleasure": *EC*, 200.

114 **FGL and others invent Capdepón:** C. B. Morris, "Granada in García Lorca's *Romancero gitano*," *Siglo XX / 20th Century* 6, 1–2 (1988–1989), 20; FM, 106–12; Andrés Soria Olmedo, "Más sobre don Isidoro Capdepón, personaje lorquiano," in *Federico García Lorca. Saggi critici nel cinquantenario della morte*, ed. Gabriele Morelli (Fasano: Schena, 1988), 137–42; AFFGL.

114 **FGL begins sketching:** FM, 433; FGL, *Dibujos*, 119–25.

115 "The Lyrical World of García Lorca": Melchor Fernández Almagro, "El mundo lírico de García Lorca," *España* (Madrid), 391, October 13, 1923, 7–8.

115 "I know that you love me": *EC*, 256.

115 "When I'm not on close terms": *EC*, 197.

115 "strolled through the secret": *EC*, 208, trans. FGL, *Selected Letters*, 44. For discussion of

FGL's deviation from the facts of the original Mariana Pineda story, see Morris, *Son of Andalusia*, 108–15.

116 **"symbol of a revolutionary ideal"**: Pinto.

116 **"exalt"**: OC, III, 358.

116 **"very close to the event"**: OC, III, 359.

116 **"at the age of nine"**: EC, 208.

116 **"few notes . . . understand?"**: EC, 187.

116 **"absurd"**: EC, 188.

116 **"poetry"** and **"emotion"**: OC, III, 490–92.

116 **"Since childhood . . . meet her . . ."**: EC, 208.

116 **"Mariana the lover"**: OC, III, 361.

116 **"Juliet without Romeo"**: EC, 209.

116 **"poetic truth"**: Melchor Fernández Almagro to FGL (September 15, 1923), AFFGL.

116 **1923 coup d'état**: Military coups were nothing new to Spain. From 1814 to 1923 no fewer than forty-three took place; the bloodless coup, in fact, was the country's preferred form of changing government. The system did not change until 1981, six years after Franco's death, when King Juan Carlos boldly defied a military insurrection to preserve the country's fledgling democratic government.

117 **"The political circumstances"**: Melchor Fernández Almagro to FGL (September 15, 1923), AFFGL.

117 **"a man's movement"**: ABC (Madrid), September 14, 1923, in Díaz-Plaja, 9.

117 **"People, King and Military"**: "Primo de Rivera escribe sobre Mussolini," El Sol (Madrid), February 9, 1924, 1.

117 **"step backward"**: Melchor Fernández Almagro to FGL (September 15, 1923), AFFGL.

117 **"strident politics"** and expulsion of Unamuno: El Sol (Madrid), February 22, 1924, in Díaz-Plaja, 33–35. Unamuno went into exile in France.

117 **De los Ríos prosecuted**: El Sol (Madrid), March 1–3, 1924.

117 **FGL signs 1924 manifesto**: G, I, 381, citing Pedro Sainz Rodríguez, *Testimonio y recuerdos* (Barcelona: Planeta, 1978), 345–46. In the spring of 1924, FGL told his parents, "The political situation is the same if not worse; because in Africa I think they're eating us alive" (EC, 229). On his dislike of "official documents" see EC, 260.

118 **FGL attends Pirandello play**: Juan Gutiérrez Cuadrado, "Crónica de una recepción: Pirandello en Madrid," Cuadernos Hispanoamericanos 333 (March 1978), 347–86.

118 **"a reality more real"**: Heraldo de Madrid, December 24, 1923.

118 **FGL and new literary generation**: For instance, poems by five members of the generation—Lorca, José Bergamín, Jorge Guillén, Gerardo Diego, and Pedro Salinas—appeared in an issue of the *Berliner Tageblatt* (December 1924) devoted to "young literature of the different European nations" ("El 'Berliner Tageblutt.' La joven literatura español en Alemania," El Sol [Madrid], December 11, 1924, 5).

118 **"tremendous dark laugh"**: Vicente Aleixandre, "Federico," Hora de España 7 (Valladolid, July 1937), 43–45.

119 **"Stupendous"**: Jorge Guillén to Germaine Guillén, Papers of Jorge Guillén, Wellesley College Archive. Parts of this letter are reprinted in EC, 230n. I am grateful to Christopher Maurer for alerting me to this extraordinary collection of letters.

119 **"Federico's here"**: Francisco García Lorca, introduction to FGL, *Three Tragedies*, 11–12.

119 **"It's no use"**: Guillén, "Federico en persona," xix.

119 **"Federico continues to make us laugh"** and **"court of friends"**: Jorge Guillén to Germaine Guillén, Papers of Jorge Guillén, Wellesley College Archive.

119 **"the tram"**: Salazar, "Federico en La Habana," 30. See also Buñuel, *Mi último suspiro*, 64.

119   **FGL as "last bard"**: Torre, 61–62; see also Guillermo de Torre, "Federico García Lorca. Boceto de un estudio crítico inconcluso," AFFGL, and *FM*, 285.

119   **"he gave the impression"**: Luis Rosales, "Evocación de Federico," *Cuadernos Hispanoamericanos* 475 (January 1990), 32–33.

119   **"When I correct proofs"**: Pinto.

119   **"Here's a poem"**: Paul Patrick Rogers, "García Lorca and His Friends: Some Anecdotes Recalled by Pictures," *The Library Chronicle* (Austin, Tex.), New Series 113 (1980), 13.

120   **"García Lorca state of mind"**: Miguel Pérez Ferrero, "Un libro de García Lorca. *Romancero gitano*," *La Gaceta Literaria* (Madrid), August 15, 1928, 2.

120   *lorquismo*: Rafael Martínez Nadal, introduction to FGL, *Poems*, xii–xiii; Ontañón; Río, "El poeta Federico García Lorca," 174; Ángel del Río, "A los sesenta años del nacimiento de un poeta que no llegó a cumplirlos," *Estudios sobre literatura contemporánea española* (Madrid: Gredos, 1966), 242; Auclair, 274.

120   **"With these portraits"**: Gregorio Prieto, *Lorca y la Generación del 27* (Madrid: Editorial Biblioteca Nueva, 1977), 48; Penón, 180.

120   **"virgin"**: Mora Guarnido, 115.

120   **FGL meets Rafael Martínez Nadal**: Martínez Nadal, *Cuatro lecciones*, 13–19; Auclair, 168; Nicholas de Jongh, "Protector of *The Public*," *The Guardian* (London), October 3, 1988, 20.

120–21   **"really good . . . criticize them"**: Martínez Nadal, *Cuatro lecciones*, 22–23.

121   **FGL's friendship with Martínez Nadal**: Martínez Nadal, *Cuatro lecciones*; Martínez Nadal, *Lorca's The Public*, Auclair, 168–69; see also Rafael Martínez Nadal correspondence to FGL, and Vicenta Lorca correspondence to FGL, AFFGL.

121   **"Jesus, you know a lot!"**: Martínez Nadal, *Lorca's The Public*, 218.

121   **FGL's reading**: Fernández-Montesinos, "Descripción"; Martínez Nadal, *Cuatro lecciones*, 65–66, 82–83; Martínez Nadal, *Federico García Lorca: Mi penúltimo libro*, 96, 182; Martínez Nadal, *Lorca's The Public*, 218–19; Zalamea, "Federico García Lorca," 1509; Río, "Federico García Lorca"; Eutimio Martín, "Testimonio de Luis Rosales sobre *Poeta en Nueva York* de García Lorca," *El País* (Madrid), Art and Ideas section, January 29, 1978; Rodrigo, *García Lorca*, 196.

121   **"the Bible has Heaven"**: César Tiempo, "Homenaje a García Lorca," *Argentores* 31 (Buenos Aires, July–December 1966).

121   **"as an intellectual exercise"**: Proel.

122   **"Lorca would deftly separate"**: Crow, 14.

122   **"Oh, I can smell the thyme!"**: Juan Gutiérrez Padial, introduction to Jiménez, *Olvidos de Granada*, 14–15.

122   **Jiménez visits Granada**: Juan Gutiérrez Padial, introduction to Jiménez, *Olvidos de Granada*; Jiménez, *Cartas (primera selección)*; Jiménez, *Olvidos de Granada*. According to a letter from Jorge Guillén to his wife, Germaine, FGL and Jiménez were scheduled to leave for Granada on June 21, 1924 (Papers of Jorge Guillén, Wellesley College Archive). Jiménez's lyrical response to the city was in contrast to that of another prominent Spaniard who visited Granada in late June, Miguel Primo de Rivera. During his swing through the city, the country's new dictator told its inhabitants: "Anyone who is truly masculine must have two great loves—the fatherland, and women" ("El viaje del presidente. Las visitas a Granada y Málaga," *El Sol* [Madrid], June 26, 1924, 3).

122   **"to the gills . . . deep affection"**: Jiménez, *Cartas (primera selección)*, 267–69.

122–23   **"intimately . . . doesn't it?"**: EC, 236.

123   **FGL writes poem on Jiménez**: Hernández, introduction to FGL, *Canciones*, 86–87.

123   **"since I believe"**: EC, 241.

123   "fountain," "I was able," and "preserves an eternal feeling": EC, 238–40. On Ciria's death, see EC, 236.

123   "And you above": FGL, Collected Poems, 727.

123   "From time to time": EC, 238.

123   "the vessel best shaped": FGL, "Conferencia-recital del Romancero gitano," in OC, III, 179.

123   "river of the Spanish language": Juan Ramón Jiménez, El romance, río de la lengua española (University of Puerto Rico: De la Torre, 1959).

124   FGL begins Gypsy Ballads: For the timing and manner of FGL's composition of Gypsy Ballads see FGL, Autógrafos I, and Hernández, introduction to FGL, Romancero gitano, 18–30. See also EC, 241; C, I, 55; and FGL, Collected Poems.

124   "truest and purest thing": OC, III, 179.

124   "worn away by time": "García Lorca presenta hoy tres canciones populares escénificadas," Crítica (Buenos Aires), December 15, 1933, trans. Maurer, introduction to FGL, Collected Poems, xlvi.

124   "Pena is not anguish": OC, III, 183.

125   "completely for my own enjoyment": EC, 241.

125   "for the first time": OC, III, 178.

9. DALÍ: 1924-25

126   FGL returns to Madrid: Santos Torroella, Dalí residente, 68; Alberti, Federico García Lorca: Poeta y amigo, 272–73; Alberti, La arboleda perdida, 168.

126   FGL meets Rafael Alberti: Alberti, La arboleda perdida, 168–70; Alberti, Federico García Lorca: Poeta y amigo, 272–73. On Rafael Alberti see Auclair, 18; Luis García Montero, introduction to Alberti, Federico García Lorca: Poeta y amigo, 30–36.

127   "younger brother": Alberti, Federico García Lorca: Poeta y amigo, 243.

127   FGL writes "Thamar and Amnon": FGL, Romancero gitano, 33–34; FGL, Autógrafos, I, 181–89; Auclair, 78, 153–55; Umbral, 101; author interview with José Antonio Rubio Sacristán.

127   "chunks of incest": Dalí, Salvador Dalí escribe a Federico García Lorca, 88, 145n; FGL, Collected Poems, 833.

128   "meetings of the desperation": Martínez Nadal, Cuatro lecciones, 19–21.

128   FGL and others embrace avant-garde: Moreno Villa, Vida en claro, 114; Morris, A Generation of Spanish Poets, 84–86; Buñuel, Mi último suspiro, 63–67.

128   "anaglyphs": Moreno Villa, Vida en claro, 113; Alberti, La arboleda perdida, 214–15.

128   "fart meter": Alberti, La arboleda perdida, 215.

128   Buñuel's "Order of Toledo": Buñuel, Mi último suspiro, 72–74; Alberti, La arboleda perdida, 215–18; Aub, 272–73; José de la Colina and Tomás Pérez Turrent, Objects of Desire. Conversations with Luis Buñuel, ed. and trans. Paul Lenti (New York: Marsilio Publishers, 1992), 7.

128   "surrealist at heart": Santos Torroella, Dalí residente, 222.

128   FGL compares Bello to El Greco: FGL said Bello possessed "a personality as distinctive as El Greco's" (Santos Torroella, Dalí residente, 156).

128   "putrefaction": On putrefactions and Dalí's proposed book of putrefactions, see Santos Torroella, "Los putrefactos"; José María Moreiro, "Dalí, en el centro de los recuerdos," El País Semanal (Madrid), October 23, 1983, 15–21; Santos Torroella, Dalí residente, 80; Alberti, La arboleda perdida, 172–73; Dalí, Salvador Dalí escribe a Federico García Lorca, 32–34, 126.

129   "EMOTION" and "lied a lot": Years later, recalling FGL's penchant for lies, Bello said
      that for FGL "lying was creation. His lies were poetry or art. He lied a lot, and with pleasure.
      And he was good at it" (Santos Torroella, "Los putrefactos," 34–38).

129   FGL's and Dalí's antics in Madrid: Dalí, Vida secreta, 216; Suero, "Crónica"; Ontañón;
      Ontañón and Moreiro, 121; Giménez Caballero; Moreno Villa, Vida en claro, 112; Chas de
      Cruz, "Han pasado dos Poetas," Primer magazine argentino (Buenos Aires), April 25, 1934,
      supplement.

129   "one of those girls . . . the ideas I have": EC, 267–68.

130   Atheneum invites FGL to Barcelona: Rodrigo, García Lorca, 21; Dalí, Salvador Dalí es-
      cribe a Federico García Lorca, 151.

130   "both eternal and actual": Ana María Dalí, 101; EC, 277.

130   "My friend . . . had always known one another": Rodrigo, Lorca-Dalí, 39.

130   Dalí's father memorizes FGL's poems: EC, 269.

130   "without doubt": G, I, 408. On FGL's response to Ana María Dalí, see Rodrigo, Lorca-
      Dalí, 40–41.

130–31 "What pretty breasts . . . Touch them!": Agustí, 25.

131   Relationship between Salvador and Ana María Dalí: Not long after their mother's death
      in 1921, their father married Catalina Domènech Ferrés, his late wife's sister (Gibson
      et al., 23).

131   FGL and Dalí siblings play with "Little Bear": Rodrigo, Lorca-Dalí, 116–18; EC, 485.

131   "You don't love me . . . felt loved": Rodrigo, Lorca-Dalí, 40.

131   FGL's gloom: Rodrigo, García Lorca, 342.

131   FGL parodies own death: Dalí, Diario, 81; Dalí, with Parinaud, Confesiones, 17.

132   "a hive of golden bees": Ana María Dalí, 46.

132   "perfectly elegant . . . transformed": Ana María Dalí, 102–3.

132   FGL reads Mariana Pineda to Dalí family: Ana María Dalí, 101–2.

132   "the cream of the progressive": G, I, 409.

133   "It requires as much effort": G, I, 399.

133   "clichés and devices": González Olmedilla, "Los autores después del estreno," Heraldo de
      Madrid, October 15, 1927, 2.

133   "My play is naive": FM, 290, trans. in GM, 160.

133   "Oh, what a sad day": This and other passages from Mariana Pineda are taken from OC, II,
      81–174.

133   "a nocturnal, lunar": FM, 290, trans. GM, 160.

134   "intense maturity": "Un poeta granadí a Figueres," La Veu de L'Empordá (Figueres),
      April 18, 1925, 5.

134   "loved the most": G, II, 286.

134   "I have a portfolio . . . niece of the sea!": EC, 276–77. Christopher Maurer concludes that
      FGL returned to Granada on or about June 16, 1925 (EC, 279).

134   "I sing a common belief": This and other passages from the "Ode to Salvador Dalí" are
      taken from FGL, Collected Poems.

134–35 "AH, MY ODE! . . . Your socks": Dalí, Salvador Dalí escribe a Federico García Lorca, 20.

135   "What are you doing . . . I've ever known": Dalí, Salvador Dalí escribe a Federico García
      Lorca, 24.

135   "little son": Dalí, Salvador Dalí escribe a Federico García Lorca, 20–34.

135   "My Beloved Darling": Dalí, Salvador Dalí escribe a Federico García Lorca, 49.

135   "an abundant correspondence": EC, 318.

135   "the ineffable Dalí," "Salvadorcito," and "They will live": EC, 293.

135   FGL watches sunset: EC, 289.

136 "The hotel is lively": FGL to José Murciano (September 25, 1918), *EC*, 54.

136 FGL and homosexuality: Auclair, 94–98; Arturo Barea, *Lorca: The Poet and His People*, trans. Ilse Barea (New York: Grove Press, 1949), 56–58; Mora Guarnido, 57; *FM*, 143; Penón, 115; Sahuquillo, 44, 184–85; Fernández-Montesinos, "Descripcíon," 170–71.

136 "impassioned force," "I wanted him," and "When I eventually": Rivas Cherif, January 27, 1957.

136 "I'm getting into problems": *EC*, 302.

136 FGL sketches clowns and harlequins: FGL, *Dibujos*.

136 "The young ladies": *EC*, 362; see also Maurer, introduction to FGL, *Collected Poems*, xiv–xv. Despite the problematic dating of this letter (see *EC*, 361n), its imagery reflects FGL's state of mind in the summer of 1925.

137 "saved" his life: *EC*, 297.

137 "Dionysus rubs your head": *EC*, 293.

137 FGL writes erotic poetry: *EC*, 302; Piero Menarini, introduction to FGL, *Canciones y Primeras Canciones*, ed. Piero Menarini, Clásicos Castellanos (Madrid: Espasa Calpe, 1986), 30–34; FGL, *Collected Poems*; *OC*, I, 390–93.

137 "a distinguished field . . . never going to be *old*": *EC*, 302.

137 FGL begins *Perlimplín*: *EC*, 300.

138 "Pure poetry. Naked": *EC*, 283–84.

138 FGL writes dialogues: FGL, "Tres diálogos," ed. Manuel Fernández-Montesinos (Granada: University of Granada, 1985); Fernández-Montesinos, "Federico García Lorca en la Residencia de Estudiantes," 7; *OC*, II, 177–92.

138 "Goodbye Dalilaitita": FGL to Dalí (n.d.), AFFGL.

138 "more *universal*": *EC*, 284.

138 "I've gone through a terrible": *EC*, 299.

138 "very poor" and "My parents are angry": *EC*, 300.

138 "You don't tell me why": Melchor Fernández Almagro to FGL (September 25, 1925), AFFGL.

138 "the way water dissolves": *EC*, 292.

138 "to Italy" and "some qualifying exams": *EC*, 300. Francisco García Lorca had visited Paris in 1924 (*EC*, 220n).

138–39 "unspeakable laziness": Melchor Fernández Almagro to FGL (September 25, 1925), AFFGL.

139 "You've been too distracted": Alberti, *Federico García Lorca: Poeta y amigo*, 244.

139 "It's not right": Christopher Maurer, "Correspondencia entre Benjamín Palencia y Federico García Lorca," *Poesía* 38 (1992), 282.

139 "the impossible and doubtful": *EC*, 379n.

139 "without realizing it": *EC*, 344n.

139 "I work in order to die living": *EC*, 283.

10. INCORRIGIBLE POET: 1926-27

140 "one of the latest inventions": Fernando Vela, "El suprarealismo," in Fernando Vela, *Inventario de la modernidad. Ensayos* (Gijón: Biblioteca de la Quintana, 1983), 49–54.

140 "dream and reality": Reprinted in C.W.E. Bigsby, *Dada and Surrealism* 23, *The Critical Idiom*, gen. ed. John D. Jump (London: Methuen, 1972), 37.

140 "Foreign waters": *EC*, 319.

140 "all the news": *EC*, 308.

140   "the best one!" and "rare, surprising *unity*": *EC*, 329.

140   "In four months time": *FM*, xxii, trans. *GM*, xxii.

140–41   "of creating a great" and "I have seen *completed*": *EC*, 330, trans. *GM*, xxii.

141   FGL writes "The Unfaithful Wife": FGL, *Romancero gitano*, 173–75; *EC*, 334.

141   "You can't say": *EC*, 338.

141   "I want to be a Poet": *EC*, 319.

141   "poetic transcription": This and subsequent passages from Torre's review of the ode appear in Guillermo de Torre, "Federico García Lorca: Boceto de un estudio crítico inconcluso," *Defensor de Granada*, March 13, 1927, 1.

141   "Ode to Salvador Dalí": Quotations from the "Ode to Salvador Dalí" are taken from FGL, *Collected Poems*, 588–95.

141   "must be clear": *OC*, III, 75.

141   "almost ARITHMETIC": Dalí, *Salvador Dalí escribe a Federico García Lorca*, 32.

142   Ortega's "The Dehumanization of Art": José Ortega y Gasset, "The Dehumanization of Art," trans. Helene Weyl, in *The Dehumanization of Art and Other Essays on Art, Culture and Literature*, 2nd ed. (Princeton, N.J.: Princeton University Press, 1972).

142   "I'll never forget": *EC*, 330.

143   FGL's lecture on Góngora: On the writing and delivery of the lecture see Maurer, introduction to C, I, 18; *EC*, 333–34; and "En el Ateneo: 'La imágen poética de don Luis de Góngora.' Conferencia de García Lorca," *Defensor de Granada*, February 14, 1926, 1. On the lecture itself see Belamich, 97–98, and Laffranque, 119–30. Quotations from the lecture are taken from *OC*, III, 53–77.

143   "brilliant dissertation . . . emotion": "En el Ateneo: 'La imagen poética de don Luis de Góngora.' Conferencia de García Lorca," *Defensor de Granada*, February 14, 1926, 1.

143–44   "My voice . . . Old age!" and "You tell me": *EC*, 334.

144   "as I believe I will": *EC*, 255.

144   "that bastard" and "Will anyone want": *EC*, 331–32.

144   "*deadly*": *EC*, 346.

144   "few friends": *OC*, III, 82.

144   "We must love Granada" and "a joyful, lively": *OC*, III, 190.

144   "is a symbol of youth": "Una comida literaria: Gallo y sus simpatizantes en la Venta de Eritaña," *Defensor de Granada*, March 9, 1928, 1.

144   "I'll make you all the covers": Dalí, *Salvador Dalí escribe a Federico García Lorca*, 34.

145   FGL visits Madrid, April 1926: *EC*, 340–42; and Guillén, *Federico en persona. Carteggio*, 96.

145   "total admiration": *EC*, 416.

145   "I'm not intelligent": *EC*, 438.

145   "to the Poet Federico García Lorca": Jorge Guillén to FGL (August 1925), AFFGL.

145   "clean and beautiful," "excessively cerebral," and "the gift of tears": *EC*, 415–16.

145   "I have too much chiaroscuro": *EC*, 333.

145   Guillén introduces FGL in Valladolid: Guillén, "Federico en persona."

145–46   "almost adolescent" and "whisper his songs": Francisco de Cossío, "Ensayos. Una lectura," *El Norte de Castilla* (Valladolid), April 11, 1926, 1. The *Defensor de Granada* reprinted Cossío's account on page 2 of its April 13, 1926, edition.

146   "well taken care of . . . *gratis*": *EC*, 344.

146   "We think of you constantly" and "Another hug": Dalí, *Salvador Dalí escribe a Federico García Lorca*, 40. On FGL's probable encounter with Dalí in Madrid, see also *EC*, 349n.

146 **Dalí meets Picasso:** "I've come to see you first, before visiting the Louvre," Dalí told Picasso in Paris. "You've done well," replied the Andalusian (Dawn Ades, *Dalí* [London: Thames and Hudson, 1982], 32).

146 **Dalí expelled from Academy:** Dawn Ades, *Dalí* (London: Thames and Hudson, 1982), 29; Rodrigo, *Lorca-Dalí*, 85–87.

146 **"definitively seize power!":** Dalí, *Vida secreta*, 218.

146 **"the harshest criticism . . . enthusiastic":** Gibson et al., 27.

146 **"Little son!":** Dalí, *Salvador Dalí escribe a Federico García Lorca*, 32.

146 **"Do you love me?":** Dalí, *Salvador Dalí escribe a Federico García Lorca*, 36.

147 **"This business of dealing":** EC, 346.

147 **"slightest worry"** and **"That's how I've freed myself":** EC, 351–52.

147 **"delicious"** agony and **"Saint Objectivity":** Dalí, *Salvador Dalí escribe a Federico García Lorca*, 42–46; Dawn Ades, "Morphologies of Desire," in Gibson et al., 140.

147 **"love, effort, and *renunciation*":** EC, 370.

147 **"In the country":** EC, 355.

148 **Buñuel writes to FGL from Paris:** AFFGL.

148 **The Huerta de San Vicente:** The word *huerta* literally means "vegetable" or "kitchen" garden. Don Federico García Rodríguez purchased the Huerta de San Vicente in July of 1925 and took possession of the property on October 30, 1925 (Registro de Propiedad, Granada, no. 7, bk. 635, fol. 182).

148 **"a lyrical headache":** EC, 367.

148 **"the most beautiful":** EC, 587.

148 **"divinely unbreathable":** EC, 363.

148 **"I was in the city . . . direct reality":** OC, III, 472; FM, 305.

148 **"was like slamming my fist":** *La Razón* (Buenos Aires), November 28, 1933, in OC, III, 468.

149 **"as though I were holding":** OC, III, 472.

149 **"the exceedingly tiresome,"** "I know her mother died," and **"My parents see":** EC, 365.

149 **"disastrous venture,"** "bad faith . . . with my family," and **"What do I do? . . . *drowning*":** EC, 384.

149 **"For the first time":** EC, 375.

150 **"I think I have a vocation":** EC, 366.

150 **"You have to start":** Guillén, *Federico en persona. Carteggio*, 110.

150 **"What fantastic notes":** EC, 375.

150 **"Because I need to have a job . . . imminent?":** EC, 369.

150 **Concha García Lorca announces engagement:** Don Federico insisted that Concha secure her brother Paco's permission to marry Montesinos, and she did so. It is not known whether she also consulted FGL (Concha García Lorca to Francisco García Lorca [June 26, 1926], AFFGL).

150 **"a tranquil and sweet life":** FGL, *Cristo. Tragedia religiosa*, AFFGL.

150 **"Let me stay":** EC, 367. The childhood rhyme appears in EC, 367n.

150 **"Paris would be ideal . . . (a good for nothing!)":** EC, 375.

151 **"My private opinion":** Pedro Salinas to FGL (October 2, 1926), AFFGL, in Pedro Salinas, *Dos cartas a Federico García Lorca*, facsimile ed. (Fuente Vaqueros: Casa-Museo Federico García Lorca, 1991).

151 **"You won't take examinations":** Dalí, *Salvador Dalí escribe a Federico García Lorca*, 44.

151 **"Federico (incorrigible poet)":** EC, 375.

151 **Litoral press:** Altolaguirre, *Obras completas I*, 231; Morris, *A Generation*, 8; Alberti, *La arboleda perdida*, 231.

151 **Emilio Prados visits Granada**: Hernández, introduction to FGL, *Canciones*, 19; Santos Torroella, *Dalí residente*, 154; EC, 378–83.

151 **"paradise closed to many"**: OC, III, 83.

152 **"twenty thousand unknown"**: Emilio Prados to Jorge Guillén, in Maurer, "De la correspondencia," 68. On the state of FGL's manuscripts in general, see Hernández, notes to FGL, *Libro de poemas*, 243, and AFFGL.

152 **"more than ten!" and "even if it's just"**: EC, 415.

152 **"It's disgusting"**: EC, 391. On Xirgu's presumed reason for producing the play, see Andrew A. Anderson, "¿Entre prodigio y protegido? El joven Lorca en Madrid (1919–1920)," *BFFGL* 17 (June 1995), 100.

152 **"peripheral to my work"**: EC, 435.

153 **"just where it wants"**: EC, 430.

153 **"I'm happy . . . not of worth"**: EC, 418.

153 **"surprises for many"**: EC, 427.

153 *Songs* **published**: FM, xxiv; Hernández, introduction to FGL, *Canciones*. All quotations from *Songs* are taken from FGL, *Collected Poems*, 412–515.

153 **"my three weaknesses"**: EC, 417.

153 **"book of friends"**: EC, 416.

153 **Guillén praises *Songs***: Jorge Guillén to Germaine Guillén, papers of Jorge Guillén, Wellesley College Archive.

154 **"new, new, new"**: Lluís Montanyá, "Canciones de Federico García Lorca," *L'Amic de les Arts* (Sitges), July 31, 1927, 55–56.

154 **"the higher algebra"**: José Ortega y Gasset, "The Dehumanization of Art," trans. Helene Weyl, in *The Dehumanization of Art and Other Essays on Art, Culture and Literature*, 2nd ed. (Princeton, N.J.: Princeton University Press, 1972), 32.

154 **"everything . . . true person"**: EC, 395.

155 **FGL's "Three Portraits with Shadow"**: See D. Gareth Walters, " 'Comprendí. Pero no explico.' Revelation and Concealment in Lorca's *Canciones*," *Bulletin of Hispanic Studies* LXVII (1991), 265–79.

155 **"genuine anguish" and "The songs remain girded"**: EC, 417.

155 **"a poetry of codes and arabesques"**: Ricardo Baeza, "De una generación y su poeta," *El Sol* (Madrid), August 24, 1927, 1.

155 **"pure poetry"**: Luis Montanyá, "Canciones de Federico García Lorca," *L'Amic de les* (Sitges), July 31, 1927, 55–56.

155 **"penetrating poetic vision"**: Enrique Díez-Canedo, [Canciones], *La Nación* (Buenos Aires), August 28, 1927.

155–56 **"a nickel-plated motor," "delightful songs," and "Your songs . . . we already know!"**: Dalí, *Salvador Dalí escribe a Federico García Lorca*, 58–59. Lindbergh's crossing took place on May 21, 1927, four days after the publication of *Songs*.

II. CELEBRITY: 1927

157 **1926 Dalí exhibition**: Ana María Dalí, 131–32; G, I, 465.

157 **"*Carísimo amigo* . . . our hunger!"**: Dalí, *Salvador Dalí escribe a Federico García Lorca*, 48.

157 **"I'm saying goodbye"**: EC, 475.

157–58 **FGL's financial problems**: EC, 469–70; Aub, 99.

158 **"Send me fifty pesetas"**: EC, 218.

158 **"You know that we want"**: Vicenta Lorca to FGL (March 29, 1921), AFFGL.

158   "more than repay . . . upsetting you": *EC*, 469–70.
158–59   "exuded 'south' " and "I'm from the Kingdom": Gasch, 39.
159   "shrewdly intuited": *EC*, 496.
159   "sophisticated sentimentality": Rafael Moragas, "Durante un ensayo, en el Goya, de *Mariana Pineda*, cambiamos impresiones con el poeta García Lorca y el pintor Salvador Dalí," *La Noche* (Barcelona), June 23, 1927, 3.
159   FGL attends *tertulias* at Barradas apartment: Rodrigo, *Lorca-Dalí*, 122–26; Mario Verdaguer, *Medio siglo de vida íntima barcelonesa* (Barcelona: Barna, 1957), 295–97; Gasch, 36–37.
159   "so terribly interesting . . . impulsive character": Gasch, "A la luz del recuerdo," 38.
159   FGL's mood swings: Luis Capdevila, "Unas horas de la vida de Federico," *La Vanguardia* (Barcelona), December 1, 1972, 55; Rodrigo, *García Lorca*, 342. On FGL's general moodiness see Sánchez Vidal, 53; Auclair, 16; Celaya, 145; Penón, 178, 185.
159   "aroma . . . olive": Sebastian Gasch, Prologue to FGL, *Cartas a sus amigos* (Barcelona: Ediciones Cobalto, 1950), 10–11.
159   "nervously, easily": Joaquín Montaner, "Discos. Recuerdos de García Lorca," *El Día Gráfico* (Barcelona), December 20, 1935, 1.
160   "these old things" and "Perhaps": Rafael Moragas, "Durante un ensayo, en el Goya, de *Mariana Pineda*, cambiamos impresiones con el poeta García Lorca y el pintor Salvador Dalí," *La Noche* (Barcelona), June 23, 1927, 3.
160   "picturesque": *EC*, 496.
160   "wonderful": *Heraldo de Madrid*, October 15, 1927.
160   Xirgu spends money on *Mariana*: *EC*, 488.
160   FGL's first meeting with Xirgu: Rodrigo, *García Lorca*, 58–60.
160   Margarita Xirgu, background: Rodrigo, *Margarita Xirgu*; [Trillas Blásquez], "Hablando con Margarita Xirgu, que se va a América y recuerda su vida," *Crónica* (Madrid), December 22, 1935.
160   "the actress who breaks": "En el hotel Alhambra Palace. En homenaje a Margarita Xirgu y a Federico García Lorca," *Defensor de Granada*, May 7, 1929, 1, in OC, III, 194.
161   "Even the old folks": Rodrigo, *Margarita Xirgu*, 144.
161   "But without speaking": Rodrigo, *Lorca-Dalí*, 120.
161   "Huge success": *EC*, 489.
161   FGL telegraphs family: Francisco García Lorca to FGL (n.d.), AFFGL.
161   "luminous": "Goya: La obra de un poeta granadino," *El Día Gráfico* (Barcelona), June 25, 1927, 11. On the quality of FGL's verse, see also *El Noticiero Universal* (Barcelona), June 25, 1927, 4.
161   "delicate and sentimental": M. Rodríguez Codolá, "*Mariana Pineda*, romance popular en tres estampas, en verso, original de don Federico García Lorca," *La Vanguardia* (Barcelona), June 26, 1927, 15.
161   "with nothing more": Doménec Guansi, "El teatre," *La Publicitat* (Barcelona), June 26, 1927, 6.
161   "now join the list": Francisco Madrid, "Teatro Goya. Se estrenó, con éxito, 'Mariana Pineda,' romance en tres estampas de Federico García Lorca, por la compañia de Margarita Xirgu," *La Noche* (Barcelona), June 25, 1927, 3.
162   "the most important daily": Collection of William Layton, displayed in the exhibition *Federico García Lorca y su teatro*, Teatro Español, Madrid, 1984–85.
162   FGL's family cannot tolerate stains: Author interview with José Caballero.
162   "aphrodisiac": Salvador Dalí, "Federico García Lorca: Exposició de dibuixos colorits (Galeries Dalmau)," *La Nota Revista* III, 9 (Barcelona, September 1927), 84–85.

162   **FGL shows drawings at Dalmau Galleries:** Rodrigo, *Lorca-Dalí*, 140; Mario Verdaguer, *Medio siglo de vida íntima barcelonesa* (Barcelona: Barna, 1957), 303; Helen Oppenheimer, *Lorca: The Drawings. Their Relation to the Poet's Life and Work* (London: The Herbert Press, 1986), 31–37; FGL, *Dibujos*, 147–53.

162   **FGL's drawings, c. 1927:** Rodrigo, *Lorca-Dalí*, 144; FGL, *Dibujos*; Helen Oppenheimer, *Lorca: The Drawings. Their Relation to the Poet's Life and Work* (London: The Herbert Press, 1986); Isabel García Lorca, "Recuerdos," in FGL, *Teatro de títeres y dibujos*, ed. Mario Hernández (Santander: Universidad Internacional Menéndez y Pelayo / Fundación Federico García Lorca, 1992), 11; Sebastian Gasch, "Lorca dibujante," *La Gaceta Literaria* (Madrid) 30, March 15, 1928, 4; author interview with José Caballero.

163   **"for the duration":** Dalí, *Vida secreta*, 217.

163   **"Lorca saw me":** Robert Descharnes, *Dalí. La obra y el hombre* (Barcelona: Tusquets, 1984), 21.

163   **"Cadaquééééś!":** Rodrigo, *Lorca-Dalí*, 161.

163   **FGL's friendship with Ana María Dalí:** Rodrigo, *Lorca-Dalí*, 177–78; Ana María Dalí, 127–28.

163   **FGL's fear of death:** Ana María Dalí, 126–27.

164   **"grave throat illness":** *EC*, 506.

164   **"babouet":** Rodrigo, *Lorca-Dalí*, 174–75.

164   **"the same pure emotion . . . cradle":** *EC*, 544.

164   **FGL signs "Anti-Artistic Manifesto":** *EC*, 492; Rodrigo, *García Lorca*, 195. On the significance of the manifesto, see Jaime Brihuega, *Manifiestos, proclamas, panfletos y textos doctrinales. Las vanguardias artísticas en España. 1910–1931* (Madrid: Ediciones, 1979), 157–61; Dawn Ades, *Dalí* (London: Thames and Hudson, 1982), 41; and *Los vanguardistas españoles (1925–1935)*, ed. Ramón Buckley and John Crispin (Madrid: El Libro de Bolsillo, Alianza, 1973), 38–42.

164   **"materialistic, irreligious, and objective":** Sebastian Gasch to FGL (n.d.), AFFGL, in Rodrigo, *García Lorca*, 177.

165   **"Your Saint Sebastian":** Dalí, *Salvador Dalí, escribe a Federico García Lorca*, 48.

165   **"I'm sending you this card":** Dalí, *Salvador Dalí escribe a Federico García Lorca*, 63.

165   **"one of man's":** FGL, "Lecture: A Poet in New York," 186.

165   **"Saint Objectivity":** Dalí, *Salvador Dalí, escribe a Federico García Lorca*, 42.

165   **Dalí publishes prose poem on Saint Sebastian:** Rodrigo, *Lorca-Dalí*, 94; *EC*, 506.

165   **"is you . . . We'll see":** Dalí, *Salvador Dalí escribe a Federico García Lorca*, 48.

165   **"unwounded ass":** Dalí, *Salvador Dalí escribe a Federico García Lorca*, 44.

165   **"Saint Sebastian's arrows":** *EC*, 511.

165   **FGL's relationship with Dalí, c. 1927:** Santos Torroella, *La miel*, 84–85; Santos Torroella, "Los putrefactos," 54; Martínez Nadal, *Federico García Lorca. Mi penúltimo libro*, 50, 91n; Buñuel, *Mi último suspiro*, 66, 180; Angela Rodicio, "José Bello, testigo de excepción, recuerda sus años en la Residencia de Estudiantes," *Diario 16* (Madrid), January 9, 1988; "Altoaragoneses en lo alto. José Bello, comentarista y degustador de la Generación del 27. El surrealismo es una teoría del humor," *Diario del Altoaragón* (Huesca), October 28, 1990, 12. Dalí made repeated boasts about FGL's sexual advances toward him; see, for example, Ian Gibson, "Con Dalí y Lorca en Figueras," *El País* (Madrid), January 26, 1986, Sunday section, 10–11. In his *Vida secreta*, Dalí—never a reliable witness—claims he was a virgin until he became involved with Gala Eluard in 1929 (259).

165   **Dalí's paintings of FGL:** Santos Torroella, *La miel*, 94–97. On Dalí's sexual malaise, see especially Santos Torroella, "Los putrefactos," 48–54.

166 "Federico is better than ever," "extreme narcissism . . . ill-fated influence": Buñuel, *Obra literaria*, 36.

166 "black," "a new kind of poetry," and "I long more than ever": EC, 495–96.

166 FGL writes to Dalí from Barcelona: EC, 498–500.

167 Dalí's *Honey Is Sweeter than Blood*: Santos Torroella, *La miel*, 85–88, 96–98; Dawn Ades, *Dalí* (London: Thames and Hudson, 1982), 45.

167 "historic melancholy": EC, 506.

167 "I think about you": EC, 502.

167–68 "not one decent curvaceous thigh" and "grace in the midst of torture": EC, 511–12.

168 FGL's prose poems, 1927: OC, I, 487–507; G, I, 507–9; Terence McMullan, "Federico García Lorca's Santa Lucía y San Lázaro and the Aesthetics of Transition," *Bulletin of Hispanic Studies* LXVII (1990), 1–20; Miguel García-Posada, introduction to FGL, *Poesía* II, 2nd ed. (Madrid: Akal, 1982), 56–60.

168 "wonderful . . . putrefaction": G, I, 527.

168 "Act of FAITH": Dalí, *Salvador Dalí escribe a Federico García Lorca*, 85.

168 "poetically stale": EC, 508.

168 "I live moments": EC, 513.

169 "unforgettable drawings": Ricard Salvat i Ferrer, "Federico García Lorca y las vanguardias catalanas," BFFGL 19–20 (December 1996), 184.

169 "to choose the essential traits": EC, 519.

169 "perpetual dream," "the great dark mirrors," and "I am . . . terrible and fantastic": EC, 518–20.

169 "nor a member" and "romantic, but ironically": Juan González Olmedilla, "Los autores después del estreno," *Heraldo de Madrid*, October 15, 1927, 2.

169 "with a vengeance": Enrique Díez-Canedo, "*Mariana Pineda* de García Lorca," *El Sol* (Madrid), October 13, 1927, 12.

170 "It had to come": Fernández Almagro.

170 "a most enjoyable family": Salinas and Guillén, 75.

170 "trick from the old theater": Enrique de Mesa, *El Imparcial* (Madrid), October 13, 1927, 8, cited in María Francisca Vilches de Frutos and Dru Dougherty, *Los estrenos teatrales de Federico García Lorca (1920–1945)* (Madrid: Tabapress [Grupo Tabacalera; Fundación Federico García Lorca], 1992), 45.

170 "intentional ingenuousness": Francisco Ayala, "*Mariana Pineda*," *La Gaceta Literaria* (Madrid), October 15, 1927, quoted and translated in Morris, *Son of Andalusia*, 120.

170 *Mariana Pineda* sparks polemic: Some feared that in the political climate of the time, FGL's play might even be banned (Alberti, *La arboleda perdida*, 255). On the general debate over the play, see Salinas and Guillén, 75, and *La Gaceta Literaria* (Madrid), November 1, 1927, 5.

170 *Mariana Pineda* fails commercially: G, I, 513; Josep María Balcells, "Cartas de Margarita Xirgu sobre Lorca y Alberti," *Cuadernos Hispanoamericanos* 433–36, (July–August 1986), 197; María Francisca Vilches de Frutos and Dru Dougherty, *Los estrenos teatrales de Federico García Lorca (1920–1945)* (Madrid: Tabapress [Grupo Tabacalera; Fundación Federico García Lorca], 1992), 45.

170 "It must be something written": Gonzalo Torrente Ballester, "*Mariana Pineda*, 1927," *Primer Acto* 50 (February 1963), 27, quoted and translated in Morris, *Son of Andalusia*, 120.

170 "great success": EC, 565.

170 "an embarrassment": FGL to Pepín Bello, in Luis Martínez Cuitino, introduction to FGL, *Mariana Pineda*, ed. Luis Martínez Cuitino (Madrid: Cátedra, 1991), 70–71.

170 **"I'd do it another way"**: Juan González Olmedilla, "Los autores después del estreno," *Heraldo de Madrid*, October 15, 1927, 2.

170 **"ANTIARTISTIC magazine"**: Dalí, *Salvador Dalí escribe a Federico García Lorca*, 80.

171 **"Did you see"**: *EC*, 564.

171 **FGL achieves celebrity**: For evidence of his growing renown see, for example, Enrique Díez-Canedo, "Los poetas jóvenes de España," *La Nación* (Buenos Aires), October 5, 1924, 5; *Mercure de France*, July 1, 1926, 235; *EC*, 354; *G, I*, 414; "Letras españolas en Alemania," *El Sol* (Madrid), May 8, 1926, 4; *Heraldo de Madrid*, October 20, 1927.

171 **Baeza's "A Generation"**: Ricardo Baeza, "De una generación y su poeta," *El Sol* (Madrid), August 24, 1927, 1.

171 **"must have produced"**: *EC*, 521.

171 **"medieval and random"**: Gerardo Diego, "Federico García Lorca. Canciones. Suplementos de 'Litoral,'" *Revista de Occidente* XVII (1927), 380–81.

171 **"a game"**: Juan González Olmedilla, "Los autores después del estreno," *Heraldo de Madrid*, October 15, 1927, 2.

171 **"Ah, how talented I am"**: Ontañon and Moreiro, 110; author interview with Santiago Ontañón.

171 **"let himself be adored"**: Guillermo de Torre to Jorge Guillén, papers of Jorge Guillén (shelf mark bMS span 100 [484]), Houghton Library, Harvard University.

171 **Rivalry between FGL and Alberti**: Aub, 549; Altolaguirre, *Obras completas I*, 66; Luis García Montero, introduction to Alberti, *Federico García Lorca: Poeta y amigo*, 29–30; *EC*, 370n; Salinas and Guillén, 76, 117; Joaquín Amigo to FGL (June 5, 1927), AFFGL; Alberti, *Federico García Lorca: Poeta y amigo*, 72. In February 1926, Enrique Díez-Canedo wrote of FGL's "undoubted influence" on Alberti ("Revista de libros. Rafael Alberti—*Marinero en tierra*," *El Sol* [Madrid], February 20, 1926, 2). In 1928, José Mora Guarnido referred to Alberti as a "García Lorca in a minor key" ("Dos poetas andaluces: Federico García Lorca y Rafael Alberti," *Pluma* IV [1928], 56).

172 **"You don't know"**: Rafael Alberti to FGL (February 1927), AFFGL.

172 **"go with him"**: Santiago.

172 **FGL insults Gómez de la Serna**: Ontañón.

172 **Guillén praises FGL**: Guillén, "Federico en persona," li–lvii.

172 **"We're the captains"**: *EC*, 597.

173 **"the filthiest beast"**: Buñuel, *Obra literaria*, 36.

173 **Góngora tricentennial**: Alberti, *La arboleda perdida*, 237–61; Morris, *A Generation*, 10–11, 22; *Lola, amiga y suplemento de Carmen* (Santander), April 1928; Paloma Ulacía Altolaguirre, *Concha Méndez. Memorias habladas, memorias armadas*, introduction by María Zambrano (Madrid: Mondadori España, 1990), 50–51; Dámaso Alonso, *Poetas españoles contemporáneos*, 3rd ed. rev. (Madrid: Gredos, 1969), 169–70.

173 **"Brilliant Pleiad"**: "Coronación de Dámaso Alonso," *Lola, amiga y suplemento de Carmen* (Santander), April 1928.

173 **Guillén describes trip to Seville**: Jorge Guillén to Germaine Guillén (December 15, 1927), papers of Jorge Guillén, Wellesley College Archive.

173–74 **Ignacio Sánchez Mejías, background**: S. Morales Jiménez, *Buscando una muerte de luz* (Motril: Copartgraf, 1979), 59; Nicholas J. Collins, "Reality in Lorca's 'Llanto por Ignacio Sánchez Mejías,'" *Reflexión* 21, 1, 2nd series (Ottawa, July [May–August] 1972), 99–104; William Lyon, "La rebelión de Ignacio Sánchez Mejías," *El País* (Madrid), August 13, 1984, 9; Alberti, *La arboleda perdida*, 241; *FM*, 202–3, 240–41.

174 **"seduction itself"**: Auclair, 19.

174 **Revelry in Seville:** Jorge Guillén to Germaine Guillén (December 15, 1927), papers of Jorge Guillén, Wellesley College Archive; Alberti, *La arboleda perdida*, 243, 258–61; Dámaso Alonso, *Poetas españoles contemporáneos*, 3rd ed. rev. (Madrid: Gredos, 1969), 155; *G, I*, 525–26.

174 **FGL reads poetry in Seville:** Alberti, *Federico García Lorca: Poeta y amigo*, 275–77.

174 **Luis Cernuda meets FGL:** Luis Cernuda, "Federico García Lorca (recuerdo)," *Hora de España* 18 (June 1938), 13–20; Luis Cernuda, "Notas eludidas: Federico García Lorca," *Heraldo de Madrid*, November 26, 1931, 12.

175 **Generation of '27:** Ricardo Baeza, "De una generación poética," *El Sol* (Madrid), August 24, 1927, 1; Morris, *A Generation*; Dámaso Alonso, "Una generación poetica (1920–36)," *Poetas españoles contemporáneos*, 3rd ed. rev. (Madrid: Gredos, 1969); Juan Marichal, "La universalización de España (1898–1936)," in Soria Olmedo, 11–23; Luis García Montero, introduction to Alberti, *Federico García Lorca: Poeta y amigo*, 18–21. FGL knew his fellow poets' work so well that in 1928 he wrote a witty series of pastiches of their poems (see "Antología 'modelna,' " *OC*, I, 781–93).

175 **"We love each other":** Pinto.

175 **"astronomical maps . . . satellites":** "Coronación de Dámaso Alonso," *Lola, amiga y suplemento de Carmen* (Santander), April 1928.

12. MADNESS OF BREEZE AND TRILL: 1928

176 **"at peace with myself":** *EC*, 543.

176 **"an absolute scandal":** *EC*, 551.

176 **FGL publishes first issue of *gallo*:** "Una comida literaria: *gallo* y sus simpatizantes en la Venta de Eritaña," *Defensor de Granada*, March 9, 1928, 1; *EC*, 547–62; Martínez Nadal, *Federico García Lorca. Mi penúltimo libro*, 247; Antonio Gallego Morell, "Ilusión y kikirikí de *gallo*," in *gallo. revista de granada*. 1928, facsimile ed. (Granada: Comares, 1988), xiv, xviii. On the magazine's distribution in Madrid, see *EC*, 553n.

177 **"who have given":** Gallego Morell, "Ilusión y kikirikí de *gallo*," in *gallo. revista de granada*. 1928, facsimile ed. (Granada: Comares, 1988), xvi.

177 **"the way you hold":** "Una comida literaria: *gallo* y sus simpatizantes en la Venta de Eritaña," *Defensor de Granada*, March 9, 1928, 1.

177 **"As I'm its father":** *EC*, 551.

177 **"hostile new cock"** and **"chicken coop":** "Silueta del día: Gallismo," *Defensor de Granada*, October 30, 1928.

177 **FGL publishes *Pavo*:** "*Pavo* en la calle," *Defensor de Granada*, March 18, 1928, 1; *Pavo* (Granada), March 1928.

177 **"succulent . . . prosperous life":** "*Pavo* en la calle," *Defensor de Granada*, March 18, 1928, 1.

177 **Dalí's "Anti-Artistic Manifesto":** In March 1928, Dalí had printed the inflammatory document in Catalan and mailed it to Barcelona's cultural and business elite, who were scandalized. One critic labeled the manifesto "Futurist crap." In the document, Dalí and his cosignatories aligned themselves with the great artists of the day; these included Picasso, Tzara, Cocteau, Stravinsky, André Breton, and FGL (Sebastian Gasch, *L'Expansió de l'art català al mon* [Barcelona: Private edition, 1953], 206; Jaime Brihuega, *Manifiestos, proclamas, panfletos y textos doctrinales. Las vanguardias artísticas en España. 1910–1931* [Madrid: Ediciones, 1979], 157–61).

177 "To me": Salinas and Guillén, 88.

178 "anti-art": Sebastian Gasch, *L'Expansió de l'art catalá al mon* (Barcelona: Private edition, 1953), 142.

178 "to the four winds": *FM*, xxiv.

178 "marvelous . . . disappoint my parents": *EC*, 437.

178 **Relationship between FGL and Francisco García Lorca**: *FM*, iv; Francisco García Lorca, prologue to FGL, *Three Tragedies*; José Méndez, "Las dos raíces de Laura García Lorca," *ABC. Semanal* (Madrid), June 9, 1985, 6–8.

178 "Yes . . . life is hard": Francisco García Lorca, *Poesía*, ed. Mario Hernández (Madrid: Editora Nacional / Libros de Poesía–9, 1984), 90.

178–79 "If I don't go": *EC*, 545.

179 "write to me": Emilio Aladrén to FGL (summer 1925), AFFGL.

179 "I knew you wouldn't come": Emilio Aladrén to FGL (January 6, 1928), AFFGL.

179 "ten or twelve conflicts": *EC*, 548–49.

179 "emotional conflicts" and "cleansed": *EC*, 543.

179 **FGL begins ode to Christ**: *EC*, 550; *FM*, 156; Miguel García-Posada, introduction to FGL, *Oda y burla*, 51; Martín, *Federico García Lorca, heterodoxo*, 264; Auclair, 159; Javier Herrero, "The Father Against the Son: Lorca's Christian Vision," in *Essays in Hispanic Literature in Honor of Edward Diley*, ed. Jennifer Low and Phillip Swanson (Edinburgh: Department of Hispanic Studies, 1989), 170–99.

179 "Here I am in Pitres": *EC*, 555, trans. FGL, *Selected Letters*, 129–30.

179 "erotic feeling . . . inviolable heights": *OC*, III, 72–73, trans. FGL, *Deep Song*, 81.

180 **FGL writes and publishes "Two Norms"**: FGL, *Diván del Tamarit*, 95, 171–72; Martínez Nadal, *Cuatro lecciones*, 104.

181 **FGL rereads Plato's *Symposium*; "If oneness"; and "We are born"**: Rafael Martínez Nadal, *El público, amor y muerte en la obra de Federico García Lorca*, 2nd ed. (Mexico City: Joaquín Mortiz, 1974), 87. FGL owned a 1923 edition of Plato's *The Banquet* (*El banquete o del amor*); the volume, inscribed "Federico García Lorca," is heavily underlined, including the passage that begins "We are born with one type of love," from Pascal's "Discourse on the Passions of Love" (Fernández-Montesinos García, "Descripción," 85, 167).

181 "between Russian and Tahitian": Martínez Nadal, *Cuatro lecciones*, 28–29.

181 **Emilio Aladrén, background**: Penón, 105–6; G, I, 544–47, 561–62; Madrid, Universidad Complutense, School of Fine Arts, Records of Emilio Aladrén, no. 1.266; Martínez Nadal, *Cuatro lecciones*, 28–30; author interview with Santiago Ontañón.

181 "Federico, I'd like to be frank . . . put up with me": Emilio Aladrén to FGL (n.d.), AFFGL, in G, I, 548–49.

182 "fabulous" and "Russian temperament": G, I, 544–45.

182 "my springtime friend": Emilio Aladrén to FGL (n.d.), AFFGL.

182 **Aladrén performs circus stunts**: Martínez Nadal, *Cuatro lecciones*, 29–30.

182 "I'd like it to be a surprise": *EC*, 580.

182 "one of the most brilliant": Unidentified article by Valentín Álvarez Cienfuegos, AFFGL.

182 "Isn't it true": Emilio Aladrén to FGL (n.d.), AFFGL, in G, I, 548–49.

183 "You're a Christian tempest": Dalí, *Salvador Dalí escribe a Federico García Lorca*, 86. Dalí, who knew and disliked Aladrén, nicknamed him "Aladreniño" (G, I, 546).

183 **FGL travels to Zamora**: G, I, 550; Christopher Maurer, introduction to *Federico García Lorca escribe a su familia*, 11; "Coral Zamora. Ciclo de conferencias. Soto de Rojas visto por el poeta granadino don Federico García Lorca," *Diario Católico* (Zamora), July 11, 1928, AFFGL.

183 "like a flower," "volcano of joy," and "Look! Look": Author interview with José Antonio Rubio Sacristán.

183   "You know that in Zamora . . . against bitterness": *EC*, 573.

184   "reached [Federico's] heart": Author interview with José Antonio Rubio Sacristán.

184   FGL confronts Ortega y Gasset: *EC*, 563.

184   "I think it will be beautiful": *EC*, 567.

184   "congealed blood": Juan Chabás, review of *Romancero gitano*, in *La Libertad* (Madrid), September 1, 1928, 6–7.

184   *Gypsy Ballads* published: Hernández, introduction to FGL, *Romancero gitano*, 10–14, 188; FGL, *Autógrafos I*, 257n. The book's official title was *First Gypsy Ballads*. While it is possible FGL was contemplating the publication of a "second" ballad book, there is little evidence to support this. More likely, he simply meant to emphasize that the collection was the first of its kind.

184   "I believe in your authentic poetry": Vicente Aleixandre to FGL (September 7, 1928), AFFGL.

184   Reviews of *Gypsy Ballads*: Ricardo Baeza, "Los 'Romances gitanos' de Federico García Lorca," *El Sol* (Madrid), July 29, 1928, 2, and "Poesía y gitanismo," *El Sol* (Madrid), August 3, 1928, 1; Miguel Pérez Ferrero, "Un libro de García Lorca. Romancero gitano," *La Gaceta Literaria* (Madrid), August 15, 1928, 2; Luis Montanyà, " 'Romancero gitano' de Federico García Lorca," *L'Amic de les Arts* (Sitges), October 31, 1928, 226–27.

185   "Although the book": *EC*, 570.

185   "I want and rewant": *EC*, 577.

185   FGL's hatred of "The Unfaithful Wife": Auclair, 315; Neruda, *Confieso*, 73; Ontañón.

185   "greatest proof": Neruda, *Confieso*, 73.

186   "poem" of Andalusia and "sorrow": *OC*, III, 179.

186   "is a drama in brief": Ricardo Baeza, "Poesía y gitanismo," *El Sol* (Madrid), August 3, 1928, 1.

186   *Gypsy Ballads*: All quotations are taken from *OC*, I, 415–54, trans. FGL, *Collected Poems*.

186   "Andalusian altarpiece . . ." and "truest and purest thing": *OC*, III, 179.

187   "wild unruly hair" and "big eyes": Morris, *Son of Andalusia*, 312.

187   "ragged and dirty": "El recital de García Lorca i Margarida Xirgu a la Residencia," *La Humanitat* (Barcelona), October 12, 1935, 5.

187   "harmonize the *mythological Gypsy*": *EC*, 334, trans. FGL, *Selected Letters*, 73.

187   "who calls me by name": *OC*, III, 184.

188   FGL and Camborio: Couffon, 31; Higuera Rojas, 168; Morla Lynch, 23–24; C. Brian Morris, "Granada in García Lorca's *Romancero gitano*," *Siglo XX / 20th Century* 6, 1–2 (1988–89), 21.

188   FGL and Civil Guard: Binding, 60; FGL, *Autógrafos I*, 256n; Auclair, 372; Mora Guarnido, 26–30; and *EC*, 330–31. For an account of the episode FGL and Ángeles Ortiz witnessed in 1919, see Rodrigo, *Memoria*, 169–71, and "Gitanos y civiles. Los guardias asesinados en Ugíjar. Como se realizó el crímen," *El Sol* (Madrid), November 5, 1919, 1.

189   "Molière was right": Alardo Prats, "Los artistas en el ambiente de nuestro tiempo," *El Sol* (Madrid), December 15, 1934, in *OC*, III, 546.

189   "How can that be?": Author interview with José Antonio Rubio Sacristán.

189   "The Gypsies are a theme": *EC*, 414, trans. FGL, *Selected Letters*, 94.

189   "I am not a Gypsy": Giménez Caballero.

189   "glory and end," "washed up," "passé," and "pure . . . possibilities": Martínez Nadal, *Cuatro lecciones*, 32–33. On FGL's refusal to attend Alberti's reading, see Salinas and Guillén, 94.

189   "a vision of trees": *EC*, 571.

189   "I am tormented": *EC*, 579.

189   "beset by love": *EC*, 581.
189   "fast and furiously": *EC*, 590.
189–90   "sheer willpower," "I'm going through . . . should never see it," "reasons of disci-
        pline," and "eroticism": *EC*, 582.
190   "I am a slave": Quoted in Jack J. Spector, *Delacroix: The Death of Sardanapalus*, in the se-
        ries Art in Context, ed. John Fleming and Hugh Honour (London: Allen Lane, 1974),
        61–91.
190   "Ode . . . Sesostris and Sardanapalus": *OC*, I, 744–47; Miguel García-Posada, introduc-
        tion to FGL, *Oda y burla*; Paul Verlaine, *Selected Poems*, trans. C. F. McIntyre (Berkeley:
        University of California Press, 1948), 3.
190   "full of humor": *EC*, 579.
190   "the exact opposite": *EC*, 590.
191   "I'm going through": *EC*, 576.
191   "You'll always be": *EC*, 586.
191   "Don't get involved . . . Don't stop writing": *EC*, 575.
191   "They'll bring me," "I love you," and "As for E": Jorge Zalamea to FGL, AFFGL, cited in
        G, I, 558.
191   "I too have had": *EC*, 587.
191   "I want to be": *EC*, 589.
191–92   "internal conflicts . . . all of it is shit": Martínez Nadal, *Federico García Lorca. Mi
        penúltimo libro*, 219.
192   "unconscious erotic inspiration": *G, I*, 571.
192   **Dalí criticizes *Gypsy Ballads***: Dalí, *Salvador Dalí escribe a Federico García Lorca*, 88–94,
        trans. Gibson et al., 36–38.
192   **Dalí's "Reality and Surreality"**: Jaime Brihuega, *Manifiestos, proclamas, panfletos y textos
        doctrinales. Las vanguardias artísticas en España. 1910–1931* (Madrid: Ediciones, 1979),
        295–302.

13. RAIN FROM THE STARS: 1928-29

194   "intelligence, grace, and acuity": Martínez Nadal, *Federico García Lorca. Mi penúltimo li-
        bro*, 52.
194   "a sharp and arbitrary letter" and "It died": *EC*, 585.
194   "All day long," "vein-opening poetry," and "which gives me life": *EC*, 587.
194   "new *spiritualistic* manner": *EC*, 588.
195   "another ism": Sebastian Gasch, "Superrealismo," in Jaime Brihuega, *Manifiestos, procla-
        mas, panfletos y textos doctrinales. Las vanguardias artísticas en España. 1910–1931* (Madrid:
        Ediciones, 1979), 304.
195   **FGL delivers "Imagination, Inspiration, Escape"**: Mario Hernández, "De la correspon-
        dencia epistolar lorquiana," unpublished typescript, 23; Laffranque, 171; Maurer, introduc-
        tion to FGL, *Poet in New York*, xvi–xvii. All passages from this lecture are taken from *OC*,
        III, 98–112.
196   "If you ask me why I wrote": *OC*, III, 105–8.
196   "a complete aesthetic theory": "Vida cultural. El Ateneo de Granada inaugura el curso
        1938–1929: Conferencia de Federico García Lorca," *Defensor de Granada*, October 12, 1928.
196   *gallo* **Night**: "Gallismo," *Defensor de Granada*, September 21, 1928; "En el Ateneo–Noche
        de 'Gallo,'" *Defensor de Granada*, October 28, 1928, 1; Christopher Maurer, "Adios a este
        gallo," in *gallo. revista de granada. 1928*, facsimile ed. (Granada: Comares, 1988), xxx–xxii;

EC, 595. On the proposed third issue of *gallo* see correspondence from Joaquín Amigo to FGL, AFFGL, and *EC*, 579.

196 **"Sketch of the New Painting"**: *OC*, III, 88–97; Christopher Maurer, introduction to *C*, I, 20; Laffranque, 116; María Clementa Millán, "Líneas de una biografía," in FGL, *Dibujos*; and Mario Hernández, "Ronda de los autorretratos con animal fabuloso y análisis de los dibujos neoyorquinos," in FGL, *Dibujos*.

197 **"great tribute . . . I hope to go"**: *EC*, 595.

197 **"more affected"**: Jorge Guillén to Germaine Guillén (November 24, 1928), papers of Jorge Guillén, Wellesley College Archive.

197 **"What do you mean"**: Ontañón and Moreiro, 122.

197 **FGL gives talk on lullabies**: [Residencia de Estudiantes], 115; Francisco García Lorca to parents (December 1928), AFFGL; and Margarita Ucelay, "Homenaje a Federico García Lorca," talk given at Instituto Internacional, Madrid (March 11, 1986). All passages from the lecture are taken from *OC*, III, 113–31.

198–99 **FGL interview**: Giménez Caballero.

199 **"the faggot poets"**: Buñuel, *Obra literaria*, 30.

199 **"son of a bitch" and "pederastic news"**: Josep Playà Maset and Victor Fernández, "Buñuel escribe a Dalí," *La Vanguardia* (Barcelona), April 1, 1996, Culture and Entertainment section.

199–200 **Buñuel collaborates with Dalí**: Alberti, *La arboleda perdida*, 277; Aub, 67; Rodrigo, *Lorca-Dalí*, 209; Buñuel, *Mi último suspiro*, 102–3; Buñuel, *Obra literaria*, 40; and Sánchez Vidal, 183–89.

200 **"complete"**: Buñuel, *Mi último suspiro*, 102–3.

200 **"stupendous screenplay" and "Dalí and I are closer"**: Luis Buñuel to Pepín Bello (February 10, 1929), in Santos Torroella, *Dalí residente*, 218.

200 **FGL and Aladrén separate**: Martínez Nadal, *Cuatro lecciones*, 32–33; Penón, 186; *G*, *I*, 594.

200 **Cipriano Rivas Cherif, background**: Enrique de Rivas Ibáñez, introduction to Cipriano Rivas Cherif, *Retrato de un desconocido. Vida de Manuel Azaña*, ed. Enrique de Rivas Ibáñez (Barcelona: Grijalbo, 1980); Josep Pla, *Madrid—El advenimiento de la República* (Madrid: Alianza, 1986), 24; Rodrigo, *Margarita Xirgu y su teatro*, 167; Cipriano Rivas Cherif, *Heraldo de Madrid*, August 7, 1926, 4; Cipriano Rivas Cherif, "El teatro de la Escuela Nueva," *La Pluma* (Madrid), April 1921, 236–44; and "Conferencia de Cipriano Rivas Cherif," *Defensor de Granada*, April 7, 1929, 3.

201 **FGL attends rehearsals for Don Perlimplín**: Margarita Ucelay, "Amor de don Perlimplín con Belisa en su jardín, de Federico García Lorca. Notas para la historia de una obra: Textos, ediciones, fragmentos inéditos," in *Essays on Hispanic Literature in Honour of Edmund L. King* (London: Tamesis, 1983), 233–39.

201 **Don Perlimplín**: All quotations are taken from *OC*, II, 238–64; see also *FM*, 314–20; 200 Cifuentes, 117; Miguel García-Posada, introduction to FGL, *Teatro* I (Madrid: Akal, 1980), 52; Ucelay, "De las aleluyas de Don Perlimplín a la obra de Federico García Lorca," in *Federico García Lorca. Saggi critici nel cinquantenario della morte*, ed. Gabriele Morelli (Fasano: Schena, 1988), 96–104; and J. G. Cummins, ed., *The Spanish Traditional Lyric* (Oxford: Pergamon, 1977).

202 **"human puppet play," "grotesque tragedy," "anti-hero," and "a lot of fun"**: "Un estreno de García Lorca en el Español en gran función de gala," *Heraldo de Madrid*, April 4, 1933, in *OC*, III, 406.

203 **"And this"**: *G*, *II*, 383.

203 **"This is a mockery!"**: Río, "Federico García Lorca," 203.

203–4 *Don Perlimplín* cancelled: G, I, 591; Río, "Federico García Lorca," 203; *FM*, 313; Rivas Cherif, January 27, 1957.

204 FGL signs open letter: José Ortega y Gasset, *Obras completas* XI (Madrid: Ediciones de la Revista de Occidente, 1969), 102–6; *EC*, 607–10.

204 "piece of shit" and "Buñuel's made a shit of a film": Buñuel, *Mi último suspiro*, 101, 154.

205 Dalí refrains from publishing FGL letter: *L'Amic de les Arts* (Sitges), March 31, 1929; Sebastian Gasch, *L'Expansió de l'art català al mon* (Barcelona: Private edition, 1953), 154.

205 Dalí meets Gala Eluard: Dalí, *Salvador Dalí escribe a Federico García Lorca*, 154; G, I, 589; José María Moreiro, "Dalí en el centro de los recuerdos [Entrevistas con Ana María Dalí, Pepín Bello, Cristino Malloy y Rafael Sánchez Ventura]," *El País* Semanal, October 23, 1983, 19, 21; Buñuel, *Mi último suspiro*, 179.

205 Dalí joins surrealists: Rodrigo, *Lorca-Dalí*, 217; Ana María Dalí, 136–39.

205 "He's a disgrace": Dalí, *Salvador Dalí escribe a Federico García Lorca*, 95.

205 "a self-destructive rage . . . from everything": Salvador Dalí, with André Parinaud, 81.

205 "As the authentic poet": OC, III, 104.

205 FGL meets Carlos Morla Lynch: Auclair, 162; Morla Lynch, 22–29; author interview with Veronica Morla.

205–6 Carlos and Bebé Morla Lynch, background: Morla Lynch, 312; Auclair, 164–65; Martínez Nadal, *Federico García Lorca. Mi penúltimo libro*, 66; Escobar; author interview with Veronica Morla.

206 "very seductive": Jorge Guillén to Germaine Guillén (August 3, 1934), papers of Jorge Guillén, Wellesley College Archive.

206 "He comes and goes": Morla Lynch, 28–35.

206 "Even if" and "Always that deep obsession": Morla Lynch, 44.

206–7 FGL and Morla Lynch discuss sorrow: Morla Lynch, 39–40. Information on the death of Colomba Morla Lynch is drawn from Auclair, 167; "Colomba Morla Vicuña," *El Imparcial* (Chile), August 1928, Veronica Morla Archive; and author interview with Veronica Morla.

207 "used to get angry": Altolaguirre, *Obras completas I*, 287–88.

207 "I'm an aesthetic . . . anarchic Catholic": Altolaguirre, *Obras completas I*, 214; Santiago Ontañón, quoted in "Federico García Lorca," *La Clave* 160, Spanish Television, June 21, 1980.

207 "with photographs": *Revista de Occidente* XXII, LXVI (October–December 1928), 294.

208 "decorative bad taste" and "grandeur": Jorge Guillén to Germaine Guillén (November 14, 1928), papers of Jorge Guillén, Wellesley College Archive.

208 "Ode to the Most Holy Sacrament": All passages from this poem are taken from OC, I, 463–69, trans. FGL, *Collected Poems*, 598–609.

209 "surrealistic things . . . but false ones" and "a stinking ode": Buñuel, *Obra literaria*, 36.

209 "tormented by God . . . concerns": Fabienne Badu, *Antonieta, 1900–1931* (Mexico: Fondo de Cultura Económica, 1991).

209 "Were I to write . . . rest of the poem": *FM*, 155, trans. *GM*, 127–28.

209 "Gold, frankincense, and myrrh": See Maurer, notes to FGL, *Collected Poems*, 836.

209–10 FGL marches in Holy Week procession: José Martín Campos, "Federico García Lorca fue cofrade activo de Santa María de la Alhambra de Granada," *Ideal* (Granada), May 17, 1972.

210 FGL battles cold and "I'm not to blame . . . spiritual rest": FGL to parents (April 1929), AFFGL.

210 FGL in Bilbao: *El Liberal* (Bilbao), April 16 and 17, 1929, 1; "García Lorca en el Ateneo," *El Pueblo Vasco*, April 16, 1929, 1; *EC*, 604–5.

211 "It could earn me lots": *EC*, 602–3.

211 **FGL's father talks to Martínez Nadal:** Martínez Nadal, *Cuatro lecciones*, 33–34. Another friend of FGL's, Santiago Ontañón, believed that Don Federico was aware of his son's involvement with Emilio Aladrén and deliberately sent FGL to New York to remove him from Aladrén's influence. "Don Federico was no fool," said Ontañón (author interview).

211 "elegant lecturer's outfit . . . as a lecturer": *EC*, 606.

211 **De los Ríos agrees to accompany FGL:** See *Defensor de Granada*, June 11, 1929, 1.

211 "I find myself full of responsibility": "En el hotel Alhambra Palace. En homenaje a Margarita Xirgu y Federico García Lorca," *Defensor de Granada*, May 7, 1929, 1, in *OC*, III, 195.

211 *Mariana Pineda* **produced in Granada and "the frail work of a beginner":** *Defensor de Granada*, April 23, 28, and 30, 1929; May 3 and 4, 1929. AFFGL contains a clipping of Francisco Oriol Catena's review of *Mariana Pineda*, "Impresiones. 'Mariana Pineda,' " *Defensor de Granada*, May 3, 1929.

212 **FGL and Xirgu attend banquet and "If by the grace . . . incandescent joy":** "En el hotel Alhambra Palace. En homenaje a Margarita Xirgu y Federico García Lorca," *Defensor de Granada*, May 7, 1929, 1, in *OC*, III, 194–96.

212 **"Keep it or tear it up," "New York seems horrible," and "Papa . . . practical life":** *EC*, 612.

213 **FGL leaves Spain:** *Defensor de Granada*, June 9, 1929; *La Gaceta Literaria* (Madrid), June 15, 1929, 6; *La Voz* (Madrid), June 14, 1929; *Heraldo de Madrid*, June 14, 1929; and *G*, I, 607.

213 "Onward!": *EC*, 611.

14. NEW WORLD: 1929-30

214 "She's a bourgeois!": *G*, I, 607, and Río, "Federico García Lorca," 204. On FGL in Paris see also Mathilde Pomès, "Españoles en París. Federico García Lorca," *ABC* (Madrid), November 22, 1967.

214 **FGL in London:** *G*, I, 608–11; Río, *Vida y obras*, 37; Río, "Federico García Lorca," 204; Salvador de Madariaga, "Tres estampas de Federico García Lorca," in *De Galdós a Lorca* (Buenos Aires: Sudamericana, 1960), 221.

214 "black as blackest": FGL, "The Poet Writes," 205. Except where noted, all quotations from FGL's letters home from the United States are taken from "The Poet Writes"; the letters appear in Spanish in *EC*, 613–88.

214 "I don't know why": *EC*, 614.

214–15 "into the belly . . . the ocean": FGL, "The Poet Writes," 205–6.

215 **FGL arrives in New York:** The date of FGL's arrival appears on page 8 of FGL's passport, AFFGL. For FGL's response to arrival see FGL, "The Poet Writes," 205–6, and FGL, "Lecture: A Poet in New York," 185.

215 **New York City, 1929:** See, in particular, Robert A.M. Stern, Gregory Gilmartin, and Thomas Mellins, with David Fishman and Raymond W. Gastil, *New York 1930. Architecture and Urbanism Between the Two World Wars* (New York: Rizzoli, 1987). Among many Spaniards to publish their impressions of New York in the 1920s and early 1930s was FGL's old Residencia colleague José Moreno Villa, whose 1927 book *Pruebas de Nueva York* offered a dismaying account of the "violent" American city. FGL was also familiar with the French writer Paul Morand's *New-York* (1930) (Leslie Stainton, " '¡O Babilonia! O Cartago! O Nueva York!': El europeo ante Manhattan, Manhattan ante el europeo," *BFFGL* 10 [February 1992], 192–211).

215   **FGL enrolls in Columbia:** Eisenberg, *Textos y documentos*, 21; FGL, "The Poet Writes,"
      207, 215–16, 224; Adams, 91, 119.
216   **FGL visits Times Square:** FGL, "The Poet Writes," 208–9.
216   **FGL's initial response to America:** In general, see FGL, "The Poet Writes," 206–8; FGL,
      "Lecture: A Poet in New York," 187–88; Adams, 120–21; and Crow, 44. On FGL's reaction to
      Prohibition see Adams, 126–27, and FGL, "The Poet Writes," 245, 273. On his response to
      the Protestant faith see FGL, "The Poet Writes," 219–21. On his reaction to Americans see
      Crow, 6, and FGL, "The Poet Writes," 233–34.
216–17 **"shishpil":** Eisenberg, "Cuatro pesquisas," 536. On sexual mores in America and FGL's
      response to American sexuality, see Crow, 4; Luis de Oteyza, *Anticípolis*, (Madrid: Com-
      pañía Ibero-Americana de Publicaciones, 1931), 101, 226–27; and John K. Walsh, "The So-
      cial and Sexual Geography of *Poeta en Nueva York*," in C. Brian Morris, ed., *"Cuando yo me
      muera . . ." Essays in Memory of Federico García Lorca* (Lanham, Md.: University Press of
      America, 1988).
217   **FGL's buoyant letters home:** FGL, "The Poet Writes," 206, 224–25.
217   **FGL teaches popular songs:** FGL, "The Poet Writes," 216–17; Río, *Poeta en Nueva York*, 259.
217   **FGL's inability to learn English:** Adams, 119–21; Río, "Federico García Lorca," 228; Eisen-
      berg, *Textos y documentos*, 20; FGL, "The Poet Writes," 217–18, 222; Andrew A. Anderson,
      "Una amistad inglesa de García Lorca," *Ínsula* 462 (May 1985), 3–4; Ontañón; and Daniel
      Solana, "Federico García Lorca," *Alhambra* (New York), vol. 12 (August 1929), 24.
218   **Sofía Megwinoff tutors FGL:** Daniel Eisenberg, introduction to FGL, *Songs*, 11; FGL,
      "The Poet Writes," 215–16; Eisenberg, "Cuatro pesquisas," 533–36; "Lorca in New York,"
      WGBH-TV, Boston (May 10, 1986).
218   **Description of FGL in New York:** Río, *Vida y obras*, 37, and AFFGL.
218   **FGL feigns lameness:** Eisenberg, "Cuatro pesquisas," 537.
218   **"I don't see much":** FGL, "The Poet Writes," 222.
219   **FGL attends *tertulias*:** Author interview with Amelia Agostini del Río; B. Bussell Thomson
      and J. K. Walsh, "Un encuentro de Lorca y Hart Crane en Nueva York," *Ínsula* 479 (Octo-
      ber 1986), 1; author interview with Ángel Flores.
219   **FGL visits Hart Crane:** B. Bussell Thomson and J. K. Walsh, "Un encuentro de Lorca
      y Hart Crane en Nueva York," *Ínsula* 479 (October 1986), 1; author interview with Ángel
      Flores.
220   **"terrific poet":** Author interview with Ángel Flores.
220   **Felipe and FGL discuss Whitman:** Río, *Poeta en Nueva York*, 37; Luis Rius, *León Felipe,
      poeta de barro*, 2nd ed. (Mexico: Colección Málaga, 1974), 161. Felipe later described his
      own six-year American sojourn as a search for "Whitman / and I did not find him."
220   **FGL frequents Harlem:** Benumeya; FGL, "Lecture: A Poet in New York," 189–92; Christo-
      pher Maurer, "Los negros," in *Federico García Lorca escribe a su familia*, 143–50; Adams,
      130; FGL, "The Poet Writes," 218–19; Crow, 3. On homosexuality in Harlem see Michael
      Bronski, *Culture Clash: The Making of Gay Sensibility* (Boston: South End Press, 1984), 73.
221   **FGL writes first New York poems:** FGL, *Poet in New York*; Christopher Maurer, "Los ne-
      gros," in *Federico García Lorca escribe a su familia*, 146–50; FGL, "The Poet Writes," 219,
      226–27.
222   **"a world shameless and cruel enough":** Tiempo.
222   **"enriched and changed":** FGL, "Nota autobiográfica," in *OC*, III, 307.
222–23 **"and I believe . . . don't tell anyone":** FGL, "The Poet Writes," 226.
223   **"time to feel lonely":** FGL, "The Poet Writes," 228.
223   **"melancholy":** Concha Espina, *Singladuras. Viaje americano* (Madrid: Companía Ibero-
      Americana de Publicaciones, 1932), 150–53.

223   "shadow of absence": Río, *Vida y obras*, 37–38. Privately, Río may have known more than he claimed. Years later his wife, Amelia, remembered confronting her husband one day with a rumor that FGL was homosexual. "Forget you've heard anything about it," Ángel told her, "because Federico is doing everything he can to overcome it" (author interview with Amelia Agostini del Río).

223   **FGL roams Manhattan at night:** FGL, "The Poet Writes," 230; Crow, 6, 44.

223   **FGL writes childhood poems:** FGL, *Poet in New York*; García-Posada, introduction to FGL, *Poesía*, I, 2nd ed. (Madrid: Akal, 1982), 23; Eisenberg, "A Chronology," 236; FGL, "Lecture: A Poet in New York," 186; Isabel García Lorca, 12–13; Christopher Maurer, introduction to FGL, *Poet in New York*, xxiii.

224   **"I love him":** Author interview with Ángel Flores.

225   **FGL travels to Vermont:** Daniel Eisenberg, introduction to FGL, *Songs*; author interview with Philip Cummings; Río, *Poeta en Nueva York*; FGL, "The Poet Writes," 231, 235–41.

226   **"Ay! I've left the dungeon!":** Author interview with Philip Cummings.

226   **"barcarole of tenderness":** FGL wrote this on the back of a photograph of himself with the Cummings family (FGL, *Federico García Lorca escribe a su familia*, 23).

226   **FGL with Cummings family:** Cummings; author interview with Philip Cummings; FGL, "The Poet Writes," 235–40; Kessel Schwartz, "García Lorca and Vermont," *Hispania* 42 (1959), 50–55.

227   **FGL writes poetry in Vermont:** FGL, "The Poet Writes," 237; Kessel Schwartz, "García Lorca and Vermont," *Hispania* 42 (1959), 50–52; author interview with Philip Cummings; Daniel Eisenberg, introduction to FGL, *Songs*, 11; FGL, *Poet in New York*. In an earlier version of "Double Poem of Lake Eden," FGL was even more direct: "I want to cry speaking my name, / Federico García Lorca, on the shore of this lake."

228   **"It doesn't stop raining":** *EC*, 642–43.

228   **"You're going to bury me":** Author interview with Philip Cummings.

228   **FGL arrives in Bushnellsville:** Río, *Poeta en Nueva York*, and Angel del Río, "Fotos de Federico García Lorca en Norteamérica (1929)," *PSA* XLII (1966), 66–69.

228   **FGL in Bushnellsville:** Angel del Río, "Fotos de Federico García Lorca", 66–69; Eisenberg, "A Chronology," 238; Eisenberg, "Cuatro pesquisas"; FGL, "The Poet Writes," 242–43; author interview with Amelia Agostini del Río; FGL, *Federico García Lorca escribe a su familia*, 27; Adams, 118.

229   **FGL describes "Mary's" death:** FGL, "Lecture: A Poet in New York," 194–98; Río, *Poeta en Nueva York*; Eisenberg, "Cuatro pesquisas," 531; Río, "Federico García Lorca," 256; G, I, 50; *Defensor de Granada*, March 27, 1928; Isabel García Lorca; C. Brian Morris, " 'Aqua que no desemboca,' " in C. Brian Morris, ed., *"Cuando yo me muera," Essays in Memory of Federico García Lorca* (Lanham, Md.: University Press of America, 1988), 168–69.

229   **FGL moves into John Jay Hall:** *EC*, 646–49; Angel del Río, "Federico García Lorca vivió como un colegial en Nueva York," *La Prensa* (New York), October 15, 1937, 4; FGL, "The Poet Writes," 244–51; Eisenberg, *Textos y documentos*, 27.

229–30   **FGL befriends Crow and Hayes:** Crow, 3–5, 44, 54; FGL, "Nota autobiográfica," in *OC*, III, 306–7; and Onofre di Stevano and Darlene Lorenz, "Conversations with Three Emeritus Professors from UCLA: John A. Crow, John E. Englekirk, Donald F. Fogelquist," *Dester, Revista Literaria de los Estudiantes Graduados*, UCLA Department of Spanish and Portuguese, VIII, 1 (January 1979), 29–42.

230   **FGL meets Brickells:** Brickell; Adams, 123; Christopher Maurer, "Presentación," in FGL, *Federico García Lorca escribe a su familia*, 13; *EC*, 668.

230   **"phenomenal":** Ian Gibson, *Un Irlandés en España* (Barcelona: Planeta, 1981), 183. On FGL's piano-playing in general see FGL, "The Poet Writes," 228; Adams, 123; Crow, 3;

Brickell, 390; and Dámaso Alonso, "Federico García Lorca y la expresión de lo español," in *Poetas españoles contemporáneos*, 3rd ed. (Madrid: Gredos, 1978), 260–61.

231   **FGL continues writing poems:** Crow, 44–47; Eisenberg, "A Chronology," 238–42; FGL, *Poet in New York*; *Autográfos I*, xxxv, 243.

231   **"so you can see"**: FGL, *Autógrafos I*, xxxv, 243.

231   **"rapid progress"**: EC, 652.

231   **"I am *more responsible*"**: FGL, "The Poet Writes," 258.

231   **"soup, a platter of meat"**: FGL, "The Poet Writes," 232, 255–56.

232   **FGL and American theater:** FGL, "The Poet Writes," 231–32, 256, 258–59, 265–66; Christopher Maurer, "El teatro," in FGL, *Federico García Lorca escribe a su familia*, 137–39; Benumeya. José Antonio Rubio Sacristán, who coincided with FGL in New York, remembered attending plays with FGL—including works by Chekhov and O'Neill, and productions at Eva Le Gallienne's Civic Repertory Company (author interview with José Antonio Rubio Sacristán). During FGL's stay, the great Peking actor Mei Lan-Fang paid a two-week visit to New York and galvanized the city's theater world with his costumed impersonations of female characters. Mei was the talk of the town, and if, as is probable, FGL saw him perform (Mei Lan-Fang opened his two-week run in New York on February 17, 1930, during FGL's last full month in the city), he would have been struck by what critic Brooks Atkinson called the "unalloyed imagination" of Mei's performance (*The New York Times*, February 18, 1930, 18).

232   **FGL and American movies:** FGL, "The Poet Writes," 258–59. FGL's piece on Chaplin appears in *OC*, I, 748–51, trans. FGL, *Collected Poems*, 784–86 (see also discussion of the work in FGL, *Collected Poems*, pages 858–59).

233   **FGL drafts filmscript:** OC, II, 266–78. See also Richard Diers, "A Filmscript by Lorca," *Windmill Magazine* (spring 1963); Marie Laffranque, introduction to FGL, *Viaje a la luna (Guión cinematográfico)*, ed. Marie Laffranque (Loubressac: Broad Editions, 1980); FGL, *Viaje a la luna* (Guión cinematográfico), ed. Antonio Monegal (Valencia: Pre-Textos, 1994).

233   **"I need to be in touch"**: Auclair, 84.

234   **FGL's New York drawings:** Crow, 7, 43n; Mario Hernández, "Ronda de los autorretratos con animal fabuloso y análisis de los dibujos neoyorquinos," in FGL, *Dibujos*, 99; FGL, *Dibujos*, 170–76.

234   **"What do you mean?"**: Mathilde Pomès, "Une visite à Federico García Lorca," *Le Journal des Poètes* 5 (May 1950), 2.

234   **FGL spends autumn in New York:** FGL, "The Poet Writes," 250–57.

235   **"pure hero" and "valiant, poetic"**: FGL, "Presentación de Ignacio Sánchez Mejías," in *OC*, III, 199.

235   **"He has taken me"**: FGL, "The Poet Writes," 275.

235   **FGL witnesses Wall Street Crash:** Adams, 121; FGL, "The Poet Writes," 260–62; FGL, "Lecture: A Poet in New York," 192–93; Suero, "Crónica," in *OC*, III, 438; Daniel Eisenberg, *"Poeta en Nueva York": Historia y problemas de un texto de Lorca* (Barcelona: Ariel, 1976), 213.

236   **FGL reads poems to friends:** FGL, "The Poet Writes," 274; Brickell, 392; Río, *Poeta en Nueva York*, 251, 264.

236   **Poet in New York:** Quotations from this collection are taken from FGL, *Poet in New York*; see also OC, I, 509–81. For commentary see Crow, 43–45; Christopher Maurer, introduction to FGL, *Poet in New York*; García-Posada, introduction to FGL, *Poesía* II, 2nd ed. (Madrid: Akal, 1982), 66; García-Posada, introduction to FGL, *Poesía* I, 2nd ed. (Madrid: Akal, 1982), 63, 91; Laffranque, 214–28; Río, "El poeta Federico García Lorca," 183; Morris, *A Generation*, 217; FM, 169.

236–37   **"What I will give," "escape," "event," and "respond to"**: FGL, "Lecture: A Poet in

New York," 186–88. The lecture also appears in *OC*, III, 163–73. See also Miguel Pérez Ferrero, "Voces de desambarque," *Heraldo de Madrid*, October 9, 1930, in *OC*, III, 370.

238 **"Cry to Rome"**: FGL's "Cry to Rome" was most likely inspired either by the pope's 1929 signing of the Lateran accords with Mussolini or by his refusal in the summer of 1929 to intervene on behalf of the Cristeros rebels in Mexico, a decision that led to the savage murder of the group's leader, Father Pedroza. See Eisenberg, "A Chronology," 250; Juan Cano Ballesta, "Historia y poesía: Interpretaciones y sentido de 'Grito hacia Roma,' " *Revista Hispánica Moderna* XXXIX (New York, 1976–77), 210–14; García-Posada, introduction to FGL, *Poesía* I, 2nd ed. (Madrid: Akal, 1982), 57.

238 **FGL recalls brother Luis**: FGL, *Poeta en Nueva York. Tierra y luna*, 152n.

238 **"Adam"**: FGL, *Collected Poems*, 731, in *OC*, I, 186.

240 **"He amuses me"**: Rivas Cherif, January 13, 1957.

240 **"since Paco and I"**: FGL, "The Poet Writes," 257.

240 **FGL celebrates Christmas**: FGL, "The Poet Writes," 268–74; Adams, 124–25; Brickell, 391.

240 **FGL delivers lectures**: According to Amelia Agostini del Río, FGL sent his $100 lecture fee to his father, "to show him that poetry, too, makes money" (author interview with Amelia Agostini del Río). See also FGL, "The Poet Writes," 277–79; *EC*, 676–84; Eisenberg, *Textos y documentos*, 23–26; Andrew A. Anderson, "García Lorca at Vassar College: Two Unpublished Letters," *García Lorca Review* XI, 1 and 2 (spring 1983), 100–9.

241 **FGL travels to Cuba**: Eisenberg, "A Chronology," 24; *G*, *II*, 81, citing "Barcos llegados ayer" and "Los que llegaron en el Cuba," *Diario de la Marina* (Havana), March 8, 1930; FGL, "The Poet Writes," 279–84; FGL, "Lecture: A Poet in New York," 199–201; FGL to parents (March 8, 1930), AFFGL. FGL later told a group of young Spanish writers that leaving New York was like "escaping from the atrocious nightmare of a tortured night into the joy of a sunny day" (Luciano del Río, "García Lorca en Pontevedra," *Diario de Pontevedra*, August 12, 1973, 16).

242 **"new layers"**: Río, *Poeta en Nueva York*, 257.

242 **"to Russia"**: FGL, "The Poet Writes," 268.

15. SPANISH AMERICA: 1930

243 **FGL arrives in Cuba**: Suero, "Crónica," 438; *EC*, 681–84; *Diario de la Marina* (Havana), March 8, 1930.

243 **"exaggerated"**: *EC*, 681.

244 **"I've spent the happiest"**: Marinello, 15.

244 **FGL gives lectures**: Nicolás Guillén, "Recuerdos de García Lorca," *Triunfo*, June 12, 1976, 17; [Quevedo], 21–22; *OC*, III, 109–10; *Diario de la Marina* (Havana), March 10, 11, 12, 17, 19, and 30, 1930; April 7 and 9, 1930; June 6, 1930.

244 **"lightness and ease"**: Cardoza y Aragón, 347.

244 **"doesn't lend" and "He is bursting . . . of Adam"**: *Revista de Avance* 46 (Havana), May 15, 1930, 159.

244 **"This is called"**: Nicolás Guillén, "Recuerdos de García Lorca," *Triunfo*, June 12, 1976, 17.

244–45 **FGL reads New York poems**: Arciniegas; Luis Cardoza y Aragón, "Federico en Nueva York," *Romance* I, 13 (Mexico, 1940).

245 **Salazar encounters FGL**: Salazar, "Federico en La Habana," 30.

245 **"scene from an Athenian"**: [Quevedo], 17.

245 **"Local, I take it?"**: Jesús Sabourín, "Federico García Lorca en Santiago de Cuba," *Santiago de Cuba. Universidad de Oriente. Revista* I, 2 (March 1962), 2.

245 "If you write to me": [Quevedo], 37.

245 "I've forgotten": [Quevedo], 36.

245 "three or four hours" and "I am going to give": FGL, "The Poet Writes," 285–86.

245–46 FGL disappears: FGL, "The Poet Writes," 286; [Quevedo], 18; Guillermo Cabrera Infante, "Brief Encounters in Havana," *World Literature Today* 61, 4 (Norman, Okla., autumn 1987), 519–25.

246 "without tragedy": FGL, "Lecture: A Poet in New York," 201. On FGL's interest in Cuban blacks see also *G, II*, 102, and Isabel Cuchí Coll, *Del Madrid literario . . . Madrid 1933–1934* (San Juan: Venezuela, 1935), 80.

246 "drop of Negro blood . . . better": FGL, "The Poet Writes," 285.

246 "Oh, Cuba": *EC*, 691.

246 "gone native": *Social* (Havana), May 1930, 6.

246 FGL embraces Cuban culture: [Quevedo], 17, 25, 30–35; FGL, "The Poet Writes," 284–85; Auclair, 399; Marinello, 20; Emilio Ballagas, "Recuerdo de García Lorca," *Carteles* (Havana), July 24, 1938, 55.

246 FGL participates in strike: Emilio Ballagas, "Recuerdo de García Lorca," *Carteles* (Havana), July 24, 1938, 55. On FGL's sympathy with the Cuban opposition see [Emilio Roig de Leuchsening], "Habladurías por 'El Curioso Parlanchín.' Federico García Lorca, poeta ipotrocasmo," *Carteles* (Havana), April 27, 1930, 30, 46–47.

247 "What will become": *EC*, 668.

247 "What's happening over there": *EC*, 688.

247 FGL and Cuban music: *Heraldo de Madrid*, October 9, 1930; Mathilde Pomès, "Une visite à Federico García Lorca," *Le Journal des Poètes* 5 (May 1950), 1; *FM*, 68; Adolfo Salazar, "El mito de Caimito," *Carteles* (Havana), February 20, 1938; and Nicolás Guillén, "Recuerdos de García Lorca," *Triunfo*, June 12, 1976, 17.

247 FGL writes "Son": Pérez Coterillo, 41; Auclair, 397; Marinello, 17–18, 20. It was in Santiago harbor that the Spanish fleet succumbed to the United States Navy in 1898, the year of FGL's birth. As a result of the defeat, Spain lost Cuba, a fact that may account for the elegiac tone of FGL's poem.

247 FGL with Quevedos: [Quevedo]; *G, II*, 93, 98; Ciro Bianchi Ross, "Aniversario. Federico en Cuba," *Cuba Internacional* XII, 130 (Havana, September 1980), 26; E. Dobos, "Nuevos datos sobre el viaje de Federico García Lorca por Cuba en el año 1930," *Acta Litteraria. Academiae Scientiarum Hungaricae* XXII (Budapest, 1980), 397–98.

248 "invitation and surrender": Joseph Hergesheimer, *San Cristóbal de la Habana* (New York: Alfred A. Knopf, 1927), 197.

248 FGL with Cardoza y Aragón: Cardoza y Aragón, 328, 350–58.

248 FGL rumored to have had love affairs: *G, II*, 92, 105–6; [Quevedo]; Guillermo Cabrera Infante, "Lorca hace llover en La Habana," *Cuadernos Hispanoamericanos* 433–36 (July–August 1986), 247–48; AFFGL (photograph archive).

249 FGL begins *The Audience*: The title of FGL's *El público* is typically translated as "The Public"; because the Spanish "público," however, means both "public" and "audience," and because the notion of "audience" is at the heart of FGL's play, I have elected to translate the title as *The Audience*. For details on the manuscript of *The Audience* see Martínez Nadal, *Lorca's The Public*, 21–23; Martínez Nadal, introduction to FGL, *El público y Comedia sin título*, 26; and FGL, *Autógrafos II*.

249 "some sort of obese": Cardoza y Aragón, 352–53.

249 FGL with Loynaz family: Pérez Coterillo, 40–42; *G, II*, 99–101; E. Dobos, "Nuevos datos sobre el viaje de Federico García Lorca por Cuba en el año 1930," *Acta Litteraria. Academiae Scientiarum Hungaricae* XXII (Budapest, 1980), 398–99; Ciro Bianchi

Ross "Aniversario. Federico en Cuba," *Cuba Internacional* XII, 130 (Havana, September 1980), 29–30; Dulce María Loynaz, "Comentarios" (unpublished ms., May 2, 1988), AFFGL.

250 **FGL has surgery:** Auclair, 399; Eisenberg, "A Chronology," 248; Fernández-Montesinos García, "Descripción," 27; Dulce María Loynaz, "Comentarios" (unpublished ms., May 2, 1988), AFFGL; Salazar, "Federico en La Habana," 30; Emilio Ballagas, "Recuerdo de García Lorca," *Carteles* (Havana), July 24, 1938, 55; Luis Cardoza y Aragón, "Federico García Lorca," *El Nacional* (Mexico), September 30, 1936.

250 **FGL departs Cuba:** *G, II,* 121–22; [Quevedo], 39; Pérez Coterillo, 42; Ciro Bianchi Ross, "Aniversario. Federico en Cuba," *Cuba Internacional* XII, 130 (Havana, September 1980), 30; Marinello, 15; *Diario de la Marina* (Havana), June 11 and 12, 1930. FGL's ticket for the *Manuel Arnus* is stamped "departure" on June 12, 1930 (AFFGL).

250 ***Manuel Arnus* stops in New York:** Eisenberg, "A Chronology," 249; *The New York Times,* June 18 and 19, 1930; *EC,* 689; Salazar, "La casa," 30; Brickell, 394–95; Adams, 137.

16. AUDIENCE: 1930-31

252 **FGL writes to Martínez Nadal:** *EC,* 689–90. On FGL's plans to revisit America see *EC,* 669, 693; and FGL interview with Miguel Pérez Ferrero, *Heraldo de Madrid,* October 9, 1930, in *OC,* III, 368–73.

252 **Priest encounters FGL:** Vásquez Ocaña, *García Lorca: Vida,* 269–70.

253 **"You could stay . . . charm":** *EC,* 692–93.

253 **"terrible washing machines":** *EC,* 671.

253 **FGL's typical behavior at Huerta:** Rodrigo, "La huerta," 824–28; José Manuel Fajardo, "Granada: La sombra de García Lorca es alargada," *Cambio 16,* April 7, 1986, 123.

253 **"keep up his spirits":** FGL, "The Poet Writes," 223.

253 **FGL's affection for mother:** Cano, 87–88; Penón, 90.

253 **Lorca family follows political developments:** *G, II,* 124–25.

254 **"It consists" and "Marvelous":** FGL interview with Miguel Pérez Ferrero, *Heraldo de Madrid,* October 9, 1930, cited in Martín, "Lorca y Nueva York."

254 **"greater decisiveness . . . rite had ended":** Cernuda, 15.

254 **"to recognize his nature . . . cynical":** Author interview with José Antonio Rubio Sacristán.

254 **"I've done the most difficult":** Joaquín de Entrambasaguas, "Nota preliminar," in FGL, *Poeta en Nueva York* (selection), *Anthology of Contemporary Literature* I (Madrid: First supplement of "Cuadernos de Literatura Contemporánea" of the CSIC, 1945), 4.

255 **"I have to defend":** Martínez Nadal, "Guía al lector," in FGL, *El público y Comedia sin título,* 260–61. Martínez Nadal also describes FGL's recitals of his New York poems.

255 **FGL reads *The Audience* to Morla Lynch and friends and "They haven't understood":** Martín, "Lorca y Nueva York," 48; Auclair, 199; Martínez Nadal, *Lorca's The Public.*

255 **Manuscript of *The Audience*:** Most editions of *El público* remark on the uncertain state of the manuscript. On the placement of "Song of the Idiot Shepherd," see José Rubio Barcía, "Ropaje y desnudez de *El público*," *Cuadernos Hispanoamericanos* 433–34 (July–August 1986), 385–97.

255 ***The Audience*:** Passages from this play are taken from *OC,* II, 279–327.

256 **FGL writes brief sketch in adolescence:** Margarita Ucelay, "La problemática teatral: Testimonios directos de Federico García Lorca," *BFFGL* 6 (December 1989), 35.

258 **"would be sensational":** *EC,* 706. On Rivas Cherif's plans to produce *The Audience* see "Noticias teatrales," *Luz* (Madrid), May 6, 1932, 2; "Sección de rumores," *Heraldo de*

Madrid, May 4, 1932, 6; and Juan G. Olmedilla, "Al margen de la escena consuetudinaria," *Heraldo de Madrid*, November 21, 1933, 13.

258   **"I don't think any company"**: "Llegó anoche Federico García Lorca," *La Nación* (Buenos Aires), October 14, 1933.

258   **"A poem to be hissed"**: Pinto. On FGL's publication of scenes from *The Audience* see Martínez Nadal, *Lorca's* The Public, 19.

259   **FGL reportedly gives nude reading**: José María Alfaro, "Hombres, aconteceres y nostalgias. Federico y *El público*," ABC (Madrid), June 18, 1978, Sunday Cultural section, 28.

259   **Xirgu decides to premiere** *Shoemaker's Wife*: Rodrigo, *Margarita Xirgu*, 168; FGL to parents (January[?] 1929), cited in Antonio Monegal, "Federico García Lorca–Luis Buñuel: Cartas inéditas," *Plaza, Revista de Literatura* 11 (Cambridge, Mass., autumn 1986), 60.

259   **Rehearsals for** *Shoemaker's Wife*: Rodrigo, *Margarita Xirgu*, 168; FM, 301–5; "Sección de rumores," *Heraldo de Madrid*, December 4 and 5, 1930, 7; Hernández, introduction to FGL, *La zapatera*, 29–36.

260   **"As you can see"**: EC, 702. In his letter, FGL mentions that he was considering having an aviator friend fly him home for the holidays.

260   **FGL encounters Aladrén**: Carlos G. Santa Cecilia, "La insoportable levedad de Federico," *El País* (Madrid), August 19, 1986, x–xi; G, *II*, 128–29.

260   **"Emilio Aladrén Perojo"**: Emilio Aladrén to FGL (August 30, 1930), AFFGL.

260   **"absolutely pre-revolutionary"**: Salinas and Guillén, 122.

261   *Shoemaker's Wife* **opens**: Fernández Cifuentes, 98; FGL, *La zapatera*, 192.

261   **"compensate"**: EC, 701n.

261   **"real work"**: "Antes del estreno. Hablando con Federico García Lorca," *La Libertad* (Madrid), December 24, 1930, 9.

261   **Francisco García Lorca attends** *Shoemaker's Wife*: Francisco García Lorca, introduction to FGL, *Five Plays*, 15.

261   **"share the anxiety"**: "Antes del estreno. Hablando con Federico García Lorca," *La Libertad* (Madrid), December 24, 1930, 9.

261   *The Shoemaker's Prodigious Wife*: Passages from this play are taken from OC, II, 191–237.

261   **"violent" and "vulgar"**: FGL, *La zapatera*, 48.

262   **FGL collects folk sayings**: Auclair, 263; Rodrigo, *Memoria*, 60; Altolaguirre, "Recuerdos," 603.

262   **"Ask a duchess"**: Auclair, 171.

262   **"a simple farce"**: *La Nación* (Buenos Aires), November 30, 1933, 11, in OC, III, 471.

263   **"dramatic material . . . for later"**: *Crítica* (Buenos Aires), December 1, 1933, in OC, III, 477.

263   **"grotesque"**: "Una interesante iniciativa," *El Sol* (Madrid), April 5, 1933, in OC, 407–10.

263   **"malice and bad will"**: EC, 355.

263   **"the voice of conscience" and "indispensable"**: "Antes del estreno. Hablando con Federico García Lorca," *La Libertad* (Madrid), December 24, 1930, 9, in OC, III, 374.

264   **Autobiographical elements in** *Shoemaker's Wife*: FM, 46; Hernández, introduction to FGL, *La zapatera*, 15.

264   **FGL adds prologue**: Hernández, introduction to FGL, *La zapatera*, 29–36; Anderson, *García Lorca: La zapatera prodigiosa*, 13.

264   **FGL performs prologue**: During the first performances of *The Shoemaker's Prodigious Wife* in Madrid, Xirgu's company presented a brief Chinese legend as a prelude to FGL's play. In January 1931, the Chinese legend was dropped in exchange for Calderón's auto sacramental *The Grand Theater of the World* (Anderson, *García Lorca. La zapatera prodigiosa*, 64).

265 **Critical response to *Shoemaker's Wife***: For general discussion of critical response see Anderson, *García Lorca: La zapatera prodigiosa*, 14, and Fernández Cifuentes, 98.
265 **"simple, entertaining"**: Salinas and Guillén, 124.
265 **"the struggle between" and "a compendium"**: *La Nación* (Buenos Aires), November 30, 1933, 11, in *OC*, III, 472–73.
265–66 **Xirgu closes *Shoemaker's Wife***: See *G*, *II*, 131, and María Francisca Vilches de Frutos and Dru Dougherty, *Los estrenos teatrales de Federico García Lorca (1920–45)* (Madrid: Tabapress, Fundación Federico García Lorca, 1992), 65.
266 **"I don't know"**: Dalí, *Salvador Dalí escribe a Federico García Lorca*, 95. For FGL's response see Ontañón and Moreiro, 158.

17. REPUBLIC: 1931

267 **"republic based on national sovereignty"**: Díaz-Plaja, 180.
267 **"writers and artists . . . Republic"**: *El Sol* (Madrid), February 10, 1931, in Díaz-Plaja, 197–98.
267 **"rumors . . . about each other"**: Salinas and Guillén, 130–31.
268 **"They're preoccupied"**: Morla Lynch, 45.
268 **Gatherings at Morla Lynch home**: Escobar, 84; Morla Lynch, 51–61, 118–19, 290, 319; Auclair, 165–69; Martínez Nadal, *Federico García Lorca. Mi penúltimo libro*, 68; author interview with Veronica Morla; correspondence from Veronica Morla to author (July 18, 1985).
268 **"volcano"**: Morla Lynch, 48.
268 **"Your mother . . . already started"**: Carlos Morla Lynch to FGL (July 30, 1931), AFFGL.
268–69 **FGL and brother**: Fernández-Montesinos, xi; Escobar, 83; Andrés Ruiz Tarazona, "La generación musical del 27 y Federico," *Primer Acto* 205 (September–October 1984), 19; Morla Lynch, 165; *G*, *II*, 153.
269 **"We were doing"**: Emilio Garrigues Díaz-Cañabate, "Al teatro con Federico García Lorca," *Cuadernos Hispanoamericanos* 340 (Madrid, October 1978), 106–7.
269 **"always off somewhere"**: Salinas and Guillén, 133.
269 **"an absurd Charlus . . . minors?"**: Jorge Guillén to Germaine Guillén (August 3, 1934), papers of Jorge Guillén, Wellesley College Archive.
269 **"I'm just crazy"**: Escobar, 84.
269–70 **FGL's behavior at Morla Lynch home**: Morla Lynch, 118–19, 128–29, 143–44; Salinas. On FGL's fondness for Morla's bathroom, see *EC*, 718.
270 **"a glass, a pencil holder"**: Ernesto Guerra da Cal, "Federico García Lorca en el recuerdo," *Punto y Coma* 11 (Madrid, winter 1988–89), 50–54.
270 **"*chorpatélico*"**: Altolaguirre, *Obras completas I, Estudios literarios*, 282.
270 **"*pimpavonillas* . . . typical of Federico"**: Salinas.
270–71 **Morla Lynch's diary**: Auclair, 96, 164–65; Morla Lynch, 159–60; Ontañón and Moreiro, 117–18; author interview with Veronica Morla; correspondence from Veronica Morla to author (July 18, 1985).
271 **FGL discusses death with Morla Lynch**: Morla Lynch, 158–60.
271 **"These months"**: Salinas and Guillén, 134.
271 **April 12 elections**: For FGL's activities on April 12, see Morla Lynch, 54; Rivas Cherif, January 6, 1957; Francisco Vega Díaz, "Una anécdota del poeta en la calle," *El País* (Madrid), June 5, 1980; Luis Lacasa, "Recuerdo y trayectoria de Federico García Lorca," *Literatura soviética* (Moscow, 1946), 41; Auclair, 228.

272 **Republic declared**: Thomas, 39–41; Jackson, 7, 24–26; Josep Pla, *Madrid — El advenimiento de la República* (Madrid: Alianza, 1986), 13–27; Alberti, *La arboleda*, 311–12; Díaz-Plaja, 217.

273 **"Federico—1931—Republican April"**: FGL, *Dibujos*, 206.

273 **First weeks of Republic**: Thomas, 42; Jackson, 28; Byrd, 17; Auclair, 230; Díaz-Plaja, 246–47. For Cardinal Segura's letter see Thomas, 50, citing *El Sol* (Madrid), May 7, 1931. On FGL and the convent school, see V.S., "Estudiantes de la F.U.E. se echarán a los caminos con 'La Barraca,' " *El Sol* (Madrid), December 2, 1931, 1, in *OC*, III, 381–82; Gregorio Prieto, *Lorca en color* (Madrid: Editora Nacional, 1969), 54.

274 **"economic position" and "all my things . . . All the publishers"**: EC, 694–95.

274 **FGL makes recording with La Argentinita**: EC, 695; Pedro Vaquero Sánchez, " ' La Argentinita,' García Lorca y las canciones populares antiguas," liner notes, *Colección de Canciones Populares Españoles*, FGL piano, La Argentinita voice (Madrid: Sonifolk, 1990, J-105); Mario Hernández, introduction to FGL, *Primeras canciones*, 37–38, 229; *FM*, 33; Adolfo Salazar, "Discos," *El Sol* (Madrid), November 27, 1931; Pedro Massa, "Fiesta de arte. Federico García Lorca, el romancillo popular y 'La Argentinita,' " *Crónica* (Madrid), March 20, 1932; Federico de Onís, "La Argentinita," *Revista Hispánica Moderna* (January–April 1946), 183.

274 **"at all hours"**: EC, 711.

275 **FGL publishes *Poem of the Deep Song***: Rafael Martínez Nadal, introduction to FGL, *Autógrafos I*, xiii–xv, 251n; Mario Hernández, *Cronología*, in FGL, *Poema del cante jondo*, 191–203. On advertising for the book, see *El Sol* (Madrid), June 18, 1931, 2. For prefatory note to collection, see FGL, *Poesía* I, ed. Miguel García-Posada, 2nd ed. (Madrid: Akal, 1982), 598–99.

275 **FGL friendship with Martínez Nadal**: Vicenta Lorca to FGL (n.d.), AFFGL; Morla Lynch, 81, 228; Martínez Nadal, *Cuatro lecciones*, 24; Auclair, 168–69; Martínez Nadal, *Federico García Lorca: Mi penúltimo libro*, 200, 275, 298–99; Rafael Martínez Nadal to FGL (n.d.), AFFGL.

276 **Critical response to *Deep Song***: Azorín, "Los cuatro dones," *Crísol* (Madrid), July 2, 1931; Sebastian Gasch, "Un libre de García Lorca, *Poema del cante jondo*," *Mirador* (Barcelona), August 20, 1931, 6; Agustín Espinosa, "Escaparate de libros," *La Gaceta Literaria* 111 (Madrid), August 1, 1931, 14.

276 **"intense attacks . . . myrtles"**: EC, 712.

276 **"frozen . . . on its surface"**: EC, 715.

276 **FGL's niece Vicenta**: EC, 695, 700–2, 719; Rodrigo, "La huerta," 828.

277 **"I can imagine . . . each thread"**: EC, 713–14.

277 ***Poems for the Dead***: EC, 716; Gil Benumeya, "Estampa de García Lorca," *La Gaceta Literaria* (Madrid), January 15, 1931, in *OC*, III, 377; Andrew A. Anderson, "Lorca's 'New York Poems': A Contribution to the Debate," *Forum for Modern Language Studies* XVII (July 3, 1981), 264–65.

277 **FGL writes *Once Five Years Pass***: FGL, *Autografos III*, 214; *FM*, 333; EC, 712, 716.

277 ***Once Five Years Pass***: All quotations are taken from *OC*, II, 329–93, trans. FGL, *Once Five Years Pass*, trans. William Bryant Logan and Angel Gil Orrios, in *American Theatre* 3, 9 (December 1986), Special Insert, 1–15.

278 **"To [Federico], the living mystery"**: *FM*, 137, trans. GM, 112–13.

278 **"entirely of my brother's"**: Auclair, 206.

279 ***Theater of Souls***: Margarita Ucelay, "La problemática teatral: Testimonios directos de Federico García Lorca," BFFGL 6 (December 1989), 35; and *OC*, IV, 884–89.

279 **"a mystery play"**: "Llegó anoche el poeta Federico García Lorca," *La Nación* (Buenos Aires), October 14, 1933, 9, in *OC*, III, 444.

279 "personal vision": *FM*, 333, trans. *GM*, 199.

280 **Jorge Manrique:** In *Coplas a la muerte de su padre* (c. 1477–79), Manrique wrote, "Our lives are the rivers / that flow into the sea / which is death" (Jorge Manrique, *Coplas a la muerte de su padre* [Madrid: Castalia, 1983], 48).

280 **Fuente Vaqueros names street in FGL's honor:** Andrés Soria Olmedo, introduction to FGL, *Alocución al pueblo*, 8–11; Marie Laffranque, "Bases cronológicas para el estudio de Federico García Lorca," in Gil, 442.

280 **FGL speaks at library dedication:** All quotations are taken from FGL, *Alocución al pueblo*, in *OC*, III, 201–14. For additional information on the dedication, see *FM*, 23–24, trans. *GM*, 13–14; and Andrés Soria Olmedo, introduction to FGL, *Alocución al pueblo*.

281 "to escape into lost corners . . . orator!": *FM*, 24, trans. *GM*, 14.

18. A PEOPLE'S THEATER: 1931-32

282 "more *granadino* than ever": Morla Lynch, 77.

282 "magnificent . . . madness, come on!": Morla Lynch, 106–7.

282 **Government drafts constitution:** Jackson, 45–54; Thomas, 72–74; Josep Pla, *Madrid—El advenimiento de la República* (Madrid: Alianza, 1986), 135.

283 **FGL attends Cortes session:** Juan-Simeón Vidarte, *Las Cortes Constituyentes de 1931–1933. Testimonio del primer secretario del Congreso de los Diputados* (Barcelona: Grijalbo, 1976), 189–96; *G*, II, 157–59.

283 **Manuel Azaña:** Jackson, 46–56; Thomas, 43–45; Cipriano Rivas Cherif, *Retrato de un desconocido. Vida de Manuel Azaña*, ed. Enrique de Rivas Ibañez (Barcelona: Grijalbo, 1980), 153; León.

283–84 **FGL announces plans for La Barraca:** Morla Lynch, 127–28; Anderson, "Los primeros pasos"; Aub, 279; Saenz de la Calzada, 43. On FGL's choice of name for the company, see Byrd, 15–16; Aub, 279; Enrique Moreno Báez, "La Barraca. Entrevista con su director, Federico García Lorca," *Revista de la Universidad Internacional de Santander* (1933), in *OC*, III, 426; *FM*, 439.

284 **"To give back to the people":** V.S., "Estudiantes de la F.U.E. se echarán a los caminos con 'La Barraca,' " *El Sol* (Madrid), December 2, 1931, 1, in *OC*, III, 384.

284 **"We will remove plays":** *FM*, 449–50.

284 **De los Ríos named minister of education:** Antonio Campoamor González, "La Barraca y su primera salida por los caminos de España," *Cuadernos Hispanoamericanos* 433–36, vol. II (September–October 1986), 782–83; "Actividad de los estudiantes. Creación de un teatro universitario para la divulgación de obras clásicas," *Heraldo de Madrid*, November 26, 1931, 2; Saenz de la Calzada, 42–43; Fernando de los Ríos, "Programa y presupuesto de Instrucción Pública," *El Liberal* (Madrid), March 25, 1932, 11.

284 **"was like a dazzling toy":** *FM*, 452.

284–85 **La Barraca sparks controversy:** *G*, II, 164–66, citing José Luis Tapia, "Romance del Federico," *Gracia y Justicia* (Madrid), January 23, 1932, 10; and *Gracia y Justicia* (Madrid), March 12, 1932; Fernando de los Ríos, "Programa y presupuesto de Instrucción Pública," *El Liberal* (Madrid), March 25, 1932, 11.

285 **Eduardo Ugarte:** Ontañón; *El exilio español en Mexico. 1939–1982* (Mexico City: Salvat 38; Fondo de Cultura Económica, 1982), 868; Buñuel, *Mi último suspiro*, 125; Saenz de la Calzada, 23–24, 184–85; Auclair, 240; author interview with Arturo Saenz de la Calzada; "La política y las tendencias en las obras de hoy. Hay que crear un teatro de ensayo," *El Imparcial* (Madrid), May 2, 1932, in *OC*, III, 413–16.

285   **FGL and Ugarte select company members:** Emilio Garrigues Díaz-Cañabate, "Al teatro con Federico García Lorca," *Cuadernos Hispanoamericanos* 340 (October 1978), 106–7; author interview with María del Carmen Lasgoity; Saenz de la Calzada, 66; Octavio Ramírez, "Teatro para el pueblo," *La Nación* (Buenos Aires), January 28, 1934, Arts and Letters section, in *OC*, III, 494–95.

285   **"effective" and "positive":** Author interview with Arturo Saenz de la Calzada.

285   **"incredibly malleable":** Penón, 66.

285–86   **FGL at rehearsals:** Saenz de la Calzada, 110–16; Auclair, 246; "Entrevista con María del Carmen Lasgoity. 'Federico nos dirigía por radar,' " *Centro Dramático Nacional: Noticias* 2 (December 1986), 12; author interviews with Álvaro Custodio, María del Carmen Lasgoity, and Arturo Saenz de la Calzada; *G, II*, 171; Mario Hernández, "Música para La Barraca," in *FM*, 495–96; Luis Fernández-Cifuentes, "García Lorca: Historia de una evaluación, evaluación de una historia," in *Estelas, laberintos, neuvas sendas. Unamuno, Valle-Inclán, García Lorca. La Guerra Civil*, ed. Angel G. Loureiro (Barcelona: Anthropos, 1988). Information on FGL's knowledge of Stanislavsky comes from J. G., "Margarita Ucelay: Recuerdos de la profesora y de la actriz," *El Público* 68 (Madrid, May 1989), 9, and author interview with Álvaro Custodio.

286   **"And to hell":** Auclair, 235. On FGL's camaraderie with his actors, see also "El carro de la farándula," *La Vanguardia* (Barcelona), December 1, 1932, in *OC*, III, 396–400; Saenz de la Calzada, 150; and author interview with María del Carmen Lasgoity.

286   **FGL fires actor:** Author interview with Álvaro Custodio.

286   **La Barraca repertoire:** Saenz de la Calzada, 49–126; Estelle Trépanier, "García Lorca et La Barraca," *Revue d'Histoire du Théâtre* 18 (April–June 1966), 165; *FM*, 445–50; Dru Dougherty, "El legado vanguardista de Tirso de Molina," *V Jornadas de Teatro Clásico Español* II (Almagro, 1982), 14–21; Celaya, 148; Suzanne W. Byrd, *La Fuente Ovejuna de Federico García Lorca* (Madrid: Pliegos, 1984), 13; Fernández Cifuentes, 24; Enrique Moreno Báez, "La Barraca. Entrevista con su director, Federico García Lorca," *Revista de la Universidad Internacional de Santander* 1 (Santander, 1933), in *OC*, III, 426–27.

286   **"German, Russian . . . propaganda, of course":** "Nuevo tabladillo popular. Una hora de ensayo con los estudiantes de la Barraca. Y unos minutos de charla con Federico García Lorca," *La Voz* (Madrid), February 1, 1932, 9, in *OC*, III, 386.

287   **"river of meringue" and "true national theater . . . representative poets":** FGL, "Presentación de *Peribáñez o el Comendador de Ocaña*, de Lope de Vega, representado por el Club Teatral Anfistora," in *OC*, III, 251–52.

287   **FGL's admiration for Calderón:** FGL, "Presentación del auto sacramental *La vida es sueño* de Calderón de la Barca, representado por La Barraca," in *OC*, III, 218–21; Saenz de la Calzada, 57; "En la Universidad. La Barraca," *La Libertad* (Madrid), November 1, 1932; Byrd, 117.

287   **"Earth . . . present, and future":** FGL, "Presentación del auto sacramental *La vida es sueño* de Calderón de la Barca, representado por La Barraca," in *OC*, III, 219.

287   **"as dark as his costume":** Altolaguirre, *Obras completas I, Estudios literarios*, 295.

287   **"a Tibetan widow":** Ontañón and Moreiro, 147; Ontañón.

287   **"La Barraca keeps him":** Morla Lynch, 234.

288   **"He couldn't be more serene":** Morla Lynch, 209.

288   **FGL gives lecture-recital:** All quoted passages are taken from FGL, "Lecture: A Poet in New York."

288   **"I'll publish it later":** "Llegó anoche Federico García Lorca," *La Nación* (Buenos Aires), October 14, 1933, 9, in *OC*, III, 443.

289   **"greatest achievement":** Victor de la Serna, "El Poeta en Nueva York. Conferencia y lec-

tura de versos por Federico García Lorca en la Residencia," *El Sol* (Madrid), March 17, 1932.

289   **FGL on lecture circuit:** *G, II,* 172–73; Morla Lynch, 245–58; *El Liberal* (Seville), March 31, 1932, and April 1, 1932; Carlos Martinez-Barbeito, "García Lorca, poeta gallego. Un viaje a Galicia del cantor de Andalucía," *Griál* 43 (March 1974), 90; Eduardo Rodríguez Valdivieso, "Un dios gitano," *El País* (Barcelona), June 12, 1993, 4; *El Adelanto* (Salamanca), May 31, 1932, 1.

289–90   **FGL in Galicia:** Eduardo Blanco-Amor, "Los poemas gallegos de Federico García Lorca," *Ínsula* (July–August 1959), 9; "Cronología gallega de Federico García Lorca y datos sincrónicos," *Griál* 45 (July–August–September 1974), 288; Carlos Martínez-Barbeito, "García Lorca, poeta gallego. Un viaje a Galicia del cantor de Andalucía," *Griál* 43 (March 1974), 90–98; Ernesto Guerra da Cal, "Federico García Lorca en el recuerdo," *Punto y Coma* 11 (Madrid[?], winter 1988–89), 52–53; *El Eco de Santiago*, May 7, 9, and 12, 1932; Xesús Alonso Montero, "Encontro en Madrid con García Lorca e Francisco Lamas," *Faro de Vigo*, January 9, 1981, 22.

290   **FGL befriends Martínez Barbeito:** *EC,* 731–41; Carlos Martínez-Barbeito, "Garcia Lorca, poeta gallego. Un viaje a Galicia del cantor de Andalucía," *Griál* 43 (March 1974), 90–98; "Federico García Lorca. Seis cartas a Carlos Martínez Barbeito," *BFFGL* 3 (June 1988), 77–87; correspondence from Carlos Martínez-Barbeito to FGL, AFFGL.

291   **FGL and Ernesto Pérez Guerra:** Ernesto Guerra da Cal, "Federico García Lorca en el recuerdo," *Punto y Coma* II (Madrid[?], winter 1988–89), 52–59; José Landeira Yrago, *Viaje al sueño del agua. El misterio de los poemas gallegos de García Lorca* (La Coruña: Edicíos do Castro, 1986), 15; *G, II,* 177–78; Morla Lynch, 451; Eduardo Blanco-Amor, "Federico, otra vez; la misma vez," *El País* (Madrid), October 1, 1978, vii; Eduardo Blanco-Amor to [Marie Laffranque] (August 10, 1979), and correspondence from Ernesto Pérez da Cal to Eduardo Blanco-Amor (September 14, 1958), Eduardo Blanco-Amor Archive, Orense.

291   **FGL writes Galician poems:** Mario Hernández, introduction and notes to FGL, *Primeras canciones*; Anderson, *Lorca's Late Poetry,* 237–74; *G, II,* 180–82; Carlos Martínez-Barbeito, "García Lorca, poeta gallego. Un viaje a Galicia del cantor de Andalucía," *Griál* 43 (March 1974), 94; Eduardo Blanco-Amor, "Los poemas gallegos de Federico García Lorca," *Ínsula* (July–August 1959), 9; Ernesto Guerra da Cal, "13. Federico García Lorca (1898–1936)," in Rosalía de Castro, *Antología poética. Cancioneiro rosaliano, Centenary Homage,* ed. Ernesto Guerra da Cal (Lisbon: Guimaraes, 1985), 193–95; Ramón González Alegre, "Los 'seis poemas gallegos' de Federico García Lorca," *Poesía gallega contemporánea* (Pontevedra: Colección Huguin, 1954), 220; *FM,* 186; Luis Manteiga, "Seis poemas galegos," *Heraldo de Galicia* (Orense), February 3, 1936; Ernesto Pérez da Cal to Eduardo Blanco-Amor Archive, Orense; FGL, *Diván del Tamarit. Seis Poemas galegos. Llanto por Ignacio Sánchez Mejías,* ed. Andrew A. Anderson (Madrid: Espasa Calpe, 1988); Xesús Alonso Montero, "Blanco-Amor e García Lorca," *La Voz de Galicia,* December 4, 1980. All quoted passages are taken from *OC,* I, 607–14, trans. FGL, *Collected Poems.*

293   **Rehearsals for Barraca debut:** Saenz de la Calzada, 28–29; Antonio Campoamor González, "La Barraca y su primera salida por los caminos de España," *Cuadernos Hispanoamericanos* 433–36 (September–October 1986), 785; Pablo Suero, "Hablando de 'La Barraca' con el poeta García Lorca," *Noticias Gráficas* (Buenos Aires), October 15, 1933, in *OC,* III, 451–53; Morla Lynch, 276–77.

293   **Méndez-Altolaguirre wedding:** Morla Lynch, 266; Paloma Ulacía Altolaguirre, *Concha Méndez. Memorias habladas, memorias armadas,* introduction by María Zambrano (Madrid: Mondadori España, 1990), 89–90.

293–94   **FGL and Ortega y Gasset:** *EC*, 732–33; Ontañón and Moreiro, 123; author conversation with José Bello and Isabel García Lorca.

294   **La Barraca's first outing:** *G, II*, 167, 189–93; Estelle Trépanier, "García Lorca et La Barraca," *Revue d'Histoire du Théâtre* 18 (April–June 1966), 172; José María Martínez Laseca, "Gracia y desgracia de 'La Barraca' de Federico García Lorca por tierras de Soria," *Campo Soriano*, December 28, 1981, 12–13; Auclair, 242; "El carro de la farándula," *La Vanguardia* (Barcelona), December 1, 1932, *OC*, III, 398; "El ensayo de 'La Barraca' estudiantil. En busca del teatro español," *Luz* (Madrid), July 25, 1932, 9; *La Libertad* (Madrid), July 17, 1932, 8; Jorge Guillén to Germaine Guillén (July 11, 1932), papers of Jorge Guillén, Wellesley College Archive; Antonio Campoamor González, "La Barraca y su primera salida por los caminos de España," *Cuadernos Hispanoamericanos* 433–36, vol. II (September–October 1986), 785; Saenz de la Calzada, **128**, 170; Cipriano Rivas Cherif, "Apuntaciones por el teatro dramático nacional," *El Sol* (Madrid), July 22, 1932; FGL, "Al pueblo de Almazán," in *OC*, III, 215; Enrique Moreno Báez, "La Barraca. Entrevista con su director, Federico García Lorca," *Revista de la Universidad Internacional de Santander* 1 (Santander, 1933), in *OC*, III, 426–27.

296   **Truck accident and aftermath:** Antonio Campoamor González, "La Barraca y su primera salida por los caminos de España," *Cuadernos Hispanoamericanos* 433–36, vol. II (September–October **1986**), 790; Hermenegildo Lanz, "Misioneros de arte, La Barraca," *Defensor de Granada*, October 5, 1932, 1; *Heraldo de Madrid*, July 25, 1932, 5; *G, II*, 196.

296   **"Loca . . . Andalusian ballad":** "La silueta de la semana. Federico García Loca o cualquiera se equivoca," *Gracia y Justicia* (Madrid), July 23, 1932, 10.

296   **"daring . . . simply theater":** Antonio Agraz, "El Teatro Universitario. La primera salida y lo que hará, según García Lorca, en su próxima campaña," *Heraldo de Madrid*, July 25, 1932, in *OC*, III, **392–95.**

296   **"fundamentally political":** "La política y las tendencias en las obras de hoy. Hay que crear un teatro de ensayo," *El Imparcial* (Madrid), May 2, 1932, in *OC*, III, 415.

296   **"noble":** "Noticias teatrales," *Luz* (Madrid), May 23, 1933, 6.

19. APPLAUSE AND GLORY: 1932-33

297   **Concha gives birth to second child:** Auclair, 267; Carlos Martínez-Barbeito to FGL (August 1, 1932), AFFGL; Rodrigo, "La huerta," 828.

297   **FGL writes *Blood Wedding*:** Hernández, introduction to FGL, *Bodas de sangre*, 21–24; Auclair, 266–68; Maurer, "Lorca y las formas," 245–47; Christopher Maurer, "Bach and *Bodas de sangre*," in *Lorca's Legacy: Essays on Lorca's Life, Poetry, and Theatre*, ed. Manuel Durán and Francesca Colecchia (New York: Peter Lang, 1991), 103–14; Francisco García Lorca, introduction to FGL, *Five Plays*, 17; Francisco García Lorca, prologue to FGL, *Three Tragedies*, 23.

298   **Sources for *Blood Wedding*:** Auclair, 265–66; *G, II*, 554; *FM*, 67, 334–42; Hernández, introduction to FGL, *Bodas de sangre*, 28–29, 175–77, quoting from *Defensor de Granada*, July 25, 1928, and *ABC* (Madrid), July 25–28, 1928; C. B. Morris, *García Lorca: "Bodas de sangre"* (London: Grant and Cutler, 1980), 16–17; "Los auténticos protagonistas del 'crimen de Níjar' no quisieron ver sus *Bodas de sangre*," *El País* (Madrid), October 15, 1985, 38; Fernando Vals Guzmán, "Ficción y realidad en la genesis de *Bodas de sangre*," *Ínsula* 368–69 (1977), 24. FGL's friend Miguel Cerón has recalled reading Synge's *Riders to the Sea* to FGL in adolescence, translating the work into Spanish as he read (Auclair, 262); FGL talked

of staging Synge's *Playboy of the Western World* with La Barraca (José R. Serna, "Charla amable con Federico García Lorca," *Heraldo de Madrid*, July 11, 1933, in *OC*, III, 419).

298 **"a long, constant, exhaustive" and "I spend three or four years"**: Nicolás González-Deleito, "Federico García Lorca y el teatro de hoy," *Escena* 1 (Madrid, May 1935), in *OC*, III, 565.

298 **"to be written in Spain"**: F. Lluch Garín, "*Bodas de sangre*," unidentified clipping (1933), AFFGL, cited in Hernández, introduction to FGL, *Bodas de sangre*, 19.

299 **"Without a tragic sense"**: Suero, "Crónica."

299 **"must return to tragedy"**: "Federico García Lorca y la tragedia," *Luz* (Madrid), July 3, 1934, in *OC*, III, 436.

299 **"with freedom . . . in the people"**: "Antes del estreno. Hablando con Federico García Lorca," *La Libertad* (Madrid), December 24, 1930, in *OC*, III, 374.

299 ***Blood Wedding***: All quoted text is from *OC*, II, 413–75.

300 **"flavor of the earth . . . boyhood years"**: Luna, "La vida."

300 **"holiday"**: Francisco García Lorca, prologue to FGL, *Three Tragedies*, 19.

301 **"the realism that dominates"**: Pedro Massa, "El poeta García Lorca y su tragedia *Bodas de sangre*," *Crítica* (Madrid), April 9, 1933, in *OC*, III, 410.

301–2 **FGL and the moon**: Martínez Nadal, *Cuatro lecciones*, 41; Javier Herrero, "The Father against the Son: Lorca's Christian Vision," *Essays on Hispanic Literature in Honor of Edward Diley*, ed. Jennifer Low and Phillip Swanson (Edinburgh: Department of Hispanic Studies, 1989), 184; FGL, *El Retablillo de Don Cristóbal*, in *OC*, II, 399; FGL, *Impresiones y paisajes*, in *OC*, IV, 160; FGL, "El primitivo auto sacramental" (December 4, 1918), AFFGL; Ángel Álvarez de Miranda, *La metáfora y el mito* (Madrid: Taurus, 1963), 38–70; Alice M. Pollin, ed., *A Concordance to the Plays and Poems of Federico García Lorca* (Ithaca and London: Cornell University Press, 1975), 1141.

302 **"freedom . . . revolution"**: "Cronología gallega de Federico García Lorca y datos sincrónicos," *Grial* 45 (July–August–September 1974), 288.

302 **FGL's love of people, scorn for bourgeoisie**: Saenz de la Calzada, 225; Octavio Ramírez, "Teatro para el pueblo," *La Nación* (Buenos Aires), January 28, 1934, Arts and Letters section, in *OC*, III, 495–96; author interview with María del Carmen Lasgoity; García-Posada, "García Lorca en Uruguay," 84–85; Suero, "Crónica"; author interview with Arturo Saenz de la Calzada; Alardo Prats, "Los artistas en el ambiente de nuestro tiempo," *El Sol* (Madrid), December 15, 1934, in *OC*, III, 544–46.

302 **"She was so and so!"**: Author interview with María del Carmen Lasgoity.

302 **"How I'd love to travel"**: Luis Saenz de la Calzada, "Noticia sobre La Barraca," in Suzanne W. Byrd, *La Fuente Ovejuna de Federico García Lorca* (Madrid: Pliegos, 1984), 123n.

302–3 **Typical ambience and events on Barraca tours**: Auclair, 245–46; Saenz de la Calzada, 22, 134–40, 219; author interview with María del Carmen Lasgoity; author interview with Arturo Saenz de la Calzada; Morla Lynch, 216.

303 **FGL's Barraca productions**: Juan Chabás, "La Barraca en el teatro María Guerrero," *Luz* (Madrid), December 8, 1933, 6; Enrique Moreno Báez, "La Barraca. Entrevista con su director, Federico García Lorca," *Revista de la Universidad Internacional de Santander* (1933), in *OC*, III, 426–27; Byrd, 47; Salinas, 6; *FM*, 440; Auclair, 246; Saenz de la Calzada, 22, 42–43, 52–67; *G, II*, 167.

303 **"For me La Barraca"**: Octavio Ramírez, "Teatro para el pueblo," *La Nación* (Buenos Aires), January 28, 1934, Arts and Letters section, in *OC*, III, **494**.

303 **"No . . . I haven't set it aside"**: José María Salaverría, "El carro de la Farándula," *La Vanguardia* (Barcelona), December 1, 1932, in *OC*, III, 397.

303 "set up a theater . . . to life": Salinas, 6.

304 "song of the little lice": Saenz de la Calzada, **219**.

304 **Actors resent FGL's bombast:** Emilio Garrigues Díaz-Cañabate, "Al teatro con Federico García Lorca," *Cuadernos Hispanoamericanos* 340 (October 1978), 106n.

304 "I've got a drama": Ontañón; Auclair, 268.

304–5 **FGL reads Blood Wedding to friends:** Mario Hernández, "Cronología de *Bodas de sangre* (1928–1939)" (unpublished ms., 1985); Auclair, 268, 272–73; Ontañón; Jorge Zalamea, "Sobre el teatro de García Lorca," *Boletín Cultural y Bibliográfico* VIII, 7 (Bogota, 1965), 996; Jacinto Grau, "Federico García Lorca," in *Don Juan en el tiempo y en el espacio* (Buenos Aires: Raigal, 1953); Morla Lynch, 285–87.

305 **Membrives rejects Blood Wedding:** Ontañón; *El Imparcial* (Madrid), February 16 and 17, 1933.

305 **Díaz agrees to stage Blood Wedding:** Fernando de la Milla, "Teatro. Retorno a la escena de Josefina Díaz de Artigas. Y concede a *Crónica* la primera interviú, después de su voluntario retiro," *Crónica* (Madrid), September 25, 1932, 9–10, cited in *G, II*, 214; Mario Hernández, "Cronología de *Bodas de sangre* (1928–39)" (unpublished ms., 1985); Pedro Massa, "El poeta García Lorca y su tragedia *Bodas de sangre*," *Crítica* [Madrid], April 9, 1933), in *OC, III*, 411; "Sección de rumores," *Heraldo de Madrid*, October 19, 1932, 8.

305 **La Barraca in Granada:** "El IV Centenario de la Universidad," *Defensor de Granada*, October 7, 1932; "La agrupación universitaria 'La Barraca' representa 'La vida es sueño,' " *Defensor de Granada*, October 8, 1932, 4; "La 'Barraca' en Granada," *Defensor de Granada*, October 9, 1932, 1; *G, II*, 216–17.

305 **La Barraca in Madrid:** Miguel Pérez Ferrero, "Teatro de hoy antiguo," *Heraldo de Madrid*, October 26, 1932, 5; Morla Lynch, 300–1; *Blanco y Negro* (Madrid), November 6, 1932; Saenz de la Calzada, **166**.

306 "I remember with distant" and "tired and rather alone": *EC*, 744–48.

306 **FGL in Barcelona:** "Conferencia Club, Federico García Lorca," *Mirador* (Barcelona), December 22, 1932, 8; "Conferencia Club. Federico García Lorca," *El Día Gráfico* (Barcelona), December 16, 1932, 1; *El Diluvio* (Barcelona), December 14, 1932; Agustí, 77–79; "Conferencia Club. 'Poeta en Nueva York,' " *La Vanguardia* (Barcelona), December 17, 1932, 7; Guillermo Díaz Plaja, "García Lorca y su Nueva York," *Luz* (Madrid), December 23, 1932, 3.

307 "You've captured me": Gerardo Diego, "El llanto, la música, y otros recuerdos," in FGL, *Llanto por Ignacio Sánchez Mejías*, facsimile ed., with texts by Dámaso Alonso, Jorge Guillén, Gerardo Diego, Rafael Alberti, José María de Cossío, Rafael Gómez (Cantabria: Institución Cultural de Cantabria / Diputación Regional de Cantabria, 1982), 29.

307 "I will burn down": Gerardo Diego, ed., *Poesía española contemporánea (1901–1934)* (Madrid: Taurus, 1979), 403, in *OC, III*, 308.

307 "No house is more joyful": Nicolás González Deleito, "Federico García Lorca y el teatro de hoy," *Escena* 1 (Madrid, May 1935), in *OC, III*, 562. On the family's Calle Alcalá apartment, see also *G, II*, 230–31; author interviews with Isabel García Lorca and Jose Caballero; Fernández-Montesinos, "Descripción," xi.

308 "joy of being able to collaborate": FGL, "Presentación del auto sacramental *La vida es sueño* de Calderón de la Barca, representado por La Barraca," in *OC, III*, 221.

308 "socialist tuxedos": "Antena literaria," *Gracia y Justicia* (Madrid), December 24, 1932, 10.

308 **FGL defends Barraca:** José María Salaverría, "El carro de la Farándula," *La Vanguardia* (Barcelona), December 1, 1932, in *OC, III*, 397–98; author interview with María del Carmen Lasgoity; Luis Araquistaín to FGL (November 15, 1932), AFFGL.

309 **Rehearsals for Blood Wedding:** *FM*, 154 and 335, trans. *GM*, 201; Josber, "Cuatro breves

preguntas, al pasar, a Josefina Días de Artigas," in FGL, *Bodas de sangre*, ed. José Monleón, 2nd ed. (Barcelona: Aymá, 1975), 65–66; Auclair, 274–75; Luis Fernández Cifuentes, "García Lorca y El éxito: El caso de *Bodas de sangre*," in Soria Olmedo, 87–88; *El Imparcial* (Madrid), March 3 and 28, 1928.

309   **"full force"**: Hernández, introduction to FGL, *Bodas de sangre*, 34, citing *El Imparcial* (Madrid), March 28, 1933.

309   **"Tell me I'm great"**: Guardia, 79.

309   **"No!! Any one of my actresses"**: Saenz de la Calzada, 110.

309   **"secondhand artists"**: Remarks by FGL to José Weissberger, cited in Christopher Maurer, "Bach and *Bodas de sangre*," in *Lorca's Legacy: Essays on Lorca's Life, Poetry, and Theatre*, ed. Manuel Durán and Francesca Colecchia (New York: Peter Lang, 1991), 107–9.

309   **"Don't pull that Lorca business"**: Ontañón.

310   **"The Spanish theater . . . so desires"**: *El Imparcial* (Madrid), January 7, 1933, and February 5, 1933.

310   **Opening night of *Blood Wedding***: Hernández, introduction to FGL, *Bodas*, 33–6; Auclair, 274–76; *GM*, 201; *Luz* (Madrid), March 9, 1933; Morla Lynch, 330–34.

310   **Reviews of *Blood Wedding***: Fernández Cifuentes, 135–41; "Beatriz: *Bodas de sangre*," *ABC* (Madrid), March 9, 1933, 43; Antonio Espina, "Estreno en el Teatro Beatriz," *Luz* (Madrid), March 9, 1933; Melchor Fernández Almagro, "Teatros. Beatriz. Estreno de 'Bodas de sangre,'" *El Sol* (Madrid), March 9, 1933, 8; "Un éxito teatral de García Lorca," *Defensor de Granada*, March 11, 1933, 1; Auclair, 276; María Francisca Vilches de Frutos and Dru Dougherty, *Los estrenos teatrales de Federico García Lorca (1920–45)* (Madrid: Tabapress [Grupo Tabacalera; Fundación Federico García Lorca], 1992), 774–75. On additional performances of *Blood Wedding*, see *G, II*, 230, citing "Cartelera," *Heraldo de Madrid*; *FM*, 336; Andrew A. Anderson, "Representaciones provinciales de dramas de García Lorca en vida del autor," *Segismundo* 41–42 (Madrid, 1985), 270–75; *La Vanguardia* (Barcelona), May 31, 1933, 10; M. Rodríguez Codolá, "Teatro y conciertos. Poliorama. *Bodas de sangre*, tragedia en tres actos, divididos en siete cuadros, original de Federico García Lorca," *La Vanguardia* (Barcelona), June 2, 1933, 10; Ignacio Agustí, "*Bodas de sangre*," *Mirador* (Barcelona), June 8, 1933, 5.

311   **"a member of the bourgeoisie . . . reality"**: "Charlando con García Lorca," *Crítica* (Buenos Aires), October 15, 1933, in *OC*, III, 447.

311   **"magnificent tragedy"**: Antonio Machado to FGL (March 12, 1933), AFFGL.

311   **"I feel calm and content" and "Why haven't you written"**: *EC*, 753.

311–12   **"these days . . . applause and glory"**: *EC*, 754–56. On FGL's loneliness, see also Eduardo Vílchez to FGL (c. 1935), AFFGL.

20. VOICE OF LOVE: 1933

313   **FGL's typical daily behavior, 1933**: Author interview with Isabel García Lorca; Martínez Nadal, *Lorca's The Public*, 11; author interview with José Caballero; author conversation with Rafael Martínez Nadal; Ontañón y Moreiro, 107–8; Ontañón; Cernuda, 16; Suero, "Crónica"; *FM*, 442.

313   **"true noctambulist"**: Salvador [García Picossi] to FGL (December 12, 1935), AFFGL.

314   **"No, fortunately"**: "Llegó anoche Federico García Lorca," *La Nación* (Buenos Aires), October 14, 1933, 9, in *OC*, III, 445.

314   **"it was as if"**: Higuera Rojas, 58.

314   **"She formed me"**: *EC*, 735.

314   "One feels . . . eloquence": Morla Lynch, 164.

314   "a gentleman . . . delightful": Suero, "Crónica."

314–15   **FGL collaborates with Ucelay on** *Don Perlimplín*: José Gordon, *Teatro experimental español (Antología e historia)* (Madrid: Escelicer, 1965), 21; *FM*, 313–14; author interview with Margarita Ucelay; Margarita Ucelay, introduction to FGL, *El amor de don Perlimplín y Belisa en su jardín*, ed. Margarita Ucelay (Madrid: Cátedra, 1990); Auclair, 219–21; Margarita Ucelay, "Federico García Lorca y el Club Teatral Anfistora: El dramaturgo como director de escena," in Soria Olmedo, 54; J. G., "Margarita Ucelay: Recuerdos de la profesora y de la actriz," *El Público* 68 (Madrid, May 1989), 8–9; Agustín de Figueroa, "El Club teatral 'Anfistora,' " *Ahora* (Madrid), December 29, 1934; Mario Hernández, introduction and notes to FGL, *La zapatera*, 41, 333–61; author interview with Santiago Ontañón.

316   "kitsch . . . won't allow," "chamber opera," and "The work is built": "Una interesante iniciativa: El poeta Federico García Lorca habla de los clubs teatrales," *El Sol* (Madrid), April 5, 1933, in *OC*, III, 407–9.

316   **Critical response to** *Don Perlimplín*: Review by M. Nuñez de Arenas in *La Voz* (Madrid), April 6, 1933, 3; Enrique Azcoaga, "Perlimplín y Belisa," *Hoja Literaria* (Madrid), April 1933, 10. On Ontañón's inaudibility, see *La Voz* (Madrid), April 6, 1933, 3; and Juan Chabás, "Función de gala en honor de García Lorca," *Luz* (Madrid), April 6, 1933, 6. Information on Marañón's response to the play comes from author interview with Margarita Ucelay.

317   "In Spain no one": *G, II,* 383.

317   **FGL correspondence with Eduardo Valdivieso**: *EC*, 754–59; Eduardo Rodríguez Valdivieso, "Hijo del tiempo. El amigo de Federico García Lorca comenta algunos episodios de su amistad con el poeta," *El País* (Madrid), December 24, 1993, 5.

318   **Growing fascist presence in Spain**: Letter by José Antonio Primo de Rivera, *ABC* (Madrid), March 22, 1933, in Díaz-Plaja, 555–56; Corpus Barga, "¿Se inicia el Fascismo español?" *La Nación* (Buenos Aires), April 8, 1933, 4; Thomas, 99; *G, II,* 226; Southworth, 1–3. On Hitler and Jewish persecution, see Payne, 30; Morla Lynch, 346; Rafael Alberti, "Entre el clavel y la espada," *El País* (Madrid), July 21, 1985, 11.

319   **Alberti launches** *Octubre*: FGL signed a manifesto "vigorously" protesting Hitler's persecution of writers, intellectuals, and proletariats (*Octubre* [May 1, 1933]).

319   "Politics is the ugliest": Luciano del Río, "García Lorca en Pontevedra," *Diario de Pontevedra*, August 12, 1973, 16.

319   "pathetic end . . . to eat": *EC*, 738.

320   "has turned communist . . . voice of art": Ricardo F. Cabal, "Charla con Federico García Lorca," *La Mañana* (León), August 12, 1933, in *OC*, III, 423.

320   **FGL and La Argentinita collaborate with Alberti**: "En el Español: La poesía popular en la lírica española," *Luz* (Madrid), May 8, 1933, 6; Miguel Pérez Ferrero, "Unas palabras de La Argentinita, García Lorca y Alberti," *Heraldo de Madrid*, May 5, 1933, 5; Miguel Pérez Ferrero, "Federico García Lorca," in *Algunos españoles* (Madrid: Ediciones Cultura Hispánica, 1972), 107; Morla Lynch, 347.

320   **FGL with La Argentinita**: [Residencia de Estudiantes], 145, 149; Sáenz de la Calzada, 152; Mario Hernández, introduction to FGL, *Divan*, 103; Morla Lynch, 202; Armando María y Campos, *Un ensayo general sobre el teatro español contemporáneo visto desde México* (Mexico, 1948).

320   *The Cuckolds' Pilgrimage*: Rivas Cherif, January 27, 1957; [Residencia de Estudiantes], 111; *Heraldo de Madrid*, November 10, 1933; review by Adolfo Salazar, *El Sol* (Madrid), November 10, 1933; *FM*, 356–57; *GM*, 217–19; Auclair, 281; Mora Guarnido, 32.

321   **Méndez birth**: Morla Lynch, 336–38; Aub, 249.

322   **FGL begins** *Yerma*: Morla Lynch, 354; Mario Hernández, introduction to FGL, *Yerma*, 10;

Mario Hernández, "Cronología y estreno de *Yerma*, poema trágico de García Lorca," *Revista de Archivos, Bibliotecas y Museos* LXXXII, 2 (April–June 1979), 290; José L. Serna, "Charla amable con Federico García Lorca," *Heraldo de Madrid*, July 11, 1933, in OC, III, 418–19; "Mercurio literario. *Yerma*," *Heraldo de Madrid*, August 3, 1933, 7.

322 **"Get my room ready"**: EC, 760.

322 **La Barraca presents *Fuenteovejuna***: Sáenz de la Calzada, 71, 126, 167; Suzanne W. Byrd, *La Fuente Ovejuna de Federico García Lorca* (Madrid: Editorial Pliegos, 1984); Carmen Diamante, "Recuerdo," *Retama* 3 (Cuenca, May 1986), 13; "Mascarilla," "Teatros. Libertad. Fuenteovejuna," *El Mercantil Valenciano*, July 1, 1933, 7.

323 **"nasty imputations . . . just theater"**: Enrique Moreno Báez, "La Barraca. Entrevista con su director, Federico García Lorca," *Revista de la Universidad Internacional de Santander* (1933), in OC, III, 426.

323 **La Barraca in Santander:** Sáenz de la Calzada, 167; EC, 763; Celia Valbuena Morán, *García Lorca y "La Barraca" en Santander* (Santander: Publisher unknown, 1974); *El Cantábrico* (Santander), August 9–20, 1933; Byrd, 133–35; *La Voz de Cantabria*, August 16, 1933, 1.

323 **"a theater by and for swine . . . European theater"**: Ricardo F. Cabal, "Charla con Federico García Lorca," *La Mañana* (León), August 12, 1933, in OC, III, 424.

324 **"better than ever"**: Jorge Guillén to Germaine Guillén (August 19, 1933), papers of Jorge Guillén, Wellesley College Archives.

324 **"*Vaya con Dios* . . . Shelley plain"**: Herschel Brickell, "Federico García Lorca: A Biographical Note," in FGL, *The Poet in New York and Other Poems of Federico García Lorca*, trans. Rolfe Humphries, introduction by José Bergamín (New York: W. W. Norton, 1940), 9–10.

324 **"every hour"**: Rafael Rodríguez Rapún to FGL (October 12, 1933), AFFGL.

324 **Rafael Rodríguez Rapún:** Tomás Rodríguez Rapún Archive, Madrid; author interview with Tomás Rodríguez Rapún; correspondence from Tomás Rodríguez Rapún to author (December 22, 1988); Morla Lynch, 351, 363–66; Sáenz de la Calzada, 21, 130, 188; Auclair, 254; G, II, 242; Marie Laffranque, "Bases cronológicas para el estudio de Federico García Lorca," in Gil, 447; author interview with José Caballero; author interview with Santiago Ontañón; Ontañón and Moriero, 146.

325 **"immersed . . . tremendous"**: G, II, 243.

325 **"the passion"**: Author interview with Santiago Ontañón.

325 **Friendship between FGL and Rapún:** Rafael Martínez Nadal, "Presentación," in Sáenz de la Calzada, 12; Sáenz de la Calzada, 140, 178–80, 187–89; Auclair, 250–51; José Caballero to FGL (1935), AFFGL; Gibson, *Federico García Lorca: A Life*, 353; Rivas Cherif; author conversation with Modesto Higueras; author interview with María del Carmen Lasgoity.

325 **FGL inscribes books for Rapún:** Tomás Rodríguez Rapún Archive, Madrid.

325 **FGL's plans to publish *The Audience*:** José L. Serna, "Charla amable con Federico García Lorca," *Heraldo de Madrid*, July 11, 1933, in OC, III, 418; Martínez Nadal, *Lorca's The Public* 19; FGL, *El público*, 109.

325–26 **Rapún confronted by father:** Author interview with Tomás Rodríguez Rapún.

326 **"Having a good friend"**: Auclair, 106.

326 **"Federico was so open"**: Author interview with José Caballero.

21. OUR AMERICA: 1933-34

326 **Membrives opens *Blood Wedding*:** Letter from Juan Reforzo to FGL, requesting rights to produce *Blood Wedding* in Buenos Aires (March 30, 1933), AFFGL; Hernández, introduc-

tion to FGL, *Bodas de sangre*, 42; "En el Maipo se aplaudió ayer *Bodas de sangre*," *La Nación* (Buenos Aires), July 30, 1933, 10; "Hay valores destacados en *Bodas de sangre*, estreno del Maipo," *La Prensa* (Buenos Aires), July 30, 1933, 15; "Beneficio de Lola Membrives," *La Nación* (Buenos Aires), January 12, 1934, 9; Guardia, 83–84; "Esta noche se despedirá Lola Membrives. Volverá al Maipo en los primeros días de octubre," *La Nación* (Buenos Aires), August 7, 1933, 10.

327 **"That's how it goes"**: "Charlando con García Lorca," *Crítica* (Buenos Aires), October 15, 1933, in *OC*, III, 447.

327 **"Your name"**: Juan Reforzo to FGL (August 2, 1933), AFFGL, cited in Mario Hernández, introduction to FGL, *Bodas de sangre*, 44.

328 **"very large ship"**: "Tres testimonios," *La Nación* (Buenos Aires), August 10, 1986, section 4, 1.

328 **"As soon as I've consulted"**: FGL to Santiago Ontañón (August 1933), AFFGL, cited in Mario Hernández, introduction to FGL, *Bodas de sangre*, 45.

328 **"immediately"**: "El poeta español García Lorca," *El Diario Español* (Buenos Aires), October 25, 1933, 3.

328 **FGL travels to Argentina**: Morla Lynch, 370–72; FGL passport (September 23, 1933), AFFGL; "Federico García Lorca embarcó ayer en nuestro puerto, a bordo del *Conte Grande*, para Buenos Aires," *El Noticiero Universal* (Barcelona), September 30, 1933, 8; "El teatre. Escenaris," *La Publicitat* (Barcelona), September 30, 1933, 8; Hernández, notes to FGL, *Bodas de sangre*, 191; *EC*, 765–69; Suero, "Crónica." On FGL's petition to exempt Rapún from military service, see letter from Rafael Rodríguez Rapún to FGL (October 12, 1933), AFFGL.

329 **FGL stops in Montevideo**: Erre, "Pasó ayer por Montevideo una de las figuras más representativas de la intelectualidad española," *El Diario Español* (Buenos Aires), October 15, 1933, in *OC*, III, 433–35; Hernández, introduction to FGL, *Bodas de sangre*, 48; Suero, "Crónica"; *El Plata* (Montevideo), October 13, 1933, 4; *EC*, 773.

329 **Suero interviews FGL**: Suero, "Crónica."

330 **FGL arrives in Buenos Aires**: Guardia, 94; Suero, "Crónica"; "Hoy llegará el poeta y autor García Lorca," *La Nación* (Buenos Aires), October 13, 1933; "Apático y de mal humor llegó anoche el embajador R. Mexía. Al saludo fascista de unos pocos, contestó quitándose el sombrero. Llegó el poeta español García Lorca, quien dijo que no vio sonreír ni una vez en todo el viaje al embajador," *República Ilustrada* (Buenos Aires), October 14, 1933, cited in FGL, *Bodas de sangre*, 193; "Llegó a esta capital el escritor español Federico García Lorca," *La Prensa* (Buenos Aires), October 14, 1933, 15; *EC*, 770–76; photograph in AFFGL; Laffranque, 280–81; "Llegó anoche Federico García Lorca," *La Nación* (Buenos Aires), October 14, 1933, 9.

330–31 **FGL's first days in Buenos Aires**: *EC*, 770–76; Guardia, 93; John K. Walsh and Bussell Thompson, "García Lorca en Buenos Aires: Entrevista con D. Edmundo Guibourg," *García Lorca Review* XI, 2 (1983), 61; Villarejo, 61; *G*, II, 266–67; "Los señores García Lorca y Fontanals, en nuestra casa," *El Diario Español* (Buenos Aires), October 22, 1933, 2; "Visitaron *La Prensa*, Federico García Lorca y Manuel Fontanals," *La Prensa* (Buenos Aires), October 17, 1933, 17. On FGL's presence at German play, see "Una obra vigorosa y cruda" and "García Lorca en el Smart," *Noticias Gráficas* (Buenos Aires), October 14 and 15, 1933.

331 **"Here in this enormous"**: *EC*, 772.

331 **FGL gives *Duende* lecture**: Christopher Maurer, introduction to C, I, 33; Lence, "Un rato de charla con García Lorca," *Correo de Galicia* (Buenos Aires), October 22, 1933, in *OC*, III, 458–61; Narciso Robledal, "El duende si hizo carne," *Aconcagua* (n.d.), in *OC*, III, 465–67.

331 "Play and Theory of the *Duende*": All passages are taken from *OC*, III, 150–62, trans. FGL, *Deep Song*, 42–53.

333 "extraordinarily successful . . . too much!": *EC*, 776.

333 "How a City Sings": FGL, *How a City Sings from November to November* in *OC*, III, 137–49.

333 "It's expensive": *EC*, 784.

333 "invaded": "El sortilegio de la palabra," *Crítica* (Buenos Aires), November 15, 1933, cited in Christopher Maurer, introduction to *C*, I, 33.

333 **FGL attends gala performance of *Blood Wedding***: "Lola Membrives apareció ayer en el Avenida. Federico García Lorca habló y fue muy aplaudido," *La Nación* (Buenos Aires), October 26, 1933, 11; AFFGL; *El Diario Español* (Buenos Aires), October 26, 1933, 5; *EC*, 777–78.

334 **FGL's popularity**: *G*, II, 268–69; *EC*, 777–84; Mario Hernández, "Cronología de *Bodas de sangre* (1928–1938)" (unpublished ms., 1985); *Crítica* (Buenos Aires), November 30, 1933, 20; *La Nación* (Buenos Aires), November 8, 9, and 12, 1933; "La función del Avenida para la gente de teatro," *La Nación* (Buenos Aires), November 14, 1933, 10; *La Prensa* (Buenos Aires), November 19, 1933, 23; "Los españoles fuera de España," *Heraldo de Madrid*, April 14, 1934, in *OC*, III, 530–34; John K. Walsh and Bussell Thompson, "García Lorca en Buenos Aires: Entrevista con D. Edmundo Guibourg," *García Lorca Review* XI, 2 (1983), 213; "En honor de Federico García Lorca," *Correo de Galicia* (Buenos Aires), November 19, 1933, 2. On FGL's friendship with Victoria Ocampo, and supposed seduction, see Victoria Ocampo, *Testimonio. Segunda serie* (Buenos Aires: Sur, 1941), 393; *G*, II, 275, 324.

334 **FGL's detractors**: Arturo Cambours Ocampo, *Teoría y técnica de la creación literaria. (Materiales para una estética del escritor)* (Buenos Aires: Pena Lillo, 1966), 136–37; Richard Burgin, *Conversaciones con Jorge Luis Borges* (Madrid: Taurus, 1974), 93–94; Fernando Sorrentino, *Siete conversaciones con Jorge Luis Borges* (Buenos Aires: El Ateneo, 1996), 197 (I am most grateful to Miguel de Torre Borges for having alerted me to this volume of his uncle's conversations).

335 **FGL befriends Pablo Neruda**: José González Carbalho, *Vida, obra y muerte de Federico García Lorca* (Santiago de Chile: Ediciones Ercilla, 1938), 34; Neruda, *Confieso*, 157–58. For background on Neruda, see Teitelboim, 11–146; Philip Ward, ed., *The Oxford Companion to Spanish Literature* (Oxford: Clarendon Press, 1978); Alastair Reid, "Personal History: Neruda and Borges," *The New Yorker*, June 24 and July 1, 1996, 56–72; Robert Pring-Mill, introduction to *Pablo Neruda: A Basic Anthology*, ed. Robert Pring-Mill (Oxford: Dolphin Books, 1975), xvii–xxii; and E. Rodríguez Monegal, *El viajero inmóvil. Introducción a Pablo Neruda* (Buenos Aires: Losada, 1966), 11–80.

336 "gastronomic": *Crítica* (Buenos Aires), November 30, 1933, 20.

337 "like a decadent Roman": Bernardo Arias Trujillo, "Remembranza de Federico García Lorca," in *Federico García Lorca bajo el cielo de nueva Granada*, ed. Vicente Pérez Silva (Bogota: Instituto Caro y Cuervo [Serie "La Granada Entreabierta," 42], 1986), 27–28.

337 "Come on in . . . full moon face": Narciso Robledal, "El duende si hizo carne," *Aconcagua* (n.d.), in *OC*, III, 463.

337 "reporters, authors, actors": Lence, "Un rato de charla con García Lorca," *Correo de Galicia* (Buenos Aires), October 22, 1933, in *OC*, III, 461.

337 "I don't want to force": "El poeta español García Lorca," *El Diario Español* (Buenos Aires), October 25, 1933, 3.

337 **Ocampo publishes *Gypsy Ballads***: "Los españoles fuera de España," *Heraldo de Madrid*, April 14, 1934, in *OC*, III, 533.

337   "This is a triumph": *EC*, 794.

337   **FGL's earnings:** John K. Walsh and Bussell Thompson, "García Lorca en Buenos Aires: Entrevista con D. Edmundo Guibourg," *García Lorca Review* XI, 2 (1983), 220; *EC*, 780, 782, 784, 789; Eulalia-Dolores de la Higuera, "Habla el chofer de García Lorca," *Gentes*, April 1977, 31; *G*, *II*, 274; H. E. Pedemonte, "El primer monumento a Federico García Lorca," *Nueva Estafeta* (December 1978), 59; Federico García Rodríguez and Vicenta Lorca to FGL (November 23, 1933), AFFGL; Mora Guarnido, 108; Penón, 157–58.

338   **FGL visits cousin Máximo:** *EC*, 778, 782–87; Máximo Delgado to FGL (November 17, 1933, and March 13, 1934), AFFGL; Máximo Delgado to Federico García Rodríguez (December 1, 1926), AFFGL.

338   "My brother and sisters, yes": *G*, *II*, 297.

338   "because you are the only": *EC*, 784.

339   **FGL and political situation in Spain:** Vicenta Lorca to FGL (December 1, 1933), AFFGL; Eduardo Ugarte to FGL (November 28, 1933), AFFGL; *G*, *II*, 267, 283–84; *EC*, 774–94; "Vengo de torero herido a dar 4 conferencias," *Crítica* (Buenos Aires), October 14, 1933, 10; Pura Ucelay to FGL (October 24, 1933), AFFGL; José González Carballho, *Vida, obra y muerte de Federico García Lorca* (Santiago de Chile: Ercilla, 1938), 33, 79.

340   **Rapún writes to FGL:** Rafael Rodríguez Rapún to FGL (October 12, 1933), AFFGL.

340   **Rumors about FGL liaisons:** *G*, *II*, 287; Gibson, *Federico García Lorca: A Life*, 374; Alberto Nin Frías, *Alexis o el significado del temperamento urano* (Buenos Aires: 1932), 179–82.

341   "LOVE BUENOS AIRES": *G*, *II*, 286.

341   "because among other things": *G*, *II*, 285–86.

341   "I'm a little drunk": FGL to parents (no date), AFFGL.

341   **FGL and sailors:** FGL, *Dibujos*, 144, 183–84; *EC*, 287; Sahuquillo, 105–6; David L. Loughram, *Federico García Lorca. The Poetry of Limits* (London: Tamesis Books, 1978), 17–18.

342   **FGL sketches in Buenos Aires:** Mario Hernández, "Ronda de los autorretratos con animal fabuloso y análisis de los dibujos neoyorquinos," in FGL, *Dibujos*, 94; *FM*, 433–34; *EC*, 782; FGL, *Dibujos*, 222–29; Salvador Novo, "Prólogo" to FGL, *Libro de poemas, Poema del cante jondo, Romancero gitano, Poeta en Nueva York, Odas, Llanto por Ignacio Sánchez Mejías, Bodas de sangre, Yerma* (Mexico: Porrua, 1973), xvii–xviii.

343   **Membrives presents *Shoemaker's Wife*:** "El estreno de *La zapatera prodigiosa* se dará mañana a conocer en el teatro Avenida," *La Nación* (Buenos Aires), November 30, 1933, 11, in *OC*, III, 471–73; *G*, *II*, 288; Mario Hernández, introduction to FGL, *La zapatera*, 45–48, 150–57, 203; *FM*, 302–3; Anderson, *García Lorca: La zapatera*, 18–22; "La compañía Membrives dio a conocer anoche 'La zapatera prodigiosa,' " *La Prensa* (Buenos Aires), December 2, 1933, 17; "Una nueva obra de García Lorca. 'La zapatera prodigiosa,' " *Correo de Galicia* (Buenos Aires), December 3, 1933; *EC*, 782–92.

344   **FGL and Membrives stage *Fin de Fiesta*:** "El fin de fiesta se estrenará hoy en el Avenida: Es un grato espectáculo," *La Nación* (Buenos Aires), December 16, 1933, 11; FGL, *La zapatera*, 166, 181–86. For FGL's thoughts on songs, see FGL, *La zapatera*, 187; Maurer, "Lorca y las formas," 237–40; John K. Walsh and Bussell Thompson, "García Lorca en Buenos Aires: Entrevista con D. Edmundo Guibourg," *García Lorca Review* XI, 2 (1983), 218–19; César Tiempo, "Conversaciones con García Lorca en Buenos Aires," *NacionalC*, July 11, 1957, 8–9; Marcelle Schveitzer, "Souvenir sur Federico García Lorca," in Louis Parrot, *Federico García Lorca*, with Marcelle Schveitzer and Armand Guibert (Paris: Seghers, 1947), 196; Suero, "Crónica"; Mora Guarnido, 89.

344   **FGL gives interview to Jewish magazine:** Marcelo Menasché, "El autor de *Bodas de sangre* es un buen amigo de los judíos," *Sulem. Revista social ilustrada para la colectividad is-*

raelita I, 2 (Buenos Aires), December 25, 1933, in *OC*, III, 486–89. On FGL's Christmas plans, see *EC*, 790.

345   **Membrives presents *Mariana Pineda*:** "Beneficio de Lola Membrives," *La Nación* (Buenos Aires), January 12, 1934, 9; "Lola Membrives celebra hoy su velada de honor con *Mariana Pineda*," *La Prensa* (Buenos Aires), January 12, 1934; *EC*, 789–95; Guardia, 84–86; "García Lorca habla de su obra 'Mariana Pineda,' " *Crítica* (Buenos Aires), January 10, 1934, 20; "La nueva obra de García Lorca," *La Nación* (Buenos Aires), December 29, 1933, in *OC*, III, 490–93; FGL, "Agradecimiento al público de Buenos Aires," *Noticias Gráficas* (Buenos Aires), January 13, 1934, in *OC*, III, 236.

346   **Membrives plans to premiere *Yerma*:** "La compañía de Lola Membrives. Reaparecerá en el Teatro Avenida el 1° de marzo," *La Nación* (Buenos Aires), January 22, 1934, 11; *EC*, 791; "Inesperadamente se despidió la compañía de Lola Membrives," *La Prensa* (Buenos Aires), January 22, 1934; "El teatro español en 1934," *La Nación* (Buenos Aires), February 8, 1934, 11.

346   **"to the country":** *La Razón* (Buenos Aires), November 28, 1933, in FGL, *La zapatera*, 150.

346   **"in the country":** "La compañía de Lola Membrives. Reaparecerá en el Teatro Avenida el 1° de marzo," *La Nación* (Buenos Aires) January 22, 1934, 11.

346   **FGL travels to Montevideo:** *EC*, 795–800; Anderson, "García Lorca en Montevideo," 167–79; Esther H. de Amorím, "Recuerdos de la estadia de Federico en Montevideo, 1934" (untitled ms.), AFFGL; García-Posada; Hortensia Campanella, "Profeta en toda tierra. Federico García Lorca, en Uruguay," *Ínsula* 384 (November 1978), 10; "Federico García Lorca está ya en Montevideo," *El Plata* (Montevideo), January 30, 1934, AFFGL; Erre, "Llegó ayer a Montevideo, el gran poeta y dramaturgo español Federico García Lorca," *El Diario Español* (Montevideo), January 31, 1934, AFFGL; "F. García Lorca en Montevideo," *El Ideal* (Montevideo), January 30, 1934, AFFGL.

347   **"Just as I need music":** Ferreiro.

348   **FGL sees Mora Guarnido:** Mora Guarnido, 209–12; correspondence from José Mora Guarnido to FGL, AFFGL; "Encuentro con Federico García Lorca," *El Ideal* (Montevideo), February 1, 1934.

348   **FGL befriends Juana de Ibarbourou:** Anderson, "García Lorca en Montevideo," 172–73; Juana de Ibarbourou, "Federico García Lorca," in Ibarbourou, *Obras completas* (Madrid: Aguilar, 1968), 1264–67.

348–49   **"Don't ask . . . telling me where?":** ' "Boy.' Ronda gitana. Persecución, captura y secuestro del poeta Federico García Lorca," *El Plata* (Montevideo), February 12, 1934, in *OC*, III, 506–7.

349   **"a fugitive":** Enrique Díez-Canedo, untitled reminiscence reproduced on jacket of *Trece de Nieve*, 2nd. series, 1–2 (Madrid, 1976). See also Enrique Díez-Canedo, "Federico García Lorca," in *Escritos y poemas* (Malaga: Fundación Pablo Ruiz Picasso, Ayuntamiento de Málaga, 1990), 22; Mora Guarnido, 211–12; Norah Giraldi de Deicas, "La gira de Federico García Lorca por el Río de la Plata: 18 días en Montevideo," in *Homenaje a Federico García Lorca*, ed. Jorge Arbaleche, *Cuadernos de Literatura* (Montevideo: Fundación de Cultura Universitaria, 1976), 113; *G*, II, 295.

349   **FGL visits Barradas's grave:** Mora Guarnido, 213; Anderson, "García Lorca en Montevideo," 179; *El Diario* (Montevideo), February 18, 1934; "Homenaje de García Lorca a Barradas," *El Ideal* (Montevideo), February 16, 1934. On FGL's departure from Montevideo, see Mora Guarnido, 213.

350   **FGL reads *La dama boba*:** Anderson, "García Lorca en Montevideo," 179; Villarejo, 105; "Mañana se reunirá en el Teatro de la Comedia la compañía de Eva Franco," *La Nación* (Buenos Aires), February 16, 1934, 9. On Eva Franco's production of the play, see "Tres testimonios," *La Nación* (Buenos Aires), August 10, 1986, section 4, 1; Villarejo, 103.

350   "You can do whatever": *EC*, 799.

350   "Wrap up your affairs . . . not even here": Vicenta Lorca to FGL (February 16, 1934), AFFGL.

350   "where an author's dreams . . . as you can see": "Discurso al despedirse de Buenos Aires," *Crítica* (Buenos Aires), March 2, 1934, in *OC*, III, 238.

350   "I've cut it": Octavio Ramírez, "Lope de Vega en un teatro nacional," *La Nación* (Buenos Aires), February 23, 1934, in *OC*, III, 520–22.

351   "marvel of nature": "García Lorca ofrenda aplausos a Lope de Vega," *Crítica* (Buenos Aires), March 4, 1934, in *OC*, III, 240.

351   "spied upon": Villarejo, 107.

351   "Lola balls": Eduardo Blanco-Amor, "Federico, otra vez; la misma vez," *El País* (Madrid), October 1, 1978, vi.

351   "distinguished actress" and "an art, a great art": "En el homenaje a Lola Membrives," *Crítica* (Buenos Aires), March 16, 1934, in *OC*, III, 242–46.

351–52   **FGL and Fontanals present puppet show**: FGL, *Retablillo*; *OC*, II, 398–411; "García Lorca presentará un ensayo de teatro de títeres," *Crítica* (Buenos Aires), February 19, 1934, 8; "Una obra inédita de García Lorca se daría en el Odeón," *Crítica* (Buenos Aires), February 22, 1934, 18; "Diálogo del poeta y Don Cristóbal," *Crítica* (Buenos Aires), March 26, 1934, in *OC*, II, 707–8; Guardia, 86–87; César Tiempo, "Conversaciones con García Lorca en Buenos Aires," *NacionalC*, July 11, 1957; *FM*, 282–84; *GM*, 146, 154.

353   "triumph for the Spanish": Juan Chabás, "Federico García Lorca y la tragedia," *Luz* (Madrid), July 3, 1934, in *OC*, III, 535.

353   "You can't imagine": Eduardo Blanco-Amor, "Evocación de Federico," *La Nación* (Buenos Aires), October 21, 1956.

353   **FGL visits Neruda**: Chas de Cruz, "Han pasado dos poetas," *Primer magazine argentino* XV, 562 (Buenos Aires), April 25, 1934, Supplement, in *Cuadernos Hispanoamericanos* 433–34 (July–August 1986), 35–36.

353   **FGL departs Buenos Aires**: *G*, *II*, 304–5, citing Enrique Jascalevich, "El amigo de Federico García Lorca. 'Después de la fiesta a las cinco de la mañana, escuchaba misa en San Carlos,' nos dice Amado Villar," *El Hogar* (Buenos Aires) (undated clipping); "Partirán García Lorca y Fontanals. Embarcarán mañana para su patria. Formarán un conjunto para cultivar un teatro artístico," *La Nación* (Buenos Aires), March 26, 1934, 13; H. E. Pedemonte, "El primer monumento a Federico García Lorca," *Nueva Estafeta* (December 1978), 59.

353   "To myself, I still feel" and "Do you know him . . . But it was mine": Luna, "La vida."

354   **FGL receives butterfly case**: Alardo Prats, "Los artistas en el ambiente de nuestro tiempo," *El Sol* (Madrid), December 15, 1934, in *OC*, III, 541.

354   **FGL writes poetry**: Mario Hernández, introduction and notes to FGL, *Divan*, 71–74, 192; Anderson, *Lorca's Late Poetry*, 67–87.

355   **FGL talks about death**: Luna, "La vida."

22. SAD BREEZE IN THE OLIVE GROVES: 1934

356   **FGL returns to Spain**: "Movimiento del puerto. Día 11," *La Vanguardia* (Barcelona), April 12, 1934; Salinas, 7; Sáenz de la Calzada, 147–50, 171–75; Moises Pérez Coterillo, "En Galicia con E. Blanco-Amor, y al fondo . . . Lorca," *Reseña* 73 (March 1974), 18; Antonio Ramos Espejo, "En Valderrubio, Granada. La casa de Bernarda Alba," *Triunfo* XXXIV, 6th series, 4 (Madrid, February 1981), 62; Higuera Rojas, 26; *G*, *II*, 309–10; José María Moreiro, "Viaje a

García Lorca. Reencuentro con sus personajes vivos," *Los domingos de ABC* (Madrid), August 1, 1971, 23; Morla Lynch, 381; "Los españoles fuera de España," *Heraldo de Madrid*, April 14, 1934, in *OC*, III, 530–34.

357 **Political troubles, spring 1934:** "El tercer aniversario de la proclamación de la República," *ABC* (Madrid), April 15, 1934, 39; Thomas, 113–16; Jackson, 53, 123–36, 159; Payne, 57–59; "Un mitin de la Juventud de Acción Popular," *Defensor de Granada*, April 17, 1934, 1.

358 **Right-wing press attacks Barraca:** Byrd, 67; "Teatro para el pueblo," *La Nación* (Buenos Aires), January 28, 1934, Arts and Letters section, in *OC*, III, 496.

358 **La Barraca stages puppet plays:** FGL, *Retablillo*, 17; Valentín de Pedro, " 'El guiñol que a Federico le regalaron en Buenos Aires,' relato de María del Carmen García Lasgoity," ¡*Aquí Está!* X, 940, May 21, 1945, 3; Auclair, 21; Sáenz de la Calzada, 105, 151–52; Alberti, *Federico García Lorca: Poeta y amigo*, 224.

358 **Neruda arrives in Madrid:** E. Rodríguez Monegal, *El viajero inmóvil. Introducción a Pablo Neruda* (Buenos Aires: Losada, 1966), 80–82; Teitelboim, 146–59; Miguel García-Posada, "Malva Marina," *ABC* (Madrid), July 12, 1984; author interview with Tomás Rodríguez Rapún; Sáenz de la Calzada, 26–27; Morla Lynch, 386; "Ochenta años de Pablo Neruda," *ABC* (Madrid), July 12, 1984, 55.

358–59 **"punch concoctions":** Rodrigo, *Memoria*, 283; see also Auclair, 260; author interview with José Caballero; José Caballero, "Recuerdos surrealistas con un perro andaluz," in *El surrealismo*, ed. Antonio Bonet Correa (Madrid: Cátedra, 1983), 202–3; Sáenz de la Calzada, 29.

359 **"closer to death":** FGL, "Presentación de Pablo Neruda en la Facultad de Filosofía y Letras de Madrid" (December 6, 1934), in *OC*, III, 249–50.

359 **"the guiding spirit":** Neruda, *Passions and Impressions*, 63.

359 **"in the turbid waters":** *FE* (Madrid), July 5, 1934, 11, cited in Gibson, *El asesinato*, 336–37.

359 **"What's more . . . of making things":** Juan Chabás, "Vacaciones de La Barraca," *Luz* (Madrid), September 3, 1934, in *OC*, III, 539; Juan Chabás, "Federico García Lorca y la tragedia," *Luz* (Madrid), July 3, 1934, in *OC*, III, 535–37.

359 **"Since I've got it all":** *EC*, 803.

360 **FGL in Granada, summer 1934:** "García Lorca," *Defensor de Granada*, July 22, 1934, 1; "D. Francisco Soriano de Lapresa," *Defensor de Granada*, July 18, 1934, 3; *EC*, 802–3.

360 **FGL writes *Divan at Tamarit*:** Anderson, *Lorca's Late Poetry*, 16–28; Mario Hernández, notes to FGL, *Diván*, 158–70, 192–93; Emilio García Gómez, "Nota al 'Diván del Tamarit,' " in FGL, *Divan*, 53–58; Emilio García Gómez, *La Silla del moro y nuevas escenas andaluzas* (Madrid: Colección Austral Espasa Calpe, n.d.), 87–88; Mario Hernández, introduction to FGL, *Primeras canciones*, 13; C, I, 76–79, trans. FGL, *Deep Song*, 36–39. On FGL and the Huerta del Tamarit, see Andrés Soria, *García Lorca y Granada* 47, Topics of Our Andalusia (Granada: Obra Cultural de la Caja de Ahorros de Granada, 1978), 4; author interview with Vicente López; Auclair, 307; Higuera Rojas, 104; Antonina Rodrigo, "La auténtica 'Doña Rosita la soltera,' " *El País Semanal* (Madrid), August 17, 1980, 4; Penón, 163.

360 **The *Divan at Tamarit*:** All passages taken from *OC*, I, 591–614, trans. FGL, *Collected Poems*. On the links between FGL and Arab poets see Luis Cernuda, "Notas eludidas," *Heraldo de Madrid*, November 26, 1931, 12.

364 **Ignacio Sánchez Mejías dies:** "Ayer falleció Ignacio Sánchez Mejías," *ABC* (Madrid), August 14, 1934, 27–29; Eduardo Palacio, "El porqué de la vuelta a los toros," *ABC* (Madrid), August 14, 1934, 29; *FM*, 203; Antonio Garrigues, "Yo estaba allí," *ABC Semanal* (Madrid), August 12, 1984, 13; Anderson, *Lorca's Late Poetry*, 153–58; *ABC* (Madrid), August 15 and 16, 1934; "Sánchez Mejías ha muerto," *El Cantábrico* (Santander), August 14, 1934, 4 (see also

August 13–20, 1934); Sáenz de la Calzada, 167; Auclair, 24–28, 257; author interview with María del Carmen Lasgoity.

365 "valiant": FGL, "Presentación de Ignacio Sánchez Mejías en Nueva York," in *OC*, III, 199.

365 "Ignacio has just announced": Auclair, 21.

365 "through what minuscule chink . . . mystery": Auclair, 29–30.

365 "elegy I never wanted": Manuscript copy of *Llanto por Ignacio Sánchez Mejías*, Biblioteca Nacional, Madrid, Mss. N.A., 180.

365 FGL drafts *Lament*: Auclair, 31; Rafael Gómez, "El manuscrito del 'Llanto,'" *ABC Semanal* (Madrid), August 12, 1984, 19; Mario Hernández, introduction to FGL, *Divan*, 104; Juan de Loxa, "Con José Caballero en Fuentevaqueros. Recordando a Federico," *Federico García Lorca–José Caballero*, ed. María Fernanda Thomas de Carranza (Granada: Patronato Cultural Federico García Lorca, 1987), 32; *FM*, 203.

365 FGL and the bullfight: Anderson, *Lorca's Late Poetry*, 158–71; FGL, *Sun and Shadow*, trans. Kathleen Raine and R. M. Nadal (London: Enitharmon Press, 1972); author interview with José Caballero; Eutimio Martín, "La actitud de Lorca ante el tema de los toros a través de cuatro cartas a José María de Cossío," *Ínsula* 322 (September 1973), 3; *C*, II, 106; FGL, *Alocuciones argentinas*, 20–23; FGL, "Presentación de Ignacio Sánchez Mejías en Nueva York," in *OC*, III, 199–200; Miguel García-Posada, "Nota," in FGL, *Oda y burla*, 102; Giovanni Papini, "Coloquio con García Lorca (o de las corridas)," *El libro negro*, trans. Mario Verdaguer (Barcelona: Plaza y Janés, 1962), 401–3.

365 *Lament for Ignacio Sánchez Mejías*: All passages are taken from *OC*, I, 615–24, trans. FGL, *Collected Poems*.

367 "When I was composing": Vázquez Ocaña, *García Lorca: Vida*, 338.

369 "I was proud": Auclair, 31.

369 "dear friend Encarnación": *OC*, I, 616.

369 "A bull from the stable": José Caballero, "Recuerdos surrealistas con un perro andaluz," in *El surrealismo*, ed. Antonio Bonet Correa (Madrid: Cátedra, 1983), 201.

369 "those who want to know him": Review by Miguel Pérez Ferrero, *Heraldo de Madrid*, May 9, 1935, 5.

369 "clear and strong . . . bad taste": Don Tertuliano, "Del momento. Llanto de Federico García Lorca, por la muerte de Ignacio Sánchez Mejías," *La Provincia* (Huelva), May 14, 1935, 5.

369 "What I've written . . . other shore": Auclair, 32–33.

23. REVOLUTION: 1934-35

370 "last as long . . . upon sand": Silvio D'Amico, "Incontro con Federico García Lorca," *Il Dramma* (Turin), May 15, 1946 [1935], in *OC*, III, 572.

370 "enormous sense": Alardo Prats, "Los artistas en el ambiente de nuestro tiempo," *El Sol* (Madrid), December 15, 1934, in *OC*, III, 542.

370 "I go on with my life": Alfredo Muñiz, "En los umbrales del estreno de Yerma," *Heraldo de Madrid*, December 26, 1934, in *OC*, III, 548.

370 "profound movement": Miguel de Unamuno, "Hablemos de teatro," *Ahora* (Madrid), September 19, 1934, 5.

370 "Come to Paris": Auclair, 258.

371 "The Congress invites": *EC*, 804. On Levi's invitation to FGL, see Auclair, 258; Ezio Levi, "La Barraca di García Lorca," *Scenario* 3 (Milan, 1934), 528–30; and Juan Chabás, "Vacaciones de La Barraca," *Luz* (Madrid), September 3, 1934, in *OC*, III, 539.

371 **Political troubles, fall 1934:** Thomas, 116–17; Jackson, 122, 143–47; Southworth, 3.

372 **Asturian revolution:** Southworth, 7; Thomas, 117–28; Jackson, 161; Carlos Bauer, introduction to FGL, *The Public and Play without a Title*, xix; Peter Weyden, *The Passionate War* (New York: Simon and Schuster, 1983), 42; Jackson, 160; Preston, 29–30, 101–6.

373 **"My God, why are these things":** Luis Lacasa, "Recuerdo y trayectoria de Federico García Lorca," *Literatura soviética* (Moscow, 1946), 42. Information on FGL's fear of bullets comes from Vázquez Ocaña, *García Lorca: Vida*, 318, and author interview with Tomás Rodríguez Rapún.

374 **"culminating moment" and "the liberation of Spain":** *Literatura y compromiso político en los años 30: Homenaje al poeta Juan Gil-Albert*, exhibition catalogue (Diputación Provincial de Valencia, 1984), 34, 79.

374 **"cruel poison":** Moreno Villa, 208.

374 **FGL's response to Asturian revolution:** Saenz de la Calzada, 167; correspondence from Pujades to FGL (January 11, 1935), AFFGL; Frank Sedwick, *The Tragedy of Manuel Azaña and the Fate of the Spanish Republic* (Columbus: Ohio State University Press, 1963), 136; Proel.

375 **FGL encounters Primo de Rivera:** *G, II*, 324–25. On Primo de Rivera see Thomas, 99–100, and Payne, 24–25. Others have recalled less dramatic encounters between FGL and Primo de Rivera at *tertulias* and football games (see Gabriel Celaya, "Recordando a García Lorca," *El País* [Madrid], June 10, 1976, and Margarita Saenz de la Calzada, *La Residencia de Estudiantes. 1910–1936* [Madrid: CSIC, 1986], 76).

375 **Neruda's daughter:** Teitelboim, 168–72; *OC*, I, 643.

375 **"at all hours":** Proel. On FGL's typical behavior, see Mariano Tudela, *Aquellas tertulias de Madrid* (Madrid: Avapiés, 1984), 90, 105; "Tertulias literarias," *Almanaque Literario* (Madrid, 1935), 181; Saenz de la Calzada, 177; Altolaguirre, *Obras completas I*, 241; Moreno Villa, 148–49; Martínez Nadal, *Lorca's The Public*, 11; Cernuda, 16; author interview with José Caballero.

375 **"an irresistible urge":** "Llegó anoche Federico García Lorca," *La Nación* (Buenos Aires), October 14, 1933, in *OC*, III, 442.

375 **"is most important":** "Un reportaje. El poeta que ha estilizado los romances de plazuela," *El Debate* (Madrid), October 1, 1933, in *OC*, III, 430.

375 **"institution . . . climate":** Salinas, 7.

376 **"celestial court":** José Caballero, "Recuerdos surrealistas con un perro andaluz," in *El surrealismo*, ed. Antonio Bonet Correa (Madrid: Cátedra, 1983), 199; author interview with José Caballero. On FGL's need to be surrounded by friends, see María Teresa León, *Memoria de la melancolía* (Barcelona: Laia-Picazo, 1977), 198.

376 **"big, square, majestic head":** Luis Rosales, "Evocación de Federico," *Cuadernos Hispanoamericanos* 475 (January 1990), 34. On his appearance in general see Gil-Albert, 181–82; Ontañón; Ernesto Guerra da Cal, "Federico García Lorca en el recuerdo," *Punto y coma* 11 (Madrid[?], winter 1988–89), 49–59.

376 **FGL's drinking and smoking habits:** Author interviews with Vicente López and Bernardo Olmedo; Molina Fajardo, 93; Martínez Nadal, *Lorca's The Public*, 14; Auclair, 169, 237; Nicholas de Jongh, "Protector of *The Public*," *The Guardian* (London), October 3, 1988, 14, 20.

376 **"synonym for joy":** Gil-Albert, 181. On FGL's mood swings, see Penón, 178, 185.

376 **"a renewed impetus . . . intolerable":** Ernesto Guerra da Cal, "Federico García Lorca en el recuerdo," *Punto y coma* 11 (Madrid[?], winter 1988–89), 55.

376 **"No, I've got a cold":** Teitelboim, 198.

376 **FGL's compartmentalized life:** Author interview with José Caballero; author interview

with Santiago Ontañón; Luna, "La vida"; *G, II*, 324; Aub, 311–12; Nicholas de Jongh, "Protector of *The Public*," *The Guardian*, (London), October 3, 1988, 20; Altolaguirre, *Obras completas I*, 289; Luis Cernuda, "A un poeta muerto," in *El compañero. Los poetas de la Generación del 27 en homenaje a Federico García Lorca* (Granada: Excma. Diputación Provincial, 1985), 24; Auclair, 98; Penón, 111–12, 180.

377 *"los ambiguos"*: *El Duende* (Madrid), June 25, 1933, 21.

377 **"Sodom on the road"**: Penón, 186.

377 **"They say you poets . . . poets?"**: Moises Pérez Coterillo, "En Galicia con E. Blanco-Amor, y al fondo . . . Lorca," *Reseña* 73 (March 1974), 17–18.

377 **"They say it's good"**: " 'Vengo de torero herido a dar 4 conferencias,' dice García Lorca," *Crítica* (Buenos Aires), October 14, 1933, 10.

377 **FGL attends *Yerma* rehearsals**: José Caballero, "Con Federico en los ensayos de *Yerma*," *ABC* (Madrid), December 29, 1984, Saturday Cultural section, I; Mario Hernández, introduction to FGL, *Yerma*, 28; Auclair, 284, 296. On FGL's chronic tardiness and unreliability, see Ontañón; María Teresa León, *Memoria de la melancolía* (Barcelona: Laia-Picazo, 1977), 198; León; author interview with José Caballero; Auclair, 38; Eduardo Blanco-Amor to FGL (November 15, 1934), AFFGL; Ontañón and Moreiro, 119; Morla Lynch, 58–60.

378 **Talk of *Yerma* permeates Madrid press**: *El Pueblo* (Madrid), December 8, 1934, 3; *El Sol* (Madrid), December 28, 1934, 2.

378 **FGL at final dress rehearsal**: José Caballero, "Con Federico en los ensayos de *Yerma*," *ABC* (Madrid), December 29, 1984, Saturday Cultural section, I; Rodrigo, *Margarita Xirgu*, 205–6; José Luis Salado, "Antes del estreno," *La Voz* (Madrid), December 29, 1934, 3; *Defensor de Granada*, December 30, 1934, 1; *Heraldo de Madrid*, December 31, 1934, 4; Rivas Cherif, January 13, 1957.

378 **"We must return to tragedy"**: Juan Chabás, "Federico García Lorca y la tragedia," *Luz* (Madrid), July 3, 1934, in *OC, III*, 536.

378 *Yerma*: All passages are taken from FGL, *Yerma*, in *OC, II*, 478–526.

380 **"with the timidity"**: Alfredo Muñiz, "En los umbrales del estreno de *Yerma*," *Heraldo de Madrid*, December 26, 1934, in *OC, III*, 548.

380 **"poems"**: Victor Ruíz Iriarte, "Teatro. La nueva tragedia: *Yerma*," *Labor* (Madrid), January 5, 1935, AFFGL; Ramón J. Sender, "El poeta en la escena. Sexta representación de *Yerma*," *La Libertad* (Madrid), January 5, 1935, 1, AFFGL.

381 **FGL tends niece**: Rodrigo, "La huerta," 828–29.

381 **"The work is Federico's own tragedy"**: Trend, 23n.

381–82 **"I want to take topics" and "In this world I am . . . accept it"**: Alardo Prats, "Los artistas en el ambiente de nuestro tiempo," *El Sol* (Madrid), December 15, 1934, in *OC, III*, 545.

382 **Xirgu's friendship with Azaña**: Rodrigo, *Margarita Xirgu*, 181–83.

382 ***Yerma*'s opening night**: Morla Lynch, 431–36; Auclair, 284–89; Eduardo Blanco-Amor, "Federico, otra vez; la misma vez," *El País* (Madrid), October 1, 1978, vi; Ricardo Gullón, "*Yerma*, ayer y hoy," *ABC* (Madrid), December 29, 1934, Saturday Cultural section, I; José Caballero, "Con Federico en los ensayos de *Yerma*," *ABC* (Madrid), December 29, 1984, Saturday Cultural section, I; "El estreno de la obra de García Lorca constituye un éxito extraordinario," *Defensor de Granada*, December 30, 1934, 2; Rodrigo, *Margarita Xirgu*, 207–8.

383 **Government censor approves *Yerma***: Antonio Gago Rodó, "Los ejemplares de cuatro estrenos de García Lorca (1927–1934)," *BFFGL* 18 (December 1995), 101.

383 ***Yerma* receives mixed reviews**: Fernández Cifuentes, 163–69, 180–81; Auclair, 290; Ramón J. Sender, "El poeta en la escena. Sexta representación de *Yerma*," *La Libertad* (Madrid),

January 5, 1935, 1, AFFGL; Enrique Díez-Canedo, "*Yerma*, el poema trágico de Federico García Lorca, obtuvo un extraordinario éxito en el Español," *La Voz* (Madrid), December 31, 1934, 3; Ian Gibson, *Un Irlandés en España* (Barcelona: Planeta, 1981), 196–97; *Informaciones* (Madrid), December 31, 1934, 8; *La Nación* (Madrid), December 31, 1934, 11; Eduardo Haro review in *La Libertad*, December 30, 1934, AFFGL; Luis Araujo Costa, in *La Época* (Madrid), December 31, 1934, 5; Melchor Fernández Almagro review in *El Sol* (Madrid), December 30, 1934, 8; *Ahora* (Madrid), December 30, 1934, 41; *Heraldo de Madrid*, December 31, 1934, 4; *El Pueblo* (Madrid), January 1, 1935, 3; "El arte escénico en 1934. García Lorca cierra el año con un alarde magnífico de inspiración y de técnica," *La Tierra* (Madrid), December 31, 1934, AFFGL; "Español: *Yerma*," *ABC* (Madrid), December 30, 1934, 53; *El Debate* (Madrid), December 30, 1934, 4, and January 3, 1935, 6; "La temporada teatral," *Gracia y Justicia* (Madrid), January 5, 1935, 8; Arturo Mori, "Crónica de Madrid. *Yerma*," *El Pueblo* (Valencia), January 4, 1935, AFFGL; [Eduardo Blanco-Amor], "*Yerma* en el Español," *Ciudad Madrid* (Madrid), January 9, 1935; "Paris: El Sr. Oulmont habla de *Yerma* y de Margarita Xirgu," *El Sol* (Madrid), January 27, 1935, 1.

384   **Public response to *Yerma***: Auclair, 291; Morla Lynch, 455; "Barcelona. La moral de *Yerma*," *El Día Gráfico* (Madrid), September 15, 1935, 13; Luengo; Mario Hernández, introduction to FGL, *Yerma*, 11; Alberti, *La arboleda perdida*, 312–13; Corpus Barga, "Tragicomedia. *Yerma* y la política," *Diario de Madrid*, January 6, 1935; Isaac Pacheco, "La vida y el teatro. Las pasiones naturales," *El Liberal* (Bilbao), January 4, 1935, and *El Luchador* (Alicante), January 2, 1935, AFFGL; "De madrugada en el Español," *El Pueblo* (Madrid), February 3, 1935, 3.

385   **"May it please you to know"**: Martín, *Federico García Lorca, heterodoxo*, 399–400.

385   **"As you know, I'm liberal"**: Carmen Diamante, "Recuerdo," *Retama* 3 (Cuenca, [May] 1986), 14.

385   **"conservative," "politically insurgent," and "I'm a Christian"**: Luengo.

385   **Catholic paper disapproves of *Yerma***: *El Siglo Futuro* (Madrid), December 31, 1934, and January 1, 1935.

385   **Granada officials ban *Yerma***: Rodrigo, *Margarita Xirgu*, 217.

2 4 . THEATER OF POETS: 1935

386   **"audacious . . . disappointed" and "greatest feelings"**: "Después del estreno de *Yerma*," *El Sol* (Madrid), January 1, 1935, in *OC*, III, 552.

386   **FGL lists plays**: *Heraldo de Madrid*, January 17, 1935, 5; Mario Hernández, introduction to FGL, *La casa de Bernarda Alba*, 13–14; *OC*, II, 808.

386   **"crudeness . . . archangels"**: Luengo.

386   **"I have no interest"**: Proel.

387   **"must capture"**: Nicolás González Deleito, "Federico García Lorca y el teatro de hoy," *Escena* 1 (Madrid, May 1935), in *OC*, III, 563.

387   **"a man of national tradition" and "theater of love, adventure"**: *OC*, III, 56.

388   **FGL addresses audience at *Peribáñez***: Antonio Espina, "Escena y bastidores," *El Sol* (Madrid), January 26, 1935; FGL, "Presentación de *Peribáñez y el Comendador de Ocaña*, de Lope de Vega, representado por el Club Teatral Anfistora," in *OC*, III, 251–53.

388   **"necessary anachronism"**: Enrique Díez-Canedo, "En el Capitol," *La Voz* (Madrid), January 26, 1935, 3.

388   **FGL and Ucelay visit Castile**: Auclair, 222–23; Antonio de Obregón, "*Peribáñez y el*

Comendador de Ocaña, de Lope de Vega. Hablando con García Lorca," *Diario de Madrid*, January 26, 1935, in *OC*, III, 553; Margarita Ucelay, "Federico García Lorca y el Club Teatral Anfistora: el dramaturgo como director de escena," in Soria Olmedo, 61–62.

388   **FGL witnesses lamb slaughter:** Auclair, 222; Neruda, *Passions and Impressions*, 62–63.

389   **FGL and Xirgu present "actors-only" *Yerma*:** "Escena y bastidores," *El Sol* (Madrid), January 30, 1935, and February 1, 1935, 2. FGL's talk was published in the Madrid press (see "La *Yerma* extraordinaria de Margarita Xirgu y unas cuartillas admirables de García Lorca," *El Liberal* [Madrid], February 3, 1935, 5). Passages from the talk are taken from *OC*, III, 254–57.

390   **Azaña attends *Yerma*:** *La Libertad* (Madrid), February 21, 1922.

391   **"Success never satisfies":** Armando Bazán, "Con el poeta García Lorca en Madrid," *Todos* I, 1 (Castellón, May 1935), in *OC*, III, 560.

391   ***Blood Wedding* produced in New York:** Morla Lynch, 363–64; Christopher Maurer, "Bach and *Bodas de sangre*," in *Lorca's Legacy: Essays on Lorca's Life, Poetry, and Theatre*, ed. Manuel Durán and Francesca Colecchia (New York: Peter Lang, 1991), 107; Adams, 170–72; *The New Republic*, February 27, 1935, 78; Luis Fernández Cifuentes, "García Lorca y el éxito: El caso de *Bodas de sangre*," in Soria Olmedo, 87; Christopher Maurer, "Adelfa amarga en Nueva York," *El País* (Madrid), August 19, 1986, vii; Río, "Federico García Lorca," 208, citing *The New York Sun*, February 12, 1935; Percy Hammond review in *New York Herald Tribune*, February 12, 1935, 16; " 'Bitter Oleander' and 'The Eldest' Presented in Broadway Playhouses," *New York Post*, February 12, 1935, 11; Robert Benchley review in *The New Yorker*, March 2, 1935; Mario Hernández, introduction to FGL, *Bodas de sangre*, 60, citing "Campo de armino y *Bodas de sangre*, en inglés, no agradan," *Ahora* (Madrid), February 26, 1935. For FGL's remarks on the production, see J. Palau-Fabre, "D'una conversa amb García Lorca," *La Humanitat* (Barcelona), October 4, 1935, in *OC*, III, 603.

391   **"You're going to find yourself":** José L. Salado, "Con Lola Membrives a propósito del lorquismo puro," *La Voz* (Madrid), February 7, 1935, 5.

392   **FGL delivers radio talks to Argentina:** FGL, *Alocuciones argentinas*, 9; *OC*, III, 260–68.

392   **"Because now it's *my* turn":** On FGL's financial status, see "Información teatral. Lola Membrives está muy contenta con el éxito de *Bodas de sangre* en el Coliseum," *La Voz* (Madrid), March 6, 1935, 3; Auclair, 278; Guillén, "Federico en persona."

392   **"I realize you must be giving":** Carlos Morla Lynch to FGL (March 12, 1935; November 26, 1935), AFFGL.

392   **"Now, yes":** Guillén, "Federico en persona."

392–93   **"shackle . . . true to yourself" and "That's the secret":** Proel. On FGL and money see also Penón, 90.

393   **"if I don't, I'll rot inside":** "García Lorca ante el teatro, sus recuerdos de Buenos Aires," radio interview broadcast by Transradio Española from Madrid to Buenos Aires (May 1935), in *OC*, III, 566.

393   **FGL's shoes:** Morla Lynch, 460.

393   **"romantic tenderness":** Morla Lynch, 462–64.

393   **"rest . . . temperament":** "Abans de l'estrena. L'autor ens diu," *La Humanitat* (Barcelona), December 12, 1935, in *OC*, III, 619.

393   **FGL writes *Doña Rosita*:** FGL, *Dibujos*, 239–40; Felipe Morales, "Conversaciones literarias. Al habla con Federico García Lorca," *La Voz* (Madrid), April 7, 1936, in *OC*, III, 631; FGL, *Teatro inconcluso*, 179–81; Moreno Villa, 120–21; *FM*, 362; "Escena y bastidores," *El Sol* (Madrid), May 23, 1935; *EC*, 813; Rodrigo, *García Lorca*, 290, 317.

393   ***Doña Rosita*:** All passages are taken from FGL, *Doña Rosita*, in *OC*, II, 527–79.

394 **"profound drama"**: "Abans de l'estrena. L'autor ens diu," *La Humanitat* (Barcelona), December 12, 1935, in *OC*, III, 619.

394 **"maidens . . . Spanish spinster" and "How long"**: Massa; on *Rosita* as elegy, see also Morales, 203.

395 **"elegy . . . for families" and "where there isn't one"**: Luengo.

395 **Sources for Doña Rosita**: In his review of *Rosita*, critic Antonio de Obregón noted that FGL often said, "I copy everything from life" (Antonio de Obregón, "Un estreno en el Principal Palace de Barcelona," *Diario de Madrid*, December 14, 1935, 2). On sources for *Rosita*, see *FM*, 85, 363–65; "Abans de l'estrena. L'autor ens diu," *La Humanitat* (Barcelona), December 12, 1935, in *OC*, III, 619; Antonina Rodrigo, "La auténtica 'Doña Rosita la soltera,'" *El País Semanal* (Madrid), August 17, 1980, 4–5; Francisco García Lorca, prologue to FGL, *Three Tragedies*, 17–18; Auclair, 299.

396 **"vulgar" and "ordinary"**: Morales, 209.

396 **"magnificent bad taste"**: "La mort de la rosa," *Ultima Hora* (Barcelona), December 13, 1935, 6.

396 **"the whole tragedy . . . pretentiousness"**: *FM*, 367, trans. *GM*, 227; Massa.

396 **"Perhaps"**: Morales, 203.

396 **"if in certain scenes"**: Francisco García Lorca, prologue to FGL, *Three Tragedies*, 18.

396 **FGL and Chekhov**: *FM*, 143; Helen Sheehy, *Eva Le Gallienne: A Biography* (Alfred A. Knopf, 1997), 181–84. According to José Antonio Rubio Sacristán, FGL saw productions by Eva Le Gallienne during his stay in New York (author interview with Sacristán).

396 **"tight-fitting skirts"**: Massa.

397 **Blanco-Amor visits Granada**: *Defensor de Granada*, June 19 and 20, 1935; Eduardo Blanco-Amor, "Evocación de Federico," *La Nación* (Buenos Aires), October 21, 1956; Eduardo Blanco-Amor, "Federico, otra vez; la misma vez," *El País* (Madrid), October 1, 1978, vi; Eduardo Blanco-Amor to FGL (September 22, 1935), AFFGL. For background on Blanco-Amor, see *G*, *II*, 234–36; Moises Pérez Coterillo, "En Galicia con E. Blanco-Amor, y al fondo . . . Lorca," *Reseña* 73 (March 1974), 14–18; Guerra da Cal, 194; L. Pérez Rodríguez, "Cartas inéditas de Blanco-Amor a Lorca," *La Región* (Orense), November 15, 1994.

397 **"spiritual representative"**: Eduardo Blanco-Amor to FGL (November 29, 1935), AFFGL.

397 **"artificial"**: José L. Franco Grande to Andrew A. Anderson (April 23, 1986); I am grateful to Andrew Anderson for having allowed me to consult this letter.

398 **"tiny, gracious"**: Eduardo Blanco-Amor, "Evocación de Federico," *La Nación* (Buenos Aires), October 21, 1956.

398 **"For Eduardo"**: Eduardo Blanco-Amor, "Federico, otra vez; la misma vez," *El País* (Madrid), October 1, 1978, vi.

398 **Ruiz Carnero assaulted**: *Defensor de Granada*, July 6 and 7, 1935; *G*, *II*, 370; Moises Pérez Coterillo, "En Galicia con E. Blanco-Amor, y al fondo . . . Lorca," *Reseña* 73 (March 1974), 18.

399 **Barraca loses funding**: Byrd, 79; Saenz de la Calzada, 155.

399 **"an authentically Spanish . . . communist type"**: E.R.L., "Ante el centenario de Lope," *Haz* (Madrid), March 26, 1935, 2–3.

399 **"Go on performing"**: Silvio D'Amico, "Incontro con Federico García Lorca," *Il Dramma* (Turin), May 15, 1946 [1935], in *OC*, III, 571.

399 **"will not die . . . secret theater"**: Miguel Pérez-Ferrero, "La commemoración del Tricentenario de Lope de Vega," *Heraldo de Madrid*, August 22, 1935, 7, in *OC*, III, 578.

399 **The Barraca in Santander**: Auclair, 259; Saenz de la Calzada, 102–4; Celia Valbuena Morán, *García Lorca y "La Barraca" en Santander* (Santander: Publisher unknown, 1974), 30; *El Cantábrico* (Santander), August 29, 1935, 5; Valentín de Pedro, "'El guiñol que a

Federico le regalaron en Buenos Aires,' relato de María del Carmen García Lasgoity," *¡Aquí Está!* X, 940, May 21, 1945, 2–21.

399   **Xirgu presents *Fuenteovejuna*:** Byrd, 88; Rodrigo, *García Lorca*, 245–46; Rivas Cherif, January 6, 1957; Vázquez Ocaña, *García Lorca: Vida*, 336.

400   **Xirgu presents *La dama boba*:** *El Liberal* (Madrid), August 28, 1935, 3–4; "El teatro. Margarita Xirgu y E. Borrás conmemoran en el Español la Semana de Lope. *La dama boba*," *La Libertad* (Madrid), August 29, 1935, 3. On Xirgu's work in general see Fernández-Cifuentes, 144n; "Las més gran actualitat," *La Rambla de Catalunya* (Barcelona), September 16, 1935, 5; Rodrigo, *Margarita Xirgu*, 164; Byrd, 62–63; "El arte de Margarita Xirgu," *El Día Gráfico* (Barcelona), September 25, 1935, 13; and Juan Chabás, "El ejemplo de Mérida," *Luz* (Madrid), June 20, 1933, 6.

400   **"so long as it's always done":** Joan Tomás, "A proposit de *La dama boba*. García Lorca i el teatre classique espanyol," *Mirador* (Barcelona), September 19, 1935, in *OC*, III, 586–87.

401   **"The contemporary Spanish theater":** *El Imparcial* (Madrid), January 7, 1933, 5.

401   **"because some man . . . disaster" and "blue-blooded ladies . . . resolved":** Alardo Prats, "Los artistas en el ambiente de nuestro tiempo," *El Sol* (Madrid), December 15, 1934, in *OC*, III, 544–45.

401   **"the contemporary Spanish theater is unquestionably":** "García Lorca ante el teatro, sus recuerdos de Buenos Aires," radio interview broadcast by Transradio Española from Madrid to Buenos Aires (May 1935), in *OC*, III, 566.

401   **"is the theater of poets":** Nicolás González Deleito, "Federico García Lorca y el teatro de hoy," *Escena* 1 (Madrid, May 1935), in *OC*, III, 563–64.

401   **"poetic, and always poetic":** "García Lorca ante el teatro, sus recuerdos de Buenos Aires," radio interview broadcast by Transradio Española from Madrid to Buenos Aires (May 1935), in *OC*, III, 568.

401   **"I believe in and fervently hope":** Armando Bazán, "Con el poeta García Lorca en Madrid," *Todos* I, 1 (Castellón, May 1935), in *OC*, III, 561.

401–2   **"true mission . . . multitudes":** "Federico García Lorca parla per als obrers catalans," *L'Hora* (Palma de Mallorca), September 27, 1935, 4, in *OC*, III, 600.

402   **"Nietzschean":** Luengo.

402   **"If I've momentarily . . . even more so":** "Federico García Lorca parla per als obrers catalans," *L'Hora* (Palma de Mallorca), September 27, 1935, 4, in *OC*, III, 598.

25. TO ENTER INTO THE SOUL OF THE PEOPLE: 1935

403   **"delicate and careful":** *El Liberal* (Madrid), August 28, 1935, 3.

403   **"my sex, my status, my soul":** *EC*, 240. On FGL's stay at Xirgu's home, see FGL to family (October 7, 1935), AFFGL; and "Hablando con Margarita Xirgu, que se va a América y recuerda su vida," *Crónica* (Madrid), December 22, 1935.

403   **"the eyes and the feet":** "El teatro al día," *El Día Gráfico* (Barcelona), September 17, 1935, 18.

403–4   **"ordinary . . . not a poet":** Agustí, 83.

404   **"And if it is":** Joan Tomás, "García Lorca parla de *Yerma*," *La Publicitat* (Barcelona), September 17, 1935, 6, in *OC*, III, 582.

404   **_Yerma_'s opening night crowds:** María Luz Morales, "*Yerma*, poema trágico," *La Vanguardia* (Barcelona), September 19, 1935, 10; *La Vanguardia* (Barcelona), September 18, 1935, 27; *Mirador* (Barcelona), September 26, 1935; Agustí, 82.

404   **"baptism of blood"**: María Luz Morales, "Teatro Barcelona. Un sensacional estreno. *Yerma*, poema trágico en tres actos, de Federico García Lorca," *La Vanguardia* (Barcelona), September 19, 1935, 10.

404   **"I give all this"**: Josep Palau-Fabre, "D'una conversa amb García Lorca," *La Humanitat* (Barcelona), October 4, 1935, in *OC*, III, 595.

404   **Critical and audience response to *Yerma***: G. Sánchez Boxa, "Los estrenos, Barcelona. *Yerma*, drama en tres actos de Federico García Lorca," *El Día Gráfico* (Barcelona), September 19, 1935, 17; María Luz Morales, "Teatro Barcelona. Un sensacional estreno. *Yerma*, poema trágico en tres actos, de Federico García Lorca," *La Vanguardia* (Barcelona), September 19, 1935, 10; Valentín Moragas, *Diario de Barcelona*, September 19, 1935, 5; Mario Hernández, introduction to FGL, *Yerma*, 10; Aguirre, "Crónica de Barcelona. *Yerma* y Margarita Xirgu" (no source, no date), AFFGL.

404   **"We authors"**: *La Noche* (Barcelona), September 26, 1935, in Mario Hernández, notes to FGL, *Yerma*, 173.

404   **"more than sixty thousand"**: Jou.

404   **"trivial words"**: Sebastian Gasch, prologue to FGL, *Cartas a sus amigos* (Barcelona: Cobalto, 1950), 14.

404   **"*Yerma*'s success . . . these days"**: *EC*, 816.

404   **"to be careful"**: Vicenta García Lorca to FGL (October 4, 1935), AFFGL.

405   **FGL gives reading to commemorate Asturian revolution**: *EC*, 816–17; *La Rambla de Catalunya* (Barcelona), October 7, 1935, 4; "Margarita Xirgu i García Lorca donaren diumenge, a les onze del mati, al teatre Barcelona, un recital de poesíes organitzat per l'Ateneu Enciclopèdic Popular," *La Humanitat* (Barcelona), October 8, 1935, 2; Juan G. Olmedilla, "García Lorca y su romancero del pueblo," *Defensor de Granada*, October 12, 1935, 1.

405–6   **"It's too frivolous . . . for our civilization"**: Jou.

406   **Italian invasion of Abyssinia**: *La Publicitat* (Barcelona), October 5, 1935, 1, 4; "World War II: International Relations," in *The New Encyclopaedia Britannica* 21, Macropaedia. Knowledge in Depth, 15th ed. (Chicago: Encyclopaedia Britannica, 1997), 834–36. For FGL and Xirgu's response to the news, see Miguel Pérez-Ferrero, "La commemoración del Tricentenario de Lope de Vega," *Heraldo de Madrid*, August 22, 1935, 7; "Para el entreacto. Margarita Xirgu no irá a Italia, en cambio volverá a actuar en Barcelona," *El Día Gráfico* (Barcelona), October 12, 1935; "Los intelectuales y la paz: Los pueblos que presencien impasibles la ruina de Etiopía siembran la suya propia," *Diario de Madrid*, November 9, 1935, 3. On FGL's desire to write "work of peace" see Morales, 208–9.

406   **Xirgu tribute**: "El vinent dia 2, a l'Olympia: Gran homenatge popular a Margarida Xirgu," *La Publicitat* (Barcelona), October 11, 1935, 8; "Homenatge popular a Margarita Xirgu," *La Publicitat* (Barcelona), October 24, 1935, 1; "Anoche, en el Olympia . . . El homenaje a Margarita Xirgu," *El Día Gráfico* (Barcelona), October 24, 1935.

407   **FGL reunited with Dalís**: Dalí, *Salvador Dalí escribe a Federico García Lorca*, 96–97, 149, 155; Rodrigo, *Lorca-Dalí*, 218–21; Rodrigo, *García Lorca*, 263; "Ecos," *La Humanitat* (Barcelona), October 1, 1935, 5; *G*, *II*, 384; "Obertura de curs dels 'Amics de la Poesía,'" *La Publicitat* (Barcelona), October 5, 1935, 4; Josep Palau-Fabre, "D'una conversa amb García Lorca," *La Humanitat* (Barcelona), October 4, 1935, in *OC*, III, 604; Luengo; Jou.

408   **Xirgu goes on tour**: *El Día Gráfico* (Barcelona), October 26, 1935, 17; *Diario de Valencia*, October 24–November 13, 1935; *El Mercantil Valenciano*, November 6–12, 1935; *EC*, 815; "Federico García Lorca en Valencia," *El Mercantil Valenciano*, November 10, 1935, 4; *El Sol* (Madrid), November 5, 1935; Morla Lynch, 469; "Teatro Principal *Yerma*," *El Mercantil Valenciano*, November 6, 1935, 7; Rodrigo, *García Lorca*, 288; *G*, *II*, 391, 553.

408   **"fragility . . . face-to-face with death"**: Morla Lynch, 79.

408 **"social and sexual"**: Luengo.

408 **"influence the historic destiny"**: "Los actos políticos del domingo en Valencia. Conferencia de Augusto Barcia," *El Mercantil Valenciano*, November 12, 1935, 4.

409 **FGL writes "Sonnets of Dark Love"**: Anderson, *Lorca's Late Poetry*, 305–10, 447; Mario Hernández, "Jardín deshecho: Los 'Sonetos' de García Lorca," *El Crotalón* I (1984), 200–1; Miguel García-Posada, "Un monumento al amor," *ABC* (Madrid), March 17, 1984, 43–44; AFFGL; Gil-Albert, 185–86; Luis Antonio de Villena, *El razonamiento inagotable de Juan Gil-Albert* (Madrid: Anjana, 1984), 28–29; Celaya, 146–47.

409 **"the love of difficult passion . . . suffer!"**: G, II, 393–94; José Luis Cano, *Los cuadernos de Velintonia* (Barcelona: Seix Barral, 1986), 284–85; Aleixandre, 43–45.

409 **Popularity of love poetry**: Jaime Brihuega, *Manifiestos, proclamas, panfletos y textos doctrinales. Las vanguardias artísticas en España. 1910–1931* (Madrid: Ediciones, 1979), 68–72; Anderson, *Lorca's Late Poetry*, 650; Ernesto Giménez Caballero, "Literatura española, 1918–1930," in *Los vanguardistas españoles (1925–1935)*, ed. Ramón Buckley and John Crispin (Madrid: El Libro de Bolsillo, Alianza, 1973), 54. On FGL's waltz poems, see Mario Hernández, "Antología y prólogo a 10 poemas sobre el vals," *Poesía* 29 (Madrid, October 1987), 118–21; Morla Lynch, 309; Suero, "Crónica."

410 **"crusade . . . meter and rhyme"**: Felipe Morales, "Conversaciones literarias. Al habla con Federico García Lorca," *La Voz* (Madrid), April 7, 1936, in OC, III, 633, trans. Anderson, *Lorca's Late Poetry*, 490.

410 **"apparently cold" and "an eternal feeling"**: EC, 240.

410 **"You can't be a poet"**: Martínez Nadal, introduction to FGL, *Poems*, xxv.

410 **"One hundred sonnets"**: As told to Joaquín Romero Murube, in Miguel García-Posada, "Un monumento al amor," *ABC* (Madrid), March 17, 1984, 44.

410 **"could not have been written"**: Author interview with José Antonio Rubio Sacristán.

410 **"never stopped being"**: Vázquez Ocaña, *García Lorca: Vida*, 338.

410 **"Sonnets of Dark Love"**: All quotations are taken from OC, I, 627–34, trans. FGL, *Collected Poems*, 712–35. On FGL's visit to Cuenca see Florencio Martínez Ruiz, "El día que García Lorca estuvo en la Ciudad Encantada," *El Día de Cuenca*, April 14, 1991, 24–25.

413 **"tragedy" and "drama"**: "García Lorca i la gairebé estrena de 'Bodas de Sangre' per Margarida Xirgu," *L'Instant* (Barcelona), November 21, 1935, in OC, III, 617. On Xirgu's production see *El Día Gráfico* (Barcelona), November 22, 23, and 26, 1935; *La Vanguardia* (Barcelona), November 24, 1935, 11; and Rivas Cherif, January 27, 1957.

413 **Rapún in Barcelona**: Letter from José Caballero to FGL (late November–early December 1935), AFFGL; Rivas Cherif, January 13 and 27, 1957. On FGL's jealousy, see G, II, 553.

413 **FGL meets with Rivas Cherif**: Rivas Cherif, January 13 and 27, 1957.

414 **"realist drama . . . Don't write it"**: Rivas Cherif, January 27, 1957; see also FGL, "La bola negra," in OC, II, 766–67.

414 **FGL goes to Madrid**: Rodrigo, *García Lorca*, 310; *La Noche* (Barcelona), December 4, 1935, 9, and December 10, 1935, 9; Saenz de la Calzada, 97, 102; G, II, 400–1; Byrd, 86; *El Sol* (Madrid), December 1, 1935, 6.

414 **Doña Rosita opens in Barcelona**: *Crónica* (Madrid), December 15, 1935; José Monleón, "García Lorca y su 'Doña Rosita la Soltera,' " in FGL, *Doña Rosita*, 34–35; Hernandez, introduction to *FM*, xxv; G, II, 401; unidentified press clipping, Library of the Institut del Teatre, Barcelona; author interview with Isabel García Lorca.

415 **"What magnificent bad taste!"**: Rodrigo, *García Lorca*, 311.

415 **"marvelous" and "An intense emotion"**: "Para el entreacto," *El Día Gráfico* (Barcelona), December 14, 1935, 15.

415 **Critical response to *Rosita***: Fernández Cifuentes, 213–26; Antonio de Obregón, "Un es-

treno en el Principal Palace de Barcelona," *Diario de Madrid*, December 14, 1935, 2; María Luz Morales review in *La Noche* (Barcelona), December 14, 1935, 9; Cruz Saudo, "En Barcelona. Margarita Xirgu. Estreno de una obra de García Lorca," *Política* (Madrid), December 15, 1935, 2; Marín Alcalde, "Margarita Xirgu estrena en Barcelona una comedia de García Lorca," *Ahora* (Madrid), December 14, 1935, 29; Andreu A. Artis review in *Última Hora*, December 13, 1935, 7; *El Día Gráfico* (Barcelona), December 14, 1935, 15; Antonio Espina, "Estreno de la última obra de Garcia Lorca en el Principal Palacio de Barcelona," *El Sol* (Madrid), December 15, 1935, 4; Ignasi Agustí review in *L'Instant* (Barcelona), December 16, 1935, cited in Luis Fernández Cifuentes, "Doña Rosita la soltera o el lenguaje de las flores," *Cuadernos Hispanoamericanos* 433–34, vol. I (July–August 1986), 322.

416 **"I don't do anything well"**: Agustí, 88–90.

416 **"a real novice . . . like a dense orb"**: Luengo.

416 **"youngest and dearest daughter"**: Morales, 180; "A proposit de 'Doña Rosita la soltera.' García Lorca; les floristes de la Rambla," *La Publicitat* (Barcelona), December 25, 1935, 8, in *OC*, III, 269–70.

416 **FGL becomes toast of Barcelona:** "En Miramar. Margarita Xirgu ofreció un banquete a los críticos teatrales de Madrid y Barcelona," *El Día Gráfico* (Barcelona), December 14, 1935, 15; Rodrigo, *García Lorca*, 322. On FGL's homage to Albéniz see *El Día Gráfico* (Barcelona), December 15, 1935, and *La Noche* (Barcelona), December 14, 1935, 2.

416 **"I'm now writing"**: Celaya, 147.

416 **Xirgu gives performance for florists:** "A proposit de 'Doña Rosita la soltera.' García Lorca; les floristes de la Rambla," *La Publicitat* (Barcelona), December 25, 1935, 8, in *OC*, III, 269–70; "Margarita Xirgu y las floristas," *El Día Gráfico* (Barcelona), December 19, 1935, 17; Morales, 210; Rodrigo, *Margarita Xirgu*, 231.

416 **"This is the revolution"**: Antonio Serrano Plaja, "En la muerte de Federico García Lorca," in *Homenaje al poeta Federico García Lorca*, cited in *Federico García Lorca y su teatro* (Madrid: Concejalia de Cultura—Ayuntamiento de Madrid, 1984), 57–58.

416 **Barcelona honors FGL:** *Renovación*, December 22, 1935, 7; "Banquete de homenaje a García Lorca," *El Día Gráfico* (Barcelona), December 25, 1935, 17; *La Vanguardia* (Barcelona), December 25, 1935, 11; *FM*, 286.

417 **"how I feel . . . it's fine as it is"**: Luis Góngora, "Apostillas a una cena de artistas," *La Noche* (Barcelona), December 24, 1935, in *OC*, III, 623.

26. THE DREAM OF LIFE: 1936

418 **Fuente Vaqueros sends greetings to FGL:** FGL, *Alocución al pueblo de Fuentevaqueros*, 13, 78.

418 **"gushing"**: Salinas and Guillén, 168.

418 **Xirgu leaves for South America:** "Adiós a Barcelona de Margarita Xirgu," *La Vanguardia* (Barcelona), January 4, 1936, 17; Rodrigo, *García Lorca*, 333. On FGL's plans to accompany Xirgu, see "Conversaciones," *La Voz* (Madrid), January 25, 1936, in *OC*, III, 632–33; Luis Góngora, "Apostillas a una cena de artistas," *La Noche* (Barcelona), December 24, 1935, in *OC*, III, 624; and Agustí, 90, 94.

418 **FGL inscribes *First Songs* for Rapún:** Tomás Rodríguez Rapún Archive.

419 **"I'm so lazy"**: Otero Seco.

419 **"take all his papers"**: Suero, "Los últimos días."

419 **"I don't believe"**: Jou.

419 **FGL projects, early 1936:** Mario Hernández, introduction to FGL, *Primeras canciones*, 13;

Armand Guibert and Louis Parrot, eds., *Federico García Lorca* (Paris: Seghers, 1964), 6; Maurer, "De la correspondencia," 80–85; Martínez Nadal, *Lorca's The Public*, 13; Mario Hernández, notes to FGL, *Bodas de sangre*, 222; Mario Hernández, introduction to FGL, *Yerma*, 12–16, citing "Apuntes," *Eco, Revista de España II*, 8 (May–June 1934); Otero Seco.

419 "**will be so heavy**": Otero Seco.

419 "**feverish**" **and** "**ultramodern**": "Sección de rumores," *Heraldo de Madrid*, February 12, 1936, 9.

419 **FGL titles play *The Dream of Life***: "Sección de rumores," *Heraldo de Madrid*, May 29, 1936, 9. Prior to Ian Gibson's publication of this interview in 1986, *The Dream of Life* was commonly known as "Play without a Title," a title by which some critics still refer to the work.

419 "**comedy,**" "**drama,**" **and** "**political tragedy**": Marie Laffranque, introduction and notes, in FGL, *Teatro inconcluso*, 87. See also "García Lorca en la Plaza de Cataluña," *El Día Gráfico* (Barcelona), September 17, 1935, in *OC*, III, 584; and Otero Seco.

419 **FGL writes *The Dream of Life***: "Sección de rumores," *Heraldo de Madrid*, February 12, 1936, 9; Marie Laffranque, introduction to FGL, *El Público y Comedia sin título*, 284; Marie Laffranque, introduction and notes, in FGL, *Teatro inconcluso*, 93–94; Suero, "Los últimos días"; César Tiempo, "Homenaje a García Lorca," *Argentores* xxxi (Buenos Aires, July–December 1966), 20.

419 *The Dream of Life*: All quotations from the play are taken from *OC*, II, 769–86.

420 *Dragon*: *OC*, II, 762–64.

420 "**completely subversive act**": Luengo. On FGL's admiration for Erwin Piscator, see "Federico García Lorca parla per als obrers catalans," *L'Hora* (Palma de Mallorca), September 27, 1935, 4, in *OC*, III, 599–600.

420 "**my constant anguish**": Luengo.

420 **Xirgu hears script**: Rodrigo, *García Lorca*, 291–92; León.

421 **Political developments in Spain, early 1936**: Thomas, 128–29; Jackson, 176–77; Southworth, 8–9; *ABC* (Madrid), January 14, 1936; Preston, 109–14.

422 **FGL's support of communist causes**: Molina Fajardo, 358–59; Morla Lynch, 293; Jou; "Federico García Lorca parla per als obrers catalans," *L'Hora* (Palma de Mallorca), September 27, 1935, in *OC*, III, 597–98; *Nuestro Cínema* IV, 17, 2nd series (August 1935), cited in Rafael Utrera, *García Lorca y el cínema*. "*Lienzo de plata para un viaje a la Luna*," prologue by Miguel García-Posada (Sevilla: EdiSur, 1982), 40. On his desire to know Russia personally, see *EC*, 821.

422 **Alberti homage**: "En honor de dos poetas," *El Sol* (Madrid), February 8, 1936, 2; *La Libertad* (Madrid), February 8, 1936, 9; *El Socialista* (Madrid), February 9 and 11, 1936; *Mundo Obrero*, February 11, 1936, 5; *FM*, 403–4; Robert Marrast, *Rafael Alberti en México* (1936) (Santander: La Isla de los Ratones, 1984). For photo of FGL and others see FGL, *Antología comentada (I, Poesía)*, ed. Eutimio Martín (Madrid: Ediciones de la Torre, 1988).

423 **Valle-Inclán homage**: *La Libertad* (Madrid), February 15, 1936, 4; *El Sol* (Madrid), February 15, 1936, 8; Agustí, 94; *El Socialista* (Madrid), February 14, 1936, 5; *Mundo Obrero*, February 15, 1936, 5; "Ha muerto Valle-Inclán," *El Sol* (Madrid), January 7, 1936, 1, 6.

423 "**If we don't win**": Suero, "Los últimos días."

423 **February 1936 elections**: Thomas, 129–37; Preston, 114–24; Jackson, 186–97; Southworth, 9–10; *ABC* (Madrid), February 18, 1936; Pablo Suero, "Los jovenes poetas están con la España nueva," in Eutimio Martín, "Un testimonio olvidado sobre García Lorca en el libro *España levanta el puño*, de Pablo Suero," *Trece de Nieve*, 2nd series, 3 (Madrid, May 1977), 80–82.

425 "**more poisoned**": Salinas and Guillén, 171.

425   **FGL signs manifestos and contributes to liberal causes:** *Mundo Obrero*, February 15, 1936, 3, and March 31, 1936, 6; *El Sol* (Madrid), February 23, 1936; Juan Cano Ballesta, "Peripecias de una amistad: Lorca y Miguel Hernández," *Cuadernos Hispanoamericanos* 433–36 (July–August 1986), 220; "En Madrid hay un club infántil," *Ahora* (Madrid), February 16, 1936; *El Socialista* (Madrid), March 29, 1936, 4; Gibson, *El asesinato*, 352–55; *FM*, 403; Hortensia Campanella, "Profeta en toda tierra. Federico García Lorca, en Uruguay," *Insula* 384 (November 1978), 10.

425   **"As an observer of life":** "Federico García Lorca parla per als obrers catalans," *L'Hora* (Palma de Mallorca), September 27, 1935, 4, in *OC*, III, 600.

425   **"the social trap" and "scorchingly communist drama":** Salinas and Guillén, 171.

426   **"an anarchist-communist-libertarian":** Rafael Martínez Nadal, *El público, Amor y muerte un la obra de Federico García Lorca*, 2nd ed. (Mexico City: Joaquín Mortiz, 1974), 276.

426   **"Look, I greet some people":** Penón, 188.

426   **FGL receives court citation:** Otero Seco; Manuel Iglesias Corral, "Recuerdos históricos," *La Voz de Galicia* (La Coruña), August 24, 1983, 3, cited in *G*, *II*, 411–12; *FM*, xxv; author interview with Santiago Ontañón.

426   **FGL travels to San Sebastián:** "En el Ateneo. El poeta García Lorca y su Romancero Gitano," *El Pueblo Vasco* (San Sebastián), March 8, 1936, 2; FGL, [Conferencia-recital del *Romancero gitano*], in *OC*, III, 184.

426   **Cernuda tribute:** "Homenaje a Luis Cernuda. García Lorca leyó un bello trabajo sobre el poeta y su obra," *El Sol* (Madrid), April 21, 1936; Gil-Albert, 192, 201; Paloma Ulacía Altolaguirre, *Concha Méndez. Memorias habladas, memorias armadas*, introduction by María Zambrano (Madrid: Mondadori España, 1990), 97–98; Altolaguirre, *Obras completas I, Caballo griego*, 86–87, and *Estudios literarios*, 235; Antonio Aparicio, "Federico García Lorca y su época," *Atenea XCIII*, 286 (1949), 58.

426   **"Envy and petty grievances":** Jou.

427   **"as if in a dream":** Paloma Ulacía Altolaguirre, *Concha Méndez. Memorias habladas, memorias armadas*, introduction by María Zambrano (Madrid: Mondadori España, 1990), 97–98.

427   **Escalating violence:** Thomas, 138–45, 153; Preston, 128–31; Jackson, 197–98; Payne, 100; Southworth, 10; *Heraldo de Madrid*, April 7 and 14, 1936; May 2 and 9, 1936; *El Socialista* (Madrid), May 9, 1936; *La Libertad* (Madrid), May 10, 1936.

427   **FGL's social life, spring 1936:** Morla Lynch 479–81; Felipe Morales, "Conversaciones literarias. Al habla con Federico García Lorca," *La Voz* (Madrid), April 7, 1936, in *OC*, III, 631–33.

427   **"richer than ever":** Torre, 69.

427   **FGL projects and publications, spring 1936:** Mario Hernández, introduction to FGL, *Yerma*, 14–15, citing *Cruz y Raya* 23–24 (Madrid, February–March 1935); *Heraldo de Aragón* (Zaragoza), January 21, 1936, 2; Morla Lynch, 90–92; "Universidad Internacional. Matilde Pomés habla de la mujer española, del arte de traducir, de los novelistas y de los poetas españoles," *El Sol* (Madrid), July 19, 1936, 4; *La Barraca y su entorno teatral* (Madrid: Gráficas Oviedo, 1975), 43.

428   **"religious and socioeconomic" and "I see it clearly . . . aren't I?":** Felipe Morales, "Conversaciones literarias. Al habla con Federico García Lorca," *La Voz* (Madrid), April 7, 1936, in *OC*, III, 631–32.

428   **FGL takes part in May Day celebrations:** Carlos G. Santa Cecilia, "La insoportable levedad de Federico," *El País* (Madrid), August 19, 1986, xi; ¡*Ayuda!* (Madrid), May 1, 1936, 5.

428   **"I've come here as a friend":** Torre, 69; Guillermo de Torre, "Presencia de Federico García

Lorca," in *La aventura estética de nuestra edad* (Barcelona: Seix Barral, 1962), 266.

428   **FGL relinquishes La Barraca**: *EC*, 820; Byrd, 86; Auclair, 261; *G, II*, 431; "Una declaración de Federico García Lorca relativa a La Barraca," *La Noche* (Barcelona), April 9, 1936, 15; Valentín de Pedro, " 'El guiñol que a Federico le regalaron en Buenos Aires,' relato de María del Carmen García Lasgoity," *¡Aquí Está!* X, 940, May 21, 1945, 5–21.

429   **Club Anfistora rehearses *Once Five Years Pass***: Auclair, 320–21, Penón, 183; Margarita Ucelay, "Federico García Lorca y el Club Teatral Anfistora: El dramaturgo como director de escena," in Soria Olmedo, 56–59; J. G., "Margarita Ucelay: Recuerdos de la profesora y de la actriz," *El Público* 68 (Madrid, May 1989), 8–9; Ana Mariscal, *Cincuenta años de teatro en Madrid* (Madrid: Avapiés, 1984), 33–34; author interview with Margarita Ucelay.

429   **FGL's "impossible theater"**: Auclair, 321; J. G., "Margarita Ucelay: Recuerdos de la profesora y de la actriz," *El Público* 68 (Madrid, May 1989), 8; "Conversaciones literarias. Al habla con Federico García Lorca" *La Voz* (Madrid), April 7, 1936, in *OC*, III, 631; "Llegó anoche Federico García Lorca," *La Nación* (Buenos Aires), October 14, 1933, in *OC*, III, 444.

429–30   **FGL writes *Bernarda Alba***: "Sección de rumores," *Heraldo de Madrid*, May 29, 1936, 9; Salazar, "La casa de Bernarda Alba," 50; Morla Lynch, 483–88; *FM*, 372; José Bergamín, " 'La luz de esta memoria' (Cuando han pasado cuarenta años)," *Sábado Gráfico* (Madrid), March 17, 1976, 20–21; author interview with José Caballero.

430   **Factual basis for *Bernarda Alba***: Morla Lynch, 488–89; *FM*, 376–78; C. B. Morris, *García Lorca. La casa de Bernarda Alba*, Critical Guides to Spanish Texts, 50 (London: Grant and Cutler, 1990), 15; Morris, *Son of Andalusia*, 133–44; Antonio Ramos Espejo, "En Valderrubio, Granada. *La casa de Bernarda Alba*," *Triunfo* XXXIV, 6th series, 4 (Madrid, February 1981), 58–63; Antonina Rodrigo, "La auténtica 'Doña Rosita la soltera,' " *El País Semanal* (Madrid), August 17, 1980, 5; author visit to the cemetery of Valderrubio (formerly Asquerosa), Granada province. Although town records list Frasquita Alba as "Francisca," her contemporaries have always referred to her as "Frasquita," a name I have chosen to retain in the text. I am grateful to José Pérez Rodríguez and Francisco Padilla Martín for having enabled me to consult FGL's confirmation records (Church Archive, Valderrubio, Confirmations [August 15, 1907]) and Frasquita Alba's death certificate (Church Archive, Valderrubio, Burials, no. 25 [July 23, 1924]).

431   **"The only topics that interest me"**: Antonio Aparicio, "Federico García Lorca y su época," *Atenea* XCIII, 286 (1949), 59.

431   ***The House of Bernarda Alba***: All quotations from the play are taken from *OC*, II, 581–634. For commentary on the play see C. B. Morris, *García Lorca. La casa de Bernarda Alba*, Critical Guides to Spanish Texts, 50 (London: Grant and Cutler, 1990); Hernández, introduction to FGL, *La casa de Bernarda Alba*; Fernández Cifuentes; Francisco García Lorca, introduction to FGL, *Three Tragedies*; Altolaguirre, *Obras completas I, Estudios literarios*, 210; *FM*, 376, 435–36; Umbral, 182–83; Arturo Barea, *Lorca: The Poet and His People*, trans. Ilse Barea (New York: Grove Press, 1949). FGL's ideas for the set design come in part from an author interview with José Caballero.

433   **"It's because women are more passionate"**: García-Posada, 86.

433   **"too daring"**: Jean Gebser, *Lorca, poète-dessinateur* (Paris: GLM, 1949), 16, quoted in Hernández, notes to FGL, *La casa de Bernarda Alba*, 168.

433   **"cannot be a Spanish wife"**: *La Alhambra* (Granada), June 15 and 30, 1919, 358.

433   **FGL's trilogies**: On FGL's "trilogy of the Spanish land," see Hernández, introduction to FGL, *La casa de Bernarda Alba*, 29. On his proposed Biblical trilogy, see Marie Laffranque, introduction and notes, in FGL, *Teatro inconcluso*, 13, 51–60; Hernández, introduction to

FGL, *La casa de Bernarda Alba*, 33–34; Salazar, "La casa de Bernarda Alba," 50; Rafael Martínez Nadal, *El Público, Amor y muerte en la obra de Federico García Lorca*, 2nd ed. (Mexico City: Joaquín Mortiz, 1974), 259–62.

434   **Political situation, June 1936:** Thomas, 24–30, 141–59; Jackson, 218–29; Payne, 103–6; Preston, 131–32.

434   **"My laughter today":** Angel Lázaro, "Galería. Federico García Lorca," *La Voz* (Madrid), February 18, 1935, in *OC*, III, 558.

434   **FGL's fear of old age:** FGL, "Los ojos de los viejos" (March 20, 1918), in *OC*, IV, 311–12; Auclair, 206; Luna, "La vida"; "Encuentro con Federico García Lorca," *El Ideal* (Montevideo), February 1, 1934; Isabel Cuchí Coll, *Del Madrid literario . . . Madrid 1933–1934* (San Juan: Imprenta Venezuela, 1935), 80.

434–35   **FGL interview with Luis Bagaría:** Bagaría. On FGL's request that an exchange be deleted from the interview, see *EC*, 823–24.

436   **"I don't want that":** Edgar Neville, "La obra de Federico, bien nacional," *ABC* (Madrid), November 6, 1966.

436   **"abusive":** *G, II,* 447–48.

436   **"Those of us who have mothers like you and I":** Author interview with José Antonio Rubio Sacristán.

436   **FGL continues to contemplate trip to Mexico:** *FM*, xxvi; Felipe Morales, "Conversaciones literarias. Al habla con Federico García Lorca," *La Voz* (Madrid), April 7, 1936, in *OC*, III, 632–33; *El exilio español en México. 1939–1982* (Mexico City: Salvat y Fondo de Cultura Económica, 1982), 636–37; La Argentinita to FGL (May 2, [1936]), cited in Maurer, "De la correspondencia," 85; Auclair, 317; Penón, 117; Morla Lynch, 489; Pablo Suero, *Figuras contemporáneas* (Buenos Aires: Sociedad Impersona Americana, 1943), 54–55; Ian Gibson, "Poeta en Nueva York, Poeta en La Habana," *América* 92, 7 (Madrid, August–September–October 1986); *G, II,* 448; Mario Hernández, "Ochocartas inéditas [Comentario]," *Trece de Nieve*, 2nd series, 1–2, 2nd ed. (Madrid, December 1976), 52. On the possibility of Rapún's accompanying FGL to Mexico, see Rivas Cherif; *G, II,* 409; and author letter from Tomás Rodríguez Rapún (December 22, 1988).

436   **Daily strikes and political killings:** Thomas, 166; Preston, 131–32.

436–37   **FGL's behavior, June–July 1936:** *G, II,* 449–50; AFFGL; Auclair, 322–24; Mario Hernández, "Ocho cartas inéditas [Comentario]," *Trece de Nieve*, 2nd series, 1–2, 2nd ed. (Madrid, December 1976), 52; Martínez Nadal, *Lorca's The Public,* 12; Morla Lynch, 491–92; "El comité español de Amigos de Portugal se dirige a Oliveira Salazar protestando de la política que desarrolla," *Heraldo de Madrid*, July 4, 1936, 15; Cernuda, 16; Neruda, *Passions and Impressions*, 95; Mario Hernández, "Jardín deshecho: Los 'Sonetos' de García Lorca," *El Crotalón* I (1984), 209–10. On FGL's fear of traffic, see José Caballero, "Con Federico en los ensayos de *Yerma,*" *ABC* (Madrid), December 29, 1984, Saturday Cultural section I; Ernesto Guerra da Cal, "Federico, na lembrança," nos. 4-5-6 (Pontevedra, September 1986–March 1987), 65; Cano, 87; Alberti, *La arboleda perdida*, 258; Ontañón.

437   **"I'm a diplomat":** Teitelboim, 197–98.

437–38   **Calvo Sotelo's murder:** Thomas, 169–76; Jackson, 230; Payne, 115.

438   **"What's going to happen?":** Gil-Albert, 185. On the whereabouts of FGL's family, see Fernández-Montesinos, "Descripción," xi–xii.

438   **"Rafael . . . come what may":** Martínez Nadal, *Lorca's The Public,* 14–15.

438   **FGL visits Méndez and Altolaguirre:** Altolaguirre, *Obras completas I, Estudios literarios,* 281; and Paloma Ulacía Altolaguirre, *Concha Méndez. Memorias habladas, memorias armadas,* introduction by María Zambrano (Madrid: Mondadori España, 1990), 99–100. In-

formation on Rapún's whereabouts comes from author interview with Tomás Rodríguez Rapún.

438   **FGL visits sister:** Martínez Nadal, *Lorca's* The Public, 16–17; *G, II,* 454.

438–39   **FGL visits Rodríguez Espinosa:** Rodríguez Espinosa, 110. FGL often visited Rodríguez Espinosa in Madrid (Couffon, 90). For the precise date of FGL's departure, see *G, II,* 453–55, and Molina Fajardo, 26–27. Ian Gibson has convincingly disproved Martínez Nadal's contention (*Lorca's* The Public, 17) that on the night train to Granada FGL encountered the man who would eventually arrest him, Ramón Ruiz Alonso (see *G, II,* 471–72, and Gibson, *El asesinato,* 50–52).

27. FOUNTAIN: 1936

440   **"The soul went back":** *FM,* xxvi.

440   **News coverage of FGL's arrival:** *Defensor de Granada,* July 15, 1936, 1; *Ideal* (Granada), July 16, 1936, 6; *El Noticiero Granadino,* July 17, 1936, 4. For installation of telephone in Huerta, see Gibson, "La 'Huerta de San Vicente,' " 21–30.

441   **"in a state of unrest":** *Ideal* (Granada), July 1, 1936, 3; for a general account of Granada in early July 1936, see *Historia de la Cruzada Española.*

441   **FGL writes Aurelia:** *FM,* xxvi; Marie Laffranque, introduction and notes, in FGL, *Teatro inconcluso,* 68; FGL's interview with Antonio Otero Seco was published posthumously in *La Voz* (Madrid), October 8, 1936, in *OC, III,* 626; Gregorio Prieto, "Historia de un libro," *Cuadernos Hispanoamericanos* (July–August 1949), 21; Gregorio Prieto, *Lorca en color* (Madrid: Editora Nacional, 1969), 29–33.

441   *The Dreams of My Cousin Aurelia: OC, II,* 787–807.

442   **"therapeutic slap . . . of her house":** "Sección de rumores," *Heraldo de Madrid,* May 29, 1936, 9.

442–43   **First days of war, July 17 and 18:** Thomas, 165, 181–88; *Historia de la Cruzada Española,* 276–78; Preston, 141.

443   **FGL's saint's day:** Gibson, "La 'Huerta de San Vicente,' " 24; Gibson, *El asesinato,* 173; Antonio Valverde, " 'Lorca tenía miedo al inicio de la guerra,' " *El Día de Granada,* August 17, 1986, 5; author interview with Vicente López.

443   **"García Lorca. 'Precious child' ":** *Heraldo de Madrid,* July 18, 1936, 3.

443–44   **Conflicting radio reports, July 18:** *Historia de la Cruzada Española,* 183, 278; Thomas, 191.

444   **Events on the Spanish mainland, July 19 and 20:** *Ideal* (Granada), July 19, 1936, 1–3; Thomas, 194–206; Brenan, *The Spanish Labyrinth,* 314.

445   **Nationalists seize Granada, July 20–23:** *Historia de la Cruzada Española,* 280–89; Thomas, 204–5, 211–13; Helen Nicholson, *Death in the Morning* (London: Loval Dickson, 1937), 20–24; "Mass Executions and Air Raids in Spain Related in Neville Diary. Granada Incidents of Civil War Are Described by *Herald Tribune* Bridge Editor; Victims of Firing Squad Hauled Alive to Cemetery," *New York Herald Tribune,* August 30, 1936, section II, 1 and 6; *Ideal* (Granada), July 21, 22, 23, and 24, 1936; *El Correo de Andalucía* (Seville), July 21, 1936, 1; author interview with Bernardo Olmedo. For an eyewitness account of the insurrection, see Gallego Morell, *Antonio Gallego Burín,* 81–82.

446   **Executions begin in Granada:** "Mass Executions and Air Raids in Spain Related in Neville Diary. Granada Incidents of Civil War Are Described by *Herald Tribune* Bridge Editor; Victims of Firing Squad Hauled Alive to Cemetery," *New York Herald Tribune,* August 30, 1936, section II, 1 and 6; Helen Nicholson, *Death in the Morning* (London: Loval Dickson, 1937),

20–24; *Ideal* (Granada), August 1, 8, and 11, 1936; Gibson, *The Assassination*, 99–100, 103–5, 109–11; Couffon, 127; Molina Fajardo, 50, 308–11, 404, 421; author interview with Enrique Lanz Durán.

447 **FGL nightmare:** Gibson, "La 'Huerta de San Vicente,' " 26.

447 **Lorca family's response to events:** Gibson, *The Assassination*, 114; author interview with Vicente López; author interview with Carmen Perea.

447 **Republicans bomb Granada:** Penón, 88; *Ideal* (Granada), July 30, 1936, and August 1, 1936, 1; Helen Nicholson, *Death in the Morning* (London: Loval Dickson, 1937), 28–32; Gibson, *El asesinato*, 106.

447 **Falange squad searches Huerta, August 6:** Gibson, "La 'Huerta de San Vicente,' " 26; Molina Fajardo, 347.

447 **Rodríguez Orgaz seeks help from Lorca family:** Penón, 83, 199; Molina Fajardo, 31; Gibson, *El asesinato*, 175.

448 **Falangists interrogate Huerta residents, August 9:** Gibson, "La 'Huerta de San Vicente,' " 27–28; Molina Fajardo, 347; Gibson, *El asesinato*, 177–79; *Ideal* (Granada), August 10, 1936; author interview with Carmen Perea.

449 **FGL elects to go to Rosales home:** Tico Medina, "Introducción a la muerte de Federico García Lorca," *ABC* (Madrid), August 20, 1972, 20; *G, II*, 463–64; Auclair, 334–36; Gibson, *El asesinato*, 181–82; Gibson, "La 'Huerta de San Vicente,' " 28; Ian Gibson, "Luis Rosales aclara su actuación y la de su familia," *Triunfo* (Madrid), February 24, 1979, 43; *FM*, xxvii; Molina Fajardo, 33–34. For background on Luis Rosales, see Molina Fajardo, 35; Auclair, 178; Augustín Martínez, "Entrevista con Luis Rosales," *Diario* 16 (Andalucía), August 19, 1986, 4; Eutimio Martín, "Testimonio de Luis Rosales sobre *Poeta en Nueva York*, de García Lorca," *El País* (Madrid), January 29, 1978, Art and Ideas section; Antonio Valverde, " 'Federico era una persona casi acosada por todos sus conocidas,' " *El Día de Granada*, August 17, 1986, 4; Gibson, *Federico García Lorca: A Life*, 452; author interview with Vicente López; author interview with Carmen Perea.

449 **Chauffeur drives FGL to Rosales home:** Penón, 155; Auclair, 336; Molina Fajardo, 34; Eulalia-Dolores de la Higuera, "Habla el chofer de García Lorca," *Gentes*, April 1977, 31. For Falange searches of Huertas de San Vicente and Tamarit see Gibson, *El asesinato*, 182–85.

450 **FGL in Rosales home:** Luis Rosales Camacho, *El contenido del corazón* (Madrid: Cultura Hispánica, 1969), 110; Penón, 66, 200–4; Auclair, 336–37; *G, II*, 465–67; Molina Fajardo, 35–43, 185; Higuera Rojas, 195–98; Gibson, *El asesinato*, 189–201; Tico Medina, "Introducción a la muerte de Federico García Lorca," *ABC* (Madrid), August 20, 1972, 20. On Lorca's possible writing activities at the Rosales home, see Mario Hernández, "Jardín deshecho: Los 'Sonetos' de García Lorca," *El Crotalón* I (1984), 206–8, 220–22; Mario Hernández, notes to FGL, *La casa de Bernarda Alba*, 168–69; Couffon, 117; Ian Gibson, "Luis Rosales aclara su actuación y la de su familia," *Triunfo* (Madrid), February 24, 1979, 42; Auclair, 337; and Gibson, *El asesinato*, 202.

451 **Montesinos execution:** Gibson, *El asesinato*, 202–4; *G, II*, 468; *FM*, xxvi.

452 **FGL arrested:** Gibson, "La 'Huerta de San Vicente,' " 28; Auclair, 337–46, 377; Molina Fajardo, 41–42, 187; Gibson, *El asesinato*, 206–16; *G, II*, 472–73; Higuera Rojas, 198; Penón, 47, 200–4. Eduardo Molina Fajardo has uncovered an undated official report noting that Lorca was "arrested and accused" by Ruiz Alonso, and that the charges against the poet "were numerous and made in writing" (Molina Fajardo, 375). For further discussion of Ruiz Alonso's role in Lorca's arrest see Penón, 32; Gibson, *El asesinato*, 148–64; *G, II*, 470–71; Molina Fajardo, 47, 375; and Auclair, 338.

453   Don Federico and Mr. Rosales see lawyer: Gibson, *El asesinato*, 222–23; Auclair, 346.

453   FGL in Civil Government building: Penón, 33–34; Gibson, *El asesinato*, 218–22; Molina
       Fajardo, 44–45, 347–48; Auclair, 347–49; Higuera Rojas, 201.

453   Rosales family contributes to Falange: *Ideal* (Granada), August 19, 1936, 6, and August 20,
       1936, 4.

453   Angelina Cordobilla visits FGL: Penón, 87; Gibson, *El asesinato*, 223–26.

453–54 FGL driven to Víznar: Penón, 42, 53–56; G, II, 481–86; Ian Gibson, "El último día de
       García Lorca," *El País* (Madrid), August 19, 1986, 11; Gibson, *El asesinato*, 235–39; Auclair,
       356–59; Molina Fajardo, 51, 61. There is conflicting evidence about the precise date of
       Lorca's departure from the Civil Government building and subsequent murder in Víznar;
       the most compelling and consistent testimony, however, points to the early morning of Au-
       gust 18 as the correct date for both events (see G, II, 481–82).

454   FGL in La Colonia: Auclair, 360; Molina Fajardo, 52, 244; Gibson, *El asesinato*, 241–44.

454   Fuente Grande: Gibson, *El asesinato*, 255–56; Antonio Gallego Burín, *Guía de Granada*
       (Granada, 1946); José Acosta Medina, *La Granada de ayer* (Granada: Imprenta Márquez,
       1973); Molina Fajardo, 52. Lorca himself alluded to the fountain in his 1926 lecture on Soto
       de Rojas, where he mentioned that Granada's gardens are "irrigated by the waters of Al-
       facar" (OC, III, 79).

454   FGL's death: According to Molina Fajardo, deaths at the Víznar execution site usually took
       place at approximately 4 a.m. (Molina Fajardo, 63). José Jover Tripaldi claimed that it was
       shortly before dawn when he heard the shots that killed FGL and his colleagues: "It was ap-
       proximately 4:45 in the morning, and daylight was just beginning to break" (Penón, 56, 172).
       See also Gibson, *El asesinato*, 245–58; Molina Fajardo, 65; Río, "Federico García Lorca," 210.

EPILOGUE

455   Angelina Cordobilla visits Civil Government building: Penón, 85; Gibson, *El asesinato*,
       223–26.

455   Manuel de Falla visits Civil Government building: Mora Guarnido, 199–200; Auclair,
       346–47, 408; Molina Fajardo, 69–70; Gibson, *El asesinato*, 260–61.

455   Lorca family learns of FGL's death: FM, xxvii.

455   Don Federico receives FGL letter: EC, 825. See also Penón, 77, 85, and 156; Eulalia-
       Dolores de la Higuera, "Habla el chofer de García Lorca," *Gentes*, April 1977, 30–33; G, II,
       488. Accounts differ as to whether the requested sum was 1,000 or 2,000 pesetas; the note it-
       self has not been preserved.

455–56 Friends respond to news of FGL's death: Lilice Valenzuela, "Los pasos cubanos de
       García Lorca," *La Habana*, August 23, 1986, 5; Neruda, *Passions and Impressions*, 59–60;
       Juan Ramón Jiménez, "Federico García Lorca, cárdeno," in *Españoles de tres mundos*,
       ed. Ricardo Gullón (Madrid: Aguilar, 1969), 343; Salinas; Teitelboim, 205–7; Antonio
       Machado, *Selected Poems*, trans. Alan S. Trueblood (Cambridge, Mass.: Harvard University
       Press, 1982), 265.

456   "stupid regime . . . hatred for intelligence": José Bergamín, "Unamuno, testigo excep-
       cional. Dos cartas inéditas en víspera de su muerte," *Historia* 16, 1, 7 (1976), trans. GM, xxvi.

456   The Spanish Civil War: See Peter Weyden, *The Passionate War* (New York: Simon and
       Schuster, 1983, and Thomas.

457   Rapún's death: Tomás Rodríguez Rapún Archive.

457   False reports of Benavente's and others' deaths: *Ideal* (Granada), August 21, 1936, 2, and
       August 22, 1936, 1; G, II, 479–80; Gibson, *El asesinato*, 229–30.

457   **Government issues death certificate:** Gibson, *The Assassination*, 124.

458   **Lorca family's post-war activities:** *FM*, xxviii–xxx; author conversation with Manuel Fernández-Montesinos.

458   **Generation of '27 in exile:** C. B. Morris, *A Generation of Spanish Poets*, 233–46.

459   **"The moment I learned . . . the most apolitical person on earth":** Alain Bosquet, *Entretien avec Salvador Dalí* (Paris: Pierre Belfond, 1966), 50, and Salvador Dalí, *The Secret Life of Salvador Dalí*, 3rd ed. (London: Vision Press, 1968), 361.

459   **"an extraordinary creature":** Guillén, "Federico en persona," xvii.

459   **"something that walks," "unpredictable path," and "Poetry has no limits . . . of oil":** María Luz Morales, "Conversaciones," *La Voz* (Madrid), April 7, 1936, in *OC*, III, 628–29.

461   **"four thousand five hundred":** "García Lorca ante el teatro. Sus recuerdos de Buenos Aires," Transradio Española (May 1935), in *OC*, III, 566.

461   **"I'm in love":** Nicolás González-Deleito, "Federico García Lorca y el teatro de hoy," *Escena* 1 (Madrid, May 1935), in *OC*, III, 565.

BIBLIOGRAPHY

WORKS BY FEDERICO GARCÍA LORCA

Alocución al pueblo de Fuentevaqueros. Facsimile ed. Ed. Manuel Fernández and Andrés Soria Olmedo. Prologue by Andrés Soria Olmedo. Granada: Edición del Cincuentenario, 1986.

Alocuciones argentinas. Madrid: Fundación Federico García Lorca, 1985.

Autógrafos I. Facsímiles de ochenta y siete poemas y tres prosas. Ed. Rafael Martínez Nadal. Oxford: The Dolphin Book Club, 1975.

Autógrafos II. El Público. Facsímil del manuscrito. Ed. Rafael Martínez Nadal. Oxford: The Dolphin Book Club, 1976.

Autógrafos III. Facsímil de Así que pasen cinco años. Ed. Rafael Martínez Nadal. Oxford: The Dolphin Book Club, 1979.

Bodas de sangre. Ed. Mario Hernández. Madrid: Alianza, 1984.

Canciones. 1921–1924. Ed. Mario Hernández. Madrid: Alianza, 1982.

Collected Poems. Ed. Christopher Maurer. Trans. Francisco Aragon, Catherine Brown, Will Kirkland, William Bryant Logan, David K. Loughran, Christopher Maurer, Jerome Rothenberg, Greg Simon, Alan S. Trueblood, Elizabeth Umlas, John K. Walsh, and Steven F. White. New York: Farrar, Straus and Giroux, 1991.

Conferencias. Ed. Christopher Maurer. 2 vols. Madrid: Alianza, 1984.

Deep Song and Other Prose. Ed. and trans. Christopher Maurer. 3rd ed. New York: New Directions, 1980.

Dibujos. Ed. Mario Hernández. Madrid: Ministerio de Cultura, 1986.

Diván del Tamarit. Llanto por Ignacio Sánchez Mejías. Sonetos. Ed. Mario Hernández. Madrid: Alianza, 1981.

Doña Rosita la soltera o El lenguaje de las flores. Poema granadino del novecientos dividido en varios jardines con escenas de canto y baile. Madrid: Centro Dramático Nacional, 1981.

"[Dos cartas a sus padres]. Ateneo de Madrid, 1920; Residencia de Estudiantes, 1921." Ed. Christopher Maurer. *El País* (Madrid), April 11, 1992, Babelia section, 6.

El público. Ed. María Clementa Millán. Madrid: Cátedra, 1987.

El público y Comedia sin título. Dos obras póstumas. Ed. Rafael Martínez Nadal and Marie Laffranque. Barcelona: Seix Barral, 1978.

Epistolario. Ed. Christopher Maurer. 2 vols. Madrid: Alianza, 1983.

Epistolario completo. 1 vol. Bk. I (1910–26), ed. Christopher Maurer. Bk. II (1927–36), ed. Andrew A. Anderson. Madrid: Cátedra, 1997.

Federico García Lorca escribe a su familia desde Nueva York y La Habana [1929–30]. Ed. Christopher Maurer. Special issue of *Poesía* 23–24. Madrid: Ministerio de Cultura, 1986.

Five Plays. Trans. J. Graham-Luján and R. O'Connell. Introduction by Francisco García Lorca. New York: New Directions, 1961.

How a City Sings from November to November. Trans. and ed. Christopher Maurer. San Francisco: Cadmus Editions, 1984.

Impresiones y paisajes. Facsimile ed. Granada: Editorial Don Quijote, 1981.

La casa de Bernarda Alba. Ed. Mario Hernández. 2nd ed. Madrid: Alianza, 1984.

La zapatera prodigiosa. Fin de fiesta. Ed. Mario Hernández. Madrid: Alianza, 1982.

"Lecture: A Poet in New York." Trans. Christopher Maurer. In FGL, *Poet in New York*, 185–201.

Libro de poemas. Ed. Mario Hernández. Madrid: Alianza, 1984.

Lola la comedianta. Prologue by Gerardo Diego. Ed. Piero Menarini. Madrid: Alianza, 1981.

Obras completas. Ed. Miguel García-Posada. 4 vols. Barcelona: Galazia Gutenberg / Círculo de Lectores, 1996.

Oda y burla de Sesostris y Sardanápolo. Ed. Miguel García-Posada. Ferrol: Sociedad de Cultura Valle-Inclán, 1985.

Poema del cante jondo. 1921. Ed. Mario Hernández. Madrid: Alianza, 1982.

Poesía inédita de juventud. Ed. Christian de Paepe. Preface by Marie Laffranque. Madrid: Cátedra, 1994.

Poeta en Nueva York. Tierra y luna. Ed. Eutimio Martín. Barcelona: Editorial Ariel, 1981.

Poet in New York. Trans. Greg Simon and Steven F. White. Ed. Christopher Maurer. Rev. ed. New York: Farrar, Straus and Giroux, 1998.

"The Poet Writes to His Family from New York and Havana." Trans. Christopher Maurer. In FGL, *Poet in New York*, 204–86.

Primeras canciones. Seis poemas gallegos. Poemas sueltos. Canciones populares. Ed. Mario Hernández. Madrid: Alianza, 1981.

Prosa inédita de juventud. Ed. Christopher Maurer. Madrid: Cátedra, 1994.

The Public and Play Without a Title. Trans. Carlos Bauer. New York: New Directions, 1983.

Retablillo de Don Cristóbal y Doña Rosita. Aleluya popular basada en el viejo y desvergonzado guiñol andaluz. Unpublished Buenos Aires version, 1934. Ed. Mario Hernández. Granada: Diputación Provincial de Granada, 1992.

Romancero gitano. Ed. Mario Hernández. Madrid: Alianza, 1981.

The Rural Trilogy: Blood Wedding, Yerma, The House of Bernarda Alba. Trans. Michael Dewell and Carmen Zapata. Introduction by Douglas Day. New York: Bantam, 1987.

Season in Granada, A. Uncollected Poetry and Prose. Trans. and ed. Christopher Maurer. London: Anvil Press Poetry, 1998.

Selected Letters. Ed. and trans. David Gershator. New York: New Directions, 1983.

Songs. Trans. Philip Cummings. With the assistance of Federico García Lorca. Ed. Daniel Eisenberg. Pittsburgh: Duquesne University Press, 1976.

Suites. Ed. André Belamich. Barcelona: Ariel, 1983.

Teatro inconcluso. Fragmentos y proyectos inacabados. Ed. Marie Laffranque. Granada: University of Granada, 1987.

Teatro inédito de juventud. Ed. Andrés Soria Olmedo. Madrid: Cátedra, 1994.
Three Tragedies. Blood Wedding, Yerma, The House of Bernarda Alba. Trans. James Graham-Luján and Richard L. O'Connell. Introduction by Francisco García Lorca. Harmondsworth: Penguin, 1969.
Yerma. Ed. Mario Hernández. 2nd ed. Madrid: Alianza, 1984.

OTHER REFERENCES

Adams, Mildred. *García Lorca: Playwright and Poet.* New York: George Braziller, 1977.
Agustí, Ignacio. *Ganas de hablar.* Barcelona: Planeta, 1974.
Alberti, Rafael. *Federico García Lorca: Poeta y amigo.* Introduction by Luis García Montero. Granada: Biblioteca de la Cultura Andaluza, 1984.
———. "Imagen primera de . . ." In *Federico García Lorca: Poeta y amigo,* 107–33.
———*La arboleda perdida. Libros I y II de memorias.* 6th ed. Barcelona: Seix Barral, 1981.
Aleixandre, Vicente. "Federico." *Hora de España* (Valencia) VII, July 1937, 43–45.
Altolaguirre, Manuel. *Obras completas I. El caballo griego. Crónicas y artículos. Estudios literarios.* Ed. James Valender. Madrid: Ediciones Istmo, 1986.
———. "Recuerdos de Federico García Lorca." *Previsión y Seguridad* (Monterrey) 1944, 601–6.
Anderson, Andrew A. "García Lorca en Montevideo: Una cronología provisional." *Bulletin Hispanique,* LXXXVII, 1–2 (January–June 1985), 167–79.
———. *García Lorca: La zapatera prodigiosa.* Critical Guides to Spanish Texts, 53. London: Grant and Cutler, in association with Tamesis Books, 1991.
———. *Lorca's Late Poetry: A Critical Study.* Liverpool Monographs in Hispanic Studies, 10. Leeds: Francis Cairns, 1990.
———. "Los primeros pasos de 'La Barraca': Una entrevista recuperada, con cronología y comentario." In *L'Imposible / Posible di Federico García Lorca.* Ed. Laura Dolfi. Naples: Edizioni Scientifiche Italiane, 1989. 177–99.
———. "Some Shakespearean Reminiscences in García Lorca's Drama." *Comparative Literature Studies* 22, 2 (summer 1985), 187–210.
Aranda, Francisco. *El surrealismo español.* Barcelona: Lumen, 1981.
Arciniegas, Germán. "Federico García Lorca." *Diario de la Marina* (Havana), April 1, 1930, 16.
Aub, Max. *Conversaciones con Buñuel.* Prologue by Federico Álvarez. Madrid: Aguilar, 1985.
Auclair, Marcelle. *Vida y muerte de García Lorca.* Mexico: Era, 1972.
Bagaría, Luis. "Diálogos de un caricaturista salvaje." *El Sol* (Madrid), June 10, 1936. Reprinted in *OC,* III, 634–39.
Belamich, André. *Lorca.* Paris: Gallimard (Collection Idées), 1983.
Benumeya, Gil. "Estampa de García Lorca." *Gaceta Literaria* (Madrid), January 15, 1931. Reprinted in *OC,* III, 377–80.
Binding, Paul. *Lorca: The Gay Imagination.* London: GMP Publishers, 1985.
Brenan, Gerald. *The Literature of the Spanish People: From Roman Times to the Present Day.* Harmondsworth: Penguin, 1963.
———. *South from Granada.* Cambridge: Cambridge University Press, 1980.
———. *The Spanish Labyrinth: An Account of the Social and Political Background of the Spanish Civil War.* 2nd ed. London: Cambridge University Press, 1969.
Brickell, Herschel. "A Spanish Poet in New York." *The Virginia Quarterly Review* 21 (1945), 386–98.
Buñuel, Luis. *Mi último suspiro. Memorias.* 5th ed. Barcelona: Plaza y Janés, 1985.

———. *Obra literaria*. Ed. Agustín Sánchez Vidal. Zaragoza: El Heraldo de Aragón, 1982.

Byrd, Suzanne. *García Lorca: "La Barraca" and the Spanish National Theatre*. New York: Abra, 1975.

Cabrolié, Martine. *Enquête sur le milieu socio-économique de la famille de Federico García Lorca*. University thesis. University of Toulouse–Le Mirail, 1975.

Cano, José Luis. *García Lorca. Biografía ilustrada*. Barcelona: Destino, 1962.

Cardoza y Aragón, Luis. *El río. Novelas de caballería*. Mexico: Fondo de Cultura Económica, 1986.

Carr, Raymond. *Modern Spain: 1875–1980*. Oxford: Oxford University Press, 1980.

———. *Spain: 1808–1975*. 2nd ed. Oxford: Clarendon Press, 1990.

Casa Museo de Manuel de Falla. 2nd ed. Granada: Exmo. Ayuntamiento de Granada, 1984.

Celaya, Gabriel. "Un recuerdo de Federico García Lorca." *Poesía y verdad*. Barcelona: Planeta, 1979. 120, 146–47.

Cernuda, Luis. "Federico García Lorca (recuerdo)." *Hora de España* 18 (June 1938), 13–20.

Comincioli, Jacques. "En torno a Lorca." *Cuadernos Hispanoamericanos* 139 (July 1961), 37–76.

Couffon, Claude. *À Grenade, sur les pas de García Lorca*. Paris: Seghers, 1962.

Crow, John A. *Federico García Lorca*. Los Angeles: University of California, 1945.

Cummings, Philip. "August in Eden: An Hour of Youth." In FGL, *Songs*, 125–66.

Dalí, Ana María. *Salvador Dalí. Visto por su hermana*. Barcelona: Juventud, 1949.

Dalí, Salvador. *Diario de un genio*. Ed. Robert Descharnes. Barcelona: Tusquets, 1983.

———. *Salvador Dalí escribe a Federico García Lorca (1925–1936)*. Ed. Rafael Santos Torroella. Special issue of *Poesía* 27–28. Madrid: Ministerio de Cultura, 1987.

———. *Vida secreta de Salvador Dalí*. Trans. José Martínez. Figueras: Dasa, 1981.

Dalí, Salvador, with André Parinaud. *Confesiones inconfesables*. Barcelona: Mundo Actual de Ediciones, 1975.

Devoto, Daniel. "Notas sobre el elemento tradicional en la obra de García Lorca." *Filología* (Buenos Aires) II, (1950), 292–341. Reprinted in Gil, *Federico García Lorca*, 23–72.

Díaz-Plaja, Fernando. *El siglo XX. Dictadura República (1923–1936)*. Madrid: Instituto de Estudios Políticos, 1964.

Dougherty, Dru, and María Francisca Vilches. *La escena madrileña entre 1918 y 1926. Análisis y documentación*. Madrid: Fundamentos, 1990.

Eisenberg, Daniel. "A Chronology of Lorca's Visit to New York and Cuba." *Kentucky Romance Quarterly* (1978), 233–50.

———. "Cuatro pesquisas lorquianas." *Thesaurus. Boletín del Instituto Caro y Cuervo*, XXX (Bogotá, 1975).

———. *Textos y documentos lorquianos*. Tallahassee: Dept. of Modern Languages, Florida State University, 1975.

Escobar, Luis. "Cuento y no acabo: capítulo V." *Semana*, December 15, 1984, 82–87.

Fernández Almagro, Melchor. "Primer estreno de Federico García Lorca." *ABC* (Madrid), June 13, 1953.

Fernández Almagro, Melchor, and Antonio Gallego Burín. *Epistolario: 1918–1940*. Ed. Antonio Gallego Morell and Cristina Viñes Millet. Granada: Excma. Diputación Provincial, 1986.

Fernández Cifuentes, Luis. *García Lorca en el teatro: La norma y la diferencia*. Zaragoza: University of Zaragoza, 1986.

Fernández-Montesinos García, Manuel. "Descripción de la biblioteca de Federico García Lorca (catálogo y estudio)." Unpublished thesis, Madrid, Universidad Complutense, 1985.

———. "Federico García Lorca en la Residencia de Estudiantes, 1919–1928." In *Federico García Lorca en la Residencia de Estudiantes*. Fundación Federico García Lorca, Amigos de la Residencia de Estudiantes. Madrid: Tabapress, 1991.

Ferreiro, Alfredo Mario. "García Lorca en Montevideo." In FGL, *Poema del cante jondo*. Santiago de Chile: Veloz, 1937. 135–47. Reprinted in *OC*, III, 508–17.

Gallego Morell, Antonio. *Antonio Gallego Burín*. Madrid: Moneda y Crédito, 1973.

———. *Sobre García Lorca*. Granada: University of Granada, 1993.

García Lorca, Francisco. *Federico y su mundo*. Ed. Mario Hernández. 3rd ed. Madrid: Alianza, 1981.

———. *In the Green Morning: Memories of Federico*. Trans. Christopher Maurer. Prologue by Mario Hernández. New York: New Directions, 1986.

———. Introduction to FGL, *Five Plays*.

———. Prologue to FGL, *Three Tragedies*.

García Lorca, Isabel. "Recuerdos de infancia." In *L'imposible / posible di Federico García Lorca. Atti del convegno di studi Salerno, 9–10 maggio 1988*. Ed. Laura Dolfi. Naples: Edizioni Scientifiche Italiane, 1989. 11–19.

García-Posada, Miguel. "García Lorca en Uruguay." *Triunfo* 21–22 (July–August 1982), 82–88.

Gasch, Sebastian. "A la luz del recuerdo. Las artes y las letras en la Barcelona de los años veintitantos." *San Jorge* (Barcelona) 18 (April 1955), 35–41.

Gibson, Ian. *The Assassination of Federico García Lorca*. New York: Penguin, 1983.

———. *El asesinato de García Lorca*. 2nd ed. Barcelona: Plaza y Janés, 1987.

———. *Federico García Lorca I. De Fuente Vaqueros a Nueva York, 1898–1929*. Barcelona: Grijalbo, 1985.

———. *Federico García Lorca II. De Nueva York a Fuente Grande, 1929–1936*. Barcelona: Grijalbo, 1987.

———. *Federico García Lorca: A Life*. London: Faber and Faber, 1989.

———. "Federico García Lorca, su maestro de música y un artículo olvidado." *Ínsula* XXI (1966), 14.

———. "La 'Huerta de San Vicente.' Los últimos días de García Lorca en Granada." *El País Semanal* (Madrid), August 17, 1986, 21–30.

———. *Lorca's Granada. A Practical Guide*. London: Faber and Faber, 1992.

———. "Salvador Dalí: The Catalán Background." In Gibson et al., *Salvador Dalí: The Early Years*, 49–64.

Gibson, Ian, Rafael Santos Torroella, Fèlix Fanés, Dawn Ades, and Agustín Sánchez Vidal. *Salvador Dalí: The Early Years*. Ed. Michael Raeburn. New York: Thames and Hudson, 1994.

Gil, Ildefonso-Manuel. *Federico García Lorca*. Madrid: Taurus, 1973.

Gil-Albert, Juan. *Memorabilia*. Barcelona: Tusquets, 1975.

Giménez Caballero, Ernesto. "Itinerarios jóvenes de España: Federico García Lorca." *Gaceta Literaria* (Madrid), December 15, 1928. Reprinted in *OC*, III, 364–67.

Guardia, Alfredo de la. *García Lorca, persona y creación*. 4th ed. Buenos Aires: Schapire, 1961.

Guerra da Cal, Ernesto. "13. Federico García Lorca (1898–1936)." In *Rosalía de Castro, Antología poética. Cancioneiro rosaliano*. Centenary homage. Ed. Ernesto Guerra da Cal. Lisbon: Guimaraes, 1985. 193–95.

Guillén, Jorge. "Federico en persona." In vol. 1 of FGL, *Obras completas*. 20th ed. 2 vols. Madrid: Aguilar, 1980. xvii–xxxiv.

———. *Federico en persona. Carteggio*. Milan: All'insegna del Pesce D'Oro, 1960.

Hernández, Mario. "Francisco y Federico García Lorca." Prologue to FM. (Trans. in GM, vii–xxviii.)

———. Introduction to FGL. *Bodas de sangre*.

———. Introduction to FGL, *La casa de Bernarda Alba*.

———. Introduction to FGL, *Poema del cante jondo*. 1921.

———. Introduction to FGL, *Romancero gitano*.

————. "Retablo de las maravillas: Falla, Lorca y Lanz en una fiesta granadina de títeres." In *Federico García Lorca, Teatro de títeres y dibujos. Con decorados y muñecos de Hermenegildo Lanz.* Ed. Mario Hernández. Santander: Universidad Internacional Menéndez y Pelayo / Fundación Federico García Lorca, 1992. 33–52.

Higuera Rojas, Eulalia-Dolores de la. *Mujeres en la vida de García Lorca.* Madrid: Editora Nacional y Excma. Diputación Provincial de Granada, 1980.

Historia de la Cruzada Española. Ed. Joaquín Arrarás. Vol. III. Bk. XI. Madrid: 1939/1943.

Jackson, Gabriel. *The Spanish Republic and the Civil War: 1931–1939.* 3rd ed. Princeton: Princeton University Press, 1972.

Jiménez, Juan Ramón. *Cartas (primera selección).* Ed. Francisco Garfias. Madrid: Aguilar, 1962.

————. *Olvidos de Granada.* Introduction by Juan Gutiérrez Padial. Granada: Padre Suárez, 1969.

————. *Olvidos de Granada.* Facsimile of the 1945 original with various unpublished texts by the poet. Ed. Francisco Giner de los Ríos. Madrid: Caballo Griego para la Poesía, 1979.

————. *Selección de cartas (1899–1958).* 2nd ed. Barcelona: Picazo, 1973.

Josephs, Allen. *White Wall of Spain: The Mysteries of Andalusian Culture.* Ames, Iowa: Iowa State University Press, 1983.

Jou, Jordi. "La poesía vista per un poeta. Parlant amb Federico García Lorca." *La Humanitat* (Barcelona), October 6, 1935. Reprinted in *OC,* III, 605–10.

Laffranque, Marie. *Les Idées Esthétiques de Federico García Lorca.* Bordeaux: Institut d'Études Hispaniques, 1967.

La música en la Generación del 27. Homenaje a Lorca, 1915 / 1936. Exhibition catalogue. Madrid: Ministerio de Cultura, 1986.

Lecturas del 27. Granada: University of Granada, 1979.

León, María Teresa. "Federico y Margarita." *El Nacional* (Caracas), October 11, 1956.

Los vanguardistas españoles (1925–1935). Ed. Ramón Buckley and John Crispin. Madrid: El Libro de Bolsillo / Alianza, 1973.

Luengo, Ricardo G. "Quiero provocar revulsivos, a ver si se vomita de una vez todo lo malo del teatro actual." *El Mercantil Valenciano,* November 15, 1935. Reprinted in *OC,* III, 611–16.

Luna, José R. "El poeta que ha estilizado los romances de la plazuela." *El Debate* (Madrid), October 1, 1933. Reprinted in *OC,* III, 428–31.

————. "La vida de García Lorca, poeta." *Crítica* (Buenos Aires), March 10, 1934. Reprinted in *OC,* III, 523–29.

Marinello, Juan. *García Lorca en Cuba.* Havana: Belic, 1965.

Martín, Eutimio. *Federico García Lorca, heterodoxo y mártir. Análisis y proyección de la obra juvenil inédita.* Madrid: Siglo XXI, 1986.

————. "Lorca y Nueva York. Las primeras declaraciones de Lorca a su regreso de Estados Unidos." *Triunfo* (Madrid) 858, July 7, 1979, 48–50.

Martínez Nadal, Rafael. *Cuatro lecciones sobre Federico García Lorca.* Madrid: Fundación Juan March and Cátedra, 1980.

————. *Federico García Lorca. Mi penúltimo libro sobre el hombre y el poeta.* Madrid: Casariego, 1992.

————. Introduction to FGL, *Poems.* Trans. Stephen Spender and J. L. Gili. Oxford: Oxford University Press, 1939. vii–xxvi.

————. *Lorca's The Public: A Study of His Unfinished Play* (El Público) *and of Love and Death in the Work of Federico García Lorca.* London: Calder and Boyars, 1974.

Martín Martín, Jacinto. *Los años de aprendizaje de Federico y Francisco García Lorca.* Granada: Excmo. Ayuntamiento de Granada, 1984.

Massa, Pedro. "Una gran solemnidad teatral en Barcelona. Estreno de Doña Rosita la soltera o el lenguaje de las flores, nueva obra de García Lorca, interpretada por Margarita Xirgu." *Crónica* (Madrid), December 15, 1935.

Maurer, Christopher. "De la correspondencia de García Lorca: Datos inéditos sobre la transmisión de su obra." *BFFGL* yr. I, 1 (January 1987), 58–85.

———. Introduction to FGL, *A Season in Granada. Uncollected Poetry and Prose.*

———. Introduction to FGL, *Collected Poems.*

———. "Lorca y las formas de la música." In Soria Olmedo, 237–50.

———. "Sobre la prosa temprana de García Lorca: 1916–1918." *Cuadernos Hispanoamericanos* 433–34 (July–August 1986), 13–30.

Molina Fajardo, Eduardo. *Los últimos días de García Lorca.* Barcelona: Plaza y Janés, 1983.

Mora Guarnido, José. *Federico García Lorca y su mundo.* Buenos Aires: Losada, 1958.

Morales, María Luz. *Alguién a quien conocí.* Barcelona: Juventud, 1973.

Moreno Villa, José. *Vida en claro.* 2nd ed. Mexico: Fondo de Cultura Ecónomica, 1976.

Morla Lynch, Carlos. *En España con Federico García Lorca. Páginas de un diario íntimo, 1928–1936.* Madrid: Aguilar, 1957.

Morris, C. B. *A Generation of Spanish Poets: 1920–1936.* Cambridge: Cambridge University Press, 1971.

———. *Son of Andalusia: The Lyrical Landscapes of Federico García Lorca.* Nashville: Vanderbilt University Press, 1997.

Neruda, Pablo. *Confieso que he vivido. Memorias.* Barcelona: Seix Barral, 1976.

———. *Memoirs.* Trans. Hardie St. Martin. 2nd ed. New York: Penguin, 1982.

———. *Passions and Impressions.* Ed. Matilde Neruda and Miguel Otera Silva. Trans. Margaret Sayers Peden. New York: Farrar, Straus and Giroux, 1984.

Ontañón, Santiago. "Semblanza de García Lorca." *El Comercio* (Lima), June 7, 1946. Reprinted in FGL, *Dibujos.*

Ontañón, Santiago, and José María Moreiro. *Unos pocos amigos verdaderos.* Prologue by Rafael Alberti. Madrid: Fundación Banco Exterior de España, 1988.

Otero Seco, Antonio. "Una conversación inédita con Federico García Lorca. Índice de las obras inéditas que dejó el gran poeta." *Mundo Gráfico,* February 24, 1937. Reprinted in OC, III, 625–27.

"Para los anales de nuestra Facultad. Excursiones de estudios artísticos." *Lucidarium* (Granada) 2 and 3 (1917), 81–84 and 84–94.

Payne, Stanley. *Falange: A History of Spanish Fascism.* Stanford, Calif.: Stanford University Press, 1961.

Penón, Agustín. *Diario de una búsqueda lorquiana (1955–56).* Ed. Ian Gibson. Barcelona: Plaza y Janés, 1990.

Pérez Coterillo, Moises. "La Habana: Donde Lorca escribió 'El público.' " *El Público* 10–11 (July–August 1984).

Pinto, Ernesto. "Federico García Lorca: Gitano auténtico y poeta de verdad." *La Mañana* (Montevideo), February 6, 1934. Reprinted in OC, III, 497–502.

Prados, Emilio. *Diario íntimo.* Ed. José Luis Cano and Juan Such. Málaga: Publicaciones de la Librería Anticuaria El Guadalhorce, 1966.

Preston, Paul. *Franco: A Biography.* New York: HarperCollins, 1993.

Proel [Angel Lázaro]. "Galería. Federico García Lorca." *La Voz* (Madrid), February 18, 1935. Reprinted in OC, III, 554–58.

[Quevedo, Antonio.] *El poeta en La Habana.* Havana: Consejo Nacional de Cultura, 1961.

[Residencia de Estudiantes]. Monograph dedicated to the Residencia de Estudiantes (1910–36) on the centenary of the birth of its director, Alberto Jiménez Fraud (1883–1964). *Poesía* 18–19 (January 1984).

Río, Angel del. "El poeta Federico García Lorca." *Revista Hispánica Moderna* I, 1935.
———. "Federico García Lorca." *Revista Hispánica Moderna* (July–October 1940), 193–260.
———. *Poeta en Nueva York*. Madrid: Taurus, 1958.
———. *Vida y obras de Federico García Lorca*. Madrid: Zaragoza, 1952.
Rivas Cherif, Cipriano. "Poesía y drama del gran Federico. La muerte y la pasión de García Lorca." *Excelsior* (Mexico), Cultural Diorama section, January 6, 1957; January 13, 1957; January 27, 1957.
Rodrigo, Antonina. *García Lorca: El amigo de Cataluña*. Barcelona: Edhasa, 1984.
———. "La huerta de San Vicente." *Cuadernos Hispanoamericanos*, vol. II (September–October 1986), 433–36, 817–33.
———. *Lorca-Dalí. Una amistad traicionada*. Barcelona: Planeta, 1981.
———. *Margarita Xirgu y su teatro*. Barcelona: Planeta, 1974.
———. *Memoria de Granada: Manuel Ángeles Ortiz, Federico García Lorca*. Barcelona: Plaza y Janés, 1984.
Rodríguez Espinosa, Antonio. "Souvenirs d'un vieil ami." In Marie Laffranque, *Federico García Lorca*. Paris: Seghers (Théâtre de Tous les Temps), 1966.
Sáenz de la Calzada, Luis. *"La Barraca." Teatro Universitario*. Prologue by Rafael Martínez Nadal. Madrid: Biblioteca de la Revista de Occidente, 1976.
Sahuquillo, Ángel. *Federico García Lorca y la cultura de la homosexualidad. Lorca, Dalí, Cernuda, Gil-Albert, Prados y la voz silenciada del amor homosexual*. Stockholm: The author, 1986.
Salazar, Adolfo. "Federico en La Habana." *Carteles*, January 13, 1938, 30–31.
———. "La casa de Bernarda Alba." *Carteles*, April 10, 1938, 50.
Salinas, Pedro. "Federico García Lorca." Unpublished manuscript. Papers of Pedro Salinas. Houghton Library, Harvard University.
Salinas, Pedro, and Jorge Guillén. *Correspondencia (1923–1951)*. Ed. Andrés Soria Olmedo. Barcelona: Tusquets, 1992.
Salobreña, José. *Tierra natal de Federico García Lorca*. Granada: Pública Comisión de Cultura de la Excma. Diputación Provincial, 1982.
Sánchez Vidal, Agustín. *Buñuel, Lorca, Dalí: El enigma sin fin*. Barcelona: Planeta, 1988.
Santiago, Magda. "García Lorca." *Excelsior* (Mexico), Cultural Diorama section, January 6, 1957, 1.
Santos Torroella, Rafael. *Dalí residente*. Madrid: Publicaciones de la Residencia de Estudiantes (CSIC), 1992.
———. *La miel es más dulce que la sangre. Las épocas lorquiana y freudiana de Salvador Dalí*. Barcelona: Seix Barral, 1984.
———. *"Los putrefactos" de Dalí y Lorca. Historia y antología de un libro que no pudo ser*. Madrid: Publicaciones de la Residencia de Estudiantes (CSIC), 1995.
———. "Pepín Bello, o la amistad." *ABC Literario* (Madrid), November 14, 1987, 9.
Sopeña, Federico. *Atlántida. Introducción a Manuel de Falla*. Madrid: Taurus (Cuadernos Taurus), 1962.
Soria Olmedo, Andrés, ed. *Lecciones sobre Federico García Lorca. Granada, mayo de 1986*. Granada: Edición del Cincuentenario, 1986.
Southworth, Herbert Rutledge. "The Falange: An Analysis of Spain's Fascist Heritage." In *Spain in Crisis*. Ed. Paul Preston. Hassocks, Sussex: The Harvester Press, 1976.
Suero, Pablo. "Crónica de un día de barco con Federico García Lorca." *Noticias Gráficas* (Buenos Aires), October 14 and 15, 1933. Reprinted in *OC*, III, 436–40.
———. "Los últimos días con Federico García Lorca. El hogar del poeta." In *España levanta el puño*. Buenos Aires: Noticias Gráficas, 1936. Reprinted in Eutimio Martín, "Un testimonio

olvidado sobre García Lorca en el libro *España levanta el puño*, de Pablo Suero." *Trece de Nieve*, 2nd series, 3 (May 1977), 79–88.

Teitelboim, Volodia. *Neruda*. Madrid: Ediciones Michay (Libros del Meridión), 1984.

Thomas, Hugh. *The Spanish Civil War*. Harmondsworth: Penguin Books, 1968.

Tiempo, César. "Conversaciones con García Lorca en Buenos Aires." *NacionalC*, July 11, 1957, 8–9.

Torre, Guillermo de. "Federico García Lorca." In *Tríptico del sacrificio: Unamuno, García Lorca, Machado*. 2nd ed. Buenos Aires: Losada, 1960.

Trend, J. B. *Lorca and the Spanish Poetic Tradition*. Oxford: Basil Blackwell, 1956.

Umbral, Francisco. *Lorca, poeta maldito*. Madrid: Biblioteca Nueva, 1968.

Vázquez Ocaña, Fernando. *García Lorca, asesinado: Toda la verdad*. Barcelona: Planeta, 1975.

———. *García Lorca: Vida, cántico y muerte*. Mexico. Biografías Gandesa, 1957.

Villarejo, Pedro. *García Lorca en Buenos Aires. Una resurrección anterior a la muerte*. Buenos Aires: Libros de Hispanoamerica, 1986.

Walsh, John K. "The Social and Sexual Geography of *Poeta en Nueva York*." In *"Cuando yo me muera." Essays in Memory of Federico García Lorca*. Ed. C. Brian Morris. New York: University Press of America, 1988.

Ward, Philip, ed. *The Oxford Companion to Spanish Literature*. Oxford: Clarendon Press, 1978.

Zalamea, Jorge. "Federico García Lorca, hombre de adivinación y vaticinio." *Boletín cultural y bibliográfico* (Bogota) 2, 8 (1966), 1507–13.

ACKNOWLEDGMENTS

Without the encouragement of Stephen B. Oates and the late Sumner M. Greenfield, I would not have embarked on this biography. Exemplary teachers both, they showed me, as Martín Domínguez Berrueta showed Lorca, that writing books is a sublime pursuit.

I am also grateful to Glenn Banner, Gordon Wickstrom, Doris Abramson, Ed Golden, Virginia Scott, and Richard Trousdell, who, together and separately, taught me to respect the demands of language and scholarship.

Manolo Montesinos and the staff at the Fundación Federico García Lorca in Madrid expertly answered my many requests and inquiries, and granted me unrestricted access to the Lorca archive. Without their support, this biography would not exist. I am especially thankful to Araceli Gasso, Sonia González García, and Rosa María Illande Haro for their prompt and cheerful help. Isabel García Lorca has been unfailingly cordial and cooperative. Additional members of the Lorca family, especially Manolo Montesinos's wife, Ana, have made my task easier through their friendship.

Critical support from a Fulbright research grant enabled me to live in Spain from 1984 to 1986, and to consult archives, conduct interviews, and retrace Lorca's steps through the country he knew and loved best. I am particularly indebted to Tony Chillura of the United States Information Agency and to Patricia Zahnisser and Thomas Middleton of the Fulbright Commission in Madrid for their perceptive advice and thoughtful assistance throughout my stay in Spain.

I am also grateful to the United States–Spanish Joint Committee for Cultural and Educational Cooperation for a grant that allowed me to complete a key phase of research on the biography in 1992.

From the start of my work, Christopher Maurer has been a model of scholarship and collegiality. He readily shared his time, knowledge, and insight. For their friendship and hospitality, my profound thanks to both Christopher and his wife, Estrella. I am similarly indebted to Mario Hernández, who provided generous counsel throughout my two years in Spain, and who valiantly gave me his out-of-print copy of Mora Guarnido's *Federico García Lorca y su mundo* in exchange for "my" Lorca. My thanks as well to Mario's wife, Alicia, for her many kindnesses. Andrew Anderson lent his support to this biography during much of its development; his contribution to the whole is inestimable.

Spud Baldwin, Laurie Benton, Manuel Camarero, Dru Dougherty, Daniel Eisenberg, Marie Laffranque, Francisco Martín, Jacinto Martín Martín, David Maves, Ricardo Pereira, Antonina Rodrigo, José Salobreña García, Andrés Soria Olmedo, Bob Spires, and Ed Stanton provided help in the early stages of my research. Frank Casa assisted with translations. Ian Gibson graciously offered his advice and assistance at critical junctures; his books on Lorca are an indispensable reference, and his courageous investigation of Lorca's murder—at a time when it was extraordinarily dangerous to do so—has been an inspiration.

For their willingness to answer my questions and share their memories, my deep-felt thanks go to Amelia Agostini del Río, José Alemán Marín, Conchita Burgmann, José Caballero, José Luis Cano, Álvaro Custodio, Philip Cummings, Ana María Dalí, Angel Flores, Antonio Gallego Morell, María del Carmen García Lasgoity, Eulalia Dolores de la Higuera, Paz Jiménez de Marquina, Houston Kenyon Jr., Enrique Lanz Durán, Vicente López, José Martín Campos, Rafael Martínez Nadal, Gonzalo Menéndez Pidal, Veronica Morla, Santiago Ontañón, Henry Rickard, José Antonio Rubio Sacristán, Arturo Sáenz de la Calzada, Margarita Ucelay Maórtua, Antonio Velázquez, and Dionysio and María Venegas Heredía. I am abidingly grateful to Tomás Rodríguez Rapún and his wife, Margarita Bernis, for their friendship.

Gabriel Nuñez Ruiz and Carmina Ruiz García introduced me to Almería and to the landscape that inspired *Blood Wedding*. During walks through Granada with Bernardo Olmedo, I came to know Lorca's hometown and to glean a sense of what it was like to live there during the shocking first days of the Spanish Civil War. Carmen and Fermín Guzmán and their extended family taught me to appreciate the subtleties of Andalusian life. On countless occasions, Francisco Padilla Martín and his family—in particular his grandfather, Manuel Padilla Fernández—welcomed me into their home in Valderrubio (formerly Asquerosa) and introduced me to others whose lives were touched by Lorca's, among them Carmen Perea Ruiz, José Pérez Rodríguez, and Francisco "Frasco" Santalla Sánchez. Without the friendship and fine cooking of the late María Trescastro de Correal, and the affection of her family, I would not have known the true magic of Lorca's Huerta de San Vicente, nor the "sweet domestic air" that, as Lorca understood, suffuses Granada.

The following archivists and librarians provided invaluable assistance, and I am in their debt: the reference staff at the Houghton Library, Harvard University; Wilma Slaight of the Wellesley College Archives; the staff at the Fundación Juan March in Madrid; staff members at the Hemeroteca Municipal and the Hemeroteca Nacional in Madrid, and at the Hemeroteca Municipal in Barcelona; Juana de Dios of the Hemeroteca Municipal de Granada (Casa de los Tiros); the staff at the Biblioteca Nacional in Madrid; Jennifer Campbell of the Cleveland Public Library; staff members at the Archivo Parroquial in Fuente Vaqueros and the Archivo Parroquial de Nuestra Señora de las Angustias, Granada; staff members at the Archivo del Excmo. Ayuntamiento, Granada, and the Juzgado, Granada; the reference staff at the University of Granada Archives; Anita Solak at the Hispanic Society of America; Laura García Lorca de los Ríos of the Huerta de San Vicente, Granada; and the staff at the Universidad Cumplutense, Madrid. Special thanks go to Antonio Manjón of the Hemeroteca Municipal de Granada (Casa de los Tiros), for lightening my hours at the library by letting me visit his beautiful *granadino* garden, and to Juan de Loxa of the Casa-Museo Federico García Lorca in Fuente Vaqueros, for his unstinting help and generosity.

I am grateful to those friends and fellow writers who read portions of this book and offered commentary: Sandra and Bill Katz, William Kimbrel, Elizabeth Lloyd-Kimbrel, Ann and Michael Meeropol, and Stephen Oates of the Amherst Biography Group; as well as Donald Lamm, Victoria Wilson, Nicholas Delbanco, John Ware, Jennifer Dix, Diane Moroff, Patricia Simpson, Madeline Diehl, Sylvia Watanabe, Zach Lowe, and Michael McClure. I owe particular thanks to Sandra Katz and Hank Meijer for their insightful criticism of early drafts of the manuscript. Helen Sheehy read the manuscript during the final stages of writing, and with passion, intelligence, and clarity provided advice, encouragement, and inspiration in equal measure. Tom Sheehy was an ongoing source of cheer.

I thank my agent, Carol Mann, and her assistants, Marc Baller and Yumi

Ota, for their expertise, hard work, and welcome wit. I am indebted to Stu Abraham for his efforts on my behalf, and to Liz Calder and Jonathan Galassi for their enthusiastic support of the book. Through his exacting eye, gentle humor, and steady deadlines, my editor at Bloomsbury, Bill Swainson, did much to strengthen the biography. I am equally grateful to Ethan Nosowsky, my editor at Farrar, Straus and Giroux, for his careful reading of the book and astute observations. Chris Wood in London and Karla Reganold in New York did a superlative job of copyediting.

Finally, and with particular happiness, I thank Steven Whiting, who shared the last leg of this journey with incomparable grace and joy.

INDEX

NOTE: Titles of works are by Lorca unless otherwise identified.

Núñez de Arenas, M., 316–17
Nuns of Granada, The, 441

Obregón, Antonio de, 415
Ocampo, Victoria, 334, 337
Octubre. Escritores y Artistas Revolucionarios
(magazine), 319
"Ode and Mockery of Sesostris and Sardana-
palus," 190, 460
"Ode to Injustice," 238
"Ode to Salvador Dalí," 134, 142, 208, 209, 407
"Ode to the Fighting Bull," 366
"Ode to the Most Holy Sacrament of the Al-
tar," 207–9, 231
"Ode to Walt Whitman," 239, 250, 325, 330
Odets, Clifford, 391
"Old Spanish Songs (For Piano and Voice),"
418
Olmedilla, Juan, 265
Olympia Theater (Barcelona), 406
Once Five Years Pass, 277–82, 297, 301, 304,
305, 321, 330, 351, 396, 420, 429, 437, 442,
459, 460
O'Neill, Eugene, 232, 286, 301, 501n
Onís, Federico de, 215, 218
"On Love. Animal Theater," 68
Ontañón, Santiago, 172, 313, 315–17, 376,
507n
Order of Toledo, 128
Orgaz, Gen. Luis, 443, 446
Origin of Species (Darwin), 23
Ortega, Manuel ("El Caracol"), 100
Ortega y Gasset, José, 29, 141–43, 153, 160, 184,
195, 204, 267, 283, 294, 318, 427
Orwell, George, 456
Ovid, 23
Oxford University, 149

Pacheco, Isaac, 384
Palacios Ríos, Matilde, 9, 321, 381
Palencia, Benjamín, 135, 137, 139, 188
"Palimpsests," 85
Paris, Luis, 265
Pascal, Blaise, 181
"Patriotism," 374
Pavo (magazine), 177
Pavón, Tomás, 297

Paysan de Paris, Le (Aragon), 168
Pedrell, Felipe, 93, 124
Pedroza, Father, 511n
Perea Ruiz, Gabriel, 448, 450
Pérez Barradas, Rafael, 66–67, 159, 350
Pérez de la Riva, Juan Ernesto, 248
Pérez de Roda, Ramón, 471n
Pérez Ferrero, Miguel, 254, 305, 356–57, 369
Pérez Guerra, Ernesto, 291–93, 376, 397
*Peribáñez and the Knight Commander of
Ocaña* (Lope de Vega), 387–88
Persistence of Memory, The (Dalí), 278
Philip II, King, 371
Picasso, Pablo, 90, 110, 162, 168, 173, 196, 197,
307, 457, 488n, 495n, 501n
Pineda, Mariana, 115–18, 132–34, 160
Pinter, Harold, 460
Pirandello, Luigi, 118, 258, 278, 370–71, 406
Piscator, Erwin, 420
Pittaluga, Gustavo, 320
Plato, 23, 42, 181
"Play and Theory of the *Duende*," 331–33
Playboy of the Western World, The (Synge),
521n
"Play without a Title," *see Dream of Life, The*
Poe, Edgar Allan, 218, 236
Poemas arábigos-andaluces (García Gómez),
361
Poem of the Deep Song, 96–101, 140, 141,
154, 155, 237, 275–76, 300, 337, 347, 460,
486n
"Poem of the Gypsy Siguiriya," 97, 98
"Poem of the Saeta," 97–98
"Poem of the Soleá," 97
Poems for the Dead, 277
"Poet Asks His Love for the Enchanted City of
Cuenca, The," 412
"Poet Asks His Love to Write Him, The,"
409
"Poetic Image of Don Luis de Góngora, The,"
143
Poet in New York, 236–40, 361, 419, 427, 459,
460
"Poet in New York," 288–89, 333
"Poet Speaks with His Beloved on the Tele-
phone, The," 409, 412
"Poet Tells the Truth, The," 411
Polignac, Princesse de, 488n
Popular Front, 422